The 2001

GOOD CURRY GUIDE

Where to find the
1000 best Curry Restaurants in Britain

PAT CHAPMAN

Author of the CURRY BIBLE
and founder of the CURRY CLUB

SIMON &
SCHUSTER

Assistant Editor and Database Management: Dominique Chapman (DBAC)
Design: Peter Ward
Statistics: Taylor Nelson, Sub Continent Publishing
Researchers: Roshan Ali, Pieter Badenhorst, Biren, Jonelle Folscher, Asher Frank, Michelle Harewood, Iqbal, Jason, Gabriel Jindeau, Stephen John, Zeville Narbutis, Buela Samuels, Diana Sebastian, Samson Sohail and Greg Wilson.

Edited and typeset: Grapevine Publishing Services, London

Good Curry Guide Reporters of the Year:
Ralph Warrington, Hyde, Cheshire (GM) and
Bill Parkes-Davis, Tunbridge Wells, Kent
with last Guide's Hilary Chapchal of London and
Malcolm Wilkins of Gravesend, Kent both still deserving special mention,
plus many hundreds of others, without whom
this Guide would not exist, and whose names appear on page 604

First published in Great Britain by Simon & Schuster UK Ltd, 2000
A Viacom company

1 3 5 7 9 10 8 6 4 2

Simon and Schuster UK Ltd
Africa House
64–78 Kingsway
London WC2B 6AH

Typeset by Grapevine Publishing Services
Printed and bound in Finland

A CIP catalogue record for this book is available from the British Library

ISBN 0 743 20840 4

CONTENTS

THE ENTRIES

Author's Notes

Sponsorship The continuing sponsorship of Cobra Beer, the *Guide*'s sole sponsor, enables the author to finance the considerable costs of operating and producing this *Guide*, which include: maintaining the restaurant database on computer; subscribing to a press-cutting service and other information suppliers; printing a detailed questionnaire and mailing it to all 8,000 restaurants twice a year; mail-shotting the 1,500-plus restaurants that are selected to appear in the *Guide*; telephoning many for verification of information; producing, supplying and mailing the selected restaurants (free of charge) their wall certificates and window stickers; printing and mailing restaurant report forms for interested parties; collating and recording the info received (some 5,000 reports per annum) and operating the Awards Ceremony.

Accuracy The contents of this *Guide* are as up-to-date and accurate as possible, but we cannot be held responsible for any changes regarding quality, price, menu details, decor, ownership, health offences or even closure, following our processing of the reports.

Connections Pat Chapman, the publishers of this *Guide* and the proprietors of The Curry Club wish to make it quite clear that they have absolutely no financial or ownership connections with any restaurants, including those mentioned in this *Guide*.

False representation Restaurant reports are welcomed from any bona-fide source. We do not pay for reports – they are sent in spontaneously and voluntarily. Our own research and restaurant testing is normally done anonymously, the bill is paid, and often no disclosure is made as to our presence. On some occasions, such as openings, we accept invitations to visit restaurants as 'guests of the house'. Under no circumstances do we tout for free hospitality, and anyone doing so in the name of The Curry Club is an impostor. We have heard of cases where people claiming to be members of The Curry Club, or *Good Curry Guide* 'inspectors', request payment and/or free meals in return for entry into this *Guide*. In such cases, we would recommend that restaurants threaten to call the police. We would also like to be informed of any such incidents and we will not hesitate to take action against people acting illegally in our name.

Discounts We invite all restaurants selected to appear in this *Guide* to participate in a discount scheme for members of The Curry Club. Those restaurants who agree to participate are indicated by the symbol © on their entry. The terms of this scheme are clearly spelled out to all parties. We cannot be held responsible if, at any time, the restaurant declines the offered discount. *See also page* 626.

County Index

See page 614 for Town Index

Certificates and window stickers We send all restaurants appearing in this *Guide* a 2001 certificate, hand-signed by Pat Chapman, and a 2001 window sticker. These items are supplied free of charge. Some choose not to display them, others display them proudly and prominently. You may observe that our certificate is not displayed alone. There may well be a host of others, some bigger and flashier than ours, including the Dome Grading certificates issued by Peter and Colleen Groves, which are genuine, as are certificates issued by London's *Time Out*, Ronay, local council health departments and certain others. Unfortunately, some certificates are a pure sham. They are issued to any restaurant who cares to pay for them, in some cases with a promise of entry into a *Guide* which does not even exist. We reported last time on a scam by *Good Food Guide*, yet again, but this is not The *Good Food Guide*. There is no *Guide* and this is the same outfit that were sued by the Consumers' Association some time ago and have now re-emerged at a different address. Masterchef returned after being exposed by BBC 'Food and Drink' in June. Certificates are on offer for £67.50 (£10 for extra copies) and £5 for window stickers. The *Asian Food Guide* was caught out on Radio 4. There are others on the bandwagon. Like Peter Groves, we would like to see this scam stopped.

But how do you know that the *Good Curry Guide* certificate you see is genuine? Earlier this year, we were sent a fax by one of the award-winning restaurants in the *Good Curry Guide*. It was a copy of a fax they had just received. Its heading in large type was *THE GOOD CURRY GUIDE*, with 'a new idea to make your restaurant more popular'. It told of a new website called *The Curry Guide*. Strange that, because we have registered *The Good Curry Guide.com* and *The Good Curry Guide.co.uk* as domain names and we've not been sending anyone any such faxes. It seems this fax is offering a *Good Curry Guide* certificate for a cost of £30. Funny that! We give our certificates free of charge. So who is this plagiarist?

It seems the person responsible is one Ian Cowan of Inc Software, Paisley, Scotland. We doubt that he will actually make any money, but if even one restaurant is mug enough to hope to fool his customers with a dazzling *Good Curry Guide* certificate, it's bad news for the customer and for the industry, because I do not believe that Mr Cowan will stop at offering only entrants to our *Guide* the chance of a £30 certificate. He'll offer it to every UK restaurant. The problem is that selling a certificate is not illegal. And restaurateurs are anxious to impress their customers. In the last year you have flooded us with information on which certificates restaurants display. We'd like you to continue with this intelligence.

And, apparently, you've been telling your restaurants that you are aware of the scam, and prefer awards which are given free on merit.

About this Guide

The Good Curry Guide broke new ground when it was first published in 1984, by being the first restaurant guide to specialise only in the British curry. This, its seventh edition.. As usual, there there have been demotions and promotions since last time. We want continuity in each edition of the *Guide*, and because we do expect changes, we feel it is important that each restaurant completes our questionnaire. For one thing, it means the restaurant actually wants to be in the *Guide*. It also verifies its current name, address, telephone number, and above all, prices. Despite our earnest endeavours, not all restaurants reply, even if they did so last time. So if we have not received a reply from a restaurant that was in the previous edition, after it has been sent a form three times, should it be delisted? I believe it should if it cannot be bothered, for whatever reason, to talk to us. But curry restaurants are a peculiar trade; communications aren't always easy and normal rules don't apply.

A completed form from a restaurant does not guarantee entry to the Guide. We rely on various other sources of information. We can only visit a handful of restaurants each year, and do not have a team of paid inspectors. Most important to us are the opinions of the customers – you, the diners. We do not pay for such reports, though from time to time The Curry Club gives prizes for your efforts. The report itself can be a simple short note, though we have a special form (*see* final page) for all who want one. A report may deal with a single restaurant or several. Some reporters write to us only once, others write repeatedly. For this *Guide*, we received about 5,000 reports, yielding information on up to 50,000 restaurant visits. We read and record every report, although it is becoming increasingly difficult to reply to all of them. I would like, therefore, to thank all those who have taken the time to tell us where they have found the best, good, mediocre and even bad curries.

Of course reporting standards vary, and the The Wind of India, Puddle-come-on-the-Marsh may well be reported as the best in the world by an ardent, novice, local fan (and I want such opinions), but may not rate highly if compared with London's best. Nevertheless, it will be a competent curry house in that area, serving standard formula curry. Numerous entries in this *Guide* come into this category, and they are here because someone, maybe more than one person, has taken the trouble to write in and praise the place, and to exclude it would be wrong. We want to know what you know.

Answering the question 'Name your favourite curry restaurant(s)' may not always be as easy as it sounds. It is worth quoting Sutton Coldfield's John Brockingham, a retired college lecturer: 'My favourite restaurants,' he wrote, 'range from opulent establishments like Rajdoot, Birmingham, where I might take the family on special occasions, to cheap and cheerful places like Erdington's Balti Express, where a meal costs £11 a head. I have a favourite posh curry restaurant, when I can afford it, and a favourite posh Balti. But I have a favourite plonk version of both, and a favourite takeaway, and then there's a favourite lucky dip. Some of my favourites are good enough to tempt me in whenever I'm in the district, but could not be nominated for the highest accolade.'

Of course we do not receive reports on every single establishment. On occasion a restaurant we normally receive good reports about gets damned. If this is the exception, we will probably still carry that restaurant. Some will have closed, and others should perhaps have been omitted. But none get into this *Guide* unless we have had at least one recent good report on it, preferably several. To get into the TOP 100 we need several detailed excellent reports, including at least one by one of our elite 60 or so regular reporters. As editors we visit a TOP 100 restaurant anonymously whenever we can, but it's impossible to go to them all within one year. We do our best to filter out 'good' reports on bad restaurants, particularly those written by their hopeful owners. This time we requested that restaurants selected for entry get their customers to write to us, and many did. This way, we have almost weeded out the few restaurants who previously sent us phoney reports, purportedly from adoring customers. However, even after fifteen years in the editor's chair, it is possible that I've been conned and a 'bad' restaurant has slipped in. Equally, I'll guarantee that we've missed someone's favourite, and that there are a few *faux pas* too. Please let us know about these. No doubt, we'll continue to get irate letters from people who won't have bothered to read this section, telling us that, because this or that restaurant was awful when they visited, 'it casts doubt on the credibility of the entire *Guide*'.

We certainly do not enter restaurants just because they ask us to. After seventeen years of bona-fide operations, you would imagine that curry house owners would clamour to be in the *Guide*. Indeed some do. As I have said in previous *Guides*, more than one restaurant has made veiled references to the benefits that would be made available to the editors if that restaurant were declared the UK's number one. The very idea is abhorrent. Besides, if one did accede to such bribery, word would soon get round risking the credibility of both author and publication. The book is paid for through book sales and sponsorship, not through bribes.

So what's new in this edition? Regular readers will know that we go alphabetically by county, then within that, by town and then restaurant. We are continuing with this system, since it is easier to see at a glance what alternative choices are nearby. We have also continue with the town index at the end of the book (*see page* 614). At the start of each county's entry, we have also improved our thumbnail county maps, which help pinpoint the location of that particular county, along with a new feature, which lists adjacent counties, and a few statistics. It should make this *Guide* more informative and finding your way around it easier. And that, after all, is what this *Guide* is all about – finding good curries easily, and nothing else.

Curry in Decline?

Pat Chapman hits back at the dripping tap of scepticism

Last summer, I was furious to find myself quoted in a respected broadsheet newspaper. My 1999 *Good Curry Guide* was quoted as saying that for every new curry restaurant opening, three are closing. From this the journalist deduced that the industry has peaked and is in decline! Neither I, nor *The Good Curry Guide* said any of that. Firstly, it is not true. Secondly, I would not give a bad-news generalisation for the media to quote me on. I always give upbeat quotes. Newspapers have a duty to report accurately, or they did once, but now, it seems, anything goes. It's not the first time I've been misrepresented by that newspaper. Previous protestations led to no action, so I didn't bother this time. Besides I was about to go on holiday, and complaints take time and effort. But the phone started to ring, with journalists wanting confirmation of what I was alleged to have said. I told them all what I've just told you – and emphasised the positive things happening in our industry – new openings, increased consumption of curry, and new up-and-coming personality chefs, such as Atul, Cyrus, Merenosh, Udit and Vineet.

The ultimate journalistic probe came two days into my holiday, while Dominique and I were lounging round the pool in Spain. At around 3pm my mobile rang and a journalist from Canada wanted to know my opinion about the 'collapsing UK curry market', quoting what he had read in the British press. When I told him what I told you, he said 'so you disagree?' I told him again that not only had I never made that statement, but that curry consumption figures are increasing. In fact I spent several minutes giving him upbeat positive facts. After listening to all that, he then said 'so why do you think the trade is declining?' At that I hit the roof. 'What exactly do you think I've been saying to you for 5 minutes?' I exploded. 'Not once have I said that. And there you are, just like all your kind, with your pen poised, ready to write the next curry market Pat Chapman doom and gloom piece. I won't have it. Why is it you journalists never listen?'

I did go on a bit, so much so that Dominique was in stitches of laughter, hugely enjoying this poolside spectacle. As luck would have it my journalist did not hang up. He actually apologised, and said 'so there's no story then?' I said: 'If you mean that the market is not collapsing, then no there's no story.' He said his goodbyes, and as far as I know, Canada got no story. The sad fact is that no one, it seems, wishes to publish good news. It's boring.

Although I thought I'd heard the end of the misquote, it was not to be. *Time Out's Eating and Drinking Guide* 2000 appeared late last year. For those of you outside the capital, *Time Out* publishes a weekly listings magazine, with a number of spin-off annual guides, of which this guide to London's best cafés restaurant and bars, is one. I'm a fan of *Time Out* – it is a brilliant original concept. But this year it has really annoyed me. In the 'Indian' chapter, they assiduously tell us that the curry market is in decline. As proof, they offer one statistic from the 'Economic and Social Research Council' (who?), reporting that three restaurants close every week in the UK.

Writing that three 'Indian' restaurants are closing every week sounds dramatic. It reminds me of the spurious facts doled out by the media in the early days of the beef crisis. 'Thousands,' they claimed 'are turning away from meat and flocking to vegetarianism.' The figures to substantiate this were, if I recall, something like 10,000 people per week are becoming vegetarians. Sounds a lot doesn't it? But what they don't bother to tell us is that of the 60 million people in Britain today, 5.3 million are said to be vegetarians. Most of those eat eggs, many eat fish and some eat white meat like chicken, so very few are true vegetarians. That figure has been more or less static since I researched it a decade ago, for my first *Vegetarian Indian Cookbook*, and again for my new *Vegetable Curry Bible*, just published. It means that less than 9% of the population claim to be vegetarian. So does 10,000 conversions per week mean that vegetarianism is vastly increasing? Let's see! 10,000 x 52 weeks equals 520,000 people per annum. And that's less than 1% of the population! And those quoting this figure neglect to advise us that it has been constant for at least ten years. It also omits to tell us of the many converts who change their mind and revert to their meat-eating former ways.

So *Time Out*, how much in decline is the curry restaurant industry with your three-per-week closure figure? The figure is accurate, but sadly, you too have fallen into the trap of failing to analyse it in print, resulting in your inaccurate and potentially damaging 'decline' statement. Here's why: 3 x 52 weeks equals 156 closures. Sounds bad, but is it? 156 out of the 8,000 curry restaurants known to exist in this country, is under 2%. *Time Out* fails to mention that, nor that this rate has not changed for well over a decade. *Time Out* also fails to tell its readers how many new openings there are each week. Surprise, surprise, if 2000 is anything like 1998 and 1999 there will be at least double that figure, indeed a fair few appear in *Time Out*'s own 2000 *Guide*!

And it's not just 'decline' figures' which obsess the media. How many times have they told us that the curry business employs more people than the coal, steel and shipbuilding industries? But this fact is wrong. Lucy Kellaway's *Financial Times* piece earlier this year enjoyed trotting out this remarkable fact, backed up, it seems, by even more remarkable figures. Lucy must have been in the Sky with Diamonds when she said that there are 80,000 curry restaurants, employing 200,000 staff. [There are only 51,000 pubs in the land, so 80,000 curry restaurants has to be wrong, but even if it were true, what restaurant employs 2.5 employees?] But Lucy thunders on to inform her readers that steel, ship-building and coal together employ some 150,000 people. We know the facts to be 8,000 restaurants and *c.*80,000 staff; ergo another erroneous fact slips into historical concrete.

Incidentally, another over-hacked headline, that curry-eating exceeds fish and chips, has been dredged by Kathryn Trivert from where? Now let me see, ah yes – the British Potato Council, at (what did I say about there being a glut of awards ceremonies) the 'British Fish and Chip Shop Awards' at the Café Royal. Well, she would say that, wouldn't she? But, guess what the most popular vegetable dish at the curry house is? Bombay Potato, of course!

I have great respect for Jonathan Meads, he's been kind about this *Guide* on several occasions, but really, Jonathan, calling a dish a 'ring burner' in the *Times Magazine* isn't really you, is it? (I'll publish your answer on these pages next *Guide*.) It encourages others with like minds, and of course the editor decided that nothing could suit the piece better than a cartoon of a waiter squirting a soda siphon (do they still exist?) at a customer's said ring.

As one who has been doing all things curry for 19 years, I have been a beneficiary of media goodwill, but in the last 18 months, I find myself vehemently defending our industry. If the curry issue of the week is not food colouring, it's staff shortages, non-authenticity, a curry chef cooking contest row, or some other negative topic. Now it's closures and decline. The blame for this situation is complex and might be just a reflection of the nation's delight in putting down British successes, following a period of building them up. It happens to people, business and industry. Whatever the reason, the curry industry's honeymoon period is over. But I'm damned if I'm just going to sit around doing nothing about it. Fortunately, neither are the British public. One only has to look at a good favourite curry restaurant's performance as a reminder of just why curry is still number one.

Cobra Curryholics' Directory

This *Guide*'s purpose is to give a selective critique of the UK's 1000 best curry restaurants. Popular though this *Guide* is, it does not tell the full curry story, and for some years, we have been asked if we would produce a nationwide listing of every curry restaurant. The *Cobra Curryholics' Directory* is a new product from The Curry Club, aimed at the enthusiastic curry restaurant diner. It lists all the Indian, Bangladeshi, Pakistani, Nepalese and Sri Lankan restaurants. And we decided to go further and include Thai, Malaysian and Indonesian restaurants as well. There is no commentary, just name, address and one telephone number. The book is the same size as a phone directory (A4), and is printed on golden huldi-coloured pages – a very appropriate colour in the curry business. It covers the whole of England, Scotland, Ireland and Wales in one book, with a listing of the 8,000 restaurants.

But we know you want more. We are often asked 'what curry products are on the market, and where I can buy them?' The Directory lists manufacturers and details their products. In addition we give numerous information service addresses, publications, shows, festivals and exhibitions, all dedicated to CURRY. The Directory also contains a colour section with plenty of fun, facts and features to entertain and inform, including sponsor, Cobra India Beer's icon, award-winning Dave the Curryholic. The *Cobra Curryholics' Directory* is the companion to the *Guide*: it is a must for all curry lovers.

Currystats

Some 2,300 restaurants responded to our Cobra Good Curry Guide survey, by answering detailed questions on the forms we sent them in April. We combine our results with those of *Tandoori Magazine*'s survey, which was completed a few months earlier. We also measure selected data (prices, favourite dishes etc.) from restaurant information sent to us by curry diners (*see page* 604).

Since our last survey, two years ago, there has been a net increase of 487 'Indian' restaurants and takeaways. And some of these are of a high enough quality to go straight into our TOP 100 (*see page* 27). Our database, last updated in September 2000, now gives us a total of 8,018 venues, of which 6,298 are restaurants. This is thousands more 'Indian' restaurants than there are in India. They are a major UK revenue earner. Closures are harder to measure, because such events are not publicised by the unfortunate restaurateurs. Since the last *Guide* the closure rate has dramatically slowed to 1.5% (*see page* 9) while the opening rate has doubled to 3%. But our surveys have revealed a more remarkable finding: 90% report an increase in numbers both of dining-in and takeaway customers. To cope, 70% of restaurants have refurbished their premises since our last survey two years ago. But this is not just a lick of paint and a new carpet. Most tell of better utilisation of existing space to increase seating. Some report that they have carried out more extensive building works, by doing large conversions and/or by acquiring further units, or building conservatories, etc.

The national average seating has increase from 53 to 56. This doesn't sound like a lot, but it totals 24,000 seats nationwide. Converted to money this is some £60m gross extra revenue per annum. And still the popular restaurants report turning away trade on Fridays and Saturdays. Prices have risen in most areas in the last 2 years, by as much as 8% in some cases, though the average is just under 5%. The average spend, however, is £14.50 per customer (including drink) – up by 12%. And restaurants tell of more dining-in customers than before. This concurs with the National Food Survey 1999 issued by MAFF which indicates a tiny drop in national expenditure on food. Some basic ingredients fell by 9%, but this was offset by an 8% rise in ready meals. Pasta continues to soar ahead with 24% growth. Dining out, says MAFF, continues to rise (by 9%) and if this trend continues the market will have increased by 50% in less than 10 years.

Most restaurants do takeaway, representing 30% of their trade. Remarkably, given the above statistic, under 200 restaurants report that they don't do takeaways at all. As it happens, we do not know of any restaurants which refuse such business, including the pricey London ones, and if you know of any, please tell us, and their reasons.

The increase in home delivery is very significant since we last reported on this figure in 1998. Then, only 20% of all restaurants home-delivered. Now the figure is 58% and rising. Asked if home deliveries have detracted from their existing dining-in and takeaway business, the average response was 'no' to the former (it has increased) and 'yes' to the latter, in that less people come to collect takeaways, although coupled together takeaway and delivery sales have significantly increased. As yet, only 9% deliver alcoholic beverages. 1,033 outfits charge to deliver (the highest £5, another, the taxi fare). One impressive new takeaway, the Bombay Romna, NW1 (*see page* 85) home-delivers not only drink and Indian food, but Italian, Japanese, French, Chinese, and Thai food and puddings. They also deliver flowers, candles, chocolates, cigarettes and cigars. Service like this could be the way forward for many in the Indian sector. 1,469 venues on our database are takeaway only outlets. 10% of these intelligently have an off-license. Half of these deliver.

Over 70% of us pay by credit card. Less than 10% of restaurants impose a service charge. Of those 30% leave the slip open! 11% of customers visit twice a week; a further 21% of customers visit once a week. 25% visit once a fortnight. 30% visit regularly around every three weeks or once a month. 60% are couples. 19% are families with children under 16. 5% are singles. 63.4% of the venues turn over under £5,000 per week. Only 7.5% turn over more than £10,000. Only a handful turn over £80,000 and more per week. As for profits, average industry margins were just 2.8%; 20% made in excess of 10% pre-tax profit, though 75% of these borrowed to do so.

Every year we eat 200 million popadoms and 21 million kilos of rice in the Indian restaurant. Beer/lager is still the no. 1 drink with curry. We wash our meals down with an average 84 million pints of lager a year, but wine is on the increase, with 15 million bottles of wine drunk at the curry house in 1999 (up by 10% in the year) of which 44% of which was red.

Despite attempts to get more authenticity in the curry house, little has changed in the popularity stakes for over a decade: Tikka Masala is still the no. 1 dish, followed by Korma (the mildest curry), though Jalfrezi has taken the no. 3 crown from Madras, however, it being as hot or hotter with the application of fresh green chilli. Vindaloo is still at no. 10!

And finally, yes they do like curry at no. 10! The Blairs have their favourite curryhouses, in and around Islington, their former home. And there is a branch of The Curry Club at the Houses of Parliament, with prominent MPs from Red Ken to Michael Fabricant extolling the virtues of curry.

*Facts here and elsewhere in this Guide from the 2000 Curry Club User survey and the 1999 *Tandoori Magazine Restaurateurs survey. Subsidiary information: Taylor Nelson AGB, Mintel, Gallup, National Food Survey 1999, Market Power, and Plimsoll Portfolio Analysis and CACI population projections.*

*(*Pat Chapman is Associate Editor of Tandoori Magazine, which is owned by Cobra beer, the Guide sponsor)*

CurriNation 2000

One of our wittier correspondents, Brian Sylvester, asks 'Did you know that "Leonardo da Vinci" is an anagram of "vindaloo and rice"?' It certainly wasn't on the menu for the Last Supper, although if that event had been held 2 millennia later, it most certainly would be – in the UK at any rate.

Predictions of the demise of the UK curry were, as Mark Twain might have said, greatly exaggerated. So too were the end-of-the-world predictions, due as we entered the 21st century. The much vaunted 'millennium' came and went – no bugs, no crashing aircraft, no sinking ships, no bankrupt banks, no shut down microwaves, nothing at all really. The Dome puffed itself into life with a politarati celeb do and a self-conscious Queen singing 'Auld Lang Syne', then subsided into derision. The London Eye did work, eventually, but the nation celebrated everywhere 'on the night'. But life, it seems, goes on as before and to prove it here's our first *Guide* of the new century. True the world is changing more rapidly than before – take the mobile phone. In 1995, there were just some 2 million mobiles, the preserve of business men and women. Most mobiles were fairly cumbersome, did not stay charged up long and easily went out of range of a transmitter. They were expensive and exclusive status symbols. Five years on, the top 1999 Christmas present was a mobile. They are now cheap, light, super powerful, and available for all – a triumph of technology... It appears that 24 million of us own one. At the November *BBC Good Food Show* in Birmingham, I was in transit between Safeway and Tesco theatres. En route, I passed a group of about ten 14-year-old school girls. As I came close, one said 'Where's Tracy?' All ten simultaneously reached for their mobiles to find her. It was like the quick-draw scene from *High Noon*. Who could have predicted that five years ago?

It's the same with computers and the internet – 30% of the nation, it seems, have home computers, thus access to the internet. Doubtless this will increase dramatically in the next year or two as the net will be accessed by the new generation of mobiles and television sets. However, shopping on the net seems to me to be a much-hyped activity. True, one can place an instant order by e-mail. At some restaurants, I can actually order my curry online. But from then on, it still relies on someone actually reading my communication, cooking, packing and delivering it, and me paying for it. And therein lies the problem. Just how long do you wait in for your 'instant' order to be delivered? In that respect, internet ordering is no different from a phoned, faxed, or written order sent by post. As Angus Deayton says 'no change there then'! Unless your e-mail is processed immediately and efficiently, with priority over all other forms of order, it will not reach you any quicker. No one can deny that the internet is a phenomenally powerful tool, but until it does the housework, and delivers my curry instantly, I remain a little cynical.

Cyber-squat

Incidentally, there's a new scam afoot, called 'cyber-squatting'. Perpetrators hijack a name or brand in the hope that they can hold the legitimate name-holder to ransom in a pay-off deal. Pinching names is, it seems, fair game on the Web. I'm told that 95% of the names in the English dictionary have been registered in the US on the Web, presumably in the hope of selling your own copyrighted name back to you. The case of Marks & Spencer and Al Fayed come to mind – both registered without the owners/copyright-holders permission, and 'leoblair.com' was announced within hours of his birth. US and British courts are uncertain which way to judge on such issues, so the practice is rife. I find that The Curry Club has been registered four times: with and without the 'The' and in '.com' and '.co.uk' form. Only one is legit. Ah me! Looking positively ahead, during this year our own web site will come on line, and Pat intends to have a regular 'open-house' session where he can answer your queries 'on-line'.

Dome and out

Talking about the millennium, pubs and restaurants which tried to overcharge for the big night came to earth with a jolt when the crowds they'd hoped to rip off did not materialise. Fortunately, most curry restaurants remembered that they had to face their regulars from 1st January, and little rip-off was reported in the curry sector. One restaurateur is thankful to have made the right decision about the dreaded Dome. Initially Ranjit Mathrani was exasperated that his request to be the sole Indian restaurant on site had been overlooked for several months. He was forced to cobble together a business plan demanded at the last minute by the Dome. Against all odds he won the contract, and in November 1998 was making plans for a 2,000 meal per day operation. He was cock-a-hoop but, as the weeks and months went by, this joy turned to ash as more and more conditions were imposed upon him. Amongst a long list of impositions, he found that his contract could be terminated with just 10 days notice, that his menu was subject to debate, and above all that the Dome had ultimate say over hirings and firings. The writing for the events to come was clearly on the wall, and now we know that a bigger waste of money could not be envisaged. Public money is one thing, but with a potential personal £250,000 investment at risk, with no public subsidy, and nothing but bureaucrats producing crass rules, Mathrani cancelled the contract. Who's laughing now?

One of the most preposterous events concerns Nadim Butt of the TOP 100 Best Chef 1998 restaurant Shamaina, at 14 Brougham Street, Edinburgh, who has been given appalling operating restrictions by his local council planning department's officers and elected officials. In an attempt to expand his business, he sought planning permission to move to nearby premises across the road. His application has been refused on the grounds of 'bad neighbour usage' and 'excessive concentration of commercial uses'. Not only that, this same council has also imposed a new 8am–8pm operating hours restriction, if Butt were to move. I find this restriction incredible and unique to this council. According to our database, the average last-orders time around Britain (including Scotland) is 11–11.30pm. Far from being a bad neighbour, the Shamiana is welcomed for its quality by the locals. We hope that the issue is resolved by the time we are published, but mention it because decisions made by elected council planning departments are not always popular with their voters, and are by no means final. They can be appealed at the DETR. But above all, the real decision comes on polling day. Watch this space!

Currioke

Japanese businessmen Ohashi Sachiyo and Hiriyama Makato, owners of the Japanese manufacturers 'House of Food' astonished the world in general and India in particular, by filing a patent application [No. 06090838] claiming a world patent on the curry-making process. Not the first time such things have been attempted. India managed to prevent such a claim on turmeric, though the outcome of a similar US attempt to patent basmati rice is not settled, with the issue considerably muddled by US producer Rice Tec branding their rice 'Jasmati'. Much of this is patent opportunism, like internet squatting (*above*). In a limp face-saver, Makato said 'We were misquoted. We were trying to patent a food additive (ugh!! Ed) and not curry as a whole.' He then destroyed his argument by adding 'in any case the [curry-making process] patent would only have applied to our Japanese home products.' Ah, so!

Researchers at the University of Tokyo found that people who ate curry showed dramatic increases in blood flow to their brains. They also observed a rise in brain-wave activity in the area of the brain that governs vision and there are surprising indications that curry can help in cases of senile dementia. 'The effect of curry in raising blood flow was higher than any commercial medicines for senile dementia,' said JC Cyong, assistant professor at the University of Tokyo, who led the study. 'These results clearly showed that curry stimulates neural activity.' The results also suggest that, by activating the brain, curry may help raise the body's metabolism and influence immune and endocrine functions, he maintains.

The study was conducted on 12 healthy women aged 25–39 years old. Half of the women received curry soup. The other half, the control group, was given the same amount of rice porridge. Both the curry and porridge groups showed similar levels of blood pressure and oxygen saturation in their arteries. But 30 minutes after eating, women in the curry group showed dramatic rises in the level of blood flow to the brain – 10 to 20 percent – while no such change was detected in the control group. His group is planning to do a similar experiment on senior citizens involving the effect of curry on their quality of life.

'Curry can help relieve flu and colds,' says professor Ron Eccles, director of the Common Cold Centre at Cardiff University. 'Hot spices such as chilli and cummin, garlic and onion kill bacteria when eaten. The idea,' he says, 'is to promote saliva by stimulating the taste receptors, thus producing mucus in the nose and mouth, which is part of our natural protection against infection.' However, alcohol negates the effect, so the traditional pint should be avoided. Better have words with Cobra about that, Ron.

Cancer Research Campaign's Prof Gordon McVie has declared that an Indian diet of rice, veg and fruit is higher in roughage than its western counterpart and can help prevent bowel, heart and lung cancer. According to British biotech company Phytopharm, turmeric prevents cancer. Experiments with a new drug using turmeric oleoresin are very promising in inhibiting cancerous growth, say the company.

We're delighted that Tokyo University has just 'discovered' what India has known for ever. Did Tokyo refer to the identical research done in 1988 by Professor Prescott of Sydney University, or that done by Paul Bosland of New Mexico University in 1992? Or our own West Midlands Health Authority in 1996? Or the research by aforementioned Ron Eccles? Or indeed what the CurriNation's Curryholics have known for years.

Here are some of the year's antics:

Currindipidy

Bath's Nigel Bodman, 31, persuaded his local (the Desh, Lower Weston, Bath, to make a curry 10 times hotter than phal (it was boosted by copious naga chillies – *see* **A to Z of the Curry Menu**) in an attempt to get Nigel into *The Guinness Book of Records*. Guinness rejected the attempt on the grounds that it could be hazardous to health. Scientist Maureen Cooper, lecturer in Chemistry at Stirling University, has researched why 'bachelors' like eating the remains of the night-before's takeaway CTM for breakfast (the mind boggles). She reckons it's the tomato puree in the recipes which awakens the digestive juices. Couldn't be that the lads are just too bone idle to make something fresh, like toast, could it? Madras-mad Keith Dickinson has to have a morning-after breakfast fix. But he never seems to have enough left-over rice. His solution – he mixes cold Madras curry with Kellogg's Rice Crispies, and thus, he claims, delights in a Snap-Crackle-Hot Biriani. Maybe we should put Keith and Maureen together.

Ian Mirrelson was so nervous about his bridegroom speech that new bride Kim had local restaurant, The Jamuna, Pemberton, near Wigan, G Man, deliver a 'seriously hot' vindaloo right to the bridal breakfast table to 'calm Ian's nerves'. What, one wonders, did he need to sort him out on his wedding night? Phal practice maybe? Ask us in nine months time – it may bring a whole new meaning to home delivery service. Incidentally, Kim, you can now get married in an Indian restaurant. Gulu Anand, owner of Southall's Brilliant, is now a registrar, so get wed, get fed, get married, get curried. We've catered for a wedding ourselves. Suffolk's Tony and Jenny Stockman sealed the union with a six-course curry meal. Only two of the guests couldn't face curry, and we made them something different, but most adored it. Body builder Mark Nichols, 32, is having a go at becoming Mr Britain. Masala-mad Mark claims to visit his local, the Curry Centre, High Wycombe, Bucks once a week (is that all?) to eat a curry. Says Mark: 'It puts a fire in my belly and builds up my biceps.' The floor opened up, literally, at the Lahore Karahi, Harrow when the kitchen floor collapsed into a hitherto unknown basement, taking cookers, pots, pans and curry with them. Owner Fiaz Ansari was said to be Kormatose about it. Birmingham's Raj Bangladesh Cuisine Chef Noor Khan extinguished a cooker fire by pouring a large pan of yoghurt over it. Raita kind of cool thinking. Cunard's QE2 has 17 Indian chefs amongst its 140 kitchen brigade, but not one specialises in Indian cooking. They are all trained in continental cooking – one specialises in sauces and roasts, another in salads, another in patisserie, and so on. Pat Chapman's regular appearance as demonstrator and guest chef makes up for this deficiency. His curry lunch at sea between Malaysia and Bombay went down a storm (it was calm actually): 800 passengers (out of 1,200) forsook their assigned restaurants, and came to the self-service Lido restaurant to enjoy Pat's curry. Interesting international stuff, especially as most were Americans. By contrast, P&O's Oriana chefs had a curry-cooking contest which was won by Lester Carnello, who will enter this year's CIEH National Curry Chef contest at the Southampton area contest. Another example of an international culinary cross-over winner was brought to light by Judy and Richard in their 'This Morning' quest for the ITV chef of the year. Winner is Tony Singh, executive chef of the Royal Yacht *Britannia*, now permanently moored at Leigh Docks in Edinburgh. The ship's restaurant is open to all, but unlike Wali Udin's nearby Britannia Spice, don't expect Indian food from Singh. Like his QE2 counterparts, he is 'continental-trained' and his ITV winning dish was roasted leg of lamb with aubergine compote. 'I did throw in some curry powder (ugh), garlic, ginger and chillies,' he confessed.

Former chef at the Maharani, Sittingbourne, Kent, Yakuz Miah won £4.6m on the lottery. He apparently chose his numbers by using the most popular ordered items on the menu: onion bhajis (13), naan (17), CTM (25), lamb roghan josh (29), madras (45) and pullau rice (49). Having got over the shock of winning, Miah handed in his notice and retired to Sylhett a very rich man. Bet he's already bored! Gwent's Bombay Bicycle Club's chef Iftekhar Harris cooked a kangaroo curry in an attempt to weaken the Australian rugby team's winning resolve when they visited his restaurant prior to a match against Wales. Far from weakening them, the Aussies not only loved roo roghan, they asked for seconds, then the next day went on to beat Wales resoundingly, with a hop, skip and jumparooni. A mighty backfire that, isn't it, boyo?

German car maker BMW's heart-stopping crash of the Rover business was given a new slant with the news that one of their cars smashed through the window of Peterborough's Shah Jahan during a busy evening session. Fortunately no one was hurt. The driver said later he was not hoping to speed up collection of his takeaway. Like BMW , he apparently just lost control. Owner Mohammed Younis now keeps a watchful eye out of his window, wondering 'Who's coming-to dinner'.

Currivision

The BBC announced that they have sold Madhur Jaffrey to India. The English-trained actress, now full-time resident in New York, rarely visits the country of her birth, but her *Flavours of India* series has earned the Beeb £700,000. The series, screened in 1995, took Ms Jaffrey to many regions of India for its location shooting. Despite its photogenic backgrounds, the series did not fare as well as Madhur's previous *Indian Cooking* series, screened six times in the early 1980s. But in spite of numerous impassioned pleas from your editor, nothing, it seems, can convince the Beeb and ITV for that matter, that what the nation wants to see is a stonking good series on curries, as found at the nation's favourite waterholes up and down the country. Still, I'll keep trying. Incidentally, Delia continues to reign supreme, but despite being the best-seller of all time, I wish she'd keep off the ethnic. Her Thai recipes are more than somewhat lacking, and as for her leaning tower of 'doapiza' (*sic*) in Basics 2, I think she was referring to Do piaza, but you wouldn't recognise it from either her pronunciation or the recipe.

At least Delia tries, but perhaps it is the continual downmarketing of the nation's favourite food that seals curry's fate as a serious subject for a cooking series. The title of Channel Four's latest offering by Twenty Twenty Vision, *Argie Bargie*, gave one the sinking feeling that bad news was to follow, and sure enough, it did, picking on three unfortunate Wilmslow Road, Manchester restaurants – The Darbar, Lal Qila and Mughal. The equally unfortunate three groups of customers, mug enough to appear, were 1) lager louts, 2) enthusiasts made to look foolish and 3) foul-mouthed adolescent girls. Need I say more? Yes! Colleen Grove (editor of *Menu Magazine*) admitted that I had helped the programme researchers with statistics and venues. She bemoans the outcome in a well-written piece addressed to the trade and I concur with her sentiments exactly. Twenty Twenty Vision did indeed approach me for information. And, if I know TV researchers, not content with the hour-long free brain-picking session from me, during which they disregard my information in favour of their preconceived ideas, off they flit, without as much as 'can we reimburse you for your time?' let alone 'thank you', to the next 'source' (if not all and sundry).

Hardly a week goes by without my being approached by some earnest young researcher, working for peanuts for the giant, highly profitable TV companies. Indeed in the three days it has taken me to write this very intro in June 2000, I've had no less than three such approaches. A popular chat show wanted me to supply a list of curry eaters and restaurants and a family who eat vindaloo takeaways regularly. 'Oh, and where are the bad curry restaurants?' You can see where that one was going! *Changing Rooms* wanted me to suggest two neighbouring Indian restaurants wanting a make-over. I suggested that running a restaurant was a serious business, and only if they were desperate for publicity would restaurants allow the *Changing Rooms* mob in, rather than professional builders. That went down like a lead balloon, of course! But the researchers continue to ask. The third in as many days asked me to supply a list of curry-lovers who'd be willing to cook a curry dinner party and be filmed before, during and after for a proposed BBC TV series *Friends at Dinner*? The information they want would take me hours to locate, type and send. What I'm tempted to say is 'Look here, I'm not the NHS, paid for by the government. Think of me as a lawyer. You want information or help, and I'll charge you for it.' Mention the subject of a fee, and it's amazing how fast they all disappear, presumably to phone you, Colleen.

Balti appeared on the boards this spring when a play toured Britain to critical acclaim. *Balti Kings* is a play devised by the Tamasha Theatre company, set in a mythical restaurant in Birmingham's thriving Balti land, where Indian restaurants have reached saturation point. Curry wars abound with price-slashing, chef-poaching and style-mimicking being the order of day. Yahsin Anwar, the pioneer of Balti, and his sons, Shakeel and Shalab, are on the verge of being swallowed up by the mighty KK from Karachi Karahi Restaurant.

Curry appeared in print in more than one novel. *The Corpse at Haworth Tandoori* by Robert Barnard is a right spicy whodunnit. Set at a real Indian restaurant, West Yorks' Haworth Tandoori, Mill Hey Road, Haworth, Barnard not only got owner Fotik Miah's permission, he also held his book-launch party there. According to a new book, *Close to the Edge – the story of Yes,* while at the Manchester Free Trade Hall some years ago, Rick Wakeman decided he wanted a curry so badly, that a roadie was despatched to Wilmslow Road. Rick, unable to overcome his drooling, ate it on stage, mid-performance. Good job he isn't a wind player.

The latest Bond novel *High Time to Kill* (written under license by Raymond Benson) has 007 eating curry and drinking none other than Cobra Beer – neither shaken nor stirred, we trust. Scary Spice (Mel G) announced that the birth of daughter Phoenix was helped by copious curry eating, even while she was in labour. Ready-meal manufacturer Authentic Foods claimed a rise in sales at the supermarkets following Mel's amazing announcement. Scary, eh?

The Curryfree zone

Not everyone behaved correctly during the year, and some are enjoying a curry-free time at Her Majesty's pleasure. Katherine Barnes, 39, copped six months following her failed attempt to blackmail innocent members of a Carlisle curry house. In her defence, she claimed that staff had exposed themselves and invited her to lick ice cream off their genitals. It is reported that the police were keen to get the problem licked at once, and there was no shortage of volunteers to mount a surveillance operation. Funny how sex is never far from the headlines. Mohamed Aktar of Strood's Bengal Balti scored with his local media with the introduction of a Viagra Curry, served, he claims, only to male customers, made apparently from 'erect sausages'. I feel something there isn't politically correct! Heather Inns, 20, attempted to blackmail the owners of the Kashmir Balti House, Sparkhill, but failed when she posed as an Environmental Health Officer. She demanded an on-the-spot cash fine of £400 because a vegetable storage bin was left unlidded. However, canny Habib Malik was suspicious and performed a citizen's arrest. Ms Inns was fined by magistrates. Stephen Chamberlain was jailed after attempting to blackmail the Aagrah group for £50 per week 'protection' money to prevent an arson attack on the Aagrah Doncaster. Japan's Masumi Hayashi, 37, murdered four people by poisoning them with arsenic in their curry noodles. She denied this, of course, but was sent down nonetheless, also accused of fuelling a number of copy-cat killings in Japan. Brawling seems to attract certain politicians (reminds me of the good old Kinnock days with his more-than-one punch-up at his local Ealing curry house – remember?). Anyway, the Labour Party's conference in Llandudno hit the news when the *Mirror*'s political journalists, Don Mackay and Paul Starling came to blows over an argument which got out of hand (or is that fist?): £50 worth of damages were inflicted upon the innocent award-winning Bengal Dynasty in front of a full house of Labour gliteratti. Starling subsequently resigned over the issue.

Currybusiness

Café Spice Namaste's Cyrus Todiwalla has opened his Asian & Oriental School of Catering, in Upper Street Islington N1, and Thames Valley University opened theirs in St Mary's Road, Ealing.

National Curry Day raised many thousands of pounds for the Bangladeshi charity, Mother and Child, with hard-working restaurants producing the usual round of biggest and best. Faisal Chowdhury Veena Scholes Cleckheaton cooked the world's biggest bhaji (59.4kg/1.83m dia). For any one wishing to replicate or better this feat, it used 60kg onions, 20kg gram flour, 5 litres oil, 150 eggs, 5kg spices. Cabaret Angels, W Mids, made a naan 10m sq that covered a car park. Newcastle's Cuisine des Indus produced a chapatti at a mere 94cm diameter, while Spice Plaza, London, made a gigantic samosa.

The Curry and Oriental Restaurant Show at Wembley (May 99) flopped despite William Hague's opening and confessions that he liked curry and that his favourite local was in his home town in North Yorkshire. Cobra's 'Dave' ad campaign by Team Saatchi (Saatchi and Saatchi) won the FAB award for the Best Press Campaign for Alcoholic Drinks and the Best Press Campaign overall. Pat Chapman was declared Curry Personality of the Year at the BIBA Awards. The ridiculous EU ban on Bombay Duck was finally lifted.

Beleaguered M&S, presumably searching for alternative headlines, following their dismal profits declarations, and their extraordinary choice of name for their new chain of in-store coffee shops ('Revive') have announced that their research shows that the further south you go, the milder the curries. This, they say, indicates that northerners are 'harder' than southerners. (Could this have anything to do with the fact that their curry ready-meals are supplied by a multi-million pound company called Northern Foods? Indeed Northern Foods shares crashed following M&S poor results. This may not be fair since M&S's food is not the problem – its clothes are – but Northern supply 30% of M&S food.) M&S have been sending staff to India to research regional food (lucky them). Result: a chilli rating on the new range's packaging (wow, that's original). Incidentally, M&S say they sell 18 tonnes of CTM per month. S&A's Perween Warsi is Britain's richest Asian woman, helped no doubt by her deal with Shell petrol stations to supply 12 ready meals to 940 Shell forecourt shops. Shell discovered that 64% of the adult population prefer 'exotic' takeaways to traditional items (f&c); 66% say curry make them romantic mood; 10% of 18–29-year-olds find vindaloo eaters more attractive than mild curry eaters.

Meena Pathak is close behind: she was awarded Asian Woman of the Year award. Wali Udin JP (owner of Edinburgh's Verandah and Britannia Spice) has been made an honorary Doctor of Business Administration at Queen Margaret University, Edinburgh. First Great Western trains introduced CTM (supplied by Anwar Ali of Nahin Spice Centre, Cardiff) and Cobra beer to the buffet/ restaurant car menus. Richest Asians include Amin Ali (7m) and Charan Gill of the Harlequin Group. Overall richest is Lakshmi Mittal £2.2bn. And since biggest is best, at least according to Glasgow's Abdul Sattar, here is the ultimate record breaker: his Top 100 Café India restaurant seats 560 and Sattar claims it recently catered for 1,160 covers in one day.

Currywars

There are, it appears, no shortage of Restaurant Award Ceremonies and Chef Contests these days. There are almost as many different annual winners as there are certificates. Indian Restaurant of the Year shows include our own Curry Club Awards ceremony, which, I believe, pioneered the ceremony business back in 1991. Other ceremonies include Carlton TV Awards, the glamourous London ceremony, which has one Indian prize. It listed Sarkhels as best Indian in 1999 while this year it was Zaika with Quilon, Vama and Gifto's Lahore Kebab House, Southall, all short-listed. The *Evening Standard* Award went to Vama (previous winners Sitara and Raj Vogue, both N19). Trevor Gulliver won Best Restaurant with the non Indian St John. He also owns the Pukkabar, SW13 (relocated from Sydenham). The Booker Prize also got in on the act with the Excellence Awards which included Best Restaurant (The Aagrah) at their ceremony at the Hilton, London, in April.

As for Chef Contests, we mentioned ITV's Chef of the Year earlier. Viresh Patel, 15, won the Junior Masterchef Midlands heat with a curry meal. The CIEH Curry Chef contest is being sponsored by Patak and held in Harrogate. The 1999 winner was Tabaq's Manzoor Ahmed. *Harpers'* magazine Young Restaurant Manager of the Year 2000 award has Jabbar Khan of Shanee restaurant Birmingham on the shortlist.

Sumit Malik (Noon's chef) was crowned International Chef of the Year Feb 1999 and Chef Shamin Syed of the Durbar, W2, won it for 2000. Syed found the aftermath of winning can have its downside. He's been at the Durbar for two decades, indeed, his prize-winning Oriental Chicken dish has been on the menu for over 15 years. It's the sort of restaurant we all love – a bog-standard formula place of long standing. As *Evening Standard* restaurant critic Fay Maschler pointed out it isn't (until now) listed in this *Guide*. Many similar restaurants aren't. Anyway, post-win, Syed was described as a 'Standard bearer for the 21st century'. No, I don't understand it either, but I don't think it was a pun on 'standard'. *The Times* elevated his status to that of Marco Pierre White or Gordon Ramsay – if that is elevation, poor chap. You won't find anyone more affable. Fay Maschler trotted in a few days later, but was far from pleased, vowing you'd get better food from the Royal Navy chef runner up, Kevin Williams. Rule Britannia! But therein lies the problem. Including the BBC Mega Mela contest last November (winner Miff, 23, chef partner winner of Salaam, George Street, Warminster, Wilts) and the two new proposed Ethnicity contests due this autumn, there are no fewer than five annual Indian Chef Contests and six Restaurant of the Year contests. With all of them heralded as the 'ultimate' that's a lot of ultimate chefs and restaurants. The problem is similar to the Eurovision Song Contest. Do you dare to enter? (The BBC Mega Mela contest attracted only four entrants, and it is not alone in such paucity.) Not only do the entrants risk not winning – even if they do win, they risk their reputation at the hands of the media. It also has the potential to create a bitter war as to which ceremony/award caries the most prestige. I suppose it's the same in every industry, but too much can be confusing to the public, and all it achieves is to devalue everything.

Curryfree Guides

The mainstream food guides remain virtually curry free and at best refuse to acknowledge that Indian food can be as sublime as French cuisine. Quite why British chefs are so in awe of French Michelin escapes me. Michelin conspicuously fails yet again, to give our Indian restaurants the accolade they deserve. Not one got a single rosette, let alone two or three. Chutney Mary, Quilon's, the Bombay Brasseie and Sarkhel's don't get mentioned. Fay Maschler was right when she said 'Michelin inspectors don't have a clue when it comes to any cuisine east of Venice'. Maybe it's time for more chefs to join Marco and Nico in asking to be excluded. Maybe even Gordon would calm down if he did the same, instead of being so, well, Ramsayish about wanting three stars.

At least the *AA* gives Zaika three rosettes – the first time for an Indian restaurant. *AA* Chief Inspector David Young rather pompously said 'this award takes restaurants into the big league' [something the *Cobra Good Curry Guide* has been doing for Indian restaurants since 1984]. But even if it has taken the *AA* this long to get there, the move must be applauded. Before we recommend that David goes back on the beat, at least it's a start, particularly when he continues so enthusiastically: 'We've seen over the last five years, that your typical formula curry house is making way for innovative cooks trying to do more authentic and imaginative dishes.' The *2000 Good Food Guide*'s Jim Ainsworth was equally enthusiastic about Zaika, naming it one of the Restaurants of the Year and he also names London's Barbur, New Tayab, Old Delhi and Soho Spice (all long-term entrants in our *Guide*) as well. Square Meal's Mark de Wessleo names Zaika and Café Spice Namaste as two-star venues (high ratings) recommended for business lunches. *Time Out* appears to be far more critical of formula curries this year, which is probably a good thing. If only the Bangladeshi sector would offer real food, instead of, or, if you prefer, as well as, the onion gravy-pot standards, then *Time Out* would have less to carp about and maybe even Michelin would sit up. However, I do have one gripe about *Time Out* (*see* page 9).

Whatever these *Guides* list this year, you can be sure that we've been there and done it in this *Guide*, with, of course, the help of you, our readers. After all, who else can the other *Guides* trust?

Cobra Beer

Karan Bilimoria, the man behind Cobra Indian Beer, has a passion for good beer and good Indian food. Horrified with fizzy, bloating Euro-lagers he decided to develop an Indian lager which perfectly complemented curry. That was ten years ago. Today Cobra Beer is the biggest selling bottled Indian lager in the UK and has been ranked in the Sunday Times Virgin Atlantic Fast Track 100, the definitive list of the one hundred fastest growing companies in the country.

Born in Bangalore, Cobra is double filtered and less gassy, creating an extra smooth brew that allows one to eat more. Cobra is stocked in the majority of Indian restaurants and for take-home sales it is also available in Tesco, Safeway, Asda, Waitrose, Morrison's, Europa, Cullens and Budgens. Cobra can also be found at Harrods, Selfridges, Terrence Conran's Bluebird Foodmarket and nation-wide in Victoria Wine Cellars, Bottoms Up, Threshers Wine Shop, Victoria Wine, Haddows, Drinks Cabin, Wine Rack, Martha's Vineyard, The Firkin Off Licence, Drinks Direct, Hutton's, Home Run and other independent off licences and grocers.

Introducing Swift Lager

Cobra Beer is proud to announce the launch of a new, lighter bodied, draught lager to accompany Indian cuisine. Swift Lager is a 3.8% abv quality lager that has been specially brewed for people who want a lighter bodied drink but who don't want to compromise on quality or taste. Swift Lager is anything but a standard lager. Swift Lager is refreshingly smooth and less gassy, which makes it the perfect accompaniment to Indian cuisine and it is also very refreshing, very thirst quenching and very drinkable.

The perfect **Wine** to accompany Indian Cuisine

General Bilimoria

Lt. General F.N. Bilimoria, PVSM, ADC, affectionately known as General Billy, was commissioned into the 2nd Battalion of the 5th Gurkha Rifles (Frontier Force), a battalion that won three Victoria Crosses in the Second World War. Two of the VC holders served with the General, who later rose to General Officer Commander-in-Chief in the Indian Army. He can remember the days when, as a young officer, only the finest French wines were served in the officers' messes.

After he retired the General commissioned his son, the founder of Cobra Beer, to find a wine to complement Indian cuisine. Following a dedicated world-wide search on his father's behalf, he found something very special – two extra smooth, finely balanced wines, which taste as good on their own as they do with spicy food.

Both wines are from the Languedoc region of France. The red is a Merlot – a rich wine with soft and plummy flavours, and underlying tannins providing the structure required for a wine of this type, with a good length on the finish. The white is a Terret-Sauvignon blend, with the Terret providing a smooth, rich, peachy base, while the Sauvignon adds herbaceous aromas and a citrus fruit lift on the finish. They are exported to the world (and to General Bilimoria) by Cobra Beer.

Swift Lager, General Bilimoria and Cobra Beer are distributed by Cobra Beer Ltd., 21 *The Coda Centre,* 189 *Munster Road, London,* SW6 6AW.

If you would like more information about any of the Cobra brands, please call their head office on freephone 0800 146 5300. *Tel:* 020 7385 5300. *Fax:* 020 7385 2474.

email: cobrabeer@cobrabeer.com

Or visit their websites: www.cobrabeer.com, www.generalbillys.com or www.swiftlager.com.

Our TOP 100 Restaurants and Award Winners

Only one in every eight of the nation's curry restaurants achieve entry into this *Guide*, so by definition they are all top restaurants and a cut above the remaining 7,000.

But, naturally, we are always asked to identify the best of the best, so to speak. And it is true that there is an élite of really excellent restaurants including, by definition, those establishments about which we receive many consistently good reports. We first introduced such a list in 1987 (as our TOP 30). In our next edition we expanded the list to our TOP 100 restaurants. A decade on, with restaurant numbers increasing and standards improving, we find ourselves unable to contain our TOP 100 list to an exact 100. In fact we've not done so in last two editions. This time the total is somewhat in excess, but TOP 100 is a *Curry Club/Guide* brand name, understood by the public and the restaurants alike, so for now, it stands.

As ever, this year there has been change. Sixteen have been demoted from the list, two as the result of closure for financial reasons, Jehangir SE26 and Zujumas SW19, and three resulting from ownership change. Eleven have lost their TOP 100 cachet because of a decline in performance. Fortunately, from the many you have brought to our attention, we are able to promote a remarkable 49 'new' entrants (indicated *) to the list. Some are indeed new, although some are long-established. Seven are previous TOP 100 entrants, returning after receiving many good reports this year (indicated •).

The *Guide's* editors and researchers visit TOP 100 restaurants (or nominees) anonymously whenever we can, but it's impossible to go to them all within one year. We also need several detailed excellent reports about the restaurant concerned, including at least one by one of our 60 or so prolific regular reporters. Anyone is free to send us such a report. The criteria to confirm or nominate a TOP 100 are largely instinctive, but it is essential that you have had a flawless occasion. Venue cleanliness, customer care and food must be exemplary. Think of it as a recommendation to a friend – would it stand up to their unsentimental, critical gaze? So if you feel we have missed a restaurant you believe to be a TOP 100, it may be just a case of telling us. And if you feel a restaurant no longer deserves to remain in our TOP 100 list, we also need your views. There is a further, even more élite list, the cream of the cream, where everything is as good as it get. Winners of our National Awards are highlighted in bold capitals. For the record, all previous award winners are also indicated, because, as with the Oscars, once a restaurant becomes an an Award winner, it remains an Award winner.

London

E1	**CAFÉ SPICE NAMASTÉ** (BEST CHEF 1992/5 & 1996/8. CULINARY EXCELLENCE 2001)
	SHAMPAN (BEST BANGLADESHI 2001)
	*Tiffin Indian
E14	***MEMSAHEB ON THAMES (MOST PROMISING NEWCOMER 2001)**
	*Tabla
EC1	*City Café Lazeez
EC2	*Shimla Pinks
N3	**RANI (BEST VEGETARIAN 2001)**
N6	Kiplings
N16	Rasa Vegetarian
N21	***JIM THOMPSON'S THAI (BEST ETHNIC PUB CHAIN 2001)**
NW1	DIWANA BHEL POORI HOUSE (BEST VEGETARIAN 1995/1998)
	GREAT NEPALESE (BEST NEPALESE 2001)
NW4	**PRINCE OF CEYLON (BEST SRI LANKAN 2001)**
NW5	Bengal Lancer
NW6	*Geeta South Indian
	*Vijay
SE1	*Bengal Clipper
SE13	Spice of Life
SE23	Babur Brasserie
SE24	*Three Monkeys
SW1	***QUILON'S (BEST IN UK 2001)**
	Saloos
	•Woodlands Vegetarian
SW3	*Haandi
	Tandoori of Chelsea
	***ZAIKA (MOST INNOVATIVE CHEF 2001)**
SW5	Star of India
SW6	Nayab
SW7	BOMBAY BRASSERIE (BEST IN UK 1995/7)
	*Café Lazeez
	*Memories of India
	*Shezan Indian
SW10	CHUTNEY MARY (BEST IN UK 1991/4 AND 1999/2000)
	*Saffron
	*Vama The Indian Room
SW11	*Cafe Spice Namaste
SW12	**TABAQ (BEST PAKISTANI** 1998/99, 1999/2000 and **2001)**
SW15	Ma Goa
SW17	Jaffna House
	*Radha Krishna Bhavan
	Sree Krishna

SW18	**SARKHELS (BEST NEWCOMER 1999/2000, BEST INDIAN 2001)**
W1	Anwars
	*Café Lazeez
	Caravan Serai Afghan
	CHOR BIZARRE (BEST NORTH INDIAN 2001)
	•Gaylord
	LA PORTE DES INDES (BEST INDIAN AND BEST IN UK 1998/9)
	Ragam South Indian
	*Rasa South Indian
	*Rasa Samudra
	TAMARIND (BEST NEWCOMER 1995/97, BEST INDIAN 1998/9 BEST CHEF 1999/2000)
	VEERASWAMY (BEST NEWCOMER 1998/9)
	•Woodlands
	*Yatra
W2	Bombay Palace
	Khans
	Old Delhi
W5	*Clay Oven
	Monty's
W8	Malabar
W13	SIGIRI (BEST SRI LANKAN,1998/99 & 1999/2000)
WC1	MALABAR JUNCTION (BEST SOUTH INDIAN 1999/2000)
	Mandeer Vegetarian
WC2	INDIA CLUB (SPECIAL AWARD WINNER 1995/97)
	*Mela
	PUNJAB (BEST NORTH INDIAN 1999/2000)

England

BERKSHIRE

Cookham	*Malik's
Theale	CAFE BLUE COBRA (BEST IN THE WEST 1995/7)
Wokingham	*Sultan Balti Palace

BRISTOL

Bristol Centre	RAJDOOT (BEST RESTAURANT CHAIN 1991/4 & 1995/7)

BUCKINGHAMSHIRE

Milton Keynes	JAIPUR (BEST RESTAURANT OUTSIDE LONDON)
Woburn Sands	*Jalori
Newport Pagnell	*Mysore

KEY

*New entrant to TOP 100 •Return to TOP 100 † Branch of similarly named restaurant(s)

CAPITALS – PREVIOUS AWARD WINNER **BOLD CAPITALS** – CURRENT AWARD WINNER

CHESHIRE	
Ellesmere Port	(THE) TAJ OF AGRA FORT (BEST IN THE NORTH 1998/9)
DORSET	
Poole	Rajasthan
ESSEX	
Ilford GL	Curry Special
	Jalalabad
HAMPSHIRE	
Fleet	GURHKA SQUARE (BEST NEPALESE 1998/9)
Liss	Madhuban
Port Solent	*Indian Palace
HERTFORDSHIRE	
Abbots Langley	Viceroy of India
St Albans	Mumtaj
KENT	
Bromley GL	TAMASHA (BEST IN THE SOUTH 1998/99)
Chislehurst GL	•Bengal Lancer
Folkestone	The India
Halstead	*Bengal Mangrove
Welling GL	Tagore
Westerham	*Pitts Cottage
	*Tulsi
LANCASHIRE	
Adlington	Sharju
	*Polash
LEICESTERSHIRE	
Leicester	**CURRY FEVER (BEST IN THE MIDLANDS 2001)**
	Friends Tandoori
LINCOLNSHIRE	
Boston	•Star of India
MANCHESTER (GTR)	
Atherton (M46)	Savar
Manchester	Gaylord
MERSEYSIDE	
Liverpool	**GULSHAN (BEST IN THE NORTH 1999/2000 & 2001)**
MIDDLESEX	
Southall	BRILLIANT (BEST PUNJABI RESTAURANT 1998/9)
	MADHU'S BRILLIANT (**SPECIAL AWARDS 1991-2000**)
	Omi's
Twickenham	*Pallavi South Indian
Wembley	Chetna's Bhel Puri
	Clay Oven
	Curry Craze
	•Woodlands

NORTHUMBERLAND

Berwick	*Magna
Corbridge	THE VALLEY (BEST IN THE NORTH 1995/7)

NOTTINGHAMSHIRE

Nottingham	Chand
	Saagar

OXFORDSHIRE

Oxford	Aziz

SOMERSET

Bath	(The) Eastern Eye

STAFFORDSHIRE

Kingsley Holt	Thornbury Hall Rasoi
Lichfield	Eastern Eye

SUFFOLK

Woodbridge	Royal Bengal

SURREY

Croydon	*Planet Spice
Epsom	Le Raj
Oxted	GURKHA KITCHEN (BEST NEPALESE 1999/2000)
Woking	Jaipur

SUSSEX

Worthing	Ma'hann

TYNE & WEAR

Gateshead	The Last Days of the Raj
Newcastle	Sachins
	VALLEY JUNCTION 397 (MOST ORIGINAL 1999/2000)
	Vujon

WARWICKSHIRE

Kenilworth	*The Coconut Lagoon

WEST MIDLANDS

Birmingham	MAHARAJAH (BEST IN THE MIDLANDS 1998/9 & 1999/2000)
	ADIL 1 (BEST BALTI HOUSE 1999)
	ROYAL NAIM (BEST BALTI HOUSE1995-98)
Coventry	*Monsoon
Solihull	*Rajnagar International

WILTSHIRE

Swindon	*Rafu's Tandoori

WORCESTERSHIRE

Worcester	*Monsoon
	*Spice Cuisine

KEY

*New entrant to TOP 100 •Return to TOP 100 † Branch of similarly named restaurant(s)

CAPITALS – PREVIOUS AWARD WINNER **BOLD CAPITALS** – CURRENT AWARD WINNER

NORTH YORKSHIRE

Skipton	†AAGRAH (BEST RESTAURANT CHAIN, 1998/99 &1999/2000)
Tadcaster	†AAGRAH (BEST RESTAURANT CHAIN, 1998/99 &1999/2000)
York	*Jinnah

SOUTH YORKSHIRE

Doncaster	†AAGRAH (BEST RESTAURANT CHAIN, 1998/99 &1999/2000)
Sheffield	*Ashoka
	Nirmal's

WEST YORKSHIRE

Garforth	†AAGRAH (BEST RESTAURANT CHAIN, 1998/99 &1999/2000)
Leeds	Darbar
	•Polash
Pudsey	†AAGRAH (BEST RESTAURANT CHAIN, 1998/99 &1999/2000)
Shipley	†AAGRAH (BEST RESTAURANT CHAIN, 1998/99 &1999/2000)
Wakefield	†AAGRAH (BEST RESTAURANT CHAIN 1998/99 &1999/2000)

Scotland

FIFE

St Andrews	NEW BALAKA BANGLADESHI (BEST IN SCOTLAND 1995/7. BEST BANGLADESHI 1999/2000)

LOTHIAN

Edinburgh	Far Pavillion
	Lancers Brasserie
	SHAMIANA (BEST CHEF 1998/99)
	Verandah
Leith	**BRITANNIA SPICE (BEST IN SCOTLAND 2001)**
	GULNAR'S PASSAGE TO INDIA (BEST IN SCOTLAND 1999/2000)

STRATHCLYDE

Glasgow	THE ASHOKA (BEST IN SCOTLAND 1998/99)
	*Ashoka at the Mill
	Café India
	*La Creme de la Creme
	*Koh-i-noor
	*Mister Singh's India
	*Murphy's Pakora Bar
	•Shish Mahal

Wales

CLWYD

Colwyn Bay	**† BENGAL DYNASTY (BEST IN WALES 2001 – THIRD TIME)**

GLAMORGAN

Cardiff	JUBRAJ 2 (BEST IN WALES 1999/2000)
Swansea	Moghul Brasserie

GWYNEDD

Llandudno	**† BENGAL DYNASTY (BEST IN WALES 2001 – THIRD TIME)**

KEY

*New entrant to TOP 100 •Return to TOP 100 † Branch of similarly named restaurant(s)

CAPITALS – PREVIOUS AWARD WINNER **BOLD CAPITALS** – CURRENT AWARD WINNER

Wolfe on Wine

Geography versus variety

The geography of wine is a simple matter. A wine's place of origin used to be a reliable (well, usually) guide to its character. Most older generation wine drinkers knew (roughly) where Beaujolais and Chablis were from, and how they tasted. But few had heard of their Gamay or Chardonnay grape types. Today there are many varietals – wines named for their grapes – and even the French may soon change their current policy, that varieties must not be named on labels of *appellation controlleé* wines from classic regions.

Variety is much more dependable than geography in defining the style of a wine, but it is not always entirely accurate, because of mis-identification, or incorrect naming, of the variety (*see* Sauvignon in Chile, and Gamay in the US). Variety is now the first thing to consider when choosing wines to accompany Indian food because of its particular demands. This A-Z of varieties is a short list of names most likely to appear on the label, or descriptive back label. It excludes many countries' indigenous grapes some of which are particularly well matched with Indian food. We name few Portuguese grapes for example, because the rest mean little in the wider world, and are unlikely to be on the label.

WHITE WINE GRAPES

Aligoté The second grape (far behind Chardonnay) of white Burgundy. It makes fruity light wines with a crisp balancing acidity. It should be the basis of the Kir apéritif made by adding a little Crème de cassis, or black-currant liqueur, to the wine.

Alvarinho (Portuguese) makes the best Vinho Verdes. Across the Spanish border in Galicia it becomes Albariño and makes fine fruity dry wines.

Chardonnay is the world's favourite fine white wine grape. Its home is Burgundy where the great Chablis and Cote de Beaune wines exhibit its deep, rich flavour sometimes described as 'vegetal' or 'cabbagey'. The flavour is often complemented by the taste of oak from barrels of that wood (or more commonly today by oak chips, or planks, put in the wine).

Chenin Blanc comes from the Anjou-Touraine region of the Loire where it makes wines ranging from ordinary to superlative. It is the basis of Vouvray which can be either still or sparkling, and dry to ultra-sweet. Pleasant but unambitious medium-dry Chenin now comes from Australia, New Zealand and California. In South Africa it is called Steen and ranges from decent basic dryish wine to intensely sweet.

Colombard which makes thin wines for distillation into Cognac and Armagnac, also makes acceptable light, dry vin de pays des Cotes de Gascogne.

Furmint is one of two main varieties used for the Hungarian dessert wineTokay, and increasingly for strong dryish table wine.

Gewürztraminer There is no real difference between this and plain Traminer. The prefix *gewürz* is German for 'spice' and refers to its aromatic smell and a taste more accurately compared to that of lichees. The makers of Gewürztraminer have long traded on the word 'spicy', and say that it goes particularly well with Indian and all oriental food. In our opinion it does not – this 'happy marriage' is purely verbal. Gewürztraminer wines are usually medium-dry, quite heavy and highly alcoholic. They have spread from their home in Alsace to Germany, Italy, eastern Europe and the New World.

Grüner Veltliner (Austria), often called plain Veltliner, make pale greenish, crisp, dry, fruity wines best drunk young.

Macabeo or Maccabeo is a main constituent of white Rioja under the name Viura and in Penedes is used to make cava.

Malvasia The Malmsey of Madeira appears in central Italy, many European countries and occasionally in the New World. Its table wines are soft, dark and smoky.

Manseng, Petit and Gros The main grapes of Juranon in south-west France usually make medium dry wines of delicious floral character. Just beginning to escape to other regions.

Marsanne A main grape of the northern Rhone where its wines include Hermitage and its neighbours.

Melon de Bourgogne The Muscadet grape, now confirmed as descended from Chardonnay.

Muscat A family of grapes producing wines with a scent not unlike roses, and a taste of grapes – which is surprisingly rare in wine. It produces sweet wines all over the world. In Spain it is Moscatel, in Italy Moscato where its wines include Asti Spumante. French Muscats include the popular Beaumes de Venise and the usually dry, delicate, Alsace Muscats.

Palomino The basic grape of Sherry, it can make pleasant if unexciting dry, slightly fruity table wine.

Pinot Blanc Often confused with Chardonnay but makes less fruity, less powerful wines. Rare as a varietal except in Alsace, where it is lighter, but much less expensive than Pinot Gris.

Pinot Gris is another important Alsace varietal where it is often called Tokay or Tokay-Pinot Gris. But this has no connection with Hungarian Tokay. It also appears in northern Italy and under various pseudonyms in Hungary and other central European countries. Rare in the New World.

Rkatsiteli A Russian grape of little merit, other than the entertainment it provides in trying to pronounce it.

Riesling (pronounced *rees-ling*, not *ryes-ling*) is the great grape of Germany, also the noblest of Alsace varietals. Often found in other countries, but often confused with less noble varieties including Welsch, Olasz, Gray and Emerald Rieslings. Its characteristic aromas and tastes, in wines varying from dry to richly sweet, maintain its wide popularity despite the unfashionableness of German wine. Its qualities are increasingly recognised in the New World, especially Australia.

Roussanne accompanies Marsanne in the northern Rhone and nearby areas. It is more delicate with a distinctive herby nose.

Sauvignon Blanc The distinctive aroma and flavour are sometimes compared to gooseberry or unflatteringly to cat's pee. Pure Sauvignon wines are normally dry, as in that odd varietal from northern Burgundy, Sauvignon de St Bris; but more famously in Loire wines, especially Sancerre and Pouilly Fumé. The latter is sometimes used as an alternative name for the grape especially in California. It is also found in the New World, notably in New Zealand whose acclaimed Cloudy Bay has a reputation rivalling that of Sancerre. Sauvignon is often used with Sémillon especially in Bordeaux where this blend makes great dry white Graves as well as the intensely sweet, yet subtle wines of **Sauternes and Barsac.** Much Chilean 'Sauvignon' is not the true Sauvignon Blanc but other less favoured and less flavoured varieties.

Sémillon See above for its use with Sauvignon in Bordeaux. As a single varietal it is most often seen in Australia (where it loses the accent on the 'e' and is pronounced sem-il-on). The rich smell and opulent dry flavour are (usually) pleasantly reminiscent of wool or lanolin.

Terret-Sauvignon The blend used in *Cobra's General Bilimoria* white *(see page* 26). Terret provides a smooth, rich, peachy base, while the Sauvignon adds herbaceous aromas and a citrus fruit lift on the finish.

Tokay or Tocai are alternative names in Alsace and Italy for the Pinot Gris (Pinot Grigio). But in north-western Italy, Tocai Friulano is a different grape. None are connected with Hungarian Tokay wine.

Trebbiano (Italy) By quantity probably the world's most important grape, identical to Ugni Blanc. It makes quite ordinary light, usually dry wine.

Ugni Blanc French synonym for Trebbiano, used extensively in s-west France but with good reason rarely credited on labels. Much is distilled into brandy.

Verdelho A Madeira grape also found as a western Australian varietal, fine and delicately fruity-winey.

Vernaccia No connection, as libellously asserted, with varnish, but a whole family of Italian grapes. The best known wine is Vernaccia di San Gimignano.

Viognier Until recently the ultra-rare grape of flowery, lightly winey, heavily expensive, Condrieu in the northern Rhone. It now appears as a varietal in southern France, California and . . . where next?

RED WINE GRAPES

Barbera Originally from the Italian north-west, Barbera is now seen in California and Argentina.

Cabernet Franc Now proved to be the ancestor of Cabernet Sauvignon, it is most important in the western Loire where it is the sole or main grape of Chinon, Bourgueuil, Saumur-Champigny, Anjou Villages wines. In the clarets of St Emilion and Pomerol in the Bordeaux region it is more important than Cabernet Sauvignon. Also found in other areas including north and south

America, although rarely as a single varietal. The word 'Cabernet' on a label may mean either Cabernet Franc or Cabernet Sauvignon or a blend of both.

Cabernet Sauvignon Fine reds from all over the wine world are based on this grape. In Bordeaux, its spiritual home, it is blended with Merlot, Malbec, Cabernet Franc and others to makes the great wines of the Médoc. Few of these archetypal clarets carry any indication of their grapes, whereas in California, Australia, South America and elsewhere the presence of Cabernet Sauvignon is normally emblazoned on the label. Its taste and its aroma are reminiscent of blackcurrants, and its subtlety is unsurpassed.

Cinsaut or **Cinsault** Eastern Med grape used in north Africa and southern France. Its solid, four-square wines are of little interest. Its one distinction is that it is a parent of Pinotage.

Dolcetto makes lightish, easy-drinking wines from districts around Alba in Piedmont, north-west Italy.

Gamay In various parts of central France this grape produces light, fresh, fruity quaffing wines. But only in Beaujolais, which uses no other grape, does it fully express its charming character. So called 'Gamay' in California is hardly ever the true Gamay, and is usually not even related.

Garnacha or Grenache Originally Spanish, it is important in Rioja and other northern Spanish regions. Under its French name it is a major component of Rhone wines, where its powerful, sometimes over-heavy style calls for, and receives the refinement of Grenache to balance it.

Lambrusco and many sub-varieties in central Italy produce the semi-sparkling wine of the same name.

Malbec A minor Bordeaux grape but gaining favour as a varietal in Chile and especially in Argentina.

Mavrud Indigenous Bulgarian grape making soft, even plummy wines, regarded as that country's best but not for long keeping.

Merlot The second grape of Bordeaux, but the first in St Emilion and Pomerol. Its wines are softer and quicker developing than Cabernet Sauvignon and fuller flavoured. It is widely used in Argentina and in Chile where it vies with Cabernet Sauvignon. Merlot's characteristics make it, in this writer's opinion, the ideal choice with most Indian food. Merlot is, not surprisingly, the grape used in *Cobra's General Bilimoria* red wine. (*see page* 26).

Montepulciano A town as well a grape. The town's wine, Vino Nobile di Montepulciano, is mainly made from the Sangiovese of Chianti fame. The grape is widely used in central Italy, and in the Abruzzo is known as Montepulciano d'Abruzzo. But it makes more distinguished wines in the Marche and Emilia-Romagna.

Mourvedre Originating in Provence, used in Chateauneuf-du-Pape and many other southern French areas, and widely in Spain under its Spanish name Monastrell. It is beginning to appear as a varietal, especially in the Languedoc. The wines are strong in alcohol and tannin and the powerful flavour is sometimes described as gamey.

Nebbiolo Produces classic Barolo and Barbaresco of Piedmont in north-west

Italy. Its wines are strong and the high tannin content means they greatly benefit from long maturation.

Petit Verdot A minor Bordeaux variety, occasionally a New World varietal.

Pinot Meunier Unimportant except in Champagne where it is the third grape after Chardonnay and Pinot Noir.

Pinot Noir One of the great red varieties, its original home is Burgundy. The finesse and elegance of the best is matched by a glorious depth of flavour which has an affinity with the tangy 'sweetness' of well-hung game. Difficult to grow but sometimes succeeds in Australia (especially Western Australia) and New Zealand. Californian can be fine (especially Carneros) but some of the best Pinot Noirs outside Burgundy are from Oregon.

Pinotage One of the few varieties whose origin is fully documented, this South African cross between Cinsaut and Pinot Noir was made in 1925. It combines the burly character of the former with some of the delicacy of the latter. Sometimes reminiscent of Australian Shiraz, although it can be rather thin. A good one goes well with curry.

Sangiovese The basic grape of Chianti. The famous 'Super-Tuscans' are mostly made by including other grapes, notably Cabernet Sauvignon, to add roundness. Some would say Chianti is too delicate to go with Indian food – except for milder curries and tandooris.

Syrah This northern Rhone variety appears in such classic wines as Hermitage and in Chateauneuf-du-Pape further south. It is also an important varietal in southern France. In Australia it is called Shiraz and is successful both as a single varietal, and in blends with Cabernet Sauvignon or other grapes. It makes noble wines in the Barossa Valley, and is the sole grape of the classic Australian Grange Hermitage.

Tarrango A cross between Portuguese Touriga and the Sultana (aka Thompson Seedless table grape). In Australia it makes a soft, easy drinking would-be 'Beaujolais'.

Tempranillo As well being the main grape of Rioja, it is extensively planted in other parts of Spain and in Argentina.

Tinta Barroca Portuguese Port grape makes a dark, strong, red varietal in South Africa.

Touriga Nacional The only other well-known name in Portuguese grapes is a major constituent of Port, and sometimes a deeply powerful red table wine, superb with Indian food.

Vranac Powerful dry red from Montenegro in former Yugoslavia stands up well to Indian spicing.

Zinfandel California's 'national' grape, now believed to be the Primitivo of southern Italy, is rare elsewhere. Its wines are made in many styles – some like Port, others as 'Blush wine' sweetish rosés. But more usually it is like a fruity, pleasantly acid, distant relation of the claret family.

David Wolfe, our regular wine expert, writes for wine magazines and gourmet guides. He is also a specialist consultant to ethnic restaurants which need advice on their wine list selection and wine descriptions.

The Cuisine of the Subcontinent

Afghan Afghanistan's location had always held the strategic key to India until this century, for it was through the solitary mountain passes that the invaders came and possessed India from as early as 3000 BC. Located between Iran (formerly Persia) and Pakistan (formerly NW India), it brought the cuisine of the Middle East to India – and that of India to the Middle East. Afghan food features Kebabs and Birianis, and skewered spiced lamb over charcoal. The only UK Afghan restaurants are Caravan Serai, London W1 and Afghan Kitchen, London N1.

Balti In the high mountains of north Pakistan is the ancient state of Baltistan, sharing its border with China and India's Kashmir, and once on the Spice Route to China. These days, with Pakistan and India in a permanent state of war, the few roads connecting the two countries are permanently closed. Little may have been known about Balti food outside its indigenous area, had it not been for a small group of Pakistani Kashmiris, who settled in east Birmingham in the 1960s. There, they opened small cafés in the back streets, serving curries made aromatic with Kashmiri Garam Masala, and herbs, with plentiful coriander, in two-handled pots called the 'karahi' in India, but known here as the 'Balti pan'. Eating with no cutlery, using fingers and bread to scoop up the food, is the norm to the community, but a revelation to Birmingham's white population, who made Balti their own.

Bangladeshi/Bengali Most of the standard curry houses in the UK are owned by Bangladeshis and nearly all of those serve standard formula curries (from mild to very hot). Bangladesh, formerly East Pakistan, is located at the mouth of the River Ganges. Before Partition, the area either side of the Ganges was Bengal. Today Bengal is the Indian state that shares its border with Bangladesh. Bangladesh is Muslim, so pork is forbidden. The area enjoys prolific fresh and seawater fish – pomfret, boal, ruhi, hilsa and ayre, and tiger prawns – and specialises in vegetable dishes such as Shartkora and Niramish. Until recently, true Bangladeshi/Bengali cuisine was nigh on impossible to find in the UK. Hopefully we will find more and more of our Bangladeshi restaurants serving the delights of their own country.

Bombay Bombay curries are mellow and light and, although a favourite restaurant dish, Bombay Potato (*see page* 42) is not found as such in Bombay, but it is typical of Bombay tastes. Also in the glossary are Bombay Duck, presently banned from the UK, Bombay Mix, re-invented under this name in Southall in the 1970s. Bhel Puri, also in the glossary, is Bombay's favourite kiosk food, most famously available at the city's Chowpatti beachand now found in the Bhel Puri houses in Drummond Street, Wembley, and other places around London. It is served cold and is delicious. Most of India's Parsees (q.v), with their distinctive food, live in Bombay.

Burmese Burma, now renamed Myanmar, shares its boundaries with Bangladesh, India, China, Laos and Thailand. Its food is a combination of these styles. Rice is the staple and noodles are popular too. The curries are very hot and there are no religious objections to eating pork, beef or other meats. Duck and seafood are commonly eaten. The only UK Burmese restaurant is the Mandalay, London W2.

Goan Goa is on the west coast of India, about 400 miles south of Bombay. It was established in 1492 by the Portuguese who occupied it until 1962. It is now a state of India where Christianity prevails and there are no objections to eating pork or beef. The food of Goa is unique. Their most famous dish is Vindaloo, but it is not the dish from the standard curry house. The real thing is derived from the Portuguese dish Vino d'Alhos, traditionally pork marinated (the longer the better) in wine vinegar and garlic, then simmered until tender. To this the Goans added hot red chillies, creating a rich red curry gravy. Goa also has delicious seafood and fish dishes. There is only one true Goan restaurant in the UK, Ma Goa in London SW15, although Goan dishes do appear at the better Indian restaurants.

Gujarati Gujarat is a largely vegetarian coastal state, north of Bombay. The first British diplomat docked at the port of Surat in 1608, and the town was used as a British trading post, until Bombay was built in 1674. The soup-like dish, with gram flour dumplings, called Khadi, whose yellow gravy is made with turmeric, spices and yoghurt, may have been the very dish which gave curry its name. The food is India's least spicy. The Parsees, who lived in Gujarat for 500 years (*see* below), influenced the food, with subtleties of sour and sweet. Yoghurts and gram flour prevail. The famous Bhaji also originated here, as did the lesser known Dahi Vada, a gram flour dumpling in a tangy yoghurt sauce. Gujarati restaurants are prevalent in Leicester and Wembley, Middlesex, and they pop up elsewhere, too.

Moghul The curry from the standard curry house is based on rich, creamy dishes developed by the Moghul emperors. No one was richer than the Moghuls, and it was during their time, four centuries ago, that Indian food was perfected. Authentically, this style of food should be subtly spiced. It can be found in an increasing number of 'haute cuisine' restaurants around the country, spelt variously Moghul, mogul, moglai, muglai mugal, mugul, etc.

Nawabi The Nawabs were the rich royals of the Lucknow area of India who lived over two centuries ago. Like the Moghuls before them, they perfected a style of cooking which was spicy and fragrant. Called Dum or Dum Pukt, it involves cooking the curry or Biriani in a round pot, whose lid is sealed into place with a ring of Chapatti dough. The resulting dish is opened in front of the diners, releasing all those captured fragrances, as found in some of the better UK curry restaurants.

Nepalese Beautiful Himalayan mountains, the world's only Hindu kingdom, home of Gurkas, sherpas, yak and yeti, Kumari the living virgin goddess-princess, Everest, and unique food. Some similarities to north Indian, with curry (tarkari) rice (bhat), and wheat breads (roti haru). Kukhura (chicken), Khasi (lamb), Dumba (mutton), Bhutwa (pork), Hach Ko (duck), Jhinge (prawn) and Maccha (fish) are cooked in the clay oven (chula) or curried. Specialities include Aloo Achar – potatoes in pickle sauce, Momo/Momocha – keema-filled dumplings, and Tama Bodi – bamboo shoots and black-eye beans – a dish showing Tibetan/Chinese roots. More examples will be found in the entries for Great Nepalese, NW1, Gurkha Kitchen, Oxted, Surrey and Gurkha Square, Fleet, Hants.

Pakistani Until independence in 1947, Pakistan formed the north-western group of Indian states. Located between Afghanistan and India, it contains the famous Khyber Pass. The people are predominantly meat-eaters, favouring lamb and chicken (being Muslim, they avoid pork). Charcoal cooking is the norm, and this area is the original home of the tandoor. Breads such as Chupatti, Nan and Paratha are the staple. Balti cooking originated in the northernmost part of Pakistan (*see* earlier). In general, Pakistani food is robustly spiced and savoury. The area called the Punjab was split by the formation of Pakistan, and it is the Punjabi tastes that formed the basis of the British curry house menu (*see* Punjab, London WC2). Bradford, Glasgow and Southall have sizeable Pakistani populations.

Parsee/Persian It is quite common to see Persian dishes listed on the standard curry house menu. Dishes such as Biriani and Pullao did indeed originate in Persia (now called Iran). Bombay's Parsees came from there, having fled from Persia centuries ago. In India, they originated dishes of their own, such as Dhansak and Patia. The real thing is a subtle cooked-together combination of meat and vegetables and/or fruit. True Persian food is hard to find in the UK, although it is served at the Old Delhi, London W1. There is no Parsee restaurant in the UK but south-west London's Bombay Brasserie and Chutney Mary both have Parsee chefs who cook decent Parsee dishes.

South Indian Much of India's population is vegetarian, the southern part of India almost exclusively so. Until recently the extraordinary range of vegetarian specialities was virtually unknown in the UK. The growth in restaurants offering south Indian fare coincides with the increasing awareness of vegetarianism. Specialities include many types of vegetable curry including Avial, with exotic vegetables in a yoghurt base, and Sambar, a lentil-based curry. Other delights include huge, thin crisp rice- or lentil-flour pancakes (Dosas), with a curry filling (Masala) and Idlis – steamed rice or lentil-flour dumplings. South Indian restaurants are now springing up all over the UK.

Sri Lankan Sri Lanka is the small, pearl-shaped island, formerly Ceylon, at the southern tip of India. Its cuisine is distinctive and generally chilli hot. They eat similar fare to that eaten in south India, i.e. vegetarian dishes, but they also enjoy very pungent meat, squid, chicken and duck curries. Good Sri Lankan restaurants include Palm Paradise, Southall, Middlesex, Prince of Ceylon, London NW4, and Sigiri, London W13.

The A to Z of the Curry Menu

To the first-timer, the Indian restaurant menu is a long and complex document. This glossary explains many of the standard, and some of the specialised, dishes and items that you are likely to encounter. *See also* **The Cuisine of the Subcontinent**. Spellings of vowel sounds will vary from restaurant to restaurant, reflecting the 15 languages and hundreds of dialects of the subcontinent. (*See* Masala, Moglai, Papadam and Rhogan Josh Gosht for some examples.) Our spelling here is as near as possible to the standard accepted way of spelling, when translating phonetically from Delhi Hindi, Lahori Urdu or Dhaka Bengali to English.

A

AAM or AM Mango.
ACHAR or ACHAAR Pickle, such as lime, mango, aubergine, etc. *Achar Gohst* is meat curry, curried in a pickle base, *Achar Murgh* is the chicken version.
AFGHANI CURRY Nuts and fruit are added for the standard curry house interpretation.
ALOO Potato.

B

BAIGAN or *BEGUN* see Brinjal.
BALTI Balti originated centuries ago in north Pakistan's Mirpur, Kashmir and Skardu (Baltistan). It found its way to east Birmingham in the 1970s, where any combination of ingredients was curried in a two-handled pot known as the *karahi* (qv) elsewhere, but the Balti there. Served to the table still cooking, the art is to eat the food – which should be spicy, herby and aromatic – Indian-style, with the bread as the scoop in the right hand. In the 1990s, Balti spread rapidly all over the UK and beyond. The Balti found at the standard Bangladeshi curry house, however, owes its flavours more to Patak's acidic Balti paste than to Mirpur, and unless it is cooked in its pan and served cutlery-free, it will (correctly) never convince the Brummy purist that it is anything other than hype.
BARFI or BURFI Indian fudge-like sweet made from reduced condensed milk (*koya* or *khoa*), in various flavours.
BASMATI The best long-grained rice.
BATERA Football-sized puri (qv) becoming increasingly popular.
BATTAR Quail.
BENGAL CURRY A chicken or meat curry with chilli, sugar, potato cubes and halves of tomato.
BHAJI or BHAJEE Dryish, pan-fried mild vegetable curry.
BHAJIA Deep-fried fritter, usually with sliced onion, mixed with spiced gram

flour batter, then deep-fried. Bhajia is the correct term, meaning fried. Bhaji or Bhajee is the anglicisation. For the real thing, visit Maru's Bhajia House, Wembley, Middlesex. *See also* Pakora.

Bhel Puri This is the delicious street food snack from Bombay. It is a cold combination of those crunchy squiggles you find in Bombay Mix (qv), the smallest of which is called *Sev*. To this is added small-diced cooked potato, puffed rice (*mamra*), coriander leaf, onion and chilli. It is laced with brown sweet and sour tamarind (*imli*) sauce, yoghurt (*dahi*), coriander chutney (*dhania*) and chilli sauce, and topped with crispy puri biscuit chippings. The result is an exquisite combination of crisp, chewy and soft textures with sweet, hot, savoury and sour tastes. Variations include differing amounts of ingredients, under various similar names, such as *Sev Batata Puri, Dahi Batata Puri, Chat Aloo Papri* and *Batata Pava. Bhel* can be accompanied by Gol Goppas (qv). This delicious food is generally beyond the abilities of the average curry house, so is rarely found. Try it when you can (*see* London NW1's Drummond Street).

Bhoona or Bhuna Cooking process involving slowly frying out all the water content to produce a dry, usually mild curry.

Bindi A pulpy, rather sappy vegetable also known as okra or ladies fingers. Correct cooking of this dish is a good test of a chef's ability.

Biriani Traditionally, rice baked between layers of meat or vegetable filling, enhanced with saffron and aromatic spices, served topped with edible silver leaf (*vark*). The restaurant interpretation is a cooked rice, artificially coloured, with filling stir-fried in. It is usually heavily garnished and served with a vegetable curry sauce (*see* Pullao).

Bombay Duck A smallish fish native to the Bombay docks, known locally as *bommaloe macchi*. This was too hard for the British Raj to pronounce, so it became Bombay Duck. It is dried and appears on the table as a crispy deep-fried starter or accompaniment to a curry.

Bombay Mix An age-old traditional Indian snack nibble, called *muruku*, made from a savoury, gram-flour, spiced batter called *ompadi*, which is forced through a press straight into the deep-frier, to give different shapes and thicknesses of squiggly nibbles. Nuts, pulses, seeds and other ingredients are added. It should always be really crunchy and fresh. Re-invented by GK Noon, owner of Royal Sweets in Southall, under the catchy name Bombay Mix, it will keep you going at the bar.

Bombay Potato A popular invention of the curry house. Potatoes in curry sauce with onions and tomato.

Boti Kebab Marinated cubes of lamb cooked in a tandoor oven (*see* Tandoori).

Brinjal Aubergine, also called *baigan* or *began*. In *Baigan Burtha*, aubergine is smoked, spiced and mashed, in *Baigan Bhaji* it is chopped and curried by pan-frying.

C

CTM Chicken Tikka Masala. Invented by a British curry house chef (identity unknown) *c.* 1980, as a way to exploit his already popular Chicken Tikka by adding a creamy, pink, mild sauce made tasty by skilful blending of curry sauce, tomato purée, tandoori paste, cream, coconut, mango chutney and ground almonds. It is now ordered by 65% of all diners. Not only that, it appears in supermarket sandwiches, flavours crisps, is a pizza topping and even spices mayonnaise. If only that chef had copyrighted it, he'd be earning millions in royalties a year. *See* Makhani and Tikka.

CEYLON CURRY At the curry house, this is usually cooked with coconut, lemon and chilli.

CHANA A yellow lentil resembling, but not identical to, the split pea, used in Dhal (qv) and to make gram flour. *Kabli chana* is the chickpea. Both can be curried or dried and deep-fried as in Bombay Mix (qv). *See also* Paneer.

CHASNI, CHICKEN A central Scotland Pakistani restaurant name for CTM (qv)

CHAT or CHAAT Literally means 'snack', though often a salad.

CHILLI Fleshy members of the capsicum family, ranging in heat from zero (the bell pepper) to incendiary. All chillies start green and, if left long enough, eventually turn red, the one being no hotter than the other. The chilli normally used in Indian cooking is the narrow 7.5cm (3in) cayenne. The hottest in the world are Mexican habañeros, Caribbean Scotch bonnets and Bangladeshi nagas. People build up a tolerance to chillies, but they should never be inflicted upon the novice, not even in fun.

CHUPATTI A 15cm (6in) flat disc of unleavened bread, cooked dry on the tava (qv). It should always be served hot and pan-fresh. The spelling can vary – Chupati, Chapatti, etc.

CHUTNEY The common ones are onion chutney, mango chutney and tandoori chutney. There are dozens of others that rarely appear on the standard menu. *See* Sambals.

CURRY The only word in this glossary to have no direct translation into any of the subcontinent's 15 or so languages. The word was coined centuries ago by the British in India. Possible contenders for the origin of the word are: *Karahi* or *Karai* (Hindi) – the wok-like frying pan used all over India to prepare *masala* (spice mixtures); *Karhi* or *Khadi* – a soup-like dish made with spices, gram-flour dumplings and buttermilk; *Kari* – a spicy Tamil sauce; *Turkuri* – a seasoned sauce or stew; and *Kari Phulia* – Neem leaves, which are small and rather like bay leaves, used for flavouring. The Dutch, who were in India in the 17th century have their own derivation. They say it was used in Malaya of their Malay curries, and that it derived from the word *Lekker* meaning delicious, or in colloquial Dutch, *Lekkerie*.

CURRY HOUSE *See* Formula Curries.

D

DAHI or DOHI Yoghurt, used as a chutney (*see* Raita) and in the cooking of some curries. Most curry houses make their own, and it is delicious as an accompaniment to curry, being less sharp than the shop-bought equivalent. Incidentally, Dahi, not water, is the best antidote if you eat something that's too hot for you.

DAHI VADA South Indian savoury gram-flour doughnut, deep-fried, cooled and dunked into cold, spicy yoghurt (*see* Vada).

DAL or DHAL LENTILS There are over sixty types of lentil in the subcontinent, all packed full of nutrients. The common restaurant types are *massor* (red, which cooks yellow), *moong* (green), *chana* (also used to make gram flour) and *urid* (black).

DEGCHI or DEKHCHI Brass or metal saucepan without handles.

DHANIA Coriander leaf or spice.

DHANSAK Traditional Parsee meat dish cooked in a purée of lentils, aubergine, tomato and spinach. Restaurants use dal and methi, and sometimes chilli and pineapple.

DOPIAZA Traditional meat dish. *Do* means two, *piaza* means onions. Onions appear twice in the cooking, first fried and second raw. They give the dish a sweetish taste.

DOSA South Indian pancake made from rice and *urid* (lentil) flour, which, when made into a batter, soon ferments to give a superb sour taste. *Masala Dosa* is a Dosa filled with mashed potato curry spiced with onion, chilli, turmeric and mustard seed.

DUM Cooking by steaming in a sealed pot, invented by the Royal Nawabs (*see* The Cuisine of the Subcontinent), e.g. *Aloo Dum*, steamed potatoes. Also called Dum Pukt or Pukht (pronounced 'pucked').

E

ELAICHI Cardamom. Can major in curries – for example, *Elaichi Murgh* is chicken curried with a predominance of green cardamom.

F

FOOGATH Lightly cooked vegetable dish found in the Malabar area of South India. Any vegetable such as gourds or plantain can be used.

FORMULA CURRIES Many of our 'Indian' (qv) restaurants operate to a formula which was pioneered in the late 1940s. In those days, a way had to be found to deliver a variety of curries, without an unreasonable delay, from order to table. Since all authentic Indian recipes require hours of cooking in individual pots, there was no guarantee that they would even be ordered. So cubed meat, chicken or potatoes, dal and some vegetables were lightly curried and chilled, and a large pot of thick curry gravy, a kind of master stock, was brewed to medium-heat strength. To this day, portion by portion, on demand, these ingredients are reheated by pan-frying them with further spices and flavourings. At its simplest, a Medium Chicken Curry, that benchmark of middle ground, is still on many menus, though sometimes disguised as Masala, and requires no more than a reheat of some gravy with some chicken. For instance, take a typical mixed order for two. Chicken Korma (fry a little turmeric, coriander and cumin, add six pieces of chicken, add a ladleful of curry gravy, plenty of creamed coconut, almonds maybe and a little cream – result, a mild dish, creamy-golden in colour), with Vegetable Dhansak (fry some cumin seeds, dry methi leaves (qv), chopped onions, a little sugar, tomato, red and green capsicum with the gravy, add dhal and some cooked veg – result, colourful, and still medium-strength). Meat Korma (as for the chicken, using meat), and Prawn Vindaloo (fry spices and chilli powder, add the gravy which at once goes red and piquant, then cooked peeled prawns, fresh tomato and potato, simmer and serve). Maybe also a Sag Paneer (fry cummin, some thawed creamed spinach and pre-made crumbled paneer together, add fresh coriander – done). One cook can knock all these up, simultaneously, in five pans, within minutes. Rice is pre-cooked, breads and tandoori items made to order by a different specialist. And, hey presto, your order for two! The menu can be very long, with a huge variety of dishes, sometimes numbered, sometimes heat-graded, mild, medium and hot, hotter, hottest, and any dish is available in meat, poultry, prawn, king prawn, and most vegetables, too. That's the formula of the standard curry house. Just because this is not authentic does not make it bad. It can be, and variously is, done well. This *Guide* is full of many such restaurants, about which we say 'a standard curry house, doing the formula well'.

G

GARAM MASALA Literally meaning hot (roasted) mixture (of pepper and aromatic spices), it originated in Kashmir and is added towards the end of cooking in certain north Indian curries. *See also* Masala.

GHEE Clarified butter or vegetable oil used in high-quality north Indian cooking.

GOBI Cauliflower.

GOL GOPPAS or PANI PURI are mouth-sized puffed-up crispy biscuits, served with *Jeera Pani* (water spiced predominantly with chilli, black salt and cumin water) and *Aloo Chaat* (potato curry) at Bhel Puri (qv) houses. To eat the correct way, gently puncture the top of the biscuit, pour in some *Jeera Pani*, and pop into the mouth in one. Chew and then add some *Aloo Chaat*.

GOSHT Meat, usually refering to lamb or mutton.

GULAB JAMAN An Indian dessert of cake-like texture. Balls of curd cheese paneer, or flour and milk-powder, are deep-fried to golden and served in light syrup.

GURDA Kidney. *Gurda Kebab* is marinated kidney, skewered and cooked in the tandoor.

H

HALVA Sweets made from syrup and vegetables or fruit. Served cold in small squares, it is translucent and comes in bright colours depending on the ingredients used. Orange – carrot; green – pistachio; red – mango, etc. Has a texture thicker than Turkish Delight. Sometimes garnished with edible silver leaf.

HANDI Cooking pot, sometimes earthenware, sometimes metal.

HASINA KEBAB Pieces of chicken breast, lamb or beef marinated in a yoghurt and spice (often tandoori) mixture, then skewered and barbecued/baked, interspersed with onions, capsicum and tomato. Turkish in origin. *See* Shaslik.

I

IDLI Rice- and lentil-flour steamed cake, about the size and shape of a hockey puck, served with a light but fiery curry sauce. South Indian in origin.

IMLI Tamarind. A very sour, date-like fruit used in cooking or chutney which is of purée consistency, sweetened with sugar.

INDIAN In 1947, the subcontinent of India was partitioned. To cut a long story short, in Britain and the West we still generally erroneously refer to our curry restaurants as 'Indian'. In fact, over 85% are Bangladeshi, with only around 8 percent run by Indians and 8% run by Pakistanis. There is a smattering of Nepalese and Sri Lankan restaurants, and only a single Afghan and a single Burmese restaurant in Britain. *See* Formula Curries.

J

JALEBI An Indian dessert. Flour, milk-powder and yoghurt batter are squeezed through a narrow funnel into a deep-frier to produce golden, curly, crisp rings. Served in syrup.

JAL FREZI Sautéed or stir-fried meat or chicken dish, often with lightly cooked onion, garlic, ginger, green pepper and chilli.

JEERA Cumin or cummin seed or powder, hence *Jeera Chicken*, etc.

JINGRI or CHINGRI Prawns of any size.

K

KALIA Traditional Bengali/Bangladeshi meat, poultry or fish dish in which red-coloured ingredients are mandatory, especially red chillies and tomatoes. *See* Rezala.

KARAHI A two-handled Indian kitchen dish. Some restaurants reheat curries in small karahis and serve them straight to the table with the food sizzling inside. *See also* Curry and Balti.

KASHMIR CHICKEN Whole chicken stuffed with minced meat. *See* Kurzi.

KASHMIR CURRY Often a medium curry to which is added cream and coconut and/or lychees, pineapple or banana.

KEBAB Kebab means 'cooked meat' in ancient Turkish, traditionally cooked over charcoal, in a process over 4,000 years old. It was imported to India by the Muslims centuries ago. Shish, incidentally, means 'skewer'. *See* Boti, Hasina, Nargis, Shami and Sheek Kebab.

KEEMA Minced meat, e.g. as used in curry. *See also* Mattar.

KOFTA Balls made from ground meat, poultry or fish/shellfish or vegetables, then deep-fried and simmered in a curry sauce.

KORMA Probably derived from the Persian *Koresh*, a mild stew. The Moghuls made it very rich, using cream, yoghurt and ground almonds, fragranced with saffron and aromatic spices. But, traditionally, Kormas need not be mild. In Kashmir a popular dish is the *Mirchwangan Korma*, red in colour because it is full of Kashmiri chillies. To the curry house, Korma is terminology for the mildest curry, sometimes made sickly by the overuse of creamed coconut block, cream and nuts.

KULCHA Small leavened bread. Can be plain or stuffed, e.g. *Onion Kulcha*.

KULFI Indian ice cream. Traditionally it comes cone-shaped in vanilla, pistachio or mango flavours.

KURZI Leg of lamb or whole chicken given a long marination, then a spicy stuffing, e.g. rice and/or Keema (qv), then slowly baked until tender. This is served with 'all the trimmings'. It is many a curry house's Special, requiring 24 hours' notice (because of the long preparation, and a deposit to make sure you turn up to eat it). Often for two or four, it is good value. Also called Khurzi, Kasi, Kozi, Kushi, etc. *See also* Murgh Masala.

L

LASSI A refreshing drink made from yoghurt and crushed ice. The savoury version is *Lassi Namkeen* and the sweet version is *Lassi Meethi*.

M

MACCI or MACHLI Fish. Today, fresh exotic fish from India and Bangladesh are readily available and, when a restaurant offers them, you have the chance of getting a truly authentic dish.

MADRAS You will not find a Madras Curry in Madras. It does not exist. But the people of the south eat hot curries, firing them up with as many as three different types of chilli – dry, powdered and fresh – added to the cooking at different stages. As the Brits got used to their early formula curries, they began to demand them hotter. With no time to add chillies in the traditional way, one of the pioneer curry house chefs simply added one teaspoon of extra-hot chilli powder to his standard sauce, along with tomato and ground almonds, and ingeniously called it 'Madras'. The name stuck. *See also* Chilli, Phal and Vindaloo.

MAKHANI A traditional dish. Tandoori chicken is cooked in butter ghee and tomato sauce. Some say this was the derivation of CTM (qv).

MALAI Cream. So *Malai Sabzi Kofta*, for example, means vegetable balls in a creamy curry gravy. *See* Rasmalai.

MALAYA The curries of Malaya are traditionally cooked with coconut, chilli and ginger. In the Indian restaurant, however, they are usually based on the Korma (qv), to which is added pineapple and/or other fruit.

MASALA A mixture of spices which are cooked with a particular dish, e.g. *Garam Masala* (qv). It can be spelt a remarkable number of ways – Massala, Massalla, Masalam, Mosola, Moshola, Musala, etc.

MASALA DOSA *See* Dosa.

MATTAR Green peas. So *Mattar Paneer* is peas with Indian cheese, *Keema Mattar* is mince meat curry with peas, and so on.

MEDIUM CURRY *See* Formula Curries.

METHI Fenugreek, pronounced 'maytee'. Savoury spice. The seed is important in masalas. The leaves, fresh or dried, are used particularly in Punjabi dishes. At the curry house, the flavour of these leaves predominates in their *Dhansak*.

MOGLAI Cooking in the style of the Moghul emperors, whose chefs took Indian cookery to the heights of gourmet cuisine centuries ago. Few restaurateurs who offer Moglai dishes come anywhere near this excellence. Authentic Moglai dishes are expensive and time-consuming to prepare. Can also be variously spelt Muglai, Mhogulai, Moghlai, etc.

MULLIGATAWNY A Tamil vegetable consommée (*molegoo* pepper, *tunny* water), adapted by the Raj to create the thick, meat-based British soup.

MURGH Chicken.

MURGH MASALA or MURGH MASSALAM Whole chicken, marinated in yoghurt and spices for hours, then stuffed and roasted. *See* Kurzi.

N

NAN or NAAN Pronounced 'narn', it is flat, leavened bread, usually made from plain white flour (*maida*) dough, but sometimes from wholemeal flour (*atta*). After the dough rises, it is rolled out and baked in the tandoor (qv). It is teardrop-shaped and about 20-25cm (8-10 inches) long. It must be served fresh and hot. As well as *Plain Nan,* there are many variations involving the addition of other ingredient(s). *Keema Nan* is stuffed with a thin layer of minced, spiced kebab meat. *Peshwari Nan* is stuffed with almonds and/or cashew nuts and/or raisins. Garlic, onion, pineapple, tomato, indeed anything, can be added. Double- or treble-sized *Karak,* Elephant or Family Nans are offered at Balti houses to share to scoop your food up with.

NARGIS KEBAB Indian scotch egg – spiced, minced meat around a hard-boiled egg.

NIRAMISH A Bangladeshi mixed vegetable, often cooked without garlic, and spiced only with *Panch Phoran* – Indian Five Spice mixture.

O

OOTHAPPAM *See* Uthappam.

P

PAAN Betel leaf folded, samosa-fashion, around a stuffing of aniseed, betel nut, sunflower seeds, lime paste, etc. and eaten in one mouthful, as a digestive after a meal. The leaf is bitter, the mouth-feel coarse and the taste acquired; but more acceptable (to Westerners) small spices and seeds (*supari*), sometimes sugar-coated in lurid colours, are often offered by the curry house after the meal.

PAKORA The true pakora is a whole piece of vegetable, lightly coated in gram-flour batter and deep-fried, although at the curry house it is to all intents and purposes the same as the Bhajia (qv).

PALAK *See* Sag

PANEER Cheese made from milk by separating the whey (liquid) from the curds (solids) which, when compressed, can be crumbled, chopped, fried, tandoori-baked and/or curried (*see* Mattar). In Bengali, Paneer is called *Chhana,* not to be confused with the lentil, Chana (qv).

PAPADAM or PAPAD Thin lentil-flour wafers. When cooked (deep-fried or baked) they expand to about 20cm (8 ins). They must be crackling crisp and warm when served. If not, send them back and deduct points from that restaurant. They come either plain or spiced, with lentils, pepper, garlic or chilli. There are many ways to spell papadam, using any combination of the vowels 'a', 'o' and 'u', and double 'p' and double 'd'. But, despite many people calling it so, it should never be referred to as a pampadom.

PARATHA Dough combined with ghee (q.v) thinly rolled out and folded over itself to create a layered disc, like puff pastry. Pan-fried to create a soft bread.

PASANDA Meat, usually lamb, which traditionally is thinly beaten, then cooked in a creamy curry gravy to which some chefs add red wine. The dish and wine were both true treats of Moghul emperor Jehangir who, though Muslim, blessed the wine to make it 'holy water' thus circumventing the rules of Islam. Then he and his court proceeded to drink themselves legless while enjoying this dish.

PATIA Restaurant curry with a thick, dark, red sweet and sour sauce. Based on a Parsee prawn or fish dish.

PATRA A Gujarati speciality, in which colcasia (*patra*) leaves are rolled in gram-flour paste, like a Swiss roll, then steamed, sliced and deep-fried.

PESHAWARI NAN *See* Nan.

PHAL The hottest curry, also known as a Bangalore Phal, invented by the British curry house restaurateurs.

PICKLE Pungent, hot, pickled vegetables essential to an Indian meal. The most common are lime, mango, brinjal and chilli. Though rarely seen at the restaurant, meat and game are made into traditional and very delicious Rajasthani pickles.

PODINA Mint. A fresh chutney, puréed from fresh mint, chilli and onion. Can also be spelt Pudina.
PRAWN BUTTERFLY Usually a large or giant king prawn, cut so that it opens out and flattens, butterfly-shaped, marinated in spices and immersed in gram-flour batter, then deep-fried. A curry house invention, whose name could also have derived from 'batter-fry'.
PRAWN PURI Prawns in a hot sauce served on a Puri (qv) bread. Although sometimes described as Prawn Puree it is not a purée.
PULLAO Ancient Persia invented *Pollou,* with rice and meat and/or vegetables, cooked together in a pan until tender. Following Muslim invasions it evolved into Turkey's *Pilav,* Greece's *Pilafi,* Spain's *Paella* and, of course, India's *Pullao.* In many curry houses, the ingredients are mixed after cooking, to save time. (*See* Biriani.) There are many other ways to spell it: *Pillau, Puloa, Pillar, Pilaw, Polaw,* etc.
PULLAO RICE The restaurant name for rice fried with aromatic spices, usually with rice grains coloured yellow and/or red and/or green.
PURI Unleavened wholemeal bread: rolled out flat to about 10cm (4 ins) in diameter, it puffs up when deep-fried, and should be served at once.

Q

QUAS CHAWAL or KESAR CHAVAL Rice fried in ghee (qv), flavoured and coloured with saffron (*kesar*).

R

RAITA A cooling chutney of yoghurt on its own (*see also* Dhai) or vegetable, e.g. cucumber or mint (sometimes called Tandoori Sauce) to accompany papadoms, the starter or the main course.
RASGULLA Walnut-sized balls of paneer (qv), or semolina and cream cheese, cooked in syrup (literally meaning 'juicy balls'). They are white or pale gold in colour and served cold or warm. *See* Rasmalai.
RASHMI KEBAB Kebab of minced meat inside an egg net or omelette.
RASMALAI Rasgullas cooked in cream, served cold. Very rich, very sweet.
REZALA Bengali/Bangladeshi speciality. Lamb cooked in evaporated milk, rich and subtly spiced, it would be milder than Korma except that green chillies are mandatory. Traditionally no red- or orange-coloured ingredients should be used. *See* Kalia.
RHOGAN JOSH GOSHT Literally meaning 'lamb in red gravy'. Traditionally, in Kashmir, lamb is marinated in yoghurt, then cooked with ghee, aromatic spices and natural red colorants. It should be creamy but not hot. The curry house version omits the marinade and the aromatics, and uses tomato and red pepper to create a red appearance. There are many ways of spelling it – Rogon, Roghan, Rugon, Rugin, Rowgan, Ragan, etc., Just, Joosh, Juice, Jash, etc., Goosht, Goose, Gost, etc.
ROTI Indian bread of any type, rolled out into thin flat discs.

S

SABZI Vegetable.
SAG or SAAG Spinach, also called *Shak* in Bengali, *Palak* in the Punjab and *Rai,* although these are mustard leaves. *Lalshak* is delicious red spinach.
SAMBAL A Malayan term describing the chutneys accompanying a meal. Sometimes referred to on the Indian menu. Malays also refer to Sambal as a dish of various ingredients cooked in a hot sauce, e.g. prawn sambal.
SAMBAR A hot and spicy, runny, almost consommé-like south Indian vegetable curry made from lentils and exotic vegetables, such as the drumstick. In the Manchester/Merseyside area, the curry houses have a dish called *Samber.* It bears no resemblance to Sambar, except that lentils and a lot of chilli powder are added to meat, chicken or prawn curry.
SAMOSA Celebrated triangular, deep-fried meat or vegetable patties, supreme as starters or snacks.
SHAMI KEBAB Round minced meat rissoles.
SHASHLIK KEBAB Shashlik in Armenia means 'to grill'. Cubes of skewered lamb or chicken are marinated (in an oil, garlic and chilli mixture) then grilled. *See* Hasina.
SHATKORA A Bangladeshi citrus fruit, the size of a grapefruit but sharper in flavour. Can be eaten fresh or used in cooking.
SHEEK KEBAB or SEEKH Literally means (from Turkish *shish*) a skewer. Spiced minced meat, usually coloured lurid red at the curry house (from proprietary tandoori/kebab paste), is moulded onto the skewer, then baked in the tandoori and grilled.
STANDARD CURRY *See* Formula Curries.

T

TANDOORI An ancient style of cooking, which originated in the rugged north-west frontier of India (now Pakistan). It gets its name from the cylindrical clay oven, the tandoor, with its opening at the top, fired with charcoal in its base. Originally the ingredients were chicken and lamb, marinated for many hours in a spiced yoghurt-based sauce, traditionally slightly reddened with red chilli, then skewered and baked in the tandoor. Now the curry house product also includes fish, prawns, paneer (qv) and vegetables. But its lurid red or orange colour is created by the unnecessary use of tartrazine food colouring in proprietary ready-to-use pastes. *See* Boti Kebab, Tikka, Nan Bread and Raita.
TARKA DHAL A tasty, spicy lentil dish, the Dhal being *massoor* (red) lentils, cooked to a purée, to which the Tarka (crispy, fried caramelized onion and/or garlic) is added as a garnish. This simple-sounding dish is a great test for the cook. It should taste very slightly burnt (from the Tarka), and be subtly, yet decisively, spiced, neither too thick nor too thin.
TAVA A heavy steel, rimless, flattish frying pan, used to cook items such as Parathas.

THALI or TALI A round tray (*thali*) with a low rim, averaging about 34cm (12in) in diameter. It is a plate on which an entire meal is served. Dry items (rice, bread and even dry curries) are placed directly on the thali. Wet portions (curries, dhals, soups and sweets, etc) are placed in matching serving bowls (*tapelis*), and they too reside on the thali. They were made of gold for the Moghul emperors, silver for the Maharajas, and stainless steel for the rest of us. To be found at certain restaurants serving 'special' meals.
TIKKA Literally, a small piece. For example, *Chicken Tikka* is a filleted chunk of chicken, marinated (*see* Tandoori), skewered and baked in the tandoor. Traditionally, the marinade is identical to Tandoori marinade, and cooks a naturally russet brown colour. Proprietary Tikka paste, as used in the curry house, is lurid orange or yellow because of the tartrazine it contains.
TINDALOO *see* Vindaloo

U

UPPUMA South Indian dish. Lightly fried semolina with onion and spices.
UTHAPPAM A spicy south Indian pizza, made from rice flour and topped with onions, tomatoes and chilli.
URID A type of lentil, its husk is black, and it comes whole, split or polished. Available as a dhal dish in some restaurants, e.g. *Maharani Dhal.*

V

VADA or VADAI Lentil-flour spicy doughnut, enjoyed in Gujarat and south India. *See* Dahi Vada.
VARK Edible silver or gold leaf, made today in Hyderabad, but a Moghul speciality, said to be an aphrodisiac.
VINDALOO A fiery dish from Goa. (*See* **The cuisines of the Subcontinent**) It now means the second hottest dish (two spoonfuls of chilli powder), usually with a chunk of potato (Aloo). Also sometimes called *Bindaloo* or *Tindaloo* (even hotter). *See also* Chilli, Madras and Phal.

Y

YAKNI Literally mutton, or a meat-based stock.

Z

ZAFFRON Saffron, also known as *Kesar* or *zafron*. The world's most expensive spice.
ZEERA Alternatively called Jeera, which is cumin. *Zeera Gosht* is lamb cooked with cumin.

COBRA
नाग
INDIAN BEER

The 2001 GOOD CURRY GUIDE

THE ENTRIES

CURRY CLUB

THE ENTRIES

An explanation of our method

There is no perfect system for laying out a nationwide restaurant guide. Many guides simply list their entries in town alphabetical order. The problem here is that there is no geographical relationship between each town. The method we have adopted in our guides is to record the entries by county. We believe that most people understand the ancient British counties. We list them alphabetically. Unlike some guides, we do not group the counties in National Regions (such as 'The Midlands' or the 'West Country' etc.), since this too lacks logic. Counties are not without confusion. In some cases, their once sacrosanct borders have been altered by frequent local government tinkering. Greater Manchester is one example. When it was established as a 'Unitary Region' in 1965, it nibbled away parts of Cheshire and Lancaster. Many residents prefer to stick to these counties in their addresses, though we have adopted 'Greater Manchester' as a 'county' in this *Guide*. Other bodies, such as the post office, add to the confusion of recent years. Their postcodes are far from logical and do not follow county borders. BT also have their own system of geographical reference. It is because few people understand postcode logic, and even fewer understand phone codes, that we use the counties.

Starting on page 176, we cover the English counties. With the demise of Avon (which was, in any case, not a county, but a Unitary Region) we now start with Bedfordshire. Within each county, we record the relevant towns alphabetically, and within each town, we record each restaurant alphabetically. In Bedfordshire, for example, the first town we record is Arlesey, and its first restaurant is Raj Villa, and so on. Following England, we then look at the Isles and Islands, then Scotland and finally Wales.

We start with London, as is explained alongside. Before we are accused of London bias, it is worth giving our usual caveat: of the 8,000 British curry restaurants on our nationwide database, nearly 20% of them are in London. Naturally, with such competition, many of the country's best are in the capital. Our coverage reflects this, with a strong London section.

The international food press has recently declared London the food capital of the world, taking that crown from New York. London not only has a strong and healthy home-grown selection of excellent restaurants, it also has at least one representative of each cuisine of the world. The curry sector reflects this, with an exhaustive choice of sub continental and regional food. In addition to standard Bangladeshi curry houses, you'll find examples of every one of the regional cuisines, which are described on page 38.

CENTRAL LONDON

Area: British capital
Postcodes E, EC, N, NW, SE, SW, W & WC
Population: 5,735,000

For the purpose of this Guide we define Central London as its 1870 postal districts, now known as postcodes. We run them alphabetically as follows: E, EC, N, NW, SE, SW, W *and* WC. *Within each individual postcode, we run numerically, starting with* E1 *and ending with* WC2. *As with all postcode logic, this is not in any geographical order. For example,* W5 *Ealing, shares its borders with* W13, *West Ealing and* W3, *Acton. For 95 years these postcodes comprised all of London. In 1965 Greater London (GL) was established. It includes these postcodes and expanded its borders, absorbing Middlesex and parts of Essex, Hertfordshire, Kent and Surrey (shown in black in the drawing below).*

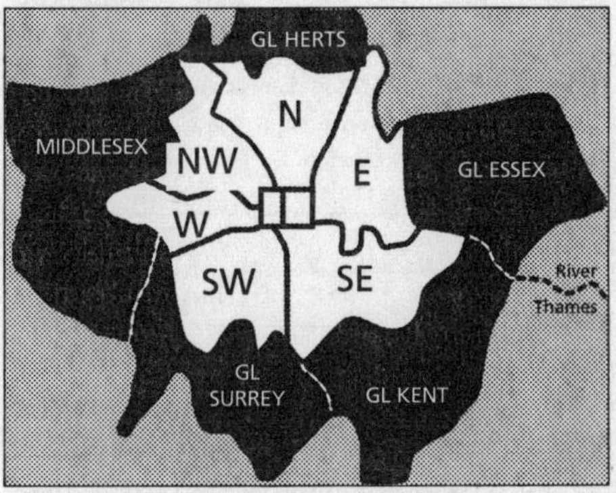

For GL towns/boroughs in these areas, please see the relevant county – see list on page 8.

London E

Area: East London, postcodes E1 to E18
Population: 1,050,000

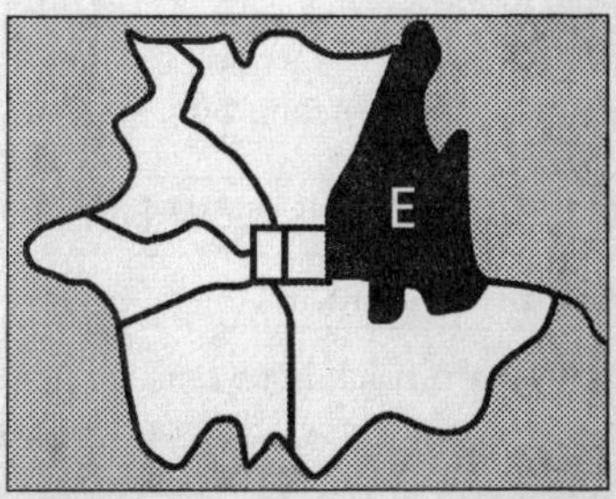

©	Curry Club Discount	U	Unlicensed
V	Vegetarian	ANP	Alcohol not permitted
e-a-m-a-y-l	Eat as much as you like	BYO	Bring your own alcohol

London E1

Docklands, Spitalfields (inc. Brick Lane), St Katherine's Dock, Whitechapel

E1 – Brick Lane

Once predominantly Jewish, and bustling with tailors, cab drivers, and salt-of-the-earth street markets, the long and narrow Brick Lane, has, since 1971, become home to the country's largest Bangladeshi community. Running between Shoreditch and Aldgate East tube stations, plans are afoot to rename it Banglatown, indicating its proliferation of cheap and cheerful curry cafés, snack bars, restaurants and provisions shops, run by the thriving community. (To emphasise its roots you'll also find an all-night, fresh-baked bagel shop where cabbies queue for sustenance.) As for curry, some of the establishments have remained fairly spartan, and unlicensed (you can BYO). Here are your favourites:

BENGAL CUISINE

12 Brick Lane, E1 — 020 7377 8405

Traditionally decorated 60-seater, well-established in Brick Lane terms (1980). Taken over in 1993 by N Choudhury. 'Food good, staff friendly, as is owner.' BBF. Price check: Methi Chicken £4.95, Sag Bhaji £2.45, Papadam 45p, CTM £6.95, Pullao Rice £2.15, Peshwari Nan £2.15 Lager £2.45. Delivery: 3-mile radius. Hours: 12pm-12am non stop! Branch: Taja, 199a, Whitechapel Road, E1. Stocks Cobra.

CAFÉ NAZ NEW ENTRANT

46-48 Brick Lane, E1 — 020 7247 0234

'Opened two years ago and rebuilt after the Brick Lane bomb. I have eaten there twice now, and will become a regular. Both meals really excellent, costing around £16 inc. starter, papadoms, main course and pudding. The feature, however, is the decor. It is presented as a modern bar style, chrome rims to the chairs, and the stainless steel kitchen is fully on view, and a/c.' BBF. Branch: Cafe Naz, 234 Old Brompton Road, SW5 (020 7370 1188). Service 12.5%. Lager £3. E-a-m-a-y-l lunch (to 3pm): £7.95. Hours 12pm-12am; Sat. 6pm-12am; Sun. 12-3pm/6pm-12am. Stocks Cobra.

CITY SPICE NEW ENTRANT

138 Brick Lane, E1 — 020 7247 1012

Long-term Brick Lane fans will remember the Clifton at no. 126. Here is the reincarnation, serving a good representation of Bangladeshi dishes: Salmon, Rui and Bekti feature amongst the fish dishes, and the use of coconut, mustard and shatkora (a kind of sweet lemon) gives the food its edge. Like many of its neighbours, City Spice offers Balti and other 'standards' on their menu. It is now licensed. 'Very appealing menu. Starter Ureebisi Biran (beans, including gatta, a regional type of runner bean) was very good. Lentils with Shatkora was very definitely different, a mixture of sweet, sharp and sour. No Indian desserts – what an omission in a street full of Indian sweet shops.' HC. Relatively inexpensive. Branch: Shampan (*see* below) 79 Brick Lane, E1. Hours: 12-3pm/6pm-12am. Stocks Cobra.

EASTERN EYE BALTI HOUSE

63a Brick Lane, E1 020 7375 1696

Pakistani Baltis cooked by Bangladeshi chef-owner Babul, in the Brick Lane heartland. Whatever next, we asked last time? Answer, Baltis cooked by Bangladeshis. But we hear they are good. Price check: Papadam 65p, BCTM £6.95 (inc. Nan or Roti), Bombay Potato £2.25, Pullao Rice £1.75, Pickles and Chutneys 65p per portion. You could buy a jar for that! Delivery: £12 minimum, 3-mile radius. Hours: 12-3pm/6-12am. Stocks Cobra.

FAMOUS CURRY BAZAAR NEW ENTRANT

77 Brick Lane, E1 020 7375 1986

'Well laid out menu with the occasional variations from the standard, e.g. Squid and Fish curry or Mooli and Pumpkin Bhajis. £33 for two, including beers.' IB.

NAZRUL BYO

130 Brick Lane, E1 020 7247 2505

The Nazrul has graced our *Guide* pages since our first edition in 1983. It's an archetypal, BYO, really cheap, café-style venue, with a huge following of curryholics – and fabulous food! It is for that you must go. Still has red banquettes and flock, long may that last ... somebody get it listed! 'Recently picked up a copy of the 1998 *Guide*, and was somewhat embarrassed to find my comments on the toilet still being reprinted. Compelled to make another visit, I have to report that the single toilet was clean and no parts of the fittings were loose! [That's my editoral jokes flushed away, then.] Balti Methi Gosht was rather more liquid than normal methi gosht. A bit on the oily side.' DMW. 'Good value, beautifully cooked, quantities fine.' BF. 'Best value for money I've ever had (maybe apart from Rusholme, Manchester). Brilliant Dhansak and Aloo Gobi. Curry paradise!' MH. Set meal average £6. Branch: Nazrul II, 49 Hanbury Street, E1, 020 7247 5656.

SHALIMAR NEW ENTRANT U

70 Brick Lane, E1 020 7247 9846

'With time to spare and Austrian friends to convert to curry, my wife, my daughter and I visited Brick Lane. They had never seen anything like it. The first venue we chose wouldn't take Visa, so we went onwards down the Lane. The Shalimar (it's no newcomer, it has the usual tatty Brick Lane decor) welcomed us and our plastic, and in we went. I explained that for some of us it was first time curry, and they made us an ultra mild Korma and Chicken Biriani (both £3.50) which had the converts and my daughter grinning from ear to ear. I had a Karali Gosht which overflowed over the edges, and the most super dhal, which had flavour, texture and real taste. Huge portions, value for money. Happy converts. What a find for the *Guide*.' CF.

SHAMPAN BEST BANGLADESHI AND TOP 100 ©

79 Brick Lane, E1 020 7375 0475

Shiraj Hoque's Shampan has always led the rest of the Lane by serving Bangladeshi dishes a decade ago, in his licensed, air-conditioned, up-market (by Brick Lane standards) surroundings. Others have copied to greater or lesser extents, and, to quote Mr Hoque 'we also do all types of curry because that's what they want'. So, if you're one of them, go for all your curry favourites, if you must, but nowhere will you get a more authentic taste of Bangladesh. Betki, Rup, Ayre and Rhui (Bengali fish) and the sour-flavoured Shatkora (Sylheti citrus fruit), Gosht/Murgh, meat or chicken, and seasonal veg such as Kakrol, Potol and Lalshak. Price check: Bangladeshi Thali £10.50, Papadam 40p, CTM £5.35, Pullao Rice £1.55. Branch: City Spice, 138 Brick Lane, E1. Stocks Cobra.

STANDARD BALTI HOUSE NEW ENTRANT

71 Brick Lane, E1 020 7247 5855

'Large, bustling restaurant, open plan fashion. Standard menu and prices. Enjoyable mixture of dishes.' RW.

SWEET AND SPICY U BYO

40 Brick Lane, E1 020 7247 1081

Little changes at this friendly, formica-tabled Brick Lane veteran caff, founded in 1969 – its roots being emphasised by the Punjabi-Pakistani food being ladled out of containers onto plates as you wait. Excellent no-nonsense food and plenty of it at low prices. 'Karahi Gosht £3.55, spicy, plenty of meat and no fatty gristly bits. Aloo Gobi and Brinjal £2.20, large portions, excellent spice and flavour. Small plate of onion, Raita and red sauce free, water provided on each table. BYO policy for drink. They clearly have a similar policy for toilet paper, something to remember if likely to need to use the facilities!' MW. 'My sort of restaurant in so many ways – decor hardly matters, self service. Our exchange party from India, two teachers with 13 students, had visited the Tower of London, and we strolled up Brick Lane. We bought snacks, made fresh for us, outstandingly good. For 22 people, cost £20.' BG. 'Lively little cafe, simple tables and chairs. Prepared food kept in Bain marie's and starters microwaved. Sheek Kebabs £1.30 – little tough, juicy, highly spiced, served with Onion Salad, Yoghurt and Chilli Sauces. Karahi Gosht £3.50 – thin but rich sauce, again without fear of chillies, good chunks of meat. Chappatis £1.40 for two – nice, though stiffened towards the end of meal. Gulab Jamans £1.10 – excellent but more sauce wouldn't have gone amiss. Good value dining.' RW. Price check: Meat and Chicken curries £2.95 or £3.55, Veg curries £2.20, Papadam 40p, Pullao Rice £1.55. No credit cards, cash preferred to cheques. Hours: 8am-10pm daily (Sun. to 6pm). Closed during Ramadan.

LE TAJ — U BYO

134 Brick Lane, E1 — 020 7247 4210

Le Taj has changed *le nom* (it used to be Taj Mahal) – we know not *pourquoi?*, except may be *le decor nouveau*, which is light and airy. *Le menu*, now including a separate Bangladeshi list, lives up to expectations, with 'the food as good as ever. My favourite being roop (pomfret) chanda £6.75.' GP. BYO no charge. Prices average under £10. Hours: 12-2.30pm weekdays/5.30-11.45pm daily, except Sun. 12-11.30pm.

Elsewhere in E1

BENGAL TRADER — NEW ENTRANT — NEW TO OUR TOP 100

44 Artillery Lane, Parliament Court, E1 — 020 7375 0072

Try the Pakura bar with its tiffin snacks and a tipple, before going into the restaurant. Average bill £25 with drink. 'I have now had two meals at the Trader. Chef Ram Das' food is first class, the surroundings pleasant, and the staff friendly. A very useful addition to the list.' BBF. With its pedigree of sound management (*see* branches), it goes straight into our TOP 100. Hours: 11.30am-3pm/5.30pm-12am; closed Fri & Sat. Branches: Bengal Clipper, SE1, Bengal Mangrove, Halstead Kent, Bengal Lancer, Chislehurst.

CAFÉ INDIYA

30 Alie Street, E1 020 7481 8288

Some love the minimalist look of this 100-seater's polished wooden floors, charcoal-coloured tables and ladder-backed chairs, set off against cream walls. Others find the high decibels of the long-lunching city chatterers resounding off these reflective surfaces unpleasantly deafening. The former home of Cyrus (*see* below), it is owned by K Mody and Vilas Palnitkar since inception in 1995, though Michael Tarat does the PR, leaving its management to Ashik Ali and the cooking to head chef Maq Sood for northern curries, and Taj-trained Antoinette D'Cruz, for Goan specialities. The limited but carefully chosen menu includes Chicken Mo Mo, a Nepalese dumpling starter £4.75, Tandoor-cooked Afghani Murghi Kebabish, chicken pieces marinated in vinegar, cashew paste, melon seeds and spices, Raan, sliced leg of lamb, from Rajasthan £9.75, Chicken Pista Korma from Hyderabad £7.95 and Chicken Pepper Fry from south India. Goan specialities are there, including a traditional Pork Vindaloo and Chicken Xacuti both £7.25, and some Goan fish dishes. Price check: Papadam 50p, CTM £5.95, Pullao Rice £1.75. Hours: 12-4pm/6-11pm; closed Sat. & Sun. Branch Rupee Room, EC2. Stocks Cobra.

CAFÉ SPICE NAMASTÉ AWARD WINNER ©

16 Prescot Street, E1 020 7488 9242

It's hard to believe that it is now over 5 years since this 110-seater restaurant was opened in 1995 by Michael Gottlieb and Cyrus and Pervin Todiwalla, a Taj-trained husband and wife team, he cooking, she managing the front. The former court house has been restored to some of its former glory, after an interim period of DSS occupation which left it more like Colditz blitz than E1 Glitz. But that's long past and the bright blues, browns and saffron colours have mellowed into maturity. So too has the restaurant's trade, with a house as busy at weekday lunch times, as it is for dinners. This enviable state of affairs is in part to do with the restaurant's city location, with Namaste being a favourite waterhole for expense account holders, though Cyrus sighs as he races against time to serve a full house in the limited time that his clients' lunch break brings. Evenings are more leisurely, and definitely the time to experiment with Cyrus' menu. It is a lengthy document and frequently changes to bring in some Cyrus innovations. Its core always includes regional dishes from Gujarat, Goa, Nepal, Kashmir and northern and southern India. You are spoilt for choice: starters like Chilli Cheese Garlic Toast, for example, or Shinanio Balchao (mussels in a Goan sauce). Main dishes include Kerla Nandu (crab curry), Galhina Xacutti (Goan chicken curry), Parsee Lamb Liver and Kidney Curry or Rawa Kalwa (oysters marinated in Goan Piri Piri Masala, dipped in dry semolina and crisply flash-fried, served with a hot garlic dip). One of the most popular ingredients is Wensleydale Wild Boar – in such guises as Jungli Maas Dhuanaar – where a haunch is marinated in a masala, smoked over whole spices such as cinnamon, cardamom, cloves, etc., then slowly oven-roasted. Last time I was criticised by some for being critical (isn't that the *raison d'etre* of a *Guide*?). Cyrus and I talked about it later, and we agreed that one can easily get misquoted in the media, and I make it quite clear that, since I first met him in Goa in the early 1980s, I've been a great fan of his. I was elated when he arrived in the UK, so much so that I gave him my Chef of the Year Award in 1991 before he opened his Namaste Restaurant, and that's putting faith in someone. Since then he has been showered with accolades, which, in a way can be detrimental, causing customer expectation to exceed human limits. Maybe that is why we get a mixture of reports – from 'very satisfied' to 'hate it', and 'downright cross' (with us for recommending the place). But it is not stopping me from giving Cyrus his third Award (and our first ever for 'Innovation') in five *Guides*. But what does this mean? Every time I write about Cyrus, I always say his food is not formula curry-house stuff. Many dishes are beautifully-produced, perfect classics. But Cyrus always has a twist up his sleeve to share with his clientèle. I'm not sure about serving croissants with curry starters, and curried emu, bison, kangaroo, ostrich, frog and alligator does little for me. But I was smitten with Cyrus' foiegras paté mixed with garam masala, and served with red currant chutney. Fabulous. So unless you want the formula, there's something for everyone. We've had many happy reports about both branches. But there is always a dissenter, and, whereas in the past it's been dissenting whites longing for their bog-standard CTM and creamed coconut Korma, and not finding it, interestingly more than one poor report has come from Indians this time. Here are two of the former and one latter. 'A wonderful evening. Couldn't fault it on welcome, decor, atmosphere, service, food, price or wine prices.' BF. 'Superb food. By the end we were ridiculously full. Prices not as bad as we had feared. One wishes more curry houses showed the daring and imagination of Cafe Spice.' RL. 'I went expecting to be impressed. Decor strange if not rather naff. Service was average and food very poor. Monk Fish had clearly left the sea long before it landed in the tandoor. Dhansak looked and tasted appalling. The bill for two without drinks came to over £50. A very mediocre restaurant described in the Guide as one of the best in the UK – is competition really that low?' NJ. Oh really, Nef Jandu. I include it because, a) we get the blame, and b) I really find it hard to agree with it, but it's what we get, so caveat emptor. Besides most Indians I know admit to being purists when it comes to Indian cuisine. When visiting Café

Spice Namasté, I say go with an open mind and an open palate – unless, you really can't bring yourself to try something new. Price check: Papadam 60p, CTM £8.95 (inc Pullao Rice), Pullao Rice £2.35, Peshwari Nan £2.25. House wine £9.75. Delivery: £35 minimum, E1 area only. Hours: 12-3pm/6.15-10.30pm; Sat. 6.30-10pm; closed Sun. & bank holiday Mon. Branch: Café Spice, 247, Lavender Hill, Battersea, SW11. Stocks Cobra.

EMPRESS TANDOORI NEW ENTRANT ©

141 Leman Street, E1 020 7702 1168

Formerly Empress of Bengal. Owned by Mr Islam since 1992. Good Bangladeshi choices here, including the restaurant's most popular dish: Skiandari Lamb – marinated and roasted £6.95. Interesting menu additions: Cox's Bazar Crab £8.95 – soft crabs cooked with ginger, garlic, coconut and fresh herbs, garnished with cucumber and lemon. Annan's Haash £6.95 – succulent roasted breast of duck, cooked in aromatic spices, served with pineapple and cherry tomatoes, fairly hot. Takeaway: 10% discount. Minimum charge: £12. Delivery. Price check: Papadam 60p, CTM £6.25, Pullao Rice £2.10. Hours: 12-3pm (closed Sat. & Sun.)/6pm-12am (Sat. & Sun. to 11.30pm). Stocks Cobra.

LAHORE KEBAB HOUSE U BYO

2 Umberton Street, E1 020 7488 2551 or 7481 9737

For anyone who has not been to either Pakistan or to Sparkbrook, the LKH is what it's all about. Despite Brum's claim to be the inventor of the currinary world, this gaff has been doing Balti, under what some say is its true name, Karahi – or Karrai (sic.) – since it opened in the seventies – serving darned good food, geared to Asian tastes, without compromising it for Westerners. At least that's what it used to be. But its relatively new-found glory as a lunchtime dive for the money boys and girls from the City has permeated into the evenings, and it's had an effect on management. The redec has now become old hat, and tatty even, much to the delight of LKH's aficionados and its Asian patrons, who were wary of such inventory as arty line drawings. Cutlery is still for wimps (though you no longer have to ask for it). But when in Rome, eat the correct way, please, using a piece of Roti to scoop up your curry, in your right hand only – too bad if you're left-handed. And expect limitations if you're a veggie. Halal mutton, chicken and quail are it, in the karahi, from the tandoor as tikkas or kebabs, or as steam roast (Choosa), with robust lentils and fragrant rice. Real veterans show their spurs by enjoying the celebrated, and very filling and satisfying, Paya (lamb's trotters), laced with the Hot Chilli Raita, followed by their gorgeous

Kheer rice pudding. Service is swift and accurate, but don't expect pampering, and don't expect to pay more than a tenner, including tip, in cash, please – nothing fancy like credit cards. It has a different atmosphere at different times of the day, different again at the weekend, depending on who's eating when. 'Not been here since the 99 Guide reported a re-dec. I read this with some concern and suspicion. Happily the food was as I remembered – very robustly spiced and excellent. Remains one of my favourites.' MW. 'We love the food that is served here. Friendly and helpful waiters and reasonably priced. We go regularly.' SR. Four visits by RE: 1. 'A return visit to an old favourite. Crowded as usual. A bit on the yuppy side, reflected in the price – three times what I paid for the first time, but food remains the best. Shame we now live 200 miles away!' 2. 'A lot more expensive than it used to be, but food quality is the same, excellent. Service is quick. Shekh kebabs: freshly cooked and spicy. Karahi Goshi: tender lamb chunks in an "out of this world sauce". Dal Tarka: bright yellow and still the best. Food is brilliant. I was only there for about 20 minutes, but each time I go it is memorable.' 3. 'This remains my all time No 2 – if I still lived closer it would be No 1. On this occasion the service was surly, but the food remains the best.' 4. 'Place was heaving, as ever. Seekh Kebabs freshly made and spicy – only 50p – no salad (thank goodness) but as many onions as you can eat. Dhal, out of this world, but a little thin £3.50. Unique Karahi Gosht £4.50. Excellent Roti – 50p. Service is fast. BYO welcome. 'What a find!' BI. Hours: 12pm-12am.

NEEL KUTER NEW ENTRANT

23-24 Shoreditch High Street, E1 020 7375 3535

Although this restaurant serves the old formula favourites, it's the Bangladeshi chef's specials to go for. Authentic Bengali cooking, with dishes which include Shatkora. Fish includes rupchanda, boal and pomfret, Golda Chingri (tiger prawns) and achari (meat of chicken with a pickle base). Great stuff. Reports please.

PRIDE OF ASIA ©

207 Mile End Road, E1 020 7780 9321

A bog-standard, 65-seater serving all the favourites by chef Amir Uddin, owned and managed by Abdul Habiz. Price check: Papadam 50p, CTM £6, Pullao Rice £1.50. Delivery: £10 minimum, 3-mile radius. Hours: 12-2.30pm/6pm-12am. Stocks Cobra.

TAJA NEW ENTRANT

199a Whitechapel Road, E1 020 7247 3866

'The problem: you come out of Aldgate East happily humming The Curry Song and looking forward to lunch. You turn into Brick Lane and then ... twelve hours later your emaciated body is picked out of the gutter by the corporation dustcart. This is because you are Aesop's Ass and you have not been able to make up your mind. Up and down the street – reading all the menus over and over again – I am sure you get the picture. The solution: do not turn down Brick Lane (if tempted, remember that it starts with Osmond Street and think revolting American pop groups). Keep straight on down the Whitechapel Road to a strange building on the outside of the pavement. This is Taja and the building is a defrocked public lavatory, giving a new meaning to the term bog-standard curry. It has been thoroughly converted and is light and airy with long wooden tables and benches. On my first visit I had the stuff-yourself-till-you-keel-over buffet. There was not much choice but it did an absolutely delicious chicken tikka – not often found in this sort of deal. My second meal started with chotpoti – peas very much al denté (may not appeal to mushy pea lovers) with bits of potato and tomato in a comforting broth and sprinkled with coriander and scraps of papadom. The accompanying tamarind sauce had attitude and bit very satisfactorily. I followed with Lamb Buna, a half portion of vegetable curry (an option on the current menu), a warm and fluffy naan and a pint of draught Cobra. There is a wine list of sorts and I noticed some bottles of Mateus Rose behind the bar. I didn't realise they still brewed the stuff. My bill was just over £12 and a decent tip is earned but not solicited. This is a good restaurant with a pleasant atmosphere and cheerful service.' BS. Stocks Cobra.

TAYYAB KEBAB HOUSE U BYO

89 Fieldgate Street, E1 020 7247 9543

A 36-seat truck-stop, according to one reporter. Well, an unlicensed (BYO tolerated, but discreetly please) caff, anyway, which now operates daytime. Owned by M Tayyab since 1974, who is also the head chef serving Southall-style Pakistani/Punjabi kebabs and curries at ludicrously reasonable prices. 'One of my favourites.' RE. Its curious operating procedure would make any accountant faint at misused resources. Hours: 12-5pm. Then the same staff open up next door ...

NEW TAYYAB U BYO

83 Fieldgate Street, E1 020 7247 9543

... at this 65-seat former pub, opened in 1995, where they curry on, in rather smarter premises. The food's the same, and it's OK with our regulars, especially the kebabs and the prices. And since the Tayyab family are the owners, accountants and cooks, it's OK with them too! 'The Old Tayyab is still a couple of doors away catering for cafe-style trade. The New is a bit more "posh". Quite crowded with a mix of Asian and European customers. Food good.' RE. Despite being in a former pub, it's unlicensed. BYO with discretion please, i.e., don't flash it around and offend strict Muslims who are the real regulars. Price check: Papadam 50p, CTM £3.40, Pullao Rice £1.50. Hours: 5pm-12am. Both branches closed for Ramadan month. Incidentally, there is the Tayab (Bengali) sweet/snack shop at no. 85, sandwiched in between.

TIFFIN INDIAN NEW TO OUR TOP 100 ©

165 Cannon Street Road, E1 020 7702 3832

Abdul Kalam describes his 42-seat venue, just off the Commercial Road, as furnished with green and black marble-topped tables, high-backed iron chairs, café-style. We applaud Mr Kalam's prices, held since our 1999 *Guide*, and the excellent menu with delights like Salmon Samosa £2.95, and Bathera, quails £8.50, £9.95, but the Tiffin Royal Tandoori £13.95 would make Meena Patak blush the same red, so much of her paste is used on the ingredients. 'Good to busting, it is.' TH. 'We found Tiffin excellent.' D&LT. Check out the menu for low cholesterol dishes, cooked with pure virgin olive oil and served with fragrant basmati boiled rice. Some Like it Hot! £9.95 – chicken from the tandoor, diced and cooked with fresh chillies, garlic, methi and Tiffin masala. Lebu Murghi £9.95 – chicken marinated in lemon, capsicum, onion, coriander, garlic, ginger, lemon grass and Tiffin masala. Such delights, superb home made chutneys, good service, and many happy reports (mainly from medics, we note) have promoted Tiffins to our TOP 100. Price check: Papadam 50p, CTM £6.95, Pullao Rice £1.95. Set meal from £8.95. Branch: Tiffin, 56-58, Balmoral Road, Gillingham, Kent – tel: 01634 570555. Hours: 12-3pm/6pm-12am; Sun. 6pm-12.30am. Stocks Cobra.

London E2

Bethnal Green

AL AMIN ©

483 Cambridge Heath Road, E2 020 7729 7415

Abdul Noor's two-room 39-seater remains a popular standard curry house, with all the trimmings, including Balti. Price check: Papadam 50p, CTM £5.55, Pullao Rice £1.65. Delivery: £10 minimum, 2-mile radius. Hours: 12-2.30pm/6pm-12am. Stocks Cobra.

London E4

Chingford, Highams Park

PURBANI

34 The Avenue, E4 020 8531 8804

54 seats in this friendly local, owned by Tony Turu Miah since 1983. Popular dishes: CTM, Balti Specials. 'I go here much more frequently now, usually for takeaways. Staff are very friendly; regular loyal clientele; good amount of family groups early evening. Food is good and portions remain very generous indeed. Chicken Korma and Lamb Chana both very good. On a recent occasion, had my school exchange group staying locally and we negotiated a meal for 25. Produced an excellent spread of Rice, Tandoori Roti, Tarka Dhal, Mixed Veg and Sag.' BG. Takeaway: 10% discount. Delivery. Price check: Papadam 50p, CTM £6.25, Pullao Rice £1.55. Hours: 12-2.30pm-6-11.30pm.

London E6

East Ham, Upton Park

EASTERN EYE ©

269 High Street South, E6 020 8470 8078

A good standard, licensed, air-conditioned curry house run by Mabud Mussain. DMCC visits here 'many times', and she never has 'any complaints'. Lunch and dinner daily. Sunday buffet 1-5pm. Average prices. Home delivery in local area, small charge. Branch: Himalaya, 178 The Grove, Stratford, E15. Stocks Cobra.

London E7

Forest Gate

MOBEEN ANP

222-224 Green Street, E7 020 8470 2419

The owners of this chain of Pakistani caffs are strict Muslims, so it's unlicensed, and no booze is permitted and it's no credit cards and no smoking too. All that aside, go for darned good, inexpensive, value-for-money Kebabs, tandoori items and curries of all sorts, selected from the counter, with specials varying from day to day. Can be heaving with local Asians, who know you won't find better food, which adds to a fab atmosphere. Being Punjabi, it's a bit short of vegetarian fodder, but for those, see next entry. Average spend: £6. Hours: 11am-10pm. Branches: 229 High Street North, E6; 725 High Road, Leyton, E10; and 80 Ilford Lane, Ilford, Essex.

VIJAY'S CHAWALLA NEW ENTRANT U BYO

268 Green, Upton Park, E7 020 8470 3535

Another Green Street gem with an equally avid Asian following, but unlike Mobeen (above) this time no meat. It's a vegetarian/vegan establishment, with a range of dishes mainly from Bombay. The Masala Dosa has that slightly sweet Gujarati taste of molasses, rather than the robustness of the Kerelan version. BYO is permitted, but please ask and dispense discretely. The Bhel Puri (£1.75) is always popular, and for value for money the thali tray with its filling selection is phenomenal at £5. No credit cards. Hours: 10.30am-8pm.

London E9

Homerton, Victoria Park

MOGUL PALACE TAKEAWAY NEW ENTRANT

247 Wick Road, E9 020 8986 259s4

Bangladeshi takeaway/delivery service managed by Syed Rahman and opened in 1989. You can fax your order by dialling 020 8533 4002 45 minutes before you want it delivered – now that's service! House special: Salam Bombay £6.95 – chicken or lamb tikka cooked with aubergine and potato. Delivery. Price check: Papadam 35p, CTM £4.95, Pullao Rice £1.25. Hours: 12-2pm (except Fri.)/5pm-12am (Sat. to 1am).

©	Curry Club Discount	U	Unlicensed
V	Vegetarian	ANP	Alcohol not permitted
e-a-m-a-y-l	Eat as much as you like	BYO	Bring your own alcohol

London E14

Docklands, Isle of Dogs, Limehouse, Poplar

GAYLORD TANDOORI NEW ENTRANT

141 Manchester Road, Isle of Dogs, E14 020 7538 9826

'The restaurant is tiny, only 34 seats around a central island. Service was friendly, and the food was delicious. All dishes were generously full of meat. My Sag Gosht the most flavourful I've had.' JLN.

MEMSAHEB ON THAMES NEW ENTRANT TOP 100

65-67 Amsterdam Road, E14 020 7538 3008

Bare wooden floors, spacious seating, a riverside view of the Thames and the Dome through the picture windows are the much-publicised hooks at this two room 100-seater restaurant (plus 8 good-weather pavement tables) which opened after our last *Guide* went to bed. And we hear plenty about it from its many supporters, some of whom are the new well-heeled Docklands residents. But others tell us they travel from Kent, Essex and up West just to come here. Salmon samosa, £3, are not original to the Memsaheb, but are now one of its most popular signature dish starters. They do regional food festivals from time to time, of which the Bangladeshi, not surprisingly, was the most accurate and most successful. Full marks, though for effort with the others, e.g. Goan, South Indian, etc. 'Open since the last *Guide*, and has now built up a very good reputation locally. Good attentive service, offering specials e.g. Lamb Xacuti (£6.95) and Bengal roast chicken, not found in usual restaurants. Recommend Chicken Bemisal (sweet, sour with green chilli) and House special rice.' JB. LS wants it in our TOP 100. OK Linda, done! Cover Charge £1. Average spend £15. Set lunch £10.95. Kids portions at special prices. Hours: 12-2.30pm (no lunches Sat. & Sun.)/6-11.30pm.

TABLA INDIAN RESTAURANT AND BAR

NEW ENTRANT **NEW TO OUR TOP 100**
MOST PROMISING NEWCOMER

Dockmaster's House, West India Dock Gate,
Hertsmere Road, E14 020 7345 0345

Here's something to beat the drum about in ever-improving Docklands. Tabla, an Indian drum, opened in early 2000 in a grand Georgian building near Canary Wharf. The House was built in 1807 for the Dockmaster himself, and one imagines the ghost of said individual as being a rather robust Dickensian Beadle type who would adore the current use of his former home. The new masters are former *Tandoori Magazine* editor Iqbal Wahhab and Albert Ray, former Ivy Maitre D', with the kitchen led as his first venture in England by Taj-trained Chef Yogesh Datta. This combination offers a style and menu on a par with the other Top Indian restaurants in London and India. There are three elements. A 100-seat restaurant with a satisfying range of Indian regional dishes. Starters (all *c.*£4) include a soup, crab cake, smoked salmon samosas, and Mini South Indian Dosa pancake filled with spiced lamb mince. Tandoor dishes include Salmon Steak and Duck breast both £5.95/£11.95 with a vegetable option: aubergine, tomato, courgette, pepper and potato £3.95/£6.50. Main courses include Goan style haddock, Pickled king prawns with chillies and whole spices, Hot south lamb shank on the bone in a rich spicy sauce, Rajasthani style lamb in a red chilli paste with bitter gourd, all between £10 and £12, and there is a sound range of vegetable dishes and accompaniments. There is also a daily changing set menu, which includes the option of trying the day's Staff Curry – as cooked for the restaurant workers. Down in the extensive cellars, is now a 120-seat bar offering a range of spicy pub grub, the likes of Spiced burger and Lamb Rogan Josh Pie both with masala fries and Naan bread stuffed with chilli pepper and onion and a choice of Tuna, Cheese, Chicken Tikka or Minced lamb kebab. Outside there is a garden large enough to accommodate 80 seats which serves a Fridays-only summer barbecue of Indian kebabs, grills and tandooris on platters alongside pitchers of beer. Hours: 12-3pm/6-1030pm. So many good elements here, that we're giving Tabla our MOST PROMISING NEWCOMER award. Reports please.

London E17

Walthamstow

DHAKA

103 Hoe Street, E17 020 8520 5151

A bog standard safe bet curry house, the like of which is the backbone of this *Guide*. 'I used to live in E17 and my hall is littered with takeaway menus. But my winner, to whom I still return, is the Dhaka.' CJ. Stocks Cobra.

©	Curry Club Discount	U	Unlicensed
V	Vegetarian	ANP	Alcohol not permitted
e-a-m-a-y-l	Eat as much as you like	BYO	Bring your own alcohol

London E18

Redbridge, South Woodford, Woodford

BHANGRA BEAT NEW ENTRANT

49, Chigwell Road, South Woodford, E18 020 8989 0911

AG says: 'England had been knocked out of Euro 2000 – we needed cheering up. Bangra Beat has intrigued me for some time and I've never seen it in the *Guide*.' [You're right, Andy, though its Essex branch (*see* below) has been entered continuosly from our 1995 edition to date. At that time Shamin (Sam) Khan gave a CC discount. Strangely we've not heard from him since, but we know a further branch in Streatham has since closed, and this one has opened.] AG. goes on: 'Overall, we were impressed. The Kingfisher lager was not that good but the food was consistently fine. Tarka Dhal and Garlic Nan were excellent. Vegetable Jalfrezi exactly as I requested – Vindaloo hot! Well worth a visit.' AG. Hours: 12-2.30pm/6-11.30pm. Branch: Bhangra Beat, Chadwell Heath, Essex.

MEGHNA GRILL ©

219 Woodford High Road, E18 020 8504 0923

Siddiqur Rahman's long-established (1971), competent Bangladeshi curry house. 'Restaurant packed, waited 20 minutes for table. Decor superb – almost art deco. Vegetable Dhansak, hot and served with Pullao Rice, excellent King Prawn dishes, Garlic Nan superb. Good value. £74 for four including £20 for drinks.' AG. Takeaway-only branch down the road at no. 249.

THE ROSE ©

65-67 Woodford High Road, E18 020 8989 8726

Formerly Rose of India, The Rose has been operated for 22 years by Messrs Miah and Hoque, who offer all the favourite tandooris and curries at sensible prices. 'Closed for refurbishment – what a transformation, no flock wallpaper any longer, nor the average CTM dishes. Food delicious, service exemplary. Chef's Rallwa – chicken or lamb tikka with prawns, keema and spring onions in ginger sauce £8.95, very tasty. Generous portions and rice served in little china dishes (Villeroy and Bosch) with matching lids.' SSTC. Be more adventurous and try the Garlic Mussels on Puri – mussels cooked in a garlic, red onion and white wine sauce, served on a puri £4.95. 20% discount on collected takeaways. Price check: Papadam 60p, CTM £7.95, Pullao Rice £2.25. Hours: 12-2.30pm/6-11.30pm.

London EC

Area: The City of London
Postcodes EC1 to EC4
Population: 145,000

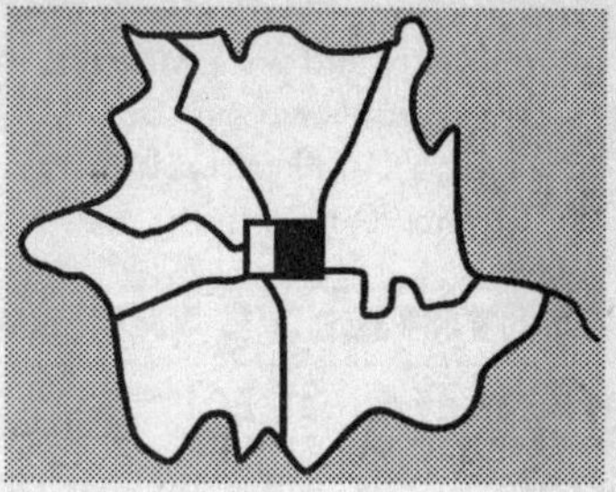

London EC1

Angel, Clerkenwell, Farringdon, Old Street, Smithfield

CITY CAFÉ LAZEEZ

NEW ENTRANT **NEW TO OUR TOP 100**

88 St John Street, EC1 — 020 7253 2224

See Café Lazeez, London SW7 and W1.

RAVI SHANKAR — V BYO

422 St John Street, Clerkenwell Road, EC1 — 020 7833 5849

DRC loves its south Indian vegetarian menu: 'choosing is always agonising. The Vegetarian Thali and a starter of yoghurt, spices, and what appeared to be small pieces of idli, was delicious, spicy, sweet and sour all at once. Our Paper Dosa, with usual relishes, was absolutely marvellous and served very eye-catchingly, vertically, curved around the back of the stainless steel platter with the relishes in front, rather than the more usual roll laid on the plate. How do they get it to stand upright?' 'Service not over friendly, but quick, polite and efficient. BYO is a plus point, but the real selling point is the food – beyond compare. Paneer Dosa, full of cheese, very spicy Bhindi Dupiaza and equally spicy Bombay Potato with a smoky mustardy Tarka Dall. Stuffed full for £20. Superb – his partner and I are both vegetarian and this is our favourite in the country.' AG.

SEMA INDIAN BALTI — U BYO ©

141 Whitecross, EC1 — 020 7253 2927

Proprietor, Abdul Khalique Choudhury. Unlicensed, but you can bring your own wine or lager and Mr Choudhury says he will provide the glasses. Special: Chicken or Lamb Pasanda – thin fillets marinated in masala with

©	Curry Club Discount	U	Unlicensed
V	Vegetarian	ANP	Alcohol not permitted
e-a-m-a-y-l	Eat as much as you like	BYO	Bring your own alcohol

cream, spices and pistachio nuts. Liver Hazarh £2 – exclusive starter, cooked chicken liver served on roti. Balti King £22.50 for two people – normally served at a Royal party. Delivery. Price check: Papadam 50p, CTM £4.95, Pullao Rice £1.60. Hours: 12-2.30pm/5.30-11.30pm.

SMITHFIELD'S TANDOORI NEW ENTRANT

4 Lindsey Street, EC1 020 7606 3868

'The decor has had a complete facelift. The menu is fairly standard and the prices are on the low side for central London, but the portions are average and the cooking well above average. The staff were very attentive, and the whole meal was most enjoyable and very professional.' and 'Had Tandoori King Prawns, a meal I haven't have for years. The prawns were gorgeous, well spiced, moist, small areas of burned tandoori patches, lots of sizzling onions. Full marks – they had several Indian sweets – I had Gulab Jamun, served warm, lovely. Danny made to feel welcome even though he wasn't eating. An unplanned and unexpected Indian meal turned out to be a real pleasure. A real pleasure, exceeded expectations. Service really good, particularly one waiter who really added to the evening. Full marks.' HC.

London EC2

Barbican, City, Liverpool Street, Moorgate

RUPEE ROOM

10 Copthall Avenue, EC2 020 7628 1555

Owned by K Mody and Vilas Palnitkar since inception in 1995. Restaurant seats 52 in the basement, where rupee's the name, rupee's the decor, and rupee's the game. Its City-suit brigade don't, it seems, mind forking out mucho dinero while they fork up. Menu features authentic Indian dishes, by chef Abdur Rob, not the usual Bangladeshi curry house fare. Authentic dishes: Sikandari Raan (for two) £22.95 – braised leg of lamb marinated in a mixture of malt vinegar, dark rum, cinnamon, cummin and served with Dal Makhani and Nan. Takeaway: 10% discount. Price check: Papadam 75p, CTM £7.95, Pullao Rice £2.25. Hours: 11.30-3pm/5.30-10.45pm; closed Sat. & Sun. Discount scheme. Branch: Café Indiya, E1.

SHIMLA PINKS NEW ENTRANT TOP 100

7-8 Bishopsgate Churchyard (between Bishopsgate and Old Broad Street), EC2 020 7628 7888

Open since the last *Guide*, as another branch in the Oriental Group led by

Kal Dhaliwal; before that it was the Sri India, but it was its life before that which gets everyone talks about the building – it was a Turkish Baths. But it was not to be just another branch, it was to be the be all and end all branch. Daliwal boasted of spending close to £1m on it. 'My shareholders are all city men', he said, and he wanted a flagship to impress them. A rich man's local so to speak. Sadly, but maybe with little wonder, his group is in administration as we write. We wish it well, and will update next time. Meanwhile go to enjoy the venue. Built in 1895, the small upstairs reception belies the huge basement area, housing 110 seats and the bar. It was here that housed the baths, and the old mosaic tiling pillars, walls and ceiling supports could have been designed for their current use. The money went on installing the remainder of the decor, furnishings and kitchens. Shimla Pinks spin is to deliver upmarket Indian food. The food is above average, but not the average formula stuff. Specials include Paneer Ka Khass Tikka £3.75 – cubes of spiced paneer with raw mangoes, Dum Pukht cuisine which originated in the Nawabi courts (*see* page 39). Joojeh Seekh £4.50 (cardamom laced tandoori minced chicken kebab), Tikhey Jhinghey £10.95 (king prawns with peppercorns and coriander seeds), Chandi Kaliyan £7.95 (picatta of lamb cooked with cashew nuts, almonds and saffron). House wine £10.95 bottle, £2.95 glass, Lager £4.95 (large bottle). Average spend £24. Unusual hours reflect its City location. Hours: 11.30-3.30pm/5.30-9.30pm; closed Sat & Sun. Branches: Shimla Pinks Birmingham, Manchester, Oxford and Johnstone, Strathclyde, Scotland. Stocks Cobra.

London EC3

Aldgate, Fenchurch Street, Tower of London

MATAB'S NEW ENTRANT

76 Aldgate High Street, EC3 020 7481 4010

Owned by the personable Matab Choudhury, one of the prime movers and Chief Treasurer of the Bangladeshi Caterers Association, this restaurant in some way acts as a flagship and example to the 12,000 other restaurants which the BCA quotes as its membership. One is struck by the vibrant wall paintings and ceilings, with contrasting crisp white tablecloths, King's cutlery and wooden floor. The deft service provides all the old favourites that one has come to expect of the Bangladeshi formula curry venue. And it is a favourite haunt of many a city regular, of which VW-P and LD-W are two. Reports please.

PLANTERS INN NEW ENTRANT

25 Great Tower Street, EC3 020 7621 1214

Owner Shohid Chowdhury and chef Masuk Miah worked together at the Red Fort (W1). Decided to start their own venture and named it after Bangladesh's major industry, tea planting. Of the 138 tea estates in Bangladesh, 128 are in Sylhet. 'We arrived promptly at 12 o'clock, as we were meeting a friend. The bar is on your right, but our friend was to found at a table sipping a chilled glass of white wine, while he waited for us. The restaurant is uncluttered, white walls, mirrors, polished wood. The floor is tiled, there are glossy palm trees in pots to divide up the tables. Our arrival was timely, as the restaurant was beginning to get busy, with suited City men (and the occasional woman) grabbing a good quick lunch before their afternoon business. The owner told us that his clients often needed to be served within an hour. When our main courses were served all tables were occupied, the restaurant buzzed. The chef has introduced some Bangladeshi specialities and they were very tasty, as was all the food.' DBAC.

London N

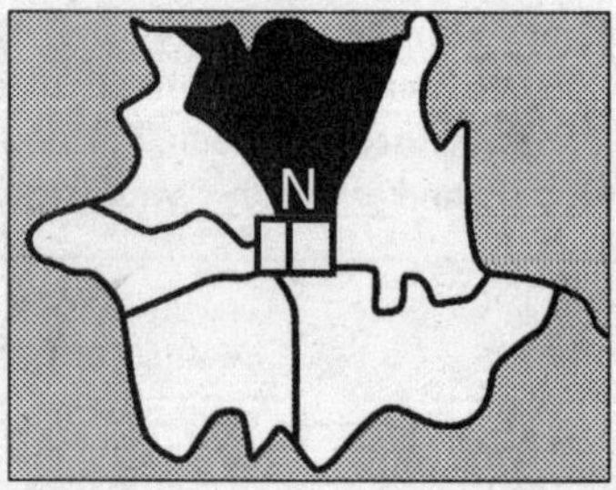

Area: North London, postcodes N1 to N22
Population: 1,250,000

London N1

Islington, King's Cross, Shoreditch

AFGHAN KITCHEN

35 Islington Green, N1 020 7359 8019

This restaurant is right there in Blair's lair – new Labour Islington, with its clutch of trendy caffs, and not cheap chomp houses. Right bang on the Green (it's the tiniest green you've ever seen, surrounded by thundering 24-hour traffic, but cherished none the less, by the rest of Islington. Anyway, it's a great site for the Afghan, and with Afghanistan now a no-go area for the sound of mind, there are only two Afghan restaurants in the UK (*see also* page 38 and Caravan Serai, W1). Afghani food is Muslim, big on Halal goat (here they use lamb) and goat's milk. Yoghurt always accompanies a meal. Try Dogh – Savoury Yoghurt with mint, and the Tourshis or chutneys. In general the food is less spicy than Indian, but the names are similar. Bread isn't Naan, it is Nane Lawash – thinner, glazed and basket-shaped. Qurma is Korma, etc, etc. GR says it all really: 'Not knowing anything about Afghan food, four of us were delighted to find that it bore a close resemblance to Indian with the Murgh Kofta – chicken meat balls in sauce, Gosht Qurma, a type of meat Korma, Suzhi Gosht – meat with spinach spiced with Char Masasa (a four-spice version of India's Garam Masala), each £4.50 with the bread as the staple, chilli pickle to liven up the delicate spicing, house wine to wash it all down.' GR. Small menu. No credit cards. Average spend £9. Hours: 12pm-12am Tues.-Sat.

BALTI MANIA NEW ENTRANT BYO

391 Liverpool Street, N1 020 7697 0407

'Wonderfully and favourably within slightly drunken walking distance of where we live. The chef is young but amazingly gifted. Service unobtrusive and welcoming. The restaurant's decor is a concern, admittedly! It's clean and brightly lit, but without any customary pretension to ambience. My wife has renamed it "The Shower Room" because of the glazed tiles that cover the floor and walls. [I know what you are getting at with the tiles, but I don't mind that austere type of decor once in a while – at least it's clean and easy to keep clean.] But don't be deceived, the surroundings are irrelevant to the main event – the food is an absolute dream. Mushroom Pullao £1.95, Sag Bhajia £1.95, Brinjal Bhaji and Tarka Dall £1.95, keep us optimistic throughout the week as we head to a regular Friday night order. You can have as many Popadoms as you want for free [the menu says 40p – you must be a special customer – Ed] with a choice of four home-made pickles and chutneys. BYO no corkage.' GB. Delivery. Hours: 5.30pm-12am.

INDIAN VEG BHEL POORI HOUSE e-a-m-a-y-l V

92 Chapel Market, N1 020 7837 4607

'Although I have sung the praises of the excellent value eighteen buffet dishes e-a-m-a-y-l £2.95, I feel I must praise it again. I now lunch there once a week and the quality is always consistent. Occasionally there is a superb mashed potato and onion curry. Always a friendly welcome and my half lager is now brought automatically.' TN. 'All the dishes are superb, and I'm no veggie. The Bhel Puri is still my favourite though.' ME. Hours: 12-11.30pm.

©	Curry Club Discount	U	Unlicensed
V	Vegetarian	ANP	Alcohol not permitted
e-a-m-a-y-l	Eat as much as you like	BYO	Bring your own alcohol

CURRY CLUB

London N2

East Finchley

MAJJOS ©

1 Fortis Green, N2 020 8883 4357

Established in 1993 by Mrs Ashraf. Manager S Mogul. A shop with a seating area for just 10 diners, so you can enjoy some spicy dishes while shopping for your Indian groceries. Kashmiri, Pakistani and Indian food. Meat curries £5.25 (large) £3.50 (small), Vegetable curries £3.50 (large) £2.30 (small). Price check: CTM £5.25, Pullao Rice £1.25. Hours: 10.30am-10.30pm (10pm on Sun.).

London N3

Finchley, Fortis Green

BALTI NEW ENTRANT

120 Ballards Lane, Finchley, N3 020 8343 2062

Owned and managed by Mr J Uddin since 1992 and seats 42. Air-conditioned. Popular dishes: Balti. Delivery. Price check: Papadam 50p, CTM £5.95, Pullao Rice £1.50, House wine £6.40. Hours: 5-11pm. Stocks Cobra.

RANI VEGETARIAN BEST VEGETARIAN TOP 100 V

7 Long Lane, N3 020 8349 4386

Jyoti Patni's Rani (queen) is tastefully decorated in shades of turmeric and red, with Georgian chairs and glass-topped tables. Its vegetarian menu features mainly Gujarati items cooked by his wife and his mother, which are tasty enough to please all but the most obdurate non veggie. India's most western state, Gujarat, is the home of mild, slightly sweet dishes, with a love of yoghurt and gram flour. The soup-like curry Khadi is one dish showing Gujarati adoration of both. The famous bhajia also originated in Gujarat, as did the lesser known Dahi Vada, a gram flour dumpling in a tangy yoghurt sauce. Kachoris – Spicy mashed potato and peas spicy ball, coated in batter and deepfried. Bhel Puri are all there along with Gujarati curries e.g. Undui – five vegetable stew, and a Gujarati national dish. Traditionally the five vegetables are beans, aubergine, red pumpkin, sweet potato and a further vegetable. These are cooked in a sauce made from gram flour, asafoetida and yoghurt. It is often served with besan kofta balls in it. Another superb dish is Lasan Bateta, £3 – literally garlic potato, but it's not that simple – it is baby new potatoes, and the stuffing includes spices and red chilli. The whole is dipped in gram-flour batter, deep-fried and served in imli (sweet tamarind chutney). Wow!!! Innovations to prevent diner boredom [I wouldn't get bored if you were in my town, Jyoti] make this restaurant different. How about pizzas (which are after all just Naan bread cooked in the oven) with Indo-Italian toppings, such as banana (plantain) methi with green chilli and mozzarella. Great stuff. 'The menu has some cold starters which are "to die for". Rashia Vall, great. Rice and breads as good as usual.' CT. Says the highly critical RL: 'Menu includes unusual and tasty dishes. Recommended to me by so many people. Aloo Shai Poori (crispy pooris, potatoes, onions with yoghurt) and Vall Papri (spicy beans and onions on pooris with tamarind and yoghurt), both a taste of heaven. This restaurant is pure quality. It's Finchley's finest curry house.' RL. We'll go further, Russell; we're giving it our Best Vegetarian Award. Thali £10, Set meal £13, min 2, Average Spend £15. Kid's menu. High chairs for the tinies. Hours: 6-10.30pm daily; Sun. 12.15-2.30pm. Stocks Cobra.

London N6
Highgate

KIPLINGS TOP 100 ©

2 North Hill, Highgate Village, N6 020 8340 1719

From the Stanley Krett and Akrim (Hussain) Ali stable (*see* Bengal Lancer, NW5), it has established a good reputation with everything 'as it should be.' JE. 'We were lucky enough to get a table for two at this packed curry house on a Friday night. Sensibly we didn't over-order for once, and shared the most unusual stuff we could see – Chilli Chicken Bayang, Rangoon Noodles and a Stuffed Kulcha. They arrived in a flash and were extremely tasty. On the price front there were pluses and minuses – they forgot to charge us for the Kukcha, but it was £4 for a pint (i.e. two bottles) of Kingfisher!' RL. But it is Highgate! Stocks Cobra.

London N7
Tufnell Park

BENGAL BALTI HOUSE NEW ENTRANT ©

6 Brecknock Road, N7 020 7609 7075

Owned by Ashik Ali since 1994. Air-conditioned restaurant seats 86 in two rooms, decorated in green ragroll paint. Takeaway: 10% discount. Delivery. Price check: Papadam 45p, CTM £5.25, Pullao Rice £1.45, House wine £5.95.

Hours: 12-2.30pm/6pm-12am (Sat. to 12.30am). Branch: Hillmarton Tandoori, Hillmarton Terrace, N7. Stocks Cobra.

London N8

Crouch End, Hornsey, Turnpike Lane

ELAHEE NEW ENTRANT

218a Middle Lane, Holloway, N8 020 8348 0741

'First impressions are not too great, it has to be said, but food is excellent. Particularly good are the papadom dipping sauce, Lamb Chana, Chicken Dupianza, Chicken Sag, Chicken Ceylon and Bindi and Brinjal Bahjis.' R&RS.

London N10

Muswell Hill

TASTE OF NAWAB ©

93 Colney Hatch Lane, N10 020 8883 6429

Taken over in 1996 by Mujibur Rahman, the comfortable air-conditioned Nawab has 'all the old favourites plus exciting dishes. The Chicken Kori is a must – really delicious, spicy and full of flavour. All dishes are large, reasonably priced and tasty. Service great!' SM. We attended a buffet dinner in aid of Breast Cancer Campaign. Mujibur's an energetic chap, holding many fund-raising do's for deserving courses. The place was packed, with people queuing outside on the pavement. Buffets can sometimes be a total let down – but the chefs had pulled out all the stops to create a fresh, hot and appetising selection of dishes. Price check: Papadam 50p, CTM £5.95, Pullao Rice £1.75, Peshwari Nan £1.75, Lager £2.10 pint, House wine £6.95. Delivery: £10 minimum. Hours: 12-2.30pm/6pm-12am. Sunday buffet 12-5.30pm.

London N11

Friern Barnet, New Southgate

BEJOY ©

72 Bounds Green Road, N11 020 8888 1268

Established 1995, Abdul Sukur's restaurant seats 54, party room 16. Bangladeshi standards and side dishes cooked by chef M Rahman. Price check: Papadam 50p, CTM £6.30, Pullao Rice £1.60, Peshwari Nan £1.75. Delivery: £8 minimum, 2-mile radius. Hours: 12-2.30pm (Sat.-Thurs.)/6pm-

12am. Sunday buffet £5.95 per person, 12-11pm. Branch: Sunderban, N4. Stocks Cobra.

London N12

North Finchley, Woodside Park

FINCHLEY PAN CENTRE

15 Woodhouse Road, N12 020 8446 5497

A tiny, unlicensed Indian snack bar, frequented by Indians. Kebabs, samosas, veg rissoles, etc., very inexpensive. Friendly service. Cash please. Oh, and as for Pan or Paan, it's not a cooking vessel, it is a collection of edible ingredients, ranging from very bitter to very sweet wrapped in the paan or bright dark green paan or betel leaf. Paan is an acquired taste, used as an aid to digestion. The observant visitor to India will have noticed very busy street kiosks dispensing paan all hours. We only know of a few other Pan houses (in Asian communities such as Southall). *See* page 49 for more about Paan. Hours: 12-10pm (Fri. 3.30-10pm); closed Tues.

London N13

Broomfield Park, Palmers Green

DIPALI INDIAN NEW ENTRANT ©

82 Aldermans Hill, N13 020 8886 2221

Owned and managed by Muzahid A Choudhury, since 1972. Mr Choudhury has re-opened the Dipali Restaurant in Palmers Green, a former *Guide* entrant, following the fire which tragically claimed the lives of his business partner and close friend Shajahan Miah and Miah's young family. Mr Choudhury is still trying to come to terms with his loss, but he took the brave decision to set up again on his own, to ensure that his friend's memory lives on and that Shajahan's local charity work can continue. The popular Dipali restaurant appeared in the first and subsequent *Guides* until the appalling tragedy. We are delighted it is back, and would like reports please. Specials: Murghi Shassle £5.50 – piece of spring chicken marinated in mint sauce, cooked with selected spices and topped with salad. Murghi Tamatar £3.95 – chicken cooked in fresh green chilli and coriander ginger, very spicy hot. Achar Murghi £4.75 – cooked with pickle, slightly hot. Sunday Buffet 12-3.30pm. Delivery. Price check: Papadam 50p, CTM £5.95, Pullao Rice £2.15. Hours: 12-2.30pm/6pm-12am. Stocks Cobra.

London N14

Oakwood, Southgate

BEKASH NEW ENTRANT ©

6-8 Hampden Square, N14 020 8368 3206

Owned by Nazrul Miah (manager) and Harun Ali (chef), decorated in yellow, seats 55. Delivery. House wine £7.80. Price check: Papadam 50p, CTM £6.25, Pullao Rice £1.60. Hours: 5.30-11.30pm (Sat. to 12am). Stocks Cobra.

London N15

Seven Sisters, South Tottenham

BOMBAY SPICE NEW ENTRANT

440 West Green, N15 020 8881 1636

Taken over in October 1999, by Abdul Ullah. Formerly Cottage Tandoori. You will find all the curry house favourites here at very competitive prices. Delivery. Price check: Papadam 40p, CTM £5.25, Pullao Rice £1.50. Hours: 5pm-12am.

London N16

Stamford Hill, Stoke Newington

LE TAJ ©

56 Stoke Newington Church Street, N16 020 7249 0799

Formerly Spice of Asia opened in 1989, taken over in 1997 by Abu Chowdhury. The 46-seater Le Taj serves le curry and les side-dishes. Decorated in clean cream with pink tablecloths. Indian art hangs from the walls. Notable specials include: Achar Goshti, pickled meat, Muglai Murgh, creamy chicken, Hash Masala, duck curry and Fish Jalfrezi, fish dry stir-fried. Delivery, 3-mile radius. Price check: Papadam 50p, CTM £5.70, Pullao Rice £1.55. Hours: 6-11.30pm; closed Tues.

RASA TOP 100 V

55 Stoke Newington Church Street, N16 020 7249 0344

This is the first of three restaurants established by Shiva Das Sreedharan – Das to you and me and his wife Alison. Decor is very relaxing, with about fifteen tables. They specialise in southern Indian cooking from Kerala,

India's most southerly state. To be precise it is Nair cuisine. Nair's the most respected of the five Kerelan ethnic groups. Descended from the original Kerelan warriors, they are contrarily, non-vegetarian; contrarily, because at Rasa it is all vegetarian. Since, from economic necessity, much of Kerela's food is vegetarian, the food you get at Rasa is expert exposition of the vegetarian art. Cooking uses coconut, mustard, curry leaves, curds, chillies, lentils and rice. Exotic vegetables include plantains, drumsticks, gourds, sour mango, and beans. The differences between the cooking of the five Kerelan groups is intensely subtle, including the names of the similar dishes. But differences there are, so try it out. 'My favourite North London restaurant. On last trip had Dhal Soup, a curry made with Indian shallots, a side dish called Ulli Theeyal with cabbage and coconut and Mango Lassi. There is a 10% service charge and the total cost for this wonderful meal was £13.59.' DS. 'Purely veg restaurants not really my bag, but it's hard to fault the quality of the food here. I had Achappam, nice change from usual papadom. Accompanying chutneys fantastic.' RL. The continued understated 'very good' from DrCF and his tribe of highly critical Indian medics is, as we say, praise indeed! We continue to include this restaurant in our TOP 100, though in truth it doesn't need this accolade – it's always full. So book! Branches: Rasa, Dering Street, and Rasa Samudra Charlotte Street, both W1.

London N19

Archway, Tufnell Park, Upper Holloway

THE PARSEE NEW NAME NEW ENTRANT

34 Highgate Hill, N19 020 7272 9091

Was Raj Vogue until Mr Choudhury died early in 2000. Now run by his son with Dr CF and Adam Metha and some other doctors, whose critical comments have graced these pages for years. They are putting their money where their mouths are, literally! As we write the menu is being prepared by Cyrus Todiwalla, of Café Spice Namasté, E1, himself a Parsee, and we anticipate very high quality here, so reports please.

London N21

Winchmore Hill

JIM THOMPSON'S THAI PUB NEW ENTRANT TOP 100

Green Lanes, N21 020 8360 0005

One of a chain of Thai theme pubs. Fun decor. Good ambience. Well-trained management and staff. Good Thai food. 7 branches mostly London.

London N22

Alexandra Palace, Wood Green

AKBAR TAKEAWAY NEW ENTRANT

13 Salisbury Road, N22 020 8881 7902

'Superb quality food, good sized meals, all at a very good price. Large selection of different rice and vegetable dishes. Chicken Madras is my favourite, King Prawn dishes are really good value.' SM.

London NW

Area: North West London,
Postcodes: NW1 to NW11
Population: 680,000

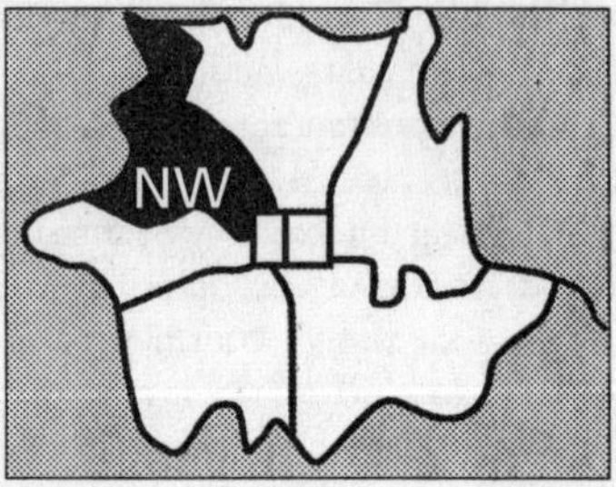

London NW1

Camden Town, Chalk Farm, Drummond Street, Euston, Marylebone, Regent's Park

NW1 – Drummond Street

I am often asked where the best restaurants are. It's the reason for producing this Guide. Drummond Street is one such area. West of Euston Station, it will not win any beauty awards, and it lacks the ethnic glamour of Southall and Wembley, or the intensity of purpose of Brick Lane. Its assets are a concentrated selection of extremely good, mainly inexpensive Indian food vendors. There are greengrocers, a Halal butcher and ingredient stores, such as Viranis, where Pataks began trading in the 60s. It is open all hours for all things Indian including Cobra (useful for the nearby BYOs), a dozen or so takeaways and restaurants. Here in alphabetical order is our Drummond Street selection:

AMBALA SWEET CENTRE TAKEAWAY

112 Drummond Street, NW1 020 7387 3521

Ambala started trading in 1965. It specialises in takeaway-only savoury snacks (Pakoras and Samosa, etc.), Indian sweets (Halva, Jalebi, Gulab Jamun, Barfi, etc.) and a few vegetarian curries such as chickpea. Established initially for Asians, it now has branches in Birmingham, Bradford, Derby, East Ham, Finchley, Glasgow, Leicester, Leyton, Luton, Manchester, Slough, Southall,

Tooting and Wembley. Drummond Street is the flagship. All branches serve identical items at identical prices. The quality is first-class and the prices are always reasonable. Be prepared to queue, and pay cash. Open daily 10am-11pm

DIWANA BHEL POORI HOUSE TOP 100 V BYO

121 Drummond Street, Euston, NW1 020 7387 5556

Established in 1971 by Kris Patel, who manages, assisted by Eddie Labak, and describes his gem as serving 'authentic Gujarati, Bombay and south Indian food'. It's functional, more or less café-style, unlicensed, open all day, still very cheap, highly successful. 100-seat restaurant, divided into two ground-floor sections plus a further floor. The food is all vegetarian, with much vegan, and above all, it's all fabulous, and it's most certainly all authentic. And Diwana is an original. As is often the way, the originator of a concept (in this country at any rate) usually remains the best. Diwana pioneered Bombay pavement kiosk snack food in the UK and is now much copied. And it is undoubtedly still the best of its kind. It is one of DBAC S 'favourites, not to be visited for the decor, nor for a long and relaxing meal – sitting on the floor would be more comfortable than sitting on the bolted-down benches, so opt for chairs if you can. I have the same thing every time I visit, Papadam with Coconut Chutney, Rasam, a soup, whose chillies without fail give me attention-drawing hiccups, then a Dosa £3 to £4.60 depending on type, with more Coconut Chutney, with its mustard seed and chilli and Sambar. If Pat and I share, I try to get all the drumsticks before him. And of course I never miss out on one of their adorable Bhel Puris, their masthead and their most ordered dish.' Bhel Puri, or Poori, is defined on page 40. Diwana offers several types -Batata Puri, Dahi Batata Puri, Chat Aloo Papri and Batata Pava, all £2.10. Bhel can be accompanied by Gol Goppas (*see* page 43). A super alternative starter is Dahi Vada (*see* page 42). By now you've spent £5 or £6, and you're probably full. But try to leave a little space for the Diwana's desserts. Their legendary Kulfi, perhaps, or 'the highlight of our meal, the Falooda – an Indian knickerbocker glory – probably the best in London. The quality of the food outweighs the numbness in your backside!' DB. 'All first class. Reasonably priced.' MW. 'Consistently good quality and low prices. Never changes.' JR. 'On one of the hottest days in July, I needed lunch in Drummond Street. I chose Diwana because of the jug of water that is automatically provided. It was too hot for alcohol and lassis is too filling when there is serious eating to be done.' BS. 'The back of the bill has a questionnaire. I was pleased to tick excellent for everything.' HC. Booking is hit and miss, and they won't even try on Fri. to Sun. so expect a queue (especially at peak hours). Probably the best value in London and don't forget to BYO (no corkage charge). Off-licence with chilled Cobra available at Viranis up the street. Thali from £4 to £6. E-a-m-a-y-l lunch to 2.30pm, £4.50. Hard to exceed £12 for a good veggie blow-out! It remains very high in our TOP 100. Hours: 12pm-11pm. Daily buffet: £3.95 till 2.30pm.

GUPTA CONFECTIONERS TAKEAWAY

100 Drummond Street, Euston, NW1 020 7380 1590

Overshadowed, perhaps, by the nearby Ambala, Gupta is nonetheless a very good, long-established, less flashy vegetarian snack and sweet takeaway. Samosas and Pakoras, plus their unique, delightful, and often still-hot Pea Kebab, a Gujarati speciality, are freshly cooked in the kitchens behind. Their sweets achieve a lightness of touch, and seem to avoid the taste of tinned evaporated milk that sometimes spoils those made by others. Cash or cheque. Branch: Watford Way, Hendon, NW4.

RAAVI KEBAB HALAL ANP

125 Drummond Street, Euston, NW1 020 7388 1780

Kebab tells you it's very much a meat place, Halal that there's no pandering to Western tastes, as one can tell by its local mostly Muslim patronage (so no alcohol permitted). 'Had three Roti which were freshly made, very good and moist. Main course – Haleem, the rarely encountered Hyderabadi/ Pakistani dish, cooked with meat, wheat, lentils and spices – very nice and spicy. The rest of the menu wasn't extensive with five grills, four specials, four meat, three curry, four vegetable dishes.' GH. 'One of my favourites. Cheap and cheerful. Food superb. Sheek Kebabs amongst the best anywhere.' RE. Cash only. 'Superb food in a cosy little café-style curry house. Service was casual, meal presented in the authentic way. Only disappointing dish was the chicken curry which was a little thin in taste. Karahi Gosht though was perfection. They are seeking to extend the hours of trade into the night.' RW. 'A stone's throw from Euston Station. A small restaurant, clean, but in danger of being overrun by plastic foliage. Staff a bit on the surly side, but food is excellent. Tarka Daal was thick and tasty, Tandoori Roti was piping hot and made to order.' RE. Hours: 12.30-11pm.

RAVI SHANKAR

133-135 Drummond Street, NW1 020 7388 6458

The least pretentious of the Drummond trio (inc. Chutneys, and Haandi) and the first, it is slightly (but only just) more up-market than, but otherwise similar in most respects to the Diwana which it followed into Drummond

Street. Prices are still very reasonable and it is usually busy at peak hours. Recommended are the two Thali set dishes, the Mysore and the Shankar, and the Shrikand dessert. Vegetarian restaurant serving excellent, authentic food. Bhel Poori, Potato Bonda, Mysore Masala Dosa, Mixed Vegetable, Bombay Aloo. Every dish was excellent – flavoursome, spicy and delicious. Prices are extremely reasonable. Daily special at under £3 mid-week (£3.20 Sat. & Sun.) which look excellent. This one must be knocking on the door of the "TOP 100". Two visits within a week.' MW. Hours: 12pm-11pm. Branches: Chutneys, and Haandi, both on Drummond Street. Stocks Cobra.

SHAH NEW ENTRANT

159 Drummond Street, Euston NW1 020 7383 5677

A reincarnation, in name and street if not street number. The original Shah, est. 1951 was London's fourth Indian, and fathered Fulham's Star of India, SW5, literally, because that restaurant is still going strong, with son Reza at the helm. The original Shah closed a decade ago and Chutney's took its well-known corner site at 124 on the street. So what, you say? Just facts, say I, and that's what I like dishing up, so there! And so what does this new Shah dish up? RW says it's a: 'light and airy restaurant. Lunchtime special advertised at £4.60, but subject to 10% service charge [naughty, naughty]. Enjoyable but thin lentil soup, followed by two rather insubstantial and watery basic mild curries. Taken for what it was, a varied and complete meal for the price of something unpleasant from one of the multinational burger chains.' I simply don't know what you mean, Ralph.

Remainder of NW1

BOMBAY ROMA NEW ENTRANT ©

Arch 78, 30 Randolph St, Camden Town, NW1 0800 195 0690

Takeaway opened in 1999, catering in world food. There are sections on Indian, Italian – pasta and pizza, Japanese – sushi and tempura, French, Chinese, Thai with canapés, salad and puddings. AND they have an off-license (Cobra £3.80), so drinks can be delivered with your food. AND you'll never believe it but they sell flowers – roses, orchids or lilies, candles – scented, coffee and chocolate chip cookies (and for those who want lung cancer – cigarettes and Havanas). All this can be delivered to your door. What a service! What a takeaway! The Indian menu includes all your favourites: Vegetable Samosa £2.90, Chicken Tikka £4.80 and Lamb Rogan Josh (most popular) £6.80. In the snack menu there are two great dishes: Bombay Fishcakes £5.90, Scottish salmon flavoured, potato, ginger, garlic, coriander and mustard seed, served with mint sauce and Bhel Puri £4.30 (my favourite – shame only a few restaurants do it – never mind it makes going to Bombay, sitting in the Sea Lounge at the Taj Mahal Hotel and sipping a Gimlet even more exiting!) – cool mix of crispy puri, puffed rice, potato, shallots, combined with tangy tamarind. Price check: Papadam 50p, CTM £6.80, Pullao Rice £2.10. Hours: 5.30-11pm (Sat. to 11.30pm). Stocks Cobra.

GREAT NEPALESE BEST NEPALESE AWARD TOP 100 ©

48 Eversholt Street, Euston, NW1 020 7388 6737

There have been a number of Nepalese restaurants opening recently around the country, partly as a result of disbanding so many Gurkha regiments (bad move that – like throwing out the baby with the bathwater). But the army's loss is a culinary gain – though real authentic Nepalese food is still hard to find. One Nepalese restaurant that has stood the test of time is The Great, started by Gopal P Manandhar in 1982, and recently joined as chef by son Jeetendra, whose charming wife Mandira also adds her culinary expertise, especially with Nawari (an Nepalese ethnic group) food, for example the starter, Momo, or Momocha – steam-cooked meat-filled pastries, £3.50. Other Nepalese specialities include Masco Bara, black lentil pancakes with curry sauce £3.45, Kalezo Ra Chyow (chicken liver). Main courses include Dumba (mutton), Pork Bhutwa (the Nepalese have no proscriptions of either pork or alcohol) and Hach Ko (duck) curries. There is also a range of eleven Nepalese vegetable dishes. Add those to sixteen 'standard' curry house vegetable dishes and the vegetarian will be spoilt for choice. In addition, the Great does all the standard curries and tandooris, from Phal, 'very very hot', to Shahi Korma, 'very very mild', though why you'd go there for these is beyond me. Go for Nepalese food, and if virgin to it, tell the 'friendly, knowledgeable and efficient staff who take the time to explain the dishes. Pancake starters were smooth but spicy in taste served with a delicious red sauce. Main meal was an aromatic and beautifully balanced rich sauce with cuts of moist lamb. Perfectly cooked Basmati rice, naan delightfully laced with chunks of garlic, soft and moist. Very pleasant meal.' RW. Set Nepalese meal £13.50. Service 10%. Average spend: £15. Price check: Papadam complimentary, CTM £8.25, Pullao Rice £1.95, Peshwari Nan £1.95, Lager £2. Takeaway: 10% discount. Delivery: £12 minimum, 5-mile radius. Hours: 5.30-11.30pm (Sat. to 12am). It's time for us to put the Great in the Great and give it our Best Nepalese Award. Stocks Cobra.

TAWA INDIAN NEW ENTRANT

108 Parkway, Regents Park, NW1 020 7485 6507

Formerly Tandoori Nights, opened in 1988 and taken over by Zafar Uddin and Abbas Karim in 1999. Seats 52 diners. Popular dishes: Chicken Tikka Special £7.95 – chargrilled chicken, green pepper, onions, tomato, mushroom, flambéed at the table with brandy. House wine £7.95. Delivery. Price check: Papadam 50p, CTM £6.95, Pullao Rice £1.95. Hours: 12-2.30pm/6-11.45pm (Sat. to 12am). Stocks Cobra.

VICEROY OF INDIA RE-ENTRANT

3-5 Glentworth Street, NW1 020 7486 3515

Once in our TOP 100, then sadly delisted altogether last time, we return the Viceroy because we're fed up with trying to explain its absence. Once the doyen of Indian business people and High Commission officials, and seemingly the daily meeting place of Air India's directors, it has simply been overtaken by a decade of advancement elsewhere. Its brick and marble decor, redolent of the once sumptuous, and now equally jaded Mughal Sheraton Hotel in Agra, and its once original window kitchen are not enough to please CF and his group of Parsee, Goan, Bombay, Bangladeshi and Delhi doctors. But it does please others: 'we thought the Biriani (£10.50) in its sealed Dum Pukht pot was just lyrical' ME. Set 2-course lunch £10, 3-course £13. Average spend £25. Evening min. spend £16. Set meals from £19-22. Service 12.5%. Hours: 12-3pm (not Sat & Sun)/6-11pm daily. Stocks Cobra.

London NW2

Cricklewood, Neasden

FINCHLEY PAN CENTRE

15 Woodhouse Road, NW2 020 8446 5497

No, it doesn't sell utensils, and I never said it did. But one American *Guide* purchaser told me I did not make this fact clear, and she wasted hours trudging here to buy Indian cookware. Pity she saved her blast for a belated e-mail. One phone call at the time... So what does go on at the Pan Centre? Well, let me repeat my previous remarks. It's a takeaway only, owned and managed by S Sayed serving Kenyan Asian curries and accompaniments – Biryani being the most popular dish. Pan is indeed on offer. Pan or Paan is bright dark green paan betel leaf, folded samosa-fashion around a stuffing of sweet spices such as aniseed, shredded betel nut, sunflower seeds, lime paste, etc. It is eaten in one mouthful, as a digestive. The leaf is bitter, the mouth-feel coarse and the taste acquired. The observant visitor to India will have noticed the ubiquitous, very busy paan street kiosks with their leaves and dozens of silver pots containing all sorts of weird and wonderful ingredients. In the subcontinent, everyone takes paan daily. British Asians are virtually deprived of this pleasure, there being just a handful of paan shops, and then only where there are large Asian communities (such as Southall). No credit cards. Price check: Vegetable Samosa (2) 90p, Meat Samosa (2) 90p, Chicken Biryani £4.25, Mutton Masala £3.60. Hours: 12-10pm; 3.30-10pm Fri; closed Tues.

KHANA NEW ENTRANT

68 Cricklewood Broadway, NW2 020 8452 4789

'A fantastic meal. Chicken Chat full of flavour. Khana Fish, an East African talapia, was one of the nicest dishes I have ever tasted. Service was friendly and polite, atmosphere was happily busy. By far the best of the seven curry houses in the vicinity and we eat in all of them throughout the course of the year!' RP.

London NW3

Belsize Park, Hampstead, Finchley Road, Swiss Cottage

FLEET TANDOORI ©

104 Fleet Road, NW3 020 7485 6402

'A good restaurant for those seeking a dependable, quiet and inexpensive meal. The Sunday buffet is a must for those who wish a cheap alternative to meat and two veg. An additional attraction is the Special on the menu – Pomfret Fish, which comes either tandoori or, for those with a rich palate, bathed in a curry sauce flavoured with a multitude of spices. Good prices enhanced by a 10% discount to Curry Club members at any time!' AD. Stocks Cobra.

London NW4

Hendon

PRINCE OF CEYLON BEST SRI LANKAN AWARD ©

39 Watford Way, NW4 020 8202 5967

Abdul Satter has been here since 1979. And he's been beavering away since we last reported. He's bought next door and extended his empire by another 30 seats, giving a total of 150 seats, including a party room. Now split over five rooms, you don't feel you are eating in nearby RAF Hendon's aircraft hangars. It's a kind of bamboo/coir jungle with yellow-ochre and brown linen, olive green leather seats, and a lot of natural dark wood – tables given privacy by carved wood screens. The Prince's standard menu of tandooris, kebabs, curries and all the business, all perfectly competently cooked, are not what you go there for. It is the Sri Lankan specials. And if these items are unfamiliar, ask the waiter's advice, but be patient if explanations are unclear at first. It is a rice (Buth) cuisine. Jaffna Thossai, soft pancake made of soaked and ground urid dal, served with coconut chutney. Devilled curries are there, including Squid curry. Fried Cabbage with onion £2.75. Coconut Chutney £1.50. Hoppers or Appas are rice and coconut-flour pancakes; String Hoppers, like string made of wheat or rice flour dough, but resembling vermicelli nests (10 for £3); or Pittu – ditto dumpling. These or straight rice are accompanied by pungent watery curries, in which coconut, turmeric, tamarind, curry leaves and chillies feature. But they can be mild, too. Look out for aromatic black curries and fragrant white ones. Fish dishes, such as Ambul Thial (a Sri Lankan national dish – a sour, spicy tuna fish dish) and the Ceylon Squid (Dhallo) curry are popular. And there are substantial curries such as Lumpri (chicken, meat and egg). Sambols, or relishes, include dried fish and chilli (Seeni Sambol is a cooked version). We've not received any blaster reports this time (phew!) so we now tempt fate by keeping it in our TOP 100, aided and abbetted by DR CF and his subcontinental doctor super group who declare the Prince: 'Excellent every time'. Average spend £13. Sunday buffet, noon-5pm, £8.50. Hours: 12-3pm/6pm-12am; Sat. & Sun. 12pm-12am. Serves Cobra.

SITARA INDIAN NEW ENTRANT

105 Brent Street, NW4 020 8202 6986

'Standard curry house. Good portions, food and service, and reasonably priced. Busy most times.' JB.

London NW5

Kentish Town

BENGAL LANCER TOP 100 ©

253 Kentish Town Road, NW5 020 7485 6688

We've always thought of Stanley Krett and Akram (Hussain) Ali's Lancer as your absolutely perfect example of a local curry house. Albeit, it's in densest central London, but it's a local, nonetheless. And it's spot on. Decorated with sepia prints of regimental men, and a kind of jungle theme, it may have pioneered reminiscence-theme restaurants, and may have suited the end of the last century, but the owners are aware that a redec is needed, and are plotting expansion and planning permission when we met with them recently. Meanwhile, the Lancer soldiers on, presenting a menu of old favourites and innovative variations. 'Menu interesting, ample and informative. Food very good – nice dumplings and shahi.' MT. 'This is a restaurant whose standard has remained consistently high. Always a pleasure to visit. The service is efficient, but not obtrusive, and the quality of food very high, thus guaranteeing that we will be visiting again shortly.' DM. 'A genuine classy restaurant with an excellent menu range. Liver Hazra, liver cooked and tossed in spices, rich and almost a meal in itself. Unusual, good and great taste. Tiger Wings are chicken drumsticks tandoori-style. Service first-class, attentive and despite a packed peak-time Saturday night they kept checking up to see if we required anything else. Food up among the best for quality, portions more than adequate and at value-for-money prices. Deserves its rating in the TOP 100.' AS. Branch: Kiplings, N6.

INDIAN BRASSERIE ©

56 Chetwynd Road, NW5 020 7482 2803

Established as the Indian Lancer in 1990, this 42-seater was taken over and name-changed by Muktadir Miah in 1999. It serves all your favourite curry house items, and we are pleased to note, it continues to use authentic ingredients. Specials include Punjabi Tinda (gooseberry-sized marrow) Gosht, Shalgam (Turnip) Gosht, Maachi Tamatar – dish curry speciality of south east region of Cox Bazaar and Paneer Tikka. 'Wide menu, fairly conventional with some unusual choices. Service polite and attentive, but only brought two papadoms and not three, and forgot to bring the chapati ordered. Tandoori Lamb Chops were plentiful, and well marinated if a little too salty and lacking in piquancy. Lamb Gosht was just right.' GP. Price check: Papadam 45p, CTM £5.50, Pullao Rice £1.75, General Billy's wine £7.95. Service 10%. Delivery. Hours: 12-2.30pm/6-11.45pm; Sun. 12-10.45pm. Stocks Cobra (on tap).

London NW6

Kilburn, West Hampstead

GEETA SOUTH INDIAN NEW TO OUR TOP 100

57-59 Willesden Lane, NW6 020 7624 1713

Yes, you can get standard meat and chicken curries, et al, here, though we cannot for the life of us imagine why you'd want to. But a lot of Geeta's diners order the formula stuff, and I for one can only presume it's done better than average. I say that because as a *Guide* writer, I should know. But I confess I've not tried these delights at Geeta's. Slapped wrists (if that's still legal)! But I can't bring myself to and it's a free world. So for heaven's sake go there and try the mainly south Indian vegetarian food at which Geeta excels, and has done since the 70s, with never a decline in standard. Dosas, Idli, Sambar, Upamas Karela (bitter gourds), drumsticks (long pithy marrow which you suck to extract the tender flesh), Ravaiya – baby aubergine and plantains stuffed with a coconut spicy filling Rasam – and more. And with most of these around the £2 mark, and providing you keep off the carnivorous items, you'll fill up for less than a tenner, with drink. It's all fine stuff, served in less than glamorous, but typically Indian surroundings, to a thoroughly devoted following. 'This and Vijay (below) are different and should not be missed.' DMW. Hours: 12-2.30pm/6-10.30pm (Fri & Sat. to 12am). It's high time we recognised Geeta's with a long-service medal, and promoted it to our TOP 100. Stocks Cobra.

GOLDEN BENGAL ©

73, Fairfax Road, South Hampstead, NW6 — 020 7372 4646

Owned and managed by Mr R Khan, since 1998. Delivery. Price check: Papadam 40p, CTM £5.45, Pullao Rice £1.60, House wine £6.95. Hours: 12-2.30pm/6-11.30pm (Sat. to 12am). Stocks Cobra.

SURYA V ©

59 Fortune Green Road, NW6 — 020 7435 7486

Mr (front of house) and Mrs Tiwari (chef) really pack 'em in at this tiny, 34-seat vegetarian, licensed restaurant – there's no room to move, almost literally – it's always full. The dish of the day (it changes daily) excites several of our regulars. We hear well of Gujarati dishes such as Patra and Kaddu Kari and inexpensive prices. Hours: 6-10.30pm, and Sun. lunch. Branch: Shree Ganesha, 4 The Promenade, Edgwarebury Lane, Edgware, Middlesex.

VIJAY NEW TO OUR TOP 100

49 Willesden Lane, NW6 — 020 7328 1087

Vijay was founded in 1966, and predated nearby Geeta (*see* above) by several years, so it can take the crown for being the earliest to provide south Indian food for NW6, and its menu contains all the vegetarian items listed in Geeta's entry, at much the same prices. Indeed my remarks are the same, since Vijay like Geeta does carniverous dishes too. Vijay has its own clan of loyal regulars who know they'll get 'very nice tasty food.' B&WW. 'This and Geeta (above) are different and should not be missed.' DMW. Prices are much the same, perhaps just a tad higher here, but again, even with the ridiculous 10% service charge (please get rid of it) you'll only spend a tenner if you stick to the scrumptious vegetarian delights. Hours: 12-2.45pm/6-10.45pm (Fri & Sat to 11.45pm). Like Geeta, we rather belatedly promote Vijay to our TOP 100. Stocks Cobra.

London NW7

Mill Hill

DAYS OF THE RAJ ©

123 The Broadway, NW7 020 8906 3477

Established in 1989 by S Miah, who tells us that he changes the wallpaper every six months to 'maintain standards'. M Miah manages the 100-seater, whose extensive menu appears to be formula stuff from Kurma to Phal, etc. But a closer look provides a number of 'unique' dishes. What are Noorane, Sherajee, Kushboo, Dilkush and Bakhara curries, for example? Each available in chicken, lamb, beef, prawn, king prawn and vegetables (the menu explains their attributes), they are clearly house inventions. So is the dish Days of the Raj, gently cooked with pineapple, lychees and sultanas in a thick creamy sauce sprinkled with nuts. It sounds like a fruit salad but is, we're assured, 'really quite delicious, the chicken quite succulent, and mild enough for my boss who is a curry novice.' GC. It is more than a 'safe-bet' curry house. It is very smart indeed and is a place to go for an enjoyable meal out. Price check: Papadam 50p, CTM £7.50, Duck Bakhara £8, Pullao Rice £2, Peshwari Nan £2.20. Service 10%. E-a-m-a-y-l lunch buffet daily £7. Delivery: £12 minimum, 3-mile radius. Hours: 12-2pm/5-11.30pm. Stocks Cobra.

London NW10

Harlesden, Kensal Green, Willesden

ANN MARIE AT THE TASTE OF THE TAJ ©

4 Norbeck Pde, off Hanger Lane, Ealing, NW10 020 8991 5366

Ann Marie won't mind if I repeat myself about location, location, location. Her Taste, which has been going since 1989, is in Ealing. It's also in NW10, which Ealing isn't (but it used to be W5). The North Circular Gyratory rebuild caused mayhem with Ann Marie's access, if you follow me, not to mention with her postcode. She says herself it's 'essential to phone and ask for directions, because the access to the front is now closed from the NCR'. As in Birmingham, you can see it, but you cannot touch it. But find this 64-seater you should. Relax to the warm and cosy red decor, admire the many tiger pictures on the walls, then avail yourself of a personalised service and advice that some of Ann Marie's regulars have known and delighted in for a staggering 35 years, here and at the now-closed Taj. Enjoy the memsahib's personal touches that turn this very ordinary-looking menu into a welcoming taste experience. Chef Nazrul converts it all into stimulating cuisine. CR tells of: 'fabulous fresh Chicken Dapeaza (*sic*) floating in fresh glistening onions, cooked original-style with crispy fried onion.' While RG tells of a 'mean' Dhansak and very succulent Tandoori dishes – basically curries with attitude and a rather unexpected delicacy of touch in the Courgette Bhaji served with fluffy Nans. BYO on champagne only, but please ask. Delivery: £12 minimum. Hours: lunch weekdays only/6pm-12am daily.

RAJ BALTI NEW ENTRANT ©

146 High Street, NW10 020 8965 6036

Managed by Mr Hoque. Formerly Harlesden Tandoori. Seats 50 and serves Bangladeshi formula curries. Specials: Stuffed Bengal Mirch £2.50 – barbecued green pepper stuffed with spiced minced meat or vegetable. Delivery: £8.95, 4-mile radius, hours 6-11.45pm. Price check: Papadam 40p, CTM £5.25, Pullao Rice £1.50, Peshwari Nan £1.75. Hours: 12-2.30pm/6pm-12am.

SABRAS V

263 High Road, NW10 020 8459 0340

What's this? New decor at Hemant and Nalinee Desai's 27-year old Sabras. Hope it's not cos of something we said last time. What we do say is that afficionados simply don't care about trivia like decor. No one does in India except the tourist hotels. What Sabra's regulars (of which our postbag tells us there are many) admire and keep returning for, is the truly home-cooked authenticity of the food. We also admire the menu repertoire which we are sure ranges wider than any other vegetarian Indian we know, and that includes India. Here you can get really accurately flavoured Punjabi, Kashmiri, Gujarati, Maharashtran and Kerelan dishes, and as if that's not enough, the Desai's throw in snippets from Kenyan Asia too. The menu describes all the dishes, and it's worth perusing if it's new to you. One way in is to try the deluxe thali (£15.50). For 'deluxe' read gargantuan, so don't order anything else – it gives so much variety. If you're one of those lucky regulars, you've no doubt trucked through each and every dish. Specials include, from north to south: Kashmiri Kofta Punjabi Alu Chole (Chickpeas in tangy chaat masala) or a varietal Paneer version. From Gujarat are Kadais, vadas, pakoras and kachoris while Maharashtra is represented by those two Bombay favourites, Bhel Puri and the fabulous Ravaiya – baby aubergine and plantains stuffed with a coconut spicy filling. Dosa, samosas, home-made chutneys, and heavenly curries redolent with curry leaves and fluffy rice.' DN. The prices are still really attractive, and help is at hand if you are unfamiliar with the food. Even with the silly 10% service charge, expect to pay between £12 and £15 for a worthy meal. Hours: 6-10.30pm Tues.-Sun. Stocks Cobra.

London NW11

Golders Green, Temple Fortune

ZAIKA NEW ENTRANT ©

113 Golders Green Road, NW11 020 8731 7389

Zaika is a buzz name, after the success accrued by Vineet in SW3. This Zaika also opened in mid '99 and is one of the many club-type Indian establishments opening around the Middlesex/London NW area. It has a large downstairs area, complete with large bar, stage and dance floor, and some 30 tables, enough for at least 120 diners. Upstairs is a smaller dining area with its own bar. Manageress Meena enthuses about the popular karaoke sessions she leads personally at busy weekends, and the Asian wedding traffic the place generates. It serves authentic well-spiced Punjabi food. Specials include Murgh Channa Lahori – chicken with chickpeas, Biryani, Baby Lamb Chops, Whole Stuffed Chicken, Hara Kerekla – stuffed bitter gourd and much more. Hours: 12-3pm/6pm-12am.

London SE

Area: South East London, postcodes SE1 to SE28
Population: 910,000

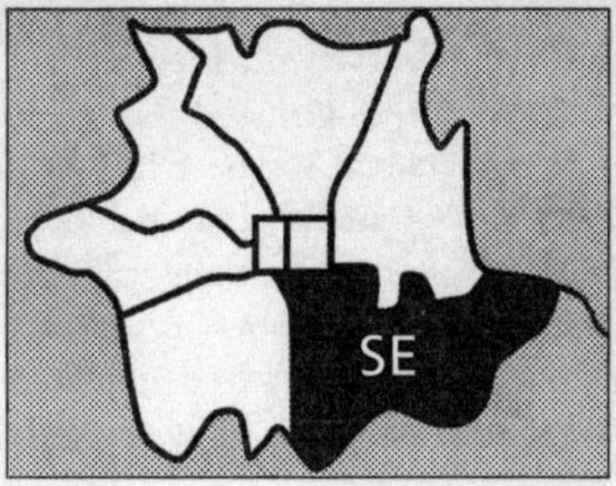

London SE1

Borough, Elephant and Castle, London Bridge, Old Kent Road, Southwark and Waterloo

BENGAL CLIPPER NEW TO OUR TOP 100

11-12 Cardamom Building, 31 Shad Thames, Butlers Wharf, SE1 020 7357 9001

Finding it is the problem. It's a fair walk from the tube! Taxis will find it (it's behind Conran's). If you're driving, and you've squeezed through the narrow one-way streets, you'll then have to find a parking space (min. £4). Once inside, you'll find Kenneth Lynn's sophisticated and expensive interior. The grand piano is still in evidence, and the ivories are tinkled at busy times, we hear, when it is less obtrusive on nearby diners. Chef Ram Das seems to have sorted out the samey taste that once emanated from the kitchens. From reports received, there is no doubt that cooking quality has gone up: 'At last I felt the food bore less resemblance to curry house and more to individual spicing.' ME. There is no doubt that the venue has always been popular and profitable. Witness the branch list with its two new ventures(*). The Choudhury's have always spent immeasurable sums of money on this and their newer creations, and it was only the cooking which let them down [only!!]. Now, having seemingly overcome this, we are finally please to welcome the Clipper aboard our TOP 100 list. Expect to pay more than usual here. Average £25-30. Branches: Bengal Trader*, E1, Bengal Mangrove*, Halstead Kent, and the original Bengal Lancer, Chislehurst. Stocks Cobra.

CASTLE TANDOORI

200 Elephant & Castle Shopping Centre, SE1 020 7703 9130

Mr Uddin's Castle is a spirited place, and a regular entrant in our *Guide*. He once told us, and will tell you, if you care to be entertained by him, that he's outlived twenty-two Hoovers, two recessions, and several prime ministers, and served enough nan bread to stretch from Waterloo to Paris. No update on this yet; but I expect he's calculating anew. The menu is pretty much formula (135 items) but includes duck, lamb chops and trout in various guises. Reports tell of the value for money. We know of no longer hours in London (let us know if you know better). So, if you're an insomniac curryholic, or just a late-night reveller, note this place well. Hours: Lunch Mon.-Fri./6pm-1am daily (Fri. & Sat. to 2.30am). Stocks Cobra.

IMPERIAL TANDOORI ©

48 Kennington Road, SE1 020 7928 4153

'MPs love it' winks Mohibad Rahman, though, despite attempts, he still doesn't elaborate. 'Lamb samosas were powerful (I think they use mutton for greater flavour), Chicken Tikka Bhuna was nicely spiced, Chicken Vindaloo was sneaky (2-3 minute time lapse for shock). With the coffee and liqueurs came a nice selection of supari dishes with fragrant, palette-cleansing seeds and sweets (nice touch). Attentive service. High quality cuisine. Good value.' TE. Price check: Papadam 40p, CTM £6.45, Tandoori Shashlik £5.95, Pullao Rice £1.75. Minimum charge £7.95. Stocks Cobra.

SHAKTI NEW ENTRANT

41 Tower Bridge Road, SE1 020 7403 5387

Owned by Shailas Ali since 1993. Restaurant seats 50 and serves Bangladeshi curries. Service: 10%. Sunday buffet lunch: £4.95. Delivery: £6, 3-mile radius. Price check: Papadam 35p, CTM £4.95, Pullao Rice £1.35, Peshwari nan £1.40, Lager £4 pint, House wine £6.95 bottle. Hours: 12-2.30pm/6pm-12.30am. Stocks Cobra.

THAMES TANDOORI

79 Waterloo Road, SE1 020 7928 3856

Established in 1985, Kalkur Rahman's 52-seater is still doing it under the railway bridge, and, yes, its neighbour, the Fishcotheque [it's a fish & chip shop for those who keep asking] is still doing it too, flashier than ever! And still no name-change to Tikkatheque! Mind you the frontage is smarter than ever. And HC's still doing it there too: 'This restaurant looks so ordinary from outside and the menu has just the usual items, but overall it is very well run and the food is well above average. Helpful, friendly and professional service. People kept piling in, mostly seemed like local office workers. Very pleasant meal' and 'Most of the tables were occupied and most of the diners business-suited men, working late [that's what they tell their wives – Ed]. Pleased to report the welcome, service and food well up to standards. I had a very pleasant meal. King Prawn Tandoori served on a sizzling platter with lots of onions.' Delivery: £20 minimum, 2-mile radius. Hours: 12-2.30pm/5.30-11.30pm. Branch: Strand Tandoori, WC2. Stocks Cobra.

London SE3
Blackheath

TASTE OF RAJ NEW ENTRANT

9 Royal Parade, SE3 020 8244 2823

'Continues to offer excellent service and beautifully prepared food. Packed at 7pm on Sunday, a testament to its popularity. Vegetable Dhansak, £3.60, was hot and quite sweet, full of fresh vegetables. Tarka Dall, £2.40, wonderfully smoky and the Garlic Nan, £1.90, light and fluffy.' And, 'Extremely reliable.' AG. Delivery. Hours: Fri.-Sat. 12-2.30pm/6pm-12.30am; Sun. 12pm-12am.

London SE9
Eltham

CROWN TANDOORI TAKEAWAY ©

7, Lingfield Crescent, Falconwood, SE9 020 8294 1313

Owned and managed by Saiful Abedin, since January 1997. Set meal excellent value from £3.85 for Chicken Tikka and Nan to £7.50 for Onion Bhajia, Chicken Bhuna, Bombay Aloo, Pullao Rice and Nan. Complimentary Popadoms, Mint Sauce and Onion salad with all orders – well that's very kind. Delivery: 3-mile radius. Price check: Papadam 40p, CTM £4.65, Pullao Rice £1.40. Hours: 5-11.30pm. Discount scheme.

CURRY GARDEN NEW ENTRANT ©

144 Westmount Road, SE9 020 8850 2250

Opened in 1992, taken over in 1999 by A Miah (manager), F Haque, S Miah and K Miah. Interesting menu additions: Koleze Puree £1.95 – chicken liver delicately prepared and served with pancake, Bahari Nan £1.65 – with green chilli and coriander. Delivery: 5-mile radius, £15 minimum, no delivery to high rise buildings. Price check: Papadam 40p, CTM £5.45, Pullao Rice £1.55. Hours: 5-10.30pm (Sat. to 11pm). Discount scheme.

RUCHITA TAKEAWAY ©

31 Avery Hill Road, SE9 020 8850 1202

Unusually for a takeaway-only, Miss Salma and Mohammed Yousuf's and Chef A Mukid's Ruchita is licensed. It's been going since 1975, so they know what they're doing. Their Chicken Tikka at £5.95 is still easily their most popular dish (surprise, surprise). Price check: Papadam 40p, CTM £5.50, Pullao Rice £1.50, Peshwari Nan £1.70. Delivery: £10, 3-mile radius. Hours: 5.30pm-12am. Stocks Cobra.

London SE10

Greenwich

TASTE OF INDIA NEW ENTRANT

57 Greenwich Church Street, SE10 020 8858 2668

'A standard, competent curry house, reliable but not special. Vegetable Dhansak £5.50 lightly spiced with excellent variety of vegetables. Happy to find a Chilli Nan £1.95 and that DID have a kick!' ES. Sunday Buffet Lunch £7.95 – children under 6 free. Price check: Papadam 40p, CTM £6.50, Pullao Rice £1.75.

London SE13

Hither Green, Lee, Lewisham

BENGAL BRASSERIE ©

79 Springbank Road, SE13 020 8461 5240

This 60-seater restaurant, prettily decorated in pale shades of pink, is owned and managed by Syed Ahmed. CT describes chef M Chowdhury's efforts as 'a nice little menu, now containing a few originals'. 'The spinach in Lobster Saghee (£6.95) makes this a fine dish.' ES. And others enjoy the Sea Thali (£8.50) – clever name. Most popular dish Sali Ana Roshi, chicken or meat with pineapple and honey, lightly spiced £4.75. Price check: Papadam 40p, CTM £5.50, Pullao Rice £1.30. Peshwari Nan £1.50, House wine £6.50. Minimum charge £15. Parties of 20 diners, eat and drink as much as you like for £25 per diner! Service 10%. Cover charge £1. Delivery: 3-mile radius. Hours: 5.30-11.30pm (12am on Sat.). Stocks Cobra.

GREEN CABIN SRI LANKAN NEW ENTRANT ©

244 Lewisham High Street, SE13 020 8852 6666

Opened in August 1996 by SE Jebarajan. Restaurant seats 40 and serves Sri Lankan and South Indian food – lovely. I would love a Sri Lankan restaurant to open near us, but unfortunately middle England just isn't ready for it – shame. Maybe SE13 isn't either, because the Green Cabin does the safe-bet Korma-through-Vindaloo range. I suggest you forget all that and go for the real stuff – you won't be disappointed. Meat Roll £2.25 (diced lamb, onions, chillies and potato wrapped in a pancake, bread crumbed and deep-fried, served with spicy sauce), Potato Kulambu £1.75 (deep-fried cubes of potato cooked in coconut milk with dry roasted chilli powder), Cabbage Mallung £2 (shredded cabbage stir-fried with mustard seed, turmeric and other light spices), Kotthu Roti £3.75 (a personal favourite of mine – soft and thin as a silk cloth rotti sliced into pieces and mixed with shredded chicken on a hot griddle and blended together). Delivery: 2-mile radius, £15 minimum, dinner only. Takeaway: 10% discount, £15 minimum. Price check: Papadam 30p, CTM £4.95, Pullao Rice £1.50, House wine £6.95. Hours: 12-3pm/6-11pm; closed Mon. Stocks Cobra.

SPICE OF LIFE TOP 100 ©

260 Lee High Road, SE13 020 8244 4770

It's amazing – yet again, we've not heard from this restaurant, despite elevating them last time to our TOP 100, and despite repeated attempts. Ah me! So we rely on you, yet again, to tell us about this Guide-shy establishment. Owned by Syed Ahmed since 1989, it seats 58. 'Small, cosy restaurant which is hard to fault. Its special gourmet nights and daily blackboard specials lift it well above average.' [The latter are still so rare in the curry business. But it's such a simple way of varying the menu, and everyone loves that. It's one of my bones of contention, and we should go on nagging at the other curry restaurants until they all do it.] 'Friendly atmosphere, service excellent, food delicious and well presented.' RL. 'It's indeed superb, gets better and better. Lately have ordered "Hot" Vegetarian Specialities, with Garlic Chilli Vegetables the best of the lot. Definitely a favourite. Tarka Dall very thick, Garlic Nan soft and fluffy.' AG. '10pm on a Saturday night, we were the only diners, but it was football England versus Germany!! [Andy – if only you'd told us, Pat and I would have joined you.] Another fantastic meal at this wonderful restaurant. Tried a Dhal Samba, as good as Tarka Dal. Made our Vegetable Chilli Masala and Garlic Chilli Chicken hotter than usual ... and they were hot! Garlic Nans, Bindi Bhaji and three bottles of Chablis!! everything was great. To cap it all – when we were told we had an hour to wait for a taxi, a waiter drove us home and refused to take any money... it doesn't get much better than that.' AG. 'Thought it was a long time since I'd written about our favourite restaurant! New vegetarian menu available. Gourmet Special is excellent value at £10 each. We had Duck Puri and Machli Kofta Rezala (boneless mackerel fishballs cooked in yoghurt, aromatic herbs, spices and green peppers). Extremely tasty, succulent, well presented, hot and flavoursome. When I first wrote about visiting "Spice of Life" I said every occasion was a party – it still is!' GM.

London SE18

Plumstead, Woolwich

MEGHNA

287 Plumstead High Street, SE18 — 020 8312 2091

'A takeaway only, yet I can say without doubt the food is the best I've ever had. My verdict: go there. You will not be disappointed.' DP.

London SE22

East Dulwich

AL AMIN TANDOORI — NEW ENTRANT ©

104b Forest Hill Road, SE22 — 020 8299 3962

Owned and managed by Kabir Khan since October, 1999. Tikka Masala most popular dish. Delivery: £12. Price check: Papadam 50p, CTM £5.25, Pullao Rice £1.60, Peshwari Nan £1.65, Lager £2.95 pint, House wine £7.10 bottle. Hours: 1-2pm/6pm-12am. Stocks Cobra.

London SE23

Forest Hill, Honor Oak

BABUR BRASSERIE — TOP 100 ©

119 Brockley Rise, SE23 — 020 8291 2400

Babur established the Moghul Empire in 1483 through his courage and daring in capturing Delhi. This restaurant captured Forest Hill in 1985, though its ownership by the dynamic Rahman brothers did not occur until 1992. Quite simply, it's in our TOP 100 because everything the Rahmans do, they do well. Enam Rahman's cooking is bright and fresh, while front of house is equally so, under the careful supervision of co-owner manager Emdad Rahman. Regulars get frequent mail-shots telling of festivals and alfresco dining. Talking about outside, the front is really attractive, with white Mogul arches, each one enhanced by hanging baskets and floor tubs. The white decor continues inside, offset by 56 air-force-blue chairs. Dining is intimate in a screened area or in the conservatory. The menu is interesting with no formula stuff done here. Starters include some real treats: Ros Tos Crab £5.25 – fresh white crab meat, white wine, mango juice and cheese, served in its shell. Main courses include: Raan Gulnar £7.95 (shank of lamb, spiced, marinated and pot roasted to melt in the mouth, served with masala sauce), Caldin £8.75 (medallions of monkfish, jeera, tamarind, coriander and coconut milk), Oonbhariu £4.95 (bananas, sweet potato, baby aubergines, shallots, lovage seeds, cummin and asafoetida), Mausami Murgh Subze £10.95 (baby vegetables and chicken morsels in a Thai style sauce), Chicken Peri Peri £7.50 (hot Goan dish), Salmon an Babur £8.95 (poached salmon cutlet, a timbale of spicy mashed potatoes and onions, and a serving of caramelised baby tomatoes). And for the vegetarian, Paneer Kurma £7.75 (curry sauce with home-made cheese and baby tomatoes), Beans Porial £3.75 (runner beans and peanuts partnered with onion seeds, coriander and garam masala). 'Comfortable, well-appointed, welcoming restaurant. Special Kerala menu included squid in a spicy tasty sauce and Nilgri chicken.' G&CM. Delivery: 2-mile radius. Sunday e-a-m-a-y-l lunch £8.95, kids under seven free. Price check: Papadam 50p, CTM £6.95, Pullao Rice £2.10, House wine £7.95. Hours: 12-2.30pm/6-11.30pm. Branches: Planet Spice, Addington, Surrey; Babur Takeaway, 443 Brockley Road, Crofton Park, SE4. Stocks Cobra.

London SE24

Herne Hill

THREE MONKEYS NEW ENTRANT ©
NEW TO OUR TOP 100

136-140 Herne Hill, SE24 020 7738 5500

Opened in December 1998 by Jan Peacock and Matt Gormley, and so it just missed being in our previous (1999) *Guide*. First point of interest, both men were apparently something to do with EuroDisney, but it's monkeys here not mice. Second point of interest – it's housed in a former bank (told you – interest!) and entry is via a bridge variously described as glass, bright metal, painted scaffold and a causeway. Take your pick. And pick which level you wish to sit in – it's on two levels, below and same floor, and the decor is variously described as clean, modern, bright, light and austere. Both floors, the bar and the open kitchen are all on view giving an airy spacious feel to the place despite the considerable seating of 110. The most interesting feature: Udit Sarkhel (*see* Sarkhel's, SW18) is consultant chef, and with protegée Prem Singh installed as Exec Chef, what you get is perfect Indian food. Authentic dishes to be tried: Kashmiri Shorba (a warming lamb broth simmered with spices, fresh herbs and saffron), Macchi Til Tinka (crispy fried fish in a light sesame flavoured marinade served with a chilli dip), Goan fish curry (boneless fish simmered in a fresh stone-ground coconut, chilli and spice masala), Bhindi Jaipuri (crispy fried slivers of okra and onions tossed with dry mango powder), Peri Peri £14.75 (pan-fried prawns marinated in spicy Goan masala, topped with flamed onions, tomatoes and chillies), Sev Puri £5.50 (one of my faves, makes me think of Bombay, gram flour straws, flour crackers, spiced cubes of potato, green mung beans and tangy chutney), Patrani Macchi £5.75 (Pat likes this dish, I don't like fish – seasonal fish cooked with mint, coriander, coconut and steamed in a banana leaf); Indian puddings: Gajar Ka Halwa £4.25, Rasmalai £4.95 (soft dumplings soaked in sweetened milk and pistachio nuts – fantastic)! I agree with Jan – a great way to end a meal. Delivery. Service: 12.5%. Average spend: £22. Price check: Papadam 75p, CTM £8.95, Pullao Rice £3.50, House wine £12.95. Hours: 12-3pm (Sun. only)/6-11pm. Stocks Cobra.

London SW

Area: South West London
Postcodes SW1 to SW20
Population: 705,000

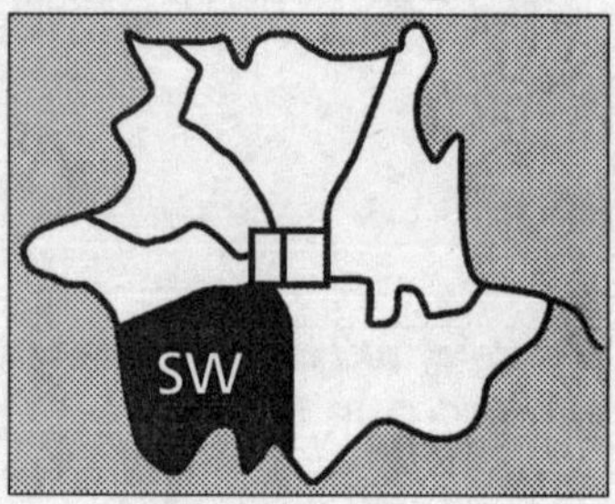

London SW1

Belgravia, Pimlico, St James's, Sloane Square, Victoria, Westminster

GREAT INDIA

79 Lower Sloane Street, SW1 020 7730 5638

'Situated in a parade of shops and several restaurants. Decor is completely plain cream, modern and could be any cuisine – no Indian artifacts or pictures at all. At 10.15pm the restaurant was almost full and had the most wonderful atmosphere. The menu is very large but standard with extremely reasonable prices for Chelsea. Average Papadam with relishes. Onion Bhajia, very good, flat disc-style with a wonderful flavour. Excellent Prawn and Bean curry, Butter Chicken Tikka Masala, an unusual combination which turned out to be spectacularly good, a sort of Chicken Tikka Masala with a butter chicken sauce, rich with coriander and coconut, over the top. Good Brinjal Bhajia, large chunks. Pullao Rice good and generous. Altogether a very enjoyable meal with good service.' HC.

KUNDAN

3 Horseferry Road, SW1 020 7834 3434

There are 117 seats at the Kundan (and 200 or so at the House of Lords and 632 at the Commons). And like as not you'll spot many a political face in here, all enjoying right-wing-raitas with Commons seeds and red-Vindaloos or Matar Peers, perhaps. Our Honourable and Right Honourable members enjoy curry so much that some years ago, they even formed a branch of The Curry Club at their House, and are frequently seen practising at the Kundan. We've not heard of Blair Biriani, or Mandelson Madras, Prescott Patia, or Kinnock (remember him?) Kebab, but I wouldn't put it past owner Nayab Abbasi, who just loves all this, of course. Given half a chance, if he's not at his San Francisco branch, he'll explain that they, and many other politirati, have been seen tucking in here, as often as not. Ask him to explain about the loud bell that rings here from time to time. And since so many of you have asked me to explain, I will: it's not the fire alarm, so don't make a move! It's an extension of the division bell. In times of tight majorities, it means a mad exodus of smart, dark Armani suits (unless it's Gordon Brown, of course), leaving half-eaten plates of curry. Standard food, with some nice specials from Chef Mohamed Aziz Khan. Not cheap, but such delights wouldn't be, and it is Westminster! Hours: Lunch, dinner from 7pm; closed Sun. and bank holidays. Stocks Cobra.

PIMLICO TANDOORI NEW ENTRANT

38 Moreton Street, SW1 020 7834 3375

'Quantities and quality above average. Only popped in for a late main course. Pullao Rice was of perfect texture, and the two main courses were so generous in amounts, we were pleased not to have ordered starters.' CC.

QUILON'S NEW TO OUR TOP 100 BEST IN UK AWARD

St James's Crt Hotel, 45 Buckingham Gate, SW1 020 7821 1899

When the Taj group first set up in business in London in 1982, they did so at Bailey's Hotel, SW7. The hotel restaurant was of course the Bombay Brasserie, the BB. But the hotel always lacked a prestigious address, and was somehow scruffy in an almost charming, but colonial way. This image was not what the rapidly expanding Taj Group wanted for a London flagship, and within a few years they upped sticks and acquired and refurbished the St James's Court Hotel. This most elegant hotel is still the Taj Group's only London hotel, but what a hotel. (Rooms start at £159.) Unexpectedly at the start, neither of the two restaurants were Indian. One was Chinese, the other French. The group felt that their award-winning BB filled the Indian position. The problem is that the BB is quite some way from St James' Court and, even after its enlargement, it was always overbooked. Finally, bending to demands, the position has been addressed with the 1999 opening of the 92-seater Quilon's. Curiously, direct access to/from the hotel has been closed off, so the restaurant is only accessible from the street. It is modern, with clean lines and sparkly mosaics running discreetly around the room. The banquette seating is lovely, soft and immaculately clean. The restaurant's name comes from Quilon, an unremarkable town on the coast road in the south of Kerala, not far from India's southern-most tip. This is the clue that the food is from the various states of south India. Indeed, the restaurant reflects what has been happening in Taj Hotels across India, where regional food of a high order is on their menus. Chef Shreema Vatan is the specialist the group chose to head this prestigious operation, and what a choice. The man is a master. His spicing lyrical, his balance of flavour dreamlike, his menu a super choice of meat, fish and vegetable dishes. Unlike others in town, Vatan proves that there is no need for flamboyance, or new wave, or spin. In typical understated Taj style, he simply and quietly goes about his business of producing perfect Indian cooking.

On our first visit, we were able to park on a single yellow line outside the door (it was just 6.30pm). We were politely shown to our pre-booked table. We nibbled on a collection of fried popadoms, mini popadoms, spiralled crackers (similar to an oriental prawn cracker) and deep-fried, crispy, black (but not burnt) lotus root served in an expensive, woven, highly varnished basket. Two little plates of chutney came with the basket, pale green Coconut Chutney, flavoured with mustard and curry leaf and a spicier version, orangey-red in colour. For these we were charged £1. Our assigned waiter poured sparkling water (£3.95 a bottle) and house wine (Baron Philippe £14.95) while we checked out the menu. Tomato Rasam (with compliments of the kitchen) was served in small, tall-stemmed glasses –

warm, spiced with peppercorns, red chillies, fresh coriander and tamarind – delicious. Starters include Drumstick and Lentil Soup £3.95 – containing adorable drumsticks, which must be the sucked across the teeth to enjoy their flesh – diner participation. Top starter must be Coorg Chicken (Koli Barthade) £4.75 – a tangy preparation of chicken marinated in dark-roasted and ground coriander, peppercorns, mustard seeds, cinnamon, cumin, laced with Coorg toddy vinegar. Coorg is one of Karnatka's most beautiful regions. It is just north of Mysore. Its cuisine is unique – robust and primarily non-vegetarian. Coorg dishes are rare to find in Britain, though they appear at Chutney Mary sw10. The Koli Barthade chicken is sautéed in a manner reminiscent of Cajun 'blackened' cooking. The result is a very black (actually very dark reddy-brown) exterior, contrasting when cut, with the white flesh. The whole is very aromatic and succulent, and just how it should be. This makes an interesting comparison with Zaika's sw3 version where the black is too black and seems artificial. Here at Quilon's it is aromatic and perfect, and was there faintly evident the taste of the rare south Indian spice muruki murkus? Pat spotted his beloved Coconut Lamb (Erachi Varathada) £4.95 – lamb chop pot-roasted with onions, curry leaves and diced coconut, spiced with whole garam masala, chilli, turmeric and coriander (it brings back memories of Shells Restaurant in Kovalum, south India). The lamb was juicy and fell off the bones it clung to. Both dishes were accompanied by a spicy coleslaw – which I have only ever come across in southern India and makes a good change from the usually mundane green leaves. As our starters were served, we momentarily just stared at them – enormous is an understatement. Feeling quite full, we bravely launched into our main courses: Southern Canara Lamb Curry £12.25 – cubes of tender lamb smothered in a reddish-brown spicy gravy – delicious, hot, yet subtly spiced, and Guinea Fowl Salan £12.50 – chunky big bits of fowl, in rich sauce – lovely flavour, accompanied by Spinach Poriyal £5.25 – cooked with mustard seed, whole red dried chillies, split Bengal gram (soft and nutty) and freshly grated coconut, Tamarind Rice £2.50 – nutty, with roasted peanuts and Vegetable Dish of the day – diced courgette in a lentil based sauce – mild but good. We ended with a slice of Goan Bibenca. This is a Goan layer cake made of sugar, coconut, eggs yolks and flour with precisely 10 layers. When cooked its dark brown layers have a texture like a very firm mousse. It is a perfectly accurate rendition of the authentic Goan dish. All Quilon's food is produced to this level of accuracy, and with Taj management and service, it is an exemplary restaurant. Hours: 12-2.30pm (Mon. to Fri.)/6-11pm (closed Sun.). Branch: Bombay Brasserie, sw7.

Indisputably a TOP 100, indeed we are delighted to give Quilon's our Best UK Restaurant Award.

©	Curry Club Discount	**U**	Unlicensed
V	Vegetarian	**ANP**	Alcohol not permitted
e-a-m-a-y-l	Eat as much as you like	**BYO**	Bring your own alcohol

SALOOS TOP 100

62 Kinnerton Street, SW1 020 7235 4444

I continue to get more praise about Saloos from my Indian friends than about any other restaurant, and I do mean Indian. Saloos is very much Pakistani, owned by M Salahuddin. As I say, it is immensely popular with London's well-educated wealthy Indians, who ignore politics when it comes to good food. And what about the food? Meat, meat and more meat predominates ('A vegetarian-free heaven' says RA who, like Bernard Shaw, despises vegetables). There is a comprehensive tandoori section providing succulent, natural-coloured, divinely flavoured offerings. Chicken Shashlik superb. Lamb chop and Shami Kebab were both lean and melt-in-the-mouth. Hard-to-find, acquired taste Haleem, pounded meat cooked with wheat, supplied complete with a DIY spice kit of chillies, ginger, garam masala and onion tarka, which you add yourself, was well spiced this time. The Chicken Jalfrezi was fresh and pungent. The Pullao Rice was, again, superb and definitive. Aloo Paratha was fantastic. 'I was impressed with Saloos and I didn't think it was over expensive, although I did have the set lunch. Food and service were both very good. Waiter kindly informed me the Seekh Kebab was a spicy dish, he needn't have bothered!' RC. It is essential to book. The elegant Farizeh Salahuddin (daughter of the house – she can be heard out of hours on the answer machine) handles bookings with considerable aplomb. Our bill for two with an aperitif, wine, starter, main course and coffee came to £120 (up £20) which still makes it probably the most expensive Pakistani, Indian or Bangladeshi restaurant in the UK, if not the world. The place is an institution and is worth at least one visit. Cover charge £1.50. Service 12.5%. Hours: Mon.-Sat., 12pm-2.30pm/7-11.45pm. Remains in our TOP 100.

TAJ MAHAL NEW ENTRANT

3, Panton Street, Leicester Square, SW1 020 7930 2777

'All dishes were well cooked, flavours good, portions good to generous.' HC. 'A small restaurant that filled very quickly – non smokers may find it a little intimate. Chicken Tikka – small portion. Chicken Madras, dry but Sag Aloo fresh.' MK. Price check: Papadam 40p, CTM £6.30, Pullao Rice £2.20, Peshwari Nan £2.10. Hours: 12pm-12am.

WOODLANDS RETURNS TO OUR TOP 100 V ©

37 Panton Street, Haymarket SW1 020 7930 8200

Long-established (1985) licensed, vegetarian, south Indian 55-seat restaurant, just off Haymarket, is managed by Mr Valaiya, head chef Mr Bhatt. It is the tiniest of three UK Woodlands (there are branches in India, Singapore and LA, each serving identical excellent vegetarian food). 'I particularly like southern Indian food, and find the menu so appealing, it makes choice difficult. We chose one exceptionally good-value set meal, Thali, £6.50, which was quite generous, with good variety, and the Paper Dosa, £3.95. Upma, £2.95, Lhassi, £1.25, and Channa, £3.75 are as good as ever. Also glad to have a choice of Indian desserts. Good value.' HC. 'Enjoyed my lunchtime visit, indulging in the vegetarian buffet. Plenty of flavoursome dishes.' RL Service 12.5%. Price check: Papadam £1, Pullao Rice £2.75, House wine £8. Hours: 11-2.45pm/5.30-10.45pm. Branches: London, W1, Wembley, Middlesex. Stocks Cobra.

London SW3

Chelsea, King's Road, Knightsbridge

HAANDI NEW ENTRANT **NEW TO OUR TOP 100**

136 Brompton Road, SW3 020 7823 7373

Haandi is the traditional round-bellied narrow-necked pot widely used for cooking in many parts of India, and especially Gujarat. Pottery shards have dated it from 2500BC. Rather newer (it opened in 2000) but equally awe-inspiring, is the Haandi in Knightsbridge, for size as much as anything. It has a back entrance a block away in Ceval Place. Its well-established sisters have been reported to us for many years by our overseas scribes as being the best Indian restaurants in East Africa. AR, now living in New York, is one such. His wish for a UK Haandi is now upon us. The Brompton Road entrance has a bright, clean and tidy reception. Downstairs on the right is the bar, which serves snacks, and on the left is the restaurant. The lemony-yellow decor, with inviting tables and chairs, give a cheerful sunshine welcome. The menu is by group Chef Arjun Singh. Specials: Machli Naryal Pani £8.70 – fish fillets simmered in coconut gravy. Murgh Malai Tikka £8.80 (BBQ breast pieces in yoghurt, cheese and cream marination), Gosht Kabuli £8 (mutton with split chickpeas in mint curry sauce), Dum Aloo Kashmiri £4.70 (stuffed potatoes in gravy), Onion Masala Pullao Rice £3, Cheese Kulcha £2.80 (stuffed Nan). Price check: CTM (Haandi Chicken Makhini) £8.10, Pullao Rice £2.80, Nan £1.80. Hours: Bar: 12-10.30pm, bar snacks: to 7pm; restaurant lunch: to 3pm/6-11pm (Fri. to 11.30pm).

SHAHEEN OF KNIGHTSBRIDGE ©

225 Brompton Road, SW3 020 7581 5329

'Decor is an odd mix of Indian and modern – anything but pleasant. Menu has some lovely touches – the naans and other breads were described as "sprinting straight from the oven"; the Bombay Potatoes were "smacking" hot. Fish Pizi Masala was a really well cooked dish of lovely moist white fish in a very spicy sauce. Full marks for the dessert menu, they did have three Indian desserts. The Gajar Halwas was really delicious. I haven't enjoyed an Indian restaurant so much for ages. Its claim of "simply superb Indian cuisine" is perhaps a bit of an overstatement, but it is very, very good.' hc. Being patronised by tourists, it's more expensive than average at £35 per head, with drink, service and cover charges. Delivery. Hours: 12-3pm/6-11.30pm; Sat. & Sun. 12-11.30pm. Stocks Cobra.

TANDOORI OF CHELSEA TOP 100 ©

153 Fulham Road, SW3 020 7589 7617

This elegant 72-seat basement restaurant, recently refurbished to a very high standard, quietly goes about its business without fanfare or hype. It is, and always has been, since it opened in 1965, a leader in style, from its carefully selected small number of dishes to its decor and wine list. Owner A Rajan, whose timeless quote cannot be omitted: 'Do not drink lager with Indian food – spice and gas don't mix!' he explodes. 'Good wine does go with well-cooked Indian food. It is not overpowered by subtle spicing. That is why we have Château Latour on the menu.' 'How much?' say I. '£130 a bottle!' 'Who the heck can afford that?' 'Arabs,' he winks knowingly. The wine list is exemplary, and a leader in its field. The restaurant specialises in Northern Indian cuisine. The menu features a beautiful painting of a Lancer, seated on a horse, galloping towards a marker in the sand. The short menu makes it easy to make a choice. Try starting with King Prawn Karahi Kebab £9.95 (sizzling prawns with tomato and green peppers) and Aloo Chat £4.20 (diced potato, chick peas in yoghurt topped with mint and date chutney – homemade). Follow with main courses of Sali Jardaloo Boti £7.50 (tender lamb with whole baby apricots and honey, sprinkled with straw potatoes) and Machchi Masalla £10.85 (halibut fillets marinated in lemon and spices, steamed and topped with a rich masala). House wine and house champagne – a bargain (for Chelsea) at £10.95 and £22 respectively. Hours: 12-2.30pm/6.30pm-12am (Sun. to 11.30pm). Stocks Cobra.

ZAIKA TOP 100 MOST INNOVATIVE CHEF AWARD

257 Fulham Road, SW3 020 7351 7823

Usually this *Guide* is in the vanguard of opinion-forming. But Zaika, meaning 'flavours' had us wrong-footed by opening six months after we published our previous *Guide*. This timing glitch leaves us coming over the finishing post last, behind *Michelin, Time Out, GFG,* and the many other guides/food critics who have lavished praise on Zaika, and in particular, its chef Vineet Bhatia, over the last year or so. It does, however, allow us to judge for ourselves whether all these accolades are appropriate. Before we do, let's set the scene. Vineet is no newcomer to this *Guide*. He was chef at Fulham's Star of India for some six years. While there he came to public notice. He made a short-lived move in '98 to Hammersmith's 'Rafique's Fine Dining'. Despite owner Rafiq Miah renaming it to 'Vineet Bhatia's Fine Dining', Vineet was soon wooed by bigger guns. Trevor Gulliver was one such, but it was Claudio Pulze and Raj Sharma who got Vineet as a partner, into their new 60-seater which opened in May 99.

'Eat early here – you can park on the single yellow lines at 6.30pm. The outside is chocolate brown, so you can easily miss it, as did a group of young Japanese on the next table to ours. We were the first diners that night and were shown to our pre-booked table by one of the suited managers and sweet, smiling waiters. At once we were served a Woolies-type (i.e cheap) basket of mini Popadoms (far too many for us and we wondered how many other licked fingers had preceded us) and a white plate containing three small white bowls of undistinguished chutneys. We perused the short menu which veers heavily to fish and seafood, which I don't eat, thus reducing my choice enormously. We started with Kala Murgh (Grilled Black Spiced Chicken) £5.50 – coal-black strips of chicken, slightly sweet, very good, if a little unnaturally black, served with milk fritters – three golden eye-balls, delicate and creamy. Cheese Samosa £5.25 – crispy pastry, stuffed with Goats cheese, sealed with a clove, served with salad and pickle – very pretty, very tasty, but not at all Indian. Both white starter plates had lines of a yellow yoghurt sauce zig-zagged on before our food had been placed on top. Our main course was Murgh Makhanwala (Butter Chicken) £9.50 – good chunks of chicken, smothered in a red, mildly spicy sauce (OK so it's CTM) – tasted of Heinz tomato soup, but I expect Vineet's minions had spent hours pushing fresh toms through a sieve! I liked it very much. Talking of minions, the rapidly filling room hushed with the first appearance of an apparation adorned in a shaven-head and seemingly unironed white tee-shirt and grubby crumpled apron. Resembling an escapee from the pot-wash department, he, and a near-identical escapee, were there, it seemed, to dispense the food, leaving the smart waiters free to watch the proceedings.

No, I lie, an apparition carrying a wobbling shield-like round tray delivered Pat's Gilafi Dum Biryani, £11.75 – a pastry-topped pot of Lamb Biryani – and yes, the waiter did have a job to do. He cut through the crust and placed it on Pat's plate. This dish, a benchmark Hyderabadi classic, looked and tasted good – steaming meat with stock-coloured rice – though it was slightly spoiled with far too much mint (which traditionally has no place in this dish). Naan £1.95 – lightly painted with butter ghee – excellent, weightless and crisp – great way to mop up all that sauce. Stuffed Mushroom £4.25 – four field mushrooms, stalks removed, lightly spiced spinach neatly placed on top, gratinated with cheddar and given "the zig-zag treatment" with minty green sauce. I don't care for spinach, but those who do – order it, you'll love it. Nor do I care for zigzagging – I thought that went out with the ark. But is it this which makes 'em rave? Many chefs would like to see the presentation of Indian food elevated beyond wet curries in bowls. And there is no doubt that at Zaika much thought has gone into the design and look of each dish, with colour contrasts, textures and positioning of each ingredient paramount. As we ate the restaurant began to fill, no wonder they wanted our table back by 8.30pm.' DBAC.

There is no doubt you agree with the pundits: 'Vineet Bhatia is a culinary genius. An excellent choice and a gourmet menu. Must try Dunghar Machli Tikka, £4.50 – Tandoori-smoked salmon kebab, flavoured with honey and mustard. Jhinga Khichdi, £4.25 – described as Indian risotto, with crispy prawns and Mali Naan – it was outstanding!' PC. 'The best my friends and I have been to, atmosphere and food. The former elegant and food exceptional. Service first-class, discrete and friendly. Ate the suggested menu, small portions of nine dishes, all tasty, including a complimentary taste of melon soup between the mini Popadoms and pickles. A great experience.' BF.

Vineet certainly can cook, and innovation is fine, particularly in presentation, where it is overdue. Does it matter if Vineet is moving ingredients and methods beyond authentic Indian? The debate about authenticity of British curry rages never-ending in the media. True this refers to the average curryhouse, and Zaika is certainly not the average curryhouse. But authenticity is a valid argument in all cuisines. Because if Vineet/Zaika does become the first Indian restaurant to achieve a Michelin star, it will not be for authentic Indian food, as is found at, say Quilon's SW1. This may be academic, and we'd love to have your views on the subject. In the meantime, we therefore place Zaika high in our TOP 100, in addition we give Vineet our Most Innovation Chef Award. Average charge £30. Set 2-course lunch, £9.90, 3-course £11.95; set 5-course dinner £20, with wine £28. Service 12.5% – declared as optional. Pleased to report the credit card slip was closed. Hours: 12-2.30pm-6.30-10.30pm. Stocks Cobra.

London SW4

Clapham

CLAPHAM TANDOORI ©

10 Clapham Common South Side, SW4 020 7622 4470

Clapham's second oldest (1971), owned by Abdur Rhaman Choudhury. His restaurant seats 72 diners, and head chef Shiraze Ahamed serves well-liked curries and side dishes and has some Indo-French specials up his sleeve, £6.25-8.95. Sunday lunch e.a.m.a.y.l £5.95, children (under 12) £3.25. Delivery: 3-mile radius, £10 minimum. Price check: Papadam 50p, CTM £5.95, Pullao Rice £1.75. Hours: 12-2.30pm/6pm-12am. Stocks Cobra.

MAHARANI

117 Clapham High Street, SW4 020 7622 2530

The 104-seat Maharani was established in 1958, at which time there were under 200 curry houses in the whole of the UK. It was not only Clapham's first curry house, opened long before Cla'am became trendy ma'am, it was one of the first to open in a London suburb. It has always earned its keep by providing good, bog-standard, formula curries; indeed, owner SU Khan was one of the pioneers of the formula. Under the same ownership for all these years, Khan has kept up with the trends, though, and everything is as it should be. Hours: 12-2.30pm/6pm-12am; Sun. 12pm-12am.

London SW5

Earls Court

LOOF'S NEW ENTRANT ©

234 Old Brompton Road, SW5 020 7370 1188

Opened in 1999 by Lesley Cornell-Wash and Luthfur (Loof) Rahman. Formerly Cafe Naz. Forget the curry-house food, you must try the Bangladeshi dishes. Specials: Singara £4.95 (triangle pastry filled with cottage cheese and spiced chicken, served with chunky pineapple chutney), Pepe Bhaji £3.25 (green papaya diced and tossed with light chillies and spices). I'll have both of those for my starter! Aloo Chops £4.75 (potato paté blended with coriander and dried chillies, served with tomato chutney). Leboor Gosht £6.50 (with Bangladeshi limes), Lau Gootha £10.95 (pumpkin and king prawns, served with Pullao Rice). Delivery available. Price check: Papadam 50p, CTM £6.95, Pullao Rice £2.25, Peshwari nan £2.45. Hours: 6pm-12am. Branch: Viceroy, 100, Middle Street, Yeovil, Somerset.

NEW ASIA NEW ENTRANT

7 Hogarth Place, SW5 020 7373 0112

'Tucked away in the heart of residential, mews cottages. We were disappointed to find a fully booked restaurant and had to make do with a takeaway, but all the diners looked very happy with what they had ordered. Takeaway was superb, and despite the affluent setting, the prices were surprisingly reasonable. Definitely worth a visit but book early!' TE.

NIZAM ©

152 Old Brompton Road, SW5 020 7373 0024

The Nizam was the former ruler of Hyderabad. Until partition he was the richest man in the world, and his dining table seated 101 guests, yes, at one table! On it was a silver model railway which chugged around the table dispensing whisky et al to the guests. M Mian's 1989 vintage Nizam is rather smaller, seating 65 on several tables in two rooms. 'Attractive appearance and warm reception. The food was varied and excellent with a number of dishes new to me and my guests. Chicken and prawn main courses with excellent vegetables, especially the smoked aubergine. Service was superb throughout.' RH. Miss Sumaira Lateef-Mian's service is exemplary, with smartly waistcoated waiters, exuding expertise. North West Frontier and Moghul cuisine is carefully executed by chef M Riaz. Specialities include smoky Baingan Bharta, £4.95 (charcoal-grilled aubergine, its flesh then mashed to a purée), Prawn Piri Piri, £8.50 (coconut milk and chilli). Price check: Papadam 60p, CTM £8.50, Pullao Rice £2.50. Cover charge £1. Takeaway 10% discount. Delivery: £12 minimum. Hours: 12-2.30pm/6-11.45pm. Stocks Cobra.

STAR OF INDIA TOP 100

154 Old Brompton Road, SW5 020 7373 2901

Next door to the Nizam, Reza and Azam Mohammed's Star, the direct descendant of the benchmark Drummond Street Shah (1950–1985, rip). The double doors open up to a small curtained (grey velvet) area, to protect the diners at the surrounding tables. The decor, painted pillars etc. are, in my opinion, a little strange if not rather naff. Once the talk of the town, times have changed and decor has moved on, but obviously not at the Star. New chef with impeccable pedigree, from Vama, we hear, has restored the quality that took a dip when Vineet walked. Starters: Rava Ar Kaju Talee Jhinge £6.50 (prawns marinated in spiced batter, coated with semolina and cashewnuts, fried till golden brown, served with a ginger and kokum sauce),

Baingan E Bahar £5.25 (baked aubergine steaks stuffed with paneer and herbs, topped with diced tomatoes, tempered with curry leaves and mustard seeds, served with a garlic dip). Main courses: Murghabi Tawe Wale £13.50 (escalopes of mallard marinated with garlic, nutmeg, lemon and chilli oil, panfried on an iron griddle), Raan Mussallam £19 (roasted leg of baby lamb marinated in a mixture of spices, then cooked over a gentle flame in a rich onion and tomato gravy, flavoured with nutmeg and flambéed with rum – serves two), Subz Kaju Thoran £5.50 (green asparagus and cashew nuts, tossed with tempered mustard seeds, green chilli, fresh coconut and curry leaves), Bhindi Aur Pyaz Karare £5.75 (crispy fried sliced okra and red onions coated in a light batter with spices), Arhar Dal Kairi Ki £4.95 (yellow lentils cooked with chopped green mangoes tempered with ginger, tomato and chilli oil), Chilgoza Aur Pyaz Pulao £2.50 (pine nuts and caramelised onions cooked with Himalayan basmati rice). 'Exciting menu, but, being a vegetarian, I found the list lacking in choice. Standard of food was good. A pricey establishment, but will definitely visit again.' RM. Prices around £30 inc. £1 cover. Hours: 12-2.45pm/6-11.45pm; Sun. 7-11.15pm. Stocks Cobra

TAMANA'S NORTH INDIAN CUISINE — NEW ENTRANT

237 Earls Court Road, SW5 — 020 7244 9977

'A Canadian colleague and I decided to test this restaurant out and had a most agreeable result! Interior is spacious with "post-modern" decor, service was swift and attentive. Papadoms were beautifully warm and fresh. Complimentary CTM (chef wanted us to try his pride and joy!). Mr Tamana has been open for two years in London, and owns a chain of nine Indian restaurants in Australia. Plans to open in Richmond. Service, food quality and price are spot on.' TE.

London SW6

Fulham, Parson's Green

NAYAB — TOP 100 — ©

309 New Kings Rd (jnct'n Munster Road), SW6 — 020 7731 6993

Owner Praveen Rai's upmarket menu is full of 'some dishes you won't recognise and some that you will.' The former are Indian and Pakistani specials cooked by head chef Akeel Ghani. These include: Nihari Kohe Avadh, pot roast shank of lamb, £7.95. Most popular dish ordered is Goan Galinha Xacutti (Sha-Coo-Tee), browned onion, fresh coconut, £6.95. Meat Dhaba Wala Lamb cooked in bone marrow stock and mince (ask Rai to tell you about this). This is all dedicated stuff, and well spoken of by the regulars. For the if-you-must-brigade, Mr Rai offers 'old curry-house favourites' which include everything except Phal (he'll explain how it came to be 'invented by chefs as a revenge against the lager lout – and he'd never serve it or them!'). So if you are chilli-addicted, as Praveen himself is, then choose the hotter specials. Price check: Papadam 50p, CTM £5.95, Pullao Rice £2.75, Peshwari Nan £2.25, House wine £8.95. Set menus for two at £13 and £16 pp. Delivery: Fulham area only. Hours: 12-2.30pm/6-11.45pm (11.30pm on Sun.). Stocks Cobra.

London SW7

Kensington

BOMBAY BRASSERIE AWARD WINNER AND TOP 100

14 Courtfield Close, Courtfield Road, SW7 020 7370 4040

The Bombay Brasserie (aka the BB by its fans) is managed by Adi Modi with Arun Harnal, and for 18 years was the Taj Hotel Group's only UK Indian restaurant, until the arrival of Quilon's SW1. Opening in 1982, as an experiment, it was the brainchild of Taj director Camelia Panjabi, who explains: 'I wanted to launch regional Indian cuisine in England'. After handing your coat, umbrella etc. to the cloakroom attendant, you enter a large and friendly bar awaiting your presence with lots of chairs clustered around dainty tables for your pre-dinner drinks (the barman can mix a very good cocktail or two). The large main restaurant has a colonial atmosphere, preferred by some to the conservatory, which, since its major facelight and size increase has balanced demand for seating preference. It is pretty with hand-painted murals and cascading tropical plants in brass tubs, creating intimate dining spaces. Once the doyen of the critics, it is now ignored by some and panned by many who say it's passé, dated, unexciting, and expensive. It simply doesn't deserve this. True, pricing here is eyebrow-raising, even for quite simple menu items. But it is only expensive by Indian standards. And it sure is cheaper than flying to India to experience the same quality. How is it diners are prepared to pay double and more for the same ingredients or less, in the hands of Blanc, Roux, Stein, Ramsay or Pierre White and be happy to do so, but whinge when it comes to a cuisine, which to be done properly, requires great skill indeed? And that skill is there in abundance in the Taj Group. As we reported last time, the formidable task of taking over the kitchens from Udit Sarkhel (*see* SW19) fell to Vikram Sunderaha. Since then he has undoubtedly found his feet with a new menu embracing the BB tradition, and the Taj imperative for dispensing the best Indian regional cuisine, while injecting life of his own. His kitchen is, as always, shared by specialist chefs from Goa, Bombay, south India and elsewhere. What they output is simply the best. The best of the old has been retained (Hooray!) with a good mix of new. Starters average £7 and include the divine Sav Batata Puri, Chaas (a Gujarati yoghurt drink), Goan Scallops Peri Peri (hot, hot), and Patrani Macchi (pomfret coated in coriander/chilli/mint purée, wrapped in a banana leaf and steamed), Parsee Murgi Ni Salli (chicken curry with straw potatoes). Main courses start at £15 and top at £23. Dum Kas Battar (Lucknowi-dum-cooked quail with yoghurt, almond and cashew nut paste and garam masala) is £7.25 as a starter and £15.25 doubles up as a main course. Hyderbadi and Goan dishes are represented, the former with, for example, Chicken Biryani, dum-cooked in the handi, and the latter with Chicken Xacutti – pronounced *shacute-eey* (chicken with ground peanut, cashew and coconut paste with Goan red chilli), Fish Kozambhu, £17.25, from the Tamil Nadui Chetiyars who have been resident in the Madras area since the earliest times. And for the carnivores there is Lamb Nehari – a Punjabi dish – marinated leg piece (shank) of lamb served with a spicy gravy in which the marrow is extracted from the bones. Top of the price-tree comes Masala Fried Lobster £22.95. Many reviews summed up simply by LH: 'Out of this world.' Lunch: buffet £15.95 (under 12's, half price). Parking is difficult, but it's opposite Gloucester Road tube. Hours: 12.30-3pm/7.30pm-12am. As ever, the Bombay Brasserie is the yardstick at the top of our TOP 100.

CAFÉ LAZEEZ NEW TO OUR TOP 100

93-95 Old Brompton Road, SW7 020 7581 9993

Lazeez, meaning 'delicate and aromatic', describes itself as a 'new type of Indian restaurant'. It operates in true café mode, with nonstop opening hours. It has a striking frontage, with 26 good-weather seats outside. Inside are 130 seats, on two floors. Downstairs in stark, minimalist surroundings, is a short-menu café (which changes to full menu after 7pm). Upstairs is decorated with an illuminated, white, tented roof, and a full menu. Its owners are Pakistani, in the persons of the elegant Ms Sabiha Kasim and her brother Zahid. They were undoubtedly ahead of their time with their bar/new-wave concept. Despite criticism in earlier years about the evolved nature of some of their food, they've stuck to their guns. Suddenly, and at long last, we're getting the good reports we've always longed Lazeez to achieve. HC glows: 'Spicing different, and not necessarily Indian. A good place to take people who say they don't like Indian food. Succulent prawns, sizzling lamb chops, well-spiced vegetables, rich and creamy Korma, the Lamb Sag, not enough lamb, but good flavour, Saffron Rice fantastic, firm, fresh and spicy mushrooms, star dish, aubergine – superb – and the Nan, small, round, lightest and crispest I've had. Expensive, but first class. Overall, a wonderful meal.' That Korma is a good example. It's authentic, as done in the Pakistani heartlands where the meat is marinated in yoghurt to tenderise it, resulting in a mild, aromatic dish with subtle spicing, including a hint of garam masala, ergo Lazeez! It's a lively place. Average snack price £6, meal price £30, inc. service and cover charge. Hours: 11am-11pm. (10.30pm on Sun.). Stocks Cobra. Branches: Café Lazeez London EC1 & W1.

DELHI BRASSERIE

134 Cromwell Road, SW7 020 7370 7617

Owner Mr A Jabber says 'shop out and pop in' (it's near Sainsbury's). A bright comfortable spacious 60-seater. Chef Ram Singh's food and service excellent. Hours: 12-11.30pm. Stocks Cobra.

KHAN'S OF KENSINGTON

3 Harrington Road, SW7 020 7584 4114

60-seater, est. 1991 by Mr Khan (no relation to Khan's, W2). 'A lovely experience all round. Reasonable cost (for this part of the world), great food, first-class service, highly recommended. "Tandoor Cocktail" starter was a knockout – marinated minty lamb chops, chunks of lamb and chicken tikka, 2 shamis, chutney and small naan. Murgh Makhni and Naniyal Gosth (lamb in coconut) truly delicious.' MS. Definitely a 'would go back' restaurant and probably the best of the several Indian restaurants in the area. Menu has some unusual items, such as scallops and a stuffed green pepper. There was no mushroom rice or any mention of brinjal on the menu, but the waiter offered to see what the kitchen had and could do. A lovely mushroom rice and a very good brinjal bhaji turned up – we were very impressed.' HC. 'My starter was two smallish, light and crispy Onion Bhajia's with a little salad. Followed by dry Chicken Adrokwala – cooked with ginger, lemon juice and hot spices, complemented by Vegetable Curry and Pullao Rice. All in good quantity. Overall excellent, fresh and very palatable.' MK. Plenty for veggies, and fishies e.g. Machli Gowala (pomfret). Price check: Papadam 55p, CTM £6.95, Pullao Rice £1.90. Delivery: £20 minimum. Hours: 12-2.30pm/6-11.30pm; Sat. 12pm-12am; Sun. 12.30-11pm. Stocks Cobra.

KHYBER PASS NEW ENTRANT

21 Bute Street, SW7 020 7589 7311

'Small and busy restaurant, but you are made welcome and the food is particularly good.' JL. 'No frills – decorative or culinary, serving formula curries of high standard. I have been going there with friends – two of whom served in India during the War – for over twenty years and have never had cause to complain. Service is efficient and friendly, they serve very drinkable wines and prices are very reasonable.' CB.

MEMORIES OF INDIA NEW TO OUR TOP 100

18 Gloucester Road, SW7 020 7581 3734

Managed by N Islam, seating 70, with a 30-seat party room. Curries and side dishes cooked by head chef M Uddin. 'Outstanding. The meal was a really marvellous experience. All dishes were very, very good or excellent.' HC. 'Excellent formula curry house at a very good price for Kensington. Highly recommended.' NI. Price check: Papadam 50p, CTM £6.95, Pullao Rice £1.95. Hours: 12-11.30pm. Stocks Cobra.

MOTI MAHAL ©

3 Glendower Place, SW7 020 7584 8428

Opened way back in 1956 – and amazingly this restaurant pioneered curry in Kensington. Owner patrons BA and T Rahman's 40-seater is 'very lively'. 'We'd been here some years ago and been pleased, this time it was even better. Made very welcome, service attentive, helpful and friendly, food outstandingly good. Mushroom Rice – not on menu, but made for us. Onion Bhaijia – two lovely, flat style, crip bhajis, just as they should be but rarely are. Brinjal Bhajia, excellent. Mattar Panir. Fish Tikka Chilli Masala – really superb and made with boal, no compromising. Sizzling BBQ Malabar Chicken – large pieces still on the bone in a spicy rich BBQ sort of sauce, dryish like a Bhuna. Two main courses were fairly hot, waiter did advise, quite sensibly, marvellous, fabulous flavours, beautifully cooked. Excellent value.' HC. Delivery: 3-mile radius, £10 minimum. Takeaway: 15% discount. Sunday lunch £6.95. Price check: Papadam 60p, CTM £6.90, Pullao Rice £2.30, Lager £2.60 pint, House wine £8.95. Hours: 12- 11.30pm. Stocks Cobra.

SHEZAN INDIAN NEW TO TOP 100

16 Cheval Place, Montpelier Street, SW7 020 7584 9316

To find this old hand (1966) very traditionally elegant 120-seat Pakistani restaurant, go up the street opposite the world's number one store. [That's Harrod's, ma'am, for the benefit of the lady from Connecticut who emailed me to ask!] and turn left into Cheval Place. It's 100 yards on your right. Parking is difficult so take the tube (subway, ma'am) to Knightsbridge, or walk. It'll probably be all you can afford when you get the bill, so be warned!

The plate-glass door is secured by a geezer, straight from a Rajasthani movie, his silver hair matching his immaculate white robes. He doesn't speak English, so a dialogue about the cost of living etc. is wasted. The downstairs dining room, past the bar, is elegantly simple, with its downlighters, pewter plates, long-rolled napkins, traditional Pakistani chairs, all made theatrical by strategic lighting and candlelight. Chef Khan's food is as sophisticated as the service. We love all this. And we hope it lasts as long as Indian civilisation has. But then we love going against the trend, especially with this new wave of exceedingly tedious minimalism and bright new colours, to us already passé. And, because we never want to see traditional authentic food drowned by new-wavism, we are promoting the Shezan to our TOP 100, where, perhaps it should have been all along. We warned about the prices (it is Knightsbridge) though we're please to say they haven't risen since last time. Still, are you sitting comfortably? Price check in ascending order: Papadam free, Naan £2, Raita £3, Paratha £3.50, Pullao Rice £4.50, CTM (sorry, Makhni) £11.75, Choosa e Shezan – a chicken (whole poussin)-and-egg story described on the menu as a speciality of our dear old Khansama (cook), and billed at a dear old £15! Jhinga Masala King – Prawn curry to you and me – £17.50. Set lunch £12.95. Minimum charge dinner £25. Service 10%. Cover charge £1.50. Takeaway 20% off. Shezan branches in New York and Washington. Stocks Cobra.

London SW8

South Lambeth, Vauxhall

BOMBAY BICYCLE CLUB DELIVERIES NEW ENTRANT

28 Queenstown Road, SW8 020 7720 0500

See same name branch at SW12 for details.

HOT STUFF NEW ENTRANT

19 Wilcox Road, SW8 020 7720 1480

New to the *Guide* but opened in 1989 by Bele Ghafoor, who runs it with her husband Abdul, son Raj, daughter Romana and sister Farida. It's a tiny 24-seater serving Kenyan Asian food, so look out for Casava chips, Chilli or Jeera Chicken £2, and a cast-list of 8 chicken dishes, inc. CTM £3.50 and 9 meat curries, Sag Gosht, £3. Star dish, rolled out only Wed.-Fri. is Masala Fish, £3.50. Using Kenyan Tilapia, it is chill-marinated for 24 hours in briny lime juice, then on demand it is stir-fried with dhania, jeera, tomato, and ginger, creating a thick tasty curry. Less choice for the veggies, but what there is is expertly spiced and cooked. 'Put it in the *Guide* please' says ME: 'It's home cooking at its best.' Average spend £7. Credit cards accepted. Hours 12-10pm; closed Sun. Closed Aug. for summer hols.

London SW9

Brixton, Stockwell

OLD CALCUTTA RE-ENTRANT ©

64a Brixton Road SW9 020 7582 1415

Old Calcutta and its prececessor (Oval Tandoori) were in this *Guide* from 1984 to 1998 editions. We're glad to welcome it back under the new ownership of Abdul Mazid who says: 'We're situated at the Oval tube end of the road (the A23) an area sometimes described as a gourmet desert. My chef and I have spent some time revamping our menu and we extend a warm welcome to everyone.' Can't say fairer than that. Reports please. Price check: Papadam 50p, CTM £5.95, Pullao Rice £1.75. Takeaway 10% discount. Free delivery, 3-mile radius, min £12. Hours: 12-2.30pm/6pm.-12am; Sun. e-a-m-a-y-l 12-12pm. Stocks Cobra.

London SW10

Chelsea, West Brompton

CHUTNEY MARY AWARD WINNER AND TOP 100

535 Kings Road, SW10 020 7351 3113

Established in 1990 by Ranjit Mathrani and Namita Panjabi, this 150-seater is easy enough to find, near Lots Road, though it's not near a Tube, so it's taxi, bike or shanks. Parking is iffy, but worth a try. The ground floor is now a fully-fledged extension of the downstairs main restaurant. Downstairs, (now described by some as passé) is gorgeous with its murals, Indian props and conservatory. Chutney Mary would be dull without its conservatory (though not everyone opts for it – some tell us they prefer the interior). This husband-and-wife team will not accept second best. They are true professionals, and do everything by the book, punctiliously, down to the last detail, without the hype and spin to be found elsewhere on the block. There is a large highly-trained house-team headed by GM Eddie Khoo, and assisted by Neeraj Mitra, delivering impeccable service. The menu is a brief document. Nothing on it resembles formula curry house, of course, but I believe most diners are aware of that. Namita despises the formula with its one-pot (of curried onion purée gravy). 'If you go down that road,' she says, 'everything ends up tasting the same. Every dish we make has its own unique spice mixture. All the curries are freshly cooked from scratch in their own pan. Wet masalas are ground on our own motorised stone grinder, imported from India.' The six chefs are each from a different region of India. Between them they can accurately cook dishes from Kashmir, the Punjab, Lucknow, Goa, Bombay, Mangalore, and Kerala. Each has his own work-station and his own ingredients. 'We supply them whatever they need,' continues Namita. 'It means flying-in certain ingredients unobtainable in Britain, such as Kashmiri chillies, Goan coconut and palm sugar, to mention just three items. It's very hard work for chefs used to having plentiful kitchen help back home, but the economics of the west preclude a large kitchen and oodles of helpers. The brigade has learnt to cover for each other for holidays and days off – no mean feat with such specialist dishes. There can be no stricter quality control than Namita's kitchen taste, face-to-face with the chefs, whenever she feels like it. 'Anyway, it's my local, so I expect it to be good,' she told me. 'Why own a restaurant if you don't dine in it?' And dine she does, in the company of her co-owner husband Ranjit and friends. Chutney Mary must be doing something right. It's packed full of aficionados, mostly regulars, who delight in its real Indian food. Starter specials: Moong Bhel £4.50 (a sprouted bean salad with spicy chutneys), Bhutta Kebab £4.50 (fresh baby corn wrapped with a spiced mash of fresh corn and potato), Salmon Tikka £6 (mustard and cumin marinated fresh salmon, roasted in tandoor), Lobster Samosa £7.75. Main course specials: Lamb Shank Xacuti £12.50 (slow roasted in a robust blend of Goan spices, served with Basmati Rice), Duck Vindaloo £13 (Barbary duck marinated and cooked in real Vindalho spices including Goa red chillies, garlic, palm vinegar and cumin), Malabar Chicken £11.50 (coconut milk, red chillies and cinnamon, served with Basmati Rice), Seafood Coriander Avial £13.75 (mussels, salmon, crab and prawns smothered in coconut sauce – a seafood lover's dream), Prawn Malai Curry £15.75 (mild and creamy, jumbo prawns, cashew purée, served with Caramelised Onion Pullao Rice), Crispy Fried Okra and Banana £3.75. Try the 'Tasting Menu', dinner only, four courses – good value at £32. Get on their mailing list and you'll be advised about their food festivals and discounts. They have a superb wine list, and for the can't-drink-wine-with-curry brigade, what do you think Namita and Ranjit delight in? Good red wine, of course! Oh, and just in case your visit to the toilet mystifies you, a Pickle John was the derogatory, arrogant term bestowed by both snooty Brits and Indians upon young Indian men who dared to wear western clothes and adopt western attitudes in the 1920s and 1930s Raj. The equivalent female was called a Chutney Mary! For the reasons given above, Chutney Mary is a one-off. It remains at the very top of our TOP 100. Price check: Set lunch £12.50 for two courses, £14.50 for three courses, Lager £2.80 and £5.80, House wine £10.95. Cover charge £1.50 – includes ample spicy Papadams with home made chutney and pickle. Service: 12.5%. Late dinner: after 10pm,

£12.50 for two courses. Average spend £38. Hours: 12.30-2.30pm (Sun. brunch with jazz band to 3pm)/7-11.30pm (Sun to 10.30pm). Stocks Cobra.

EXOTIKKA OF INDIA ©

35 Stadium Street, SW10 020 7376 7542

Someone had to think of the name! And it may as well be owners Hye and Hussain. Competent curries from chef A Kalam at this 40-seater. Price check: Papadam 40p, CTM £5.95, Pullao Rice £1.75. Set lunch £6.95. Hours: 6-11.30pm (Sat. to 12am). Stocks Cobra.

SAFFRON NEW ENTRANT NEW TO OUR TOP 100

306b Fulham Road, SW10 020 7565 8183

This first floor air-conditioned venue is a long restaurant with bleached wooden flooring and decorated with modern works of art. Opened in 1998, at a former Chinese restaurant, next to Brompton cemetery (owner Sunny Dewan and his crew have heard all the food-to-die-for gags – actually, there are some dishes on the menu, which anywhere else might well be described as such). Punjabi Fish Tikka £4 and Saffron Prawn Kebab £3.25 – small potato cakes (two in portion) spiced with prawns will excite the fishheads, but not Dep Ed DBAC, who dislikes all things fishy. She's suspicious of rabbit too, but those with catholic tastes will delight in Khand Kahrgosht £10.25 – rarely seen rabbit in a sweetish but tangy tamarindy sauce. The only other place I've had rabbit is in Udaipur, which gives the clue that there are Rajasthani specialities. Another is Laal Maas, £5 – a variant of Jungli Maas, i.e. a hunter's stir-fry made with ghee, goat (sadly, lamb over here) and red chilli. It appealed to your Ed, particularly because the chilli measure was stepped up to authentic (so tell 'em if you want it hot). Bhuna Duck Nagpuri £6.95 – chunks of duck meat in a tomato-based sauce. Kofta Dil Bahar, £5 – mutton Dhal Maharani, dark brown and creamy, is a dish which Indians measure as a mark of a chef's competence. It sure was competent. And if you've never seen a Romali Roti, £1.50, being made, ask to see it. Known as the 'handkerchief bread' this is a clue to the fact that it's handkerchief size and thinness, and to achieve it they throw it into the air pizza-fashion. Rarely seen outside India. Oh and for pud, if you're not full to bustin', having observed the bizarre 'good-health-corner' advice on the menu, go for the Firni, £3 – nutmeg/cardamom-laced rice pudding, or Dep Ed's favourite (she's purring now) Gulab Jamun. A commendable restaurant. Welcome to our TOP 100. Hours: 12-2pm (Sun. only)/6pm-12am.

VAMA THE INDIAN ROOM TOP 100 ©

438 Kings Road, SW10 020 7351 4118

Established in 1997 by Andy and Arjun Varma, and Ritu Dakmia. Their sophisticated, stylishly decorated restaurant seats 110 and serves classic North West Frontier cuisine. Specials: Mahi Salmon Tikka £8.75. Tandoori Jhinga, Tiger prawns marinaded in cream, yoghurt, mustard oil, garlic, ginger and Kashmiri chilli, roasted on charcoal, £10, being the most popular dish ordered. Also from the tandoor, you may wish to try crab, lobster, paduck, partridge or quails. 'Expensive, 3 scallops £7.75. £88 for two including one bottle of wine. Poor service, missing one meat and bread.' DW. When we recently met Andy, he told of his celeb clients and parties, including Prince Charles, Rowan Atkinson, a regular, it seems, and the recent Millennium party he was catering for. We were guests of the BBC at their Network East Asian Awards ceremony (NEC) – these type of 10-per-table functions look so great on the TV – but alas in real life are not so glamorous. We were stuck down at one end where the sight-lines to the stage were partly obscured, and it was hard to hear. It emphasised that we were sitting in the middle of an exhibition hall screened by black felt drapes hanging from the roof supports. Vama was the caterer, and it was not good. I felt quite sorry for his crew – they had over-stretched themselves – in a venue with zero adjacent facilities and jobsworth resident disinterested kitchen help. The mostly distinguished Asian attendees had paid £125 per ticket, and those on our table were far from happy. This has nothing to do with the restaurant, but it does show that catering in venues where one is not in control is dodgy. We certainly rate Vama's and are delighted to keep it in our TOP 100. Incidentally, English weather permitting, you may sit outside on the patio – four tables to choose from. Ring for entertainment schedule – cabaret and belly dancer. Price check: Papadam 75p, CTM £8.75, Pullao Rice £2.50, House wine £8.75. Service 12.5%. Cover charge £1. Hours: 12.30-3pm/6.30-11.30pm. Stocks Cobra.

London SW11

Battersea

CAFE SPICE NAMASTE NEW TO OUR TOP 100 ©

247 Lavender Hill, Battersea, SW11 020 7738 1717

The western outpost branch of Cafe Spice Namaste, E1. Cyrus is one of this *Guide*'s few award-winning chefs. His innovative menus never stand still. As we write, these are some of the delights on offer: Murgh Kay Tikkay £3.35s/£7.25m (tikkas of chicken marinated in yoghurt, ginger, garlic, cummin and chilli), Poleku Masu (Nepal) £6.25s/£11.95m (prime fillet of Scottish Highland beef marinated in puréed garlic, fenugreek, lime juice, green chilli and mint), Leeli Chutney Ma Salmon (Parsee) £4.25s/£8.95m (fillet of salmon, marinated in fresh green chutney, skewered and chargrilled in Tandoor – main courses – served with Garlic Pullao), Aloo Tamater rassa (Avadh) £3.25s/£5.95m (baby potatoes sizzled with lovage seed, curry leaves, garlic, shredded ginger, mustard and cummin, in tangy spiced tomato sauce), Vegetable Dahi Kadhi (Keralan) £3.95s/£6.45m (whipped yoghurt is cooked with roasted chickpea flour, tempered with mustard seeds, curry leaves, cumin and asafoetida simmered with vegetables – mild and flavourful). Cyrus has developed a wine guide, so there is no excuse for drinking the wrong wine with the right curry. Good value Pickle Tray: 50p per person – now that's fair. Lager £4.25. Hours: 12-3pm (Mon.-Wed. closed)/6-11.30pm (Sun. to 10.30pm). Stocks Cobra.

SPICE OF LIFE

147 St John's Hill, SW11 — 020 7924 2112

The varnished concertina folding doors (instead of plate glass window) across the entire frontage of this restaurant is open, weather permitting, giving an inviting welcome to diners. Clean, uncluttered decor, creamy walls, white, heavily starched, linen tablecloths and generous, sparkling wine glasses. No bright, vulgar colours here, suggesting a smart and upmarket appearance to this establishment. On a warm Wednesday evening, during August, it was well patronised. Formula food, at average prices. Good stuff.

London SW12

Balham

BOMBAY BICYCLE CLUB

95 Nightingale Lane, SW12 — 020 8673 6217

Great logo of a turbaned Raj-style waiter holding a serving dish while riding a penny farthing. Known to some as the BBC! 'Something wonderfully luxurious, elegant decor, massive vase of flowers dominates the room, charming staff, starched white tablecloths and napkins. In the winter, it's cosy and snug, in the summer the windows and doors are thrown open, the colonial ceiling fans whirr, and it all looks extremely pretty and atmospheric. The food is absolutely delicious, with plenty of crunchy green pepper in the main-course dishes and beautifully presented vegetable dishes. Although the Nan was a great disappointment, very dense. Masala

Papadams arrive at the table at the same time as your bottom hits the chair. However, the waiting staff feel duty bound to chivvy you along. In some restaurants you wonder what you have to do to get served. At the BBC you wonder what you have to do to get them to leave you alone. The staff are in over-drive, the message very strong and most persistent: eat up–pay up–and get up. The staff asked us for a wine order, when we were holding full pint glasses of beer. At one point they tried to remove dishes that we were eating from! It leaves you feeling miffed, when you've shelling out nearly £50 for dinner!' JM. 'When you telephone to book, it is an answerphone, which informs you to leave your details. Promptly shown to one of too many tables (insufficient room between chairs – staff tried in vain to squeeze through). Given the menu. Papadams served but no chutneys. Trying to rush us through. You could not fault the starter – absolutely beautiful. Tellicherry Squid, in a non-greasy batter, very delicate spicing, excellent. No plate warmers. Portions small compared to cost. Waitress cleared table, when one in our party hadn't finished, height of bad manners. Disappointing ice creams and luke-warm coffee. Expensive.' MW. Hours: 7-12pm Mon.-Sat. Branches: SW8 and SW20. Stocks Cobra.

TABAQ AWARD WINNING RESTAURANT AND TOP 100 ©

47 Balham Hill, SW12 020 8673 7820

Run by the brothers Ahmed. Mushtaq is front-of-house manager. His domain consists of pale walls giving a spacious feel, enhanced by richly embroidered tapestries of rural Lahore, and tables with pink cloths, around which are just 50 seats, so booking is necessary, and good old-fashioned silver service. The other Ahmed brother, Manoor, is head chef, and the culinary magic emanates from him and his brigade. But don't expect quick food from him. He cooks everything freshly, and a 30-minute wait is not uncommon. The menu is pure Lahori cuisine. Lahore, now in Pakistan, was once one of four major palace cities, resided in by rotation by the great Moghul emperors, rather in the way that QEII rotates round Buck Pal, Windsor, Sandringham and Balmoral. Agra, Delhi and Srinagar, Kashmir were the others, all linked by still-extant tree-lined trunk roads. Lahore is famous for its cuisine. Grills and tandoori, meat and chicken predominate, and there are fish, prawn and vegetable dishes too. At Tabaq, they do it all well. Specials include: Chagra – the Lahori steam-roasting technique where meat goes over a pan of water then into the oven is uniquely available here. For that special occasion, try a whole Chagra Lamb, £140, which will serve at least 12; or Chagra lamb leg, £35 – enough for 6-8, both 24-hrs notice. Chagra whole chicken, £13, in 30 mins is a reality for two + doggie bag.

Tabaq means large serving dish from which the family helps itself, and these specials are served on such a dish. Masala Machli Lahori is robustly spiced white fish, Quail Masala, £9, Baby Chicken Tabaq, £10. 'Excellent meal for group of five. Good Bindi Ghost, Muree (Pakistani) beer very interesting. Glad to receive 10% discount due to my Curry Club Membership.' MT. 'My partner and I shared a thoroughly delicious meal consisting of Shish Kebab, Palak Gosht I particularly enjoyed – a personal favourite – Daal Gosht, Pullao Rice Masaledaan and Naan-o-Punjabi. Restaurant is comfortable despite waiting 30 minutes to be served. The menu assured us that it would be worth it, we were not disappointed.' DM. Deservedly in our TOP 100. Price check: Papadam 60p, CTM £7.25, Pullao Rice £3, Peshwari Nan £3. Set lunch £7.95. Hours: 12-2.45pm/6-11.45pm; closed Sun. Stocks Cobra.

London SW13

Barnes

PUKKABAR AND CURRY HALL NEW ENTRANT

21 Barnes High Street, SW13 020 8878 3904

It's moved from SE26. Owned by Trevor Gulliver (of Fire Station, Putney and Waterloo and St John, Smithfield, fame). 'The plan,' says the spin, is 'to roll out an innovative chain marrying the nation's favourites, curry and beer.' Sound familiar? There are 8,000 curry houses out there dispensing curry and beer. 'Innovative' sounds familiar too. Every new restaurant seems to regard itself and its concept as 'innovative'. Witness the plethora of minimalist decor venues with polished floors, open kitchens, brightly coloured high-back chairs, with walls to match, and slick menus. So what's new at Pukkabar? Great name. No actual bar though, as was at its SE26 predecessor, nor a hall – rather a smart canteen with polished floors, minimalist chairs and café-style sage-green formica tabletops. Taj-trained ex-Soho Spice chef is on show in his open kitchen. Indian window-shutters are the only clue to the cuisine, apart from, that is, the tantalising spicy smells exuding from the clattering open kitchen alongside, albeit partly obscured by frosted-glass screens. The short menu includes Tandoori Salmon for starters and Hara £3.95 – deep-fried spinach and cheese balls. Barwan £3.95 – eggplant [it's aubergine, Trevor – we're in England] stuffed with minced lamb and topped with cheese. Main courses: Lamb Chilli £5.95. Goan Prawn Coconut Curry £7.95. Takeaway: 10% discount. Delivery: 1-mile radius. Price check: Papadam 50p, CTM £5.95, Pullao Rice £1.70. Hours: 12.30-2.30pm (Sat. & Sun. to 3.30pm)/6-10.30pm. Stocks Cobra.

London SW14

Mortlake, Putney, Sheen

TASTE OF THE RAJ RE-ENTRANT

130 Upper Richmond Road West, SW14 020 8876 8271

A typically well-managed Bangladeshi formula curry house, owned by the charming and personable Shawkat Ahmed, which has been operating for years and producing a highly popular formula at reasonable prices. Such venues form the backbone of this *Guide*, up and down the country, and are much-loved locals enjoyed weekly by their regulars. There is little more to say about such venues. Except perhaps that they are much despised by foodies and trendies. Such snobbery says more about the latter than the former. Stocks Cobra.

London SW15

Putney

MA GOA TOP 100

244 Upper Richmond Road, SW15 020 8780 1767

Opened in 1993 by the Kapoor family. Deepak looks after the diners, while Sushma is the chef. In fact she's his mum, so easy on the Ma Goa gags! The restaurant seats 50 in a rustic atmosphere – wooden floors, whitewashed walls and Goan art. Goa is one of India's 24 states, not a country in its own right, as some think. It is on the western coast of India and, because it was Portuguese for nearly 500 years, it inherited different characteristics from the rest of India, including a small pork-eating, Christian population. Goan cooks were prized in the Raj (because they would handle beef and pork and could cook well). Until a few decades ago, Goan cooks were frequently to be found in merchant ships. In the 1960s Goa was 'discovered' by hippies, and more recently, it has been 'discovered' by holiday companies offering the cheap package at formerly beautiful, exclusive, caring hotels. Goan food is rarely found in Britain. And what of Sushma's food? As a regular visitor to Goa, I can vouch that it's as near to home-cooking as it gets. Goan food is unique, having that Portuguese influence – any meat goes and pork is the favourite, as is the chilli. Good examples at Ma Goa are Goa Sausage £3.95 – (Chorizo) pork meat sausage with cinnamon, cloves, garlic, palm vinegar and red chilli, topped with spicy onion salsa, and Porco Vindaloo £8 –

authentic Goan recipe. This is the real thing, based on the Portuguese dish, Vinho d'alhos. In the Goan version, pork is marinated with palm (toddy) vinegar, garlic and roasted spices and plenty of red Goan chillies. It is then slow-cooked to achieve maximum penetration of flavours. Ma Goa serve it in traditional earthenware. Offal, beef, chicken and vegetable dishes prevail e.g. Sorpotel £3.95 (lambs liver, kidney and pork in rich sauce with lime and coriander), Cha Cha's Beef Fry £8.25 (beef marinated in spices, then fried with onions, chilli and potato), Fish Caldin £8.25 (chunks of fish with coconut, palm vinegar, mustard seeds, kokum and curry leaves). The daily specials board makes this restaurant an adventure. Goan delights, with unique names such as Cafreal, Balachao, Assado, Temperado, Buffado, and Recheiado all appear at one time or another. Advice is forthcoming. If you ask for Goan heat, you'll get it hot! For loonies like Pat, look under side orders and accompaniments for Taliwi Mirch £1 (fried green chillies in mustard oil). There are even Goan puds, such as Bebinca. But a word of caution. Please be patient. Sushma will not be hurried in the kitchen. Relax with their chilled Portuguese Vinho Verde, and nibble something while you wait for your order to be cooked. 'A quick BIG rave about a restaurant which I think is just "ab-fab". Real authentic stuff with great service' SM. Booking essential. Occasional Goan musical nights. Takeaway: 10% discount. Price check: set dinner: 2-courses £8.95. Hours: 6.30-11pm; Sun. 12.30-3pm/ 6-10pm; closed Mon. A rarity, deserving our TOP 100 cachet. Sells Indian artifacts and spices. Stocks Cobra.

MUNAL ©

393 Upper Richmond Road, SW15 — 020 8876 3083

'You'll find all the standards at this 65-seater, but try some Nepalese items, such as Chicken Bhutuwa, £4.95. Ask owner-manager Khem Ranamagar for explanations, and enjoy chef Bijaya Thapa's good food. Small Nepalese restaurant. Staff always polite. We usually have Sadheko Chicken which is served hot, mixed into a salad and quite spicy, and delicious mushroom rice. Lychees and an Irish coffee topped off a gorgeous meal, as usual.' DBAC. Price check: Papadam 45p, CTM £5.50, Pullao Rice £1.90. Minimum charge £8. Delivery: £10 minimum, 3-mile radius. Hours: 12-2.30pm/6-11.30pm (12am Sat & Sun). Stocks Cobra.

London SW16

Norbury, Streatham, Streatham Hill

MEMORIES OF INDIA ©

109 Mitcham Lane, SW16 020 8677 8756

M. Iqbal's restaurant seats just 30. Specials include: Chicken Langwaki, diced chicken with herbs, fresh tomato, cucumber and French beans. Price check: Papadam 35p, CTM £5.25, Pullao Rice £1.50. Delivery: £10 minimum, 2-mile radius. Hours: 6-11.30pm, Sunday Buffet £5.95 – 6-11pm.

MIRCH MASALA BYO

1416 London Road, SW16 020 8679 1828

Now well settled in its third year, Mirch Masala, 'pepper mixture', is a good example of a London Balti house under another name, such as have dominated Southall and Wembley for years. It's an offspring of the ever-popular Karahi King, where meat is king, cutlery is out, and BYO is in, no corkage charge. This unlicensed cafe is pleasant, light and bright, air-conditioned and seats 70. Open kitchen, with unusual Kenyan-Asian specials by owner Raza Ali's brigade, who delight in bringing their own cooking straight to the horse's mouth – yours that is. Great theatre. Cassava chips (mogo) can substitute for papadoms, Patra £2.50, Kebabs 70p. Wide selection of dechi (saucepan) or karahi dishes, kebabs and all the trimmings. Main course: Karahi Methi Gosht/Murgh £4.50 (lamb/chicken with fenugreek leaves) – can't imagine a Punjabi restaurant without this dish. Good veggie stuff, too. How about Karahi Valpapdi Baigan, £4. or Matoki, plantain curry. Price check: Papadams 30p, CTM £6, Pullao Rice £1.50. Set lunch: £4 for vegetarian, £5 non-vegetarian, served from 12-5pm. Credit cards accepted. Hours: 12pm-12am Tues.-Sun. Branch: Mirch Masala Takeaway, Lavender Hill SW11.

SHAHEE BHEL POORI VEGAN ©

1547 London Road, SW16 020 8679 6275

Lebas Miah's 75-seater, opposite Norbury Station, serves Gujarati vegetarian/vegan food. Thalis and Dosas are the most popular dishes served. Specials include Chappati Chana (hot), chick peas marinated in a balanced blend of spices and sauce, served with green coriander, £1.70. Bhel poori (cold), delicious mixture of Indian savouries blended with spices and exotic sauces which make this dish unique, £1.70. Dahi Vada (Bhalle) (cold), spicy black-pea-flour fritters, with yoghurt and sweet and sour sauce, £1.70.

Rava Onion Dosa, a crispy onion vegetable pancake stuffed with delicately spiced potatoes, served with coconut chutney and Sambar, £4.10. House wine £5.50. Hours: 12-2.30.pm/ 6-11pm. Sunday buffet. Stocks Cobra.

SHAMYANA NEW ENTRANT BYO ©

437- 439 Streatham High Road, SW16 020 8679 6162

Another good value Pakistani Punjabi caff, opened by Mohammed Tanveer in 1998. No frills. Seats a huge 130 in two rooms, black-and-white tiled floor, pastel walls and table linen. Enormous menu, some 130 dishes, with no explanation (thanks be to Allah) is quite a read. Starters: Masala Fish £3 (white fish in spicy sauce), Dhal Bhajia £1.50 (spiced lentils deep-fried in chicken pea dough), Zeera Chicken Wings £2.50 (wings marinated in spicy sauce with extra aromatic jeera). Main courses: Masala Karella Gosht £4.50 (lamb cubes cooked with bitter melon), Ginger Chicken £4.40 (chicken with ginger – what a surprise!), Lamb Biriani £4.20 (home-cooked, chunks of lamb with stock flavouring the rice). 'Everything was excellent.' MRS N. 'The tastes are authentic and the food is nice and hot (temperature).' FC. The menu gives calorie and fat analysis, but I personally don't want to know that. Going out to eat should be fun; where's the fun in knowing how many grams of fat you're about to eat? 'Particularly liked the freshness of the food AND the number of waiters helping me, don't need any persuading to come back.' AM. 'Good to see open kitchen – easy to over order.' JEB. Organic Roti 60p – 300 calories, just the thought is enough to fur up your arteries! 'If only it was closer to where I live!!' FH. Daily specials: please ask. Delivery: 3-mile radius, £14 minimum. Service 10%. Car parking at rear – 50 spaces. Price check: Papadam 35p, CTM £2.50, Pullao Rice £1.75, House wine £7.50. Sunday buffet: 12-6pm, £5.50. Thur.-Sat. Happy Hour: 12-6pm for half-price drinks. Set lunch: £5. Discount scheme. Service 10%. Credit cards accepted. Hours: 12pm-12am. Stocks Cobra.

SPICE COTTAGE

78 Streatham High Road, SW16 020 8677 1719

Managed by Praful Shah with Abdul Rahim as head chef. Opened in 1991, seats 40 diners. Specialities: Seafood Masala £7.20 (stir-fried prawns, scallops and squid rings with tomato, capsicum and onions), Chicken Mughlai £5.95 (chicken with egg in a mild sauce with fruits and nuts), Mushroom Dhansak, at a very reasonable £4.80 (mushrooms in spiced lentil sauce served with Pullao Rice). Takeaway: 10% discount. Delivery: £15 minimum. Price check: Papadam 50p, CTM £6.50, Pullao Rice £1.60, Peshwari Nan £1.80, Hours: 6pm-12am; Sun. 6.30-11pm. Stocks Cobra.

London SW17

Tooting

Watch out Southall! Upper Tooting Road (UTR) just gets better and better. For years, the area has reflected the varied roots of its Asian population. In the half a mile, between Tooting Bec and Tooting Broadway tube stations, there are restaurants serving nearly every style of authentic food from the subcontinent. Nowhere else in the world has such variety cheek by jowl. South Indian restaurants include Sree Krishna, 192 UTR, Radha Krishna Bhavan, 86, and Kolam, 58. There are now several Sri Lankan outlets, the best of which is still Jaffna at the Broadway. Milan, 158 UTR and Gossip, 180 are two Gujarati vegetarian havens, and largely vegetarian Kenyan Asian food is to be found at Kadiri, 32 UTR, and Kastoori, 188, while at Masaladar, 121, you get this food plus Bhel Poori and meat curries alike. Handis, 164 and Lahore Karahi at the Broadway are Pakistani and fill the carnivore gap, Southall-style. As if that were not enough there are two formula Bangladeshi curry houses, the Peacock, 242, Calcutta Indian, 116, and Raja, 169. Veggy Indian sweet and snack takeaways include Ambala, 48, and Alaudin, 98, with Royal beyond UTR (north of Tooting Bec). The shops are getting better and more varied. Competition is rife with more and more excellent rivals opening, all displaying their wares on UTR itself, many until late, every day including Sundays. Sakoni, 204-208 UTR, is still the best Asian veg shop in London and there is no better Asian grocer than next-door Dadus, 210. There are several Sri Lankan grocers too. Utensils shops, sari boutiques and halal butchers have sprung up too. Unlike Southall and Wembley, parking has not yet reached Sunday traffic-warden proportions but I fear it will soon. Meanwhile, UTR, with the tube so convenient, is an all-day curryholic's theme park. Reports please on this exciting place. Here's more detail:

HANDIS

164 Upper Tooting Road, SW17 — 020 8672 6037

A 60-seater Pakistani restaurant owned by Mrs S Sheikh. Managed by Mr J Sheikh. Cooking down one entire side. The Handi is a clay cooking pot, and dishes are served either in this or in the karahi. 'Usual very high standard. Onion Bhajia particularly superb. Chicken Jalfrezi also great, plenty of chicken breast with onion, green pepper and lots of fresh chilli, garnished with a generous amount of ginger strips, great! Superb Chappati. Clean, unremarkable decor.' CT. Price check: Papadam 30p, CTM £5, Pullao Rice £2.25. House wine £6. Hours: 11am-11pm. Stocks Cobra.

JAFFNA HOUSE TOP 100

90 High Street, The Broadway, SW17 — 020 8672 7786

For those who must have meaty tandoori items and north-Indian curries, you've got your own side entrance and dining room, with food cooked by Aziz and Kannan. I've no idea how good it is; but do enjoy (and tell us about it, if you like). Where the serious palattes boldly go (through the front door) and into K Sivalogarajah's and M Sivanandan's caff gaff, which built its name on its authentic, no compromise, chilli hot (as-it-should-be) Sri Lankan and south-Indian dishes with its particularly popular different Friday, Saturday and Sunday specials. Tastebud-tantalising stuff like Vadai – gram flour doughnut, drenched in home made yoghurt and sprinkled with garam and (if you are lucky) chopped fresh green chilli, Masala Dosa £1.50 – must be one of the cheapest in the country – rice flour pancake, stuffed with lightly spiced (turmeric, mustard seed, curry leaves) mashed potato and onion, served with the essential coconut chutney. I like to accompany my dosa with a bowl of Sambar – lentil and vegetable stew, especially good if containing drumsticks, which you scrape the flesh off on your front teeth – sounds vulgar doesn't it, but you will soon get the hang of it. Sri Lankan specials are delightful, with Pat's benchmark crab curry scoring really high because it was searingly hot, and used fresh crab. Set lunch: £4 and £5, served from 12-3pm. Hours: 12-11pm. Stocks Cobra.

KADIRI NEW ENTRANT

32 Upper Tooting Road, SW17 020 8672 0710

A Kenyan Asian licensed restaurant, it does tandooris, kebabs, and regular curries and all the trimmings. If East African food is new to you, dip into Cassava chips (mogo) with imli as a good substitute for papadams, served with authentic imli, sweet and sour tamarind chutney. Fried fish Masala, Tali Hui Jinga – breadcrumbed, deep-fried prawns, and Tandoori King fish, that tasty fish so loved in south India, are three unusual starters. Jeera chicken or butter chicken are 'just like the Brilliant's (*see* Southall, Middlesex) according to one scribe (AN), while another (BD) was smitten by the biriani.

KASTOORI PURE VEGETARIAN

188 Upper Tooting Road, SW17 020 8767 7027

This African-Asian family specialise in both Gujarati and Kenyan vegetarian dishes. The former include Vegetable Samosas, £1.80, Dahi Vadas, Kadhi, yoghurt and besan sauce, with dumplings, and Katia Wahd, a tomato-based curry. Karela Bharah is stuffed bitter gourd. The latter gives Cassava Chips, Chilli Banana, £4.50 (green banana stuffed with chillies and served with pickle), Kasodi, £4.50 (sweetcorn in a peanut and yoghurt-based sauce), and Matoki, plantain curry. Their Bhel Poori is a crunchy snip at £2.50, and this is one of the few places where you can experience Bhatura, giant puri bread, £1, which puffs up to balloon-size when deep-fried. It's all the rage in New York's curry houses (and about the only curry thing NY does passably well) but still rare in UK. Do push the boat out and have a Thali; I know it is £15.50 but the curry selection is extraordinary. Vegan dishes available. Lager £2.10 pint. Hours: 12.30-2.30pm (Mon. & Tues. closed)/6-10.30pm.

KOLAM BYO ©

58-60 Upper Tooting Road SW17 020 8767 2514

Established in 1982 by S Rajakumar. Seats 52 in one long thin dining room which is decorated quite simply: pale pink wallpaper, beechwood chairs and red carpet. The food served is authentic South Indian, as they have it in Tamil Nadu, plus standard north Indian items. It was two years since we last ate here, but they remembered Dom, Erik and me, plus Helena taking a break from the kids, and they welcomed us like long-lost friends. And friendly they are, albeit at freeze-frame slowness. Mañana is far too fast, which again reminded us greatly of India. As ever, patience will reward you with a good inexpensive meal, and, as ever, go for the South Indian delights, which is what they know best. Masala Dosa £3, Sambar £2.50, and Coconut Chutney, still as good as ever. BYO is allowed: £1 corkage. Price check: Papadam 50p, CTM £4.25, Pullao Rice £1.75. Hours: 12-2.30pm, Tues.-Sun./6-11pm (12pm on Sat.). Stocks Cobra.

LAHORE KARAHI BYO

1 High Street, Tooting Broadway, SW17 020 8767 2477

This a/c Tooting Karahi-house has been open since late 1995 and was long-awaited, now much-patronised by Asians, and is being copied around and about the area. It's Southall in style and Southall in name. Stand at the counter and order your takeaway – if you plan to eat in, sit down and wait to be served, with the cooking on view. Typical Pakistani fodder. Starters include: Masala Fish £1.95 – chunks of marinated fish, fried. Sheek Kebabs £1. Main courses: Chicken Jalfrezi £3.95. Veggies might try the Karahi Karala, £3, bitter gourd, Mehti Aloo £2.75 or Saag Paneer £3.95. 'Exceptional flavours,' CHC. Cash preferred – no credit cards. Unlicensed: don't forget to BYO, there are plenty of off-licenses on the High Street, no corkage. Average meal around £10. Hours: 12pm-12am.

MASALEDAR ANP

121 Upper Tooting Road, SW17 020 8767 7676

What lies behind the smart frontage with its smokey plate-glass window? Terracotta tiles on split-level floor and table. Plants in pots and trailing leaves. Smart up-lighters behind large halved karahis. You can sit outside watching all this through that window, at the five pavement tables. But the food is good. Starters include Bhel Poori, and Mandazi, samosa-shaped deep-fried bread with an African-Asian name, both £1.50. 'Samosas to Tandoori for starters and Bhuna to Karahi Gosht for main courses. Specials: Seekh Kebab £1.25, Chicken wings £1.75 (mine were rather skinny practically no meat on them). Watch your meal being cooked by the chef behind the glass partition. Rich, vivid Punjabi-type curries. Ginger Chicken and Methi Gosht very good. Cumin-flavoured Pilaw Rice (just like you get in Rusholme). Reasonable prices, thoroughly recommended.' JR. Don't expect a wine list – strict Muslim rules apply and BYO is not permitted. Credit cards accepted. Price check: Papadam 40p, Chilli Chicken £3.95, Veg Thali £3.50. Hours: 12pm-12am.

MILAN VEGETARIAN ©

158 Upper Tooting Road, SW17 020 8767 4347

Taj Mehta's vegetarian café is just the sort of place we like to recommend. It's unpretentious, and unexpectedly licensed and a/c. But for the vegetarian, what more could you ask for? If I were you, I'd ask for papadams and their adorable fresh home-made relishes. Next I'd ask for their fabulous Bhel Poori. I'd avoid the Masala Dosa (they do it better at Sree Krishna), and I'd go for its subtly-spiced Gujarati curries, made largely from besan flour and yoghurt, spiced with turmeric and curry leaves. If it's new to you, ask for help. The dish of the day is always a good option. And do try the fresh Rotla (millet bread). Leave some room for the terrific Indian sweets on display. And buy some fresh 'Bombay mix' items. For a complete filling meal, try the Thali – a good selection of vegetarian curries including something sweet for pudding – at £5.25 a real feast. 'Another good one' SM. Minimum charge still a ridiculous £2. Average meal under £10. Takes no credit cards so cash preferred. Price check: Papadam 35p, Masala Dosa £3, Nan £1. Sunday lunch £5.75. Hours: 10am-10pm. Stocks Cobra.

PEACOCK TANDOORI ©

242 Upper Tooting Road, SW17 020 8672 8770

Opened in 1988, owned and managed by Mr Yogi Anand. (He's heard all the bear jokes.) The 50-seater restaurant has a Mediterranean feel, decorated simply and tastefully. Recommended starters: Paneer Pakora £2.45 (curd cheese, dipped in spiced gram batter and fried), Brinjal Pakora £2.45 (sliced brinjal coated with batter and fried, served with salad). Main courses: Sag Kamal Kakri £4.25 (lotus roots cooked with spinach and onion), Batair E Khas £7.65 (quails in mild curry sauce with fresh coriander). Weekend buffet £6.96 (under 12 – half price). Service 10%. Takeaway: 10% discount. Price check: Papadam 50p, CTM £5.60, Pullao Rice £1.90, House wine £7.95. Hours: 6pm-12am. Stocks Cobra.

RADHA KRISHNA BHAVAN NEW ENTRANT TOP 100

86 Tooting High Street, SW17 020 8682 0969

This restaurant came into being as a result of a restructuring. The 12 year Sree Krishna partnership (next entry) split up and one partner and the head chef set up this Krishna down the road. In fact it has three sisters (*see* branches). The menus at all four restaurants specialise in South Indian Keralan cuisine, with dishes from the cities of Cochin, Malabar and Travancore. Full details can be found in the entry for Malabar Junction. Suffice to say, they're good at it. Light Papadams, freshly made Coconut Chutney, Masala Dosas, Rasam, Sambar, Avial, Thoran – the list is a wonderful collection of Keralan and South Indian food. Even the Chicken Korma is given the South Indian touch – creamy, coconut with ground almond. Fantastic. Minimum charge: £6. Service 10%. Cobra £3. Credit cards accepted. Hours: 12-3pm/6-11pm (Fri. & Sat. to 12am). Branches Malabar Junction, wc2; Kerela Bhavan, Croydon, Surrey, and Palavi, Twickenham, Middx. Stocks Cobra.

SREE KRISHNA TOP 100 ©

192-194 Tooting High Street, SW17 020 8672 4250

This was the original Tooting Krishna restaurant. And now there are three (*see* Rhada and Vijaya). Whether Tooting can support all three Kerelan specialists within a dosa throw of each other (plus its innumerable other authentic curry venues) remains to be seen. We hope so, but wouldn't it be loverley if the newcomers had set up shop elsewhere in sw London? Since old habits die hard, the editorial team still go to the Sree regularly as a kind of local (round-trip 90 miles). Recently we've anxiously been looking for signs of change. To be frank we can't detect much change. But then we always follow our own advice and order the Kerelan vegetarian stuff, and not the kormas and formula curry stuff, though we observe those of our table neighbours, and listen in to their satisfied comments. And this includes many an Indian client. Last time there were visiting Kerelans from the US. We were staggered at the volume of food they consumed – Pops and picks, Dosas, curries, rice, birianis, breads. It all went, down to the last grain, with infinite relish. It remains an unpretentious 120-seat south-Indian restaurant, shows exactly how Keralan cuisine should be done at totally affordable prices. Krishna is a revered, playful Hindi god. His picture is by the bar. The slightly tacky decor transports one straight back to Kerala, and the food transports you to heaven. It's a no-frills place. Paper tablecloths, methodical but sure service, bizarre toilet location, and plenty of regulars, Indian and non-Indian alike. Cobra, Kingfisher and Kaliani Indian beers are all here, and they never seem to muddle the labelled glasses. Last time we went it was with Dep Ed's sister and her two young sons in tow. 'We ate crisp, light plain Papadams with a thali of Mixed Chutneys – creamy coconut, hot coconut, onion with mint, sweet mango and raitha, followed by Onion Bhajia's, Spinach Pakoras and Mint Raitha, served with iceberg salad, lemon wedges and more Mint Raita. The kids voted for Chicken Korma with Pullao Rice; when it arrived, Harry decided he didn't want it and sulked, so Lucas ate his. Helena, Pat and myself opted for Masala Dosa – a thin, crispy pancake made from fermented rice/urid-flour batter (wherin lies the secret of success), wrapped around a tasty mashed-potato curry, still the best in town, served with more fantastic coconut chutney) and Sambar (thin lentil curry). Pat had a helping of Rasam (pepper soup), extra hot. The meal, as usual served promptly with a smile, was wonderful and we ate the lot. The boys were, unusually, almost well-behaved, and the waiter gave them a packet of sweets each – very kind. But one thing that hasn't changed for years does annoy me – the bill, which on this occasion, with two large Cobras, a bottle of red wine, two cokes and two lemonades, came to £52.70, was presented with a service charge of 10% added. I proferred a credit card. When the bill was presented back to me, it was left open. This is not acceptable.' DBAC. Most comments are still happy: 'Had a superb meal – gorgeous chilli chicken, wonderful beetroot side dish.' RL. Only one (JAR) was not happy, and we repeat his comments, without agreeing with them: 'My first visit and very disappointing. Flavours not at all South Indian – more like very average Bangladeshi. Much inferior to the other South Indian that I patronise – Jaffna House.' JAR. Other south Indian house specials include Rava Dosa, a light and crispy pancake made of semolina, rice flour, cummin and spices, served with coconut chutney and Sambar £4.15. Uthappam: a South Indian version of pizza made of rice and lentil flour with a topping of chopped onions, green chillies, tomatoes, curry leaves and ginger, served with a special chutney and Sambar. Poori Masala: a fried South Indian puffed bread made of wheat flour, served with lightly spiced potato masala £2.45. Vadai, doughnut made of black grams, ginger, onion, curry leaves, green chillies, soft centre with crunchy exterior, served with chutney £1.35. Cashew Nut Pakora £2.95 – crunchy, nutty and filling. Beetroot Thornan £1.95. House wine £7.50. Minimum charge £5. Service 10%. Credit cards accepted. Remains in our TOP 100. Hours: 12-3pm/6-11pm; Sun.-Thurs. (12am on Fri. & Sat). Stocks Cobra.

VIJAYA KRISHNA NEW ENTRANT ©

114 Mitcham Road, Tooting Broadway, SW17 020 8767 7688

Opened in 1995 by Vijayan Mullath; he also manages front of house and keeps a watchful eye on the kitchen. His 40-seater restaurant is decorated with scenes of South India. A chef from Sree Krishna has moved here; just like the SK, ignore the Kormas etc. (though they are very good and have their own South Indian twist) and eat the Keralan specialities e.g. Dosas – you won't be disappointed. Popular authentic dishes such as Masala Dosai £2.25 (a light rice flour pancake, rolled over a firm, gently spiced potato curry), Avial £2.10 (a fluid curry made with yoghurt and mixed vegetables), and Sambar £2.10 (a runny lentil curry containing, if you are lucky, many drumsticks, with which you are to scrap the flesh off with your teeth – lovely), Kozhi Varutha Curry £3.50 – chicken in garlic and coriander sauce and Green Banana Bhajia £1.90 are served. Delivery: 2-mile radius, £12 minimum. Service: 10%. Parking may be a problem for lunch, but after 7pm restrictions are lifted. The tube's adjacent. Minimum charge £5. Price check: Papadam 35p, CTM £4.50, Pullao Rice £1.90, House wine £7. Hours: 12-3pm/6-11pm (Fri. & Sat. to 11.30pm). Stocks Cobra.

London SW18

Earlsfield, Southfields, Wandsworth

SARKHELS BEST INDIAN AWARD TOP 100

199 Replingham Road, Southfields, SW18 020 8870 1483

Udit Sarkhel was, for over a decade, Exec Chef at the Bombay Brasserie sw7. His delightful Chinese wife, Veronica, once managed the Bombay Taj Mahal Intercontinental's flagship restaurant, the Tanjore. Our 1999 award as Best Newcomer might well have been the first they received, but it looks silly now, almost patronising, overshadowed by subsequent accolades from just about everyone else. Such is the timing of a non-annual food *Guide*, but we do not feel our Awards to Sarkhel's stop here (*see* end of this piece). Also, the rule of location-location-location is completely blown. Sarkhel's is on a yellow-lined, outside curve of a bend on a busy road. It's not up-west, it's in an unfashionable part of sw, just a serve and lob from oh-so-desirable Wimbledon. Such is their success that the couple have risked all, bought the two adjacent properties and knocked them through, enabling them to accommodate the demand for seats. Not only that, they now open for lunch (*see* Hours). And bang has gone their once-sacrosanct August holiday to India. (Ah me! The joys of being self employed.) But their concern of over-stretching themselves is paying off. Even with double the seating (now 72) the restaurant is always buzzing with dignified diners enjoying a serious Indian experience. 'I like the way they've decorated the restaurant. They have avoided the trap fallen into by so many restaurants recently, which is to make a trendy fashion statement which is very out of fashion by the time the restaurant opens! No, Sarkhel's is in their own understated style which tells us about the owners' individual personalities. It is smart and simple, with stylish white walls, terracotta-tiled floor, small wooden chairs at pleasantly-linened intimate tables of 2 and 4. It is uncluttered giving a cool and relaxing feel.' DBAC. The menu, once a rather short document, has also grown, to the delight of the many regulars (oh to live in Replingham Road). And it is boosted with a specials menu, that changes with what's available fresh in the markets that day. The dishes are a collection of the very best Indian regional specialities, cooked by a highly trained brigade capable of giving everything a home-made feel without losing class. Here are a few examples: Hariyalo Murg Ke Chaap £4.25 (chicken lollipops batter fried with fresh green herbs and spices), Gurda Kaleji Sailana £4.25 (lamb's liver and kidney cooked with onions, tomatoes, black pepper and lemon), Sev Puri £3.95 (crisp round flour crackers, sprouted moong beans, cubed potatoes, onion, chillies and sauces topped with sev), Kolmi nu Patia £8.50 (Parsee prawn masala, black tiger prawns, aubergine and red sweet pumpkin), Dum ka Biryani £8.95 (lamb, aromatic rice, spices cooked in sealed pot, served with Cucumber Raitha), Chutney Paneer Shashli £6.25 (cheese sandwiches with mint and chilli chutney, onions, tomato and soaked in spices and yoghurt, grilled in tandoor), Dhansak Rice £3 (basmati, browned onions, spices and star anise). We could go on extolling the virtues of classic dishes from all over India. On one visit, Udit attempted to convert DBAC to eating prawns. He produced the most divine KP dish, part of which madam ate politely and daintily. Udit beamed and said 'Told you so'. I could have told him otherwise!. Sadly madam hasn't eaten shellfish since, and not even the master will ever convert her. However, for everyone else, no one does fish dishes better. 'Delightful restaurant. Full on both the occasions that I visited. Food really good indeed, with great subtlety.' MC. 'Spicy papadoms and home-made chutneys were excellent. Sev Puri deliciously original starter, but it's a small amount for the money (£3.95). Andhra Chicken Pulao was subtly spiced and very dry (as I had been warned). Laccha Paratha and Cucumber Raita were both quality. Service was a little flustered – but they may have been training a couple of new staff up.' RL. 'Wonderful service. Very good food.' DW. Totally reasonable prices – BB food at Southfield prices.' DBAC. Deservedly gets our Best Indian Award. Average spend: £16. Sunday lunch: 4-courses, £9.95 adults, £6.95 kids. Credit cards accepted. Hours: 12-2.30pm (Fri, Sat & Sun)/6-10.30pm (Fri. & Sat. to 11pm); closed Mon. Stocks Cobra.

©	Curry Club Discount	**U**	Unlicensed
V	Vegetarian	**ANP**	Alcohol not permitted
e-a-m-a-y-l	Eat as much as you like	**BYO**	Bring your own alcohol

London SW19

Wimbledon

RAJPUT NEW ENTRANT

277 Wimbledon Park Road, SW19 020 8780 2406

The varied menu has been created by Indian chef Manoj Vassaikar, whose culinary skills have graced kitchens such as Chutney Mary, Veeraswamy and India 2000. He is consultant chef to Rajput, which opened on the site ofNirvana in '99. Warm and soothing environment, split-level interior. Bleached wooden flooring, saffron-coloured walls. Sketches of Rajput courtesans and various artifacts. Towards the back of the restaurant is the bar. White starched table linen, blue candle holders, shining glasses, and sunken ceiling lights which give an intimate and upmarket dining experience. Chairs are all hidden under loose covers made from a material called khadi – hand woven cotton with uneven weaves. Waiters smiling, helpful and polite. Specials: Onion, Courgette and Mushroom Bhajia £2.60 – finely sliced, mixed with gram flour, deep-fried. Methi Seekh Kebabs – minced lamb kebabs with fenugreek leaves. Bindi Jaipuri £3.95 – batter fried okra, crisped and dusted with mango powder. Jat Salad £1.75 – green chilli, mouli (white radish) and onion. Fish Amritsari £3.25 – sliced Bekti marinated, gram flour, ajwain, shallow fried. Highlights of the main courses: Mewari Chicken £5.75 – chicken braised in spinach, fenugreek leaves, dill and tempered with mustard seeds in mustard oil. Lamb Chettinad – lamb cooked in south Indian spices and roasted with dry coconut in which the meat is simmered. And for the vegetarian: Malai vegetable Kofta and Palak Curry – vegetable dumplings in onion, tomato, cashewnut and spinach gravy. King Prawn Saffron Korma £9.25 – cashew and onion gravy, spiced with saffron water.. Assorted Mini Basket £3.95 – nan, parath, peshwari – good idea! To round off your meat, choose the Organic Banana Split – organic banana with toffee and roasted cashew, served with vanilla ice cream and organic honey – delicious! Sunday buffet: £8.95. Delivery service. Price check: Papadam 60p, CTM £5.95, Pullao Rice £2.25, Peshwari Nan £2.50.

SPICE OF RAJ

26 Christchurch Road, Colliers Wood, SW19 020 8542 0044

'Decor dim but tables too close. Detailed menu, quantities normal, beautifully cooked food. All in all a good night out. Surprisingly cheap, £70 for four. Recommended.' RL.

COBRA GOOD CURRY GUIDE
County Index, see page 5 Town Index, see page 614
A to Z of the Curry Menu, page 41 Contributors Key, page 604

SUVAI ARUVI NEW ENTRANT **BYO**

96 High Street, Colliers Wood, SW19 020 8543 6266

Café-type restaurant, USP for SW19 (albeit in the unfashionable area of the postcode) being that it is Sri Lankan. Unlicensed: no corkage, so BYO. Specials: Soosyam 50p (doughnut, sweet coconut and lentil stuffing), Tomato Kulambu £1 – in creamy sauce, Seafood Pittu Kothu £4.50 (one of my Sri Lankan favourites minus the seafood – a mixture of meat, vegetables and rice). No credit cards – cash only, but that's OK, the prices are very good. Impossible parking, but next to the tube. Hours: 11am-12pm.

London SW20

Merton, Raynes Park

BOMBAY BICYCLE CLUB NEW ENTRANT

302 Kingston Road, SW20 020 8540 9997

A branch of the Bombay Bicycle Club in SW12.

London W

Area: West End postcode W1
and West London W2 to W14
Population: 630,000

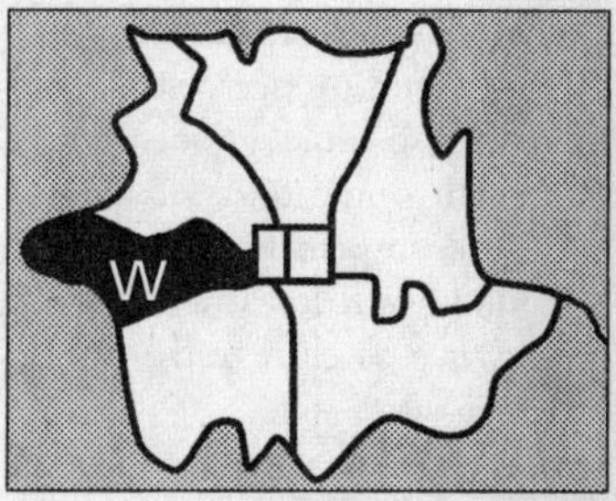

London W1

The West End

ANJUMS INDIAN CUISINE NEW ENTRANT

72 Shaftesbury Avenue, Piccadilly, W1 020 7437 9171

'Situated on the edge of Chinatown. Decor is normal, menu has no surprises. All the food was a good average, not thrilling, but no dish was disappointing. For once, it was the service that was exceptionally good.' H&DRC.

ANWARS TOP 100

64 Grafton Way, Tottenham Court Road, W1 020 7387 6664

Old hands will remember the Grafton Way's Bombay Emporium, when London had just a couple of spice stores. In 1962, Anwars opened down the street and buying spices had a new excitement. It was taken over in 1985 by Muhammad Afzal Zahid. His 52-seater serves gutsy, spicy Pakistani food and is redolent of Southall. Basic, clean café-style. Make your choice from the serving counter, from the dishes of the day (no menu as such), then carry your tray to a formica table, jugs of water in place, and enjoy it. It has good local Asian patronage. 'Café-style place. Everything, including naan bread, is microwaved and that is the downside – it was only lukewarm.' [It's how Indian's like it, Ray – they eat with their hands. But that's no excuse in these circumstances]. 'The food, however, was excellent. Seekh kebabs were excellent – no artificial colours, and good and spicy. Karahi Gosht was really tasty. Portions a bit mean. Tandoori Roti was cooked fresh to order and was excellent.' RE. 'Anwars has gone upmarket! They have replaced the old wooden chairs with a new, slightly padded variety. Thank goodness this is the only thing that has changed – the tables, layout, self-serve counter, ambience and, more importantly, the food all remain unchanged. 'Set lunch, £4.95 for Chicken Curry, ladle of mixed vegetables, ladle of Chana, ladle of Sag Aloo over a mound of rice, with a Puri and a cup of tea. The vegetarian version at £3.70 also looks good. Both excellent value. Kebab Roll (2 Kebabs in a Nan with onion and salad) at £2 was a popular takeaway. Well spiced, authentic, supremely tasty food in basic but pleasant self service cafe style surroundings at low prices. A real gem. Only problem is that this one of my favourites is so close to the Indian YMCA that I am always a little indecisive which to visit!' MW.

CAFÉ LAZEEZ NEW ENTRANT NEW TO OUR TOP 100

21 Dean Street, Soho, W1 020 7434 9393

See SW7 for menu details. This newer venture is 'a huge restaurant with a buzzing bar upstairs. Really excellent.' KB&SS. Branches: SW7, EC1 and Birmingham to come.

CARAVAN SERAI AFGHAN TOP 100 BYO

50 Paddington Street, Marylebone, W1 020 7935 1208

Because the few Afghan mountain passes offered the only entry points to land-based northern India, food methods originated in Iran and the Middle East passed through to India and vice versa. Owner Mr Nayebkhail's 50-seat

Afghan restaurant est. 1975 is one of Britain's two Afghan restaurants (*see* also Afghan Kitchen N1), and both must be treasured. Afghan food is spiced more lightly than Indian, but there are many similarities, which will appear more obvious once you have studied the menu. The Tanoor is the Tandoor, Quorma is Korma, Gosht is meat, Murch is chicken, Palaw is Pillao, and so on. Yoghurt and garlic, root vegetables and pulses are also popular. Even if you know none of this, the menu explains everything most clearly. Starters include Ashak, £4.75 – a national dish of pastries, filled with a spicy leek and mince and lentil filling, in a yoghurt sauce, and Mantu, £4.75 – mince-filled pasta parcels in sauce. 'A nice restaurant – good service, good food served in pleasant, comfortable surroundings. Homely atmosphere. Well recommended.' AN. 'Complimentary small fried filled pastry with carrot and chilli pickle (Tourshou) served at the beginning (it looks innocuous but is quite hot). Starters of Boranee Bonjon – aubergine cooked in a delicious spiced sauce – excellent. Service friendly and efficient. 10% service on bill The waiter here is always friendly, He remembers me because we talk about Afghanistan, which I travelled in years ago, when it was safe to do so.' MW. End with Carrot Kulfi or Coconut Halva. House wine £9.95, mineral water £3.50. BYO allowed: £2 corkage. 20% discount on takeaway. Hours: 12-3pm/6-11.30pm.

CHOR BIZARRE BEST NORTH INDIAN TOP 100

16 Albemarle Street, Piccadilly, W1 020 7629 8542

Owned by Rohit, Delhi's 32-room Hotel Broadway has stood the test of time. It predates most of Delhi's glamour hotels which have more stars than staff. Its has all the services at one-third the price. It is close to India Gate and Chandi Chowk, with its markets and bustling street life. Leading to the Mosque are numerous narrow twisting medieval lanes which contain many bazaars, established centuries ago, selling copper, gold, silks, flowers, food, books, artifacts, furniture, antiques – you name it. Chor Bazaar is one which has long thrilled the residents of Delhi, meaning 'thieves' markets' originally run by ex-cons pushing stolen goods. Be that as it may, today it sells anything and everything. It's a kind of permanent car-boot-sale, where you can buy anything at knock-down prices. And if you feel you've conned the cons, well it's something to tell your next dinner party. Entrepreneur Rohit Khattar hit on the idea a few years ago to exploit this image. The hotel restaurant needed a revamp, and he cannily renamed it Chor Bizarre exploiting the linguistic twist from 'Bazaar' to 'Bizarre'. The spin told Delhi it was furnished from the real Chor Bazaar. No two items were the same. It took Delhi by storm. For a while even Macdonalds and Pizza delivery took second place as the talking point. Mr Khattar set his eyes on Mayfair. When

Mahendra Kaul's 85-seat Gaylord site became available, in 1997, it was perfect. Each chair is different, some are inlaid, some are silver, some wooden carved, some are upholstered, others not. Each table is also different. Some are round, some square. Some are glass-topped cases under which are trinkets. Others are marble-topped, one is silver-topped, and the *pièce de resistance* is a table for six under an 18th-century four-poster-bed. Embroidered cushions are dotted around. The walls are adorned with wooden carvings, Rajasthani mirrors, fans, face masks, weapons and paintings of Maharajas. Even the floor has different surfaces. None of this would have been cheap. Does it work, this haphazard look? It is unexpected, and its clutter is, in a way, like a Raj/Maharaja's lounge. The room is small, maybe too small – just 50 seats in an L-shape. And it is a little dark. Some love it, other's don't. And so what of the food? Its authentic Kashmiri food is unique to London (and rare even in Delhi). Kashmir is India's most northern state in the foothills of the Himalayas. The Moghuls established their Shangrila (heaven on earth) there to take a beautiful cool retreat in the summer. Kashmiri food is highly aromatic. Saffron comes from here. Chefs Deepinder S Sondhi and Manpreet S Ahuja offers many Kashmiri dishes including Gilauati Kabab £6 (lamb kebab flavoured with saffron served with tomato and white radish salad and mint yoghurt chutney) and Marz Wangun Korma £12 (lamb cooked with Kashmiri chillies with cardamom and cloves), Goshtaba £14 (pounded lamb balls), Haaq £7 (spinach cooked with aniseed), Rajmah £6.50 (red kidney beans and Chaaman, lotus stem). A neat way to try these and other Kashmiri dishes is to order the Tarami £24. Also on the menu are dishes from Bombay, Chaat Papri, from Tamil Nadu, Chicken Chettinad £12 – flavoured with dark aromatic spices, from the Punjab, Samosa £5.50, served with channa masala, yoghurt and chutneys, from Kerala, Avial (broccoli, baby corn, cauliflower, courgette, coconut, yoghurt, curry leaves and fresh coriander), and from Pakistan, Tak-a-Tak. After the chef starts frying the dish, he takes the two steel, flat-edged spatulas and rapidly bangs them one after the other on to the pan to chop, mash and mix the ingredients. The dish gets its name from the noise made – taka-taka-taka-taka. Try the Kalega chicken-liver Tandoori, Paneer Tikka Achari £10 (large chunks of curd cheese, flavoured with a pinch of pickle), Tandoori Phool £10 (broccoli and cauliflower florets), and Wild Mushroom Methi. That very Indian soft drink Nimbu Pani £2.50 (fresh lime juice) can be served sweet, salted or plain. TV wine-expert Charles Metcalfe's wine list matches 35 dishes to a particular wine, though quite what one chooses to go with a multi-choice of dishes is not explained, so trust to your instincts. It is also very biased to white wines. The food is expertly and accurately cooked, and extremely good, each dish with its own distinct masala. Service is very amiable with a regular crew trying to please. However, with no evident system of table assignment, you can get an all-or-nothing amateurishness. At the prices you are asked to pay here, this might be forgivable, but decidedly unforgivable is the credit card billing practice. The 12.5% service charge (albeit with mini-papadoms and delicious chutneys free) is announced on the menu. Leaving the slip open with a heading for 'Gratuity' is not on, so as we said in the Brownies 'Be Prepared'. Chor Bizarre is popular with well-heeled Indians. Its site, on the edge of Mayfair, is a long trog up Albemarle Street and does not attract passing trade. This comment from one of our trusty scribes says it all: 'Not cheap. Soft, delicate flavours. Sophisticated, up-market air and decor. The sort of place to entertain business colleagues (and on a business account!).' PAW. In a wish to encourage good food, we are awarding Chor Bizare our BEST NORTH INDIAN AWARD. Average spend: £40, excluding drinks. Wine cheapest £13. Water £2.50 Buffet 2-course lunch Mon.-Fri., £12.95. Pre-theatre 2-course dinner, £11, 4-course dinner, £21 – includes car-drop to West End theatre – min. 2 people. Post-theatre – complimentary dessert and tea or coffee when you show your ticket stub. Hours: 12-3pm/6-11.30pm (Sun. to 10.30pm). Stocks Cobra.

DELHI BRASSERIE NEW ENTRANT

44 Frith Street, Soho, W1 020 7437 2613

'Small, friendly, lovely ambience. Very good and for us quite unusual choices.' CS.

DHAKA BRASSERIE ©

38 Charlotte Street, W1 020 7436 9767

'From the ashes of the Neel Akash (ex-Hanway Street – its home demolished in '98), rose Sheikh Ashik Miah's 110-seater. Run by son Zia, the new site is 'a lot nicer with additional seating downstairs.' RL. 'A delicious dinner with a party of 15 people. Everyone thought the service and food was superb.' LO. 'Always have very good meals here. Chicken Dhansak excellent. Good portions, quality meat.' AJ. Fully licensed. Takeaway: 10% discount. Service 10%. Menu specials: Chutney 20p, Chicken Tangree £2.90 – drumsticks marinated in yoghurt, grilled in tandoor – chef's recommendation. Lunch special: Thali set lunch from £3.95, 3-course set lunch from £4.95. Price check: Papadam 40p, CTM £5.90, Pullao Rice £1.70, Peshwari Nan £1.70. Hours: 12-3pm/6-11.30pm (Fri. & Sat. to 12am). Branches: Neel Akash, at 36b, basement, next door, though Colville Place divides these two, and Neel Akash Tandoori 93, Charlotte Street.

GAYLORD INDIAN RETURNED TO OUR TOP 100 ©

79-81 Mortimer Street, W1 020 7580 3615

When it opened in 1963 it was not only Britain's first upmarket Indian restaurant, it also pioneered the Tandoori oven in Britain. The name is a play on the names of the original owners Gai and Lamba, who had opened one of Delhi's very first Indian restaurants called Kwality in 1948. By the 50's there were Kwalities all over India. But they were little more than caffs. Having made a fortune producing ice-cream, the pair decided to go upmarket, with their first Gaylord which opened in Delhi in 1958. Other branches followed soon after in Bombay, San Francisco, Kowloon, Kobe Japan, Bahamas and Manchester. Still owned by Mr Lamba, it has an impressive double-frontage, decorated in blue with gold lettering, clipped bay trees in terracotta pots standing either side of the doors. Elegance extends inside and the interior has been redesigned by Ms Neetu Kohui of Bombay. Regulars enjoy the Machili Tikka, £5.25 (marinated de-boned fish), Maharaja Feast £15.95 (a vegetarian delight of Vegetable Samosa, Paneer Tikka, three vegetable curries of your choice, served with Raitha, salad, rice and bread) and Murgh Bhuna Dhania Masala £7.25 (boneless morsels of chicken cooked in spices and flavoured with green coriander), Baingan Ka Bharta £5.25 (baked aubergine mashed and cooked with tomatoes and onions), Bataire Begum Bahar £8.95 (two quails cooked with yoghurt, almond, cashew nut purée and spices). We have a wealth of satisifed comments, e.g. 'I go there because, without any doubt, they do the best Lamb Tikka I've ever had, by far. Large, moist, tender and exceptionally tasty, my mouth is watering as I type.' CP. One of our Indian scribes gives the only rather more critical report: 'Offers good choice for both meat-eaters and vegetarians. Paneer cooked in a tandoor was well cooked, but the mamra (puffed rice) in the bhel was too chewy. Overall standard of food was good, but there was too much oil in the kofta curry and the portions were on the low side. Desserts disappointing. Service attentive and unrushed, but we found the restaurant a little bit pricey.' RM. Delivery. Service 15%. Cover charge: £1.20 – includes a Papadam and pickle. Takeaway: 10% discount. Price check: Papadam 60p, CTM £7.95, Pullao Rice £2.95, House wine £10.95. Hours: 12-3pm/6-11.30pm; Sun. to 11pm. Stocks Cobra.

GOPALS OF SOHO

12 Bateman Street, Soho, W1 020 7434 1621

Gopal, real name NT Pittal, earned his spurs by cooking superb food, first at the Lal Qila, then at the Red Fort. Justifiably feeling his career was going nowhere, he opened his own restaurant in 1990, and the accolades poured in, like they are currently doing for Vineet at Zaika, SW7. And then, as they do, they stopped. Now, for some strange reason this restaurant gets a lot of adverse comment. Run by Mr Pital jnr, Gopal's son, it still serves classic well-cooked Indian food, with Gopal very much behind the scenes in the kitchen. Maybe that's it. Gopal is a really shy man. And perhaps this seeps down to the troops, because we've been hearing for years of a reserved attitude with the service, bordering (mistakenly?) on surly. Indeed it was reports about such service which have progressively downgraded Gopal's in our *Guide* editions. We had it as a TOP 100 in our 1991 edition. By '98 we had removed it from that list, then last time delisted it altogether. Yet, when we went to try out David Wolfe's fine new wine list, we found a happy place full of regulars fortunate enough to live nearby. The food on that night was superb. Tight crispy vegetable pakoras. On the whole it's a standard menu, with the full range of starters from bhaji to kebabs, tandoori and curries, but a closer look reveals rare specials. Maassa, £2.95, Parsee (capsicum pepper, its top cut off and a filling of chicken keem, rice and sweet and sour spices) and Mangalorean Crab, £4.60, cooked in coconut, are two interesting starters. Main courses include items from Goa to Kashmir, Lucknow to Hyderabad: the Murgh Massalam £24.95 (stuffed with keema , baked and served with lemon rice, vegetable curry and naan) is good value for 2. Reports please. House Thali £ 12.95. Price check: Papadam 50p, CTM £6.75, Pullao Rice £2.50, Peshwari Nan £1.70. Hours: 12-3pm/6-11.30

INDIAN YMCA CANTEEN

45 Fitzroy Street, Fitzrovia, W1 020 7387 0411

Walk (parking nigh-on impossible) north up Fitzroy Street. The large modern block on your right may already be permeating curry smells from its basement kitchen. Enter and, out of courtesy, please ask at reception, manned by gentle young Indian, if it's OK to use the canteen. By some quirk, they don't mind outsiders visiting, they say, only at lunchtime, though I've yet to see them enforce dinner time. The canteen, on your right, is clean, with brown functional formica-topped tables. It's deserted 5 minutes before opening time, then as if the school bell's rung, it's suddenly packed full with Asians, many of whom are students, and this is their residence. (Like all YMCAs, residency is open to anyone, though officially this one is subtitled Indian Student Hostel.) All students of good curry, should visit here before they can graduate as aficionados. Meal sessions last just one hour. No bookings, no licence, no BYO and no nonsense! Take a plastic tray, join the always-busy queue at the stainless steel servery. It's basic, unsophisticated but authentic expertly spiced and cooked Indian school-dinner style food, like you get at streetside Dabsa the length and breadth of India. Chicken and fish curries £2, lamb curry £2.20, vegetable curries all £1.20 and lentils £1. Your choice handed to you in bowls. Top up with chupatties, tea or coffee, and pay at the till, cash only. It's absurdly cheap – hard to exceed a fiver. Then jostle for space at a shared formica table. The food may not be five-star but the company can be, when you share your table with talkative, friendly students. Men in white coats tidy up after you. 'Marvellous.' MW. Set lunch £4.50 two courses. Hours: 12.30-1.30pm daily, prompt, and (oh yes, here's a change) Sat & Sun 7-8pm.

KERELA NEW ENTRANT

15 Great Castle Street, Oxford Circus, W1 020 7580 2125

When the bill comes, its heading is Shireef's. A few enquiries tell you Shireef's Wine Bar dates from 1935. It soon became patronised by staff and artists from newly-built nearby Broadcasting House as an extension to their BBC Club. Little had changed when in 1988 it was taken over by David Tharakan. A decade later Tharakan changed it to a 40-seater restaurant, decorated in a very Indian way, with all sorts of artifacts hanging off the walls including golden umbrellas used by temple elephants. His wife Mille took charge of the cooking. Out went English food, and in came a menu which we believe is unique to the UK. We normally think of Kerela as a vegetarian state. In fact there have been passionate non-vegetarians – Muslims, Jews and Christians – living there side by side for centuries, each with a distinctive cooking style. As for the latter, St Thomas the Apostle landed in Kerela in AD50 and made many converts to Christianity. His language was Syriac Aremenaic, his converts known as Syrian Christians. To this day they eat offal, chicken, duck, fish, shellfish, beef, and wild boar. Chef Millie Tharakan cooks Kerelan Syrian Christian food, albeit using examples of the five former, and lamb in place of beef. Erachi Olathiathu £4.95 (lamb steamed then dry fried with a paste of coconut and spices) is masterful. So is her Cochin Duck Roast, £7.95, and Karaveli (coastal) fish dishes using the tasty Kerelan king fish. Mussels Ularthu £3.75 – mussels fried, Alleppey style. As well as all this there are a number of other specialities. Starters include: a very sensibly sized mini Masala Dosa £2.75 (rice-flour pancake filled with potatoes, onions, curry leaves and mustard seeds, served with Coconut Chutney), Cashew Nut Pakora £2.75 served with Date Chutney, Meen and Mango Vevichathu £4.95 is king fish with green mango, Cabbage and Carrot Thoran £3.25 (mustard seed and curry leaves), Coconut Rice £2.20. The feature in this smallish place is its staircase with tables set around the balcony at first floor level. Some of the window tables had gone so we were placed in the narrow gangway which connects back to front. No problem. We ordered and we supped our red wine and chatted, rereading this report about Kerela from BS: 'You could stand in the middle of Oxford Circus and lob a Japanese tourist through the door it is so central. Amongst the vegetable curries was one uneatable vegetable – a thin dark green stalk which could only appeal to a broad-minded goat.' [Dom thinks it's her favourite drumsticks, Brian, and she's a bit miffed!] 'Then a couple (loud-voiced-hee-haw type) arrived, were seated at the diagonally adjacent table and proceeded to light up. With smoke now filling most of our area, and without a/c on a humid night, the one open window had no effect in pulling out the air. We asked the waitress if we were sitting in the non-smoking section. She confirmed that we were, but the table next to us was in the smoking section – bizarre or what? With a near-empty rear section, could not the smokers have been placed there? The couple stared belligerently, so we asked to move to the farthest corner, and to be fair the waitress was helpful. Our new seat had a fine view into the bar and down-stairs tables, and mine host, for I presume it was he, was rivetted to one of these, drinking red wine with a succession of friends. Not once did he patrol the restaurant or kitchen. Pat was eventually drawn to his beloved Rasam £2.75. He had pressed the waitress to make sure it was hot, like in Kerela. She patronisingly told him it was made with green chillies. Why do serving staff always think you're joking when you ask for hot? In the event, stubs of fresh raw green chillies were floating on top of the Rasam, spicy with black pepper, but hot it was not. My starter, Potato Bonda £2.50 (besan-dipped patties of potato) had been deep-fried – badly. The oil had not been hot enough, thus it seeped into the potato mixture. I was hungry and ate them anyway. The accompanying coconut chutney was good, complete with curry leaf. Main courses of Erachi Biryani £5.95 – lamb and rice cooked together, or so said the menu, but in fact not true. The tender, mildly spicy lamb had been added to a dish of coloured Pullao Rice, the give-away, small lumpy knots of white rice. Nice but not a Biryani. This came accompanied by the smallest receptacle of Sambar that you have ever seen (it contained just one piece of goat fodder) and an even smaller one of tasty Raitha. Pat's Erachi Olathiathu £4.95 was a good portion of dry-fried succulent lamb, with fried curry leaves and slices of fresh coconut shavings – delicious. Beetroot Thoran £3.25 – small chunks of firm beetroot with fried onion and more curry leaves was very tasty. The t/a menu quotes Charles Campion as saying 'jaw-dropping price'. They've gone up noticably since he wrote that, but even so £33 for two with wine and water isn't bad for Oxford Circus. We were excitedly expecting to award a TOP 100 cachet here, but for now it's a near miss. A little management effort would get there. We hope so, because its culinary concept is unique to London, bringing back great memories of Southern India. Reports please.

LA PORTE DES INDES AWARD WINNER TOP 100 ©

32 Bryanston Street, Marble Arch, W1 020 7224 0055

Still London's biggest (300 seats), and still one of the best. Opened in 1997, managed by Sherin Modi Alexander with her Taj-trained husband, Mernosh Modi, in charge of cooking. Few readers of this guide can be unaware of La Porte's £2.5m decor with its sandstone arch, 40-foot waterfall, and sweeping staircase made of white marble with pink sandstone balustrades, imported especially from India's pink city, Jaipur. Airy, domed skylights enhance La Porte's daytime atmosphere, making it a different place in darkness. There is a forest of jungle plants, a wealth of Indian artefacts and antiques, and the range of eating rooms, including the tiny private dining rooms seating 12 and 24 respectively, seating up to 60-plus. The lunch presentation of food on raised copper salvers is opulent and attractive, and you can e-a-m-a-y-l for £16.95. On Sundays it's called brunch, livened up with a jazz band. Menu Maison £31 per person without soup or sorbet, £3 with – either course (get it!). It's a great way to spend a leisurely lunch or dinner and try a little of everything. Starters: Parsee Fish (sole fillets, mint and coriander chutney, lightly steamed in banana leaf), Crab Malabar (warm salad, flaked crabmeat and corn kernels, presented in shell), Murgh Tikka Nawabi (chicken fillets, garlic, yoghurt, spices, tandoor grilled), Rasoul (pastry filled with spiced lamb and peas), Beignets d'aubergines (aubergine roundlets, filled with cheese and herb paté). And that was just your starters – now for your main courses. Adrak Ke Panje (marinated and grilled lamb chops), Poulet Rouge (shredded chicken, yoghurt, red spices, grilled, buttery cream sauce), Crevettes Assadh (prawns, mangoes, green chillies, ginger, poppy seeds, creamy coconut curry), Rogan Josh (classic lamb curry of Kashmir), Saag Paneer (spinach and cheese sautéed in butter, green chillies and ginger). Accompaniments: Kesaria Pullao Rice, Nan and Raitha. Pudding (if you can stand the thought without feeling sick!), Coupe Pondicherry (medley of fruits, ice cream and fresh mango coulis). We (I just have to confess) have eaten this menu and can tell you that we did manage all of it (me – albeit prawns) and enjoyed every mouthful. There is another set menu named 'Royal Vegetarian' with the same rules at £29 and £31 respectively. As usual, we have many contented reports from regulars and one-offs alike. But before we give examples, we retain our usual caveat about the occasional complaint from philistines unused to authentic Indian food. Malcolm Gluck is one, finding the food too un-curry-house to recommend wines for it. 'When are they going to put some spices in?' he asked. Stay on high, Malc! This is what the discerning say: 'Superb: food, comfort, decor, service, quality, quantity.' GM. 'Recommended to me by an Indian lawyer who frequently takes clients there, and by another extremely wealthy Indian lawyer who described it as being the only curry house worth eating at in the West End.' AM. 'Just as impressive as everyone has already said. Trees instead of flowers for every table! It must be seen to be believed! Staff are legion. Excellent presentation of all dishes. Food delicate and flavourful. All food excellent.' RH. 'Buffet Sunday lunch – a very lovely meal. Happy relaxed atmosphere. Goan fish curry was one of the best we've had for a long time, Tarka Dhal had a good earthy taste. Sweets were delightful and totally authentic. Drink prices ludicrously high.' CO'C. 'My personal favourite Indian restaurant.' DM. We remain impressed by La Porte. The French connection may be tenuous, but it's no more theatrical than Le Manoir. La Porte's ambience, decor, service, food is all as good as it gets. La Porte has become an Indian's Indian, with an ever-increasing clientèle from the subcontinent. We gave it our Best in UK Award in '98. This Award has only gone to two other restaurants since we started our Awards a decade ago. This Award is a permanent accolade, and does justice to Mernosh's fabulous food and Sherin's tight management. Price check: CTM (Poulet Rouge!!!) £12.80 (has to be one of the most expensive), Pullao Rice £3.80, Stuffed Nan £3.50. Average spend £43. Service discretionary. Cover charge £1.50. Hours: 12-2.30pm Mon.-Fri (to 3pm Sun)/7-11.30pm Mon.-Sat. (Sun. 6-10.30pm). Branches: Blue Elephant Thai, SW6, and others in Europe. Stocks Cobra.

MUMBAI SPICE NEW ENTRANT ©

4 Blenheim Street, off New Bond Street, W1 020 7409 0300

Formerly Bonds of Mayfair. The restaurant, opened in 1999, is owned by Vijay and Ajay Saggar, seats a discrete 36, is plainly decorated, and serves Northern Indian food – CTM is most popular. Sunday lunch £5.95. Price check: Papadam 30p, CTM £5.95, Peshwari Nan £1.20, Mineral water £1.20, Lager £2.50 (pint). Hours: 12-3pm/7-10.30pm.

NEEL AKASH NEW ENTRANT

36b Charlotte Street, Fitzrovia, W1 020 7580 9767

Sheikh Ashik Miah's popular Hanway Street Neel Akash was demolished in 1998 to make way for some capitalistic development project. Fortunately for its fans, it has been reincarnated here. Actually its next-door sister Dhaka came first. It has a similar menu but being in the basement a different atmosphere. Lunch special: Thali set lunch from £3.95, 3-course set lunch from £4.95. Price check: Papadam 40p, CTM £5.90, Pullao Rice £1.70, Peshwari Nan £1.70. Hours: 12-3pm/6-11.30pm (Fri. & Sat. to 12am); closed Sun. Branch: Dhaka Brasserie, next door, Neel Akash Tandoori, (formerly the Natraj) 93 Charlotte Street.

NEEL AKASH TANDOORI NEW ENTRANT

93 Charlotte Street, Fitzrovia, W1 020 7637 0050

Natraj, est. 1975. was an early curry contender to the street. It recently changed its name to Neel Akash Tandoori, giving the clue that it is now related to the celebrated Neel Akash of yore (*see* previous entry). It is a friendly curry house without pretentions at sensible prices, so weekdays it's busy. Takeaway 10% discount. Specials: Pumpkin Curry £2.90, Chutney Tray 20p per person – great value. Price check: Papadam 40p, CTM £5.80, Pullao Rice £1.70, Peshwari Nan £1.70. Hours: 12-3pm/6pm-12am; closed Sun.

NEEL KAMAL NEW ENTRANT

160 New Cavendish Street, Fitzrovia, W1 020 7580 6125

Located near the Telecom Tower and opposite the University of Westminster, the restaurant is decorated with creamy walls, white ornate plaster-work and a sparkling chandelier. The bar is located at the back of the restaurant. Friendly waiters. Party of tourists sat eating good helping of food which smelled delicious – I was hungry! Specials: Murgh Nilgiri £6.30 (chicken prepared with lemon juice, fried cashews, garlic, yoghurt, spices and herbs), Goan Crab £6.20 (spicy sweet and sour sauce with coconut). 'Very popular with local businessmen, myself included. Small, friendly and with good choice of well-prepared authentic-tasting food.' CP. 'Have been visiting for two years – consistently excellent. I'm surprised it's not in your guide. Good quality meat superbly cooked, good portions, good service and nice place.' AJ. Price check: Papadam 55p, CTM £5.90, Pullao Rice £1.80, Peshwari Nan £2.30. Hours: 12-3pm/6-12am. Stocks Cobra.

PALMS OF GOA

12 Charlotte Street, Fitzrovia W1 020 7636 1668

Established in 1994 by Eugene Dias, who also manages. His restaurant with its creamy walls, white linen tablecloths, and the eponymous potted palms all add to a light and bright 40-seat restaurant that serves Goan and regular curries and side dishes. House specials include: Batata Wade £1.95 (potatoes, peas, green chilli fried with gram flour), Lamb Xacutti, prepared with coconuts, vinegar and hot spices £5.95, Goan Green Fish Masala, spicy sauce with fresh coriander and chillies £5.95 and Pumpkin Curry, a speciality of nearby Mangalore £2.95. 'Caught them just as they were opening – staff still arriving. Started with plain and spicy popadom, followed by Chicken Chat

– very spicy with tender chicken. Chicken Pistachio Korma, again tender chicken with slices of Bombay Potato. Enjoyable meal.' MK. Price check: Papadam 35p, CTM £6.50, Pullao Rice £1.95, Peshwari Nan £1.75. Hours: 11.30am-3.30pm/6.30-11.30pm; closed Sun. and 2 weeks for Christmas.

RAGAM SOUTH INDIAN TOP 100 ©

57 Cleveland Street, Fitzrovia, W1 020 7636 9098

Established in 1984 this cosy restaurant seats 34 upstairs, 20 downstairs. DIY decor, stark white paintwork. Friendly waiters. Chef Nair cooks standard curries and, good though they are, our standard advice is to concentrate only on the authentic south-Indian food. Uthappam, a pizza-style pancake made of rice and lentil flour with a topping of onions, green chillies, tomatoes and herbs, served with Sambar and Coconut chutney, £4.20. Kaalan, made with yoghurt, coconut and sweet mango, goes well with rice, £2.80. Paper Dosai £3 – thin and crispy pancake, served with sambar and Coconut Chutney. Sambar Vadai £3.50 – gram flour doughnut marinated in a savoury curry made of vegetables, lentils and tamarind juice. Iddly £3.50 – steamed cake made of rice and black gram, served with sambar and coconut chutney. 'You wisely include it in your TOP 100. Have been visiting for over 10 years, always excellent.' AJ. Last note: at lunchtime you can enjoy a 'quick meal on a plate' at £4.95 for curry, rice and bread – it's a bargain! Service, 10%, not included. Delivery: minimum £10, local area only. Price check: Papadam 40p, Masala Dosa £3.80, Sambar £2.95, Chilli Chicken £7.95, Rasam £1.90, Sweet Coconut Paratha £2, House wine £9. It remains safely in our TOP 100. Hours: 12-3pm/6-11.30pm; Sat. 12-3pm; Sun. 6-11pm.

RAJ TANDOORI ©

72 Berwick Street, Soho, W1 020 7437 2897

Originally opened way back in 1969 under the name of Islamabad. Present ownership of Abdon Noor since 1993, serves Northern Indian food, all the usual curry house specials on the menu, plus some Bangladeshi specials including Ayer (Bangladeshi fish) Bhuna £6.95 and Satkora (Bangladeshi citrus fruit) Gosht £6.25. Seats an intimate 36. Air-conditioned. Takeaway: 10% discount. Price check: Papadam 60p, CTM £6.75, Pullao Rice £2.10, Peshwari Nan £2.10, House wine £8.25. Hours: 12-2.30pm/5.30pm-12am. Stocks Cobra.

RASA NEW TO OUR TOP 100

6 Dering Street, off Oxford Street, W1 020 7629 1346

Opened in 1998, this is the second of three restaurants established by Shivadas (Das) Sreedharan and his wife Alison. They specialise in southern-Indian vegetarian cooking from Kerala, south India's richest state. The prices here are high enough to deter regular visits, when the same quality can be had at several venues a stone's throw away or the original Rasa branch in scruffy north London. The place is very tiny with seating on two floors packed into the narrow rooms. It does two full sessions every night, plus a full week-day lunch trade. We've not changed our views about overcrowding and overpricing since our last report (which was in the company of a head of the Taj group and the owners of Chutney Mary, SW10). Superb cooking by Chef RS Binuraj, however, compensates for these downsides. The nibbles include papadams but also pappadavadai (thinner, crunchier), Acchappam – rice batter crisp made from a mould (acch), and chena upperi (spiced root vegetable crisps – Terence Stamp Collection style) and seven chutneys. Starters include: Banana Boli £4.25 (ripe plantain dipped in besan flour and black sesame, fried, served with peanut and ginger sauce), Vadai Selection £4.25 (fermented lentil soft dumplings, deepfried to give a crisp outside), Banana Boli £4.25 (ripe plantain dipped in besan flour and black sesame, fried, served with peanut and ginger sauce). Main courses include Xheera Parippu Curry £6.25 (spinach, too dhal, garlic cheese and tomatoes), Moru Kachiathu £6.25 (combined and spiced sweet mangoes and green bananas), Nadan Parippu £6 (lentil curry typical of Kerala, Beet Cheera Pachadi – beetroot, spinach, yoghurt, roasted coconut, mustard seeds and curry leaves), Rasa Kayi (minced vegetables, ginger, garlic and fennel seed). To experience several of these try the Keralan Feast £22.50. Tamarind, Lemon and Coconut Rice (with fresh coconut and black dhal) £3.75 each. During the evening all main courses are traditionally served on banana leaves. Puddings: Pal Payasam – like a rice pudding with cashew nuts and dried fruit – very sweet. 'All round very enjoyable, would certainly like to go back and try other dishes.' HC. Despite the caveat, we welcome Rasa to our TOP 100. Service 12.5%. Hours: 12-2.45pm/6-10.45pm. Branch: Rasa 55 Church St, N16, and next entry. Stocks Cobra.

RASA SAMUDRA NEW ENTRANT NEW TO OUR TOP 100

5 Charlotte Street, Fitzrovia, W1 020 7637 0222

The latest restaurant in owner chef Sivadas (Das) Sreedharan's trio. Outside it has the same dayglow candyfloss pink paintwork, with ice-cream yellow on the upper floor. Lovely hanging baskets burst with red flowers. Inside wooden carvings hang on pretty Wedgewood blue walls, contrasting with a naff clashing dark green carpet, of a type usually found in seaside B&Bs. His books are on sale, prominently displayed. Set on two floors, the new venture set Das back an alleged £½ mil. The menu includes many of Rasa's signature vegetarian dishes (*see* entry above). But here Das uniquely specialises in Kerelan fish and seafood, (Samudra means 'of the sea'). Special seafood starters: Rasam £4.50 (consommé with prawns, crab, mussels, squid and tomato), Meen Cutlet £4.50 (tuna and cassava mixed with spices, coated in breadcrumbs and fried), Koonthal Fry £6.95 (squid rings fried with onions and spices). Main courses include: Meen Elayil Pollichathu £9.95 (pomfret marinated in paste of Kanthari chillies, curry leaves, green pepper and fresh coconut slices), Beet Cheera Pachadi £6.25 (fresh beetroot and spinach in a yoghurt sauce with roasted coconut, mustard seeds and curry leaves), Para Konju Nirachathu (lobster) £22.50 (cut into halves and stuffed with its own meat, cooked with black pepper and Indian shallots), served whole on the plate with Lemon Rice and Beetroot Curry. Seafood main courses: Meen Manga Curry £9.50 (king fish, green mango and spice sauce). Papadams etc. with pickle and chutney tray at a ridiculously expensive £4 (Phew!). Kochi Dosa £10.95 (Phew!). Tamarind Rice £3.75. Boiled Rice £3 (treble Phew!). Puddings: Pal Payasam £3.50 (spiced rice pudding, cashew nuts and raisins). Set menus: £22.50 vegetarian, £30 seafood. Seafood Salad £8.95. Add 12.5% service charge to the phew factor and dear Das is up there in the astro-price department. Overall we get happy reports about this place, apart that is from price. This is an area devoid of tourists, and often of residents. Restaurants abound, notably Greek, and an increasing number of curry competitors in the street include the YMCA and several others (*see* above) most of whom close on Sunday, when the area is deserted. Amin Ali's superb Jamdani opened and closed a few years back. The caveat issued, for its unique menu it deserves our TOP 100 cachet. Price check: Cobra £4.50, Mineral water £3 bottle. Hours: 12-2.45pm (not Sun.)/6-10.45pm. Branch: Rasa, 55 Church Streett, N16, and previous entry. Stocks Cobra.

RED FORT

77 Dean Street, Soho, W1 020 7437 2525

What can we say about the Red Fort? Once it and its owner Amin Ali were the doyens of the press. In the early days you had to book for lunch on any of the seven days a week. Now you can get in easily without booking for lunch or evening. Pat and I recently attended a lunchtime launch/press party here. The place was packed with journalists and people in the 'trade'. The food, when it finally arrived, was very good indeed, much better than we were expecting. But service was a little strange, the table was at the very back of the restaurant, with no room to swing a cat. We diners queued at the bar area (near the front of the restaurant) and ended up going around the buffet table in opposite directions – I don't know whether this method made it quicker – I doubt it! '£12.50 – buffet was delicious and plentiful. Everything fine until the bill arrived – £28.85 (for two) including £2 cover charge and 12.5% service charge.' RL. 'Being charged for service when it is a "help-yourself buffet" does seem rather ridiculous. Menu is OK, food quality average, portions small, service is not worth £2 per cover and 12.5% service charge. We took friends and were gutted with our overall experience, and following our visit we heard the rumour that the Fort has "gone off".' RN. Amin can (and does) put on Food Festivals, as good as anyone, bringing in specialist chefs to work alongside head chef Naresh Matta, who studied in Delhi, before working in Air India's flight kitchens. He then worked in Japan, in an Indian restaurant called Gifu City. Has anyone eaten there? His Red Fort specials include: Shikmpuri Kebab £5.95 (minced lamb, ginger, deep-fried), Tiger Prawn Malabari £8.95 (crispy coated served with pickle), Guinea Fowl Maderia £14.95 (cloves, cardamom and chillies), Nalli Achari £12.50 (lamb on the bone with nigella). Try the Thalis for a good selection of dishes £15.95 – vegetarian and £19.95 for meat eaters – I hope they are good for those prices. Downstairs is more dining space which is usually used for meetings/private parties. 'People say that you will see prominent diners across from your table – well, I have never seen anyone famous – just a bunch of nobodies.' DC. Hours: 12-2.30pm/5.30-11.30pm.

REGENT TANDOORI NEW ENTRANT

16 Denman Street, Piccadilly, W1 020 7434 1134

Long-established standard curry house waving the flag for the formula. Good for a fix at sensible prices.

SOHO SPICE

124-126 Wardour Street, Soho, W1 020 7434 0808

When we dined here it was early evening – we were off to the ballet. The staff were due for a shift change – the old shift was eager to get away and the new shift was just as eager for the same reason – none of them wanted to be there. The restaurant is brightly decorated but it was dirty and scruffy. The floor was scattered with used table napkins, the table we were shown to had heavy stains on the soft furnishings. Getting service wasn't easy. Our waiter opened our wine at the table and promptly dropped the metal seal, and, instead of picking it up to deposit it in the bin, he, without any thought (obviously a regular incident), kicked it under our table. Evidently out of sight – out of mind! The chutney bowl was absolutely filthy and I mean filthy – the dirt was ingrained into the white plastic (made to look like china) container. I ordered CTM, expecting something a little authentic; what I got was Heinz tomato soup sauce around chunks of chicken. While we ate (main courses come with side dishes), a small group of 20-something Asian girls arrived. After getting past the newly-arrived bouncer (I doubt if three tiny girls are going to 'disturb the peace' and cause an afray!) they asked for a table, saying they were meeting other friends. A waiter sauntered towards a table, pointed and uttered something along the lines of 'you can have this one', rotated and sauntered back to the service station and his idle pals. The cheerful girls stood around the table, removed their coats, but there was no one to take them. They called after the waiter, 'can we sit over there instead', the waiter turned, without stopping, waved a hand in the air and said 'ok'. The group proceeded to their new table and after scrunching up their heavy coats, momentarily, sat on them. The nicest thing about the restaurant was the polite and friendly African hostess in the ladies, handing out soap and towels. 'Creative and exotic menu, fairly generous quantities, good service. Food is good but I found the tandoori vegetables disappointing.' RM. 'Menu is a modern version of Indian with a monthly changing menu featuring a particular region – this time, Goa. Fish Curry Tilapia in a spicy tomato sauce was very moist and well cooked. Soho Spice is very good, different, and for those who like the modern ambience, a good addition to Soho. Not my sort of place though.' HC. Service 12.5%. House wine £10.95, Mineral water £2.75. Hours: 11.30am-12am (Thurs., Fri. & Sat. to 3am – that's for the basement bar! And yes, it's noisy in there); Sun. 12-10pm. Branch: Red Fort, W1.

TAMARIND AWARD WINNER TOP 100

20 Queen Street, Mayfair, W1 020 7629 3561

If you come by car they'll valet it for you (evenings only), otherwise parking is horrendously difficult. Reception is polite and efficient, with coats, umbrellas etc. being taken and deposited in a private cloakroom. Down a turning staircase to the restaurant, you are met by the manager – Rajan, (with his incredible memory for people and chairs!) will show you to your table. The dining room is spacious and the 100 seats do not feel cramped. Emily Todhunter designed the interior – pale floor, gold paint, copper, brass and not forgetting the fabulous wrought-iron chairs. I particularly like the ladies, very striking, full-length mirror to check my sari (good), copper hand basins, taps etc and individual towels to dry your hands. Large white starched table linen, sparkling wine glasses and polished cutlery make for a luxurious dining experience. There can be no doubt that head chef Atul

Kochar can cook – he excels himself executing classical Indian cuisine – which I happen to adore – I even like the dreaded spinach dishes! 'Delighted to report lived up to reputation. Initial phone call, service and food all exceptional. Definitely deserves its high rating. Can't wait for another opportunity to return. Prices are high for an Indian restaurant but normal for good quality European cuisine – worth every penny.' HC. Atul's hand-made chutneys are served in three dainty glass dishes with crisp, light papadams. His kebabs: Hara Kebab £4.95 (chickpeas, lentils, spinach and potato cakes) and Murgh Kaleki Masala £5.50 (chicken livers fried with onions, cumin and coriander) have a melt-in-the-mouth consistency and are quite delicious. Tandoori cooking can be witnessed from the restaurant through a glass screen, Changezi Champen £15.50 – best end of lamb cutlets marinated with pepper and cream. The menu might feel a touch limited, but I can assure you that every dish you need is there. From the six curries try Kadhai Jhingae £17 – a little hefty, but it is Mayfair! (prawns in a light tomato sauce with coriander and fenugreek), Murgh Adraki £13.50 (ginger flavoured chicken) or Achari Saag Gosht £14.50 (lamb shanks cooked with five-spice mix and leafy spinach). Vegetables and Side Dishes include our favourites Gobi Gulistan £5.80 (florets of cauliflower tossed with ginger and onion), Khattae Jeera Aloo £5.80 (potatoes with cumin and tamarind paste) and Dal Bukhari £5.80 (black lentils). And don't forget a basket filled with slices of Pudhina Paratha £3 (unleavened bread with mint) or a plate of Punjabi Salad £2 (onion, chilli salad with toasted cumin and lemon dressing) – one of Pat's preferred choices, I believe. The average dinner will cost at least £40, assisted by a 12.5% service charge. Set-lunch prices are exceptional value (considering it is Mayfair) at £8.50 and £16.50, as are the set dinners served 6-7pm and 10.30-11.30pm Mon.-Sat., £16.50. Pre-theatre dinner: £22.50 (including a taxi to theatreland) can't be sneezed at either. Delivery: Mayfair area. Price check: CTM £13.50, Pullao Rice £4, Nan £2.50, Cobra £3.50, Mineral water £4 bottle. Hours: 12-3pm (closed Sat., Sun. to 2.30pm)/6-11.30pm (Sun. to 10.30pm).

TASTE OF MUGHAL ©

29 Great Windmill Street, Soho, W1 020 7439 8044

Established in 1987, this 50-seater is another formula curry house dispensing the standard menu at decent prices. Price check: Papadam 40p, CTM £6.45, Pullao Rice £2.25, Peshwari Nan £2.25, Lager £3.50. Takeaway: 10% discount. Hours: 12pm-12am (Sat. to 12.30am; Sun. to 11.30pm). Stocks Cobra.

VEERASWAMY AWARD WINNER TOP 100

99-101 Regent Street, Piccadilly, W1 020 7734 1401

Namita Panjabi and Ranjit Mathrani of Chutney Mary (SW10) fame bought Britain's oldest Indian restaurant (founded 1926) in 1998. The street entrance is still on the aptly-named Swallow Street. Go up the stairs one floor, or take the lift. Enter to a discrete reception desk, and you'll swiftly be shown to your table in one of the 130 seat dining areas, to your left or your right. The wine-glass display is a work of art. The walls are painted in vibrant glowing earth colours: aubergine, saffron, garam masala, coriander leaf. Discrete artefacts and etched glass take it far away from its early days. The floors are polished expensive hardwood, the lighting is modern, the view to Regent Street dominant. A few carefully selected pictures of yore are displayed on a small wall area to remind us of the Veeraswamy heritage. Management is in the hands of Preman Mohan with his deputy, Andreas Kirshnev, and is skilled and smooth. Cooking is headed by Gowtam Kumar. Start with papadam or the more unusual rice vadam with home-made chutneys. Bombay street snacks feature prominently on the starter menu – which is great, as far as I am concerned, but perhaps an acquired taste. Starters: Dahi Bhalla £5 – lentil dumpling and spiced yoghurt with tamarind and herb chutney, Pala Puri £5.25 – flat wheat biscuits layered with herbs, potatoes and three fresh chutneys, Fresh Oyster £7.70 – stir-fried with coconut and Kerala spices, Chicken Samosa £5.75 – made with filo pastry. Main courses: swordfish with turmeric, cummin and lemon £10.50, Tandoori lamb chops £13 – black pepper and ginger, served with Nan and salad. Specialities from Southern India: Mangalorean Chicken Curry £12, served with rice, Andhra Green Biryani £13 – layered basmati rice and curried lamb slow cooked in a pot with fresh herbs, served with raitha. Classical dishes from the North: Dum ka Murgh £11.50 (supreme of chicken baked in yoghurt, poppy seeds, green chillies and caramelised onion, served with rice), Avadhi Roghan Josh £12.50 (shanks of lamb cooked in an intense aromatic curry stock and spices, served with rice). Vegetarian and side dishes: Guchchi Biryani £13.50 (wild mushrooms, morels, stuffed with spiced cheese, slow-cooked with basmati rice, served with saffron curry sauce), Baghare Baingan £3 (aubergine in a tamarind and peanut sauce), Green Chilli and Cheese Nan £2.50. 'Stylish decor, wow! My Dahi Vada was delicious. My friend gave the Spicy cod and salmon fish cake a big thumbs up. We were both very impressed with the quality and standard of food. Veeraswamy thoroughly deserves its high rating. But as with other renowned Indian restaurants in the West End, first-timers should expect small portions and very high prices.' RM. 'We opted for one of the three party menus, the intermediate buffet at £27 per person. For starters, we particularly enjoyed the tangy chickpea curry (Ragada Pattice). Main course choice was equally wonderful and included: Kori Gassi (Mangalore chicken curry) and Avadhi Roghan Josh (shanks of lamb cooked slowly in bone stock and spices). Style of presentation was very much "new cuisine" with modest portions. Finishing with Gulab Jamun (warm steamed dumplings flavoured with Armagnac), this really was a wonderful meal and well worth the higher prices. Deserving of its TOP 100 status.' JL. Veeraswamy: main courses arrive plated with rice. This doesn't make for easy sharing unlike venues where the dishes are placed on the table for you to help yourself. The other thing: the wine list is an exemplary selection. Mr Mathrani is a connoisseur, and it shows. If ever there were a time to convert from beer to wine, this is it. Set lunch: £11 two courses, £14 three courses. Set dinner: 5.30-6.30pm and 10.30-11.30pm – £11 two courses, £13.95 three courses. Sunday lunch £15: e-a-m-a-y-l, 3 courses, served at the table, children under 12 – £7. Cover charge: £1.50 includes papadams and chutneys. Service 12.5%. Hours: 12-2.30pm (Sun. to 3pm)/5.30-11.30pm (Sun. to 10.30pm). Stocks Cobra.

WOODLANDS RETURNS TO OUR TOP 100 ©

77 Marylebone Lane, Oxford Street, W1 020 7436 3862

A branch of Mr Sood's well-liked, small chain of southern Indian vegetarian restaurants. Managed by My Ullur, it seats 75, is decorated in sponge-painted blue walls with Indian artifacts. The bar is made of black granite. Chef Rao's house specials include Cashewnut Pakoda (*sic.*), £2.75 (cashew nuts coated in batter with aromatic spices and deep-fried), Kancheepuram Idli, £3.25 (soft rice puffs with chilli, spices and cashew nuts), eight varieties of Dosa, £3.50-4.95. Service 12.5%. Price check: Papadam £1, Pullao Rice £3.50, House wine £9, Hours: 12-2.45pm/6-10.45pm. Branches: SW1 and Wembley, Middlesex. Stocks Cobra.

YATRA NEW ENTRANT NEW TO OUR TOP 100

34 Dover Street, Mayfair, W1 020 7493 0200

Opened early in 2000 by Sonu Lalwani with his wife Liah. Yatra, meaning pilgrimage, or journey, is so called because the couple's concept is that their diners journey into India and beyond. Decor and menu reflect this. Upon entering, you observe the wall water-feature, with its carp, and the room's warm colourings, including the flame-finish granite flooring. Another water-feature tinkles over Ganesh elephant gods. Table settings are striking, with each ivory Yatra-logoed napkin folded tusk-shape on a little red cushion. Note the low tables with cushion seating on the floor (new to Indian restaurants in Britain) but not to Thai restaurants, nor to India itself, whose maharajahs have been doing it for centuries. Choose to sit on these – they're really comfortable for those without back problems – or be a wimp and sit on conventional chairs. The kitchens are manned by Oberoi-trained chefs, which translates to superb, traditional Indian dishes, with a few of Chinese origin (e.g. broccoli in oyster sauce), which are not perhaps a snug fit, taste-wise. The delicious Patrani Machli, the Parsee favourite – pomfret coated in coriander purée and wrapped in banana leaf – £6. Those with Raj connections will delight in Railway Lamb – a kind of spicy curry stew, the like of which is still dispensed at India stations. Top of the list was Lobster and Scallop curry £24. With a menu change promised every three months, dishes will come and go, but assuming the quality is maintained we welcome Yatra to our TOP 100. Main courses arrive plated, with accompaniments in separate bowls. Average spend £40 (it is Mayfair!). House wine £13, Beer £3. Set lunch: £19, set dinner £23. Hours: 12.30-2.30pm/6-11pm.

London W2

Bayswater, Paddington, Westbourne Grove

BOMBAY PALACE TOP 100 ©

2 Hyde Park, 50 Connaught Street, Square, W2 020 7258 3507

Owned by Mr SS Chatwell since its inception in 1983. The 135-seater restaurant was last redecorated in 1997 and has a modern feel rather like that of an international hotel. We are told that there are plans in store for a refurbishment in 2001. 'We all had a thoroughly enjoyable evening, food excellent and service first-class.' William Hague, MP. 'Although in general it was okay, we were not thrilled to bits. Food was pricey, starters too expensive. Vegetarian Thali at £16 was acceptable and you would not go home on an empty stomach. My wife's Chef's Special Tandoori Vegetables, very un-Indian. Food delivery fairly quick, but took over half an hour to clear.' RM. Chef's specials include: Bagara Baigan £7 (stuffed baby aubergine with natural herbs and spices), Balouchi Raan £11.50 (grilled leg of lamb cooked in herbs and spices, served with rice), Noorani Kebab £8.50 – boneless chicken marinated with herbs and soft cheese . Service 15%. Cover charge £1 (I hope this includes a Papadam and chutneys). Takeaway: 10% discount. Price check: CTM £9, Pullao Rice £4, Peshwari Nan (with nuts, cherries and raisins) £2.50, Hours: 12-2.45pm (Sun. to 3pm)/6-11.30pm (Sun. to 11pm). Branches: Beverly Hills, Budapest, Houston, Kuala Lumpur, Mississauga, Montreal, New York, Toronto, Washington DC – please ring the London branch for full details. Discount scheme. Stocks Cobra.

DURBAR NEW ENTRANT ©

24 Hereford Road, W2 020 7727 1947

Opened when time began in 1956, by Shaimur Rahman Syed. Seats 60 diners – wicker chairs, arches, plants, Indian art, brass coffee-pots – and serves Northern Indian curries and accompaniments with a handful of specials which include: Chicken Xacuti £5.45 – very hot with dry chilli and coconut and Chicken Silla £4.95 – shredded chicken tikka. Good-value are the Thali set-meals from £8.95. Chef Shamin Syed won the International Chef of the Year Contest in Feb. 2000. He says of his winning dish – Oriental Chicken – 'it's been on the menu for over 15 years'. What more can we say about one of London's most stable and experienced venues? Price check: Papadam 45p, CTM £5.60, Pullao Rice £1.75, Peshwari Nan £1.95, House wine £7.45, Bottle mineral water £3.50. Dom Peregon (*sic.*) exceptional value at £69.95. Hours: 12-2.30pm/6pm-12am. Branch: Greenford Tandoori, Ruislip Road East, Greenford, Middlesex – tel: 020 8578 3505. Stocks Cobra.

EVEREST

41 Craven Road, W2 020 7262 3853

This 'old' venue (1961), owned by Mohammed Ali and managed by M Ahmed, has light decor, cane furniture and interesting framed photographs of old India. 'Papadoms and pickles, Meat Samosas (lean mince) and crisp salad were followed by Chicken Tikka Bhuna (one of the best I have had) and Paratha (very light) washed down by large bottles of Cobra. The bill was £14 for a small meal but the quality was good. Many of the diners were local residents who commented on their high regard for the Everest,' AE. 'Definitely as good as the reports in the *Guide*. We thoroughly enjoyed the meal. Very good value for money. My wife thought the Chicken Bhuna was one of the best she has had.' DT. Price check: Papadam 35p, CTM £5.95, Pullao Rice £1.60. Set meal £12.95. Stocks Cobra.

GANGES ©

101 Praed Street, W2 020 7723 4096

We're glad to report that this old hand reopened after a long closure for a refit. It's just a curry house, but it's very popular and it's been with us since our first *Guide*. Price check: Papadam 50p, CTM £6.50, Pullao Rice £1.95. Hours: 12-2.30pm/5.30-11pm.

COBRA GOOD CURRY GUIDE
County Index, see page 5 Town Index, see page 614
A to Z of the Curry Menu, page 41 Contributors Key, page 604

INDIAN CONNOISSEURS ©

Norfolk Place, W2 020 7402 3299

A bright and airy a/c, 46-seater with cosy interior (booking advisable). The menu has all the favourites, like Lamb Dopiaza £5.10, Murgh Sag £4.95 and much more. Interesting appetisers include Bombay Roll, ground steak coated in potato paste and deep-fried, and Ayre Cutlet, Bangladeshi fish lightly spiced and pan-fried with onion. Main-course dishes include Hass Baas (spicy duck cooked with bamboo shoots) £8.25, Potato Tilli (lamb kidney cooked with potato) £5.50, Khashi Gazar, goat's meat cooked with baby carrots £6.95, Parrot Fish, pan fried in a thick spicy sauce, £7.75, Shorisha Ayre, £5.95, is 'magnificent' DR, or Venison, pheasant, grouse and quail Bhoona. Congratulations to chef Kabir Miah for adding authenticity to the formula. Paddington sleuth AE found it to be a warm haven on a cold night and was 'swiftly served with free papadom and excellent pickles. The Meat Thali £9.50 was excellent value, good quality, nicely presented and very filling.' Set lunch: £6.95 three courses, set dinner from £8.50. Price check: CTM £5.95, Pullao Rice £1.60, Peshwari Nan £1.70. Delivery: 5-mile radius. Hours: 12-2.30pm/6pm-12am. Stocks Cobra.

Westbourne Grove – W2 and W11

This short street, whose postcode changes midway, is well-known for its many curry houses. These are worthy of mention:

KHANS TOP 100 ANP ©

15 Westbourne Grove, W2 020 7727 5420

We've always said about this 24-year-old venue 'nothing changes and it never will'. Shows how wrong we can be. Khans is no longer licensed, which has raised a few eyebrows amongst Curry Club members who were regulars and wrote to Pat asking him to speak to Mr Khan and reinstate Cobra lager – their regular tipple. ME, for example, says 'I thought restaurants were there to provide a service, not to lecture on lifestyle.' We have asked Khans why they have decided to ban alcohol, but we didn't exactly get a straight answer – only 'we've decided to become more health conscious.' Who said alcohol was unhealthy – 'cos in moderation, it isn't. So whatever do we say next? Khans was opened in 1977 by Mrs QN and Salman Khan. It seats an enormous 280 diners in two rooms (180 seats upstairs, plus 100 in the basement). The main room's high, cloud-painted ceiling is supported by a forest of gilt palm trees. There is a huge Hindi-arched mahogany bar and countless tables with pink cloths and black bentwood chairs. Here's the usual caveat: it's a love it or hate it place. They claim it is not unusual for them to do 1,000 covers a day. And therein lies the problem. This sheer volume results in a New York-style 'have-a-nice-day/take-it-or-leave-it/ don't mess with me' attitude. You'll either love that for a kind of perverse entertainment value, or you'll hate it. As first impressions count, we would not recommend it for a curry first-timer, nor to demure foreign tourist groups. Even Americans are shocked. But, for seasoned curryholics, it is an institution and decidedly not to be missed. Indeed, Khans has built up a very large customer base of frequent (some-three-times-a-week, apparently) regulars from far and wide, who certainly love Khans, and especially its north Indian food. 'I'm a regular here and if they didn't make a mistake on my order and blame me for it, I'd think I was somewhere else!' PD. 'Given the opportunity, I'd eat here every day. Their food is so fresh and full of flavour. On a purely food basis, it is the best.' RW. 'I like it although my chicken was a bit underdone. Waiter friendly (this time!). And it's still an absolute bargain for inner London.' MH. We're keeping Khans in our TOP 100 for now. Alcohol-free, it's bound to be different (orderly, even) but it's such an institution. Reports please. Children's menu. Service 10%. Price check: Papadam 50p, CTM £3.80, Pullao Rice £1.65, Peshwari Nan £1.65.

MANDALAY BURMESE

excellent

444 Edgware Road, W2 19/1/01 020 7258 3696

If Burmese food is strange to you, imagine a marriage of Indian and Chinese/Thai food – garam masala, noodles and lemon grass and, as one of our scribes slightly dubiously put it 'brothers Dwight (front) and Gary (cook) Ally's Mandalay is the only place where you can satiate your curiosity'. Burmese-born and Norwegian-educated, they wisely set up shop here in London. The decor's not up to much being somewhat café-style, but the waiters will give good heedable menu guidance. Its tiny 28 seats mean booking is advisable. Nibbles are either papadams or Prawn Crackers. Starters include Hanat-sone, a spicy chilli laden salad £3.90, spicy potato egg Samosa £1.70, and the Burmese national dish – the fishy soup Mohinga. Main course curries include the fishy Nga hin, £5.50 and Seit-tha-thay-nat, £4.90 lamb in tamarind/chilli sauce. Rice and noodles are the staples, and if you have room for pud, the Indian-style creamy Falooda, £2.50 is an example. Average meal £12, Set lunch from £3.50. Hours: lunch until 3pm/6pm-1am; closed Sun.

COBRA GOOD CURRY GUIDE
County Index, see page 5 Town Index, see page 614
A to Z of the Curry Menu, page 41 Contributors Key, page 604

OLD DELHI TOP 100

48 Kendal Street, W2 020 7723 3335

Bright spotlights accentuate this white 54-seater corner restaurant and so it stands out on this busy area of London, behind the ever-traffic-jammed Edgware Road. On a Sunday night, at around 9pm, it was teeming in its superb setting, every table occupied. This area of London is packed with Middle-Eastern grocery shops and Lebanese restaurants and many of the local population are Arabs. The Old Delhi is one of their locals. There is a centuries-long link between Persia (now Iran) and India. Dishes such as Biriani, Patia, Pullao and Dhansak had their origins in Persia. But to most curry houses these dishes are merely a modification of formula curries. Not so at the Old Delhi, whose owner is Iranian, and whose son Jay is manager. You can certainly get superbly cooked curries by Indian Chef Bhatti but venture further and try at least some of the rather less spicy but authentically cooked Iranian specials by Iranian Chef Jalalrand. Dishes like Faisenjan (chicken marinated, then cooked in a purée of pomegranate, spices and nuts) goes divinely with Saffron Rice and Doog (minty lhassi). A must for serious spicy-food aficionados. Remains high in our TOP 100. Service 15%. No children under 10 after 8pm. Hours 12.30-3-30 pm (1-4pm Sat & Sun)/ 6.30-11pm.

RYATH HALAL TANDOORI NEW ENTRANT

32 Norfolk Place, W2 020 7723 8954

'Well-cooked, flavoursome meal.' JR

SPICE OF INDIA NEW ENTRANT

12a Bathurst Road, W2 020 7262 5603

'I cannot recommend this place highly enough! Food is excellent with amazing specials, including Bengali-style Mussels and Duck Tikka Bhuna. Drawback is the location – I feel it is not getting the attention it deserves.' LMcC.

STANDARD INDIAN

21 Westbourne Grove, W2 020 7221 7502

'A pleasant surprise! Chicken Methi and Aloo Gobi were delicious. Food was better than Khan's next door.' MH.

©	Curry Club Discount	U	Unlicensed
V	Vegetarian	ANP	Alcohol not permitted
e-a-m-a-y-l	Eat as much as you like	BYO	Bring your own alcohol

London W4
Chiswick

GEETANJALI NEW ENTRANT

470 Chiswick High Road, W4 020 8994 0702

'Competent and enjoyable restaurant in an area with few curry houses. Affable, friendly staff. Chicken Chatt was pleasantly dry in taste and texture with aromatic spices. Madras thoroughly enjoyable, though a modicum of extra onion and tomatoes wouldn't have gone amiss. Good value.' RW.

London W5
Ealing

CLAY OVEN NEW TO OUR TOP 100

13 The Mall, W5 020 8840 0313

'Go for Bhadur Chelleri's cooking. Surprisingly full for Monday night. Very good spicy papadams, but chutneys poor. Excellent Paneer Tika-tak, but naans dry and disappointing. Plenty of staff on duty yet service quite poor.' DL. Branch: Ealing Cottage, 76 Uxbridge Road, W13.

MONTY'S TOP 100

1 The Mall, The Broadway, W5 020 8567 5802

Mahanta (Monty) Shrestha's 68-seater venue, managed by Donald, remains Ealing's most popular, with standard curries done exceedingly well, plus some Nepalese specials e.g. Chicken Choala, Chicken Ledo. 'Worthy of TOP 100.' RL. Price check: Papadam 50p (p & s), CTM £6.95, Bombay Potato £3.40, Pullao Rice £1.95, Pickle Tray 40p. Hours: 12-3pm/6pm-12am. Stocks Cobra.

RUBY'S NEW ENTRANT ©

185 South Ealing Road, W5 020 8560 5900

Formerly Yak and Yeti. Taken over in 1998 by Mrs S Thapa. A Nepalese restaurant, serving (along with standard curry house fayre) delights such as Momo £3.25 (meat dumplings with tomato achaar), Aloo Tama Bodi £2.95 (potatoes, bamboo shoots and black-eyed beans with gravy), Korshani Chicken or Lamb £8.95 (with green chillies and fried onion, hot). Delivery:

3-mile radius, £15 minimum. Popular dish: Chicken Bhutuwa £6.95, chicken with spring onions. Takeaway: free Papadam and Chutney. Price check: Papadam 50p, CTM £5.85, Pullao Rice £1.75, Peshwari Nan £1.75, House wine £6.25, Mineral water £2.45 bottle. Hours: 12-2.30pm/6-11.30pm. Discount scheme. Stocks Cobra.

SAMRAT

52 Pitshanger Lane, W5 020 8997 8923

Horuf Miah's formula 36-seater. Specials include: Peshwari dishes £5.95, made with diced onions, green peppers, in a thick masala. Price check: Papadam 40p, CTM £5.95, Pullao Rice £1.75, Peshwari Nan £1.95, Lager £2.30 pint, House wine £7.95. Hours: 12-2.30pm/6pm-12am.

ZAYKA INDIAN CUISINE

8 South Ealing Road, W5 020 8569 7278

Zayka opened in 1990 and has established itself as one of South Ealing's favourites, serving all the popular tandooris, starters, curries and accessories including fish specialities and an extensive vegetarian menu. Sunday e-a-m-a-y-l. Takeaway. Free local delivery on orders over £5. Hours: 12-2.30pm (Sun to 3pm)/6pm-11.30pm (Fri & Sat to 12am).

London W6

Hammersmith

AKASH NEW ENTRANT

177 King Street, Hammersmith, W6 020 8748 4567

Established in 1995 by Mr Miah. 'Ordered my standard test, could they make fresh Popadoms, interesting Pickles 45p, a good Meat Samosa £2.50 and a decent Chicken Tikka Bhuna? Samosa (2) – looked perfect and were!, absolutely fantastic, crisp, lean, spicy, plump served with a lemon wedge – drool drool! Many large chunks of Chicken breast in the Bhuna were fresh, smoky and surrounded by an excellent and subtle Bhuna sauce. Washed down with very interesting Bangla Premium. Pleasant Mango Kulfi, right texture and flavours. Bill a little above average but well worth the high quality of food and service.' AIE. Delivery: 3-mile radius, £10 minimum. Price check: Papadam 45p, CTM £6.25, Pullao Rice £1.85, Peshwari Nan £1.95. Hours: 6-11pm.

ANARKALI

303-305 King Street, W6 020 8748 1760

'Tried with trepidation, since my regular curry party had spent the previous eight years as near fixtures at the superb Rajdoot further down King Street. All starters reported as excellent. Main dishes followed likewise, with good examples of CTM, Meat Biryani, Chicken Jalfrezi etc. We were well satisfied. Recommended.' RW.

LIGHT OF NEPAL RE-ENTRANT

268 King Street, W6 020 8748 3586

'A must is the Butter Chicken. Wonderful coriander dip.' JL.

RAJDOOT RE-ENTRANT

291-293 King Street, W6 020 8748 7345

'Superb after eight years of visits with my curry party.' RW.

TANDOORI NIGHTS ©

319-321 King Street, W6 020 8741 4328

Mr Modi Udin's Tandoori Nights' 'bright white façade is as inviting as the manager, AB Choudhury, and his staff. The pink decor is relaxing, and the food from chef Mabul Miah is curry house at its best,' JW. 'Excellent food – rapidly served as requested.' HS. 'Worthy of TOP 100.' RL. 'OK the food's great, but they always pull the open credit card and 10% tip stunt.' AJ. Price check: Papadam 55p, CTM £7.95, Meat Thali £11.95, Pullao Rice £2.25. Service 10%. Set meal average for two £24.90. Hours: 12-3pm/6pm-12am. Stocks Cobra.

London W8

Kensington High Street, Notting Hill

MALABAR TOP 100

27 Uxbridge Street, W8 020 7727 8800

The simple decor and the eclectic menu haven't changed at Jo and Tony Chalmers' and Anil Bis's three-floor 56-seat Malabar since it opened in 1983. Why change a good thing? 'An old favourite of mine. Welcome and service are always of a very high standard, and the food is second to none. Among my favourites are Murg Makhni (barbecued chicken prepared with butter, cream and special spices) and Keema Aloo. Basmati Rice is a treat on its own. Also offer a delightful selection of Indian desserts including Khir (Indian rice pudding with coconut and raisins), Kulfi and Lassi. Prices not excessively higher than average.' JL. Starters include Devilled Kaleja, charcoal-grilled chicken livers, marinated in yoghurt and spices £4, Prawn Philouries, shelled prawns deep-fried in potato flour £3.80, Hiran, tamarind-marinated venison £6, and, my late gran's favourite, Bhutta sweetcorn with chillies, £3.10. Main courses include Long Chicken (medium-hot with cloves and ginger) £5.10, and Kayla Foogarth (sliced banana cooked with ginger and spices) £3.10. 'Definitely excellent, about the best in West London and no question, it should remain in the TOP 100. Chicken Dhansak is something else!' AJ. Jo Chalmers has now been joined front of house by her daughter Sophie, and we hear constant praise for their customer care. Remains secure in our TOP 100. Prices are reasonable, but the Sunday lunch buffet at £6.95 is a real bargain. Price check: Papadam 55p, Murgh Makhni £6, Pullao Rice £1.95, Peshwari Nan £1.90. Hours: 12-3pm/6-11.30pm. Closed one week in Aug. Stocks Cobra.

London W12

Shepherds Bush, White City

NEPALESE TANDOORI ©

121 Uxbridge Road, W12 — 020 8740 7551

Prabin Pradhan's cosy 38-seater's specials include: Chicken Nepal, boneless chicken with fresh fruits and cream £4.75, Nepalese Murgh Masala, chicken off the bone with sauce and boiled egg £5.75, Vegetable Nepal, seasonal vegetables with fresh fruits and cream £3.75. Price check: Papadam 50p, CTM £5.25, Pullao Rice £1.70, Peshwari Nan £1.70, Lager £2.20 pint, House wine £6.95, stocks a Nepalese brand called Iceberg. Delivery: £12 minimum, 3-mile radius. Hours: 12-2.30pm/6am-12pm.

London W13

West Ealing

LAGUNA ©

1-3 Culmington Pde, 127-129 Uxbridge Rd, W13 — 020 8579 9992

Established in 1984 by Sunil Lamba. Huge frontage, decorated with individually planted conifers in square wooden tubs. Northern Indian food is served in his 120-seater restaurant. Stylishly decorated in pastel shades, with arches and ceiling fans. Laguna Special Butter Chicken £5.25 is the most popular dish. Service 10%. Price check: Papadam 35p, CTM £5.25, Pullao Rice £1.95, Peshwari Nan £1.95, House wine £7.55. Hours: 12-3pm/6pm-12am; Sun. 12pm-12am. Branch: Laguna Banquet Hall, N Acton Road, NW10 and Khyber, W2. Stocks Cobra.

MONTY'S TANDOORI NEW ENTRANT

54 Northfield Avenue, W13 020 8566 5364

Nepalese Restaurant. Try the House specials: Chicken Safarkan (minced meat and spring onions with creamy sauce) £9. Price check: Papadam 50p, CTM £6.95, Pullao Rice £2.15. website: www.montys.uk.com

SIGIRI SRI LANKAN AWARD WINNER TOP 100

161 Northfields Avenue, W Ealing, W13 020 8579 8000

Sigiri is a landmark in Sri Lanka, which must not to be missed. If you do nothing else visit Sigiri. It is a huge mountain with a flat top (rather like Table Top mountain in Cape Town, South Africa but much more dramatic and there is no 'ski lift' to take you to the top). As you approach Sigiri you realise just how big it is and then the guide informs you that 'we' are going to climb it! It is surrounded by beautifully and symmetrically designed gardens with water pools. On top of the mountain are the ruined remains of a fabulous royal palace.

Eating here, in the unlikely setting of Northfields on a corner site with its smoked-glass windows inset in red brick, reminded us of that trip as the restaurant is decorated with pictures and wall hangings and serves delightful, authentic Sri Lankan food. We ate light Papadams, Coconut Chutney, Devilled Pork – ask for spicy, Kothu Roti chopped chapatti with onions and spicy meat – all our favourites and enjoyed them all. Don't forget other dishes such as Hoppers (Apa), Dosa and Uppaamas and that glorious pudding Wattalappam – a very sweet, jaggery-based, dark egg custard. Service is quiet and polite, you can see the workers in the kitchen through the bar, which is located at the back of the restaurant. Safe in our TOP 100. Cobra £4, Mineral water £2.75 bottle. Hours: 6.30-11pm; closed Mon. Stocks Cobra.

London W14

Olympia, West Kensington

A L'INDIENNE NEW ENTRANT

197-199 North End Road, W14 020 7610 2020

Manager: MJ Arshad. Nearest tube: West Kensington. Starters: Makhani Paneer £3.25 – is a lovely beginning but for that high price the cheese better be home-made. Main courses: Rajal Ka Saffron £5.95 (tender chicken, saffron cream sauce, green peppers), Prawn Chamberi £6.95 (prawns briskly cooked with red wine, capsicum and spices), Chana Poshori £3.25 (chickpeas with crispy potato), Nan A Magajia £1.95 – stuffed with soft curd cheese, onion and chillies. 'Good welcome and cuisine excellent. Service with smiles and food in abundance.' JL .Delivery: £5 minimum order. Sunday buffet: 12-2pm. Price check: Papadam 40p, CTM £5.75, Pullao Rice £1.95, Peshwari Nan £1.95. Hours: 5.30pm-12.30am.

London WC

Area: West End postcodes WC1, WC2
Population: 165,000

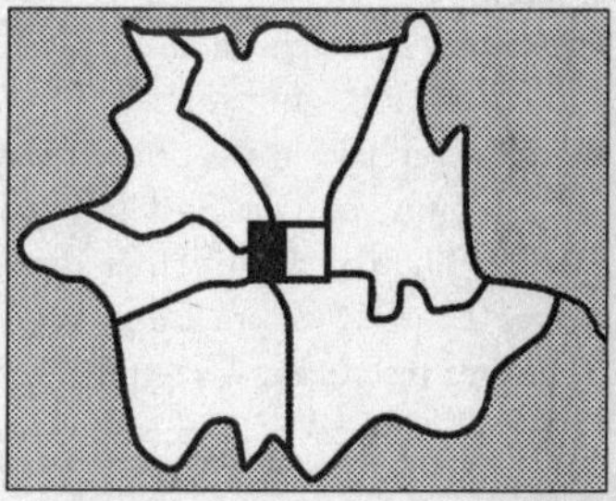

London WC1

Holborn

CHAMBELI OF RUSSELL SQUARE RE-ENTRANT

146 Southampton Row, WC1 020 7837 3925

K Shah and Anwar Hussain have been operating the formula successfully here since 1985 with help from chef Ram Das. 'A good quality, if expensive, curry restaurant. The speed of service was amazing. No rest between courses!' TE. Hours: 12pm-12am.

©	Curry Club Discount	U	Unlicensed
V	Vegetarian	ANP	Alcohol not permitted
e-a-m-a-y-l	Eat as much as you like	BYO	Bring your own alcohol

MALABAR JUNCTION

107 Great Russell Street, WC1 020 7580 5230

Light, bright and airy restaurant with Victorian-styled glass sky-light giving a good summery feel. Bamboo chairs, palm trees in polished brass pots, original paintings, a marble fountain and smiling Keralan waiters complete the scene. The menu specialises in Keralan cuisine, with dishes from the cities of Cochin, Malabar and Travancore. Hot is the norm in Kerala but they cool it for 'western tastes'! If you want it hot, tell them, the kitchen are happy to accommodate. Contrary to popular belief, meat, chicken and fish dishes are commonplace. When we lunched (we were very restrained) we chose Papadams with Coconut Chutney, Rasam (hot and spicy soup, with floating slivers of garlic, curry leaves and a red chilli!), Masala Dosa (crispy, potato curry-stuffed pancake), Sambar (thin lentil curry with drumsticks) and more Coconut Chutney; a large party of office workers were letting their hair down. But don't forget the wonderful Lamb Cutlets £4.50 (patties of spicy minced lamb, bread crumbed and fried, served with tomato sauce and salad), King Prawn Fry £7.90 (with ginger, garlic, spices and sliced coconut), Malabar Chicken £7.50 (with coconut, curry leaves, garlic and mustard), Spinach Vadai £3 (fried crunchy doughnut of channa dal, green chillies, onion, ginger, curry leaves and fresh spinach served with chutneys). And if you have any room left Banana Leaf Cake £4 – rice with sweet filling of coconut, banana and jaggery wrapped in banana leaf and steamed – divine. The bar and further dining facilities are downstairs. Minimum: £7. Lager £3 pint, Cobra £3.90 large bottle. Hours: bar – 11am-11pm; Sun. 12-10.30pm; restaurant – 12-3pm/6-11.30pm.

MANDEER VEGETARIAN TOP 100

8 Bloomsbury Way, off New Oxford Street, WC1 020 7242 6202

Mr and Mrs Ramesh Patel's original Mandeer was established in 1961 at another address. It was here that George Harrison met Ravi Shankar. Development of its site forced a move to Bloomsbury Way in 1998, aptly next to the Tibetan Studies Centre. The new 40-seater ground-floor restaurant applies Aruyvedic principles of spicing, oil and ingredients to its cooking. It's explained in the menu. The result is a collection of Punjabi, Rajasthani, Maharashtran, Gujarati and Kerelan dishes, some of which are vegan. Specials: Thali £13.75 – papadam and raitha with samosas for starters, four different curries, bread and rice for main course followed up with Shrikhand for pudding. 'Our favourite restaurant. Still as good as ever. Beyond brilliant. Wednesdays is one of my favourites, butter beans! Well deserves its TOP 100 rating.' IB and again: 'Still the best Indian vegetarian restaurant in the world. The new venue is pleasant, if a bit less atmospheric. The food is just as good as when I first found it in 1972! Buffet lunch at £3.90 for rice, dhal and curry is excellent.' IB. 'Decor of the place is very unusual and attractive. I ordered the deluxe Thali, which included a papadom, paneer cheese and peas, bombay potato, soup, a lentils dish and a sickly sweet desert. A quality restaurant, TOP 100 to be sure.' RL. 'Decor superb. Menu a delight, some unusual dishes mixed with standard items. Starters – Patra and Batata Vada, beautifully spiced, lived up to expectations. Main courses – Vadi with Onion and Panir Korma were also well spiced, but extremely oily. Service very rude, barely had drunk half our bottle of wine before we were expected to leave.' AG. Price check: Papadam 60p, Masala Dosa £5.50, Sambhar £3.25, Pullao Rice £2.60. Hours: 12-3pm buffet or à la carte/5-10pm; closed Sun. Stocks Cobra.

SIMPLY SPICE NEW ENTRANT

at the Holiday Inn, 53 Calthorpe St, London, WC1 020 7833 9787

Recently opened (1998) in the city for all those company credit card lunches/dinners and a bold venture in a Holiday Inn Hotel. This air-conditioned, 160-seater is decorated as its name suggests in spicy colours, with gold and blue upholstered chairs. Polite, friendly waiters. Chef Ms Manjula Sachdev from Goa has now moved on, but has left her impression on the menu with dishes such as Chicken Xacutti £7.95 – with chilli, coconut and peanuts, Pork Vindaloo £9.95 – cooked in a Goan Masala with pale spirits, Goan Prawn Curry £8.95 – tiger prawns simmered in a coconut and red chilli sauce, Sharabi Scallops £9.95 – succulent queen scallops marinated in dill and cognac, cooked in a light masala served flambéed in its shell, but you will also find that old favourite Rogan Josh. Great 'Spice Kids' menu – most important to start them young – Fish Cutlets, Malai Chicken Tikka with Salad priced at an amazing £2.95, that should keep the little darlings happy. Set Lunch: £7.99. Price check: Papadam 40p, CTM £7.95, Pullao Rice £2.95, Peshwari Nan £2.25. Hours: 12-2.30 pm (closed Sat., Sun. to 3pm)/6-10.30pm.

London WC2

Aldwych, Covent Garden

AKASH RE-ENTRANT

14-15 Irving Street, WC2 020 7930 0744

'It is years since we have been here. The food was outstandingly good. The menu is still very standard and the food very traditional, but the aloof and

©	Curry Club Discount	U	Unlicensed
V	Vegetarian	ANP	Alcohol not permitted
e-a-m-a-y-l	Eat as much as you like	BYO	Bring your own alcohol

impersonal service was completely unchanged and I was ashamed to see how foreign visitors were treated – no allowance was made for people with limited English and unfamiliarity with Indian menus.' H&DRC.

INDIA CLUB AWARD WINNER TOP 100 BYO

143 The Strand, Aldwych, WC2 020 7836 0650

The India Club has been here since 1950, and it's a landmark. Along the Strand, amongst the shops, you will notice a door-width entrance – there's a new (for them) sign, gold on black, saying 'India Restaurant and Hotel'. Climb the narrow stairs. (In typical Indian style, the owners do not see the need to redecorate – it's clean enough, though.) On the first floor is the hotel reception. I believe it is called the Strand Continental Hotel. With singles £29, and doubles £39 it's cheaper than Delhi. We've never dared to stay here, so reports from the courageous please! Staunch supporters know it's unlicensed so you can BYO – no corkage. On the first floor there is a 'residents' bar, where you can stock up with Cobra from a 'cackling' bar maid. From the bar return to reception then proceed up another floor. In front of you is the door to the L-shaped restaurant. It's cheap and café-style, with laidback, friendly waiters. Please don't expect modern decor, or indeed any decor. I swear nothing has changed since the India Club opened, including, I do believe, the barmaid! As in India, minimalist here means flaking plaster, no tablecloths, flies a-buzzing, bare chairs, and pictures askew. It's all part of the charm, and the regulars don't want change. 'Hadn't been here since the redecoration – phew, what a lurid yellow the walls are now. Everything else unchanged – menu is the same, still good value, service still efficient. On the minus side, the cooking smell from the kitchen still permeates the whole restaurant, and the food was not very hot on arrival.' HC. What regulars want, and indeed get, is fabulous, uncompromisingly Indian food, served in unpretentious surroundings. Head chef Puroshothaman is from south India, and it's that food at which the kitchen surpasses. 'Unique, as always, though I have to agree, the vegetable dishes are much nicer than the meat. Gorgeous Dhal!' MH. But for those of you who are unsure, you will find meat and chicken curries, which are agreeable, though the Keema Peas is excellent. If it's curry house formula you want, then go somewhere else. 'Another visit to one of the Meccas for curry freaks, and another good meal! But, oh was it crowded for 6.30 in the evening. Chilli Bhajias predictably hot, Dry Vegetable well up to standard. Prawn Pullao excellent and enormous portion, Masala Dosas delicious as ever. Still excellent, wonderful no frills ambience, and still the same elderly lady in the bar to have a quick word with (she was a dolly bird when I first went there – I'm sure she's the same one!).' MW. [Well, well Malcolm – a dhally bird even!] 'Well worth TOP 100. Even better this time around! Chilli Bhajis are not for the faint-hearted, but then neither is the decor... the waiters must keep the pictures deliberately crooked!! Waiter advised us to order a set vegetarian menu for £10 per head... he was right! were absolutely stuffed and still had food left over. Masala Dosa, superb (up there with Ravi Shankar). Amazing Dhal, Runner Bean dish good, rice and Nan, fresh and fluffy. BYO with no corkage – has to be a winner!' AG. Well done Andy, but you did have an 'experience' on another dining occasion. 'Our favourite budget Indian in London. My partner found a medium-sized bone in her Sag Aloo, manager called and profusely apologised, all staff very shocked and charged us £6 instead of £10.' AG. 'Weird, a bit expensive compared to the Mandeer (WC2). Felt authentic though, with dishes which made me think I was in Brick Lane. Cost about £6 for rice, naan, curry and veg.' IB. Ian, you were told to stick to the South Indian delights. Despite its eccentricity the Indian Club decidedly remains firmly in our TOP 100. Price check: Papadam 30p, Chicken Curry £4.60, Pullao Rice £2.20. Hours: 12-2.30pm/6-11pm; closed Sun. The last words, as always, go to PD: 'Long may the Club remain open.' Stocks Cobra.

JAKARTA INDONESIAN NEW ENTRANT

150 Shaftesbury Avenue North, WC2 020 7836 2644

Since it's next door to Mela (*see* over page) CF and the Asian Doctors wish you to know they recommended it as the best Indonesian in London. Praise indeed. Reports please.

MAHARAJA OF INDIA RE-ENTRANT

19a Charing Cross Road, WC2 020 7930 8364

'Service incredibly slow despite restaurant being virtually empty.' RL. 'The nearest Indian restaurant to the English National Opera. Staff friendly and helpful, the food was most enjoyable. Fish bhaji so good. Everything else about the Maharaja is a good average, nothing fancy.' H&DRC. And again: 'Shown to table in completely empty rear of restaurant. Commented that this wasn't nearly so congenial but were assured that it would fill up – wasn't long before 3 more tables were occupied. Popadoms arrived, complimentary to make up for seating disappointment, lovely gesture. Impressed with genuine desire to help and please. All staff smiley and efficient. Food really good, portions right and prices very modest for central London. King Prawns enormous, only two, but like mini lobsters. Pumpkin Bhajee – delicious.' H&DRC.

MELA NEW ENTRANT NEW TO OUR TOP 100

152-156 Shaftesbury Avenue North, WC2 020 7836 8635

Clean lines, huge plate window, pastel colours, bleached floor. Nothing new there. But Mela has pioneered an original idea to capture the vast potential lunch trade. Under the name 'Paratha Pavilion' Mela is the Indian equivalent of a sandwich bar. Instead of sliced loaf, choose naan, roomali, paratha, roti, puri and bhatura, appam, uttapams (served with coconut chutney), or dosa with a topping (filling) choice of chicken tikka, lamb tikka, fish tikka, mixed vegetables, prawn masala*, masala potatoes, jalfrezi chicken and spicy sliced lamb, cheese, peas, mushrooms and spring onion, aloo chana salad, jeera aloo, mixed vegetables, aloo methi, lamb keema, chicken keema and peas, tandoori salmon, oyster masala*, scallops masala*, crab masala* peppered black prawn* are just some of the many choices. There are, it seems, over 500 combination options. Prices range from £1.95 for a simple choice to £4.50 for a Gourmet Snack Lunch (*supplementary £5). For those who want a sit-down meal the restaurant seats 135 diners on two floors. Ex-Soho Spice chef Kuldeep Singh, with Sanjay Singh Sighat and Surinder Kumar Mehra have produced a fine à la carte menu. Starters: Calamari Pakhooni £3.25 (squid with Goan piri-piri red hot sauce), Junglee Murgi (guinea fowl), La Lukmi Samosas, £3.25, Mutter Adrak Ki Aloo Tikki £2.50 (patty of crushed green peas, finely chopped ginger, mashed potato with tamarind, mint and yoghurt sauce). Tandoori: Salmon £7.95, Chukandar Kalam Ke Kebab £6.95 (boned leg of chicken, marinated in beetroot and whole red chillies), Burra Champ Madiri £2.50 (lamb, soaked overnight in rum, spiced with byadgi chillies), Tawe Ki Hari Mirch Machli £6.50 (filleted tilapia, Bengali spices, green chillies and mustard seeds), Kastoori Scallops £7.95. Subz Taka Tin £4.95 (vegetables with pomegranate and fenugreek), Kadi Pakodi Curry £3.50 (natural yoghurt, gram-flour dumpling tempered with mustard seeds and garlic). Desserts: Shahi Tukra £2.95 (fried bread, saffron flavoured sweet milk, garnished with nuts), Gajjar Ka Halwa £2.95 (carrot fudge cake). 'Brilliant' KB&SS. Price check: Papadam 50p, CTM £6.95, Plain Rice £1.25, Peshwari Nan £1.75. Hours: 12-4pm/5.30pm-12am. Stocks Cobra.

PUNJAB AWARD WINNER TOP 100 ©

80-82 Neal Street, WC2 020 7836 9787

The Punjab is even older than WC2's India Club. It was London's third Indian restaurant, after Veeraswamy WC1, opening in 1947 in Aldgate. Even with its move to the present site in 1951, it is still the second oldest once Shafi closed [which MG, a music teacher from Aldershot, and one of our regular reporters, used to frequent when he was a student at Art College. Shafi's was an attraction for the great food, but the main attraction was a fellow student in a short skirt! or so he told me.] Getting back to the Punjab – it opened in 1947 in Aldgate and moved to its present site in 1951. It is still the oldest Punjabi restaurant in the UK. And for its entire life has been in the capable hands of just three men, the late founder, his son, and now his grandson Sitasl Singh Maan. Of course, by definition, the Punjab was one of the original pioneers of the curry formula. Only here it is done as it has always been done, and as it should be. 'Fabulous food. Each dish was an absolute gem, cooked to perfection and individual in its own right.' CT. The result is unlike the newer Bangladeshi clones, and is probably what old curry hands think they remember when they say 'curry isn't like it used to be in the old days'. The food is meat-orientated, spicy, savoury and very tasty. Specialities of the chef: Anari Gosht £7.50 – pomegranate and lamb, Benaam Macchi Tarkari £7.50 – nameless fish curry, Acharri Murgha £7.80 – pickled chicken. Also try the Vegetable Koofta £4.70 – diced pumpkin with spices and herbs made into balls. Regulars have their own club, the 'Punjabbers'. Remains high in our TOP 100. Service 10%. Price check: Papadam 60p, CTM £7.95, Peshwari Nan £2.30.

SITAR BALTI RE-ENTRANT

149 The Strand, WC2 020 7836 3730

HDC says: 'An exceptionally good restaurant, the food seems to get better every visit. We arrived about 10pm and it was almost full, which gave it a very marvellous atmosphere. Service is especially good and professional and the staff even show signs of recognition. Food was well up to standard with all dishes being over average in quality. Most enjoyable Vegetable Thali (even though it meant foregoing the wonderful crab dish), Butter Chicken excellent. All the portions, spicing and presentation particularly good.' On another occasion 'As usual very good, food particularly good hence many return visits. Only grumble and it is equally consistent – the size of the portions – main courses are really mean.' HC.

ENGLAND

The method in this Guide is to record our entries in alphabetical order: first the county then, within that, the town, then the restaurant. With the demise of Avon, we now start with Bedfordshire, the first town we record is Arlesey, and its first restaurant is Raj Villa, and so on. Our last English county is Yorkshire West, and Wakefield is the last recorded town.

BEDFORDSHIRE

Area: Central
Population: 557,000
Adjacent Counties: Bucks, Cambs, Herts and Northants

Arlesey

RAJ VILLA ©

27 High Street, Arlesey 01462 835145

Akthar Ali has owned and managed this 70-seater since 1996. Branches: Raj Gat, Bedford Street, Ampthill, and Raj Moni, Upper Street, London, N1.

Bedford

CHOUDHURY TANDOORI NEW ENTRANT

32 The Broadway, Bedford 01234 356162

'Good varied menu, good wine and service. Reasonable prices, recommended.' DJW

GULSHAN ©

69 Tavistock Street, Bedford 01234 355544

JS Nijjer and his wife BK are the owner/managers. 150 seats. Painted marble-effect walls and wooden lattice partitions. Chef Shanu Miah cooks

Pakistani and North Indian curries and Baltis. Specials include Lamb Sharab (lamb tikka cooked in cream and almond liqueur) served with Pullao Rice. Delivery £10 minimum, 15-mile radius. Hours: 12-2pm/6pm-1am. Stocks Cobra.

Flitwick

PEARL OF BENGAL NEW ENTRANT

2 Station Square, Flitwick 01525 713713

sw says: 'I had heard reports of wonderful unique Indian food created by an award winning chef. I am still raving about the Pearl of Indian and manager Salim, to anyone who will listen. Extensive menu, lists at least 80 dishes. Chicken Shaslik – perfectly spiced, skewered chicken breast with roasted onion, green pepper – melts in the mouth. Particularly good Tandoori King Prawns – sautéed in fresh tomato and herbs. Sag Aloo – faultless, flavour-packed. Naan – a wonderful surprise, stuffed full of finely chopped Chicken Tikka and cheese – trust me it's gorgeous. Food arrived promptly, producing a wonderful aroma. I'm impressed.' sw.

Luton

MASTER CHEF TAKEAWAY

Shop 2, 76 Hart Lane, Luton 01582 480202

'Our current favourite for takeaway food.' TK.

MEAH TANDOORI ©

102 Park Street, Luton 01582 454504

Established in 1983. Seats 50 in two rooms. Parking outside restaurant for 20 cars. Hours: 12-2.30pm/6-11.30pm. Stocks Cobra. 'Quick meal prior to a football match. Very impressed, particularly with the honesty of the proprietor, K Ahmed. Paid a bill of £32.60. He chased down the street – our bill was only £25.20. How refreshing!' AW. 'My family and friends have been enjoying the delights of Meah's since 1988. Stuffed Peppers – roasted and stuffed with minced lamb, herbs and topped with cheese. Salmon Kebabs – beautifully spiced with spring onions and potato, served with tangy sauce. Delightful.' DS. 'Very impressed with the personal service and the splendid chicken shashlick.' AW. 'A good restaurant.' TK.

BERKSHIRE

Area: Home Counties (west of London)
Population: 807,000
Adjacent Counties: Hants, Surrey, Middx, Oxon, Wilts

Bracknell

KOHINOOR NEW ENTRANT

45 Priestwood Square, Bracknell 01344 869966

Formerly Star of India. 'Always busy. James raves about the Jalfrezi.' M: email.

SPICY HUT TAKEAWAY NEW ENTRANT

Eastern Road, Bracknell No phone

'Deserves a special mention – operates from a trailer and ex-ambulance! The proprietor has the only mobile food outlet of its kind in the area. Freshness of food umatched. Vegetable Chickpea Curry with Rice, chicken added on request. Very satisfying.' M: email.

Cookham

COOKHAM TANDOORI NEW ENTRANT

High Street, Cookham 01628 522584

'Expensive but worth every penny. Service terrific, Dhansaks world-class, Papadoms always fresh.' AF.

MALIK'S NEW ENTRANT NEW TO OUR TOP 100

Royal Exchange, High Street, Cookham 01628 520085

Set in a former country pub, complete with clinging ivy, and olde beams, this restaurant takes its name from Malik Ahmed, who, with partner Mujibur Rahman, runs front of house. A huge effort is being made with the cooking. As well as popular Bangladeshi formula stuff, there are some interesting specials: Cox's Bazar Samuk – Mussels in coconut (£7.95), Haash

Poora – Duck breast (£3.95) and Annans Haash – Duck in coconut milk (£6.95), Jhanglee Horrin – Venison (£14.95) and Mixed Seafood Bhuna with scallops, cuttlefish, squid and tiger fish (£14.50). Also you'll find veal, and Bengali fish dishes. Plans are afoot for *alfresco* dining in the former pub's garden. We welcome Malik's to our TOP 100.

Crowthorne

VILLAGE TANDOORI NEW ENTRANT ©

204 Dukes Ride, Crowthorne 01344 780118

Opened in 1995. Seats 42. Lots of free parking. Bangla Night every Tuesday. Price check: Papadam 50p, CTM £6.50, Pullao Rice £1.60, Peshwari Nan £1.75, Lager £2.40 pint. Takeaway: 10% discount. Delivery: Free in local area. Hours: 12-2.30pm/5.30-11.30pm. Stocks Cobra.

Maidenhead

NABHA TAKEAWAY ©

39 King Street, Maidenhead 01628 770193

A Balti takeaway, opened in 1990, Zahire Khan taking over ownership in 1997. Parking for 4 cars in front. Specials include: Nabha Special Biryani. Unlicensed. Price check: Papadam 40p, CTM £5.20, Pullao Rice £1.60, Peshwari Nan £1.75. Delivery: £7 minimum. Hours: 5.30pm-12am (Sat. & Sun. to 1am).

Newbury

CURRY GARDEN NEW ENTRANT

18 The Broadway, Newbury 01635 528854

'Small but comfortable restaurant. All good but nothing out of the ordinary; service was polite and quick. Parking was a bit of a problem.' MB.

Reading

BINA

21 Prospect Street, Caversham, Reading 0118 946 2116

Abdul Miah won't talk to us any more since we published your criticisms of the Bina (and your criticisms of us for including it in our 'Best in the West') in previous editions. Anyway, Abdul, don't blame the messenger. But perhaps he listened. I'm very pleased to report that we've received much better comments on the restaurant: 'Being in Reading for a concert presented us with a perfect opportunity to go to the highly-praised Bina. The decor, welcome, menu and service were very good and the food was exceptional. Only one grumble and that was the long wait between ordering and food arriving. Butter Murgh absolutely marvellous, rich, but light and a lovely flavour, an excellent blend of spices. Crab Bhuna a very unusual item so had to try it – very good, but suffered the usual problem of crab, that of being so delicately flavoured itself that it couldn't really be tasted through the spices.' H&DC. 'Lived up to expectations, on the strength of one visit.' MG. 'Excellent attention to detail. Liver was the best tasted since I was five years old. Peshwari Naan very good indeed, Tarka Dall good but inordinately expensive, chicken joint well stuffed and cooked to perfection. Will definitely revisit. Best in the West? Quite probably.' RW. Anyone else agree?

THE GURKHA INN NEW ENTRANT ©

64 George Street, Caversham, Reading 0118 948 3974

42-seater, formerly La Spice Café. A&AL comment: 'Produces exquisite food of outstanding quality but has recently been affected by local council parking restrictions. We would urge you most strongly to encourage your members to rally their support – they'll not be disappointed.' Car park nearby. Price check: Papadam 45p, CTM £6.40, Pullao Rice £1.80, Peshwari Nan £1.80, Lager £2.30 pint. Delivery: £12 minimum, 3-mile radius. Hours: 12.30-2.30pm/6-11.30pm. Stocks Cobra.

INDIA PALACE ©

83-85 Wokingham Road, Earley, Reading 0118 962 2711

The Palace is jointly owned by Mrs LC Payne and chef Bhadracen, and managed by A Ahad. 'Impressed by the cleanliness, crisp linen, light ambience of lighting and decor and background music. Chicken Chatwas delicious. Palace Spring Chicken, Haandi Saag Chicken, Pullao Rice, Tarka Dal and Bombay Aloo with Kulcha Nan, all really excellent.' RT. Stocks Cobra.

STANDARD NEPALESE NEW ENTRANT ©

141-145 Caversham Road, Reading 0118 959 0093

Established in 1980. Seats 140. 8 parking places at front. Pond and fountain as centrepiece. Nepalese specials include Katmandu Aloo. 'Three of us descended on this very spacious restaurant at 6pm on a Wednesday evening;

by 8pm it was packed and queuing! Delicious spicy hot carrot chutney. Chicken tikka cooked in a specially prepared mild tomato sauce was out of this world. Chicken shashlick was brilliant. Absolutely nothing standard about this restaurant at all.' MB. Price check: Papadam 45p, CTM £6.70, Pullao Rice £1.80, Peshwari Nan £1.80. Takeaway: 10% discount. Free delivery, 10-mile radius. Hours: 12-2.30pm/6-11pm. Stocks Cobra.

Slough

ANAM TANDOORI AND BALTI HOUSE ©

1a Baylis Parade, Oatland Drive, Slough 01753 572967

A typical competent curry house owned by Javeed Ali, open evenings only. 'Baltis are a speciality here and very tasty too.' RE.

AKASH TANDOORI NEW ENTRANT

21 Burnham High Street, Burnham 01628 666601

First opened in 1982. Taken over by Foysol Ahmed in 1991. 100-seater regularly patronised by BD and CR. Price check: Papadam 60p, CTM £6.40, Pullao Rice £1.70, Peshwari Nan £1.70, Lager £2.50 pint. Hours: 12-2.30pm/6-11.30pm. Stocks Cobra.

BARN TANDOORI

Salt Hill Park, Bath Road, Slough 01753 523183

We know of restaurants in old schools, fire stations, churches, garages, Portakabins, and even an ex-ambulance (see Spicy Hut Takeaway on page 178) but the Barn takes the papadam! It's in a rather grand, ex-cricket pavilion in the middle of nowhere – well, a park, actually, and next to the tennis courts. Taken over in 1996 by Messrs Mehbub, Rahman, Alam and Kandakar. Serves formula curries. 'I have revisited this excellent Indian restaurant in the park twice with large business parties at very short notice. The staff copes admirably, delivering many different orders at the same time, maintaining high-quality cuisine with superb service.' TE. 'Masalla dosa was a great mixture of vegetables in a pancake. Chicken dhansak was tasty with an excellent balance of spices and chillies with the lentils. Worth a return visit.' RH.

SKYWAYS HOTEL AND BRASSERIE NEW ENTRANT

19-21 London Road, Slough 01753 522286

And if a curry barn isn't enough excitement, how about a curry B&B in the same town? Skyways is a family-run hotel offering an excellent 'home from home' service with lovely warm rooms, satellite television, and full English breakfast. All at half the price of the larger hotels around Slough. Nothing unusual in that, you say, but what about the restaurant? Says TE: 'It has retained the same Nepalese chefs and waiters whose excellent cuisine and efficient service put Skyways 'on the map'. New manager is Ram Panwar, from the Cookham Tandoori, who has a long track record of success in cooking and managing tandoori cuisine. Revamped menu offers a wider variety of dishes and 'special dinners'. TE. 'I stayed here and enjoyed an excellent meal at a reasonable cost. Chicken Patia was excellent, generous naan breads and free pickles and papadoms. I would recommend this hotel and restaurant to curryholic business travellers and regular diners.' RA. And so do we, it being ideal for Heathrow.

SPICES NEW ENTRANT

The Green, Datchet, Slough 01753 581008

'Chutneys excellent. Methi was tender with very tasty spices. Sabzi was a good dry mix of vegetables with mild spices. Good food and service but a bit pricy'. RH.

SPICY TANDOORI TAKEAWAY NEW ENTRANT

110 Stoke Road, Slough 01753 553316

'Friendly service, all food freshly prepared on ordering. Tasty and very authentic fare.' CP.

TAJ TANDOORI NEW ENTRANT ©

7 Upton Lea Parade, Wrexham Road, Slough 01753 521674

Established in 1993. Seats 48. Room for 20 cars at front of restaurant. Changes in decor planned. Specials include: King prawn jal frezi, chicken tikka masala, lamb pasanda, chicken jal frezi, lamb jal frezi. Price check: Papadam 40p, CTM £5.50, Pullao Rice £1.50, Peshwari Nan £1.60, Lager £1.90 pint. Free delivery, 3-mile radius. Hours: 5.30pm-12am. Stocks Cobra.

Sunningdale

TIGER'S PAD

3 Station Parade, London Road, Sunningdale 01344 621215

AF said last time: 'Expensive, minimalist, open-plan decor. Oak tables.

Perfect papadams. Onion Bhajias like tennis balls, really good. Scallops Chilli Fry and Seekh Kebab, both very good. Lamb Vindaloo £6.95, excellent, tender, very tasty. Subz Hyderabadi, vegetables roasted in the tandoor and glazed with cheese. OK but not enough cheese and too much onion. Everything was served in solid brass pots with large heavy matching spoons. Nan one of the best I've ever had. Packed full by 8pm. One complaint: wine list is outrageously expensive – £16.95 for an ordinary bottle of Australian Chardonnay. Unusual (for an Indian restaurant) 4 out of 7 staff were female.' AF. He augments his views this time, with: 'Gets better and better. They continually refine and change their menu. Sikadari Badi Lamb is out of this world. I'm convinced it is the "find of the decade".' AF. But CP doesn't agree: 'Very expensive menu. Food in small portions. Always looks nearly empty. Omit.' CP. We reserve judgement on that, but your views are welcomed. Price check: Papadam 50p, CTM £7.50, Bombay Potato £3.25, Pullao Rice £2.25, Chutney and Pickles 50p. Sunday Buffet £9.95 12-5pm.

Sunninghill

NAANU'S TAKEAWAY NEW ENTRANT

72a High Street, Sunninghill 01344 874020

'Takeaway. First class and freshly prepared food with many specialist items from a huge menu.' CP.

VICEROY NEW ENTRANT

18 High Street, Sunninghill 01344 873062

'Busy, good quality restaurant. A notch above the standard formula. I have been a regular since it opened in 1993. A little more expensive than average but good portions. Highly popular and friendly service.' CP.

Theale

CAFE BLUE COBRA TOP 100

20 High Street, Theale 0118 930 4040

A place with a real difference owned by the enterprising Abssar Waess. The venue opens at noon and operates, café-style, until midnight. The first-timer is struck by the coolness and fresh cleanliness of the decor. The bar area, with its marble and cane furnishings, seats 30. It leads on to the main dining area, whose 60 ormolu seats are designed to evoke airy oriental verandas. The light walls are a regularly changing 'gallery', home to the works of local professional artists. The Cobra Express Platter lunch can be advance-ordered by phone and served on arrival – useful for the busy exec. Those with less demanding timetables can choose à la carte until 2.30pm, or simply linger in the bar over the snacks menu until 6pm. From 6pm the full menu comes into play, and an interesting document it is. Naturally there is a wide range of Bangladeshi and Bengali dishes, some of which will be familiar to the curry aficionado. Delights include Tikka, Methi Saag Gosht and Birianis. But there are many other dishes. There is duckling, crab, venison, veal, pomfret, ayre, surma river fish and much more. The menu also includes Thai food. The Thai operation includes some classics, such as, for starters, steamed mussels, Chicken Sateh or a mixed platter. Main courses range from Thai Green Chicken Curry to Ped Pad Prik – Hot Duck with Pad Thai noodles. Expect to spend around £35 per head for a three-courser with drink and coffee. There are themed set meals from £17.90, but Waess reports that many diners happily mix and match the two cuisines. And why not? SM says: 'Service is always attentive, although it can occasionally take a while for the food to arrive. The green chicken curry is superb! Excellent food, if a bit pricey. Lately the chefs have taken to creating new traditional-style dishes, for example cinnamon chicken stuffed with surma river fish – sounds odd but works extremely well. Only two minutes off J12 of the M4. If anyone's in the area and doesn't give them a try, they're missing something real special.' And again from SM: 'Yet another trip to my local. Still as brilliant as ever – tried Thai Chicken Tom Yang soup as a prelude to the Bengali part of the meal and it worked very well.' Remains in our TOP 100.

Twyford

THE MITA'S NEW ENTRANT ©

37 London Road, Twyford 0118 934 4599

Established in 1993. Seats 32. 10 parking spaces. Specials include: Hundee dishes and Bengal fish special. Price check: Papadam 50p, CTM £6.95, Pullao Rice £1.75, Peshwari Nan £1.75, Lager £3.10 pint. Delivery: £15 minimum, 5-mile radius. Hours: 12-2.30pm/5.30-11.30pm. Stocks Cobra.

Windsor

SHARMINS OF WINDSOR NEW ENTRANT

41 Thames Street, Windsor 01753 832499

'Attractive restaurant. I like the glass separator panels with animals such as tigers and peacocks, which break up the large room. Persian Chicken Pullao was excellent. It was a Biriani-like dish with chicken, lychee and rice topped with an omelette and fresh tomatoes, cucumbers and sliced almonds. Sharmin's serves a good meal but I think the Windsor-level prices won't draw me back again.' RH.

Wokingham

ASSAM NEW ENTRANT

48-50 Peach Street, Wokingham 01189 776100

First opened in 1994, run by Helal Uddin since 1996. Seats 86. Parking at back. Jazz night every Wednesday. Price check: Papadam 70p, CTM £8.95, Pullao Rice £2.20, Peshwari Nan £2.25, Lager £2.80 pint. Hours: 12-2.30pm/6-11.30pm. Stocks Cobra.

ROYAL INDIAN TANDOORI ©

72 Peach Street, Wokingham 0118 978 0179

A 70-seater established in 1978 by T Ali, serving excellent Bangladeshi and Kashmiri-styled curries by chef M Miah. Banquets on Sundays. 'Very good food and good value, we were all very satisfied. Chicken Chilli Tandoori Masala was a superb dish, rich in colour, texture and flavour. Service friendly and attentive, some a bit slapdash.' HC. Price check: Papadam 70p, CTM £6.50, Pullao Rice £1.95, Peshwari Nan £1.95. Takeaway menu 15% cheaper than restaurant menu. Hours: 12-3pm/6pm-12am. Stocks Cobra.

SULTAN BALTI PALACE NEW TO OUR TOP 100

7 Market Place, Wokingham 0118 977 4397

In the middle of the old town, upstairs, low ceilings, black beams, white-washed walls, several small dining rooms make for an intimate and upmarket dining experience. Downstairs is modern, café-style, with its own menu, for light snacks while out shopping or between office meetings. We dined one night with Abdul and his wife Helena and enjoyed a very pleasant meal. Helena was in the process of updating waiter uniforms, throwing out the traditional white shirt and black tie for a blue shirt with yellow patterned tie, much more in keeping with the elegance of their restaurant.

BRISTOL

Area: West Country
Population: 400,000
Adjacent Counties: Glos, Soms

BRISTOL CENTRE

Consists of BS1, BS2

RAJDOOT TOP 100 ©

83 Park Street, Bristol BS1 0117 926 8033

Established in 1970 by Indian architect Des Sarda. The attractive decorations are very Indian with beaten copper tables in the bar area and bronze statues. Manager Sukhi Sharma. As always, we get contradictory reports about all the Rajdoots, despite the caveat, which I'll repeat: as most restaurants are Bangladeshi-run, Rajdoot's food may come as a surprise to some. It is much truer to the authentic food you'll find in homes in northern India. It is this very fact that leads to the disappointment which is expressed to us by some of Rajdoot's first-and-only-time diners, who simply do not find the food matching their expectations. The complaints, and I stress again that they are few but persistent, are that the food is bland and the prices high. It's the same at all three Rajdoot branches (see Birmingham; Dublin; Manchester). Here are recent examples: WOL confirms what he wrote earlier: 'really excellent meal, first class service'. Note that there is a 25% discount on food served between 1830 and 1930 hours Sunday to Thursday evenings inclusive. It was automatically applied to our bill. 'I was looking forward to renewing my acquaintance with Rajdoot, and I walked a long way through January bitter winds and sleet to reach it. But my entrance was barred by a man in evening dress, and when I asked for a table for one he just turned me away. Looking over his shoulders, I could see only empty tables. It was all too obvious that he just did not want a lone diner.' PM. 'I have eaten here on several occasions, usually before 7.30pm Monday to Friday when the restaurant runs a 25% discount Happy Hour – very much appreciated given the relatively high prices (e.g. side dishes ranging around £5). Decor has an authentic feel to it, service is friendly and helpful. Fish Tikka was pleasant but rather dry, Chicken Tikka Massalla was rather bland, Chicken Chilli Garlic had a slight vinegary taste, Aloo Gobi and Keema Naan were fine.

My first disappointing meal here, and as a result the jury is out on the merits of paying the premium prices required to visit this city centre restaurant.' JL. Perhaps it is all best summed up by DL: 'Consistently unpredictable! Sometimes wonderful, sometimes terrible, but always expensive.' DL. Hours: 12-2.30pm (closed Sun. lunch)/6.30-11.30pm.

BRISTOL NORTH EAST

Consists of BS5, BS16

BS5 Easton, Redfield

EASTERN TASTE NEW ENTRANT

94 St Marks Road, Easton, Bristol BS5 0117 952 0718

'Standard curryshop fare, but so well done and consistent. Friendly owners, relaxed atmosphere, brilliant value. Highly recommended.' JG.

BS16 Fishponds

(for adjacent Staple Hill see Glos)

RAJ MAHAL NEW ENTRANT

8-10 Frome Road, Stapleton, Bristol BS16 0117 958 6225

'Located amongst a small unprepossessing row of shops in an out of the way suburb, but worth finding. Interior is well done, seating in four person booths or open tables, lots of window seats. Dupiaza, Dhansak and Chicken Chat Masala are all particularly good. Fast and friendly service, and generally busy (unlikely to get table on Friday or Saturday evenings without booking). Reasonable prices.' CL.

SPICE OF NEPAL TAKEAWAY NEW ENTRANT ©

245 Lodge Causeway, Fishponds, Bristol BS16 0117 965 0664

A Nepalese takeaway opened in 1997 by Pradeep Karki, head chef. Dilip Karki manages front of house. Momo, dumplings filled with mince, steamed, served with Nepalese Tomato Pickle. Kastamandapa, a mild dish, flavoured with ground nuts, cream, with a hint of garlic, highly recommended. Price check: Papadam 25p, CTM £3.95, Pullao Rice £1.25, Peshwari Nan £1.40. Delivery £10 minimum, 3-mile radius. Hours: 6-11.30pm; closed on Sun.

BRISTOL NORTH WEST

Consists of BS6 to BS11

BS6 Cotham, Montpelier, Redland

DUKE OF RAJ NEW ENTRANT

376 Cotham Hill, Redland, Bristol BS6 0117 973 3733

'Service throughout was friendly, helpful and efficient. Portions good, prices cheap by Home Counties' standards, only criticism is the under-spicing of all dishes.' HC.

BS7 Bishopston, Horfield

GHURKAS TANDOORI NEW ENTRANT ©

403 Gloucester Road, Horfield, Bristol BS7 0117 942 2898

A popular local with some Nepalese dishes. Seats 46. Price check: Papadam 20p, CTM £4.50, Pullao Rice £1.50, Lager £2.50 pint. Delivery. Hours: 12-2pm/6pm-12.30am.

PUSHPANJLI e-a-m-a-y-l V

217a Gloucester Road, Bishopston, Bristol BS7 0117 924 0493

'A wonderfully informal yet smart Gujarati vegetarian restaurant fitted with formica tables and plastic chairs, with food displayed under a glass counter. All food is home-cooked. Huge variety of starters, Dal Bhajia, Samosa, Kachori, Bateta Wada, Mogo Chips, all superb. Large assorted pickle tray offering wide choice and lovely Papads. Masala Dhosas enormous with Sambar and coconut chutney. I visit this restaurant several times a month and it's truly brilliant.' DR. 'My no. 1. Can't fault the food, Sweets very indulgent.' JM.

BS9 Westbury-on-Trym

BRITISH RAJ

1-3 Passage Road, Westbury-on-Trym, Bristol BS9 0117 950 0493

Some of our scribes say this classical, upmarket restaurant, open since 1973, is one of the most highly respected in the south-west. 'Not cheap, £40 for two with drinks. Excellent service, food quality was outstanding, fresh, hot and tangy.' NO. Though DL finds it only 'adequate'. Price check: Papadam 45p, CTM £6.25, Pullao Rice £1.45. Hours: 12-2pm/6-11.30pm.

BUCKINGHAMSHIRE

Area: Home Counties (west of London)
Population: 693,000
Adjacent Counties: Beds, Herts, Middx, Northants, Oxon

Amersham

SHANTI NEW ENTRANT

16 Hill Avenue, Amersham 01494 432621

'Deceptively large place, good service and food. Closes 11pm.' JB.

Aylesbury

THE CHADNIS NEW ENTRANT

43-45 High Street, Waddesdon, Aylesbury 01296 651255

Established in 1999. Seats 70. Fully licensed and air-conditioned. 'What a wonderful evening. I am a sales manager and took my staff for an evening out. Food and drinks excellent. Mr Shah and the waiters provided first-class service in a relaxing atmosphere.' RB. Price check: Papadam 50p, CTM £6.90, Pullao Rice £1.80, Peshwari Nan £1.80, Lager £2.40. Takeaway: 10% discount on orders over £10. Hours: 12-2.30pm/6-11pm. Stocks Cobra.

EL HALAL TANDOORI HOUSE NEW ENTRANT

110 High Street, Aylesbury 01296 484454

'It's simple, offers very good value and serves great food. Excellent Murgh Shah!' AD.

GOLDEN BENGAL ©

1-2 Villiers Building, Buckingham St, Aylesbury 01296 384001

Established in 1971, taken over in 1996 by Sayad Miah and Harunur Rashid. Restaurant decorated in cream, red and gold, seats 40. Takeaway: 20% discount. Free delivery within 3-mile radius, £10 minimum. Hours: 12-2.30pm/6pm-12am. Stocks Cobra.

©	Curry Club Discount	U	Unlicensed
V	Vegetarian	ANP	Alcohol not permitted
e-a-m-a-y-l	Eat as much as you like	BYO	Bring your own alcohol

CURRY CLUB

TAJ MAHAL ©

73 Buckingham Street, Aylesbury 01296 399617

Opened in November 1993 by Abdul Khaliq. Formula curries served competently in this 50-seater curry house, CTM, Jalfrezi and Korma being the most popular dishes ordered. Delivery: £10 minimum, 3-mile radius. Hours: 12-2.30pm/5.30pm-12am. Stocks Cobra.

Beaconsfield

BUCKS TANDOORI

7 The Broadway, Penn Road, Beaconsfield 01494 674580

'I am a regular, and I mean most Friday nights. The food is Nepalese-style and is freshly prepared, so don't expect to get out in record time. Service is comfortably good with friendly, polite waiters. Sunday buffet e-a-m-a-y-l for £7.50 per person. Everything that has been tried is excellent, and well worth a visit. Watch for special events.' MS. 'Called on spec for Sunday Buffet, and what a buffet. A choice of nine dishes. An upmarket restaurant, and a strong contender for the TOP 100.' BP-D. Further good reports could achieve that.

Bourne End

LAST VICEROY

74 The Parade, Bourne End 01628 531383

'Food was quite simply superb! Bollywood Rolls – spiced lamb, chicken, king prawn and vegetables, all neatly wrapped up in pastry. Mussels cooked in herbs and spices, carefully preserving the delicate flavour of the seafood. Botikka Lamb – tender and spicy.' CF. 'Great welcome, table good, drinks quickly delivered. Large, warm Popadoms with exceptional Lime pickle. Plate warmers, superb food, excellent quantities. Hot towels. Lovely evening.' BR. 'The flavour combinations and varying degrees of spiciness of lamb, chicken and vegetables harmonised beautifully, stimulating the palate without overpowering, and the result was a tantalising visual and gastronomic delight. Well patronised, even on a Monday evening, with up to three sittings in the evenings. Reasonably priced.' CF&PC. Price check: Papadam 35p (plain) 40p (spicy), Aloo Jeera £2.20, Pullao Rice £1.60, Chutney and Pickles (per person) 50p. Hours: 12-2.30pm/6pm-12am. Stocks Cobra.

Buckingham

DIPALEE ©

18 Castle Street, Buckingham 01280 813151/813925

90-seater curry house under the watchful ownership of Salique Ahmed. Head Chef Ashik. 'Visited with friends. Offered Popadoms and drinks on being seated – excellent. Babori Mix – good value and tasty. Prawn Puree £3.50 – excellent. Onion Bhajias £1.90 – superb. Main courses took an age to be served. Hari Mirchi Bhoona Chicken £6.50 – excellent, Lamb Madras £4.95 – very disappointing. £98 for four (inc service).' DL. Price check: Papadam 50p, CTM £6.75, Pullao Rice £1.90. Hours: 12-2.30pm/6-11.30pm.

Burnham

AKASH TANDOORI ©

21 High Street, Burnham 01628 603507/602942

Foysol Ahmed's Akash is a regular entrant in these pages. Indeed, our regular correspondent of many years, who still wishes to remain anonymous, now claims to be eating his way round the menu for the sixteenth time – every dish at least once. Stocks Cobra.

High Wycombe

CURRY CENTRE ©

83 Easton Street, High Wycombe 01494 535529

Whenever the owners are personally looking after front of house (A Musowir) and kitchen (MA Mali) respectively, you can be sure of getting their best. 'Food and service of a consistently high standard.' GD.

Iver

CURRY PARADISE OF RICHINGS PARK

NEW ENTRANT

34 Thorney Lane South, Iver 01753 655262

'Everything is modern and pleasant. The spinach bhaji was excellent – dry, crisp and flavourful. Service was quite quick and commendable.' RH. Stocks Cobra.

Milton Keynes

(Includes Bletchley, Stony Stratford, Woburn Sands and Wolverton)

BALTI NIGHTS RE ENTRANT

11 Wolverton Road, Stony Stratford, MK 01908 565933

'A very popular local restaurant and I use its home delivery service regularly. I usually have Meat Thali plus Sag Bhaji or Veg Thali plus Lamb Methi. On the latter there is enough for two, or even some reserved for a cold breakfast (disgusting habits!). Under new management, but telephone staff and delivery men seem to be the same, and quality remains good and portions are large. Service is good, delivery prompt, good range of dishes. Very generous portions. Dead good, so back in the guide, please.' BG. Done, Brian!

BEKASH NEW ENTRANT

50 High Street, Stony Stratford, MK 01908 562249/568521

'Unassuming restaurant in centre of Stony Stratford. Pleasantly decorated with plenty of food and greenery. Always busy, even mid-week, speaks for itself. "Legendary" Onion Bhajia's, size of cricket balls, beautifully crisp and tasty. Good selection of unusual main courses, Duck Tikka and Whole Baby Chicken. Definitely a class above the rest.' PJ. Stocks Cobra.

BENGAL SPICE NEW ENTRANT

52 Church Street, Wolverton, MK 01908 311188

'My takeaway came in very large portions and was of good quality, all being well cooked. A comfortable interior, quite spacious albeit small. I will certainly go back for a more thorough assault on the menu. Cosy restaurant, friendly staff. Different dishes, many carrying more chilli than similar hostelries. Highly recommended.' BG. Stocks Cobra.

CHILLI GARDEN RENAMED ©

Unit 1, Agora Centre (1st Floor), Church Street,
Wolverton, MK 01908 222228

Used to be the Night of India (1988), reopened as the 80-seater Chilli Garden in June 1998. 'Grand launch with the Mayor of MK. Raita and naan both excellent.' BG. Price check: Papadam 45p, CTM £5.95, Pullao Rice £1.50, Peshwari Nan £1.30, Lager £4 pint. Takeaway: 20% discount. Free delivery. Hours: 5.30pm-12am. Stocks Cobra.

EASTERN PARADISE

8 Church Street, Wolverton, MK 01908 312969/225765

'Announces itself as the "first Balti House in Milton Keynes" and has recently been "decorated" with masses of artificial plants covering the walls and dangling from the ceiling – tasteful or naff? Service friendly, full of regulars. Went here with an Indian friend. Ordered prawn pakora (not on menu) and a very accommodating waiter and chef provided them. Meat thali very good. All dishes were in very thick sauces, nothing runny or sloppy.' BG. Stocks Cobra.

GOLDEN CURRY ©

4 Duncombe Street, Bletchley, MK 01908 377857

MK's oldest, established in 1971, taken over by Ismail Ali in 1980. Serves formula curries. Seats 58. Takeaway: 10% discount. Delivery: £10 minimum. Hours: 12-1.30pm/5.30-11.30pm. Stocks Cobra.

JAIPUR BEST OUTSIDE LONDON **TOP 100** ©

502 Elder Gate, Central Milton Keynes 01908 669796

It's public knowledge now: the Jaipur is moving within MK into a £2m detached, sumptuous, purpose-built, opulent, Maharajah-style, domed palace in its own gardens. What Mr Ahad will do with the original restaurant, operating beside the station, remains to be seen. Watch out for the cycle-rickshaw (you can have your photo taken in it with the ebullient Mr Ahad). Despite the imminent move, a brand new carpet has been installed, and it has been redecorated, in its familiar shades of pink, reflecting its namesake city, Jaipur in Rajasthan (the city where all the buildings are made from the local pink-coloured sandstone). Walls, chairs, tablecloths, ceiling (the centrepiece of which is a chandelier) are gorgeous. Life at the Jaipur never stands still. Additions to the menu, special functions. Oberoi-trained Indian chef Vijendra Singh has settled in well with the excellent resident chef Sufian Miah. We continue to get many reports singing the Jaipur's praises. Here are some recent examples: 'An old favourite. Continues to excel. Sag Paneer is especially good. I had another of our regular school parties from India with us and we sampled the Sunday Buffet. The Jaipur always seems to provide something new – this time deep fried lychees, absolutely delicious. My Indian students thought it outstanding.' BG. 'Little need to report on the excellence of the Jaipur – it remains so! Chana dal was authentically delightful, as were Bindi. Rack of lamb, marinated in spice and cooked until tender – is this the best dish I have ever had in a UK restaurant? I think so.' BG. 'Food was superb, beautifully served, presented and spiced. We will definitely try to visit again.' GM. 'Really great. Wonderful tandoori fish that I hadn't seen before. In fact the whole meal was a delight and very reasonable for the quality and setting.' BB. ' We were very impressed – a really enjoyable evening. The best Indian restaurant I have visited in a long time.' LC. 'My partner and I visited with friends expecting great things – as for the food, we were not disappointed. Subzi Jalfrezi – beautifully spiced and had green chillies in abundance. Naans wonderfully light and fluffy. Vegetable Cashew Korma – superb, rich and creamy. One criticism – service. Rushed into ordering, brisk and inattentive. Food equal to Chutney Mary (see London SW10), though unfortunately the service was not!' AG. 'Feel that the guide talks this place up a wee bit. Enjoyed my Chicken Mirch Masaledar, along with a splendid naan.' RL. Strange that! I am happy to repeat that you will not find a restaurateur who cares more about his restaurant and his customers than Mr Ahad. Everything is first-class. True the place gets exceptionally busy, 99 seats are often not sufficient to meet demand, hence the move. Price check: Papadam 50p, CTM £6.95, Pullao Rice £1.75. Look Ahad up at www.Jaipur.co.uk. Public parking to front and rear of extension. Sunday buffet £9.95 per person – children under ten £5 – children under five free. Price check: Papadam 60p, CTM £7.95, Pullao Rice £1.95, Peshwari Nan £2.50, Lager £2.50 pint. Takeaway: 10% discount. Hours: 12-3pm/6-11.30pm. Stocks Cobra.

JALORI ©

23 High Street, Woburn Sands, MK 01908 281239281226

Established in 1994 by Hai, Ahad's brother (see Jaipur, above) and managed by Abdul Kadi the 70-seater Jalori is bigger than it looks, and has a loyal following that includes Johnny Dankworth and Cleo Lane. Chef Abdul Hanaan prepares food that is 'First class.' BG. Most popular dish is Chicken Cashew Pasanda. Interesting menu addition for you to try – Cheese and Onion Naan £2.50. Delivery. Price check: Papadam 50p, CTM £6.95, Pullao Rice £1.90. Peshwari Nan £1.95, Lager £2.50 pint. Delivery: £12 minimum, 4-mile radius. Hours: 12-2pm/6-11.30pm. Stocks Cobra.

MOGHUL PALACE ©

7 St Paul's Court, High St, Stony Stratford, MK 01908 566577

'It's an old monastery school where monks once beat knowledge into the sons of local gentry.' LT. Now the local curryholic gentry beat a path through its Gothic arch, complete with wrought-iron gate, beyond which stands the imposing clerestoric building. Owners Monowar Hussain and Anfor Ali greet you and, given a chance, will tell you how much they spent in 1994 converting this Victorian former cigar-factory-cum-orphanage-cum-school into their 100-seat Palace. And impressed you will be, with the spacious reception area with its armchairs and comfortable sofas where you wait to be seated, and the scale, height, tiled floor, stonework and wood panels of the dining room. Be nice to the gargoyles, they're there to ward off bad vibes! And wonder what the monks would think of the menu offering all the familiar curry items. 'Service and food quality were both excellent although portions were on the small side. I had my usual favourite, Chicken Zalfraji. It was very tasty, as were the Chicken Madras, Thali Special – delicious – and Chicken Biryiani.' BG. Hours: 12-2.30pm/6-11.30pm.

ROSE OF INDIA NEW ENTRANT ©

6 Ducombe Street, Wolverton, MK 01908 641115

Competent formula curry house opened in 1986, taken over by A Thalis. Price check: Papadam 35p, CTM £6.45, Pullao Rice £1.40, Peshwari Nan £1.50, Lager £2.20 pint. Takeaway: 10% discount. Delivery: 8-mile radius. Hours: 12-2pm/5.30pm-12am. Stocks Cobra.

Newport Pagnell

MYSORE NEW TO OUR TOP 100 ©

101 High Street, Newport Pagnell, Milton Keynes 01908 216426

Another high-standard goodie from the Ahad stable, this one operated by brother M Abdul Odud. The dining room, cleverly housed within two cottages, seats 98, yet provides a number of secluded areas, which 'give a good feeling of privacy'. HG. North Indian curries and Balti on the menu. 'We were unsure of arrangements and numbers for a special charity dinner, so Mr Odud gave us a selection from the menu at a fixed price. Lamb Dhansak with Sag, Mixed Raitha, Pullao Rice and Paratha, all very good. The complete meal and decor (small corners and niches, then a large area with skylight, a bit colonial and glorious at full moon) to be recommended.' BG. Join the Mysore VIP Club to qualify for discounts. 10% discount for takeaways. Hours: 12-2.30pm/6-11.30pm. Stocks Cobra.

Olney

SPICE GARDEN NEW ENTRANT

2 Stanley Court, Weston Road, Olney 01234 240620

It's a very popular venue serving Bangladeshi and North Indian Tandooris, Curries, Specials, and all your favourites. 'Finished a long day in London, then sat in a seemingly even longer M1 traffic jam. Ventured off the beaten track and got lost (no map). Needed a fix. Found myself in Olney and spotted this one. The food is so good. Fixed, refreshed, destressed and satisfied, they gave me directions and I returned to the M1, now traffic-free. Before long, will map-read my return.' ME.

Princes Risborough

SHANSA NEW ENTRANT

16 Duke Street, Princes Risborough 01844 274443

'A small place in the town centre. Service pleasant and quick. Nothing special but good honest grub and we'll use it again.' MS. Stocks Cobra.

Wendover

RAJ

23 Aylesbury Road, Wendover 01296 622567

A 300-year-old listed building in a beautiful old street, in a picture-postcard town. Exposed beams, with walled partitions, dividing the 60 seats into almost separate rooms, creating agreeable ambience and comfort. 'One of the best. Another first class night. Machly Biran – spicy fried small fish with fried onions recommended. Needed a chilli buzz – Chicken Jalfrezi obliged. Shared a Naan – very fluffy. Swift service with smiles.' MS. Stocks Cobra.

Winslow

MAHABHARAT ©

25 Market Square, Winslow 01296 713611

First opened in 1979, taken over by Nurul Islam in 1990, the ground-floor restaurant seats 44 diners, plus private room for 26. Price check: Papadam 40p, CTM £6.10, Pullao Rice £1.80, Peshwari Nan £1.90, Lager £1.90. Takeaway: 15% discount. Hours: 6-11.30pm (Sat. to 12am). Stocks Cobra.

CAMBRIDGESHIRE

Area: East
Population: 729,000
Adjacent Counties: Beds, Essex, Herts, Rutland, Lincs, Norfolk, Northants, Suffolk,

Cambridge

CURRY MAHAL NEW ENTRANT

Millers Yard, Cambridge 01223 360409

'Really excellent meal.' RA.

GOLDEN CURRY ©

111 Mill Road, Cambridge 01223 329432

Shaista Miah's pleasant, air-conditioned, large 98-seater, is divided into booths. Chef Abdul Tahid creates: 'Wonderful tastes. Everything piping hot including the plate' JB. 'Top of the league. A first class meal.' RA. Price check: Minimum charge £10. Hours: 12-2.30pm/6pm-12am. Stocks Cobra.

INDIA HOUSE NEW ENTRANT

31 Newnham Road, Cambridge 01223 460173

'Location is lovely, looking across a pond or part of the river to a green and an attractively lit pub. Decor is almost all white, very light and summery. Our reserved table was not ready when we arrived, but it was laid with lightning speed – the only speedy part of the meal. Fairly traditional menu, average prices. Every dish looked different, different styles being served in different dishes and every one tasted quite distinct from the others. Portions adequate. A very good restaurant if you are not in a hurry.' HC. Stocks Cobra.

KISMET INDIAN TAKEAWAY NEW ENTRANT

71 Catherine Street, Cambridge 01223 415525

'I have been going there on and off for ten years and have never had cause to complain. Service is excellent and always on time if you phone in your order. Chicken Tikki Rogan is a favourite of mine.' RA.

KOHINOOR ©

74 Mill Road, Cambridge 01223 323639

One of Cambridge's oldest and best, serving all your favourite curries and accompaniments. Some prefer it to all others. One don, who prefers to remain anon, tells us he's been going there for decades. Stocks Cobra.

PIPASHA NEW ENTRANT

529c New Market Road, Cambridge 01223 577786

Established in 1999. Seats 60. Car parking for 40 at rear. Specials include: King Prawn Khakhri. Price check: Papadam 50p, CTM £6.95, Pullao Rice £1.85, Peshwari Nan £2.05, Lager £2.70 pint. Takeaway: 10% discount. Delivery: £1.50 minimum, 3-mile radius. Hours: 12-2pm/5.30-11.30pm. Stocks Cobra.

TAJ TANDOORI ©

64 Cherry Hinton Road, Cambridge 01223 248063

Taken over by SA Haque in 1992. Restaurant seats 72. 'Food is very good. Puri with a large helping of Prawn Bhuna on top set the scene. Excellent Chicken Tikka Jalfrezi.' RW. . Hours: 12-2pm/6pm-12am. Stocks Cobra.

Ely

SURMA TANDOORI ©

78 Broad Street, Ely 01353 662281

Established in 1979 by MA Ossi and SA Choudhury. Seats 64 in two dining rooms. 'This is the best curryhouse for miles. We regularly eat here once or twice a week.' GS. 'We have always had good meals here – the quantities and quality are always good.' JS. 'Had a very enjoyable curry.' DW. Hours: 12-2pm/6pm-12am.

Peterborough

BOMBAY BRASSERIE ©

52 Broadway, Peterborough 01733 565606

Owned by Rony Choudhury (manager) and Mahbub Khan (chef). Attractive red-brick 70-seat interior with a brass-work bar, serving generous curries. Branch: Planet Papadam, Park Road, Peterborough. Stocks Cobra.

INDIA GATE ©

9 Fitzwilliam Street, Peterborough 01733 346160/346485

Taken over in 1996 by Mohammed Farooq. This elegant 44-seater is full of Eastern trinkets and atmosphere. The menu consists of a full house of curry favourites, competently cooked by Chef Kamal Uddin. Air-conditioned. Sunday lunch buffet £7. Delivery: £13.50 minimum. Hours: 12-2pm/6pm-12am (1am on Sat.). Stocks Cobra.

KASHMIR BALTI HOUSE NEW ENTRANT U

298 Lincoln Road, Peterborough 01733 894025

'Restaurant facilities are very basic, but improving all the time. It is well out of town in a slightly run down area, but the food is simply superb. Service is friendly and efficient, and special offers such as free starters are promoted frequently.' IB.

TAJ MAHAL ©

37-39 Lincoln Road, Peterborough 01733 348840

Taken over in 1995 by Haq Nawaz, who is also the manager. Seats 100. Serving Pakistani and Kashmiri-style curries. Air-conditioned. Delivery: £10 minimum, 5-mile radius. Hours: 12-2.30pm/6pm-12am; Sat. 6-1am.

St Neots

EASTERN OCEAN TAKEAWAY NEW ENTRANT ©

2 Longsands Parade, Longsands Road, St Neots 01480 403703

Formerly Moonlight. Established in 1988 and taken over the following year by Abdor Miah. Set dinner: six meals to choose from, only £7.50 and are good value. Delivery: 5-mile radius, £7. Price check: Papadam 55p, CTM £6.30, Pullao Rice £1.75, Peshwari Nan £1.95. Hours: 5.30-11.30pm.

CHESHIRE

Area: North West
Population: 992,000
Adjacent Counties: Clwyd, Derbs, Greater Man, Mers, Shrops, Staffs

Chester

AHMED INDIAN TAKEAWAY NEW ENTRANT U

76 Brook Street, Newtown, Chester 01244 343420

Opened in 1992. House special: Jai Pur £7.00 – barbecued fillet of chicken tikka cooked in a rich sweet mango and creamy lemon sauce. Price check: Papadam 30p, CTM £5, Pullao Rice £1, Peshwari Nan £1.50. Delivery: £15 minimum, 3-mile radius. Hours: 5-11pm; Sat. lunches only, 12-2pm.

CHESTER TANDOORI NEW ENTRANT

39-41 Brook Street, Chester 01244 347410

'The place continues to be excellent with a real willingness to listen to customers to try and improve. Lamb jalfrezi consistently attains a state of perfection.' JT. Stocks Cobra.

GATE OF INDIA

25 City Road, Chester 01244 327131

Chester's second oldest (1961), and in Moinuddin Ahmed's hands since 1992. Two floors seating 64. Chef Sundar Ali serves formula curries. Hours: 6pm-2.30am (Sun. to 1am). Useful for Chester night owls and curry-insomniacs. Stocks Cobra.

SPICE BALTI NEW ENTRANT

63 Brook Street, Chester 01244 400305

Opened 1999 by Mrs Rena Begum. Formerly Arman Tandoori. Balti dishes and CTM are most popular. Price check: Papadam 50p, CTM £5.95, Pullao Rice £1.45, Peshwari Nan £1.50, Lager £1.95 pint. Takeaway: 20% discount. Free delivery: £13 minimum. Hours: 5.30pm-1am. Stocks Cobra.

Crewe

TAQUDIR NEW ENTRANT

203 Nantwich Road, Crewe 01270 215281

'I have been a regular for many years and wish to commend the very high standards of food and service which it always achieves. Easily the best.' WHF.

Ellesmere Port, Wirral

The Wirral is neither a town nor a county and until 1965 was part of Cheshire. Since then the northern part (a small, digit-like, curry-rich peninsula between the rivers Mersey and Dee) has been part of Merseyside. Ellesmere Port remains in south Wirral but is in Cheshire.

THE TAJ OF AGRA FORT AWARD WINNER TOP 100

1-7 Cambridge Road, Ellesmere Port 0151 355 1516

Spacious, clean and welcoming restaurant owned by Shams Uddin Ahmed. 'Very, very good, especially the mushroom dish from the veggie selection.' LH. 'A couple of nice touches set it apart – the waiters, in their Agra Fort jackets, ask you how long you want between starters and main courses and give you the time requested, and slices of orange were delivered with the hot towels after the main course, whether desserts were ordered or not. Pepper stuffed with small pieces of tandoori chicken and lamb, as mentioned in the guide, was excellent. Paratha was one of the best I've had. A very good evening and I look forward to visiting again.' OC. 'Heartily recommended.' RW. 'We totally recommend this restaurant to you.' MB and friends. 'Decor and service top drawer. Popadoms – warm and crisp, lime pickle needed replenishment, garlic and ginger chutney (a new one to me) was excellent. Tikka melt in the mouth, Bhajia size of tennis ball. CTM – too red, Jalfrezi – drier than normal, both excellent. Naan warm and moist. Top rate.' DB. Sunday Buffet is especially good value at £6.95 each. Monthly gourmet evenings.' RC. Price check: Papadam 45p, CTM £6.25, Pullao Rice £1.60. House wine £1.75 glass. Hours: 12-2pm/6-11.30pm (12.30am on Sat.). Sunday buffet 1-11.30pm. Stays high in our TOP 100. Stocks Cobra.

Frodsham

SHALIMAR NEW ENTRANT

25 High Street, Frodhsam 01928 739126

'Food and service excellent, staff friendly. Have no hesitation in recommending it for inclusion in your guide.' TW. Stocks Cobra.

Lymm

SAHIB

4-6 The Cross, Lymm 01925 757576

Established in 1994 and seating 50 upstairs in an old cottage. 'Excellent Onion Bhajis crisp and delicately spiced, Shami comes with "rashmi" egg wrap, is moist and delicately coriandered. Main courses good quality. Traditional village setting.' IEF-E. 'Tandoori Chicken Masala makes love to your tastebuds! King Akban Cham Cham seduces your tongue and then proceeds to nail it to the table – one for those who like a spicy kick.' JC. Price check: Papadam 60p, CTM £8.75, Pullao Rice £1.70, Peshwari Nan £1.95, Lager £2.10 pint. Takeaway: 20% discount. Hours: 4-11.30pm. Stocks Cobra.

Macclesfield

NASIB TANDOORI NEW ENTRANT

80 Chester Gate, Macclesfield 01625 617796

'Chicken Chat starter good. Keema Dish (minced lamb and chickpeas) main course good. A useful eating place.' JR. 'The extensive menu is exquisite and exciting. King Prawn Belpuri is an adventurous attempt at a Bombay street snack. Chicken Chilli Masala served in a beautiful kharai and laden with red and green chillies. Naans superb. A credit to Macclesfield, and as Arnie once said "I'll be back".' MRS SW. 'Excellent food and service.' RHD. Stocks Cobra.

Northwich

CURRY COTTAGE NEW ENTRANT ©

18-24 Chester Road, Northwich 01606 783824

Established in 1999. Originally called Castle Hill. Seats 60. 30 car parking spaces to rear. Price check: Papadam 45p, CTM £6.25, Pullao Rice £1.40, Peshwari Nan £1.60, Lager £2 pint. Takeaway: 15% discount. Hours: 5pm-12am. Stocks Cobra.

Sandbach

EASTERN SPICES NEW ENTRANT

376 Middlewich Road, Sandbach 01270 759993

'The first time I used this establishment I ordered a takeaway and gave my name. Ever since the manager has welcomed me by name, nice touch. Food cannot be faulted, concentrating on flavour instead of heat. Friendly service; if your order takes longer than expected, they offer a free beer and slip a few extra Popadoms in the bag.' DM. Stocks Cobra.

THE TASTE OF THE RAJ ©

11 High Street, Sandbach 01270 753752/763823

Opposite the old cobbled square which contains the Sandbach Cross, Anam Islam's small 38-seater 'gets very busy when the pubs close. Very neat and tidy. Panner Pakora and Fish Pakora, tasty. Chicken Lajawab with green chillies, good and spicy. Superb Brinjal.' RK. 'High class establishment with prices to match. Folded Popadoms and freshly made Raitha make it a bit special, staff could be more cheerful. Chilli Chicken – nicely spicy, uncomplicated flavour. Chicken Bhuna flavoursome, lots of large pieces of chicken breast.' DM. Price check: Papadam 40p, CTM £6.50, Pullao Rice £1.40. Minimum charge £10.50. Five-course set lunch £5. Service charge 10%. Sunday buffet £8.95. Lunch and dinner, daily, except Sat. 3pm-12.30am. Stocks Cobra.

Tattenhall

THE VILLAGE INDIAN NEW ENTRANT

Clifden House, High Street, Tattenhall 01829 770839

'Food very good, you taste the various spices. Very friendly staff, keen to explain dishes. Will certainly return.' LH. 'Menu is the best I have ever seen, and I have eaten in many UK, European and Far Eastern restaurants. Quality excellent, quantity large. Service, comfort and decor very good.' DJ. Stocks Cobra.

Upton

Adjoined to north Chester, but is part of the Wirral; see Ellesmere Port, above.

SHAH JALAL TAKEAWAY NEW ENTRANT

9 Arrow Park Road, Upton, Wirral 0151 606 1134

'We've especially enjoyed their specialities – Chicken Jhal is hot but very tasty with a citrus tang, Nadroo Kiyakni equally flavoursome but milder.' RC. Hours: 12-2pm/5-11.30pm. Fri. Sat. 5-11.30pm.

UPTON HALAL BALTI HOUSE NEW ENTRANT **BYO** ©

167 Ford Road, Upton Village, Wirral 0151 604 0166

Shofiul Miah's venture opened in 1996 and is not licensed, so BYO is a big attraction. Price check: Papadam 35p, CTM £6.80, Pullao Rice £1.60. Minimum charge £5. Set meal £9.50. Open every day except Tues., 5-11.30pm. Branch: Manzil, 73 Grange Road East, Birkenhead.

Winsford

BALTI COTTAGE INDIAN TAKEAWAY NEW ENTRANT

3 Over Square, Winsford 01606 557785

'Speedy and friendly service, generous portions with plenty of meat, complimentary coffee served while you watch your meal being prepared in an open kitchen.' JW.

CORNWALL

Area: West Country
Population: 478,000
Adjacent County: Devon

Bodmin

VIRAJ INDIAN CUISINE NEW ENTRANT

50 High Bore Street, Bodmin 01208 73480

'Very colourful meal for four and the menu featured some dishes we had never seen anywhere else. Chicken Rezella very tasty. Dishes were all hot (temperature) and the spice strength was spot-on. Service was good, although not very attentive towards the end. New and clean, but minimalist decor. A little overpriced for Cornwall.' DB. Stocks Cobra.

Bude

TASTE OF INDIA NEW ENTRANT ©

11 Queens Street, Bude 01288 356591

Established in 1995 by AM Choudhuri. 'Onion Bhajia, high onion content, ill-formed, inside undercooked – a bit like my efforts really!! [but are you charging £1.95 Malcolm?] CTM and Dhansak sauces reasonable flavours. Average Balti Vegetable Bhajee. Service very quick.' MW. Price check: Papadam 40p, CTM £6.95, Pullao Rice £2, Pickles 50p per person. Takeaway menu 20% cheaper. Delivery: £10 minimum, 3-mile radius. Hours: 12-2pm /5.30pm-12am. Stocks Cobra.

Falmouth

ASHA INDIAN RE-ENTRANT

1 The Moor, Falmouth 01326 211688

'As Viceroy of India, was in the guide but dropped out when owner changed. More stylish now, with friendly young waiters. Food still excellent, especially prawn and lamb dishes. Very good value for money.' MH. Stocks Cobra.

Newquay

RANI'S INDIAN NEW ENTRANT

49 Fore Street, Newquay 01637 850666

Under Vasant Maru's ownership. Chilli Nan £1.75 – Pat's favourite. Price check: Papadam 35p, CTM £6.25, Pullao Rice £1.70, Peshwari Nan £1.75.

Penzance

GANGES BALTI NEW ENTRANT

18 Chapel Street, Penzance 01736 333002

'A large restaurant. Superb quality Chicken Kahlin, huge chunks of chicken, the largest I've ever seen. Many different flavours in the meal, top quality stuff.' GGP. 'Chicken Karahi £6.25, cooked with black pepper, attractive sour taste. Egg Bhuna £2.95. Quality very good but slightly greasy. Very prompt, efficient service. Restaurant too dark to see my meal.' MP. Price check: Papadam 35p, Pullao Rice £1.65. Stocks Cobra.

©	Curry Club Discount	U	Unlicensed
V	Vegetarian	ANP	Alcohol not permitted
e-a-m-a-y-l	Eat as much as you like	BYO	Bring your own alcohol

St Austell

TAJ MAHAL

57 Victoria Road, Mount Charles, St Austell 01726 73716

'Spacious for two, raffia-screened alcoves may be a bit cramped for four. I've always liked it here. Menu covers all the usuals, and I've never had a bad meal in many years of visiting. Flavoursome, well cooked, nicely spiced dishes. Prices very reasonable, main dish portions enormous.' MW. Price check: Papadam 40p, CTM £6.95, Bombay potato £2.10, Pullao Rice £1.60. Hours: 12-2pm/6pm-12am. Stocks Cobra.

St Ives

RAJPOOT NEW ENTRANT

6 Gabriel Street, St Ives 01736 795301

'The quality of the food was high and the meal very tasty. Down point was the prices – quite high for an average Indian restaurant.' R&NT. Stocks Cobra.

Truro

BABA NEW ENTRANT BYO ALLOWED

32 Lemon Street, Truro 01872 262694

'The most elegant of all Truro Indian restaurants and the most expensive. By far the most interesting menu. Credit cards only accepted for amounts over £30. [Bad practice, isn't it, and nearly cost Baba its new listing?] Street level, bar and reception, attended by a sari-clad lady. Smoking and no-smoking rooms. Menu contains most of the usuals and more imaginative dishes. Wine list has a bottle of Haut Brion '86 – £275 – which I assume must be better than your average plonk, although we didn't try it! BYO allowed at £2 per bottle corkage [makes up for the credit card rubbish]. Started with Aubergine Puri £4.99 – half an aubergine, fried, topped with mild creamy mixture, raw chilli on top, cucumber and radish slices neatly arranged round the plate, very substantial and decorative. Onion Bhajia £2.35 (3) – light, crispy. Chicken Tikka Biryani £8.99 – excellent, ample, tasty chicken. Sag Aloo £4.49 – first class. Prices quite high, most expensive in Truro and considerably more than average in Cornwall. Can't complain about quality of food and decor – locals don't either – place quite full. Service a mixed bag.' MW. Price check: Papadam 60p, CTM £8.99, Pullao Rice £2.20. Hours: 12-3pm/5.30-11.30PM. Stocks Cobra.

County Index, see page 5 Town Index, see page 614
A to Z of the Curry Menu, page 41 Contributors Key, page 604

SHANAZ NEW ENTRANT

9A River Street, Truro 01782 262700

'Standard never varies, wouldn't travel 14 miles otherwise. Refurbished last year, comfortable chairs. £62.75 for three.' PW.

Wadebridge

BASH BAAGAN NEW ENTRANT

1a Molesworth Street, Wadebridge 01208 812500

Opened a year ago. Occupies prime position by the old bridge over the River Camel. Owned by the same people who own the Sagor in Launceston. Food overall was fairly average. Service efficient, portions adequate. A word of caution to future first time visitors: the toilets are situated downstairs, and the stairs start directly after the door marked "Toilets". Therefore, unless you are looking where you are going, it would be easy to open the door and fall Achar over Tikka to the bottom!' MW. [Maybe that's why its called Bash Baagan!] Stocks Cobra.

CUMBRIA

Area: Lake District
Population: 493,000
Adjacent Counties: Borders, D&G, Durham, Lancs, Yorks

Barrow-in-Furness

GOLDEN VILLAGE ©

36 Dalton Road, Barrow-in-Furness 01229 430133/430033

Owned and managed by Janet Chesherwith, head chef Aba Fateh Choudhury. The restaurant in two rooms seats 58. Price check: Papadam 45p, CTM £6.50, Pullao Rice £1.40, Peshwari Nan £1.70. Delivery: £10 minimum, Barrow area. Hours: 6pm-12am; closed Mon. Stocks Cobra.

©	Curry Club Discount	U	Unlicensed
V	Vegetarian	ANP	Alcohol not permitted
e-a-m-a-y-l	Eat as much as you like	BYO	Bring your own alcohol

MITHALI ©

252-254 Dalton Road, Barrow-in-Furness 01229 432166/431947

You give Evan Ahmed's 42-seater thumbs up for Chef Abida Choudhury. 'Excellent Thali dishes. Good selection of Biriani dishes – eight different. Curry Club members 10% discount and free bottle wine with the Kurzi Lamb (for four).' AY. Price check: Papadam 40p, CTM £5.50, Pullao Rice £1.45, Peshwari Nan £1.70. Delivery: £6.50 minimum, 10-mile radius. Hours: 12-2pm/5pm-12am (12.30am Fri. & Sat.). Stocks Cobra.

Bowness-on-Windermere

EMPEROR OF INDIA NEW ENTRANT

The Arcade, Crag Brow, Bowness-on-Windermere 015394 43991

Some interesting dishes include Banana Raitha £1.10 and Palak Nan £2.10. 'We ordered a prawn puree to start. Fresh – an even balance of spices so as not to spoil the taste of the prawns. The main course was equally well prepared and presented. Overall an excellent meal. £36 for 2 including a reasonably priced St Emilion.' DH. Price check: Papadam 60p (plain), 65p (spicy), CTM £8.95, Pullao Rice £1.90, Pickles/Chutney 50p each. Hours: 12-2pm/5.30-10.45pm (11.30pm on Fri. & Sat.). Stocks Cobra.

Carlisle

DHAKA TANDOORI ©

London Road, Carleton, Carlisle 01228 523855

Approaching junction 42 of the M6, on the edge of town, you'll find A Harid's 100-seater smart, up-market restaurant, with its marble-effect and chandeliers. Established in 1995, the 100-seater has car parking for 100 at rear and a new large front conservatory. 'Great stop-off if returning to England via M6. Lovely country setting just off motorway with pleasant conservatory tables overlooking main road. Comfortable seating and pleasant decor. Good, friendly service. Large portions of lovely food – Chicken Pasari – very unusual and reasonably priced. Much better than motorway services!' IB. [Say no more, Ian.] 'Consistently good. Try Chef M Ali's Kebab Kyberi, diced chicken in mild spices with fresh tomatoes, onions, served sizzling in iron karahi.' AY. House wine a very reasonable £5.95. Delivery: £12 minimum. Hours: 12-2pm/6pm-12am. Price check: Papadam 50p, CTM £5.95, Pullao Rice £1.55, Peshwari Nan £1.60, Lager £2.20 pint. Takeaway discount: £2 off every £12. Hours: 12-2pm/6pm-12am. Sun. 12pm-12am. Stocks Cobra.

COBRA GOOD CURRY GUIDE
County Index, see page 5 Town Index, see page 614
A to Z of the Curry Menu, page 41 Contributors Key, page 604

Cockermouth

TASTE OF INDIA ©

4-5 Hereford Ct, Main St, Cockermouth 01900 822880

F Rahman's 60-seater is divided into two rooms with a 44-seat private room. It's 'nicely decorated, and Chef NI Khan offers good choices. Judging by the number of takeaways being collected the place is very popular with the locals. All curries excellent, if slightly milder than usual. Excellent flavours/use of spices.' AY. Hours: 12-2.30pm/ 5.30pm-12am. Branches: Red Fort, Keswick, and Emperor of India, Bowness. Stocks Cobra.

Egremont

BALTI HAVEN NEW ENTRANT

8 Main Street, Egremont 01946 823186

'A most welcoming establishment. The chef Mr Mohammed Asadul Haque definitely knows his spices. I am particularly impressed by his vegetable Pullao Rice, a definite hint of the aromatics.' KD. Stocks Cobra.

Kendal

FLAVOURS OF INDIA

20 Blackhall Road, Kendal 01539 722711

Yaor Miah's 95-seater 'used to be a carpet warehouse. A huge water fountain in the centre of the restaurant refreshes the senses. Choice of dishes is bewildering. Every dish is good but many are outstanding, particularly Shahi Korma. Excellent Methi dishes. Thithir Frezi, quail marinated in herbs and spices and finished off in the clay oven, then cooked with minced meat, egg, tomatoes, onions, and capsicum, served in a hot sizzler.' AY. Stocks Cobra.

Keswick

MAHARAJAHS

6a Herries Thwaite, off Main Street, Keswick 01768 774799

Write off the pencil museum and lap up the lake, then curry on to Zahangir Ali's 56-seater, for Chef Mofiz Ali's formula delights. CTM is the most ordered dish. Takeaway menu 15% discount. Hours: 12-2pm/5.30pm-12am.

Penrith

CAGNEYS TANDOORI ©

17 King Street, Penrith 01768 867503

Established in 1987 by Messrs Imdabul (chef) and Fazul Haque (call me Hawk!). OK! Hawk manages the restaurant, so well patronised by local regulars that plans are under way to increase from 50 to 90 seats. 'Table immaculate, seating comfortable and staff courteous throughout. Lamb Masala came up trumps, encompassing a depth and range of flavours. Aloo Sag was mild and fragrant.' MR. 'Unusual decor, gold leaf wallpaper. Best Pathia.' AY. Takeaway 10% off. Hours: 12-2.30pm/6pm-12am. Stocks Cobra.

CHUINI'S NEW ENTRANT ©

19 King Street, Penrith 01768 866760

Established in 1998. Seats 70. Specials include: Exotic Balti. Price check: Papadam 40p, CTM £5.95, Pullao Rice £1.50, Peshwari Nan £1.50, Lager £2.50 pint. Takeaway: 10% discount. Delivery: £1.50 charge. Hours: 5pm-12am. Stocks Cobra.

Whitehaven

AKASH ©

3 Tangier Street, Whitehaven 01946 691171

Nurul Hoque's cooking attracts a loyal following. 'The food has much improved and the menu is more varied. This is now a curry house I would visit without worry. The staff are friendly and helpful but a bit on the shy side. Worthy of inclusion in the guide.' and 'Again, service was excellent, staff very friendly and helpful, food very tasty with good quantities. Only criticism of the Akash is that to use the toilet one has to climb some very old and narrow carpeted stairs that are pretty steep.' RE. Owners Abdul Karim and MK Rayman operate a customer loyalty scheme – 5% off the bill when dining in, and 10% off party bookings of 10 or more. Takeaway 20% discount. Delivery. Hours: 12-2.30pm/6pm-12am. Stocks Cobra.

ALI TAJ NEW ENTRANT

34 Tangier Street, Whitehaven 01946 693085

'Has recently been extended and is now a much roomier establishment. Still proving to be the most popular curry house in Whitehaven and is full most nights. There have been many changes of staff here but this does not seem to have affected Ali's too much (the present staff are just as daft on football as the last lot). Recent takeaways have included all the usual favourites and now the menu has increased to include more house specialities: Gata Bhuna, Chicken Cheese Kufta, Chooza Shashlick, Chooza Shabzi, Mutton Shashlick. Service is fast and efficient, food very good, and draft lager the best in town.' RE. And again: 'Two takeaways were first class with plenty of food crammed into the cartons. Good, quick, friendly service. Interesting to note that the Ali Taj never tries to compete with other establishments on price or cheap gimmicks. They rely on their reputation alone and it certainly works for them.' RE.

DERBYSHIRE

Area: North Midlands
Population: 975,000
Adjacent Counties: Cheshire, Leics, Greater Man, Notts, Staffs, S Yorks

Alfreton

NEW BENGAL NEW ENTRANT ©

3 King Street, Alfreton 01773 831620

Established in 1986, taken over by New Bengal Ltd in 1997, managed by F Ahmed. A cosy restaurant seating just 34 diners, decorated in cream with blue furnishings. Vegetable Thali £8.95 – Papadam, three vegetable curries, Stuffed Nan and Plain Rice. Delivery: 5-mile radius, £12 minimum. Licensed: lager £2.20 pint, 330ml Cobra £1.75, house wine £6.95. Price check: Papadam 50p, CTM £6.95, Pullao Rice £1.60, Peshwari Nan £2.15. Hours: 6pm-12am (1am on Sat.). Stocks Cobra.

SANAM NEW ENTRANT

50 King Street, Alfreton 01773 830690

'Well presented menu, good, self-confident, outgoing staff. Twelve dining – starters on the table within 10 minutes. Really excellent Chicken and Lamb Tikka/Jeera Lamb was well spiced with good flavour.' KM. Stocks Cobra.

©	Curry Club Discount	U	Unlicensed
V	Vegetarian	ANP	Alcohol not permitted
e-a-m-a-y-l	Eat as much as you like	BYO	Bring your own alcohol

Buxton

TAJ MAHAL

35 High Street, Buxton — **01298 78388**

Established in 1997, Mr Koyes Ahmed's Taj Mahal seats 50. It continues to be a popular local venue. 'We use it virtually once a week, since moving to Buxton. Favourites include Madras, Moglai and Jalfrezi, which are pretty hot! Two of us recently had the vegetarian set meal and after completely stuffing ourselves there was still sufficient left over for a light lunch the next day. Staff are young and friendly.' MR&MRS SM. Price check: Papadam 50p, CTM £5.60, Pullao Rice £1.30, Peshwari Nan £1.75, Lager £1.95 pint. Takeaway: 10% discount. Hours: 5-11.30pm. Stocks Cobra.

Castle Donnington

VILLAGE TANDOORI ©

43-45 Borough Street, Castle Donington — **01332 814455/853383**

Taken over in 1997 by Mohammed Abdul Basit. Seats 55 in two simply decorated dining rooms. Pakistani curries on the menu. Specials include: Balti Sp Cocktail. Delivery: £10 minimum, 5-mile radius. Hours: 6pm-12am.

Chesterfield

GULAB ©

207 Chatsworth Road, Brampton, Chesterfield — **01246 204612**

R Miah and A Rahman's Gulab seats 40 and serves formula curries.'Called on spec with my son after a football match at Halifax. 10% Curry Club discount agreed although I did not book previously. Fairly good all round standard curry house and inexpensive. Chicken Jalfrezi ultra hot – Thali strength. Very clean. Service good though busy (7.30 Sat night). Deserves inclusion in guide.' BP-D. Price check: Papadam 40p, CTM £5.95, Pullao Rice £1.60. Minimum charge £6. Hours: 6-11.45pm (12.45am on Fri. & Sat.).

ZAHID INDIAN NEW ENTRANT

57 Chatsworth Road, Chesterfield — **01246 558922**

Established in 1999. Seats 60. Price check: Papadam 40p, CTM £5.85, Pullao Rice £1.50, Peshwari Nan £1.65, Lager £1.90 pint. Takeaway: approximately 10% discount. Hours: 6pm-12am. Stocks Cobra.

COBRA GOOD CURRY GUIDE
County Index, see page 5 Town Index, see page 614
A to Z of the Curry Menu, page 41 Contributors Key, page 604

Derby

ABID TANDOORI BYO ©

7 Curzon Street, Derby 01332 293712/344786

Mohammed Ilyas' 90-seater serves Pakistani and Kashmiri curries. 'This particular evening the food was delicious. It always is, but tonight the dishes were really on form. The dishes are always very generous and the service is always quick and the waiters are helpful. It's comfortable but by no means up-class, just right.' NH, 'but you can BYO, £2.50 a cork.' Delivery: £15 minimum, 6-mile radius. Hours: 5.30pm-3am. Branches: Abid, Dale Road, Matlock. Abid Balti, Causley Road, Alfreton. Stocks Cobra.

SHABUZ BAGAN NEW ENTRANT

80-82 Osmaston Road, Derby 01332 296887

Established in 1997. Seats 100. Parking for 20 cars to rear, with CCTV. Specials include: Bangladeshi fish dishes cooked in traditional style. Price check: Papadam 40p, CTM £6.80, Pullao Rice £1.60, Peshwari Nan £1.90, Lager £2.50. Delivery: £10 minimum. Hours: 6pm-1am. Stocks Cobra.

Glossop

BULLS HEAD HOTEL NEW ENTRANT

102 Church Street, Old Glossop, Glossop 01457 853291

'Mahmood, the restaurant manager at this well-liked pub, has come from one of the top restaurants on Wilmslow Road, Manchester's Curry Canyon, and the food is absolutely first class. Booking is essential, as this establishment has a tremendous following all generated by word of mouth. As I write this in mid-July, the restaurant is already booked solid through the Christmas weeks.' RW.

Ilkeston

SHAH JAHAN ©

1 Awsworth Road, Ilkeston 0115 932 3036

First opened 1987, but taken over in 1994 by Abdul Aziz who is also the head chef, cooking curries and Baltis at his red-decorated 56-seater. Own car park. Takeaway: 10% discount. Free delivery: £25 minimum. Hours: 6pm-12.30am. Stocks Cobra.

Matlock Bath

ABID TANDOORI ©

129 Dale Road, Matlock Bath 01629 57400

Mohammed Bashir's 70-seater is in this delightful Peak District spa town, nestling on the River Derwent, with its many pleasant walks and even a cable car to take you to the top of the cliffs. Just the thing to work up an appetite for Chef Maroof's Pakistani and Kashmiri cooking. 'The Lamb Bhuna was huge and excellent. The rice was a little al dente and the Sag Aloo was a disappointment. Massive menu.' AGR. Delivery: £20 minimum, 5-mile radius. Hours: 6pm-12am (1am on Fri. & Sat.). Branches: Abid, Curzon Street, Derby. Abid Balti, Causley Lane, Alfreton. Stocks Cobra.

Ripley

SHEEZAN II ©

11 Church Street, Ripley 01773 747472

Opened in 1983, by N Hussain (head chef) and M Sharif (manager). Pakistani and North Indian-styled curries. Air-conditioned, 42-seater restaurant. Hours: 6pm-12am (1am weekends). Stocks Cobra.

Sandiacre

RAJPOOT BALTI HOUSE NEW ENTRANT

8 Station Road, Sandiacre 01159 491608

Established in 1993. Taken over by Umar Butt in 1998. Seats 42, parking for 30 behind restaurant. Price check: Papadam 40p, CTM £5.50, Pullao Rice £1.40, Peshwari Nan £1.80, Lager £2 pint. Takeaway: 10-15% discount. Delivery: £10 minimum, 5-mile radius. Hours: 6pm-12am/Fri. Sat. 6pm-1am. Stocks Cobra.

DEVON

Area: West Country
Population: 1,077,000
Adjacent Counties: Cornwall, Dorset, Somerset

Barnstaple

GANGES NEW ENTRANT

87 New Port Road, Barnstaple — 01271 374297

'Comfortable, warm, small restaurant, good decor, attentive staff, not bad value.' KM. Stocks Cobra.

Braunton

ROYAL BENGAL NEW ENTRANT

North Street, Braunton — 01271 817112

'Standard Indian – nothing special to report except service was quick, efficient and food was well presented. Even though it was obvious we were on holiday and therefore would not be regulars, six adults and two babies were made welcome.' SJ. Stocks Cobra.

Crediton

CREDITON TANDOORI NEW ENTRANT

137 High Street, Crediton — 01363 775548

Established in 1998. Seats 40. 'Attentive quick service without being overbearing. Garlic naan the best we have ever eaten.' TR. Price check: Papadam 30p, CTM £5.50, Pullao Rice £1.55, Peshwari Nan £1.85, Lager £2.70. Delivery: £10 minimum, 5-mile radius. Hours: 12-2.30/5.30-11.30pm; Sun. 12pm-12am. Stocks Cobra.

©	Curry Club Discount	**U**	Unlicensed
V	Vegetarian	**ANP**	Alcohol not permitted
e-a-m-a-y-l	Eat as much as you like	**BYO**	Bring your own alcohol

Exeter

GANDHI

7 New North Road, Exeter — **01392 272119**

'Remains reliable. Good-sized tables, pleasant atmosphere and friendly staff. Lamb Tikka Karahi a firm favourite. Chicken Patia in a dark, hot, sweet and sour sauce.' PJ. 'A real find, best food by far we've had in local Indians. Staff efficient and attentive, the Birianis especially tasty. Keep it in the guide!' CS.

GANGES NEW ENTRANT

156 Fore Street, Exeter — **01392 272630**

'Interesting-looking menu, but situated right in the City Centre and, if Friday night was anything to go by, would be absolutely packed. So didn't eat here.' MW. 'Our favourite, where they care for you with good food and good service.' ANON. Stocks Cobra.

TASTE OF RAJ NEW ENTRANT

106 Cowick Street, Exeter — **01392 213311**

Established in 1998. Price check: Papadam 40p, CTM £5.50, Pullao Rice £1.50, Peshwari Nan £1.50. Takeaway: 10% discount. Delivery: free, £15 minimum, 3-mile radius. Hours: 5.30-11.30pm. Stocks Cobra.

Ilfracombe

BOMBAY PALACE NEW ENTRANT ©

36 Green Close Road, Ilfracombe — **01271 862010**

Established in 1998. Seats 60. Competent formula curry house with no surprises. Specials include: Bombay Special Mosalla and Hydrabadi. Price check: Papadam 50p, CTM £5.25, Pullao Rice £1.75, Peshwari Nan £1.75, Lager £1.90 pint. Takeaway: 10% discount. Free delivery in local area, £10 minimum order. Hours: 5.30-11pm. Stocks Cobra.

RAJAH ©

5 Portland Street, Ilfracombe — **01271 863499**

First opened in 1985, Ralph Wild is the owner-chef here, assisted by his son James. Good street parking. The menu is short but comprehensive. A small restaurant, seating 28, decorated in red, with Indian ornaments. 'As regular eaters of Indian food for many years, we would thoroughly endorse your recommendation of this restaurant. The meal was unhurried, the staff were helpful, pleasant and knowledgeable. There was a good and unusual choice of menu, the food itself was excellent, and it represented very good value for money.' F&SF. 'I felt compelled to write to confirm the well-deserved listing of the above restaurant in your Guide. We visited on four out of six possible nights (during a week's holiday). Every dish was freshly prepared, authentic and the service was of the highest quality. Chicken Meghani Tandoori and Butter Chicken Tikka were favourites.' SH. Specials include: Kenya and Mombasa curries, Chittagong and Calcutta curries. Price check: Papadam 40p, CTM £4.20, Pullao Rice £1.95, Peshwari Nan £1.55, Lager £2.40 pint. Delivery: free locally, £13.50 minimum order. Hours: 6-10.30pm; open bank holidays. Stocks Cobra.

Newton Abbot

EASTERN EYE NEW ENTRANT

120 Queen Street, Newton Abbot 01626 352364

A busy, popular restaurant. 'The food is normally of a high standard although beware the sit-down-late (pub closing time) service – food quality drops in the belief that beer will affect your tastebuds. [Standard advice, I'd say!] The garlic chicken is wicked.' JM. Stocks Cobra

PASSAGE TO INDIA NEW ENTRANT

137 Queen Street, Newton Abbot 01626 688443

'A good restaurant and fairly crowded for early Sunday evening. Despite this the service was good and food excellent. Tandoori Chicken Shorati £6.10, Pullao Rice £1.85, Chutney and Pickles 35p, Nan £1.30. Still had that awful Carlsberg on draught, but had a pint of Tetley Bitter £2.30. Should be in the Guide.' BP-D. 'Food although not brilliant to start with, is improving all the time. A nightcap and a carnation for the ladies on the house, rounds the evening off nicely. Reasonably priced.' JM. 25% discount for collected takeaways. Price check: Papadam 35p, CTM £6.10, Pullao Rice £1.85. Hours: 12-2pm/5.30-11.30pm, (12am on Fri. & Sat., 11pm on Sun.).

STAR BALTI TAKEAWAY NEW ENTRANT

114 Queen Street, Newton Abbot 01626 335255

'Pleasant. Family-run. Good selection of dishes. Very tasty. Different from norm. Excellent fluffy Pullao Rice and an atypical korma not to be missed.' JM.

Plymouth

BABA INDIAN NEW ENTRANT

134 Vauxhall Street, Plymouth 01752 250677

Established by and named after EH 'Baba' Laskar, founder of Devon's Ganges chain, the 84-seat restaurant is decorated with oak panelling, Indian silk cloth paintings and brass ornaments. 'Comfortable, smart, with consistently excellent food.' SH. Menu contains all the old favourites, plus a host of unusuals. Shahi Akbari Chicken and Chicken Kahlia (both about £5) are particular favourites, presented in copper pots. There is a 9-course monthly banquet £9.95, pre-booked only. 'Good, but not ambitious enough for the discerning palate.' SH. Price check: Papadam 45p, CTM £6.95, Pullao Rice £1.85, Peshwari Nan £1.95. Delivery: £10 minimum, 4-mile radius. Hours: 5.30pm-12am; Sun. 12pm-12am, family buffet available 12-5.30pm. Stocks Cobra.

EASTERN EYE NEW ENTRANT

57 North Street, The Barbican, Plymouth 01752 262948

'Staff very helpful and friendly. Cosy alcoves with etched partitions. Nice range of dishes, some out of the ordinary. Helpings a little on the mean side. Food very good, but avoid the daals and bhajis – thin and watery.' R&NT. Stocks Cobra.

JAIPUR PALACE NEW ENTRANT ©

146 Vauxhall Street, The Barbican, Plymouth 01752 668711

Established in 1994 by Syed Abdul Wahid. The two-roomed restaurant seats 70. Chef Rumel Ahmad's cooking is 'recommended to anyone who enjoys quality food in a comfortable atmosphere. My wife says that no one cooks a lamb passanda like the Jaipur.' LC. 'I can think of no better restaurant to put in your guide for the best curry I have had the pleasure to taste.' JK. 'The menu was a good mix of all curries. The quality of food, service and comfort were all above excellent.' J&K. Price check: Papadam 50p, CTM £6.95, Pullao Rice £2.10, Peshwari Nan £2.10, Lager £2.30 pint. Delivery: free within 10-mile radius. Hours: 12-2pm/5.30pm-12am. Stocks Cobra.

KURBANI RE-ENTRANT

1 Tavistock Place, Sherwell Arcade, Plymouth 01752 266778

We are pleased to restore the Kurbani to the *Guide*, following a plethora of locals extolling its virtues. We point out that it was others who criticised the Kurbani (and criticised ourselves for recommending them – blaming the messenger). Mr Tarafder specialises in 'home-style' Indian cooking, and we point out that since this is not the formula norm, it doesn't suit everyone. But it does suit others: 'The food we find to be of excellent quality and reasonably priced, their range of menu suits the whole family (grandchildren to grandparents), including myself, a vegetarian. Staff are always friendly and the service is first class. Certainly one of the best that I visit.' PB. 'Not only is the food of high standard and very tasty and well presented, but it is also very reasonably priced. You can call me a very satisfied customer.' JT. 'I wish to show my appreciation for the superb range of foods provided by the Kurbani. The food is excellent and is only matched by the quality of the service provided by the friendly staff.' RT. 'I go to India regularly and love Indian food. Whenever in Plymouth I eat at the Kurbani where I enjoy excellent curries etc. I have done this for many years and have always been treated courteously and made most welcome.' JB. 'Excellent food and excellent service. We always recommend business friends and visitors to the Kurbani, as we can guarantee that the customers are very well looked after, and the prices are very reasonable.' P&LG. Mr Tarafder was disappointed to be removed from our TOP 100. Should the Kurbani be restored to that list? Stocks Cobra.

TAJ INDIAN ©

49 Mayflower Street, Plymouth 01752 669485

Syed Lutfus Rahman's 80-seat Taj is one of the 'old hands' of Plymouth, here since 1971. Such experience always tells. GMO talks of 'a lovely meal with really helpful waiters'. Delivery: £12 minimum, 5-mile radius. Hours: 12-2.30pm/5.30pm-12am; Sat. & Sun. open all day. Stocks Cobra.

VEGGIE PERRINS V

97 Mayflower Street, Plymouth 01752 252888

Despite the silliest name, you'll like it. At least it's obviously vegetarian. 'First impressions could put you off a little – but go for the food, not the decor, and take your own ambience. Recommend the veg tikka and madras and the aloo palau. Excellent value for money. Service was a little slow, but very friendly.' TI. Hours: 12-2.30pm (Sat. 3.30pm)/5-11pm; closed Sun.

Tavistock

GANGES

9 West Street, Tavistock 01822 616731

The popular Ganges was taken over in 1996 by N Miah. Seats 56 in two rooms, decorated with Indian mirror paintings. 'On arrival at 9pm (a Saturday) only two other tables were taken, however more arrived during the evening. No doubt things change during the summer months. Standard dishes plus some interesting variations new to me. Onion Bhaji and Chicken Chat were good, Garlic Murug was well balanced between imparting the garlic flavour without it being overpowering, and Chicken Lonkapiaza was very tasty. Service was good, friendly and efficient – my wife found a piece of plastic in her salad accompanying her Bhaji, and the waiter was most apologetic when he noticed it while clearing the plates, and refused to charge for the Bhaji despite our reassuring him that we weren't complaining.' MW. Price check: Papadam 40p, CTM £6.05, Pullao Rice £1.80, Peshwari Nan £1.75. Takeaway 20% off. Hours: 5.30-11.30pm. Stocks Cobra.

DORSET

Area: South West
Population: 698,000
Adjacent Counties: Devon, Hants, Soms, Wilts

Bournemouth

BENGAL PLAZA NEW ENTRANT

728 Christchurch Road, Boscombe, Bournemouth 01202 399945

Established in 1996, taken over by Moynul Hoque Ali in 1999. Seats 56. Specials include: Chicken Bonduhk with Pullao Rice £9.25. Price check: Papadam 45p, CTM £8.25, Pullao Rice £1.90, Peshwari Nan £2.10, Lager £2.40 pint. Takeaway: 20% discount. Delivery: £20 minimum, 3-mile radius. Hours: 12-2pm/6pm-12am. Stocks Cobra.

COBRA GOOD CURRY GUIDE
County Index, see page 5 Town Index, see page 614
A to Z of the Curry Menu, page 41 Contributors Key, page 604

BOMBAY PALACE NEW ENTRANT

286 Wimbourne Road, Winton, Bournemouth 01202 515729

First opened in 1989, taken over in 1996 by Mahmood Miah. Seats 46. Price check: Papadam 50p, CTM £6.50, Pullao Rice £1.80, Peshwari Nan £1.90, Lager £2.80. Takeaway: 20% discount. Delivery: 5-mile radius. Hours: 12-2.30pm/6pm-12am. Stocks Cobra.

BOURNEMOUTH TANDOORI ©

8 Holdenhurst Road, Lansdowne, Bournemouth 01202 296204

Shuab Ahmed's 50-seat restaurant, is 'tastefully decorated in apricot and green. Papadam and pickles arrived without asking within minutes. Started with a Madouri Kebab, new to me, diced lamb, tomato, cucumber, etc, succulent and tasty, with mint sauce in a jug to pour on, how sensible! Followed by one of my favourites, Chicken Jalfrezi and rice, bread and Mushroom Bhaji. I rate this ten out of ten. Service pleasant and swift. One of the best in Bournemouth.' MS. Specials include: Delight, cooked with Grand Marnier, fresh cream, almonds. Hours: 12-2.30pm/6pm-12am.

THE EYE OF THE TIGER ©

207 Old Christchurch Road, Bournemouth 01202 780900

'Opened in 1992 by James Dudley and Ramjan Ali. Managed by Anum Miah with Showkat Ali in the kitchen. Seats 80. 'We were a bit concerned that it was empty at 7pm on a Saturday night, but we dived in to find a pleasant restaurant with helpful waiters. It was the best curry we'd had for many a long month. I was amused to see a machine in the men's toilet selling curry-flavoured condoms! The meal (without this particular item) cost us £25 including four drinks, and by the time we left, it was packed.' CS. JS says her 'mind boggles. Imagine a Phal-flavoured version!' Really, Jane, behave yourself – this is a respectable publication! Price check: Papadam 45p, CTM £8.35, Pullao Rice £1.75. Hours: 12-2pm/6pm-12am. Stocks Cobra.

Christchurch

STARLIGHT ©

54 Bargates, Christchurch 01202 484111/470999

Ian Clasper's and Abdul Hai's eye-catching, popular Starlight is decorated with hand-painted murals. Hours: 12-2pm/6pm-12am. Stocks Cobra.

Dorchester

RAJPOOT NEW ENTRANT ©

43 High West Street, Dorchester 01305 260033

Fully air-conditioned. Established in 1981. Seats 80 in a seventeenth-century building. Specials include: duck dishes, Shahi Birianis £7.50. Price check: Papadam 50p, CTM £6.25, Pullao Rice £1.80, Peshwari Nan £1.80, Lager £2.10 pint. Takeaway: 10% discount. Hours: 12-2.30pm/6pm-12am. Stocks Cobra.

Poole

BENGALI SPICES RENAMED

69 High Street, Poole 01202 676330

'Used to be the Raj Poot, one of Dorset's finest [and a *Guide* TOP 100 subsequently altogether delisted] but has recently been taken over. It is splendid. Extensive menu including most standard dishes and interesting specialities. Shahi Mogli and Mogali Chicken (whole spring chicken dishes, cooked with almonds and moderate spices, minced meat and Pullao Rice) are satisfyingly exotic. Wide-ranging choice of mutton curries. Chicken Butter Special especially recommended. Waiters friendly, service quick.' RG. 'Parking is a nightmare. Small and a little shabby, but the service and cuisine was excellent.' MB.

THE GATE OF INDIA ©

54-56 Commercial Road, Lower Parkstone, Poole 01202 717061

Messrs Choudhurys' Gate, established in 1993, seats 80 in two rooms and regularly attracts praise: 'Welcoming staff, impressive service. Since renovations, the premises are now very comfortable and cosy yet spacious. Business is brisk and even midweek you may well have to book. Busy on weekday evenings and packed to the ceiling on Saturdays. When I talk to the customers, I am impressed by the numbers who regularly come here from quite a way – Christchurch, Wareham, Wimborne, etc – because it's worth the trip. Interesting range of dishes, generous servings. High standard of cuisine at reasonable prices. Mustard Chicken/Lamb, Razala Chicken/Lamb, Tandoori King Prawn Massala and Jeera Chicken are outstanding. At the Gate of India you are among friends who you know will look after you. Hearing us plan my birthday dinner, they offered to do us a special and prepared a Kurzi Lamb for the event – it was out of this world. Marinated for at least 24 hours, it absorbed all the mysteries of the Sub

Continent. Superb Sunday Buffets and Monday Balti Nights. The restaurant has been tireless in the causes of various charities, both international and local. They recently gave a lunch for children from a local home and have earned the personal thanks of the Indian High Commissioner.' RG. 'Extraordinarily good Indian restaurant. Mustard Chicken (highly original dish, spicy and full without being fierce) and Mojlish are wonderful. An additional reason for visiting a very pleasant part of England.' JS. 'A memorable lunch. I wish I could remember the names of the dishes we had, but I will never forget the lunch – all I can say is wonderful, wonderful, wonderful. A perfect dinner for a perfect English day. How I wish I could have taken a supply of curry back home.' MS. Price check: Papadam 45p, CTM £6.85, Pullao Rice £1.40, Peshwari Nan £1.60, Lager £2.30 pint. Takeaway: 10% discount. Hours: 12-2.30pm/6pm-12am.

MOONLIGHT ©

9 Moor Road, Broadstone, Poole 01202 605234

A Malik's restaurant seats 80, with a 30-seat function room. 'Strongly recommend a visit. No Balti but excellent food, including very interesting specials.' JL. 'Good staff, food excellent.' CC. Mr Malik tells us of a group of customers who visit five times a week. We're still waiting to hear who they are! Declare yourselves and write in! Hours: 12-2pm/6pm-12am.

RAJASTHAN TOP 100

127 Pennhill Avenue, Poole 01202 718966

Run by Kamal Mohammed (who is also in charge of the kitchen), the restaurant offers cuisine from Mohammed's native Rajasthan as well as standard high-street favourites. 'Tasteful and very spacious, napkins are of top quality, damask. There is a spacious, well-stocked bar. Tandoori meals are all very good. Shashlik and Tava Murg are blissful. Sabji Korai, green chillies and ginger, splendid experience. Chilli Chicken I had here will rank as one of the finest curry meals I have ever eaten, full, rich, spicy with a kick like a howitzer. We enjoyed a memorable evening. My wife's Rajasthani Tava Murg – a dry curry, stir-fried marinated chicken garnished with cheese (£7.50) – was exotic, fragrant and delicious. My nephew had a splendid rich Lamb Madras Curry and my Chicken Biryani was out of this world – not the usual faked-up dish with cooked rice and a few bits of chicken, but the genuine slow-cooked classic regal dish of India. All the vegetables, including the Bindhi (£2.20), are fresh. The waiters are charming, helpful, amiable and obliging without being obsequious. Value for money. Extremely impressive.' 'General tone is highly sophisticated. I would especially praise Rajasthan

Dakana – chicken drumsticks, marinated in yoghurt, spices and garnished with fried onion. Brilliant Tandoori Mixed Grill. Sabzi Pathia, hot and sour vegetables, laced with chillies and lemon, lingers in my memory. Range of different rices, coconut, lemon, mushroom, pullao and beautiful breads.' JL. 'Bill of fare is unusual, the service is exemplary and the standard is consistently very high. The Rajasthan is where good curries go when they die.' RG. 'Appears to be quickly establishing a strong reputation in the locality, and is often busy mid week. Booking recommended. Starters fairly standard, but main menu is where the specialities are, such as Zafrani, Tava, Kazana. One of my favourites is the Kebab Cocktail. Well worth a visit.' JL. Remains in our TOP 100. Stocks Cobra.

TAJ MAHAL 2 NEW ENTRANT ©

38 High Street, Poole 01202 677315

Established in 1975. Recently taken over by A Rahman in 1999. Originally called the Prince of India. Seats 52. Ample parking opposite NCP. Specials include: Asri Gost, Badami, Makani, Gost Kalyani, Morisa. Price check: Papadam 55p, CTM £6.40, Pullao Rice £1.70, Peshwari Nan £1.75, Lager £2.90 pint. Takeaway: 10% discount. Hours: 12-2.30pm/6pm-12am. Stocks Cobra.

TANDOORI NIGHTS ©

50 High Street, Poole 01202 679712

Established in 1995 by AH Choudhury. Seats 100 in two rooms. House specials: Madras Sall Samba £2.25 – vegetables with lentils in Madras curry sauce. Persian Chicken Biriani £6.00 – enveloped with omelette. Takeaway: 10% discount. Price check: Papadam 50p, CTM £7.50, Pullao Rice £1.60, Peshwari Nan £1.80, Lager £2.30 pint, House wine £7.60 bottle. Hours: 12-2.30pm/6pm-12am. Stocks Cobra.

Sherbourne

RAJPOOT ©

The House of the Steps, Half Moon St, Sherborne 01935 812455

Owned by Mizanur Rahman, managed by Fajul Hoque with Abdul Kussus in the kitchen, the spacious restaurant has lots of traditional tapestry and upholstery, seats for 58 in two rooms. Specials include Rui, Pomfret and Ayre Jalfrezi. Bangladeshi fish, 'all very good and generous. Shatkora, a tangy Bengali citrus fruit is used, when available, in chicken, meat or prawn.

Service very slow. Onion Bhaji awful, stodgy and lukewarm. Replacement the same but hot. Brinjal Bhaji absolutely wonderful, ingredients chopped very fine, no sauce, no tomatoes, superb flavour, nearly had a second helping. Butter Chicken marvellous and generous. Garlic Nan very good.' HC. Hours: 12-2.30pm/6-11.30pm. Branch: Akash Takeaway, 147, Wareham Road, Corfu Mullen, Wimbourne.

Wareham

RAJPOOT NEW ENTRANT

39 North Street, Wareham 01929 554603/554792

'All in all a good standard high street fully licensed curry house serving formula curries. Food and drinks order taken in the reception area before we were seated. Standard Popadoms with Pickles. Onion Bhajis nicely spiced but a little greasy. Chicken Chat lacked the usual bite but quite tasty. Prices average, portions sufficient, service efficient. Chicken Shatkora £4.80 – the piece of fruit I tasted on it's own was suspiciously like lime to me [*see* **A to Z of the Menu** page 46], but lent an interesting sharpness, excellent tikka chicken, very enjoyable. Chicken Dhansak £4.80 – good, flavoursome, hot to set tongue tingling. Aloo Gobi £2.70 – very good, al dente potato and cauliflower, just right! Stodgy Chapati £1.00. Efficient service, portions good, prices average.' MW. Good to see Bombay Duck 90p. Price check: Papadam 50p, CTM £7.00, Pullao Rice £1.90, Peshwari Nan £2.00. Hours: 12-2.30pm/6-11.30pm.

Weymouth

BALTI HOUSE

24 Commercial Road, Weymouth 01305 783515

100-seater opened in 1994, owned and managed by Shalim Abdul. Ample parking. Recent extension. Chef Abdul Shahid cooks Bangladeshi-style curries and Balti dishes. 'The mangoes were great.' R&CP. 'Over several years, we have been impressed by consistently high standard of service and cuisine.' M&JH. 'Lively spicy food, perfectly cooked, sensitive service.' J&JS. Price check: (unchanged since last *Guide*) Papadam 50p, CTM £6.90, Pullao Rice £1.90, Peshwari Nan £2.20, Lager £2.30 pint. Takeaway: 10% discount. Delivery: 3-mile radius. Hours: 12-2pm/5.30-11.30pm. Stocks Cobra.

COUNTY DURHAM

Area: North East
Population: 610,000
Adjacent Counties: Cumbria, Northumberland, Tyne & Wear, N Yorkshire

Bishop Auckland

THE KING'S BALTI NEW ENTRANT ©

187 Newgate Street, Bishop Auckland 01388 604222/605222

Owned by Mohammed Boshir Ali Hussan. Baltis and Bangladeshi curries on the menu. Chutneys and Pickles 50p a portion but if you buy a jar from an assortment they are £1.90 a jar – brilliant idea! Price check: Papadam 40p, CTM £4.80, Pullao Rice £1.45, Peshwari Nan £1.25. Hours: 5pm-12am (11.30pm on Sun.).

Chester-Le-Street

GOLDEN GATE TANDOORI NEW ENTRANT

11 South Burns Road, Chester-Le-Street 0191 388 2906

Established in 1993. Seats 45. Ample parking to front. House specials: Kaleeya Beef or Chicken £6.50 – hot cooked with roast potatoes, marinated in yoghurt. Sylhet Beef or Chicken £7.00 – strongly spiced, dry with eggs and tomatoes. Price check: Papadam 50p, CTM £4.80, Pullao Rice £1.50, Peshwari Nan £1.30. Takeaway: approximately 10% discount. Delivery: £10 minimum, 6-mile radius. Hours: 12-2pm/6pm-12am. Stocks Cobra.

Darlington

SHAPLA ©

192 Northgate, Darlington 01325 468920

Established in 1980, SA Khan's green and beige 80-seat restaurant has two large trees and engraved glass divisions, with a private room seating 60. 'Brilliant.' PJ. 'Excellent.' DMC. Hours: 12-2pm/6pm-12am; closed Fri. lunch. Stocks Cobra.

SPICE GARDEN NEW ENTRANT

112 Parkgate, Darlington 01325 369512

'Cosy restaurant catering for theatre goers. Nicely decorated, large mirrors. Good friendly service and varied menu. Large portions of excellent Chicken Patia and Mushroom Rice with complimentary side dish. Superb, well worth it.' IB.

Durham

RAJPOOTH TANDOORI NEW ENTRANT

80 Claypath Durham 0191 386 1495

'On a trip from Southampton, my husband popped in here for a takeaway. Service prompt and friendly, with Bombay Mix to nibble while waiting. Chilli Chicken was hot and spicy, naan bread was fresh and fluffy. This restaurant definitely warrants an entry in future editions.' CC.

Stanley

MONJU TANDOORI ©

33 Park Road, South Moor, Stanley 01207 283259/239172

Established in 1987 by Ala Miah, who is also the manager. Cooking by Moyz Uddin. A small 30-seat two-room restaurant. Delivery: £10 minimum, 8-mile radius. Hours: 12-2pm/6pm-12am. Stocks Cobra.

Stockton-on-Tees

THE ROYAL BENGAL ©

Prince Regent Street, Stockton-on-Tees 01642 674331

'Formula curry house, marginally better than the rest.' PT. Stocks Cobra.

ESSEX

Area: Home Counties, (east of London)
Population: 1,605,000
Adjacent Counties: Cambs, Herts, Kent, London, Suffolk

Part of Essex was absorbed by Greater London in 1965. We note affected towns with the letters GL.

Basildon

ASIA SPICE NEW ENTRANT

Cranes Farm Road, Basildon 01268 273787

'Opened around Xmas 98, converted small factory unit so plenty of parking. There is a Goan fish section of the menu and fish dish we had was excellent. Worth at least one visit for novelty value.' SJ. Stocks Cobra.

Benfleet *(includes Thundersley)*

MUMTAZ MAHAL RE ENTRANT ©

10 Essex Way, Benfleet 01268 751707

Opened in 1977, Abdur Rahid's Mumtaz is well respected and well liked. It has a large car park adjacent, and inside its 90 seats are split over two floors; a cosy atmosphere. It's all standard stuff, with every variation you can imagine on chicken, lamb, prawns and vegetables, and it's all done 'sumptuously' says IDB. Stocks Cobra.

TANDOORI PARLOUR

61 Hart Road, Thundersley, Benfleet 01268 793786

'Excellent curry buffet. Chicken Rougan quite nice though the chicken was very dry. Fairly pleasant meal but I have to say I was disappointed after the review in your guide. Music too loud to hold a conversation (7.30pm, Tuesday).' CF. 'My favourite restaurant in Thundersley. Food and service is as good as ever, with the menu extended to include Bangla choices, and Indian fish and game dishes, which makes choosing a dish an even longer task. Bangla Sag Gosht was delicious. Game dishes include ostrich, duck and venison. Shah and crew now do a buffet Monday to Thursday. Huge! About 40 dishes to choose from. I highly recommend this restaurant.' PE. Stocks Cobra.

Braintree

CURRY PALACE ©

28 Fairfield Road, Braintree 01376 320083

Established in 1975 by MA Noor. His restaurant seats 52 diners; warm, modern interior with framed canvas art imported from Bangladesh. House specials: Balti Chicken Tikka and Chicken Dhansak. Takeaway: 10% discount. Hours: 5.30-11pm; closed Mon.

Canvey Island

EVEREST TANDOORI NEW ENTRANT

76 High Street, Canvey Island 01268 682695

Established in 1988. Recently refurbished. Delivery: £7 minimum, anywhere in Canvey Island. Price check: Papadam 50p, CTM £5.95, Pullao Rice £1.55, Peshwari Nan £1.80. Hours: 5.30pm-12am.

Chadwell Heath GL

ESSENCE OF THE EAST

1039 High Road, Chadwell Heath 020 8598 1209

'Friendly, laid back service. Wonderful fish curry, better than Brick Lane.' IB

Chelmsford

(includes Great Baddow and Writtle)

BENGAL BLUES SHAFIQUE

30 The Green Writtle, Chelmsford 01245 422228

Mr MA Shafique has added 'Bengal Blues' to the name. Has been refurbished in a modern style. Three separate areas: lounge/bar for drinks and snacks, informal dining for Indian sandwiches – Chicken Tikka, Spicy Prawn etc – and formal dining for the house specials. It's a mile or three out of town and is in 'beautiful surroundings.' JT. 'Elegant, well decorated, large restaurant. Sunday buffet: good selection of food with fair pricing.' PEH. Seats 180. House specials: Salmon Dhaka £4.95 – fresh salmon rolled in spices, cooked in the tandoor. Tandoori Paneer Ka Sula £3.25 – home-made cheese, flavoured with mint and served with pickles. Jessore £10.95 – barbecued pepper lamb chops. Stocks Cobra.

TAJ MAHAL NEW ENTRANT

6 Baddow Road, Chelmsford 01245 259618

'Comfortable seating for 60. Standard menu with all usuals on show. Business lunch £5.95 – fairly crowded, food average high street formula. Onion Bhajias £1.65 – four reasonably sized with salad. Tandoori Chicken Wings £2.30 – generous, very tasty. Chicken Dopiaza £3.40 – bland. Chicken Korma £3.40 – very light, creamy coconut. Portions, prices and service average.' MW. Look out for Taj Mahal Butter Chicken £5.25 – cooked with white wine – scrumptious! Price check: Papadam 40p, CTM £4.55, Pullao Rice £1.50. Hours: 12 to 2.30 and 5.30 to 12. Sunday 1 to 12.

Clacton-on-Sea

BALTI HOUSE NEW ENTRANT

23 Spring Road, St Osyth, Clacton 01255 822224

Established in 1992, seats 48. Takeaway: 10% discount. Delivery: 4-mile radius. Price check: Papadam 50p, CTM £7.95, Pullao Rice £2, Peshwari Nan £1.90, Lager £2.30 pint. Hours: 12-2.30pm/ 6pm-12am. Stocks Cobra.

EAST INDIA TAKEAWAY

182 Old Road, Clacton-on-Sea 01255 436445

MA Salam's 'takeaway portions are generous. Lamb Tikka Vindaloo £4.25, hot and tasty. Only disappointment was the Nan, slightly overdone.' LG. Established in 1990. Delivery: £10.50 minimum, local. Price check: Papadam 40p, CTM £4.95, Pullao Rice £1.40, Peshwari Nan £1.50. Hours: 5-11.30pm.

Colchester

AKASH NEW ENTRANT

40 St Botolphs Street, Colchester 01206 578791

The name changed from POLASH with the advent of a new owner in May 1998. 'Waiters friendly and helpful. Food good and generous portions.' NDS.

BALTI KING NEW ENTRANT

18 Barrack Street, Colchester 01206 505151

Formerly the Churchill Arms Pub, now transformed to a 50 cover Indian restaurant by Ali Laeque. Chef Kalam Miah.

SAGARMATHA GURKHA NEW ENTRANT (RENAMED)

2 St Botolphs Circus, Colchester 01206 579438

Established in 1999. Formerly called Oriental House. Seats 42. Specialities include: traditional Nepalese 'village' meal (£9.95), the most unusual dish being Shanjali Kukhura (chicken marinated in ginger, green chilli, herbs and spinach). Two large car parks with CCTV in front and rear. Takeaway: 10% discount. Delivery: £15, 5-mile radius. Price check: Papadam 50p, CTM £5.95, Pullao Rice £2.60. Hours: 12-2pm/5.30-11.30pm. Stocks Cobra.

SPICE OF INDIA NEW ENTRANT

23b London Road, Colchester 01206 543355

Established in 1997. Takeaway: 10% discount. Delivery: £10, 5-mile radius. Price check: Papadam 40p, CTM £5.75, Pullao Rice £1.60, Peshwari Nan £1.50. Hours: 5-11.30pm.

Epping

RAJ NEW ENTRANT

75 High Street, Epping 01992 572193

Mumin Ali tells us his 40-seater is 'beautifully decorated with artificial plants with cosiness and elegance'. Chef Abdul Ali cooks formula curries. 'Recently redecorated, tastefully done. Good quality food.' SR. Price check: Papadam 45p, CTM £6.95, Pullao Rice £1.75, Peshwari Nan £1.75. Delivery: £10 minimum, 5-mile radius. Hours: 12-2.30pm/6pm-12am. Stocks Cobra.

Halstead

HALSTEAD TANDOORI NEW ENTRANT

73 Head Street, Halstead 01787 476271

Established in 1977 by Mr Abdur Rahman. Seats 34. Specials: Chicken Tikka Bhuna £5.95. Chicken & Lamb Fried Rice £2.50. Price check: Papadam 40p, CTM £5.95, Pullao Rice £1.60. Hours: 12-2pm/6-11pm. Stocks Cobra.

Heybridge

HEYBRIDGE TANDOORI NEW ENTRANT ©

5 Bentalls Centre, Heybridge 01621 858566

Abdul Rofik, Abdul Hannan and Nazrul Islam's 70-seater, decorated in bright colours with blue tablecloths, pink napkins, has a non-smoking room. The centre has ample 24hr security-guarded car parking facilities. 'Excellent. Everything well presented, fish specials were superb, attentive service. Four non-regular curry eaters have become converted.' SJ. Fish specials include Chandpuri Hilsha, Boal, Ayre and large Chingri (prawns). Price check: Papadam 50p, CTM £5.95, Pullao Rice £1.60. Minimum charge £7.95. Set meal £7.95. Delivery: £10 minimum, 3-mile radius. Hours: 12-2.30pm/6-11.30pm (Sat. to 12am.). Stocks Cobra.

Hockley

MADRAS AND SPICE NEW ENTRANT

200 Main Road, Hawkwell, Hockley 01702 207188

'Food very good, thoroughly enjoyed, prices very reasonable, fairly standard menu with a few extras.' PH, VO, Essex. Price check: Papadam 40p, CTM £6.50, Pullao Rice £1.30. Hours: 5.30-11.30pm. Stocks Cobra.

Hornchurch GL

TASTE OF BENGAL ©

194 High Street, Hornchurch 01708 477850

'Decor very swish and food surpassed expectations. The staff were really helpful and didn't mind us taking nearly three hours over our meal on a busy evening.' PW. Stocks Cobra.

Ilford GL

(inc Gants Hill, Goodmayes and Seven Kings)

CURRY EMPORIUM NEW ENTRANT

597 Cranbrook Road, Gants Hill, Ilford 020 8550 7429

'Probably worth inclusion in the guide. Good standard Bangladeshi curries. Served a dish not on menu, Vegetable Pricy, after Onion Bhajias which were just how I like them, flat, well-cooked and crispy.' DS. Stocks Cobra.

CURRY SPECIAL TOP 100 ©

2 Greengate Pde, Horns Rd, Newbury Pk, Ilford 020 8518 3005

Family-run by GL and Paul Luther, Punjabi Kenyan Asians as are their relations, the Southall Anands (*see* Madhu's Brilliant, Middlesex), resulting in a different menu from that at the formula curry house. This is the real taste of the Punjab – savoury, powerful, delicious and satisfying, and as near to Punjabi home food as you'll get in Britain. The family signature dishes are Karai Mexican Mixed Vegetables, and the renowned Butter Chicken, Jeera Chicken and Chilli Chicken. A full portion for four is £12-13. Half-portion £6.50-7. These are starters, and are huge. And the fun is to go in large parties and share each of these. That's the way the local Asians enjoy it, leaving lots of room and lots of choice for the main course. Clues to the Luthers' Kenyan background is also in the menu. Mogo Chips are fried cassava, £3 and Tilipa Masala is an African fish curry, starter £3, main £6.50.Try the Kenyan Tusker lager. 'Food brilliant, authentic and interesting. Service quite slow but well worth the wait. Definitely not run of the mill. Worth the TOP 100 status.' SJ. For the record here's our standard price check: Papadam 40p, CTM £6.50, Pullao Rice £1.50. Remains in our TOP 100. Hours: 12-2.30pm Tues.-Fri./6pm-12am daily; closed Mon.

DIDAR TAKEAWAY RE ENTRANT

686 Green Lane, Goodmayes, Ilford 020 8598 2429

'My favourite local takeaway. Fine curry dishes – all very good quality. In 98 GCG but not in 99 – what happened?' IB. Perhaps because the proprietor didn't send back his form and we didn't receive any favourable reports from diners like yourself!

HAWA BENGAL NEW ENTRANT ©

530 High Road, Seven Kings, Ilford 020 8599 9778

Mr Bashir Ullah is the owner-chef here, while Mr Hudda Kabir runs front of house. 'We visit regularly and find the staff very helpful, pleasant and knowledgeable and have sampled many of their dishes. We have also been guinea-pigs on occasions and had the opportunity to try new and tasty dishes not yet on the menu. Our favourites are Sag Chicken, CTM, Balti Chicken, Chicken and Mushroom Biriani and especially the Dilkush Special.' AN. Price check: Papadam 50p, CTM £5.80, Pullao Rice £1.50. Minimum charge £8. Hours: evenings only.

HOT SPICE TAKEAWAY NEW ENTRANT ©

36 Woodford Avenue, Gants Hill, Ilford 020 8551 6144

Formerly Tandoori Express. Owned by Mr A Rahman, since 1999. Private car parking for six cars. Delivery: 4-mile radius, £10. House specials: Rejeshori Chicken £5.95 and Chicken Delight £5.95. Price check: we can't give you these figures, Mr Rahman has struck through the form with 'n/a'. Hours: 5-11.30pm; Sat. 6pm-12am.

INDIAN PALACE HOUSE NEW ENTRANT

59 Goodmayes Road, Goodmayes, Ilford 020 8720 1995

'Standard curry house with slightly above average cooking. They also do liver. Nice thick Chicken Dhansak, King Prawn Madras oddly thin and disappointing.' IB. Stocks Cobra.

JALALABAD TOP 100

247 Ilford Lane, Ilford 020 8478 1285

55-seater established in 1977 by Nazrul Islam (head chef) and Badrul Islam (manager). It serves 'good-as-they-get' formula curries. No new comments about this TOP 100, I don't know why, so reports please. Here's a précis from last time, plus up-to-date info from the restaurant: 'Have yet to find anywhere remotely up to the Jalalabad's standard.' IB. 'Outstanding dishes of the highest quality – gorgeous.' MF. 'Starters plentiful and delicious. Waiters very attentive without being overloading. Our main course curries were all top-class. CTM the best I've tasted. When the Peshwari Nan arrived it was the best I've had. I asked the waiter if the bread had been cooked in a tandoor, at which I was invited into the kitchen to see the tandoor. Immaculate with everything laid out ready.' TL. Hopefully, restaurants as well-established as this one do not change, so we'll keep it in our TOP 100. Price check: Papadam 50p, CTM £6.90 (inc rice), Pullao Rice £1.60, Peshwari Nan £1.60, House wine £8.50. Delivery: £15 minimum, 3-mile radius. Hours: 12-2.30pm/6pm-12am (1am on Fri. & Sat.). Stocks Cobra.

LALGULAB NEW ENTRANT

43 Goodmayes Road, Goodmayes, Ilford 020 8599 3448

'Standard menu, good portion, good quality. Very, very nice staff.' IB. Stocks Cobra.

MOBEEN ANP

80 Ilford Lane, Ilford 020 8553 9733

The owners of this chain of Pakistani caffs are strict Muslims, so BYO is not permitted and it's unlicensed. Go for darned good, inexpensive, value-for-money, Punjabi, Kebabs, tandoori items and curries of all sorts, selected from the counter, with specials varying from day to day. No credit cards. No smoking. Can be heaving with local Asians, who know you won't find better food, and which adds to a fab atmosphere. Being Punjabi, it's a bit short of vegetarian fodder, but for those, see next entry. Hours: 11am-10pm. Branches: Mobeen, 229 High Street North, London E6; Mobeen, 222 Green Street, London E7; Mobeen, 725, High Road, Leyton, London E10.

Leigh-on-Sea

MUGHAL DYNASTY ©

1585 London Road, Leigh-on-Sea 01702 470373

Nazram Uddin's pretty, upmarket 68 seater, serves tandooris, starters, curries and all the favourites and is a popular local.

PIPASHA NEW ENTRANT ©

284 Eastwood Road North, Leigh-on-Sea 01702 476411

First opened 1995. Taken over in 2000 by Badrul Uddin. Seats 90. Private forecourt parking in front for 10. Takeaway: 10% discount. Delivery: £12, 3-mile radius. Price check: Papadam 50p, CTM £6.25, Pullao Rice £1.95, Peshwari Nan £2.10, Lager £2.80 pint. Hours: 12-2pm/6-11.30pm. Stocks Cobra.

TAJ MAHAL ©

77 Leigh Road, Leigh-on-Sea 01702 711006

Established in 1973 and owned by Shams and Noor Uddin, manager and chef respectively. Seats 70; it's hugely popular. Recently refurbished. 'Wide menu, generous portions, service attentive and prompt. We have never had to complain in seven years.' AGH. Specials include: Rason Mirchi, Chingri Ballichow, Chanda Fry, Lamb in Plum Sauce, Sweet and Sour King Prawns, Pomfret-Fried. 'Continues to enjoy my enthusiastic, regular patronage. Has maintained an admirable reputation for consistency of quality. Excellent reasonably priced food, produced in visibly hygienic conditions. Friendly, efficient service to both old and new customers. I personally still find the

Chicken Vindaloo my favourite.' GSH. Price check: Papadam 55p, CTM £6.25, Pullao Rice £1.85, Peshwari Nan £2.25. Hours: 12-2.30pm/6pm-12am. Stocks Cobra.

TANDOORIAN NIGHTS NEW ENTRANT

1350 London Road, Leigh-on-Sea 01702 713040

Established in 1984. Seats 17. Specialises in tandoori dishes, though if a restaurant can't put a decent plate of tandooried items together, it's a pretty poor show! Price check: Papadam 35p, CTM £5.85, Pullao Rice £1.40, Peshwari Nan £1.60, Lager £2.55 pint. Hours: 12-2pm/6pm-12am. Stocks Cobra.

Loughton GL

BENGAL SPICE NEW ENTRANT

12 Forest Road, Loughton 020 8508 7185

'Well let us tell you, the Bengal Spice is mighty damn hot (no pun intended). Both Lucy and myself feel this is our best haunt yet. Reasons for this are numerous: great decor, superb cuisine, very friendly and efficient staff, posh loos ... I could go on. When you're there, do a wee samba on your table, and Lucy and I will say hello. It goes without saying that we'll be there.' LD&SK.

Ongar

KISMET NEW ENTRANT

171 High Street, Chipping Ongar 01277 362889

'Kismet means "fate": we met here nine years ago and have come on our anniversary ever since. Always superb, quality and value. Garlic Chilli Chicken is huge and dangerously hot unless handled with care. House wine available in ½-litre carafes for drivers – no public transport unfortunately. Situated in a Tudor market house, comfortable and welcoming.' MD. Long may your anniversary celebrations remain at the Kismet. Stocks Cobra.

VOJAN NEW ENTRANT

Epping Road, Ongar 01277 362293

Proprietor Jamal Uddin. Air conditioned. Another plainly decorated restaurant, magnolia walls and lemon ceiling with brightly coloured chairs of purple, fuschia, turmeric and turquoise. I expect this much copied look will be as old fashioned at the end of this decade as flock wall paper was during the last. The restaurant has a separate bar area with comfy chairs. Menu is more interesting with Goan Crab and Mussel Puree (I think we mean Puri – or perhaps we are appealing to the baby food market). Seafood plays a big part on the menu, but there are all the usual favourites to tempt you too. Stocks Cobra.

Rayleigh

RAYLEIGH SPICY TAKEAWAY NEW ENTRANT ©

159 High Street, Rayleigh 01268 770768

Established in 1996 by Shelim Uddin and chef Moynur Miah as the Curry Palace and renamed Rayleigh Spicy. Seats 40. Specials include: Bhuna Bahar (drumstick stuffed with spicy mince in Keema sauce) £10.95, Tangar Salon (Bangladeshi fish cooked in tangy sauce) and Mancherian, mango and peach pulp, herbs, sweet and mild £6.10. Price check: Papadam 50p, CTM £6.10, Pullao Rice £1.90, Peshwari Nan £1.95, Lager £2.95. Takeaway: 10% discount. Delivery: £10 minimum, 4-mile radius. Hours: 5.30-11.30pm (Sat. to 12am, Sun to 11pm). Stocks Cobra.

SAFFRON TANDOORI NEW ENTRANT

32 Eastwood Road, Rayleigh 01268 745275

Unusual. Tented ceiling and lots of Indian jewelled work and brass pots. Family-run, very friendly, Indian rather than Bangladeshi so slightly different taste to the normal high street menu. Advisable to book as very busy at weekends. Limited parking, but parking in local supermarket car park/side roads possible.' SJ. Stocks Cobra.

Romford GL

ASIA SPICE NAME CHANGE ©

62 Victoria Road, Romford 01708 762623

Originally opened in 1970 as India Garden and under the present management (Yeabor Ali) since 1975. A medium-sized restaurant seating 54 diners. Branch: Rupali, South Woodham Ferrers, Essex. Stocks Cobra.

Shoeburyness

POLASH ©

84-86 West Road, Shoeburyness 01702 293989

The Polash and its slightly younger branch have been in our *Guide* since we began, which makes them old friends to these pages. Manager SA Motin tells us his decor is 'wonderful, air conditioned, with water fountain'. But there's a third Polash in the same ownership. Not in Essex, nor even Britain. It's in Sylhet, Bangladesh, the town where so many of our curry-house workers come from. Polash is the best hotel in town, and their restaurant, the Shapnil, has an item on its 200-dish menu that amazed us when we visited. Item 95 is no less than CTM! It is the only place in the whole of Bangladesh where it is to be found. And, says owner Sheik Faruque Ahmed, 'it sells really well!!!' His UK partner, M Khalique, agrees. 'The food was beautifully prepared, tasty and the right strength. Service excellent. Atmosphere relaxed and friendly. Despite the fact that the proprietor informed us that they did not give CC discount on a Saturday, they accepted the coupon and gave us a discount of 10%.' BP-D. Minimum charge £10. Hours: 12-2.30pm/6-12am; Sun. 12am-12pm. Branch: Polash, Burnham on Crouch. Stocks Cobra.

Southend-on-Sea

JONAKI TAKEAWAY NEW ENTRANT

383 South Church Road, Southend-on-Sea 01702 600492

'Chicken Korma delicious, Cauliflower Bhajee, Mushroom Rice and Puri all very good. Friendly, family-run takeaway with consistently good food.' PH. Parking on forecourt. Kurzi Lamb for four (24 hours required) £49.95. Delivery. Price check: Papadam 45p, CTM £5.50, Pullao Rice £1.60. Hours: 5.30pm-2am.

Southminster

VILLAGE TANDOORI NEW ENTRANT

11 High Street, Southminster 01621 772172

'Abdul deserves to be included in the new guide for his consistent quality, attention to detail and friendliness to his customers. We've never had a bad meal here yet.' SJ. Stocks Cobra.

South Woodham Ferrers

NAWAB TANDOORI

1 Chipping Row, Reeves Way,
South Woodham Ferrers 01245 321006

'Food always good, standard menu. Can get busy, they usually find us a table but service can be slow. Staff always friendly and they try very hard to please.' SJ. 'One of my favourites is "King Prawn delight with Eggs Net". Sometimes a cocktail umbrella appears on it! No quiet evening here, but do expect always excellent food served by very friendly staff.' SJ. Stocks Cobra.

IZZYS RUCHITA RENAMED

Unit 1b, Guildway, Town Square,
South Woodham Ferrers 01245 323855

Nazrul Islam (Izzy) has now added his name to the 66-seater Ruchita, which was est. in 1981; cooking by S Miah. Party room 20. SJ says 'Very slick, good decor, attentive service, expert timing. Standard menu well presented and faultlessly served.' and she continues 'Food is well cooked. Crispy samosas, really buttery Butter Chicken and large fluffy Nan. Certainly will become another regular place to visit. Undoubtedly the classiest of the three restaurants in South Woodham Ferrers.' Price check: Papadam 40p, CTM £5.50, Pullao Rice £1.50. Delivery: £10 minimum, town area only. Hours: 12-2pm/6pm-12am.

RUPALI

10 Guild Way, Inchbonnie Road,
South Woodham Ferrers 01245 322926

'The oldest Indian in town and the largest. Standard food, adequately served, always space for a last minute booking. Deserves to stay in the guide.' SJ. 'King Prawn Bhuna Puree absolutely special.Tandoori King Prawn just as good. Chicken Tikka Chillies – tikka pieces in curry sauce with as many chillies as you can stand, always excellent. The best Mushroom Bhajee I can remember – Vindaloo hot.' LG. Price check: Papadam 50p, CTM £5.80, Pullao Rice £1.50. Delivery: £10 minimum, town area only, 6-11pm. Hours: 12-2.30pm/6-11.30pm (12am on Fri. & Sat.).

Thaxted

INDIAN VILLA NEW ENTRANT

20 Watling Road, Thaxted 01371 831189

'We believe our local Indian restaurant compares more than favourably with the best in London, Bristol and Cambridge, all of which we have experienced. We are not so concerned with cost or atmosphere but more with good service and particularly the quality of taste of the food. The Guide is not complete without The India Villa.' AJ.

Tilbury

MINAR BALTI HOUSE TAKEAWAY ©

166 Dock Road, Tilbury 01375 855181

A takeaway establishment only. Price check: Papadam 35p, CTM £5.50, Pullao Rice £1.40. Hours: 5-11.30pm.

Waltham Abbey

SHUHAG ©

16 Highbridge Street, Waltham Abbey 01992 711436

21 years is how long MH Rashid has been going at his Shuhag. Everything from Roagan Goast (*sic*) to Butter Chicken is on the menu and, as you'd expect, it's all done with an experienced hand. Four-course lunch £6.95, kids half-price. Stocks Cobra.

Wickford

MARCO POLO

9-11 Lower Southend Road, Wickford 01268 764002

'Difficult to get a late booking, but well worth it if you can get in. Goan cooking excellent, very friendly and a menu that is a joy to read. Special menu page "West with East" is rather interesting.' SJ. Stocks Cobra.

GLOUCESTERSHIRE

Area: South West
Population: 566,000
Adjacent Counties: Bristol, Gwent, Somerset, Wilts

With the demise of Avon as a county in 1997, Gloucestershire has regained territory which was taken from it when Avon was formed in 1965.

Cheltenham

CURRY CORNER NEW ENTRANT ©

131 Fairview Road, Cheltenham 01242 528449

Established in 1977. Seats 40 in two rooms. Tudor style interior. Specials include: Shagar Anna, Sweet Sylheti Surprise and Mughal Shahi. Takeaway: 10% discount. Price check: Papadam 35p, CTM £5.75, Pullao Rice £1.70, Peshwari Nan £1.65, Lager £2 pint. Hours: 5.30-11.30pm. Stocks Cobra.

INDIAN BRASSERIE ©

146 Bath Road, Cheltenham 01242 231350

A pretty 56-seater in pastel shades with cane furniture, managed by A Rakib. CS still thinks it's the best in town. 'Waiters always very cheerful and friendly, there's a nice atmosphere.' Branch: Dilraj Tandoori, Dursley. Stocks Cobra.

KASHMIR RESTAURANT NEW ENTRANT ©

1 Albion Street, Cheltenham 01242 524288

Established in 1960, name change (from Raj Vooj) in 1990. Seats 42. Takeaway: 10% discount. Delivery: £15 minimum. Price check: Papadam 45p, CTM £5.75, Pullao Rice £1.75, Peshwari Nan £1.60, Lager £2.40 pint. Hours: 12-2pm/6pm-12am (Sat. to 12.30am). Stocks Cobra.

Chipping Sodbury

SULTAN RE ENTRANT

29 Horse Street, Chipping Sodbury 01454 323510

'Situated in a Georgian building which has housed a number of notable persons in the past, including Dr Edward Jenner who developed vaccination.

Despite the location and better than average accommodation, the menu is standard high street curry house and the food was very disappointing. Pickle selection was limited and a poor mix. Bhajis had too much gram flour making them rather stodgy. Chicken Madras and Lamb Dhansak were less hot than average and both contained an unusually high amount of tomato chunks. Peshwari Nan lacking in filling.' MW. Stocks Cobra.

Cirencester

RAJDOOT ©

35 Castle Street, Cirencester 01285 652651

Good reports recorded at Fozlur and Ataur Rahman's place. Stocks Cobra.

SAQHI NEW ENTRANT

36 Castle Street, Cirencester 01285 644998

'Mr KFU Ahmed is the owner of this excellent restaurant. It is the 9th restaurant he has owned and his philosophy for high-quality customer service really shines through. Full range of Indian dishes offered with additionally some Persian dishes, Pricy, Shally and Patia and a fine selection of house specials and vegetable side dishes. Tasty food, piping hot and served in timely fashion. Worth a trip into the Cotswolds.' CP. Stocks Cobra.

Gloucester

HILLTOP

19 Worcester Street, Gloucester 01452 308377

'We've taken many friends here and they have all returned, most of them the next week. The food is different but very good. The service is friendly and efficient. We particularly like the Nepalese Murgh Masala (on the bone) and the Cauliflower Bhaji.' And he continues 'Friends came from Worcester. Everyone thought the meal was excellent. Started with Onion Bhajias and Chicken Chat. For main course we had Nepalese Murgh Masalla, Chicken Sag and Hilltop Special (chicken – very enjoyable). Good sized portions.' DT. And just in case you think that the novelty might have worn off, well – it hasn't. 'Still my favourite. Chicken Chat is especially good, although you have to ask for it, because it is not on the menu. Keema is also not on menu but they are happy to cook it. I always enjoy the salad which comes with the Popadoms and Chutneys. Nepalese specials if you fancy something different.' DT. And we do fancy Nepalese Specials. Stocks Cobra.

INDIA GATE NEW ENTRANT

24-26 London Road, Gloucester 01452 501735

'A new restaurant that has opened on the site of the Bengal Lancer. Attractive. Good service. Chicken Sagorana is particularly good. Worth a visit.' DT.

INDIAN PARADISE NEW ENTRANT

42 Bristol Road, Gloucester 01452 300615

'I've been here a number of times and never had a bad meal, always get good, fast accurate service. My only complaint is that there does occasionally appear to be an over abundance of garlic added to some dishes – but that must be good for my health and keep the vampires away!' CS. I think you've been watching too much Buffy, Colin. 'Went with two friends, one was blind. Waiters particularly attentive and thoughtful. Popadoms very enjoyable. Chicken Tikka Balti – not on menu, but happy to cook. Murgh Pasanda – beautiful sauce, lovely tender chicken. Excellent service. Enjoyed.' DT. 'Chicken Tikka Bhuna the best ever. Only problem – no Cobra. Highly recommended.' CLJ. No, that's a BIG problem!

JEWEL IN THE CROWN NEW ENTRANT

88 Westgate, Gloucester 01452 310366

'It boasts that all its food is cooked fresh to order. Preparation time can be fifteen to thirty minutes. Sheek Kebab was expertly spiced, Chicken Balti was absolutely beautiful, vegetables and fresh naan all first class. The wait didn't seem too long either!' MB. Stocks Cobra.

POPPADUMS NEW ENTRANT

8-10 St Catherine's Street, Gloucester 01452 330955

'Recently opened. We have been a number of times and enjoyed each occasion. Wide menu, generous portions, food of high standard. Mon-Thurs, a four-course meal costs £7.95/person.' DG. 'They do a large number of takeaways. Service is very attentive and quality of the food is good. Particularly enjoyed the Vegetable Dhansak and Sag Bhajee. Korma the best I have ever tasted. Portions big. Value for money.' DT. Stocks Cobra.

Nailsworth

PASSAGE TO INDIA

Old Market, Nailsworth 01453 834063

'We arrived at 8.30pm, our starter arrived at 10.05, and our main course arrived two hours after our order. The food was excellent but we were too tired to enjoy it.' MC. I think, Marcus, you would have probably eaten anything by that time. 'On entering I was met with a wonderful aroma of spices. Lamb Phal and Pilau Rice well-cooked, well-balanced but so huge, I couldn't eat it all.' AEJ. 'A very tastefully decorated restaurant with friendly and courteous staff. Food is freshly cooked and mouthwatering. I will return.' ST. 'A bit expensive, but worth it, food very good.' PJ.

Staple Hill

SHADIN INDIAN AND BALTI NEW ENTRANT U

70 Broad Street, Staple Hill, Nr Bristol 0117 957 5786

Interesting menu addition for you to try – Banana Naan £1.50. Delivery. Price check: Papadam 40p, CTM £6.50, Pullao Rice £1.40. Hours: 5.30pm-12am (Fri. & Sat. to 12.30am).

Stow-on-the-Wold

PRINCE OF INDIA NEW ENTRANT

5 Park Street, Stow-On-The-Wold 01451 831198

'The weather was absolutely awful but at least it was nice and warm in this establishment, the staff was warm and friendly and the Chicken Madras kept me warm and happy until the next day.' MB.

Tewkesbury

NIRALA RENAMED

69-70 Church Street, Tewkesbury 01684 294353

First opened in 1983, taken over in 1998 by Abdul Hye. Formerly Munira. Seats 74. Fully licensed and air conditioned. 'Pleasant enough, fairly standard menu, slightly more expensive than Rajshani.' Specials include: Chicken Jefrabad – cooked with selected spices (prepared with a special blend of masala and chicken, cooked in a coriander relish sauce with a touch of garlic and ginger £6.25). Navraner Chicken Tikka – starter, diced chicken tikka cooked with curry leaves and mint £3.50. Indian Pomfret Fish – whole tandoori fish 6.96. Takeaway: 10% discount. Price check: Papadam 45p, CTM £8.25 (inc Pullao Rice), Pullao Rice £1.95, Peshwari Nan £1.95. Hours: 12-2.30pm/5.30pm-12am. Stocks Cobra.

RAJSHAHI NEW ENTRANT

121 High Street, Tewkesbury 01684 273727

Established April 1999 in a grade 2 listed building. Seats 48. Specials include: Salli Murghi Balti. 'Mr Naz converted these premises and opened in April 99, importing the manager (Mac) and the Chef (Uddin) from Birmingham to add a little spice into this old market town. Boy have they got it right! Even on a Tuesday night the place is full (plus a continuous stream of takeaways) resulting in some disappointed potential diners. Complimentary Papadoms and Pickles to kick off, then lovely, crisp Meat Samosa, followed by rich Chicken Tikka Bhuna and a delicious Chapati. I shall be revisiting soon with my family.' And 'A third return to this relatively new restaurant confirmed its increasing popularity. You now have to book a table during the week. My children commented that the Rajshahi was "buzzing, cool", probably the dynamic service of superbly presented dishes by the young waiters in their yellow shirts.' TE. 'Centrally situated and smart looking. Complimentary Popadoms and Pickles provided to begin, nice touch. Tandoori Chicken £5.50 – too much for an appetiser, marinade sauce had been smeared over chicken, not permeated. Onion Bhajia's £2.10 – two large flat hamburger type pieces, little spicing, nice salad. CTM and Chicken Pathia £4.95 – large pieces of good quality chicken, added to tasty sauces, but not cooked in them. Vegetable Pullao Rice £2.25 – superb. Peshwari Nan – enormous, nice and fresh. Portions were enormous, we took what we left (more for a second assessment). Prices average, excellent value for money. Good service friendly.' MW. Licensed: lager £2.25 pint, stocks Cobra. Takeaway: 10% discount. Delivery: 3 miles. Price check: Papadam 40p, CTM £5.95, Pullao Rice £2.50, Peshwari Nan £1.95. Hours: 6pm-12am (Fri. & Sat. to 12.30am). Stocks Cobra.

Thornbury

MOGHULS BRASSERIE

8 High Street, Thornbury 01454 416187

'Converted inn, wood panelling, low beams. Waiters very smart, food formula curry house. Tasty Sheek Kebab £2.95, Ayr-Biran £3.50 – colleague had to contend with bones [well, fish often do have bones!], removed the relish tray. King Prawn Dhansak, nicely sauced, prawns overcooked. Service OK.' MS. Price check: Papadam 50p, CTM £6.50, Pullao Rice £1.75. Hours: 12-2pm/6-11.30pm. Stocks Cobra.

MUMTAZ INDIAN ©

7 St Mary's Centre, Thornbury 01454 411764

The Mumtaz is on two levels. The downstairs seating area and small bar are for takeaway customers and perusal of the menu. The restaurant is upstairs. 'Menu not too extensive, but food extremely good and large portions. Clean European-style decor and music! Very helpful staff and friendly. Would go back.' WW. KB was less enthusiastic about the decor and other reports talk of standard curries of generous proportions. AE-J found the Phal too hot on one occasion and too mild on another, although his fiancée 'loves the Kormas'. Evenings only. Stocks Cobra.

Wooton-under-Edge

INDIAN PALACE

13-15 Church Street, Wooton-under-Edge 01453 843628

'Comfortable restaurant, good decor. Good varied menu, quantities could be a little more generous. Quality excellent, only chicken breast is used. Staff helpful and polite. Recommended.' B&PR. Stocks Cobra.

HAMPSHIRE

Area: South
Population: 1,644,000
Adjacent Counties: Berks, Dorset, Surrey, Sussex, Wilts

Aldershot

JOHNNIE GURKHA'S ©

186 Victoria Road, Aldershot 01252 328773

'Glad to see the restaurant is still as seedy as ever, although it's not quite so easy to accept since the prices are now as much as anywhere else. Mint sauce is excellent. Famous Dil Kusa Nan – an enormous bread topped with cherries and coconut.' PD. 'Food is very plentiful, beautifully cooked and spiced and nothing was left!' JW. Stocks Cobra.

SPICES NEW ENTRANT U

98 Queens Road, Aldershot 01252 323593

'I want a place I can depend on. I think I have found it – Spices Takeaway. I have tried all my old favourites, have never been disappointed. Excellent Tandoori Chicken £3.60, fresh and spicy formula Vindaloo £3.50, tasty, garlicky Sag Aloo £2. Consistently dependable.' LS. Outragous 95p for Chutney or Pickle. Delivery. Price check: Papadam 40p, CTM £4.80, Pullao Rice £1.40. Hours: 12-2pm/5.30-11.30pm.

Alresford

SHAPLA

60 West Street, Alresford 01962 732134

'A group of retired officers of The Royal Hampshire Regiment, who are addicted to curries, meet once a year as members of The Vindaloo Club (15 of us). A fortnight previously I'd visited and explained to manager, Mr Moon, what I wanted. Much pleasure in letting you know – my instructions were carried out to the letter. Popadoms the largest I have ever seen, extremely tasty Lamb Vindaloo and Garlic Chilli Chicken.' JK. Stocks Cobra.

Alton

ALTON TANDOORI ©

7 Normandy Street, Alton 01420 82154

48-seater, owned and managed by M Shahid. 'Usual menu with a few unusuals. Linda's special comprising Tikka Chicken with spinach and chickpeas was underspiced and bland. Meat Vindaloo was hot and rather good. Nice dry papadoms, flavoursome rice. Excellent service.' MG. 'Greeted by the manager like long lost friends. Service was very good. There were 14 of us, and we were treated well. Food was excellent. Madras Chicken, Meat Rogan, Chicken Morrissa (beautifully spiced and hot, succulent chicken). Rice, Bhajis, Naans, all superb. We were very impressed.' JW. Price check: Papadam 50p, CTM £8.50 (inc Special Rice), Pullao Rice £1.80, Peshwari Nan £1.90. Hours: 6-11.15pm. Stocks Cobra.

Andover

MUGHAL ©

33 Andover Road, Ludgershall, Andover 01264 790463

Owned by Towidar Rahman, managed by S Miah. 'Tucked away at the end of a modest row of suburban shops is a trip down memory lane. The food is remarkably reminiscent of the kind of curries we used to eat as students in the late 1950s. Old favourites recycled with modern subtlety, style and art. Zappy specialities such as Murgh Massala, Garlic Chicken, Acher Gosht, Jhingi Kodu. Well worth looking out for.' RG. Price check: Papadam 45p, CTM £5.95, Mughlai Kopta (fish) Dupiaza £6.10, Pullao Rice £1.50. Stocks Cobra.

Ashurst

EURO ASIA INDIAN CUISINE ©

179 Lyndhurst Road, Ashurst 023 8029 2885

Azad Miah runs the front while Mr Rahman cooks the food, which we continue to hear is fine. Hours: 6pm-12am. Branches: Prince of Bengal, Hythe, Dynasty, Brockenhurst, Lal Quilla, Lymington, all Hampshire.

Basingstoke

AGRA BALTI HOUSE

34 Winchester Street, Basingstoke 01256 475566

'Rough and ready decor. Very good and friendly service. Papadam very crisp, superb chutneys. Excellent Meat Thali. Great Nan. Great tasting Chicken Madras £3.75, right heat level. Will return.' JP. Delivery: £10 minimum, 3-mile radius, orders over £20, free bottle of wine.

BENGAL BRASSERIE ©

4 Winchester Street, Basingstoke 01256 332847

This 'old hand' originally opened in 1978 and has been under Shelim Ahmed's careful ownership since 1985. 'My favourite dish is Chicken Kashmir cooked with banana and cream in a mild sauce.' MM. Hours: 12-2.30pm/6-12am. Stocks Cobra.

KASHMIR NEW ENTRANT

4 Church Street, Basingstoke 01256 472112

'All portions were fine to generous and the cooking was far above average. Mixed Seafood Khana (prawns, king prawns and white fish in a rich, creamy sauce) was unusual and absolutely first class. The other restaurants in Basingstoke are enjoyable but the Kashmir is in a different league. Service was pleasant and efficient and overall it was a very pleasant meal.' and 'Again all dishes were excellent. People were coming in all the time we were there so the restaurant's reputation must be good amongst local residents. It deserves to be.' HC. 'A new (and clean) menu with raised prices. They had removed all the fish dishes; obviously Basingstoke diners are not fish eaters. Excellent meal, food lived up to expectations. Staff are a real credit, friendly, interested, helpful and efficient. Full marks to everyone at the Kashmir. £37 for two.' HC. Delivery. Price check: Papadam 55p, CTM £6.50, Pullao Rice £1.95. Hours: 12-2.30pm (closed Sun.)/6pm-12am. Stocks Cobra.

Botley

PURBANI NEW ENTRANT

2 High Street, Botley 01489 783161

'The service here was so swift I felt that they were trying to clear my table as soon as I sat down. The food is standard, acceptable "formula". The Maas Bora (fish kebab) was nice. The place is comfy enough. Would I come here again? Only if so desperate for a fix I couldn't make it into Portsmouth or Southampton.' MS. 'Despite some good reports from work colleagues, this restaurant failed to live up to expectations. Food was not impressive and the service was totally chaotic. I think it's another establishment to suffer from "got well known and now can't cope with the rush" syndrome. Tables are packed into the place literally inches apart, and so a private conversation over dinner was impossible. Perhaps it is a little more civilised on a weekday – we'd like to think so, but we won't hurry back to find out.' CC. Well, there is a lesson to be learned here – proprietor and staff take note! Stocks Cobra.

Brockenhurst

DYNASTY INDIAN NEW ENTRANT

59 Brookley Road, Brockenhurst 01590 624088

Located in the centre of this popular New Forest village, the Dynasty serves all the popular curries. Discount on takeaways. Stocks Cobra.

©	Curry Club Discount	U	Unlicensed
V	Vegetarian	ANP	Alcohol not permitted
e-a-m-a-y-l	Eat as much as you like	BYO	Bring your own alcohol

Cove

COVE TANDOORI NEW ENTRANT

328 Fernhill Road, Cove **01252 634192**

'Nice – probably the best Bangladeshi restaurant we have. Spicy but pricey.' MG. Stocks Cobra.

Fareham

INDIAN COTTAGE NEW ENTRANT

184 West Street, Fareham **01329 232429 / 236009**

Established in 1981. Fully licensed. Main restaurant can seat 50 diners, separate party room seats 24 plus. 'Always reliable, always enjoy the food and ambience. Popadoms, sauces, onion cachumber etc. with Chicken Tikka, followed by a lovely Prawn Pathia, Aloo Gobi, Nan and two pints of Kingfisher (not driving tonight!) Pullao Rice nice, real spices which my wife discards and I eat to release extra flavours, green cardamoms are a particular favourite! Good night.' MS. 'Nice place this. At a guess, recently decorated, all cream and burgundy. Already four tables occupied at 6.45 – good sign. Chicken Tikka starter was good, followed with Rogan Josh Lamb. Satisfaction 100%. Should be in the guide.' MS. Terrace available for alfresco lunches. Takeaway: 10% discount. Price check: Papadam 45p, CTM £7.95, Pullao Rice £1.60, Keema Nan £1.20. Hours: 12-2.30pm/6-12am.

Farnborough

GURKHA PALACE NEW ENTRANT

78 Farnborough Road, Farnborough **01252 511550**

The home of the Gurkhas, Church Crookham, is no longer. And huge numbers of Britain's favourite warriors are being disbanded. Throwing the baby out with the bathwater, we think. One legacy, fortunately for curry-lovers, is the relatively high number of Nepalese restaraunts in this area of Hampshire. This is one where the food is authentic, the staff are Nepalese, and they serve a good range of formula curries to. See branch at Gurkha Palace, Liphook, Hants, for menu details. Hours: 12-2.30pm/6-11pm. Stocks Cobra.

POPADOMS ©

33 Medway Drive, Cove, Farnborough 01252 376869

Owner Sean Usher claims to be the UK's only English owner [you're not, Sean – read this *Guide!*]. The 36-seater is painted cream and earthy red, the woodwork indigo blue, the furniture is simple wood giving an airy feeling. Swathes of cream, red and blue hang from the ceiling. Nepalese. Bikash Devkota is manager. Sanjiv Singh's specials include: Chicken Monsourri – slices of chicken tikka in a Madras-style sauce that also features sliced green chillies and soy sauce. Delivery: £8 min. Hours: 6-10.30pm. Stocks Cobra.

SPICE HUT NEW ENTRANT

72 Farnborough Road, Farnborough 01252 541419

As we say above, there are a number of good Nepalese restaurants in the area. 'Went for lunch with my wide on day off, made a nice change! Pleasantly decorated with Nepali pictures and posters. Atmosphere good. Park on back streets behind restaurant. Polite, smart waiters. Delicious food, well cooked and presented. Usual variety of chicken, lamb, etc. sufficiently unusual for us. Prices comparable to other local establishments. Went home to sleep it off!' SM.

Fleet

CHUTNEYS INDIAN TAKEAWAY NEW ENTRANT

355 Fleet Road, Fleet 01252 810330

First started in 1997. Adjacent parking for 20 cars. Price check: Papadam 50p, CTM £5.90, Pullao Rice £1.60, Peshwari Nan £1.70. Delivery: £10 minimum, 5-mile radius. Hours: 5.30-11.30pm.

GULSHAN INDIAN NEW ENTRANT

264-266 Fleet Road, Fleet 01252 615910

'Greeted in a most friendly way. The restaurant appeared to be divided into two halves, one for couples and well-behaved diners, one for noisy oiks – what a good idea. Decor was very plain, but good range and quality of food. Helpful and friendly service to the last.' CP. 'Can be fabulous, but the last time we went there the rice was hard.' MG. 'Still worthy of inclusion.' DT. 'Standard is consistently high. It has to be one of the best restaurants in Hampshire and Surrey. Orders of over £15 get a free mystery dish.' JW

THE GURKHA SQUARE TOP 100 ©

327 Fleet Road, Fleet 01252 810286

Of the several Nepalese restaurants in the area, reports received place this one at the top. And it is actually patronised by Nepalese. This 67-seater, owned by AB Gurung, managed by Om Gurung, is as good as you'll find. 'Rather twee and overrated.' MG. 'Delighted to see the Gurkha Square in the TOP 100. My wife and I can certainly back this up. Perhaps slightly on the pricey side, but superb value for money. We particularly like the Mis-Mas, and the rice and naan are quite excellent.' DT. 'Comfortable, polite service, excellent food.' GR. Delivery: 3-mile radius. Hours: 12-2.30pm/6-11.30pm

Gosport

HAPPY NIGHT TAKEAWAY NEW ENTRANT

73 Forton Road, Gosport 023 9252 1997

Formerly Dill Takeaway. 'The new management were offering a 20% discount. Meal was ordered in the premises by a smiling and very friendly gentleman from a very comprehensive 12-page A5-size menu. Lamb Patia £4.55, Pullao Rice £1.40, Plain Nan £1.40, Chupati 85p. Meat a little gristly, good flavour, nicely presented, good portion. Rice well cooked. Nan large and fluffy, delightfully sweet. The meal was packed with a complimentary Popadom and a small bag of Raita. Everything washed down very nicely with a bottle of Riesling I had chilling in the fridge, very enjoyable.' PH. Hours: 6pm (5pm on Sat.)-12am.

Hartley Wintney

MONSOON NEW ENTRANT

High Street, Hartley Wintney 01252 842743

'Colour scheme of purple and yellow. Menu quite standard with exception of Jhinga Dum Acheri and the Monsoon special fish dishes. Some of the breads were a bit pricey. Chicken and Lamb Tikkas were delicious, Jhinga was wonderful with many interesting flavours. King Prawn Korai was one of the best I've had. Friendly, helpful, efficient and polite waiters. Delighted with the restaurant.' JW. Stocks Cobra.

Hook

HOOK TANDOORI ©

1 Fairholme Parade, Station Road, Hook 01256 764979

Syed Ahmed's 67-seater is: 'Highest quality, full of flavours. Particularly the King Prawn, Chicken Vindaloo – especially good. Staff well presented and friendly.' MJBK. Hours: 12-2.30pm/6-11.30pm. Branch: Mogul, 13 London Road, Bagshot, Wiltshire.

Horndean

INDIAN COTTAGE ©

4 The Square, Horndean 023 9259 1408

Established in 1978. Taken over by Anwar Miah in 1996. Seats 48. 'Have tried this restaurant a couple of times before and have never been disappointed. Excellent parking, tasteful decor, keen staff. Garlic Chilli Chicken was excellent and not overladen with chillies. Chicken Dorai was served sizzling with large cubes of breast chicken. Peshwari Naan very nice. Well worth a visit. Will go back again.' DL. Carparking for 12. Price check: Papadam 50p, CTM £5.50, Pullao Rice £1.95, Peshwari Nan £1.95, Lager £1.75 pint. Hours: 12-2.30pm/6pm-12am. Stocks Cobra.

Liphook

GURKHA PALACE NEW ENTRANT

18 Station Road, Liphook 01428 729355

A Nepalese restaurant, newly opened this year. Liphook, rather like Haslemere, is divided by the railway, so two separate towns grew up either side. The Gurkha Palace is in the rather unglamorous part of Liphook, by the railway station. There is ample easy parking outside. The restaurant is on a corner site with large plate glass windows. On entering we were greeted and shown immediately to our table, where our coats were taken. The waiter, in strict army ceremonial manner placed our cloth napkins on our laps, making sure that we were well covered in case of any sauce mishap! Menus were given to us and while we looked at them, three chutneys (served in beaten copper katuris lined up on a wooden tray) and a basket containing two grilled, folded spicy Popadoms and Prawn Crackers were placed on the table. Nepal borders Northern India and, being land-locked, borders China on the other side. So, interesting dishes like Momo – a steamed chicken dumpling, rather like dimsum which you might find rather strange, suddenly becomes obvious, as do the Prawn Crackers. House wine (French) is good value and very drinkable at £7.95 a bottle (wanted to start with a Campari – but didn't have any – not surprising, hardly anyone likes it! – so had a G&T instead). The menu is authentically Nepalese, no pandering to the formula curry house here. As we looked around the restaurant, other diners looked bemused, ordering took some time. We chose for starters Kalejo Bhutuwa £2.95 – a generous portion of chopped chicken livers, fried in mild spices, lovely and Khasiko Bara £2.95 – three beautifully shaped spicy rissoles of minced lamb with yellow lentils, served with a yellow spicy chutney and both with a pretty salad, superb. Our main courses were served promptly, Gurkha Khasi £6.10 – a good portion of sliced char-grilled lamb, hot and spicy, Kukhurako Masu £5.50 – described as a typical Nepalese curry, tasty chicken breast in a red/orange sauce, but too mild for me. Accompanied by Bhenta Tarkari £3.10 – aubergine curry, good slices of aubergine, but too many fried onions and I dislike the use of tomatoes to bulk out a dish. Tomatoes have no place in authentic Asian cooking having arrived in the 19th century from America. Kalo Daal £3.10 – mild and creamy black lentils. Palace Bhat £3.10 – highly coloured, not saffron but food dye, had a good ghee flavour with whole bayleaf and pistachio nuts. Patina Paratha £2.20 – nicely presented, brought to the table in a basket and cut into quarters, chopped mint leaves had been rolled into the bread – very good, crispy. The restaurant is owned and managed by former Gurkhas and it shows, professional and pleased to help. Branch: Gurkha Palace, Farnborough. Hours: 12-2.30pm/6-11pm. Stocks Cobra.

Liss

MADHUBAN TOP 100

94 Station Road, Liss 01730 893363 / 894372

We are often asked what makes a restaurant good. And this is as good a place to explain as any in this *Guide*. What we are talking about is a venue, be it a pub, a shop a sports club or a restaurant, where one wants to return. It becomes one's local. As far as the Madhuban is concerned, it is my favourite Bangladeshi curry house in my area – for this type of food, it's my local. Many of our correspondents tell us about theirs with some affection. Many are listed in this *Guide*. Most are probably just as good as the Madhuban. It is located in a corner of England called the 'Three Counties' area. It is the point where Surrey, Hampshire and Sussex meet. Liss is a smallish typical southern village, which just a few years ago would have been an unlikely setting for an Indian restaurant. Now the village has two. There are no big name eateries. In the 'Location, Location, Location' stakes, none of the big boys would invest a penny in such a village. But the Madhuban stands out well above the average restaurant. What makes it so? The answer is care. If the owner cares, it shows. Firstly, many of the staff have been at the Madhuban for all its 12 years, and experience shows. Customer care begins with a prompt hello at the door, and ends with a courteous goodbye and a rose on departure. In between everything is done well, the reservation system, the service, the cooking and the ambience, And to prove it, the restaurant is busy, even on weekdays. It has a loyal following, as such places do, but untypically some come regularly from as afar afield as London and the south coast. Uncle heads the kitchen, while three brothers, including bossman Lodue Miah, head the front of house team, in smart blue monogrammed waistcoats. Blue is the house colour, used on the exterior, the chairs, the decor, and even the menu. Like everything else, this eight-page document epitomises the Madhuban's attention to detail. It is illustrated in full colour and fully describes all the dishes. There are 22 starters, 7 items from the tandoor, plus 5 nans. There is an ample choice of old favourites, and they are all done well. Unusual items include Hyderabadi Shorba, £1.60, a soup with chicken and potato, flavoured with coconut and lemon; and Hussaini Kebab, £2.50, meat stuffed with raisins; Dhaba Meat, £5.60, is a 'roadside dish of lamb'; while Elaichi Gosht, £5.60 is meat flavoured with cardamom and coriander. In addition there are specials such as Murgh Deluxe, £7.50, keema-stuffed boned chicken leg in a CTM creamy sauce; Jingha Pineapple – king prawns in a scooped-out pineapple £10.95; and sliced Raan, £7.50. 'Given the extensive menu, it took some time to make any choices. I ordered Keema Khumb for a starter (excellent and flavoursome) and Dhaba Gosht with Pullao Rice as a main course (superb). Service was friendly and attentive. A most pleasurable lunch – Madhuban deserves its laurels.' RH. 'Very stylish, great ambience. Six of us went for my daughter's 19th birthday. Food was very good as always. My Methi Gosht was very well spiced and my daughter's King Prawn Masallah superb. Pretty good value, but portions not over-generous.' MG. Says DBAC: 'Lodue rang to tell us that he had just finished building a 16-seater party room and would we like to be the first to eat in the new room. We gratefully accepted his kind invitation. Even on a Tuesday night the restaurant was busy, diners peering into the new room with a quizzical look, wondering why we were the only two eating in there. Bedar, Lodue's brother was updating the wine list and brought one of his new finds for us to sample. The delicious food, as always, was served promptly and in good portions. No wonder it's popular.' Being busy and popular (not to mention acclaiming such a place in this *Guide*) can lead to problems, as this quote from HC tells 'Eye-catching decor, spectacular food. A shame that it was all spoiled by the unreasonably long wait (arrived 7.30pm and the food arrived at 8.48pm).' [I wonder if this was a Friday or Saturday night, which as we always say, we avoid like a plague if at all possible.] True, a busy restaurant is lively and fun but serving delays can be quite annoying. MG found his teeth tested: 'On two visits I found myself chewing some very chewy lamb curry. Although overrated, meal was very good.' But JL: 'first discovered this restaurant shortly after it opened. Since that time it has gone from strength to strength, and is now on my list of top restaurants to visit when I am away on business. Special mention must be made of Murgh Deluxe (chicken stuffed with mincemeat and served in a rich red spicy sauce) and Khumbi Rice (mushrooms cooked in special selection of spices, and then added to rice) – both absolutely delicious. Thoroughly recommended. I live too far away to visit regularly, but their chilled curry sauces (Balti, Tikka Masala Korma, Madras and Bhoona) are now available nationwide (01730 891177 for further details).' [If you would like more details of the sauces, contact the restaurant or www.Madhuban.co.uk] 'Worthy of TOP 100. The food, decor, service and general ambience were still as good as ever. Good starter – Onion Bhajia, one of the best I've had. Excellent Chicken Jalfrezi, hotted up to Vindaloo strength, Pullao Rice, Mushroom Bhajia and Nan couldn't be faulted. Plus a pint of Dortmunder Union lager – very nice. Followed by Almond Kulfi – inverted it into a special glass so did not look too rude!! – not that I mind!' BP-D [and we don't either!]. Price check: Papadam 50p, CTM £5.95, Pullao Rice £2.20. Hours: 12-2.30pm/5.30-11.30pm. Remains in our TOP 100. Visit their web site on www.madhuban.co.uk. Stocks Cobra.

Lymington

LAL QUILLA NEW ENTRANT

135-136 High Street, Lymington 01590 671681257

'Only Indian in Lymington, seating 80, comfortable surroundings. Chicken Chat – large chunks of chicken in tangy sauce. Onion Bhajias – excellent, two large, crisp, spicy and round, best I've had for some time. Murgh Nhagpuri, strips of tandoori chucken in rich, thick sauce with caramelised onions and peppers, extremely tasty but at nearly £10 a little pricey. Chicken Patia, thin, light coloured sauce, quite tasty and hot. Mixed Vegetable Bhajee – reasonable, overrun with carrots! Food and drinks served efficiently but had to ask for napkins and cutlery, almost thrown on table. Raita arrived when starters finished. Portions sufficient, prices higher than average, reflects monopoly frequented by well-heeled yachting types.' MW. Price check: Papadam 50p, CTM £6.70, Pullao Rice £1.90. Hours: 12-2.30pm/6pm-12am.

Petersfield

RIVER KWAI THAI NEW ENTRANT

16-18 Dragon Street, Petersfield 01730 267077

One of the few Thai entrants in the *Guide*. Established in 1986. The restaurant is divided into smoking and non-smoking areas. During the summer months you can dine outside in the Water Garden. We had been planning to eat at the Thai Pub in Stedham, but they were closed, so we travelled a little further on to Peterfield for the River Kwai. We haven't been here for some time, but nothing has changed. Waitresses nicely dressed in traditional silk costumes. We were quickly seated and our drinks order was taken as we looked at the menu and crunched our way through a basket of Prawn Crackers £1.50. We chose starters of Por Pia Tod – Baby Spring Rolls £4.25 and Sateh Nua/Gai – Beef and Chicken Satays £4.95 – all very good. Pat asked for a dish of Nam Prik (hot chilli sauce) as he likes it hot (in fact, very hot). Soup makes a good second course, such as Tom Yam – Spicy Prawn Soup £4.95 – clear but spicy, hot and sour – lovely. Two dishes that Pat and I both really enjoy are Gaeng Panaeng Nua – Penang Beef Curry £6.95 – thinly sliced prime beef with peppers in a spicy hot curry sauce and Pud Thai – Special Thai Fried Noodles £7.50 – fried rice noodles with egg, prawns, crab meat, bean sprouts, ground peanut and chopped salted turnip, dressed with lemon and coriander. They really are fantastic and they do them so well, a must! Portions are average. Takeaway: 10% discount. Price check: Green Chicken Curry £6.50, Fried Rice £2.25.

TARA PALACE NEW ENTRANT

1 The Square, Petersfield 01730 303303

'New restaurant, visited on recommendation. Restaurant is on the first floor up steep, narrow stairs, and the whole place is on a very obvious slope due to the age of the building. Superb meal with quick, polite service. Butly Kebab, excellent, huge chunks of soft lamb. Garlic Chilli Chicken, Murag Karahi, Gosht Pasanda, all good.' MPW. Stocks Cobra.

Portsmouth

GANDHI NEW ENTRANT

139 Kingston Road, North End, Portsmouth 023 9281 1966

'Complimentary papadoms and pickles. Sheeh Kebab starter a bit bland, Chicken Chaat very sharp, main courses of Chicken Kofta Korai and Lamb

Tikka Korai were quite tasty but the Chilli Chicken Masala was hot with chilli but no taste otherwise.' TOC. Stocks Cobra.

NEW TAJ MAHAL ©

54 Kingston Road, Buckland, Portsmouth 023 9266 1021

Nothing 'new' about this 1965 curry house. It's an old hand, now owned by Lilu Miah and Abdul Matin – a safe bet on curry alley! Stocks Cobra.

STAR OF ASIA ©

6 Market Way, City Centre, Portsmouth 023 9283 7906

'Great little 40-seater restaurant, established in 1992 by Abdul Mothen, who also manages. Chef Gian Uddin cooks the curries. 'Far enough away from the circuit drinking area. Standard range of dishes. Hot and crispy Popadoms. Excellent Rashmi with large portion of succulent kebab, topped with fluffy and tender omelette. Tandoori Chicken beautifully tender. Lovely Meat Bhuna and tangy Chicken Dhansak. Late generally means 1am, I left at 2.30am and people still arriving.' RW. Delivery. Price check: Papadam 40p, CTM £5.45, Pullao Rice £1.50. Hours: 12pm-2.15am (Fri. closed)/6pm to late; Sat. & Sun. 12pm to late.

Port Solent

INDIA PALACE NEW ENTRANT NEW TO OUR TOP 100

44, The Boardwalk, Port Solent 023 9021 4444

Port Solent, just off the urban M27, is one of those new coastal developments which has grown considerably over the last few years into a marvellous marina with many restaurants, shops, bars, a pub and a shopping arcade. Residential properties include a garage at the front for the car and mooring at the back for the boat. And what boats! Hundreds of them. Fortunately for the resident and tourist curryholics, it also has a very commendable curry house. 'It was my mother's birthday and Pat and I decided to take her for an Indian. She doesn't go out very often, firstly, because that would mean father would be spending money and secondly, he's one of the 8% who don't like Indian food – "it's got garlic in it". So then we were three. It was the height of the tourist season, so by definition, as in Spain, the builders were in full disruptive dusty, lusty, noisy swing, constructing a health club with swimming pool, and around the car park it was a bit crunchy, so we ladies were careful of our high heels. Once in the complex walking is easy, decking is everywhere. The Indian Palace is on the upper level. There's a lift for those who cannot make it. After trying the wrong door (signs would be useful, please) the reception area is generous, the feel superb. On three sides, its 160 comfortable blue-upholstered chairs give wonderful views of the marina, set off by their polished dark wooden tables, plants and bamboo furniture. It was midweek and early, so we hadn't booked but the restaurant was already busy with about a dozen diners all squashed into the tiny non-smoking section. We were seated with them, but on reflection the smoking section has the better views and is in the more spacious part of the restaurant. Papadams and the Chutney Tray £1.75 (which the waiters left on the table for our starters – full marks) were served promptly. Starters: Meat Samosa £2.10 – hot and crunchy pastry. Onion Bhajia £2.10 – three golf balls, hot and crisp, Sheek Kebab £3.10 – two, sausages, good texture, a little under spiced. All were attractively served with fresh salad, lemon wedges and a nuclear red, very sweet, coconut chutney. Pat had a King Prawn extra hot Jalfrezi which contained four prawns – perhaps a little mean (KP dishes from £8.10 to £11.25), Eileen opted for Prawn Korma £5.75 – the tinest prawns you've ever seen, but a good number of them, and I, my standby Chicken Dhansak £5.10, very good, hot and sweet served with Peshwari Nan £2.15, Side dishes also very good. During our meal, diners trickled through the door – the place is a magnet. And we're told it's like this 365 days a year. We're not surprised. The complex is run very well, with not one piece of litter in evidence. It's is not for loutish youth – you need a car to get there, and the restaurants and shops are geared towards 30 plus age group, and there are security guards a-plenty checking on the facilities. Though a formula curry house, the cooking is above average, and there's the view, unique and sumptuous. We are pleased to put it straight into our TOP 100. Business lunch: 3 courses £5.95. Price Check: Popadom 50p, CTM £6.25, Pullao Rice £2.10. Hours: 12pm-12am. Branches: Indian Cottage, Horndean and Waterlooville. Stocks Cobra.

Ringwood

CURRY GARDEN ©

10 High Street, Ringwood — 01425 475075

Between them, Feroze Khan and chef Runu Miah continue to satisfy the needs of their diners. Stocks Cobra.

INDIA COTTAGE TANDOORI NEW ENTRANT

35 Christchurch Road, Ringwood — 01425 473671

'Went on a Wednesday night when they have their Banquet Night –

incredible value. Bhoona Prawn Puree, delicious with masses of prawns. All huge portions. Only complaint is the service was very slow.' JH-T. Stocks Cobra.

Romsey

LIGHT OF BENGAL NEW ENTRANT

5 Church Street, Romsey 01794 517431

'Well cooked food. The lady in the booth next to me left her sleeping five-year-old behind (apparently he likes Chicken Vindaloo but it knocks him out) and the owner ran after her with him!' MS. Price check: Papadam: 40p, CTM £5.20, Bombay Potato £1.90, Pullao Rice £1.60. Delivery: minimum £10. Hours: 5.30pm-12am.

Southampton

CHUTNEY'S CURRY HOUSE NEW ENTRANT

40 London Road, Shirley, Southampton 023 8036 6336

First opened in 1997. Seats 44. Price check: Papadam 40p, CTM £6.10, Pullao Rice £1.95, Peshwari Nan £1.80, Lager £2.30 pint. Takeaway: 15% discount. Hours: 12-2.30pm/6-12am. Stocks Cobra.

EURO-ASIA NEW ENTRANT

179 Lyndhurst Road, Ashurst, Southampton 023 8029 2885

Established in 1992. Seats 60. Decorated in pale pink with tablecloths and napkins to match. Pictures hanging on the walls from Bangladesh. Ample parking at front. Specialise in Balti dishes. Price check: Papadam 55p, CTM £6.10, Pullao Rice £1.80, Peshwari Nan £1.80, Lager £2.40 pint. Takeaway: 15% discount. Hours: 6pm-12am. Stocks Cobra.

KUTIS BRASSERIE RE ENTRANT

37-39 Oxford Street, Southampton 023 8033 3473

Exotically decorated with marble effect walls, large plants, chandelier and tented ceiling. Kurgee Lamb – a whole leg of lamb marinated in spices and slowly roasted or Kurgee Ayre – whole Bangladeshi dish marinated and roasted – 24 hours notice required for both of these dishes. Duck and venison features highly on the menu.

COBRA GOOD CURRY GUIDE
County Index, see page 5 Town Index, see page 614
A to Z of the Curry Menu, page 41 Contributors Key, page 604

NATAJ BALTI NEW ENTRANT

3 Winchester Street, Southampton 023 8036 6344

'I am vegetarian and the Vegetarian Baltis are very good. Also, according to friends that eat meat, the other Balti dishes are excellent too. The building was once a night club and the owners have kept the dance floor and they play live Indian music on Fridays and Saturdays.' MD. Hours: 12pm-2am/6-11.30pm. Stocks Cobra.

SPICE OF INDIA NEW ENTRANT

Wyndham Crt, 42 Commercial Rd, Southampton 023 8022 0201

'Location is unlikely, in a really awful concrete courtyard of an equally awful concrete block of flats, typical 1960's ugliness. Decor pale green/grey plush. Extensive menu, our dishes exceptionally competent. Popadoms served cold but very crisp and light. Batak Karai, excellent, Karahi Ayre, successful. Best ever Nan, large, light and fluffy. Generous portions, service good, most impressed.' HC. Delivery. Price check: Papadam 50p, CTM £5.95, Pullao Rice £2.20. Hours: 12-2.30pm/6pm-12.30am (Fri. & Sat. to 1am). Stocks Cobra.

Southsea

AKASH NEW ENTRANT

99-101 Albert Road, Southsea 023 9229 1813

'Not a restaurant for shrinking violets, weekend night after chucking out time. Seats 100 in two rooms. Place buzzing from 7pm onwards. Despite being busy the large number of staff provide a good level of service and manage to remain friendly and helpful. The manager walks around chatting to diners and is not afraid to clean tables or fetch drinks. Open often well past the advertised 2.30am, a little expensive, but offering half prices if you are out by midnight. Main dish – Mint Lamb £7.60, a derivation of Tikka Masala with generous chunks of lamb Tikka, addition of copious mint and lemon juice made it very tangy and piquant rather than the often overly sweet taste found in the former dish. Sauce thick enough to be easily eaten with excellent Chapatis. Thoroughly enjoyable.' RW. Licensed. Price check: Papadam 60p/30p, CTM £7.40/£3.70, Pullao Rice £2.30/£1.30. Hours: 12-3pm/6pm-2.30am. Stocks Cobra.

GOLDEN CURRY TOP 100 ©

16 Albert Road, Southsea 023 9282 0262

A few years ago, I was interviewed by local TV station Meridian here, and I sampled many dishes from the korma to the phal. As a definition of the formula, they were spot on. Colours, aromas, tastes, textures, service and price – all done right by experienced 'old hands'. In fact the 52-seater has been owned by Salim Hussein (manager) and Razak Ali (head chef) since 1979, and has a justifiably loyal following. 'An excellent restaurant which my husband and I go to for a "curry fix". Salim is a wonderful host, greeting his clients with courtesy and friendliness, the waiters follow his lead. Ali runs a wonderfully efficient and clean kitchen.' C&CH. 'Excellent food and service. Our regular curry restaurant.' DKM. House specials include: Bengal Star, chicken, king prawn, mushroom, cooked together with tomato, onion and green pepper, garnished with tomato and cucumber, medium-spiced, served with Pullao Rice £8.15; Trout Biran, a dry dish, fresh, whole trout, fried with spices, served with lightly spiced spinach, sliced lemon, served with boiled rice £8.25. Price check: Papadam 45p, CTM £7.05, Pullao Rice £1.80, Peshwari Nan £1.70. Hours: 12-2pm/5.30pm-12.30am; Sun. 12pm-12am. Stocks Cobra.

JEWEL IN THE CROWN

60 Osborne Road, Southsea 023 9282 7787

'Beautiful restaurant, helpful waiters. Kitchen is at the end of the restaurant with huge window so the chefs can be watched whilst cooking. Good Indian wine. Starters were out of this world. Trout Tandoori was great.' TJ. Chef Sikandar Ali recommends Murgh Makani, 'nice and very mild' £5.95. Price check: Papadam 40p, CTM £5.40, Pullao Rice £1.80. Delivery: £12 minimum. Hours: 12-2.30pm/6pm-12am. Stocks Cobra.

LE TAJ TANDOORI NEW ENTRANT

31 Osborne Road, Southsea 023 9275 4475

'I have only eaten in an Indian restaurant once before and that was not memorable. Due to my ignorance of Indian food, the proprietor Mr Kalam helped with the choice of dishes. It was delicious! Full of flavours and balanced from the very spicy to the very delicate. It was a revelation. I have never written to anyone about visits to a restaurant before, but on this occasion, I felt that Mr Kalam and Le Taj deserved a helping hand.' PW. Stocks Cobra.

County Index, see page 5 Town Index, see page 614
A to Z of the Curry Menu, page 41 Contributors Key, page 604

Stubbington

STUBBINGTON TANDOORI NEW ENTRANT ©

35a The Green Stubbington, Nr Fareham 01329 664615

First opened 1985. Taken over by Mr Rahman in 1997. Seats 40. Specials include: Balti £5.95, Murag Makhan £5.95 – boneless chicken cooked with butter and fresh cream. Price check: Papadam 45p, CTM £6.50, Pullao Rice £1.75, Peshwari Nan £1.95, Lager £1.95 pint, House wine £8.95 bottle. Takeaway: small discount. Delivery: £12 minimum, 4-mile radius. Hours: 5.30pm-12am. Stocks Cobra.

Waterlooville

INDIAN COTTAGE ©

51 London Road, Cowplain, Waterlooville 01705 269351

D&BR and L&AC have been coming as a foursome for many years to Sheik Shab Uddin's tiny 30-seater (exposed oak beams, blue walls and tablecloths, red velvet chairs) because chef AH Khan's 'food is excellent and the staff always attentive'. Hours: 12-2.30pm/5.30pm-12am. Branches: Indian Cottage, Port Solent Marina, and The Square, Horndean. Stocks Cobra.

SHALIMAR NEW ENTRANT ©

9 Hambledon Pde Hambledon Rd, Waterlooville 023 9225 1565

'Shalimar's greatest asset is that it does the simple things well. The Lamb Jalfrezi is a little hotter and more adventurous than usual, and the Chicken Shaslit is another highlight. A quiet, friendly establishment with young staff who are both polite and efficient.' GS. A/c 56-seater, with smoking and non-smoking sections, is managed by Mujib. 'Does the simple things well. Chicken Korma one of the best. Lamb Jalfrezi, hotter than usual. Young friendly staff – polite and efficient.' GS. Price check: Papadams 40p, CTM £5.50, Pullao Rice £1.60, Peshwari Nan £1.60. Hours: 12-2.30pm/5.30-11.30pm.

Winchester

GANDHI

163 High Street, Winchester 01962 863940

'Pleasant restaurant. All the favourites plus some less usual dishes. Chicken Milan was excellent and plentiful, Chicken Pricy also very good, Mixed

Vegetable Bhaji was delicious (lightly cooked and freshly prepared), Peshwari Naan light and tasty. Portions ample. But what of the service? Booking system totally meaningless, as everyone – booked or not – was given tables on a first come, first serve basis. Had to ask four times for a jug of water. All in all, however, a very good meal and despite the wait and poor service I would have no hesitation in using it on a regular basis if I lived in the area.' MW. 'Agree with BPD in the last GCG ...' [to remind us, he said: 'superb ambience. Most of the tables (50-60 covers) arranged for four in cabins, which can be partitioned by curtains – very unusual, but very nice for a young couple in need of a quick cuddle before a curry!' BPD]. '...ambience is very welcoming and good use is made of what is actually not a very big restaurant. Food was very good indeed. Freshly cooked Onion Bhajia, very generous portion, four pieces. Very good Lamb Tikka. Stuffed Fried Eggs, two eggs cooked and halved with the yolk replaced with some sort of whipped mixture and whole prawns, then deep-fried in batter – great!! Only table there at 6pm, waiters were prompt, attentive and polite.' CT. Stocks Cobra.

Yateley

KARAHI HOUSE NEW ENTRANT

1 Aylesham Way, Yateley 01252 890964

Fully licensed. A nicely and simply decorated restaurant in pale pink and blue. All the standard dishes served here from Korma to Vindaloo.

HEREFORDSHIRE

Area: Welsh Border
Population: 215,000
Adjacent Counties: Gwent, Powys, Shrops, Staffs, Worcs

Leominster

JALALABAD

33 Etnam Street, Leominster 01568 615656

Well promoted by the ebullient owner-manager Kamal Uddin (though, curiously not to us). Owner-chef Abdul Mukith's food menu attracts regular praise from Leominster locals. Stocks Cobra.

Ross-on-Wye

OBILASH

19a Gloucester Road, Ross-on-Wye 01989 567860

First opened 1980. Seats 40. Some unusual Bangladeshi authentic dishes on the menu include Shathkora Curry and Ada Lembu Curry. Specials include: Anderi Raat (half chicken marinated in Obilash special spices, served with rice). Price check: Popadam 70p, CTM £9.20, Pullao Rice £2.50, Peshwari Nan £2.10, Lager £2.45 pint. Takeaway: 10% discount. Delivery: £18, anywhere in Ross. Hours: 6-11.30pm (1am on Sat.). Stocks Cobra.

HERTFORDSHIRE

Area: Home Counties, (north of London)
Population: 1,028,000
Adjacent Counties: Beds, Bucks, Cambs, Essex, London

Abbots Langley

FOREST OF INDIA NEW ENTRANT

39-41 High Street, Abbots Langley 01923 270077

Seats 100. Takeaway: 10% discount. Price check: Papadam 50p, CTM £5.45, Pullao Rice £1.50, Peshwari Nan £2.10, Lager £2.25 pint. Hours: 12-2.30pm/6-11.30pm. Stocks Cobra.

VICEROY OF INDIA TOP 100 ©

20 High Street, Abbots Langley 01923 262163

Formerly Viceroy of India. Established in 1989 by Ronney Rahman. 'Has been redecorated in very modernistic style, colours dark blue and orange, gas fired lights on ceiling. Enlarged, separate non-smoking section. Food delicious, always fresh and elegantly presented. Waiters friendly and

©	Curry Club Discount	U	Unlicensed
V	Vegetarian	ANP	Alcohol not permitted
e-a-m-a-y-l	Eat as much as you like	BYO	Bring your own alcohol

attentive.' D&PM. 'Menu was full and standard with the unique addition of a number of hash (duck) dishes. Makhoni Hash – wonderfully flavourful, distinctive but mild spices in a cream and tomato sauce. Service was hesitating, a bit slow.' RH. 'I think well of the food here, however it is difficult to get in at lunchtime.' SS. House specials: Makhoni Hash (mild) tandoori grilled duck, tossed in butter, cultured yoghurt, fresh cream and mild spices £5.75 and Karahi Jhinga (hot), jumbo prawns cooked with a medium dry gravy, herbs, tomatoes, onions and green pepper, served from a iron karahi £6.95. Price check: Papadam 45p, CTM £5.75, Pullao Rice £1.70, Sunday buffet £6.95. Reports please. Hours: 12-2.30pm/6-11pm. Stocks Cobra.

Barnet GL

(inc East Barnet and New Barnet)

KING TANDOORI ©

92 East Barnet Road, New Barnet 020 8441 9272

MD Salim opened his 46-seater in 1995 and we hear well of it, especially of the Happy Hour Half Price Meal. 'It makes me happy at that price.' NL. Price check: Papadam 40p, CTM £5.30, Pullao Rice £1.50. Evenings only, except Sun. e-a-m-y-l buffet £5.95, lunch and dinner.

SHAPLA TANDOORI ©

37 High Street, Barnet 020 8449 0046

Established in 1981. SI Ahmed's smart restaurant seats 50 and is popular. 'My local, always very reliable. Standard menu. Excellent Dhansak, generous Shashlik and very good side dishes. A clean, cosy restaurant.' CT. Minimum charge £7.50. Parking in Fitzjohn Avenue. Price check: Papadam 50p, CTM £5.25, Pullao Rice £1.65, Peshwari Nan £1.60, Lager £2.30 pint. Delivery: £1.50, 4-mile radius. Hours: 12-2.30pm/6pm-12am. Stocks Cobra.

Berkhamsted

AKASH ©

307 High Street, Berkhamsted 01442 862287

'We particularly like owner Foysol Ahmed's service – greeted at the door, coats taken, napkins placed in your lap, staff are attentive without hovering.' LB. Hours: 12-2.30pm/6pm-12am.

CURRY GARDEN ©

29 High Street, Berkhamsted 01442 877867

'An old converted pub, lovely low beams and cosy booths. Very impressed. Will most definitely be back.' SW. Stocks Cobra.

Bricket Wood

VICEROY NEW ENTRANT

85, Old Watford Road, Bricket Wood 01923 672121

'A welcome surprise just off the M1/A405 junction. Prices good for location. Cuisine better than average, lightly spiced. Duck dishes make a pleasant change – Jalfrezi £5.50. Keema Nan £1.70. One of our group who does not like curry, poor fool, enthusiastically mopped up any remainders of the ample portions.' RH. Price check: CTM £5.50, Pullao Rice £1.70. Stocks Cobra.

Bushey GL

INDIA GARDEN

88 High Street, Bushey Village 020 8950 2061

At Abdul Koyes Choudhury's 52-seater, we hear of the good value: Sunday 12-course buffet lunch. Hours: 12-2.30pm/6-11.30pm. Branch: Taste of India, High Street, Kings Langley. Stocks Cobra.

RAJ GARDEN NEW ENTRANT

219 Park Avenue, Bushey 01923 493939

Established in 1997. Seats 60. Car park for 10 at rear. Price check: Popadam 40p, CTM £5.95, Pullao Rice £1.65, Peshwari Nan £1.65, Lager £2.70 pint. Delivery: £10 minimum, 3-mile radius. Hours: 5.30-11.30pm; Sun. 12-11pm. Stocks Cobra.

Cheshunt

RAJ VOGUE ©

48 High Street, Cheshunt 01992 641297

Established in 1991 by Khalek Quazi, who also manages the 82-seater restaurant. Room for 50 cars at the back. GR likes the Nawab Nargis, cooked with spicy minced chicken and fresh mint. Price check: Papadam 50p, CTM

£6.75, Pullao Rice £2.10, Peshwari Nan £2.25, Lager £3.90 pint. Takeaway: 10% discount. Delivery: £15, 3 miles. Hours: 12-2.30pm/6-11.30pm; Sat. 12-2.30pm (Sun. 1-2pm)/6pm-12am (Sun. to 11pm). Sunday lunch buffet £6.95. Stocks Cobra.

Chorley Wood

SUJOY TANDOORI INDIAN NEW ENTRANT

12, Main Pde White Lands Ave, Chorley Wood 01923 283505

Established in 1994 by Nanu Dey, who oversees front of house and the kitchens. Seats 40. Specials: Lamb Kalia £6.75 – highly spiced lamb with onions, ginger, green peppers and fenugreek leaves. Air conditioned. Easy parking at front. Price check: Papadam 50p, CTM £6.50, Pullao Rice £1.95, Peshwari Nan £1.95, Lager £3 pint. Hours: 12-2.30pm/6pm-12am. Stocks Cobra.

Hatfield

PRINCE OF INDIA ©

10 Market Place, Hatfield 01707 265977

Established in 1993, managed by SF Ali. The restaurant seats 48 diners, and is newly decorated, we are told, in a romantic and pleasant atmosphere. Delivery: £8.95 minimum. Hours: 5.30-11.30pm.

RAJ TANDOORI NEW ENTRANT

55-55 Bradmore Green, Brookmans Pk, Hatfield 01707 663259

'Recently been redecorated, giving warm and relaxed atmosphere. Seats fifty, air-conditioned. Portions on the generous side. Had my favourite Sheek Kebab and asked if the chef could add green chillies, result MOUTH-WATERING. My partner had Tandoori King Prawns WONDERFUL, full of flavour. Every dish has its own individual taste and is cooked to your requirements from mild to mind blowing. Recommended.' IJ. Interesting menu addition: Vegetable Tray £5.50 – three different vegetable dishes – great idea! Delivery. Price check: Papadam 45p, CTM £6.45, Pullao Rice £1.65. Hours: 12-2.30pm/6-11pm (Fri. & Sat. to 11.30pm).

TASTE OF INDIA ©

33-34 Salisbury Square, Old Hatfield 01707 276666

Owned by Mrs A Khatun and managed by Golam Yahna, the Taste has become a popular local haunt. Specials include: Duck Korai, and Balty (sic.) Tropical, Pullao Rice £1.40. Mondays, four-course banquet. Stocks Cobra.

Hemel Hempstead

GURU TANDOORI ©

5 Bridge Street, Hemel Hempstead 01442 254725

Owner SM Rahman. Chef S Uddin. 36 seats. MBS says he has eaten here twice a week for twenty years, and that he always recommends it to his friends, who in turn have become satisfied customers. Delivery: £15 minimum, 5-mile radius. Hours: 12-2.30pm/6pm-12am. Branch: Guru, 630, Uxbridge Road, Hayes, Middx. Stocks Cobra.

RAJA ©

84 London Road, Apsley, Hemel Hempstead 01442 252322

'Both spacious and intimate. Portions generous, brought sizzling.' JP. Delivery: 'service was fast. Large and very tasty portions arrived piping hot within 30 minutes.' JH. Branch: Paradise, above. Stocks Cobra.

Hitchin

INDIA BRASSERIE ©

36 Bancroft Road, Hitchin 01462 433001

M Chowdhury's restaurant seats 32. Specials: Chicken Makhani Tikka, Rezala Chicken and Fish Bhuna5. 'The best in Hitchin.' SW. Hours: Tues.-Thurs. 12-2.30pm/5.30pm-12am; Sun. 1-11pm, buffet £7.95. Stocks Cobra.

SPICE KING TAKEAWAY NEW ENTRANT

143 Nightingale Road, Hitchin 01462 434010

Established in 1998 by Islam Chowdhury, whose wife Mrs Rahena Islam Chowdhury keeps things shipshape front of house. House specials: Chicken Tikka Saslik Massala (with onion rings). Set Meals: Monday to Thursday – papadam, starter, main course, side dish, rice and nan – all for only £7.50. Takeaway: spend £5 and 10% discount, spend £40 and 20% discount.

Delivery: £10 minimum, 5-mile radius. Price check: Papadam 50p, CTM £5.50, Pullao Rice £1.50, Peshwari Nan £1.60. Hours: 5.30-11.30pm.

Knebworth

RAJA NEW ENTRANT

129 London Road, Knebworth 01438 813321

'We've had takeaways and eaten in this restaurant several times and return because the food is so good. They use fresh herbs and spices, and the Vegetable Biriani is superb! Staff are friendly, attentive and happy to take any special requests to the chef. Takeaway service is speedy even on a busy night. We'd like to see them in the Curry Guide, please.' MS. Stocks Cobra.

Letchworth

CURRY GARDEN ©

71 Station Road, Letchworth 01462 682820

Afiz Ullah is the head chef and owner of this 72-seater, which has a 'huge friendly menu.' MT. Hours: 12-2.30pm/6pm-12am; Sun. 12pm-12am, buffet 12-5.30pm. Branches (all named Curry Garden) at: Berkhamsted; Rickmansworth; Dunstable, Beds; Hornchurch, Essex. Stocks Cobra.

SAGAR ©

48 The Broadway, Letchworth 01462 68495

Motiur Rahman's 'Trout Masala is one of the best.' LV. Service 10%. Lunch buffet, weekdays £5.50, Sun. £5.95. Branches: Aashiana, Broadway, Beds; Ahkbar Takeaway, Abbot's Walk, Biggleswade, Beds.

New Barnet GL (*see* Barnet)

Radlett

RADLETT INDIA CUISINE

70e Watling Street, Radlett 01923 856300

'Chicken Chockro Vorty, marinated strips, grilled, served with salad, exceptional starter. Jeera Kata Garlic Chicken brilliantly tasty, no cloying curry gravies. Nan, chewy and delicious.' CJ. Stocks Cobra.

Rickmansworth

EASTERN SPICE ©

9 Penn Place, Northway, Rickmansworth 01923 711101

Ekbal Hussain's 40-seater remains popular with its local following. Hours 12-2.30pm/6-11.30pm. Branch: Gadebridge Balti, Hemel Hempstead.

MAHARAJA NEW ENTRANT

140 High Street, Rickmansworth 01923 770107

'A cold blustery night, but the welcome was very warm. Small, modern restaurant. A meal fit for a king. Starters far better than average. Chicken Chilli Massala was divine, though not a dish to be eaten by those with a delicate palette. Vegetable dishes were spicy and perfectly cooked. Naan very enjoyable, rice a little sticky. Generous portions. Definitely give this restaurant a go if and when you're passing.' SW.

Royston

BRITISH RAJ

55 High Street, Royston 01763 241471

Established in 1976 by Nazir Uddin Choudhury, whose restaurant is decorated with embossed ivory wallpaper and pictures of the Raj. Seats 44, in an L-shaped dining room. House Special: Bengali cod fish curry with tomatoes, chillies in a sauce £6.55. After your meal you can finish the night off by ordering the fifth course – Hukkah (Hubble Bubble). Takeaway: 10% discount. Price check: Papadam 50p, CTM £6.95, Pullao Rice £1.75, Peshwari Nan £1.95, Lager £2.60 pint. Hours: 12-2pm/6pm-12am. Stocks Cobra.

Sawbridgeworth

STAR OF INDIA ©

51 London Road, Sawbridgeworth 01279 726512

Established in 1981 by Dilwar and Jamal Ahmed. Seats 70 in two rooms. Free car park opposite. Specials include: Kurzi Lamb and Kurzi Chicken. Takeaway: approximately 10% discount. Delivery: £12 minimum, 5-mile radius. Price check: Papadam 50p, CTM £8.95, Pullao Rice £2.25, Peshwari Nan £2.25, Lager £2.95 pint. Hours: 12-2pm/5.30-11.30pm. Stocks Cobra.

TANDOORI NIGHT

Knight Street, Sawbridgeworth 01279 722341

'We had our wedding reception in this great restaurant. Food and service excellent.' JP. 'Chicken Tikka, excellent huge pieces, very tasty. Onion Bhajias size of tennis balls. [must be the thing round here -Ed]. Very hot and tasty Madras, plenty of Vegetable Biriani. Friendly staff.' JP. Price check: Papadam 50p, CTM £5.95, Bombay Potato £2.10, Pullao Rice £1.60, Hours: 12-2.30pm/6-11.30pm (12am on Fri. & Sat.).

St Albans

MUMTAJ TOP 100

115 London Road, St Albans 01727 858399

Originally opened as a restaurant way back in 1962. Present owner, Muklasur Rahman Mojumder took over in 1983 and has established himself as a highly regarded source of Indian cuisine. Seats 44 diners in two rooms partitioned by an archway. The owner's son Chad Rahman now runs the kitchen. He loves to try out new ideas, and has been experimenting with a new menu. He worked for some time in curry houses in Houston, Texas. We get numerous reports on this restaurant praising its qualities (and one blaster from RP). None is more interesting than PFM: 'I am lucky enough to travel widely on business, and never travel without your *Guide*. I aim to visit every TOP 100. I agree with all but one of those visited. Having visited many, many curryhouses in the UK, as well as in Brussels (ugh), Amsterdam (great), Stockholm (ugh), Riyadh (ummm), and the USA (hmmm), I am always pleased to get home to St Albans, and eat at my local, the Mumtaj. Its location and interior are not as grand as some, but its food is sublime. Many – too many – curry houses serve their food with a general brown type gravy. Everything is coated in the same sauce. But in the Mumtaj each flavour stands out on its own. I eat in, or take out there on average three times a month. It would be more if I didn't do so much travelling.' PFM. 'A very nice place to go to. Food is above average. Staff helpful and not pushy.' SH. 'I tried the Murgh Zafrani – chicken in spicy mustard, coriander chilli paste with lemon, and it was delicious. Friend similarly complimentary about his Lamb Nashilee – lamb in a rich chilli and ginger sauce, spicy hot. Everything satisfactory.' RL. Price check: Papadam 50p, CTM £7.20, Pullao Rice £1.50. Hours: 12-2.30pm/6pm-12am.

VINDALOO INDIAN CUISINE NEW ENTRANT

156 London Road, St Albans 01727 821719

Established in 1998. Seats 65, ground and basement. Price check: Papadam 50p, CTM £7.20, Pullao Rice £1.50, Peshwari Nan £1.60, Lager £2.40 pint. Takeaway: 10% discount. Delivery: £10 minimum. Hours: 12-2.30pm/6pm-12am. Stocks Cobra.

Stevenage

GATE OF INDIA ©

20 The Glebe, Chells Way, Stevenage 01438 3176195

Abdul Salam has dropped the word 'New' from his restaurant's name, but our scribes tell us not to worry, everything else is as before. Its 57 seats are divided between 4 rooms. Chef Arosh Ali cooks all the favourites. Price check: Papadam 50p, CTM £6.15, Pullao Rice £1.60, Peshwari Nan £1.70. Delivery: £10 min, 4-mile radius. Hours: 12-2.30pm/6pm-12am. Stocks Cobra.

Tring

JUBRAJ ©

53a High Street, Tring 01442 825368

Special dinners for two at Monnan Miah's 90-seater, adjacent to the town car park. Hours: 12-2.30pm/6-11.45pm. Stocks Cobra.

Ware

NEELAKASH

1-3 Amwell End, Ware 01920 487038

'Busy but service was still attentive. Slightly larger than usual menu – fish curry is quite rare to find as is a restaurant that actually has rasmali.' SJ. Stocks Cobra.

Watford

DINE INDIAN NEW ENTRANT

326 St Albans, Watford 01923 221131

'One that I have used many times and is consistently good quality at a decent price. Friendly staff go out of their way to make you welcome, especially children who they will cook specially for. Certainly worth trying and I hope it will make it into the next GCG.' NI. Stocks Cobra.

SHAPLA NEW ENTRANT

105 Longspring, Watford 01923 817876

'About two miles from town centre, I prefer it to other better known locals. Perhaps its remoteness explains its absence from the Guide.' SHS. Stocks Cobra.

Welwyn Garden City

PAVILLION NEW ENTRANT

49 Wigmore Street, Welwyn Garden City 01707 333014

'Certainly worthy of your attention.' GF. Stocks Cobra.

KENT

Area: South East
Population: 1,572,000
Adjacent Counties: Essex, London, Surrey, Sussex

Part of Kent was absorbed by Greater London in 1965. We note affected areas with the letters GL.

Ashford

CURRY GARDEN ©

31 Bank Street, Ashford 01233 620511

80 seats. House specials: Chicken Khandary – mince meat, chicken, onion, capsicum, herbs and spices. 'Sheek Kebab £2.70 – very red, good. Chicken Chat Puri £3.95 – huge, very nice. Bengal Meat Rezala £4.75 – meat chewy, otherwise good. Cheese Nan £1.70 – excellent. Good, quick service. £26.70 inc. wine.' L&CH. Takeaway: 10% discount. Sunday lunch buffet. Price check: Papadam 45p, CTM £6.95, Pullao Rice £1.70, Peshwari Nan £1.70. Hours: 12-2.30pm/6-11.30pm (Fri. & Sat. to 12am).

TANDOORI NIGHTS

9 Torrington Road, Ashford 01233 636681

First opened in 1988. Seats 32 in three rooms. Banquets Monday to Thursday. Price check: Papadam 40p, CTM £5.90, Pullao Rice £1.50, Peshwari Nan £1.75, Lager £2.20 pint. Takeaway: 10% discount. Hours: 12-2pm/5.30-11.30pm.

Barnehurst GL

JHAS TANDOORI ©

158c Mayplace Road, East Barnehurst 01322 555036

Est. 1989 by Kuldip Jhas, who is also head chef; Robinder Jhas is the manager – a family business. Seats 50. Recently refurbished. Punjabi style Chicken and Lamb Balti is a house special and most popular with customers. 10% discount on takeaways. Price check: Papadam 35p, CTM £5.15, Pullao Rice £1.55, Peshwari Nan £1.50, Lager £2.50 pint. Hours: 6-11.30pm (Fri. & Sat. to 12am); Sun. closed. Stocks Cobra.

Beckenham GL

EDEN SPICE

406 Upper Elmers End Road,
Eden Park, Beckenham 020 8650 0919/020 8658 6582

Formerly Rose of India Tandoori. Taken over in 1997 by Abdul Quadir. His simply decorated restaurant seats 40. Chicken Green Masala is the most popular dish. Price check: Papadam 40p, CTM £5.95, Pullao Rice £1.75, Peshwari Nan £1.65. Set Dinner: £7.95. Delivery: 4-mile radius. Hours: 12-2.30pm/6-11.30pm; Sat. 6pm-12am. Stocks Cobra.

THE TASTE OF INDIA NEW ENTRANT

2 Goodwood Parade, Upper Elmers End Road,
Beckenham 020 8663 1544

'Fairly small and unremarkable restaurant, clean and tidy, serving food of well above average standard. All the favourites are on the menu, but done extremely well. The shaslick was particularly good, huge chunks of meat with little or no colouring in the marinade.' CT. Stocks Cobra.

Bexley GL

AKASH NEW ENTRANT

220 Broadway, Bexleyheath 020 8304 5314

'Menu contains one or two different offerings, and the food gets off to a good start with eight choices of pickles with papadoms. Chicken Chat was unaccompanied by any garnish and was rather salty, but very tangy and a substantial portion. Onion Bhajis were light, containing plenty of mixed and fenugreek seeds. Lamb Kate was in an extremely tasty sauce. Chicken Tikka Morrisa had a deep, smoky flavour, delicious. Excellent meal, service friendly and efficient, prices about average. Not in the guide but deserves to be.' MW. Stocks Cobra.

CURRY HUT TAKEAWAY ©

166 Mayplace Road East, Bexleyheath 01322 550077

Established 1995 by Muhammed Jahangir Alam. He tells us it's very modern, with an open kitchen. Set dinner £12.95 vegetarian, £14.95 non-vegetarian. Delivery: £10 minimum, 3-mile radius. Hours: 5-11.30pm.

RUCHI NEW ENTRANT

8 Steynton Avenue, Albany Park, Bexley 020 8300 0200

Established in 1986. Seats 140 in three rooms. Takeaway: 10% discount, £12 minimum. Delivery: £30 minimum, 3-mile radius. Price check: Papadam 55p, CTM £6.75, Pullao Rice £2, Peshwari Nan £2.50, Lager £2.60 pint. Hours: 12-2pm/6-11pm; Sun. 12.30-3pm/6-11pm. Stocks Cobra.

SAGGOR ©

145 Blendon Road, Bexley 020 8303 7549

Ali Uddin's 'pleasant restaurant, had a nice ambience, appetising smell as we entered – always a good start. Good menu featuring all the usuals plus a few less common names, particularly one or two interesting looking fish dishes. One of the most tasty Chicken Chats I've had for some time. Prawn Puri also unanimously approved. Subze Tandoori – a mixture of vegetables either whole or large slices, was very different. Certainly worth going to again.' MW. Price check: Papadam 50p, CTM £6.10, Pullao Rice £1.55. Delivery: £10 minimum. Hours: 12-2.30pm/6-11.30pm (Sun. to 11pm). Stocks Cobra.

Biddenden

KUSHBOO TANDOORI BALTI HOUSE NEW ENTRANT

5-7 Headcorn Road, Biddenden 01580 291485

Formerly Maharaja. 'Situated a good half mile outside village, small car park in front. Pleasant surroundings. All dishes reasonable, nothing special, but nothing to complain about. Chicken Tikka Jalfrezi £5.95, well endowed with green chillies. Portions sufficient, prices average. Efficient service.' MW. Delivery. Price check: Papadam 50p, CTM £5.95, Pullao Rice £1.40. Hours: 12-2pm/5.30-11.30pm.

Biggin Hill

RAJ ©

187 Main Road, Biggin Hill 01959 572459

70-seater, managed by AM Crorie, decorated in an 'olde worlde' style. Delivery: £10 minimum, 3-mile radius. Hours: 12-2.30pm (3.30pm on Sun.)/6-11.30pm (12am on Sat.). Stocks Cobra.

Borough Green

RAJ NEW ENTRANT

31 High Street, Borough Green 01732 882650

'Pleasant if unremarkable meal. Vegetable dishes marginally better than average, particularly the Aloo Gobi – lightly cooked and tastily spiced. Service also pleasant and efficient, portions quite sufficient, prices about average.' MW.

Bromley GL

CAFÉ EAST NEW ENTRANT

123-125 Masons Hill, Bromley 020 8460 5452

Part of the Tamasha Group, owned by Shekor Tarat and Anil Deb, seats 76 diners. Brightly coloured menus, turquoise with orange for the food and fuschia with orange for the wine list. Somebody has rather a 'Carry On' sense of humour with starters like Tossing the Kyber £3.95 (Scottish salmon marinated with ginger and garlic, flavoured with caraway and char-grilled on the tandoor), Hey Griddle, Griddle £8.50 (chicken cooked on the tava with green peppers, onions, tomatoes and fresh herbs), Goan, Goan, Gone! £10.95 (in a trice, these Goan prawns with a Portuguese influence – hot and spicy!), It's all Fenugreek to Me £6.50 (nuggets of soya delicately spiced with garam masala and cooked with fresh fenugreek), Kebab's your Uncle! £6.95 (potato, cauliflower and paneer chunks skewered with green peppers, onion and tomatoes, then popped in the tandoor to char grill) and, probably the worst joke of the lot, Grandma, we love you! £3.00 (she may be plain, nutty or even highly scented, but we know you all love your nan). I can hear the groans already! It's perhaps not the longest menu in the world, but there are some great dishes for everyone. Sunday brunch: three courses, £9.85 per person, live jazz band, 12-3pm. House wine £8.95. House champagne £23.95. Hours: 1-2.30pm/6-11.00pm. Branch: Tamasha, Bromley. Stocks Cobra.

HOMESDALE TANDOORI NEW ENTRANT ©

28 Homesdale Road, Bromley 020 8290 0671

Established in 1986. Seats 60. Undergoing redecoration. House specials: Haryali Chicken Massalla £6.50 – baked chicken in a marinade of spinach, mint and coriander puree, served in a creamy sauce. Price check: Papadam 50p, CTM £5.95, Pullao Rice £1.50, Peshwari Nan £1.60, Lager £3.20 pint. Takeaway: 10% discount. Delivery: £10 minimum, 3-mile radius. Hours: 12-2pm/6pm-12am.

RAJ MONI NEW ENTRANT

10 Plaistow Lane, Bromley 020 8466 5561

'Good, clean decor in spacious room. Polite waiters, unintrusive and helpful. Superb, fresh Popadoms and Chutneys. Aloo Chat – very spicy, highly flavoured, garlic, excellent. Special Mixed Kebab – lamb so tender, crisp, fresh salad. Jalfrezi – very hot, chillies included seeds! Nicely cooked Pullao Rice and Peshwari Nan. Hot towels, fresh orange slices. Standard prices in affluent area.' MW. Licensed. Price check: Papadam 50p, CTM £5.25, Pullao Rice £1.80. Hours: 12-2.30pm (closed Fri.)/6-11.30pm. Stocks Cobra.

SURUCHI ©

466 Bromley Road, Downham, Bromley 020 8698 8626

Modern, simply decorated, 60-seater. North Indian curries. Recommended Kaliya Galda, tiger prawns prepared with fresh coconut, ground mustard and ghee £9.95. Sunday buffet £5.95, kids £3.95, babies free. Owner Mr Dey promises CC members a free drink as their discount. Service 10%. Delivery: £12 minimum, 2-mile radius. Hours: 12-2.30pm/6-12pm. Stocks Cobra.

TAMASHA TOP 100 ©

131 Widmore Road, Bromley 020 8460 3240

Established in 1993. Owner is Shekor Tarat and manager Pramod Dey. Attached to a small hotel, so if you need a decent curry followed by a bed for the night, now you know. Tamasha means 'something worth seeing'. And it is! There is ample car parking, and you enter past a smartly saluting geezer, via an awning flanked by tub plants. Inside, there's a well-stocked bar with a fine selection of wines and beers including Cobra. The dining room, in two parts, seats 120 in seven rooms, and is superbly decorated like a British Raj Club, with polo sticks and hats, black and white photos of polo teams, Maharajas and sumptuous banquets. Cane furniture with palms in copper planters. Head chef Rajinder Kumar cooks food from north and south India, Goa and Kashmir. Curry house formula, it certainly is not. Favourite starters include Bhajis (Pakoras), Kebabs and Tikka, and main courses Jalfrezi and Chicken Tikka Masala, both £7.95. Good they are, too. But a little exploring can yield some treasures: Chicken Nilgiri Tikka, boneless chicken marinated in spices, fresh coriander and mint, cooked in the tandoor, £4.50. Goan Fish Curry, £8.50, fish cooked in coconut and red chillies and garnished with fresh coriander leaves. Dum Pukht Gosht, marinated sliced baby lamb in a variety of spices and then steam-cooked in sealed earthenware, £7.95, and Chicken Mirchi Wala, boneless chicken cooked in strongly spiced red chilli curry with potatoes, £7.50, is popular, and Abrakebabra! so is the table magician who entertains the kids during Sunday lunch buffet. 'Crowded right through the evening and booking in advance whatever the night is to be recommended. Real orchids on the tables and everything about it shouts quality. Many unusual and imaginative dishes. Chicken Nilgiri Tikka was an intriguing shade of green, caused by being marinated in mint and coriander, flavours came through as I ate. Fish Punjabi crisp and spicy, Aloo Tikki very tasty. Raan Jaipuri and Rara Gosht equally tender and delicious. The only thing that did not suit our taste was the Peshwari Naan which was very sweet and overloaded with ground almond, but no fruit. Portions ample, service efficient and polite (but not particularly friendly, except for welcoming doorman). Prices above average, but not excessive for quality of restaurant and location. Well deserves its TOP 100 status.' MW. 'I love this restaurant to bits. Chicken a little rubbery, King Prawn Puri £4.95 – outstanding.' MR C. 'Has nothing to worry about.' MPW. Service charge 12.5%. 20 car parking spaces. Live jazz and blues on Sun., Mon. and Tues. evenings. Sunday lunch buffet with in-house magician for children. Price check: Papadam 75p, CTM £7.95, Pullao Rice £2.50, Peshwari Nan £2.25. Takeaway: 10% discount. Hours: 12-2.30pm/6-11pm. Stocks Cobra.

ZANZIBAR ©

239 High Street, Bromley 020 8460 7130

Ebullient owner Ken Modi opened his Carioca in 1971 but changed its name because 'I got fed up with Karaoke requests'. The main room seats 50, its walls and ceiling decorated with coconut matting, giving the feeling of being in a fisherman's hut – 'a very glamorous one' according to Mr Modi. The party room, which includes a mock Pullman railway carriage, seats 70. The menu contains the regular favourite tandooris, baltis, curries and accompaniments. 'After a morning shopping on a Saturday, we headed to the Zanzibar for a lunchtime buffet. The food is on view from the outside, as it is displayed on a warming table in the window. This sounds awful but it's actually well done, the dishes, polished and spanking clean, the food, fresh. We were politely served our starters first: a fresh, crisp salad with flat Onion Bhajis and half a Nan with chutneys, raita and a Coconut Chutney which was incredible, with a slight hint of heat from its mustard seed. The service became very friendly and helpful when we were given huge warm bowls for the self-serve buffet. The dishes were explained to us: Chicken Tikka Masala (smoky flavour – great), Bhoona Gosht, Mild Chicken Curry, Meat Madras, Bombay Aloo (excellent – new potatoes), Cauliflower Bhajee, Dal Makhani, Brinjal Bhajee, Plain and Pullau Rice and Nan bread. After two visits to this array of food, I was stuffed and delighted. Good food from a clean, well-decorated restaurant.' MPW. Price check: Hot buffet dinners £7.95 Hours: 12-2pm (Sun. 12.30-3.30pm)/6pm (Sun. 6.30pm)-10.30pm. Price check: Papadam 40p, CTM £5.95, Pullao Rice £1.55. Set lunch £4.95, children £2.95, dinner £9.95, children £4.95. Lunch buffet £4.95. 10% service. Dinner buffet – 20 dishes £7.95 + 10% service. Stocks Cobra.

Canterbury

TASTY SPICE NEW ENTRANT

9 Longport Road, Canterbury 01227 463326

'Smart roomy surroundings. A mature and refined clientele – certainly not a lager lout restaurant. Fairly standard menu, but food very good. Chicken Tikka Pricy just right, being quite hot with a tasty lentil based sauce which had the hint of sweetness. Smart waiters provide efficient service, portions are plentiful, prices average (very reasonable for a better than average restaurant). Deserves an entry in the guide.' MW. Stocks Cobra.

Charing

SPICES OF BENGAL NEW ENTRANT

Charing Hill, Charing Hill, Charing 01233 712286

'Comfortable furnishings with a pleasant decor and situated about a mile from the village. Window table, excellent views over North Downs. Standard menu, average prices. Chicken Tikka Dhansak £7.50 (inc. rice), thick, dark and tasty. Good service.' MW. Price check: Papadam 50p, CTM £6.25, Pullao Rice £1.60. Hours: 12-2.30pm/6-11.30pm.

Chatham

LADY CHUTNEYS NEW ENTRANT

74 High Street, Chatham 01634 400450

Opened Dec '98. 'Punjabi not Bangladeshi, only Indian open on day (Muslim Religious Festival), proprietor is Hindu. Food reasonably priced and good sized helpings. Beer rather pricey – £7 for two bottles Cobra. Very clean throughout. Nan Bread £1.50 – nearly 24" long – Sparkbrook, Birmingham size!! Very pleased with ambience and quality and I consider the quality worthy of entry in GCG.' BP-D. Stocks Cobra.

Chislehurst GL

BENGAL LANCER TOP 100 RESTAURANT

15 Royal Parade, Chislehurst 020 8467 7088

We have said before that many towns have the perfect restaurant; one which is enjoyed by local patronage, and does not look for accolades. We don't mind giving them our TOP 100 award yet again. Cooking is by Chef Ram Das, who cut his spurs at the Bombay Brasserie and the Three Monkeys, SE23, 'and is as good as it gets' ME. Since the Lancer opened, the group owned by the Choudhury family, now has four extremely good restaurants. This is the original. It is our previous Reporter of the Year (JL's) favourite. 'It is spot-on in all respects' GC. Always busy when we go, but they always remember us, and serve good food superbly well.' TG. Branches: Bengal Clipper, SE1, Bengal Trader, E1, Bengal Mango, Halstead, Kent. Stocks Cobra.

JAIPUR ©

53 Chislehurst Road, Chislehurst 020 8467 9390

Owner Abdul Mushahid and manager Abdul Hannan have put together 'an exciting, different menu.' PP. Starters include Lacy Cutless, £2.95, an Anglo-Indian Keema-stuffed potato rissole, and Fish Roe, £2.95, breadcrumbed and deep-fried. Main courses include a wealth of interesting items, such as Green Goan Chicken Curry and a Sylheti red version, both £5.95. There is a creditable selection of Bangladeshi dishes. Ayre and Roop, Bengali fish, and the super Baingan Torkari – aubergine with tamarind cooked Sylheti-style in black terracotta. Minimum charge £10. Hours: 12-2pm/6-11.30pm. Stocks Cobra.

Crayford GL

GHANDI SPICE NEW ENTRANT ©

108 London Road, Crayford 01322 559191

Established in 1997. Seats 40. Parking at front. Sunday buffet. Price check: Papadam 40p, CTM £5.50, Pullao Rice £1.40, Peshwari Nan £1.40, Lager £3 pint. Takeaway: 10% discount. Delivery: £10 minimum. Hours: 12-2.30pm/5.30-11.30pm; Sun. 12-11.30pm. Stocks Cobra.

Dartford

GREEN TANDOORI NEW ENTRANT ©

Green Street, Green Road, Darenth, Dartford 01474 708885

First opened in 1996. A pretty boring curry house from the outside, but don't be put off – inside it's really quite nice. Air conditioned, hanging plants, green (what else!) tablecloths. Seats 45. Six car parking spaces at front, 20 at rear. Specials include: Kebab Raj Bahar £3.95, Chicken Shagorana £8.50 – half tandoori chicken with keema, garlic, tomato, green pepper, onion, egg, almond, cream and butter served with Fried Rice. Chingri Raj Bahar £8.10 – king prawns with garlic, onion, green pepper, tomato and coriander, slightly hot. Price check: Papadam 40p, CTM £5.80, Pullao Rice £1.50, Peshwari Nan £1.60, Lager £2.50 pint. Takeaway: 10% discount. Delivery: 4½-mile radius. Hours: 5-12pm; Sun. 12pm-12am. Stocks Cobra.

Downham

SHANTI INDIAN CUISINE NEW ENTRANT ©

419 Bromley Road, Downham Bromley 020 8461 4819

Established in 1988. Taken over by Anwarul Azim and Rukhsana Faoir in 1998. Air conditioned. Seats 48. Specials include: Chicken Achari £5.95 – cooked in a thick sauce with hot pickles. Sunday buffet: 12.30-3.30pm, adults £6.95, children under ten £3.95. Price check: Papadam 45p, CTM £5.95, Pullao Rice £1.50, Peshwari Nan £1.90, Lager £2.40 pint. Takeaway: 10% discount. Delivery: free, 10% discount, 4-mile radius. Hours: 12-2.30pm/6-11.30pm (Sat. to 12am). Stocks Cobra.

Dunton Green

TAJ NEW ENTRANT

110 London Road, Dunton Green 01732 462277

'Probably my favourite of all time. I have tried nearly every dish. Never disappointed. King Prawn Patia the best. Ample portions. Guideworthy.' KT.

East Peckham

REDFORT TANDOORI NEW ENTRANT

14 Hale Street, East Peckham 01622 872643

'Housed in a Georgian annex with car parking. Seats 100. Comfortable seating, pleasant decor. Onion Bhajia, two, good large flat, plenty of onion and spice, bland Chicken Chat. Chicken Bakara, chargrilled meat and spices gave nice flavour, not hot. Chicken Patia and Jalfrezi, plenty of chicken but I prefer them hotter. Sag Aloo, Mixed Vegetable Bhajee fine as was rice. Peshwari Nan heavy, doughy, coconut but no fruit. Very good portions, prices marginally higher than average. Service very good, manager/owner periodically enquiring if everything was OK. Competent.' MW. Price check: Papadam 45p, CTM £6.70, Pullao Rice £1.75. Hours: 12-2.30pm/6-11pm.

Farnborough

VILLAGE CUISINE NEW ENTRANT ©

145 High Street, Farnborough, Nr Orpington 01689 860077

Established in 1991. Seats 40. Not your run of the mill curry house – check out some of these fantastic dishes on the Summer Set Menu. Samosa – choose from meat, vegetable, coconut or fish. Creamed Mussels – served in their half shells, lightly spiced with saffron cream sauce. Murg Khasthri Kebab – chicken marinated overnight in yoghurt and herbs, skewered and cooked in tandoor. Hariali Lamb – boneless meat marinated in freshly ground coriander, spinach, mint and green chillies. Cucumber Rice, Spinach Nan, Mint Paratha and this list goes on! If you are not tempted by this extraordinary menu then there are of course the usual curry house curries. Price check: Papadam 50p, CTM £5.95, Pullao Rice £1.60, Peshwari Nan £1.80. Takeaway: 10% discount. Delivery: £10 minimum, 4-mile radius. Hours: 12pm-2.30am/5.30-11pm; Sun. buffet 12-7pm. Proprietor Mr Fahim Maksud has promised to give a discount of 10% to Curry Club members; please ring him for booking confirmation. Stocks Cobra.

Faversham

RAJ INDIAN CUISINE NEW ENTRANT

105 West Street, Faversham 01795 590052

'All the usuals on the menu plus a few less common dishes amongst their specials. Service good as were the portions. Prices reasonable and they offer a good deal each Tuesday evening with any starter, side dish, rice and naan for under a tenner.' MW.

Folkestone

INDIA TOP 100 RESTAURANT ©

1 The Old High Street, Folkestone 01303 259155

Established in 1985. Seats 42. Mr Ashraf is a French-trained Indian chef and speaks French, too. In some cases he combines the French use of cream, wine and brandy with spices to provide an original interpretation of his Indian dishes. We have some contradictory reports this time: 'Sheek Kebab, delicious, Prawn Puree, lots of prawns, taste just right. Truly wonderful Beef Hyderbad, generous portion. Pullao Rice, excellent, right-sized portion. Fluffy and garlicky Garlic Nan. Chatted to the owner's wife at length. Well deserves its place in the TOP 100.' L&CH. And exactly a month later ... 'Only two other couples at 7pm on Saturday, extreme dearth of waiters – one elderly sari-bedecked lady. Whilst mulling over potential delights of menu, opted for inevitable Popadoms with chutneys. Presented stone cold and greasy, chutney selection consisted of five pots, shared amongst all diners, periodically unceremoniously whisked away. Sita's Dosha, pancakes stuffed with prawn, mushroom, crab and coriander £3.25, consisted of two cigarette sized and shaped deepfried objects, vast bed of iceberg lettuce. Pahari Chicken Gosht £5.95. Prawn Patia £5.25. Magnifying glass a useful addition to cutlery to detect contents of dishes. Mushroom Bhajee – over salted. Panir Motor – cornflour. Peshwari Nan filled with Christmas cake, not fluffy. Best part of meal were the three bottles of Cobra at £1.95 each.' CS. 'Sheekh Kebab £2.95 – very good. Lamb Tikka £3.15 – nice. Pahari Chicken £5.50 – spicy, very good. Garlic Nan £1.75 – not very garlicky but very good. Finished meal with delicious Kulfi. Service and food excellent. Got discount!! Deserves it place in TOP 100. £22.00 inc: 2 beers.' L&CH. 'Service was friendly but food sadly lacking.' RL. 'The lunch time meal my wife and I were served was certainly not TOP 100 rating – we have eaten in many of your recommendations. Frankly the food was just not freshly cooked – just warmed up. Onion Pakora was very dry and bland. Not at all impressed on this one.' IM. Price check: Papadam 50p, CTM £5.95, Pullao Rice £1.60. Hours: 12-2pm/6-10.30pm. Stocks Cobra.

Gillingham

TIFFIN NEW ENTRANT

56-58 Balmoral Road, Gillingham 01634 570555

Formerly Mango Tree, situated in town centre opposite the station. Entrance unusually but commendably provides for wheelchair access. 'Chicken Chat good, chicken with fried potato, spices, topped in tangy sharp sauce, attractively served in basket-shaped popadom. My wife had Goolar ke Kebab – two attractive bell-shaped patties of very finely minced lamb, very spicy but so dry, would have been enhanced by Mint Raitha. Achar Gosht – OK, over salted. Nilgiri Korma – lamb cooked with cashew nuts, mint and spinach, very tasty and preferable to the often sickly version. Aloo Benarsar – potato, onion, spices – dry. Jeera Rice not up to standard, Peshwari Nan – good, very rich, buttery. Not up to standards, more like a continental wine bar than an Indian restaurant.' MW. 'Four of us had eight pints of Cobra, 16 Popadoms, Chicken Tikka, Karai Murgh, Karai Ghost, Tarka Dal, Vegetable Masala, Pullao Rice, Nan Bread and Kulfi. Followed by Zambuka liqueur on the house! The meal was excellent and the proprietor Abdul Kalam visited us several times. High standard of decor, hygiene and cleanliness, including the loos!' BP-D I'm not surprised that you had a fabulous time, you certainly didn't go without! Price check: Papadams 50p, CTM £6.95, Pullao Rice £1.95. Stocks Cobra.

Gravesend

(inc. Meopham)

A LA CARTE SPICE NEW ENTRANT

Gravesend Road, Fairseat, Meopham 01732 822599

Opened by Basith Khan, who was part owner of Gandhi, Gravesend. 'Large, seating 100, light, airy, spacious and fairly comfortable with modern furnishings. Onion Bhajis (Pizau), small, nicely crisp, not particularly spicy. Prawn Puree – spiced prawns were bland, puree very good. Momocha – four large round dumplings, stuffed with minced lamb, rather stodgy, too filling for appetiser, tomato pickle suspiciously like Heinz. Podina Chicken – strong, sharp acidic mint flavour, although tasty. Murgh Roshun – mild, pleasant. Khara Massala Gosht – pieces of lamb in dark thick sauce, lightly spiced stew. Boti Achari – lamb, pickle flavoured sauce, whole green chillies. Jerra Aloo – well spiced, excellent. Good Rice and very good Peshwari Nan, hot, light and slightly crispy with good filling. Service very good. Portions large – took remainders with us. Pleasant evening in pleasant restaurant but would benefit from robust spicing.' MW. Takeaway: 10% discount. Sunday Lunch Buffet: magician for the children – £6.95 adults, £5.95 children under 12, free under 5. Business lunches: special 10% off, Mon.-Fri. 12-2.30pm. Large car park. Price check: Papadam 60p, CTM £5.95, Pullao Rice £1.90, Peshwari Nan £1.80. Hours: 12-2.30pm/5.30-11.30pm. Stocks Cobra.

CURRY EXPRESS TAKEAWAY

125 Rochester Road, Gravesend 01474 331303

Formerly Simla. 'Another good takeaway, apart from the Tarka Dal which was dreadful. This is the first poor dish I have had. However, when I telephoned to tell them, the manager was most apologetic and sent a replacement (plus a complimentary Pullao Rice) which was fine.' And on his second visit: 'All containers packed full to the brim. Still a reliable delivery service, still giving a voucher (collect 10 and get £10 off) with meals over £10, still good value and still my number one local takeaway.' MW. Price check: Papadam 40p (plain spicy), CTM £4.95, Bombay Potato £1.90, Pullao Rice £1.40, Chutney and Pickles 45p. Delivery. Hours: 5pm-12am.

GANDHI BALTI HOUSE ©

66 West Street, Gravesend 01474 536066

Owned by Abdul Basith Khan, serves Bangladeshi-styled curries. Restaurant decorated in light pinks and light green, seats 60. 'Standards as good as ever.

Chot Pote (spiced chickpea and egg mixture) tasty, Chicken Pathia always good, Vegetable Pullao had plenty of vegetables and nuts, and at £2.20 was an excellent value alternative to plain pilao rice. Service friendly and efficient and 10% Curry Club discount given without hesitation. Price average, portions ample. Usually fully booked in advance Friday and Saturday nights!' MW. Price check: Papadam 50p, CTM £5.90, Pullao Rice £1.80, Peshwari Nan £1.70. Sunday lunch buffet £6.50, children £5.50. Hours: 12-2.30pm/5.30-11pm (11.30pm on Sat.). Stocks Cobra.

MEOPHAM TANDOORI ©

2 The Parade, Wrotham Road, Meopham, Gravesend **01474 812840**

Jahir Ali's 60-seater. 'Comfortable, small fountain, glass partitions, pleasant atmosphere. Comprehensive menu, usual dishes. Onion Bhajis – four round, served with salad and mint raitha, crispy, tasty. Aloo Chat Masala, excellent, tangy, spicy. First class Chicken Dhansak, thick, spicy lentil sauce. Delicately flavoured Shahi Lamb. Aloo Gobi – fairly dry, fresh tasting, crisp coating, peppery flavour. Portions adequate with good service, much better than last visit.' MW. Sunday Buffet £6.95. Price check: Papadam 45p, CTM £5.95, Pullao Rice £1.70. Hours: 12-2.30pm/5.30-11.30pm. Branch: India Palace Balti House, Station Approach, Meopham, Kent. Mr Ali has promised a CC 10% discount. Stocks Cobra.

PUNJAB KARAHI NEW ENTRANT U

4-5 Milton Road, Gravesend **01474 322222**

'The latest Indian restaurant to open in town. Not the standard high street curry house, but more akin to those in Indian areas. Open throughout the day, spotless surroundings, no licence. Full on a Friday night, and we were the only non-Asians. Limited but sufficient selection. Good, well spiced Punjabi food cooked while you wait. Aloo Tikki and Kebab Roll starters were excellent, and main dishes were first class, gutsy and well spiced. Service interestingly amateur. All in all, a good, inexpensive meal.' And a second visit 'Plain tables now covered in tablecloths, napkins etc, and new more efficient waiters. But I am happy to report that the menu, prices and food remain the same, and the clientele was still all Asian. Food again delicious – all freshly made and extremely tasty. Reasonable prices.' MW. Delivery: £8 minimum. Price check: Papadam 45p, CTM £4.50, Pullao Rice £1.30, Peshwari Nan £1.50. Hours: 5.30-2pm; Sat. & Sun. 12pm-12am.

RICKSHAW TAKEAWAY NEW ENTRANT

164 Parrock Street, Gravesend 01474 569651

'All in all a good formula takeaway curry house. Tasty Chicken Pathia in a thick sauce with a nice underlying sweetness, Vegetable Bhaji good, with plenty of variety of vegetables, Tarka Dall a little thin, but reasonably flavoured. Good sized portions and prices average for the area. Still delivering free on orders over the very reasonable level of £8.' MW. Price check: Papadam 40p, CTM £4.90, Pullao Rice £1.40. Hours: 5.30pm-12am/5.30-11pm.

Halstead

BENGAL MANGROVE NEW ENTRANT AND TO OUR TOP 100

London Road, Halstead 01959 534688

This is the newest of four extremely good restaurants owned by the Choudhury family. Cooking is overseen by Chef Ram Das. The 180-seater, said to have cost a cool £1m, is set in a landscaped garden, overlooked by a conservatory. Decor is modern, with pastel colours, down lighters, frosted glass and chrome, and it gives a "Conran" feel. Smoking and non areas have different styles. Popadoms and three small pots of Raitha, onion and spicy Mango – all very nice. Palak Pakori Chat £3.25 – spinach fritter, chopped, mixed in strongly flavoured tomato sauce, in curled lettuce leaf. Sev Puri £2.95 – beautifully presented on large plate (very Conran). Amazing Chicken Malwari £6.95 – succulent lumps of chicken in rich, strong coconut sauce – just lovely. Bombay Potato £2.95 – perfectly cooked. Peshwari Naan £1.95 – fresh, lacking flavour. Providing Indian food with a modern slant. Portions of sufficient size. 10% service charge and still credit card slip left open.' MPW. We'll put the Mangrove straight into our TOP 100 category, despite this practice, though we'd like to hear from you that it has stopped. Sunday lunch buffet £7.95. Price check: Papadam 55p, CTM £6.95, Pullao Rice £1.95. Branches: Bengal Clipper, SE1, Bengal Trader E1, Bengal Lancer, Chislehurst, Kent. Stocks Cobra.

Herne Bay

GANDHI NEW ENTRANT

139 Sea Street, Herne Bay 01227 374763

Decorated in natural earthy colours of green and brown. Chandeliers, velvet upholstery, pink tablecloths and hanging foliage make this curry house a favourite with the locals. The menu has no surprises but all the usuals from Shami kebabs to Rogan Josh.

Hoo

SURMA TAKEAWAY NEW ENTRANT

10 Main Road, Hoo 01634 253044

'Shabby exterior. Inside, surprisingly spacious for takeaway, clean if plain. Owner, Mr Islam, extremely friendly, has been there for ten years – must be OK. All the usuals, reasonable prices, food OK. Chicken Tikka Dansak £4.60 – not particularly hot, pleasant. Mixed Dry Vegetables £1.80 – nicely cooked, not overdone, lightly spiced. Vegetable Pullao Rice £1.80 – very nice. Good sized portions.' MW. Min charge: £3.00. Price check: Papadam 30p, CTM £4.95, Pullao Rice £1.30, Peshwari Nan £1.40. Hours: 5-11pm.

Longfield

LONGFIELD TANDOORI NEW ENTRANT

77 Station Road, Longfield 01474 705735

Formerly Mahatma Cote. 'Standard menu, no specials, considerably cheaper. Food was good overall. Tangy Chicken Chat and Prawn Puri delicately spiced and of good standard. CTM – overdosed with bright red colouring, quite tasty. Lamb Dhansak – excellent, thick, spicy sauce, reasonably hot, hint of sweetness. Vegetable dishes of good standard. Particularly good Nan. Portions sufficient. Service efficient.' MW. Delivery. Hours: 12-2.30pm/6-11pm (Fri. & Sat. to 11.30pm). Stocks Cobra.

Maidstone

SHAMRAT BRASSERIE ©

36 Upper Stone Street, Maidstone 01622 764961

Est. 1989 by chef, Jamal Hussain; you say 'Chicken Jalfrezi, one of the best, appeals to me as a fire-eater!' BP-D. 'Always an excellent welcome. Good warm food on a cold night. Bottomless coffee, liqueurs, orange slices, Suchard Mints, hot towels and an excellent house white wine. How do they do it?' PS. 'The warmth of a real blazing fire and Bombay Mix helped thaw me out whilst I looked through the menu. Quality, tasty, large portions of food.' NG. Sunday lunch buffet. Delivery: £12½-mile radius. Stocks Cobra.

Margate

SIMLA BRASSERIE NEW ENTRANT

370 Northdown Road, Margate 01843 221089

First opened in 1994. Room for 50 adults, let alone children. Price check: Papadam 50p, CTM £5.95, Pullao Rice £1.70, Peshwari Nan £1.90, Lager £3 pint. Takeaway: 10% discount. Delivery: £10 minimum. Hours: 12-2.30pm/6-11pm. Stocks Cobra.

Orpington GL

CURRY HOUSE ©

24 Station Square, Petts Wood, Orpington 01689 820671

Opened 1971, since 1989 son Basth (Baz) Wahab has been running the 42-seater. 'Food good but atmosphere non-existent. Eventually won the waiters round and managed a laugh and a little conversation. Flavoursome fish tikka. Main dishes were well up to expectation.' C&GM. Hours: 12-3pm (not on Fri.) and 6pm-12am; closed Mon. Stocks Cobra.

RAJ OF INDIA ©

4 Crescent Way, Green Street Green, Orpington 01689 852170

Established in 1987. Owner-manager Muzibur Rahmanr. Seats 72. Chef recommends: Akbori Lamb, cooked with sultanas and almonds in a yoghurt sauce. Takeaway: small discount. Hours: 12-2.30pm/6pm-12am. Branches: Raj of India Sheerness, Swanley and Sittingbourne; Raj Bari Sevenoaks; Maharajah Bexley; Juboraj Brentwood, Essex. Stocks Cobra.

Rainham

RAJ RANI BALTI NEW ENTRANT

85 High Street, Rainham 01634 377144

'Papadoms served without pickles so had to ask. Extremely thin and watery mango chutney. Starters OK but on the small side. Main dishes were fine. Balti Chicken Tikka Zal was cooked with aubergine and green chillies in a light hot sauce, Meat Pathia was very good, in a thick, dark rich sauce with a good balance between hot and sweet. Crowded on Saturday night, but plenty of waiters ensured efficient service. Prices average.' MW. Stocks Cobra.

Ramsgate

RAMSGATE TANDOORI ©

17 Harbour Street, Ramsgate 01843 589134

Owned by Rezaur Rahman, managed by Mrs Rahman. Bangladeshi and Pakistani curries on the menu, cooked by head chef Joyanti Mendas. Restaurant seats 70. Sunday buffet. Delivery: £10 minimum. Hours: 12-2.30pm/6pm-12am. Stocks Cobra.

Rochester

BENGAL BRASSERIE ©

356 High Street, Rochester 01634 841930

First opened in 1993. Seats 46. Ashahin Ali (manager), Abdul Roob (chef) and Ashamim Ali (chef). 'Indian music was too loud. Good, comprehensive menu. Slightly disappointed with the spicing and flavourings of all dishes. MW. 'My favourite Indian restaurant.' BP-D. Price check: Papadam 55p, CTM £6.95, Pullao Rice £1.90, Peshwari Nan £1.95, Lager £2.45 pint. Takeaway: approximately 10% discount. Delivery: 6-mile radius. Hours: 12-2.30pm/5.30pm-12am. Stocks Cobra.

SINGAPORA ©

51 High Street, Rochester 01634 842178/686363

Dr and Mrs Shome's 150-seater spreads over three floors, with tables in odd alcoves. Specialising in Malaysian, Chinese, Indonesian, Thai and Japanese cuisine. 'Cosy, but deceptively larger with upper floors and basement. Aromatic Duck £5.95 – shredded with sliced spring onions, cucumber and plum sauce rolled in pancakes. Udang Roti £2.20 – King prawns on sesame toast – substantial flavour. Ayam Penang £4.35 – Malaysian dish, crispy chicken with ginger and onions, tasty. Ayam Iblis £4.35 – sliced chicken, chilli and ginger, very tasty. Washed down with red house wine £8.95, smooth and excellent value. Portions a little on the small side. Efficient and friendly service. Pleasant alternative.' MW. Delivery. Hours: 12-3pm/6-11pm (Fri. & Sat. to 11.30pm);. Sun. 12-10.30pm. Branch: 73, Brewer Street, Maidstone.

Sandwich

INDIAN VILLAGE

The Old Fire Station, 11 The Butchery, Sandwich 01304 611926

Fully licensed and air conditioned. Situated in the Old Fire Station. It really did once house horse-drawn fire-engines, giving reason for its gently uplit long, low ceilings. 'Very full restaurant, made room for us on a table full of spare glasses. Very good Chicken Chilli Masala. Garlic Nan – bit flat, burnt bottom. £20.70 including 2 beers.' L&CH. Price check: Papadam 40p, CTM £5.10, Pullao Rice £1.55, Peshwari Nan £1.60. Hours: 12-2.30pm/6-11.30pm. Stocks Cobra.

Seal

TANDOORI NIGHTS NEW ENTRANT

47 High Street, Seal 01732 763055

Helpful and polite waiter on the telephone. 'Continues to be a favourite.' KT. Stocks Cobra.

Sevenoaks

ASIA CUISINE NEW ENTRANT

107 London Road, Sevenoaks 01732 453153

'My local. Does a brilliant CTM with rice and always friendly service.' KT. Stocks Cobra.

PLANET SPICE NEW ENTRANT

5 Sevenoaks Road, Sevenoaks 01732 886868

Planet Spice is a favourite local restaurant, serving many favourite curries. Stocks Cobra.

RAJ BARI

7 Tubs Hill Parade, London Road, Sevenoaks 01732 743315

'Manager and waiters – so friendly. Lovely decor, space between tables. Sheek Kebab, not much flavour. Main meals cooked nicely, but too much onion in Chicken Jalfrezi. Value for money.' MR&MRS L. Stocks Cobra.

Sheerness

KOHINOOR NEW ENTRANT

6a Minster Road, Halfway, Sheerness 01795 581600

Formerly Ruby, under new management. Fully licensed, fully air conditioned. Takeaway: 10% discount. Delivery: 2-mile radius, £10 minimum or £1 extra for deliveries outside 2-mile radius. Price check: Papadam 50p, CTM £4.95, Pullao Rice £1.50, Peshwari Nan £1.80. Hours: 12-2pm/5.30-11.30pm. Stocks Cobra.

TASTE OF INDIA TAKEAWAY NEW ENTRANT

9a Minster Road, Sheerness 01795 669669

Price check: Papadam 45p, CTM £3.70, Pullao Rice £1.35, Peshwari Nan £1.75. Hours: 12-2pm/5-11.30pm (Fri. & Sat. to 12am).

Sidcup GL

BLACKFEN BALTI ©

33 Wellington Parade, Blackfen Road, Sidcup 020 8303 0013

A friendly, pleasant, competent 48-seat curry house, owned by Muzammil Ali since 1983. Stocks Cobra.

OVAL BRASSERIE ©

49 The Oval, Sidcup 020 8308 0274

Ansar Miah has owned and managed the aptly-named Oval since 1988 (head chef Mohibur Rahman). Monday and Tuesday £7.95, starter, main course, side dish, rice or Nan – excellent value. Delivery: £10 minimum, 3-mile radius, free Papadam. Hours: 12-2.30pm/6-11.30pm. All-day Sunday buffet £6.95, £4 for kids. Hours: 12-11.30pm. Stocks Cobra.

RUCHI NEW ENTRANT

56-58 Albany Park, Sidcup 020 8302 5799

Waiters very helpful and cheerful on telephone. 'Bright restaurant, staff friendly and attentive, food out of this world. Chicken Rezala and Peshwari Naan Bread are the best ever.' HL. Stocks Cobra.

Snodland

AAGRAH NEW ENTRANT

16 Holborough Road, Snodland 01634 243320

'We've generally visited this place two or three times a year, and have always had an enjoyable meal. Once again meal was good overall, but the one disappointment was the Cauliflower Bhaji, which lacked much spiciness or taste, and was clearly made from frozen cauliflower, being limp and slightly mushy. Service efficient and friendly.' MW. 'Recommended by friends, and we were not disappointed. Excellent King Prawn Bhuna on puree followed by Garlic Chicken which was as good as it gets! Service first-class.' KT.

Stone

BRITISH RAJ NEW ENTRANT

227 London Road, Stone 01322 385412

'Est. 10 years. Extensive menu containing all the usuals plus a number of more interesting dishes under the house specialities (unfortunately we only noticed these on the takeaway menu after the meal!). Well spiced bhajis, Chicken Chat in a thin but tasty sauce, Chicken Zollander extremely bland. Prices average, service efficient. If I went back it would be to try something different rather than have the same dishes again.' MW. Stocks Cobra.

Strood

CASTLE TANDOORI NEW ENTRANT

135 High Street, Strood 01634 712555/711489

'Formerly the Colonial, it spaciously seats 48. Wicker furnishings and fish pool, fresh atmosphere. Standard dishes, average formula high street fare. Pleasant tasting Chicken Patia, but not hot. Service efficient.' MW. Price check: Papadam 50p, CTM £5.75, Pullao Rice £1.50. Hours: 5.30-11.30pm (Fri. & Sat. to 12am); Sun. 12-4pm – Buffet, adults £6.95, under 16's £4. Stocks Cobra.

FRINDSBURY TANDOORI NEW ENTRANT

88 Frindsbury Road, Frindsbury, Strood 01634 718555

Delivery. Price check: Papadam 40p, CTM £4.90, Pullao Rice £1.35. Hours: 5-11pm.

SHOZNA INDIAN CUISINE ©

28 High Street, Strood 01634 710701

Established in 1978, originally called Raj Mahal. Taken over by J Ahmed in 1996. Seats 38. Parking at rear for 50 cars. Decorated in green with white plaster cornices. Specials include: Bangladeshi Chicken or Lamb Tikka cooked in butter with a fresh garlic sauce £6.90 and Jinga Masala, cooked with mincemeat, egg and spiced king prawns £7.90. Chicken Chatt is the most popular dish ordered. Price check: Papadam 50p, CTM £5.90, Pullao Rice £1.50, Peshwari Nan £1.80, Lager £2.20 pint. Takeaway: 10-15% discount. Hours: 12-1.30pm/5.30pm-12am. Stocks Cobra.

Swanley

GURKHA PALACE ©

9 High Street, Swanley 01322 663608

A Nepalese 80-seater owned by J Gautam. 'Interior very tastefully done. Nice ambience. Extremely interesting menu. Chicken Kaleja (Nepalese style fried chicken livers) was mildly spiced and tasty. Kurhura Khoransi (chicken cooked with green chillies and spring onions) was very appetising. Aloo Bodi Tama (potato, bamboo shoots, black eyed beans, tomatoes etc), apparently a traditional Gurkha dish, was superb. Plentiful portions, prices very reasonable, exemplary service. Curry Club discount willingly given. Highly recommended as something different.' and 'Another visit. Interesting to observe the clientele – wide variety of age groups and definitely none of the legendary Friday night "8 pints of lager and a curry" brigade. Aloo Char had a nice pickle flavour without being too sharp. Tandoori Chicken starter was excellent. Gurkha Lamb Karahi was a main course hit, deliciously spiced. Portions plentiful and service excellent. Very nice restaurant run by very nice people.' MW. Price check: Papadam 40p, CTM £5.10, Pullao Rice £1.75. Hours: 12-2.30pm/6pm-12am. Stocks Cobra.

RAJ OF INDIA NEW ENTRANT

23-25 High Street, Swanley 01322 613651

'Clean and spacious. The Raita was excellent – well chilled and not too minty – and the mango chutney just as I like it, all sauce and no fruit skins. Aloo chat was fabulous, tender, spicy with a slight tomato after taste. Tarka dal was poor. Service was far too quick.' MPW. Stocks Cobra.

Tonbridge

ALISHAN NEW ENTRANT

149 High Street, Tonbridge 01732 770616

A highly respected local restaurant. Good atmosphere, service and food. 'Bright and tastefully decorated, menu interesting and portions large.' NT Stocks Cobra.

SIMLA CUISINE

2 Church Road, Paddock Wood, Nr Tonbridge 01892 834515

Abdal Miah's 90-seater is air-conditioned and decorated in cream and black. Good formula curries on the menu. Price check: Papadam 40p, CTM £5.60, Pullao Rice £1.50, Peshwari Nan £1.60. Hours: 12-2.30pm/6-11pm (11.30pm on Fri. & Sat). Stocks Cobra.

Tunbridge Wells

ANGLO INDIAN NEW ENTRANT

60 The Pantiles, Tunbridge Wells 01892 526633

'Went to the opening in June 1964 as Borough Councillor and remarked on its then excellency and cheapness – a full meal under ten bob! and visited regularly up to 1973. Now a roller-coaster – sometimes fair, others downright poor. This time up. Strengths of Madras and Ceylon fairly hot – could have been hotter!! Good service. Has been structurally altered, seats about 80. 60's flock wallpaper been replaced! Grade II listed building is clean, even the lavatories. Hope they maintain current standard.' BP-D. So do we with such a pedigree. So here's our helping hand – a new mention for an old hand. Price check: Papadam 50p, CTM £6.20, Pullao Rice £1.80. Hours: 12-2.30pm/6pm-12am. Stocks Cobra.

BOMBAY MASALA ©

90 London Road, Southborough, Tunbridge Wells 01892 531056

Established in 1994 by Shamim Khandakar (manager). His 48-seater restaurant is air-conditioned and serves Bangladeshi styled curries and Balti dishes. 'We were the only customers all evening. Food nice, absolutely typical. Best dishes: Chicken Chat, Masala Dhal. Maharani. Paneer tasteless.' MM. [Paneer is tasteless!!! -Ed] Specials include: Chicken Tikka Balti, and

Chicken Shaslik. Takeaway: 10% discount. Delivery: £11 minimum. Hours: 12-2.30pm/6-11.30pm. Branches: Anglo India, Tunbridge Wells. Jubo Raj, Brentwood. Stocks Cobra.

FATEHA NEW ENTRANT

3 Castle Street, Tunbridge Wells 01892 513683

'Takeaway meal for two – four Popadoms, Chicken Jalfrezi, Madras and two Pullao Rice, Nan Bread, (inc 10% discount) £13.36. All round excellent.' BP-P. Delivery. Price check: Papadam 40p, CTM £5.50, Pullao Rice £1.50. Hours: 12-2.30pm/5.30-11.30pm.

JUNAHK NEW ENTRANT

63 St Johns Road, Tunbridge Wells 01892 615200

'A truly Indian restaurant, with Bangladesh waiters. Food brilliant, albeit up market, but "you gets what you pays for in this life." Food really tasty and different – what a change from the usual Bengali fare "Viva La Differance!" Gents spotless. As we waited – 20 minutes – offered us a pint of Kingfisher each – on the house.' BP-P. Price check: Papadam 80p, CTM £8.50, Pullao Rice £2.50.

LA LIPU CUISINE RE ENTRANT

69 London Road, Southborough, Tunbridge Wells 01892 534182

'Food very good indeed. My Lamb Tikka Masala was just the right side of green-chilli-hotness to zing my tastebuds, and my vegetarian friend had a range of excellent veggie dishes. Came away feeling very satisfied. Should go back in the guide.' MM. Stocks Cobra.

MUNA'S RESTAURANT AND BAR NEW ENTRANT ©

70 High Street, Tunbridge Wells 01892 537113

Established in 1996. Seats 38. Modern design, black and chrome. Punjabi curries – à la carte and buffet is available every evening. À la Carte – Deluxe Grill £11.95 – assortment of lamb and chicken tikka, kebab and prawns, served with potato salad and rice. Naan Toppers – warm nans topped with: Chicken Tikka Masala £7.50, Tandoori Prawn Masala £8.50, Lamb Boti £7.50. Buffet £13.95 – e-a-m-a-y-l from Papadams with Chutney and Raitha, Vegetable Pakoras, Spicy Savoy Cabbage Stir-fry, Aubergine Masala, Fried Okra and Onion in Chickpea Batter, Indian Salad in lemon and mint Dressing, Hot Stuffed Red Pickled Chillies and that's just for starters! Buffet main courses include: Lamb Rhogan Ghost, Chicken Bhoona, Vegetable Balti, Saag Aloo, Tarka Dal with Rice and Bread (menu example), tremendous value. Price check: Papadam 70p, CTM £5.20, Pullao Rice £2.10, Peshwari Nan £1.95, Lager £2.60 pint. Hours: 12-2pm/6-11pm; Sun. closed. Stocks Cobra.

RAJ PAVILION NEW ENTRANT

20 Grove Hill Road, Tunbridge Wells 01892 533153

'The best easily in town. Nepal Chicken very tasty, garlicky. Chicken Tikka Korai was served flambéed at our table and was superb.' KT. 'Appearance of luxury TOP 100 class. Large – 100+ covers on two levels, spotlessly decorated throughout. Hopes sorely dashed! Cobra £2.95, Onion Bhajia good. Pullao Rice fair. Naan rather burnt. Chicken Vindaloo, looked and tasted like a Dhansak of medium strength. Atmosphere "take it or leave it – you dine here on our terms!"' BP-D. Stocks Cobra.

TAGORE NEW ENTRANT

4 Neville Street, Tunbridge Wells 01892 615100

Established in 1997, taken over by Nur Monie in 2000. Seats 85. Price check: Papadam 50p, CTM £7.50, Pullao Rice £2.25, Peshwari Nan £1.80, Lager £3 pint. Hours: 12-2.30pm/6-11pm. Stocks Cobra.

Welling GL

FALCON ©

16 Falconwood Parade, The Green, Welling 020 8303 721

A Gofur's 54-seater is spacious, with plants all around. Chef Tamij Ali's ace is Chicken Indo Purie, a marination cooked with Tia Maria in creamy gravy, served with Special Fried Rice. 'Amazing!' LM. Hours: 12-2.30pm/6-11.30pm. (12am on Fri. & Sat.). Stocks Cobra.

TAGORE TOP 100 ©

3 High Street, Welling 020 8304 0433

Nur Monie's 40-seater is decorated with swathes of silk on the ceiling and pleated saris on the walls. Bombay-trained chef Rajendra Balmiki cooks Northern Indian curries and specials from Pakhtoomn, assisted by head waiter Tapesh Majumber. This refers to the Pathan tribal people of Afghanistan and the rugged Pakistani passes, whose name for themselves is

COBRA GOOD CURRY GUIDE
County Index, see page 5 Town Index, see page 614
A to Z of the Curry Menu, page 41 Contributors Key, page 604

Phuktana or Pukhtun. Afghan food is pretty basic, especially at tribal level, involving kebab-skewer cooking and slow-cooking in pots. This is translated at The Tagore into a select menu. Kebab Ke Karishma, a selection of kebabs £16 for two, is popular). Main dishes are divided between six chicken dishes, five meat, six from the tandoor and three fish dishes. At £6, Patrani Mahi, pomfret coated in herbal chutney, leaf-wrapped and baked, is a rarity to be treasured. Murgh Chennai, £5, is none other than Chicken Madras, and Koh-e-Avadh, £5.50, is lamb knuckles simmered in the dum method. Raan E Buzkazi, leg of lamb from the NW Frontier £19.50. The fact that it's not formula leads to adverse comment: 'Very poor meal.' DW. Others like it: 'On all occasions I have found their food to be a world apart from the traditional curry houses with the dishes being expertly cooked. Excellent value for money, service and explanation of the dishes is of a very high quality.' PG. Price check: Papadam 50p, CTM £7.50, Pullao Rice £2.25, Peshwari Nan £1.80. Average meal £20. Takeaway prices 20% cheaper. Hours: 8-11pm.

West Malling

BOMBAY CUISINE

61 High Street, West Malling, Nr Maidstone 01732 871256

A local favourite restaurant, serving formula curries. 'A good alternative to motorway slops, it being off M20, J4.' ME. Stocks Cobra.

West Wickham

DIWANA

118 High Street, West Wickham 020 8777 7159

'Very small but busy restaurant, and so people awaiting their takeaways can be standing very close to your table. However, food can't be faulted, all hot and fresh. Excellent service. Overall, superb food spoilt by its surroundings, but choose a quiet night and you will surely be impressed.' MW.

Westerham

PITTS COTTAGE NEW TO OUR TOP 100

High Street (Limpsfield Road), Westerham 01959 562125

Established in 1995. Taken over by Sujit Dey in 1997. Seats 200. 'If you do nothing else this year visit here. You dine in a 700-year-old listed cottage, once the home of William Pitt. Four separate rooms. They prepare all their own spices and grind their own masala. The menu is an absolute delight with many unusual fish dishes.' CRC. 'Very pretty and does consistently good curries.' KT. 'An interesting menu – a few of the familiar dishes, but plenty of more unusual ones. Tandoori Trout has nicely moist flesh although most of the flavour was in the crisp skin. Delicious Aloo Tikki, Mixed Vegetable Bhaji nicely flavoured. Generous portions. As one might expect, prices slightly higher than average. Service excellent. Upstairs toilets well above average.' MW. Own car park opposite, for 80 cars. Twelfth-century cottage famed for its old-world charm and tranquillity. Specials include: Prawn Massala Puree, Tandoori Trout, Mutton Cutlet, Papaya Ghosht, Rajenya (King prawns with onion and potato). Price check: Papadam 70p, CTM £5.75, Pullao Rice £2.10, Peshwari Nan £2.25, Lager £2.90 pint. Takeaway: 10% discount. Hours: 12-2.30pm/6-11.30pm; Sun. 12-3pm. Stocks Cobra.

TULSI NEW TO OUR TOP 100

20 London Road, Westerham 01959 563397

Formerly The Shapla. Tulsi (biological name *Ocimum sanctum*), is the sacred basil plant of India, where it is grown as a symbol of good luck and good health. Owned by AK Deb, it has a small waiting area with tables and chairs, and an extended, slightly elevated, well-decorated eating area, with a polished wooden floor. Walls covered by framed posters of Bollywood film stars. Ambience is good with very friendly staff, well-dressed in national costume. 'Always high quality food. Manchurian Chicken excellent.' KT. 'It hasn't quite got the opulence of the sistership the "Tamasha", but the service and quality of food are not far behind. Deserves a place in the TOP 100.' CC. Chef Anil K Hazra's specials include: Goan fish curry, cooked in coconut milk, red chillies and garnished with fresh coriander £6.95. Tandoori Paneer Shashlik, pieces of cottage cheese, mushroom, capsicum, tomatoes and onion, cooked on a skewer in the tandoor and served on a sizzler with grilled onion £6.50. Price check: Papadam 70p, CTM £6.25, Pullao Rice £1.95, Peshwari Nan £2.25. Hours: 12-2.30pm (closed Sun. lunch)/6-11.30pm. Branch: Tamasha, Bromley. Stocks Cobra.

Whitstable

INVICTA TANDOORI NEW ENTRANT

15 Harbour Street, Whitstable 01227 264700

'By far the most interesting and extensive menu (33 starters alone!) of all Whitstable Indian restaurants. Small and cosy, but rather crowded on a Saturday night. The single waiter looked extremely harassed and was not particularly welcoming. When we had not been acknowledged after five minutes, we decided to give it a miss and go to the "Shapla" instead.' MW.

Wrotham

A LA CARTE SPICE NEW ENTRANT ©

Gravesend Road, Fairseat, Wrotham 01732 822213

Present ownership commenced January 2000, originally called La Capannina. Seats 100. Own car park in front for 50 cars. Modern European decor. Price check: Papadam 60p, CTM £,5.95 Pullao Rice £1.90, Peshwari Nan £1.80, Lager £3.90 pint. Takeaway: 10% discount. 10% discount for business lunches Mon.-Fri. Hours: 12-2.30pm/5.30-11.30pm. Stocks Cobra.

Wye

JOSHAN OF WYE

2-4 High Street, Wye 01233 812231

'The visit almost fell at the first hurdle through the all-too-common problem of lack of an efficient table reservation system. Our table was booked (and confirmed) for 9.30pm. On arrival we were told it would be a couple of minutes, but we weren't seated until 10.15pm. Nowithstanding the long wait, the head waiter was very pleasant and polite, and did give us a couple of pints of Kingfisher on the house as we read the interesting menu. Food arrived quickly. Chicken Chat excellent in a spicy piquant sauce, Onion Pakora were extremely tasty morsels (smaller than normal). Kamal-ki-Murgh was a bit of a let down. Main dishes were all extremely good. As we left the waiter smiled, took my hand and said with feeling, "Thank you sir, I appreciate your patience". The evening had turned out well and the restaurant's reputation was saved by friendly service and excellent food.' MW. How very sweet and how very honest and decent – other restaurants should take note! Stocks Cobra.

LANCASHIRE

Area: North West
Population: 1,434,000
Adjacent Counties: Cumbs, Greater Man, Mers, N Yorks, W Yorks

Adlington

SHAPLA TAKEAWAY ©

178 Chorley Road, Adlington 01257 474630

Est. 1992 by Shiraz Ali (manager) and MD Rahmin Ullaj (chef). 'Addiction from an early age, satisfied on my doorstep.' AL. 'A wide range of excellent food.' AH. Hours: Sun.-Thurs. 4pm-12am.

SHARJU TOP 100 ©

Church Street, Adlington 01257 481894

Managed by BB Choudhury, this is an old favourite of our *Guide*, and of its loyal following. 'Congregation' may be a more appropriate word because this was surely the first restaurant to occupy a former church. And, yes, they've heard all the gags: from Vestry Vindaloo, RC Roghan, Baptistry Biriani, C of E Tikka to 'will they be serving papadoms with communion wine?' Now owned by Mithu Dhar, the opportunity was taken in 1984 to convert this building to its now ideal use. In fact, it is not a large room, in clerical terms, but it has made for a large number of seats in restaurant terms. Reached by an imposing staircase, the plum seats are on the balcony, which extends around the remaining three sides of the room. From here one has a view of downstairs diners. MKM says: 'It has bags of atmosphere, with its oak beams and strategically placed Indian artefacts.' Says TE: 'Having suffered from inconsistencies in food quality, decided to pay a surprise visit – boy are we glad we did! So good. Allows non-smokers to retain their sanity and lungs away from the smoking area. Pine screens and quality furniture all excellent quality. Service attentive, swift and portions generous. Lean, crisp and delicious Lamb Tikka, Onion Bhajia and Meat Samosa. Followed by Bhuna, Madras, Sag Aloo, Pullao Rice (OK we had some chips as well) – [smack wrist!] superb quality and sizzling, and the hottest hot plates ever! So £37 for three with drinks is pretty good value, my wife impressed with ambience and glitzy decor. More importantly toilets clean and kitchens can be seen from the restaurant.' 'An excellent, religious experience!' TE. And it is CC's 'Twelfth visit and still the best! Murgh Masala is superb, Tandoori Cocktail Masala was delicious. First class service. Definitely a cut above the average High Street restaurant and still very worthy of the TOP 100. Service was efficient, food excellent and well presented. Lots of unusual dishes. Prameachi Special (sizzler dish of beautifully cooked big king prawns, meat and chicken) was wonderful, and the House Special (a whole grilled trout covered in prawns with a separate Bhuna sauce as a side dish) was fabulous. Vegetable dishes were tasty and clearly cooked to order.' CC. Chef Faruk Ali's signature dishes – Chicken Shagorika and Lashuni Chicken Flambé , both with rice. The former is tikka pieces twice-cooked in a very spicy sauce with peas, the latter consists of a tandooried long fillet of chicken breast, which is flambéed in brandy, in a creamy garlicky sauce at your table. E-a-m-a-y-l Sunday lunch, 12-4.30pm, £8.95, kids (under 10) £4.50. Thursday evenings for the Candlelight Dinner. Price check: Papadam 50p, CTM £6.25, Pullao Rice £1.00. Service 10%. Minimum charge £10. Hours: 12-2pm/6-11pm; Fri. & Sat. 5.30pm-12am. Branch: Shanti, 466 Bromley Road, Bromley, Kent. Remains in our TOP 100. Stocks Cobra.

Bamber Bridge

SAGAR PREMIER

Clayton Brook Road, Bamber Bridge 01772 620200

Going north up the M6 and feeling hungry? Drive past Charnock Richard services and come off at J29. 'Disappointing exterior, rather like a community centre built onto the edge of a housing centre, but initial impression rapidly altered by the quality of the food. Very smart internally with partitioned seating. Fresh, light Popadoms with a wide range of chutneys, including a red sauce. Starters include hoppers, similar to rice pancakes, very nice and different. CTM top class.' JL.

Blackburn

HAWELI INDIAN CUISINE

32-34 Higher Road, Blackburn 01254 670265

'This was one of the best venues for service we've experienced and the food matched it.' JC&KEC.

SHAJAN ©

Longsight Road, Clayton-le-Dale, Mellor, Blackburn 01254 813640

Mohammad Ali Shaju's 144-seater is easily found on the A59. Its resemblance to a residential bungalow ceases on entry. It is stylishly decorated with cream walls, ceiling and table linen, blue carpet, and 144 wicker chairs, in two dining rooms. Wooden fretwork screens give tables privacy. 'First impressions were very good, bungalow/colonial style building, lovely decor, impressive bar. Service swift and efficient. Popadoms were fresh, pickles were pungent, the samosas, onion bhaji and (deliciously smokey) lamb tikka starters were all superbly spiced. Reasonably priced.' and ' Re-visited to celebrate my son's and daughter's graduation. When we left we felt like the keema naan – well stuffed!' TE. Price check: Papadam 30p, CTM £6.25, Pullao Rice £1.65. CC discount lunches only. Takeaway 15% off. Hours: 12-2pm/5.30-11.30pm (12am on Fri. & Sat.). Stocks Cobra.

Blackpool

BOMBAY ©

227 Dickson Road, Blackpool 01253 296144

Askor Ali's dusky pink restaurant seats 30. 'The Chilli Masala is just fabulous but, good though it is, I don't think anyone's Roghan Josh originated in Rangoon!' RT. Price check: Papadam 50p, CTM £5.90, Pullao Rice £1.80. Set meal £4.95. For delivery, you pay for the taxi!!! Hours: 12-2pm/6pm-12am (Fri. & Sat. to 1am). Stocks Cobra.

TERRY'S BALTI HOUSE NEW ENTRANT

48 Clifton Street, Blackpool 01253 622349

'Variety of food excellent. I often recommend this restaurant to friends and it always seems to please. Best to visit early as it can get very busy with late night revellers. Dish of the night was probably the Jeera Balti Special.' JC.

Burnley

SHALAMAR ©

56 Church Street, Burnley 01282 434403

'Service good – not pushy. Food presented well, portions ample, but not generous. Karahi Lamb and Chicken Bhuna – excellent with delicious side dishes of Tarka Dhal and Aloo Palak. Definitely revisit.' AC. Stocks Cobra.

Chorley

VEENA

64 Brooke Street, Chorley 01257 234235

'Smart restaurant, just outside Chorley centre. Very reasonable prices. Fish Hasina – succulent cod pieces in a rich, red, tangy masala sauce with crunchy vegetables. Also the Tikka Chicken Puri – with a rich spicy sauce, bursting with flavour. Bombay Machan, similar to Korai but laced with brandy, Chicken Kashmir a deliciously decadent mix of peaches, bananas and a rich array of herbs and spices. Indian food à la haute cuisine!' AE. 'What are Bombay Fries? Perhaps chips with a little spice – I do hope so! Our old favourite once again proved itself to be a winner. Can't seem to find much at fault, although I would like to see a few more chef's specialities. Gourmet Asam Murug was my choice.' JC. Price check: CTM £6.45, Bombay Potato £1.95, Pullao Rice 90p, Papadam relish 70p. Stocks Cobra.

Cleveleys

FAYEZ TANDOORI NEW ENTRANT

78-82 Victory Road, West Thornton, Cleveleys 01253 853562

'A few surprises on its menu such as steak mossalla, fillet steak marinated in yogurt together with a special blend of herbs and spices then cooked in brandy. A welcome watering hole.' MB. Stocks Cobra.

Clitheroe

DIL RAJ ©

7-9 Parsons Lane, Clitheroe 01200 427224

Seats 48, owned by Mr Raj. Set dinner £12.50 each, four people share. Papadams, Tandoori Chicken, Lamb and Chicken Tikka, Sheek Kebab starters, Beef Roghan Josh, Karahi Gosht, Mogulai Chicken, CTM, Vegetable Pullao, Raita, pickles and chutney, followed by desserts and coffee. 10% off takeaways. Hours: 5pm-12.30am; Sun. 12pm-12am. Stocks Cobra.

RIBBLE TANDOORI NEW ENTRANT

19 Waddington Road, Clitheroe 01200 443368

Established in 1993. Takeaway only, parking for 4. Price check: Papadam 35p, CTM £4.10, Pullao Rice £1, Peshwari £1.60. Hours: 5-11.30pm; Sun. 4-10pm.

Fleetwood

AL MINAR NEW ENTRANT ©

26 Larkholme Parade, Fleetwood 01253 777787

First opened October 1996. Three rooms with parking for 30 to 40 cars to the front. Banquets on Wednesday nights. Price check: Papadam 35p, CTM £5.95, Pullao Rice £1.25, Peshwari Nan £1.45. Delivery: £7 minimum, 4-mile radius. Hours: 5pm-12am.

Haslingden

SUNAR GAW ©

16 Regent Street, Haslingden 01204 364915

Owner-manager NA Malik and owner-chef A Quddus share ownership and roles at this popular 1987, evenings-only restaurant. RK says: 'The Kyber Murghi Maladari – chicken cooked with ginger, green chilli, onion, garlic and coriander – was out of this world.' Stocks Cobra.

Hutton

KOH I NOOR NEW ENTRANT

88 Liverpool Road, Hutton 01772 614052

'How useful the guide is when I travel on business. Local cabbie recommended this ahead of Dilshad and Sangam (both in 1998 edition). Early impressions were mixed, a picture of Pat on site, recommending the King Prawn Biryani,' [strange cos I've never been there!!! Ed.] 'but the place was cold and empty. Mobile calor gas heater seemed incongruous, but did the trick. The room was hot. The food was hot, and though average in taste, it was cheap.' HC. Stocks Cobra.

Lancaster

BOMBAY ©

16 Jubilee House, China Street, Lancaster 01524 844550

Opened in 1997 by Askor Ali, his 70-seater, plainly decorated restaurant serves chef Babul Ahmed's curries. 20% discount on takeaways. Hours: 12-2pm and 6pm-12am. Stocks Cobra.

Lytham St Annes

MOGHUL NEW ENTRANT ©

12 Orchard Road, St Annes 01253 712114

M Liaquat Ali owns and presides over a very sunny, friendly 60-seat restaurant, decorated in pastels and pine, serving all the usual Dansak, Madras, Vindaloo, Baltis and Karahis. We hear well of the Moghul Jeera Chicken (£5.90), with cummin flavour predominating, and Keema Patila (£5.90), a tasty mince curry, which one couple enjoy for takeaway – and they also like the special box provided. 'Lamb Rogan Josh was delicious. I enjoyed every last bite.' MB. Stocks Cobra.

Morecambe

MORECAMBE TANDOORI

47 Marine Road, West Morecambe 01524 832633

Opened in 1991 by MA Quadir, who is also the head chef. Butter Chicken is the most popular dish ordered. Set Dinner £13.50. Price check: Papadam 40p, CTM £6.25, Pullao Rice £1.45. Lager £1.95 pint, house wine £5.75. Hours: 12-2pm/6pm-12am. Stocks Cobra.

Preston

DILSHAD

121-123 Friargate, Preston 01772 250828

Established in 1993 by Arshad Din, 'pleasant and homely' 84-seater restaurant serving Kashmiri and Pakistani curries. 'The last time we were here (over two years ago), we were the only ones eating in the restaurant. This time it was packed. Chef's Special Jolfrenzi was heavily packed with chicken pieces at just the maximum heat level I can take comfortably.' JC. Set lunch: £4.99. Price check: Papadam 30p, CTM £7.50, Pullao Rice £1.60. Hours: 12-2pm/6pm-12am.

SANGAM

14-15 Hope Terrace, Lostock Hall, Preston 01772 628616

'The new management has injected some fire here: Wings of Fire were – wow! The main course dish, Tava Chicken Lahori, was great, as was the Pullao Rice. We didn't know whether to eat it or climb it, so big was the portion! Luckily they supplied doggy bags!' RK. 'Good menu, excellent quality/quantity of food, good friendly service, would go again often and recommend to others.' JW. Stocks Cobra.

Rawtenstall

SAMRAT ©

13 Bacup Road, Rawtenstall 01706 216183

Alkas Ali is owner-chef here, and he's proud of his cooking – so proud, in fact, that you can ring him on his mobile on 0973 328426 and he'll explain about his dishes. A unique service, we believe. 'Most fabulous night out we have had and food absolutely gorgeous. Reasonably priced.' SH. Hours: 5pm-12am. Stocks Cobra.

Rossendale

SHANAZ NEW ENTRANT

4 Burnley Road, Rossendale 01706 210606

Established in 1990. Seats 60. Price check: Papadam 50p, CTM £5.95, Pullao Rice £1.50, Peshwari Nan £2, Lager £1.75 pint. Hours: 5pm-12.30am; Sat. & Sun. 12pm-1am. Stocks Cobra.

Whalley

TRISHNA

25 King Street, Whalley 01254 822394

Mr Uddin's Trishna is: 'a very nice restaurant, bigger inside than it first appears (seats 72 diners). Food absolutely gorgeous – could not fault it. Biggest Nan bread ever seen! Polite service. On leaving, ladies get a flower, men a lollipop.' SP. 'Chicken Samber – thick curry sauce of lentils, lemon juice. Dry Vegetable Curry – good quality and quantity. Vegetable Nan and Keema Nan – doughy and undercooked, not pleasant. Otherwise enjoyable.' MK. Stocks Cobra.

LEICESTERSHIRE

Area: East Midlands
Population: 945,000
Adjacent Counties: Derbs, Lincs, Northants, Notts, Rutland, Staffs, Warks

Ashby-de-la-Zouch

RAJNI INDIAN NEW ENTRANT

48 Tamworth Road, Ashby-de-la-Zouch 01530 560349

'Smart, clean, tidy restaurant. No complaints about the quality of food, service or anything, except that they didn't serve Cobra and the restaurant was somewhat empty. I will certainly visit again.' CS.

Broughton Astley

BENGAL PALACE NEW ENTRANT ©

1 Green Road, Broughton Astley 01455 282280

First opened in 1995. Taken over by Abdul Haye and Mohibur Rahman in 1999. Seats 48, spaces for 15 cars opposite. Old cottage-style restaurant. Specials include: Palace Special (marinated chicken on the bone, with minced meat garnish with various green herbs), Chicken Jaflong. Price check: Papadam 50p, CTM £5.95, Pullao Rice £1.50, Peshwari Nan £2, Lager £2 pint. Hours: 6pm-12am; Sat. 6pm-1am.

Hinckley

BALTI RAJ NEW ENTRANT

126 Coventry Road, Hinckley 01455 890770

Established 1995, taken over by Kalim Ullah and Asmol AL. Price check: Papadam 50p, CTM £5.25, Pullao Rice £1.30, Peshwari Nan £1.40, Lager £2.50 pint. Delivery: £4 minimum, 4-mile radius. Hours: 6pm-12am (Sat. to 1am).

Leicester

Leicester is home to a good number of Gujaratis from India. In addition, many of its Asian community settled there in the 1970s when they became exiled from Africa, specifically Kenya and Uganda, where they had lived for generations, having been taken there as clerks and semi-skilled plantation labour by the British. Most contemporary Leicester Asians have little concept of the Indian subcontinent, few having ever visited it, but you would not know this from the quality of the food, particularly in the cheap and cheerful cafés, snack bars and sweet shops all over town. The first curry house, the Taj Mahal, opened in 1961 and is still there! I dined there that year, and when I asked for chilli pickle the anxious owner appeared and spent half an hour counselling me against eating hot food! (To no avail, I might add!) Now there are over 80 'Indian' restaurants on our database which, in a city of around 300,000 population, is a ratio of one 'Indian' restaurant per 3,750 people, making Leicester our second most densely curry-housed city in the UK (see Bradford, West Yorkshire). However, over a two week visit period, we found Leicester's restaurants, Indian and otherwise, to be virtually empty on weekday evenings. The City simply closes at around 6pm. What a terrible waste. We also surprised to find that Leicester council do not allow pavement trading, so vital to the charisma of London's Asian communities. They say vegetables on the street is a health hazzard! Get real Leicester, and get using your restaurants, before they close on you. Oh and yes, if you choose to have a go at me about this, your comments will be published here next time.

BOBBY'S GUJARATI VEGETARIAN V

154-156 Belgrave Road, Leicester 0116 266 2448

Mr Lakhani's long-standing Bobby's is licensed and is ever-popular with a cafeteria-type atmosphere. Mostly Gujarati food, which is light and slightly sweet. You pay (cash please) at the till. Hours: All day.

CURRY FEVER BEST IN THE MIDLANDS ©

139 Belgrave Road, Leicester 0116 266 2941

Established in 1978 by Anil Anand (head chef) and Sunil Anand (manager). They are related to the Brilliant and Madhu's Brilliant of Southall and Curry Craze of Wembley (*see* entries in Middlesex). The food is Punjabi dishes cooked just as they eat them at home. House specialities, which show the restaurant's Kenyan background, include: Jeera Chicken, Butter Chicken and Pili-Pili Chicken (most popular), all priced at full £12.60 and half £7.35, all are dry and on the bone. 'It was a Wednesday evening and we were eating early, and like all other Leicester restaurants it was disappointingly empty other than us. A yellow sign board stands out on the pavement, among other restaurants, sari shops and a lot of large, expensive-looking jewellers. The restaurant is painted in a pale, pretty pink, the bar is towards the back, tables with comfortable chairs are politely spaced, green carpet and chandeliers finish off the scene. Light, crisp and warm plain Popadoms were served with a tray of puréed mango chutney and finely chopped mint and onion chutney – very good and a nice change from the normal selection. Our waiter served us with a large bowl of their Special Salad £2.70, a combination of cubed tomato, cucumber and onion with sprinklings of chopped coriander leaves, stubs of green chilli and hot chilli powder. We ordered for starters a portion of their famous Jeera Chicken £7.35 (half). An absolute must when eating Punjabi cuisine. This is served on the bone, giving so much more flavour, but it can be rather a messy business if using your hands, though Pat and I don't care about that, so hands it was. Anil had added plenty of black pepper to the butter and jeera, making it quite delicious. Sunil recommended we follow with their Piri Piri Chicken £7.35 (half) – it was not as hot as we were expecting, but spicy never the less and Methi Lamb £7.15 – cubes of succulent and tender lamb wrapped in a pungent herby spinach sauce. To accompany our main courses we ordered Maharani Dhal £4.70 – aromatic, creamy, black urid dhal perhaps a little salty, Pullao Rice £2.30 – not brightly coloured but more natural with whole spices and peas, Nan Bread £1.45 – buttery and light, sliced in half and (Anil's surprise) a fabulous Kulchay £1.40 – a puri made of nan bread dough – absolutely delicious, crisp, light and not at all greasy which is surprising since it had been deep-fried. Everybody must try one – I insist! We drank a bottle of house red, which was very acceptable. While we were eating, Sunil chatted to us about business and Anil joined in when he wasn't in the kitchen conjuring up his next master-piece. A very satisfying evening to end a busy day.' DBAC. 10% discount on takeaways. Delivery: £50 minimum. Price check: (Unchanged since last time) Papadam 65p, CTM £7.15, Pullao Rice £2.30, Peshwari Nan £1.95. Lager £2.20 pint, house wine £8.50, mineral water £1.80. Hours: 12-2.30pm (Sun. lunch closed)/6-11.30pm (midnight on Fri. & Sat.); Mon. closed all day except bank holidays. Not just because Leicester needs a boost, but because you really will not get better food we are delighted to award the Curry Fever our BEST IN THE MIDLANDS Award. Stocks Cobra.

FRIENDS TANDOORI TOP 100 ©

41-45 Belgrave Road, Leicester 0116 266 8809

Monday evening. Pat and I couldn't wait to eat here, not just for the food but also for their incredible wine list. The restaurant is on a corner site, smokey glass windows and huge crystal chandelier. Ushered upstairs to the very spacious bar and lounge. It was completely devoid of customers. We ordered our aperitifs from the bar and sat down on one of the many comfortable sofas. We asked to see the famous 109 variety wine-list, the labour of love of owner's son Manjit Pabla, and as good an exposition of wines which go well with spicy food as you'll find. The waiter told us that it was 'all finished'. Pat replied, 'did no one buy such delightful wines?' The waiter replied 'No'. How sad. Mr Pabla had spent many hours putting it together and we were too late to try it. Also defunct is Mr Pabla's 'collection' – his 22-strong malt whisky list. The dispirited Pablas have also withdrawn their humourous menu, which has long been a talking point in this *Guide* as well as amongst his clients. No longer do we read that Gulab Jamun is 'the missing holes out of doughnuts'; Kulfi is 'a legend in its own lunchtime'; Bhindi Masala is 'fresh okra (Winfrey!)'; and it gets worse: Roti is 'Pavarotti – I mean 'ave a roti – Tandoori Roti.' The wine waiter passed Pat menus for us to peruse. Pat enquired about the long and fascinating wine list, as he could not locate it on the menu. What is the matter with you Leicester? – are there no gourmets? – don't you appreciate fine food and wine? From the small selection now offered, we chose a lovely bottle of Chilean red and were then transferred downstairs to the dining area via a large mahogany spiral staircase. The restaurant was also completely devoid of customers. Its cleanliness is quite superior – there is not a spot of dust or dirt anywhere (and that includes the toilets). We started with crispy, light Papadams 30p – served with two chutneys 30p – both green, herby, minty, yoghurty – lovely, we kept these on the table. Onion Bhajia £2.75 and Vegetable Samosa £2.75 – not the usual triangle-shaped version, but shaped rather like a pyramid, reminiscent of the samosas that I am served in India and Bangladesh. Both were served in three's with a fresh mixed salad including lemon wedges – very tasty, we ate the lot! Main courses: Tandoori Mixed Grill £8.25 – served on a sizzling dish, large prawn, chicken leg, lamb and chicken tikka and a Sheek kebab, what a portion! Chicken Tikka £6.75 – generous chicken, not the overly red marinade which is so prevalent in the south of England, succulent and I ate most of it. Enjoyed our food with a Stuffed Nan £1.50 – which Pat also ate and he's not a Nan fan (or should that be naan faan?). Waiters were efficient and friendly, chatting about the world cup England football match, on that night and about the fact that we were going to lose! We did, and so what? We always do. More to the point is how desperately sad it is to be in an empty restaurant. Not everyone is enthralled watching poor-football. We asked to say hello to the Pablas but were told they were in India. Maybe Leicester is spoilt for choice. I wish we had Friends near us. But if Leicester has lost the enthusiasm of one of its best restaurateurs, they have only themselves to blame. We'll do our bit by keeping it in our TOP 100. Stocks Cobra.

KABALOU'S NEW ENTRANT

23-25 Loughborough Road, Leicester 0116 268 2626

Here's another Leicester story. Kabalou's is an hotel and Indian restaurant residing in a very imposing building, painted in buttermilk yellow. There is parking by the side of the restaurant in a private courtyard. Creating Kabalou's has taken an enormous investment of both time and money, with the final tally being an alleged £1.8 million. And this is its problem. Repaying this investment has led to no less than three changes of ownership/management since it opened, less than a year ago in late 1999. On the night we went there was a handful of (Asian) customers. The interior of the restaurant is absolutely amazing, an incredible amount of money has been spent and the overall effect is spectacular. A mirror ball, in the centre of the restaurant, sprays sparkling light over the diners – sounds irritating? It wasn't. Pat's wine was corked. and he asked the waiter to open another bottle, again corked. Apparently this can happen, a whole case might have the same problem. The waiter handled the situation extremely well – ten out of ten – and took away the corked wine (not charged on the bill) and bottle and brought the wine list for Pat's alternative choice. He decided on a Chilean red. The head waiter, Joe (who thinks quite a lot of himself), is quite a performer; he specialises in silver service which is quite showy, when done correctly. We nibbled on crisp light Papadams 50p – with cachumber, mint yoghurt – very good, mango chutney puree and a mixed pickle, not your average pickle, authentic and hand-made. We followed this by Chicken Tikka £3.10 – not the usual bright orange/red colour, more natural and tasty, Jeera Chicken £3.95 – good pieces of chicken in a light spicy sauce both accompanied by fresh salad and served sizzling from the trolley. Jeera Chicken is actually a Punjabi dish (*see* Curry Fever, Leicester). For our main courses we chose King Prawn Chilli Chilli £8.95 – large prawns and plenty of sliced green chillies, just how Pat likes it – hot! and Chicken Butter Masala £6.75 – this dish is very similar to CTM but much nicer with Brinjal Bhaji £5.20 – not particularly smoky which I like, bulked by onions and tomatoes which I don't. Pullao Rice £1.60 – basmati, good aroma and Nan Bread £1.60 – brought to the table sliced in half, very light, butter ghee taste. A very enjoyable meal in extraordinary surroundings and not as expensive as you might expect at £40.45 inc. the wine. We asked to see the hotel rooms and can report that they are very nicely appointed and clean (we were staying at Rothley Court and their rooms weren't!). Before we left we sat in the bar with the manager, Harshad and his wife, Indira and chatted, over an Armagnac. A lovely evening and great establishment for a celebration.' DBAC.

©	Curry Club Discount	**U**	Unlicensed
V	Vegetarian	**ANP**	Alcohol not permitted
e-a-m-a-y-l	Eat as much as you like	**BYO**	Bring your own alcohol

MEMSAAB

98 Vaughan Way, Leicester 0116 253 0243

Driving around Leicester's one way system we found the Memsaab. Restaurant divided into two, with the modern café-style feel to the right, and the more stylish evening dining to the left; both have high ceiling, ornate plaster work. We sat in the modern area, which has a raised floor. We started with Onion Bhajia £2.95 – two well-cooked, crispy brown rissoles of sliced onion, served with salad, chutney and Spiced Lentils Cakes £2.95 – the two lentil cakes were of a good size, but chef had been rather timid, he needed to spice them up. They were served cold drizzled with plain yoghurt and a splash of tamarind sauce. That splash could have been bigger and it definitely needed a dollop of green herby chutney with a little chilli, otherwise they were very good. Followed by main courses of: King Prawn Palak £9.45 – good large prawns smothered in a spicy spinach sauce with green chillies. (Pat must have his chillies.) Garlic Chilli Chicken £7.65 – lots of chilli and plenty of garlic, good chunks of chicken breast, almost too hot for me but I enjoyed it very much with Keema Pullao Rice – £2.15 made a pleasant change and Garlic Nan £1.95 – not overly garlic, but that's OK, since I did have to go to work the next day. Our waiter (Scottish, possibly Glaswegian) is a credit to the establishment. He is courteous, aware of absolutely everything that surrounds him and impossibly professional. The way he serves drinks shows that he has worked the bars and nightclubs, he can spin a drinks tray on his middle finger. I couldn't eat any more food so opted to take my Gulab Jamans home; the portion was very generous – six dainty, dark brown balls, soaked in syrup, which I ate the next day (I did give one to Pat). Price check: Papadam 50p, CTM £7.45, Pullao Rice £1.65.

MONSOON ©

194 Evington Road, Leicester 0116 273 9444

Established in 1995 by Mokhtar Hussain and Monrul Huda. A pretty restaurant, seating 40. Blue hand-printed curtains with white elephants hang at the large plate-glass windows, comfortable rounded wooden chairs, square and round tables (I prefer round tables). Some unusual items. Halim (*sic*) soup is a meat- and lentil-based spicy broth, Haash Masala is half a duck on the bone, marinated and deep-fried, and Roup Chanda Bhaza is Bangladeshi fish, marinated and pan-fried. With 24 hours' notice and a deposit, you can have Shagorana (£35), a feast for two, with, amongst other things, mussels, crab, lobster and Bangladeshi vegetables. Specials include: Zalaly dishes. Takeaway: 10% discount. Delivery: £10 minimum, 4-mile radius. Hours: 12-2pm/6-11.30pm; closed Mon. Stocks Cobra

COBRA GOOD CURRY GUIDE
County Index, see page 5 Town Index, see page 614
A to Z of the Curry Menu, page 41 Contributors Key, page 604

NAMASTE ©

65 Hinckley Road, Leicester 0116 254 1778

Proprietors Dwssendra Kumar Dey (manager) and Rakhal Paul (chef) opened in April 1994, serving formula curries in a restaurant seating 52 diners. Balti Mixed is the most popular dish ordered. Minimum charge £9.50. Sunday buffet lunch £5.95. Tuesday and Wednesday £6.50 e-a-m-a-y-l dinner. Hours: 12-2pm/5.30-11pm. Stocks Cobra.

SAYONARA THALI NEW ENTRANT V

49 Belgrave Road, Leicester 0116 266 5888

Pure vegetarian Gujaraṭis restaurant owned by S and V Pandya. We visited on Tuesday for an early dinner, two other tables occupied, but the venue soon filled completely, with mainly Asian clientèle of all ages. The restaurant is quite small, it is clean and tidy though not upmarket smart in any way, but then you are not paying for it. The main attractions were the license and the Gujarati food. Our waiter welcomed us and showed us to a table. He didn't smile but wasn't grumpy, I think shy and perhaps a little fed-up (he waitered to an almost full restaurant single-handed). We ordered plain Papadams 40p – crispy and light with chutneys. Bhel Puri £2.25 – good portion (too sweet for me, though this is a typical Gujarati trait) – a combination of mamra (puffed rice), potato, onion and tamarind with a dollop of green herby chutney on top. Dhai Puri £2.25 – flying saucers (as I call them) of crispy puri topped with potato, onion, tamarind and plain yoghurt – not so sweet, good portion. We followed these with Masala Dosa £3.95 – large, light, crispy dosa, filled with mashed potato and onion, flavoured with seeds. No turmeric or curry leaves normally associated with the South Indian Dosa. These were served with Sambar – again a Gujarati version, no drumsticks (which I adore) but had a good flavour and contained a sprinkling of desiccated coconut, could have been a little thicker. Coconut Chutney, a thick sauce of coconut and yoghurt, lightly spiced. We drank glasses of Perrier water from very large brightly coloured plastic sundae glasses (bizarre) 95p with a bottle of red wine £9.50. Amazing value at £25.55.' DBAC. Brigette at local Pukka Pies thinks this restaurant is great, she orders the Thali, because 'you never know what you're going to get!' (and the portions are huge). Hours: 12-9.30pm (Sat. to 10pm). Stocks Cobra.

SHARMILEE VEGETARIAN V ©

71-73 Belgrave Road, Leicester 0116 261 0503

Opened way back in 1973 by Gosai brothers (manager, LK Goswami), this is a two-part venue. The sweet mart serves a rich assortments of Indian sweets, and such delightful items as Vegetable Samosas, Pakoras and Dahi Vadia, from 9.30am-9pm daily, except Mondays. The licensed restaurant is upmarket and vegetarian, decorated with marble pillars in shades of brown and dusky blue marble-effect walls, high-backed black chairs, white table linen. Tasty starters of Pani Puri, crispy puris served with spicy sauce, chickpeas and onion £2.25. Chanabateta, chickpeas and potatoes in a tamarind sauce garnished with onions £2. South Indian specialities: Masala Dosa, thin crispy pancake filled with potato and onion £4.25, Idli Sambhar, flat pulse balls £2.50, both served with Sambhar and coconut chutney. 'Elegantly simple surroundings, food delicately flavoured, and best recommendation of all, probably 50% of clientele were Asian. Food was beautifully cooked and incredibly cheap (Navratan Kofta, Jeera Rice, Handi Birianee, Naan and drinks for just over £12). Decor was simple, bright and cheery and the service was pleasant. The clientele comprised of mainly Asian family parties which made the atmosphere very pleasant and relaxed. My wife and I wholeheartedly recommend visiting this restaurant.' P&SM. Price check: Papadam 40p, Pullao Rice £1.50. Takeaway 10% discount. Minimum charge £4.95. Hours: 12-2.30pm/6pm-9.30pm (closed Sun.); Sat. 12-9pm; closed Mon. except bank holidays. 10% discount to CC Members. Stocks Cobra.

Loughborough

AMBER TANDOORI

5a High Street, Loughborough 01509 215754

'Decor is pleasant and clean. Food and service always good and prompt.' MG. Open 12-2.30pm/5.30pm-12.30am (1.30am on Fri. & Sat.).

Market Harborough

SHAGORIKA

16 St Mary's Road, Market Harborough 01858 464644

Ala and Ablas Uddin have been trading successfully here since 1980. Seats 70 diners. Party room seats 25 guests. Formula curries. Hours: 12-2pm/6-11.30pm. Stocks Cobra.

LINCOLNSHIRE

Area: East
Population: 630,000
Adjacent Counties: Cambs, Leics, Norfolk, Notts, E & S Yorks

Boston

ROSE OF BENGAL NEW ENTRANT ©

67 West Street, Boston 01205 363355

Established in 1996, taken over by Mr M Jay in 1998. Seats 58. Car parking for 10 cars to the rear. Specials include: Shashk Korai. Price check: Papadam 35p, CTM £5.35, Pullao Rice £1.35, Peshwari Nan £1.50, Lager £1.90 pint. Takeaway: 10% discount. Delivery: £10 minimum, 7-mile radius. Hours: 12-2pm/5.30pm-12am. Stocks Cobra.

SHAPLA NEW ENTRANT

15 Bridge Street, Boston 01205 368112

This takeaway was established in 1993. Free parking after 5pm in the Market Place. Price check: Papadam 40p, CTM £4.80, Pullao Rice £1.45, Peshwari Nan £1.40. Delivery: 5-mile radius. Hours: 5.30pm-12am; closed Tues.

STAR OF INDIA RETURN TO TOP 100

110-112 West Street, Boston 01205 360558

Owned by Tanvir Hussain. Air conditioning and completely redecorated in 1997, seating increased from 52 to 76 diners, serving Pakistani formula curries with traditional accompaniments. 'Very pleasant decor, typical Indian restaurant style enhanced by large numbers of cotton flowers. Service attentive but not intrusive. Balti Chicken was quite delicious. Keema Nan was piping hot and filled with ample quantity of minced meat. Highly recommended.' MS-R. 'Best-ever Tandoori Chicken starter followed by superb Dhansak.' AG. It continues to get plentiful one-liners of satisfaction. 'We have been to Indian restaurants all over the country and we have not come across anywhere which beats it for great food, friendliness and cleanliness. We hope to be going there every Friday for the next 18 years.' PDEP. Minimum charge: £5. Takeaway 10% discount. Price check: Papadam 35p, CTM £5.75, Pullao Rice £1.40, Peshwari Nan £1.50. House wine £5.75, Perrier £2.25. Hours: 12-2.30pm/6pm-12am. Branches (both takeaways): Chilli Master, 2 Red Lion Street, Stamford; Chilli Master, 11 Winsover Road, Spalding. Stocks Cobra.

Bourne

SHALIMAR BALTI HOUSE NAME CHANGE ©

8 Abbey Road, Bourne 01778 393959

Co-owners Ali Ashker, Ali Akbar (chef), Ali Arshad and Ali Amjad, told me last time that they have made a lot of new customer friends since they appeared in the *Guide*, and they really welcome Curry Club members for their discount, so get booking and enjoy all your favourites. Hours 5.30pm-12am (12.30am on Fri. & Sat.). Stocks Cobra.

Brigg

SHARMINS TAKEAWAY NEW ENTRANT

7 Bigby Street, Brigg 01652 657450

'We recommend our local takeaway for inclusion in the *Guide*. [OK] Admittedly there is only one curry house in Brigg, but it's good. Food's tasty and nicely presented, the staff are friendly and the prices reasonable.' DRKW

Grantham

BOMBAY BRASSERIE ©

11 London Road, Grantham 01476 576096

Large 104-seater in the town centre. Well-spaced tables achieving intimacy in a large restaurant. Festoons of red silk and satin hang from the ceiling, blue and pink chintz curtains hang by an arch dividing the dining room. Pink and white table linen, air-conditioned. 'Acknowledged as the best in the area. Wide ranging menu. I recommend the Shahi mix, a generous dish of tandoori meats in a medium sauce with plenty of herbs. Friendly and efficient staff.' RW. 'One of the best restaurants in the area. Offers a 10% discount to Curry Club members. Boti Kebab, Chicken Chaat, Murghi Jalfrezi, all very tasty. Waiters all polite.' IW. House wine £7.90, mineral water £2.50. Hours: 5.30pm-12am (1am on Sat.). Stocks Cobra.

Grimsby

SPICE OF LIFE NEW ENTRANT ©

8-12 Wellowgate, Grimsby 01472 357476

Established in 1999. Seats 100. Price check: Papadam 45p, CTM £6.95, Pullao Rice £1.50, Peshwari Nan £1.95, Lager £1.95 pint. Takeaway: 15% discount. Delivery: 3-mile radius. Hours: 12-2pm/6pm-12am. Stocks Cobra.

Lincoln

BENGALI KARAHI BAR NEW ENTRANT

94-96 Newland, Lincoln 01522 546275

Formerly the Bengal Tandoori. NTT had a 'celebration curry. Stuffed Paratha £1.50 – delicious, Mushroom Rice £1.80 – very nice as was the Vegetable Bhaji £1.70.' On another occasion he 'had a romantic Valentine's Day curry for one! [big ahhhhh Nigel, but I bet you loved it!!] Mushroom rice had a soft brown demerara sugary taste to it. Delicious.' NT. Delivery. Price check: Papadam 30p, CTM £4.50, Pullao Rice £1.40. Hours: 11.30am-2.30pm/5.30-11.30pm.

THE BOMBAY NEW ENTRANT

6 The Strait, Lincoln 01522 523264

Lincoln's oldest curry house, says NTT. Here is an amalgam of his visits: 'It was an England world cup night, and though the match failed to live up to expectations, the curry certainly did.' 'Paratha £1.30 – thick and delicious as was the Stuffed Paratha £1.50, Mushroom Rice £1.90 and Vegetable Biryani £1.90. Absolutely delicious Brinjal Bhaji. The Onion Bhajia £1.75 was disappointing as it wasn't made with real onions. .However, the Bombay remains in my Top 3 curry houses in Lincoln.' NTT. 20% discount on takeaway meals. Price check: Papadam 40p, CTM £6.95 (inc Pullao Rice), Pullao Rice £1.60.

HARI KUMAR'S NEW ENTRANT

80 Bailgate, Lincoln 01522 537000

Describes itself as a fusion restaurant. Menu includes absolutely everything e.g. Thai Style Chicken Satay £3.95, Yoghurt and Coconut Soup £2.95, Medallions of Monkfish with creamed spinach and beetroot coulis £4.75, Mussels, Mussels and more Mussels, a Goan speciality £4.75, Duck Breast

Japanese Style £10.75. It also says that Murgh Makhani Home-style Butter Chicken – which we all call CTM today – was originated in the 1950s at the Moti Mahal in Delhi. Pat tells me that there MAY be some truth in Hari Kumar's story, since the man who started the Moti Mahal brought a Tandoor oven with him from Pakistan. 'Despite the addition of Mint Raita (£1.75) the Vegetable Samosas (£2.25) were too hot and burnt my tongue. Hari's Vegetable Korma (£6.25) was full of green peppers, red pepper, sweetcorn, mushrooms and broccoli. Saffron Basmati Rice (£1.95).' NTT, Lincolnshire. Poor Nigel, how's your tongue? Price check: Papadam 50p inc. home-made chutney, CTM £6.95, Pullao Rice £1.55. Stocks Cobra.

THE ROYAL TANDOORI NEW ENTRANT

118 High Street, Lincoln 01522 514222

Nice big chunky pieces of mushroom permeated the mushroom rice. Vegetable curry was nicely augmented with mint sauce and grated carrot. 'Vegetable Korma £3.45 – very creamy and Paratha £1.20 – both delicious. Tasty Pullao Rice.' NTT. 15% discount on takeaways. Set menus exceptional value. Delivery. Price check: Papadam 35p, CTM £5.40 (inc Pullao Rice), Pullao Rice £1.50. Hours: 12-2.30pm/6pm-12am (Fri. & Sat. to 1am).

SARGA TAKEAWAY

133 Burton Road, Lincoln 01522 511777

'Well planned takeaway menu, very easy to see what is on offer, set meals good value. 'They still make the best Onion Bhajia's £1.60, best Stuffed Paratha £1.60 with thickest layers of chapati flour and the best Mushroom Rice £1.85. Still the tops in Lincoln for me.' NTT. Interesting menu addition for you to try: Garlic Rice £1.95. Naricol Chutney – coconut and mint 50p, Aloo Bonda, spicy potato burgers £1.60, 'Gandhi's Revenge' described as extremely hot and volatile curry, with special red bullet chillies; this should bring a grin to Gandhi's soul after you have eaten it! £6.25 – Sounds great! Has anyone ordered? Delivery. Price check: Papadam 30p, CTM £5.75, Pullao Rice £1.60. Hours: 5.30pm-12am.

Market Rasen

BALTI HOUSE NEW ENTRANT

5 King Street, Market Rasen 01673 843427

'An extensive menu. I have yet to taste Indian food as good. The chef/owner knows just which spice will add that extra flavour to ensure a unique taste.

Murgh Makhani (CTM!) is their particular speciality show all the flavours. The very best – we've long been customers, and eaten in other venues all over England, and failed to equal it. Excellent service. Anyone visiting Lincolnshire should make the effort to call at the Balti House.' SJL

Stamford

BOMBAY COTTAGE NEW ENTRANT

52 Scotgate, Stamford 01780 480138

'A favourite with the lads when we have the monthly night out. Food excellent. My "Brummie" friend thought the Chicken and Mushroom Balti was one of the best he'd ever had.' IW.

RAJ OF INDIA ©

2 All Saints Street, Stamford 01780 753556

Rohom Ali's well established (1982) 84-seat Raj has promised a 10% discount off the bill for CC Members. 'On being asked by friends to find a good curry house near Peterborough, I opened my trusty bible to the Raj of India. Staff very pleasant. Couldn't fault it. Fifteen of us. Xal Fari (!) very hot but very tasty, good sized portions, lovely surroundings. Another great, successful curry.' DP. 'Given I didn't have much time, I telephoned ahead and found crisp fresh Papadams waiting at my table for one. Large portion of Pullao Rice, equally big CTM – quite spicy, required a Cloret or two before my afternoon meeting, quite simply the best Mushroom Bhajee I have had, lightly spiced, thinly sliced button mushrooms, garnished with chopped fresh coriander – excellent. Clean and inviting restaurant, well worth its entry in the guide.' AG. Raj Suite for private parties. 10% discount on takeaway. Price check: Papadam 40p (plain), 50p (spicy), CTM £7.20, Pullao Rice £1.90, Hours: 12-3pm (except Sun)/6pm-12am, daily. Stocks Cobra.

Woodhall Spa

INDIA VILLAGE

6 The Broadway, Woodhall Spa 01526 352223

Dam Busters' HQ? Not the India Village, though the chaps would have loved it – the actual village, I mean. Nearby Scampton was their base. Anyway, MSLN found it 'a little slow, but the food OK'. Price check: Papadam 55p, Green Herbal Chicken Kebab £5.80, CTM £5.95, Very Hot Pili Pili Chicken £5.95, Pullao Rice £1.85. Stocks Cobra.

MANCHESTER (GREATER)

Area: North West
Population: 2,590,000
Adjacent Counties: Cheshire, Lancashire,
Merseyside, Yorkshire

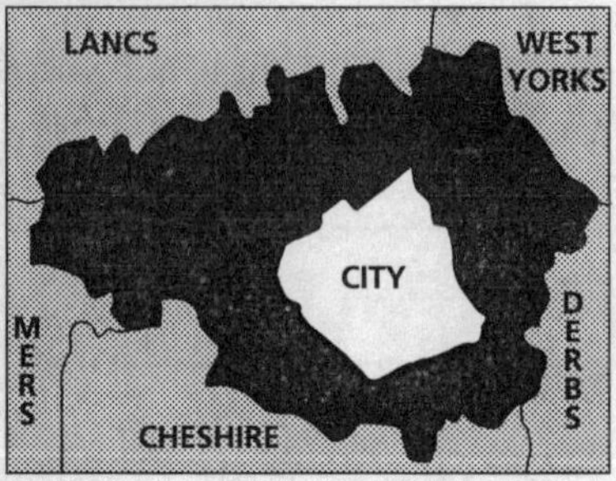

Greater Manchester was introduced as a county in 1965, though this was regarded as an imposition by many of its residents, who still prefer to refer to the counties that Greater Manchester gobbled up, e.g. parts of Lancashire and Cheshire. We have adhered strictly to the official current Greater Manchester territory for town locations in this Guide. The city area is shown in white (left), while the remainder of GM is shown in black.

Altrincham

(inc. Hale, Halebarns and Timperley)

BARINDA INDIAN NEW ENTRANT

134 Ashley Road, Hale, Nr Altrincham 0161 928 3696

First opened in 1982, taken over by Javed Akhtar in 1998. Seats 70. Chef's Specials: Began Murghi £5.25 – aubergine with chicken. Karahi and Balti dishes from £5.25. Price check: Papadam 45p, CTM £7.60, Pullao Rice £1.30, Peshwari Nan £1.60, Lager £2.20 pint. Takeaway: 10% discount. Delivery: £12 minimum, 3-mile radius. Hours: 5.30pm-12am. Stocks Cobra.

ISLAM TAKEAWAY NEW ENTRANT

8 Church Street, Altrincham 0161 929 5604

Passable takeaway, smartly furnished, in keeping with the 'Cheshire Set' locality. Very pleasant Samosas £1.60, moist, meat juices, attractive bite, served with light Raitha, small crisp salad. Biryani £4.95 – a little disappointing, dry meat, no omelette. Vegetable Curry Sauce quite good.' RW. Price check: Papadam 30p, CTM £4.95, Pullao Rice £1.30, Peshwari Nan £1.95. Hours: 5pm-12am (1am on Fri. & Sat.).

SHERE KHAN

9 Old Market Place, Altrincham 0161 926 8777

Sister restaurant to the famous Shere Khan in Rusholme. Owned by Rafiq Awan and managed by Saleem Bakir. Located next to the Orange Tree Pub (CAMRA award-winner) in an attractive old town, its reputation has grown – it's busy every night. 'Waiters pounce from all corners, service is excellent. Papadam, perfect with complimentary side salad and the usual pickles. Delicious Chicken Tikka curries, slightly spicier than expected. Breads and Rice very tasty.' TE. 'Decorated to attract the wine bar set with pale yellow, green pastel colours, fake bamboo chairs. Brusque staff. Plate of Coleslaw, Chutney, Raitha and Onion of indeterminate age on every table, charged 50p regardless whether brave enough to tackle it. Small Papadams, requested fresh tray of Chutneys. Shami Kebab £1.70 – blend of spices, onion, dall and keema bound with egg, tasty if dry, limp salad. Karahi Simla Keema £5.90 – delicious, served sizzling, tamely spiced, quality mince. Garlic Nan £1.60 – very good, plenty of chunks of garlic. Service automatically added to bill.' RW. Service 10%. Price check: Papadam (2) 60p, CTM £6.20, Pullao Rice £1.30, Peshwari Nan £1.80.

Ashton-under-Lyne

AL BALAL NEW ENTRANT

69 Penny Meadow, Ashton-under-Lyne 0161 343 1588

Better than average takeaway on a street packed with Indian takeaways and sweet centres. Starter was a good example of Shami, with plenty of meat. Dupiaza was nicely dry, with plenty of fresh onion and well balanced with a medium strength sauce. Unusually sweets are available – Ras Malai was very tasty. I intend a return visit.' RW.

INDIAN OCEAN ©

83 Stamford Street East, Ashton-under-Lyne 0161 343 3343

Pakistani curry house owned by Nahim Aslam. Seats 120. Large lounge with regular entertainments which attracts diners to stay and enjoy after dinner drinks with a cigar (there is a smoking menu). House specials: Chicken Chilli Masala – cooked with fresh green chillies. Chicken Chat Masala £5.25 – chicken pieces with chick peas, garnished with roasted cashew nuts. Minimum charge: £8. Buffet £8.95. Delivery: £7.95 minimum, 3-mile radius. Hours: 5pm (Sun. 4pm)-11pm (12am on Fri. & Sat.). Stocks Cobra.

Atherton (M46)

SAVAR TOP 100 ©

39-41 Mealhouse Lane, Atherton 01942 875544

Established in '94 by Haq (head chef), Uddin and Ali (manager), the Savar is a pleasant, unassuming restaurant, situated in a converted chapel. It seats 56 diners. 'We simply cannot contain ourselves any longer, we must tell you about our favourite restaurant in the whole wide world. My hubby and I have eaten in numerous restaurants throughout Europe – 50% at least were of the Indian variety and we cannot find a meal to equal – indeed, approach – the quality, flavour, texture and total experience of the Savar's Balti dishes. Good-quality meat and vegetables wallow in a variety of thick, rich, tangy sauces, delicately suffused with a multitude of fragrant spices and lavishly strewn with fresh coriander. The Nan breads are as light as clouds and as large as duvets, the portions reach well halfway up the side of the washing-up-bowl-sized Balti dishes – and you must try the special red sauce that arrives with the pickles and starters. The staff are lovely – especially Ranu, the chatty manager. The prices are extremely modest. All in all, this is an experience not to be missed.' IF-E. 'Has a Balti chef from Birmingham, so we expected authenticity – and we got it. Portion quantities were just about right, and the quality was superb thanks to the liberal use of fresh ingredients. King Prawn Puri quite delicious. Balti Lamb Jalfrezi was mind-blowing – love those chillies! I'm going to enjoy being a regular here.' MS. 'Papadams with fabulous Tamarind Chutney. Followed by Aloo Chat on Puri. Balti Chicken liberally covered in coriander with rice. Fabulous Tikka Chilli Masala, hot and spicy. Utterly delicious, delicately spiced Brinjal Bhajee.' RK. 'Service excellent, very friendly but not over the top. Quantities generous, quality very good, Jalfrezi the better dish. Very pleasant evening, well worth the 40-mile round trip.' PW. Decor fairly standard curry house, apart from the window into the kitchen, where the cooks worked furiously. Balti Chicken Chilli Masala nearly burnt my tongue off, temperature-wise, far too hot. I'm not a Balti man, but my friend enjoyed his Meat Balti.' RL. Price check: Papadam 40p, CTM £6.10, Pullao Rice £1.40, Peshwari Nan £1.50. House wine £6.50, mineral water £2. Minimum charge £5.50. Hours: 5-11.30pm (12.30am on Fri. & Sat.); Sun. 4-11.30pm. Remains in our TOP 100. Stocks Cobra.

COBRA GOOD CURRY GUIDE
County Index, see page 5 Town Index, see page 614
A to Z of the Curry Menu, page 41 Contributors Key, page 604

Bolton

AMIR

2 Broad Gate, Ladybridge, Bolton 01204 660525

Established in 1990, taken over by Omar Dey in 1994. Seats 186. Space for 40 cars. House specials include Jali Bhuna, served with rice for £7.95. Price check: Papadam 45p, CTM £7.15, Pullao Rice £1.60. Takeaway: 20% discount until 8pm. Hours: 5.30-10.45pm; Sun. 4-10.15pm. Stocks Cobra.

ANAZ TAKEAWAY ©

138 St Helens Road, Bolton 01204 660114

Takeaway established in 1993 by Yunus Ahmed. Specials include: Moglai, Masala, Aloo Gosht, Aloo Methi, Chilli Masala and Garlic Curries. 'Spotless, service first-class and I was offered a fresh cup of coffee whilst I waited.' MB. Delivery: £7.50 minimum, 2-mile radius. Hours: 5pm-12am (Sat. to 1am); Mon. closed.

HILAL TANDOORI ©

296 Chorley Old Road, Bolton 01204 842315

Opened in 1975 by Surat Ali, and he's still here with Anor Liiah as manager. Chef Abdul Monaf cooks the curries. A nice touch is the free liqueur at the end of the meal. Takeaways qualify for a free can of lager and Papadam. Minimum charge £5. Hours: 6pm-2am, (3am on Fri. & Sat. for the night owls). Stocks Cobra.

JITAR CURRY HOUSE NEW ENTRANT

Unit 2, 29-31 Market Street, Bolton 01204 705712

'They have some quite different items on their menu such as Malayan and Suryah dishes which are mild, and an excellent chicken samber which is hot and very tasty indeed. All very good value for money.' MB.

ROYAL BALTI HOUSE NEW ENTRANT

78 Lower Market Street, Farnworth, Bolton 01204 573515

'This smallish comfortable restaurant continues to get good reviews locally (one is the *Bolton Evening News* readers award, BEN Restaurant of the year, *Gourmet Good Food Guide* winner). Excellent and very good value for money. Service friendly and quick.' MB. Stocks Cobra.

THE SPICE ISLAND TAKEAWAY

87 Tonge Moor Road, Bolton 01204 361678

Manager Joynal and chef Mohammed Mehbub cook some intriguing unusuals. I've never seen Ekuri (£2.10) served anywhere else. It is spicy scrambled egg, served with Puri, and it's delicious. Palak Shira (£1.35) is a tasty spinach-based soup. Reporters tell of good Baltis, maybe because Mehbub professes to like them himself, especially the Garlic Special Balti, which he describes on the menu as 'recommended if you are going vampire-hunting'– presumably missable if you want to impress a new partner who's not shared your indulgence, but in all respects mind-blowing and breath-blowing! The Bangladeshi Dishes are also in demand, we hear. Shandus Baja (£4.25) is chicken or meat, roasted, then stir-fried with bamboo shoots, fresh hot chillies and other delights. Price check: Papadam 35p, CTM £4.50, Pullao Rice £1.30. Sunday Thali £4.60. Delivery: £6 order, 3-mile radius, 95p charge (!!!); £12 order, 4-mile radius, £1.95. Hours: 5-11.30pm; Sat. 4.30pm-12am.

Cheadle

ALIGARH NEW ENTRANT

202 Wilmslow Road, Heald Green, Cheadle 0161 436 8809

'Plenty to choose from on the menu, they even had twenty-two different wines on offer! Food very nice. Chicken Bhuna – best I've had. Chicken Korma – little spicy, nice. Friendly waiters and good with children (half-size portions).' GB.

Dukinfield

INDIA COTTAGE NEW ENTRANT

Foundry Street, Dukinfield 0161 343 6866

'My regular haunt so I am always pleased to report on its consistency. This time my neck was on the line – a family get-together for eight people, my older brother being very critical of service and quality. However, the staff and chef were superb. All excellent. Restaurant full at 8pm. My favourites: chicken karahi, lamb tikka, jalfrezi, vegetable rice. Always ask for naan straight from the oven.' AKD. 'Kebab was lightly spiced if a little tough, lamb was extremely tough, brinjal was bland in the extreme. Garlic naan was spot on. Platewarmers had to be requested, no hand towels, service was grumpy, bill had to be corrected.' RW. Stocks Cobra.

SPICE WORLD TAKEAWAY NEW ENTRANT

111 King Street, Dukinfield 0161 336 2525

'New takeaway, opposite Town Hall. Large, well lit, smartly decorated in tile work. Freshly cooked Seekh Kebabs £1.50, done while I waited, on the open grill, pleasantly spiced and gristle free, served with garlicky sauce and fresh salad. Chicken and Cheese Kufta £4.50 – luscious combination of chicken tikka and lamb meatballs, enveloped in tangy sauce. Paneer cannot be confirmed! Garlic Naan £1.30 – large, well cooked.' Very enjoyable.' RW. Cash and cheques only. Delivery. Price check: Papadam 30p, CTM £4.50, Pullao Rice £1.10. Hours: 4pm-1am.

Hazel Grove

THE MAHARAJ NEW ENTRANT ©

2-3 Jackson Lane, Hazel Grove 0161 439 1041

Bangladeshi restaurant and takeaway. Haroon's Specials: Shaskhick Maharaj £4.95 – Tikka with sauce of cream, cinnamon and chopped nuts. Hyderbadi Hake £4.95 – fillets in light batter with garam masala. Price check: Papadam 40p, CTM £5.95, Pullao Rice £1.50, Peshwari Nan £1.75. Hours: 5pm-12am; Sun. 1pm-12am. Stocks Cobra.

Hyde

BALTI HOUSE NEW ENTRANT

43 Clarendon Place, Hyde 0161 368 7479

'My local favourite. Some unusual dishes such as a Sour Balti Khyber Ghost feature. Enthusiastically run by owner Dilal. Smart, attentive and efficient service. Always delightful food and superb atmosphere, nearly perfect.' RW. Stocks Cobra.

GANJEES NEW ENTRANT

278 Stockport Road, Gee Cross, Hyde 0161 366 1500

'Upmarket open kitchen takeaway, wider range with many specials, but prices are generally higher. Methi gosht was very good with a robust flavour. Complimentary coffee and bombay mix available with comfy chairs and a TV while your meal is prepared.' RW.

INDIAN CHEF NEW ENTRANT

112 Market Street, Hyde 0161 367 7592

'Formerly Indian Spice, same chef, same standard, some prices reduced. Enjoyed the food, despite bad cold. Extremely comprehensive menu, with a separate balti section which includes such appealing names as Akabari Cham Cham and Silsilla. Chat was spot on. Lamb passanda was very mild, lamb chunks were large but perfectly tender and succulent. For once takeaway Pullao Rice was light and the grains separate. Naan had a good quantity of fruit and was nicely risen. Spotless open kitchen, pleasant waiting area.' RW.

NAWABI BALTI

162-164 Market Street, Hyde 0161 368 9917

'Very well-decorated 40-seater restaurant with efficient, friendly and knowledgeable staff. Starter was a well balanced medium curry with lamb, chicken, prawn and onion served on pleasantly dry puri with a tasty Chat Masalla. Karahi quite oily in appearance but well spiced. Naan well cooked and moist. Enjoyable overall.' RW. 'There is an in-house taxi service. Free home delivery.' GW. Price check: Papadam: 30p, Balti CTM £5.25, Pullao Rice £1.15. Stocks Cobra.

RAJ AUTHENTIC NEW ENTRANT

Unit 3 Pine Street, Newton Hyde 0161 368 9500

'Delivery only service operating out of an industrial unit in a suburban area. Extensive range. Good value set meals including a children's meal range (two of which are mild curries). Excellent Chat with generous amounts of garlic, Reshmi kebabs thin but high meat content, Biryani a little greasy. A great enterprising operation that deserves to flourish.' RW.

MANCHESTER CITY

(Manchester postcodes, M1 to M46
Population: 433,000)

For the purpose of this Guide, we have included M postcodes (M1 to - M46) in all our Manchester City entries. There is no geographical logic to our putting postcodes into numerical order. They are frankly a jumble. But it is the sytem which exists, and to help narrow things down, we have divided the city into Central, East, South, West and North, using major roads as our arbitrary boundaries.

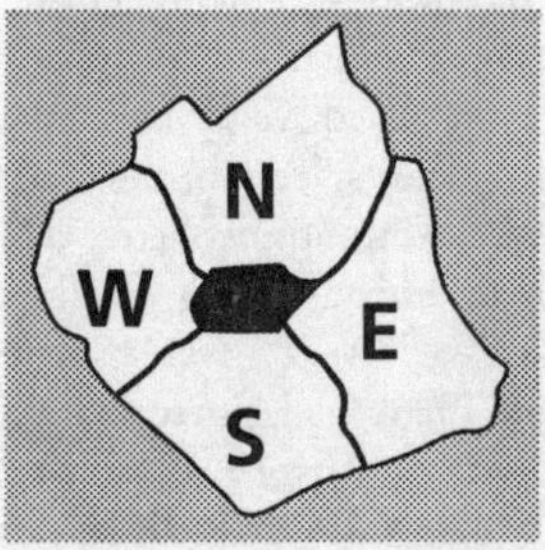

MANCHESTER CENTRAL

M1 to M4

(restaurants listed in alphabetical order)

ASHOKA

105-107 Portland Street, Manchester M1 0161 228 7550

'The service can be a little slow, but the standard of food here is well worth the wait. Rashmi Kebab – god what taste, beautiful! £19.00 for one, but worth every penny.' MB. Stocks Cobra.

CAFE MARHABA NEW ENTRANT

36 Piccadilly, off Newton Street, Manchester M1 0161 228 7377

'The best diner in the city. Difficult to find, just off Newton Street on the alley that runs behind Piccadilly, and not open at night. Seekh Kebabs are amongst the best to be had anywhere, spicy and succulent, served with incredibly hot onions. Naan breads are thin, small, crisp and exquisite.' RW.

GAYLORD TOP 100

Amethyst House, Spring Gardens, Manchester M2 0161 832 6037

Owned by PK Chadha and R Kapoor, since '93. When it opened in the 1960s it was Manchester's first up-market Indian restaurant, and it pioneered the Tandoori oven in the city. The name is a play on the names of the original owners Gai and Lamba, who had opened one of Delhi's very first Indian restaurants called Kwality in 1948. By the 50's there were Kwalities all over India. But they were little more than caffs. Having made a fortune producing ice cream, the pair decided to go up market. with their first Gaylord which opened in Delhi in 1958. Other branches soon followed in Bombay, London, San Francisco, Kowloon, Kobe Japan, and the Bahamas. This elegant Gaylord seats 92 diners, and serves northern Indian cuisine. 'Chicken Tikka and Chicken Tikka Garlic are the most succulent I've ever tasted and their Rogan Josh is my all-time favourite dish – the lamb is always tender and the sauce has to be tasted to be believed. Vegetables fresh and nowhere does a better Nan.' RC. 'Reasonable menu selection, but what they offer is excellent. Good service in a very relaxing atmosphere.' AKD. 'Chicken chilli and pullao delicious, kulcha fresh and tasty. An excellent meal. Attractive decor, service fairly good.' RL. 'Each visit never fails to impress. Karahi Chicken must be the tastiest dish I have had. Surroundings and service usual high standard.' AKD. Sunday lunch buffet £7.95. Service: 10%. Price check: Papadam 60p, CTM £7.95, Pullao Rice £2.50, Peshwari Nan £2.25. House wine £8.95, mineral water £2.50. Takeaway 10% discount. Hours: 12-2.30pm/6-11.30pm (Sun. to 11pm). Stocks Cobra.

KAILASH ©

34 Charlotte Street, Manchester M1 0161 236 6624

NP Bhattara's 75-seater basement restaurant established in 1989 is described as Nepalese and serves Northern Indian curries, but where are the Nepalese delicacies? 'Service very helpful and friendly, particularly as there was a large party already in the restaurant. Free Papadams and pickles. Lamb Rogan Josh had cashew nuts. Portions a little on the small side.' TOC. 'Food I would rate as very average, although I rate the Nan bread as one of the best I have had. Comfortable surroundings and decor.' AKD. Hours: 12-2.30pm (Sun. closed)/6.30-11.30pm. Stocks Cobra.

NAWAAB

4/5/02 ✓ excellent all round

47 Rochdale Road, Manchester M4 0161 839 0601

I'm afraid this Nawab is getting the same varying reports as its branches. For now it stays, but your reports will determine this. 'Cuisine is Kashmiri/Pakistani, and there is a tremendous range of dishes. A large number of Asian diners on my visit, as is often the case. Starter was an excellent portion of superbly cooked lamb, chicken and prawn tikkas; main course was an impressive blend of juicy chicken pieces in a mild but tasty sauce incorporating pistachio and cashew nuts with banana. For the money, the cuisine should be beyond reproach, and very nearly is, though the performance of the staff (brusque and inattentive until the bill was presented) was the reason for the downgrading of my rating (7).' RW. 'Like so many Indian restaurants, this was a mixed bag. Starters fantastic, service friendly and welcoming, ingredients second to none, but the main courses bland and lukewarm. This is a good restaurant overall, but I won't go out of my way to return.' PW. 'Overall this was excellent. We arrived as a party of seven, easily dealt with by competent staff. Extensive menu. Highlights of the main courses were Nawaabi Murgh (with two huge chicken breasts, perfectly cooked and served with a delicate sauce), Garlic Chicken, Chicken Pasanda and Lamb Tikka. Approximately £16 each. Excellent value.' CC. Takeaway 10% off. Price check: Papadam 35p, CTM £6.50, Bombay Potato £2.95, Pullao Rice £2.20. Hours: 6-11pm; Sat. 5.30pm-12.30am. Branches: Bradford, Huddersfield, Majorca. Stocks Cobra.

SHIMLA PINKS NEW ENTRANT

Dolefield, Crown Square, Manchester M3 0161 831 7099

Open since the last *Guide*, as another branch in the Oriental Group led by Kal Dhaliwal. As we write the Group is in administration, but we are keeping it in the *Guide*, although we anticipate new ownership, which may affect both its name and its branches. Near the Law Courts by Deansgate at a former Italian restaurant, with a massive 7,500 sq ft and 80 covers, with a further 40 outdoors but under cover. Plenty of money went in installing the decor, furnishings and kitchens. Shimla Pinks' spin is to deliver upmarket Indian food. The food is above average, but not the average formula stuff. Specials include Paneer Ka Khass Tikka £3.75 – cubes of spiced paneer with raw mangoes, Dum Pukht cuisine which originated in the Nawabi courts (see page 37), Joojeh Seekh £4.50 – cardamom laced tandoori minced chicken kebab. Tikhey Jhinghey £10.95 – king prawns with peppercorns and coriander seeds. Chandi Kaliyan £7.95 – picatta of lamb cooked with cashew nuts, almonds and saffron. Kalimirch aur Methiwala literally black pepper and fenugreek leg meat tikka masala (£7.95), Harrey Masaley ka gosht, green herbal masala of coriander, mint, curry leaves and green cardamom (£7.95). Tikka Maachli – salmon in dill with fennel, ginger, honey, mustard (£5.95). The minimalist design by Del Hossain and Farzana Kazi of design company, D'fusion, responsible for a number of other 'new look' Indian restaurants, includes an intelligent mural of the Himalayas, by which they mean it changes colour by varying the lighting effect; dark grey marble floor tiles and grey tables. Despite this the lighting is colourful and the venue has atmosphere, made better when it has diners. House wine £10.95 bottle, £2.95 glass, Branches: Shimla Pinks Birmingham B15, London EC, Oxford and Scotland. Hours: 11am-3pm for lunch, 3-6pm for bar and 6-11pm for dinner (Fri. & Sat. to 11.30pm). Stocks Cobra.

THIS AND THAT CAFE NEW ENTRANT ©

3 Soap Street, Manchester M4 0161 832 4971

Established in 1980. Taken over by Ismail Musa Mallu in 1992. Seats 55. Specialises in Northern Indian, Pakistani and Vegetarian meals. Different simple menu to choose from each day. Lamb and Pumpkin £2.00, Cabbage Curry £1.60, Spinach and Vegetable £1.60, Fish Curry £2.30, Lamb and Okra £2.00, Lamb Courgette £2.00, Dal £1.60. Price check: CTM £2.70. Hours: 11.30am-5.30pm (Sun. to 4pm); Sat. closed.

MANCHESTER NORTH

Consists of M7, M8, M9, M24 (Middleton), M25 & 45 (Whitefield), M25 (Prestwich), and M26 (Radcliffe)

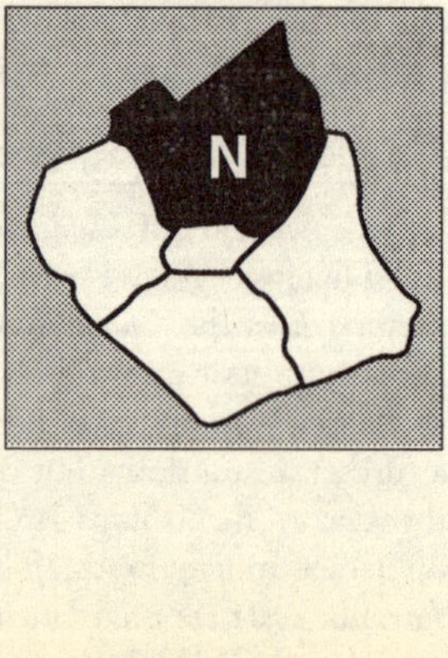

Manchester M25

Gorton (see also M45)

GARDEN OF INDIA ©

411 Bury Old Road, Prestwich M25 0161 773 7784

An 88-seat restaurant, opened in 1984 by Hafizur Rahman and managed by A Quyum. 'Chicken Samber, very reminiscent of a Dhansak, hot, but not as sweet, which was a very pleasant change and one which I shall look out for again. Chicken Paneer met with total approval.' SN&RA. 'Have visited several times and have always found it quite acceptable.' MB. TT likes the Fish Kufta Masala – fish balls in a creamy sauce. Hafizur Rahman has plans for refurbishing his 68-seater. Curries, cooked by head chef Ataur Rahman. Thalis from £10.50 to £11.90 per person, recommended. Service 10%. Cover charge £1.25. Takeaway 20% discount. Hours: 5pm-12am. Stocks Cobra.

PRACHEE NEW ENTRANT

12a Whittaker Lane, Prestwich M25 0161 798 6500

'I have been a regular here for the past seven years. Menu has nice range of all usual curries, excellent staff and exceptionally good eating. Music to your mouth! Kormas are sweet and delicious, Sambers are superb.' RB. Stocks Cobra.

Manchester M26

Radcliffe

ALISHAN

21-23 Church Street, Radcliffe, M26 0161 725 9910

Abdul Mumin's 60-seater serves formula curries cooked by Aziz Rahman. Says MB: 'It has grown an enviable reputation over the years for good food and reasonable service. The only complaint I have is that the waiters are surly and arrogant. Food is always good and quite reasonably priced – a typical meal for two with a couple of drinks around £15.' MB. Sunday lunch buffet £7. Takeaway 20% off. Price check: Papadam 40p, CTM £6, Pullao Rice £1.20. House wine £6.95. Delivery: £8 minimum, 3-mile radius. Orders over £20 – free bottle of wine. Hours: 4.30pm-12am, (1am on Fri. & Sat.); Sun. 1pm-12am. Stocks Cobra.

PASSAGE TO INDIA NEW ENTRANT

74 Water Street, Radcliffe, M26 0161 725 9129

'This one is a little bit special. Curries are absolutely superb, the Vindaloo one of the tastiest that I have ever tried. Madras is first class, prices are very reasonable.' MB.

RADCLIFFE CHARCOAL TANDOORI ©

123 Blackburn Street, Radcliffe, M26 0161 723 4870

At MLA Khan's very smart, long-standing (1966 – then the Taj Mahal) up-market 100-seater, chef SN Ali's interesting starters include: Balti Chana Masala and Puri, and Lamb Chop Tikka. 'Very comfortable restaurant but the food tends to be a little up and down. I have called in here and ordered a takeaway only to find it disappointing; on the other hand we have gone in and the food and service have been brilliant.' MB. Takeaway 30% discount. Sunday lunch £7. Delivery: 3-mile radius. Hours: 6pm-12.30am (1.30am on Fri. & Sat.); Sun. 12pm-12.30am. Branch: India Brasserie, 105, Stockport Road, Marple, Stockport. Stocks Cobra.

SHAHBAAZ

Old Barn Moor Road, Radcliffe, M26 0161 724 0000

FA Syed and Capt. NI Moshin opened this restaurant in 1989 (as the Curry Cottage) with its easy-to-remember phone number and address. Even the postcode is apt – OW1. In fact, Mr Syed should have renamed it the Owl Tandoori at the Old Barn! But we've still not heard a thing from anyone about that idea or indeed anything else. Reports please to stay in the *Guide.*

Manchester M45

Whitefield (see also M25)

DAWAT TAKEAWAY

184 Bury New Road, Whitefield, M45 0161 796 5976

'This take-away is still one of my favourites, and still up there among the very best. Mustapha has recently introduced Tikas and kebabs which are delicious.' MB. Price check: Papadam 25p, CTM £4.40, Pullao Rice £1.10.

KHAN SAAB NEW ENTRANT

117 Bury New Road, Whitefield, M45 0161 766 2148

'Fully licensed pub plus Curry House created from the converted building of Whitefield's Junction Pub (once run by one of Britain's last Hangmen). Began with Popadoms with accompaniments 50p/p/p of Mango Chutney – very pureéd, no lumps of fruit, Yoghurt, Red Onions and an interesting Cabbage and Nut Coleslaw. We skipped starters, headed straight to main meals – Khan Saab Lamb Sizzler £6.90 – medium sauce, tender, beautifully spiced, served with Pullao Rice – a treat. Mum's Chicken Kastoori £5.90 – very fruity, sweet and sour. Nan £1.00 – excellent, soft in the middle, light and crispy around the edges. Good value.' CC. Price check: Papadam (2) 60p, CTM £5.90, Pullao Rice £1.30, Peshwari Nan £1.80. Stocks Cobra.

LA IMRANS ©

Top of Elms Centre, Whitefield, M45 0161 796 0557

'Our party called for a light meal after our bowling night. Food excellent, all knocked out by the price (£53.20 for seven!), staff all knocked out by being in the 1999 *GCG*. Must return soon for a full meal. From outside, we would not have ventured in without the guide.' RN. Popular Balti Night – Tuesday and Thursday – seven dishes £7.50. Sunday buffet 1pm-6pm e-a-m-a-y-l £7.95 adult, £4.95 children. Takeaway 30% discount. Free parking at rear. Price check: Papadam 40p, CTM £6.95 (inc. rice), Pullao Rice £1.50 (with meal 75p). Lager £2.60 pint, House wine £6.50. Hours: 5 (Sun. 1)-11pm (1am on Fri. & Sat.). Stocks Cobra.

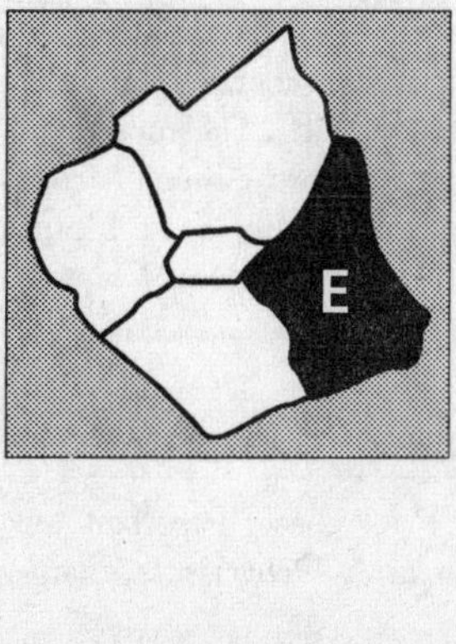

MANCHESTER EAST

Consists of M11 to M13, M18, M34, M35, M40, M43

Manchester M18

Gorton

ALISHAN TAKEAWAY NEW ENTRANT

780 Hyde Road, Gorton, M18 0161 223 3504

'No frills, but passable, standard takeaway that really tries to satisfy. Mixed special – generous chunks of chicken, beef, prawn and mushroom in a Madras style sauce with rather sticky but tasty Pullao Rice. Enjoyable and good value.' RW.

Manchester M34

Audenshaw, Denton

ABDULLAH BALTI HOUSE NEW ENTRANT

150 Hyde Road, Denton, M34 0161 320 8131

'Extremely smart, brand new custom-made interior to this bright and friendly takeaway. Real emphasis on Pakistani cuisine. Shammi Kebabs were the best tasted for a good while, thick and juicy. Lamb Rogan Josh was enjoyable, if a little on the small side.' RW.

ABDUL'S BALTI HOUSE TAKEAWAY NEW ENTRANT

77 Manchester Road, Danebank, Denton, M34 0161 337 8877

'Recently opened and brightly lit takeaway. Clean and pleasant interior, open kitchen, chatting staff. Shami Kebab £1.30 – delicious, juicy, spicy served with fried onion. Yoghurt sauce is an annoyingly additional purchase. Bhajias £1.20 – been deep-fried so many times, only useful for removing hard skin from soles of feet. Karahi £3.80 – delicious, generous chunks of chicken, well balanced sauce. Pullao Rice – light and fluffy. Substantial and enjoyable.' RW. No credit cards. Delivery. Pizzas also on the menu – from £5.50-9. Price check: Papadam 25p, CTM £3.80, Pullao Rice £1.10. Hours: 4.30pm-1am. Branch: Abduls Balti House, 853 Ashton New Road, Clayton.

BARAKAT BALTI NEW ENTRANT ©

699 Windmill Lane, Danebank, Denton, M34 0161 320 3232

Chomk Ali's Bakarat was established in 1988. Price check: Papadam 30p, CTM £4.25, Pullao Rice £1.20, Peshwari Nan £1.35. Delivery: £1 charge, 3-mile radius. Hours: 5-11.30pm (Sat. to 12am).

JAFFRIN NEW ENTRANT

116 Stockport Road, Denton, M34 No phone

'Well laid out and clean shop. Friendly staff advise on the extensive menu. Main meal was very mild in taste, with chunks of pineapple included, extremely complex in flavour. Complimented by a superbly light and fluffy Garlic Naan, sweet in taste and highly aromatic, a benchmark in takeaway breads.' RW. 'East Manchester's best kept secret. Garlic chicken tikka, sag gosht, dhansak, madras and samber all wonderful. Mushroom puri on request, even though it's not on the menu. Prices very reasonable.' I&JW

KURRY HUT NEW ENTRANT

99 Manchester Road, Denton, M34 0161 336 8844

'New takeaway, nicely decorated, light and airy atmosphere, though a few extra chairs would be welcome. Interesting selection, took too long to happen, Tikka with Chips! [WHAT, RALPH!] Samosa was taken from chiller and re-fried. Main meal – Keema Rogan Josh £3.30 – pleasant enough, good quality mince, fair sauce, though lacking refinement. Pullao Rice £1.10 – well cooked, aromatic. Tarka Dall £1.50 – high point, very garlicky.' RW. No credit cards. Delivery: 2-mile radius, £8 minimum. Price check: Papadam 25p, CTM £4.00, Pullao Rice £1.10. Hours: 4pm-12.30am (Fri. & Sat. to 1am).

SONA BANGLA NEW ENTRANT

83 Manchester Road, Denton, M34 0161 320 0559

'Standard curry house, seats 60ish. Pleasantly, simply decorated, air conditioned – handy for the Mancunian summer heat waves! Well cooked starter, pleasantly hot, though omelette on top was rather tough. Popadoms were a little on the small side, generous portion of sweet chutney and fresh tangy paprika onion salad were spot on. Chicken Rajatha (a cross between Bhuna and Jalfrezi – Chicken Tikka pieces well cooked and generous with slices of Birds Eye peppers, as hot as many a Vindaloo I have encountered) £7.75, came with Vegetable Bhajee and Pullao Rice. Bhajee not to my taste, resembling canned ratatouille with curry paste stirred in. Rice average, little aroma. Real tablecloths and hand towels.' RW. Price check: Papadam 45p, CTM £6.70, Pullao Rice £1.50. Hours: 12-2.30pm/5pm-12am; Fri. & Sat. 5pm-1am.

Manchester M40 *(formerly M10)*

Moston, New Moston

LA MIRAGE TANDOORI

67-69 Kenyon Lane, Moston, M40 0161 681 9373

'I have been a regular customer here for many years and never been disappointed, so I feel La Mirage should be given recognition for its excellent curries and tandoori dishes. The decor is not brilliant, but the meals, service and prices are. The best Madras in Manchester.' BT.

SHUHEL NEW ENTRANT

48 Old Church Street, M40 0161 947 0658

Established in 1997, taken over by Mustafa Miah in 1998. Price check: Papadam 30p, CTM £3.95, Pullao Rice £1.10, Peshwari Nan £1.25. Delivery: £8 minimum, 3-mile radius. Hours: 4.30pm-12am.

MANCHESTER SOUTH

Consists of M14 (Wilmslow Road, Rusholme) M15, M16, M20 to M23, M32, M33 and M90

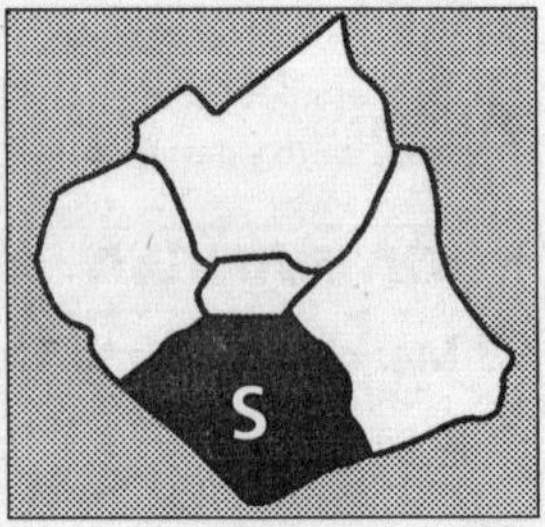

Manchester M14

Wilmslow Road, Rusholme

Wilmslow Road extends for nearly 6 miles south from Manchester Centre. It passes through Rusholme, Manchester's main Asian area. To get there from the city centre it's best to walk – parking is normally a joke. Face south on the Oxford Road, with the BBC on your left, and go for about 800 metres, passing the Uni and then the Royal Infirmary. At the Moss Lane East junction, Rusholme and Little India starts. In the last five years the expansion has been amazing and is continuing unabated. Now, in the 600 metres from Moss Lane to Claremont Road, there are no less than 35 curry eateries – Indian snack and sweet shops, cafés and restaurants. As if that's not enough, there are numerous pubs, offies, chippies, Chinese, pizza joints, kebab houses and burger bars, Asian grocers and halal butchers. Some of the cheap and cheerful all-day cafés allow BYO (but always ask – it can offend some Muslims). Some are quite expensive licensed restaurants, the largest of which seats 350 and is planning an expansion to 400! A conservative estimate on curry consumption is 50,000 curries a week here. We believe this to be the curry record for a district. Any challenges? Go a further 900 metres along Wilmslow Road, and there are some 30 more curry eateries, making this a genuine Golden Mile. With such rapid growth, we'd love full details on this phenomenon from all our scribes. Maybe it will merit a special extended feature in the next Guide. Meanwhile, here are some of your favourites:

Rusholme

AL BILAL NEW ENTRANT

87-91 Wilmslow Road, Rusholme, M14 0161 257 0006

Fully licensed. Air conditioned. 'Bright and open 150 seater restaurant on the neon artery that is Manchester's Curry Canyon. Friday night, quite full, no waiting for our party of 13. Pakistani waiters and an Italian barmaid led to consistent cock-ups with the drinks rounds. Excellent starter, generous helpings of Chicken Tikka, Lamb Tikka, Seikh Kebab and Tandoori Chop, all with crisp salad. Karahi Simla Keema £5.90, dry dish, gristle free, mildly spiced. Nan £1.60 – rather doughy, too much garlic. Excellent Almond and Pistachio Kulfi. Real tablecloths, no hand towels.' RW. Takeaway: 10% discount. Price check: Papadam 60p, CTM £6.50, Pullao Rice £1.30, Peshwari Nan £1.80.

EASTERN TOUCH BYO ©

76 Wilmslow Road, Rusholme, M14 0161 224 5665

Mohammad Akhtar took over this 72-seater restaurant in 1989. Pakistani curries, specialising in Balti. 'My favourite. Lino floor and glass-topped tables – a café, really. Warm Papadams, chutney and sauces are brought to the table immediately – free to all diners. Kebabs cooked freshly over charcoal in the corner, piping hot, highly spiced and juicy, served with a large plate of salad. Chicken Madras, prime quality, tender and succulent, very hot, sauce is rich and fiery, perfect for mopping up with a meaty Keema Nan.' P&SW, who say since they wrote that review a few years ago: 'standards have never slipped. Cheerful service. A friend of ours recommends the fish dishes. Gets the thumbs up from our Pakistani friends – especially the kharari!' P&SW. 'The decor is a little tired and shabby, but the food made up for that. Chicken Pakoras were the best we've ever tasted. The Lamb Rogan meat melted in your mouth it was so tender. We'll be back.' MB. RA however felt it was: 'a disappointing meal. Kebab starter lacked taste and texture. Chicken Tikka Rogan and Keema Naan tasted at best OK. Portions not generous.' RA. Takeaway 10% discount. Sunday lunch £7. BYO allowed, no corkage. Delivery: £5 minimum. Hours: 3pm-3am (3.30am on Sat.); Sun. 12pm-12am.

SANAM SWEET HOUSE ©

145-151 Wilmslow Road, Rusholme, M14 0161 224 8824

Despite AQ Akhtar's restaurant being huge (seating 160, plus a further 200-seat function room), it is so popular locally that it's often full, with queues waiting to be seated. 'The standard fare was very, very good . . . the Aloo Tikka was very tasty. A good first time visit.' TOC. Hours: 12pm-12am. Branches: Abdul's, 318 Wilmslow Road, and 298 Oxford Road.

SHERE KHAN

52 Wilmslow Road, Rusholme, M14 0161 256 2624

This is Manchester's version of Khan's, London W2. It is popular beyond belief and does a massive 'love-it or leave-it' trade. The decision is yours. Examples of both: 'One of the busiest restaurants on the Curry Golden Mile. Clean, a/c (sometimes) and so busy that people stand around waiting for tables, wishing you to hurry up. Food quality can vary widely on different days of the week, portions not generous and it is not cheap. Uniformly surly staff, probably a result of their constant harassment by management. Look after your valuables, had two purses and a handbag stolen. No help and sympathy from the management – only the bill. £131 for nine, no service, definitely no tip.' NSC. 'I've been there 100 times and it's great, but still they don't recognise me!' GR. 'Filling up rapidly as we sat down, and heaving within half an hour. Kitchen and meal assembly area in clear view at rear which is encouraging. Service was pleasant with smiles, but according to the local I was with, it depends where you sit in this very large place. Lamb Tikka starter was tasty and tender with Chicken Chillies, very tasty but didn't blow my brains out. Mushroom Bhaji excellent. Enjoyed it all. Seems a safe one to me out of the amazing choice of restaurants cheek by jowl in this area.' MS. Hours 12pm-12am. Branch: Shere Khan, Upper Level 3 Trafford Centre, Manchester, 0161 749 9900 – this restaurant has recently undergone a massive face lift, must be one of the trendiest if not the trendiest in the area. Seats a considerable 400. Stocks Cobra.

SPICY HUT ©

35 Wilmslow Road, Rusholme, M14 0161 248 6200

MS Mughal's simply decorated 60-seater serves traditional Pakistani curries and side dishes. Traditional Karahi Ghosht (*sic*), lamb on the bone, garlic, ginger, tomatoes, coriander, herbs and spices. Garlic and Cheese Nan. Delivery: £10 min, 3-mile radius. Hours: 5pm-2am; Sun. 3pm-1am. Stocks Cobra.

TABAK NAME CHANGE

199-201 Wilmslow Road, Rusholme, M14 0161 248 7812

Mohammad Nawab's restaurant has now reverted to Tabak again, having lost the 'New' in its name. It seats a MASSIVE 350 diners, on two floors. Pakistani curries and acompaniments on the menu cooked by chefs Raj Kumar and Abrahim Ali. 'Large, modern and trendy. Meal was rather mixed: Papadoms stale, pickles and chutneys tired, Sheeh Kebab good, Rani Chicken horrid (like a turkey burger!), Chicken Chilli very tasty, Shahi Stir-Fry Lamb delicious. Service rather poor. I would class this as a once a year place, for a change.' PW. 'The menu was one of the most varied and interesting I have ever seen, including dishes that I have not seen in other restaurants – such as Chicken Chasini, Chicken Chan Dani and Meetha Chicken. Also Nepalese curries. Tastiest Seekh Kebab I have ever had.' IM. 'My personal favourite on the Manchester trips so far. Large and chunky starters. Chicken Tikka Nantara sauce looked a bit like tomato soup, but it tasted nice.' JC&KEC. Hours: 12pm-1am. Stocks Cobra.

Manchester M19

Burnage, Kingsway, Levenshulme

THIRD EYE NEW ENTRANT ©

198 Mauldeth Road, Burnage, M19 0161 442 2900

Nepalese restaurant. First opened in 1998. Previously called Great Kathmandu. Seats 72. Cosy, traditional decor. Specials: Tangri £3.80 – chicken drumstick stuffed with saffron minced lamb and nuts. Bhutan Chara £3.95 – chicken with mushrooms and tomatoes. Kidney Masala £4.20 – lamb's kidney in spicy sauce. Price check: Papadam 35p, CTM £4.90, Pullao Rice £1.40, Peshwari Nan £1.90, Lager £2.40 pint. Takeaway: 10% discount. Delivery: £15 minimum, 3-mile radius. Hours: 5pm-12am. Stocks Cobra.

©	Curry Club Discount	U	Unlicensed
V	Vegetarian	ANP	Alcohol not permitted
e-a-m-a-y-l	Eat as much as you like	BYO	Bring your own alcohol

TONDORI ROYALE ©

682 Burnage Lane, Burnage, M19 0161 432 0930

'Bob Hoque's 110-seater is very well-established (1980) and very well spoken of by the locals. 'It was packed! It is not difficult to work out why when you taste the cuisine. Atmosphere is electric and food well worth the 40-mile trip.' MB. It has distinguished itself with a full house of familiar dishes plus some great Bangladeshi specials. Fish dishes include Boal and Ayre. NW's favourite is Zhal Golda Chingri, king prawn cooked with chilli and ginger. 'Very good. Vegetable Pasanda had excellent flavour.' RWI. 'A pleasant surprise tucked away in the Manchester suburbs. Try the Hopi for your starter – an interesting variation on the Chinese spring roll. Sizzling baltis with quality ingredients and accompanied by fluffy naans. Worth a go!' PW. Minimum charge £6. Delivery: £15 minimum, 3-mile radius. Hours: 6pm-1am; Sat. & Sun. 5pm-2.30am.

Manchester M20

Chorlton-cum-Hardy, Rusholme, West Didsbury, Withington

GREAT KATHMANDU

140 Burton Road, West Didsbury, M20 0161 434 6413

Nepalese restaurant, also serving traditional curry house food. Taken over in '96 by Chandra Kumar, who also manages his 55-seater establishment. Decorated with flowers, in red and brown, religious photos on the walls, giving a warm atmosphere. Specials include: Bhutan Chara, chicken cooked with fresh mushrooms and tomatoes, Bary Masala – mince balls with fresh onion, tomatoes and yoghurt Lobster Masala and Murghi Masala and 24-hours notice. Hours: 12-2.30pm/6pm-12am. Stocks Cobra.

GHURKA GRILL NEW ENTRANT

198 Burton Rd, West Didsbury, M20 0161 445 3461

'Arrived to find this small, friendly restaurant absolutely heaving with its strong local following. As the name suggests, the menu was a combination of Nepalese and North Indian cuisine. Our two main courses complimented each other perfectly. Lamb Chilli Masala was laden with hot green chillies and the distinctive lemon grass was an unexpected but exciting experience. Gurkha Grill Special Chicken was rich and creamy with a pleasant kick.' SW.

MOON INDIAN NEW ENTRANT

450-452 Wilmslow Road, Rusholme, M20 0161 448 8700

'A really mixed bag this one. Decor very tatty. Popadoms cold and nearly stale, but good lime pickle. But then – chicken chilli one of the best ever, very tasty. Half the waiters friendly and attentive, the others cold and indifferent. Would go again sometime for the chicken chilli.' PW 'Another excellent meal. Service was efficient and friendly. Sheeh Kebabs hot and tasty. This is better than some of the Rusholme restaurants, and is becoming a regular fixture when only a curry will do.' SW.

Manchester M21

Chorlton-cum-Hardy

PRINCESS OF HEARTS NEW ENTRANT

72 Manchester Road, M21 0161 860 0008

'Horribly lit with garish pink decor, you must overcome this and pretend you're not in a pink goldfish bowl. The food is exceptional and it's become my favourite. I'm vegetarian and there is an excellent veggie menu. Side dishes are a meal in themselves. The biggest let down is the rather bland condiments – watered down yoghurts, nasty onions. Takeaway is just as good, and 15% cheaper.' MN.

Manchester M33

Ashton-upon-Mersey, Sale

SPICE CHEF NEW ENTRANT ©

85 Washway, Sale, M33 0161 976 4577

Established 1994. Seats 50, parking for 10-15 cars. Sunday buffet: 2-6pm, five courses £5.95, children half-price. Vegetarian Night: every Tuesday, five courses £13.95. Price check: Papadam 50p, CTM £5.50, Pullao Rice £1.40, Peshwari Nan £1.90, Lager £2.40 pint. Delivery: £10 minimum, 3-mile radius. Hours: 5pm-12am. Sat. 5pm-1am. Stocks Cobra.

MANCHESTER WEST

Including M5, M6 (Salford), M17, M27 to M31, M41, M44

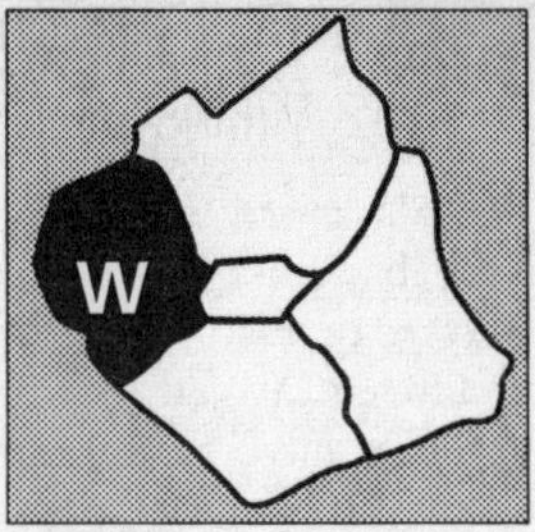

Manchester M30

Eccles, Irlam

PASSAGE TO INDIA ©

168 Monton Road, Monton, Eccles, M30 — 0161 787 7546

M Hassan Choudhury and H Uddin's serves 90 diners all the formula curries. Open 12pm-11.30pm. Branch: Gate of India, Swinton.

SHARMIN PALACE NEW ENTRANT

532-534 Liverpool Road, Eccles, M30 — 0161 789 0461

Established in 1986. Seats 65, room for about 20 cars in front. Specials include: King Aubori Cham Cham (boneless Tandoori chicken cooked like a Bhuna, but with makon and fresh cream, slightly hot). Price check: Papadam 45p, CTM £7.75, Pullao Rice £1.20, Peshwari Nan £1.50, Lager £1.80 pint. Takeaway: 20% discount. Hours: 5.30pm-12.30am. Fri. & Sat. 5.30pm-1.30am. Stocks Cobra.

REMAINDER OF GREATER MANCHESTER

Mossley

LAL QUILLA NEW ENTRANT

5 Manchester Road, Mossley 01457 839666

'Recently opened and already expanding. Friendly and helpful waiters. Standard dishes plus some specials, the Fish Massala catching my eye. A superb restaurant which I fully intend to revisit.' RW

Oldham

BALTI TASTE NEW ENTRANT

High Street, Oldham 0161 628 0400

'Good all round takeaway in small industrial town. Difficult free parking. Spotlessly clean. Friendly and efficient service. Free popadom. Lovely shami kebab. Biriani spot on. Gulabs in syrup, lovely on the tongue but terrible on waistline.' RW.

BRITISH RAJ ©

185-187 Lees Road, Oldham 0161 624 8696

Oldham's oldest (1970), taken over by Mr S Rahman in 1997, of which RK says: 'It's tasteful, right down to the Union Jacks embroidered into the chairbacks. The food is really good. The Shan Special Chicken and Bombay Chicken were both like a dream – hot and spicy and unlike the normal formula stuff. Pullao Rice exceptionally light and perfumed. The meal was finished off with hot towels and orange segments. They do special evenings with home-cooking, food as eaten by Bangladeshi families. One to return to.' RK. RW likes it too: 'Well laid out smart interior belies the tatty facade. Very polished service. Standard range of curries with large range of house specials. Started with Tandoori Fish – whole large trout, with tail and head on, dominated dinner plate, well marinated in tasty blend of spices, brought out best in flesh and served with crisp fresh salad. Handi Exotica Masala – superbly balanced curry sauce, deliciously hot, chunks of Chicken and Lamb Tikka with prawns filled a generously sized Handi. A thoroughly enjoyable meal.' Seats 50, car parking for 50 at rear. Delivery 10% discount. Takeaway 20% discount on collection. Sunday buffet – 10 courses. Hours: 5.30pm-12.30am (Fri. & Sat. to 2.30am); Sun. 4pm-1am. Stocks Cobra.

DHANA NEW ENTRANT

69-71 High Street, Lees, Oldham 0161 624 3220/3224

'Pleasant curry house (George Orwell town), comfortable, seating 55. Friendly and efficient staff. Very good Mulligatawny Soup £1.50 – plenty of lentils and garlic with a good smack of lemon. Chicken Cheese Kofta with Pullao Rice £7.50 – very generous, large chunks of chicken and meatballs in medium sauce with melted paneer. Good fluffy rice. Real tablecloths.' RW. Set meals are good value for money – three generous courses for two £18.50. Price check: Papadam 30p, CTM £4.50, Pullao Rice £1.45. Hours: 4.30pm-12.30am (Fri. & Sat. to 1am).

MILLON RESTAURANT ©

Westwood Business Centre, Featherstall Road,
South Oldham 0161 620 6445

Abdul Momin and Ashik Ullah opened their Millon, meaning 'meeting place', in 1993 in a purpose-built, elegant building. The inside is as smart as the outside. There is a pub-ish, comfortable bar and a 96-seat dining room, with alcoves and pillars and smart upholstery. Since the chef is Mr Momin, the food is of a high standard. 'Plush surroundings. Popadoms and a lovely, very tangy chutney, Amishi Chicken, very creamy and fruity and Chicken Jhali Bhuna, spicier and better. Totally approved of the Sag Paneer.' RK. Takeaway 5% off. Hours: 5pm-11.30pm (Sat. to 12.30am); Sun. 4-11pm.

NEW SAGOR NEW ENTRANT

272-274 Lees Road, Moorhey, Oldham 0161 624 9268

'Well decorated 60-seater on main road, with bonus of on-street parking directly outside. Efficient and attentive staff, who do their best – snapped Popadom and slopped soup. Good pickle tray, followed by outstanding Mulligatawny Soup £1.65 – rich stock, superb blend of lentil, garlic, onion and lemon, the best I have had for a very long time. Main dish – Balti Lamb Tikka Mashur £6.65 – exotic and well balanced hot curry sauce with a mild yoghurt based sauce topped with a sort of Salsa of cucumber, lemon and tomato. A novel and thoroughly pleasant creation made with slices of prepared Lamb Tikka which I recommend without hesitation. Complimented by light and fluffy Garlic Nan £1.65 – lovely aroma, liberal stuffing of fresh garlic, spot on. Superb meal, very good value. Real tablecloths and hot towels.' RW. Price check: Papadam 40p, CTM £5.50, Pullao Rice £1.30. Hours: 5.30pm-12.30am (Fri. & Sat. to 1.30am).

TASTE OF ASIA TAKEAWAY NEW ENTRANT

179 Lees Road, Oldham 0161 624 3666

'Clean and tidy takeaway on busy road, difficult parking. Waiting area – comfortable, TV, newspapers. Friendly, family run. Pakistani cooking. Seekh Kebab £1.20 – pair of succulent and spicy kebabs, fresh salad. Choice of sauces – yoghurt, sweet chilli or hot chilli. Chicken Cheese Kofta £4.95 – tender and juicy tikka, herby slightly gritty meatballs, garlicky medium sauce with Paneer (Mozzarella!). Pullao Rice – kaleidoscopic variety of colours, aromatic.' RW. Cheques and cash only. Kebab Sandwiches: served in a pitta bread with fresh salad and choice of sauce from £1.80. Fried Chicken, Pizzas and Burgers also available. Delivery: 3-mile radius, £8 minimum. Price check: Papadam (2) 70p, CTM £5.20, Pullao Rice £1.20, Peshwari Nan £1.50. Hours: 5pm-12.30am (Fri. & Sat. to 1.30am).

Ramsbottom

Known to residents as 'Rammy'

SHIMLA TAKEAWAY NEW ENTRANT

36 Bridge Street, Ramsbottom 01706 821110

'All excellent quality and good value for money.' MB.

Rochdale

LA TANDOOR ©

Unit A7, Bamford Precinct, Rochdale 01706 642037

Mrs S Habeeb's 68-seater is decorated with a paint effect of waves in the ocean and trees on banks. Eight spice boats have been fixed to the walls with sacks of spices in them. Fishing hammocks are tied to the ceiling. 'A superb restaurant, and be warned – book a table, as it gets very busy. We had Nargis Kebab and Vegetable Chaat for starters – a dream – and we followed with a main-course choice of Chicken Tikka Biriani and Chilli Chicken Balti, with a side dish of Malayee Kufta (vegetable balls in a coconut sauce with pineapple and peaches), Pullao Rice and Chupattis. It was all excellent, followed by ice cream, face towels, a free drink and after-meal sweets. All this cost us just £26.45. We'd eat there every day if we were locals!' RK. 'Now enlarged. Food still fab. Had forgotten this place until we read the Guide.' RN. Takeaway 20% off. Hours: 12.30pm-12.30am (1am on Sat.). Family banquets: Sunday £8.50 – 12.30-6pm. Stocks Cobra.

TANDOORI GHAR NEW ENTRANT

64 Drake Street, Rochdale 01706 646296

Established in 1985. Seats 90 in two rooms. Specials include: Handi dishes, Makni Sabzi, Vegetable Chorchara, Bengan Bhota. Hours: 6-11.30pm; Sat. 6pm-2pm; Sun. 4-11.30pm. Stocks Cobra.

Stalybridge

BRITISH RAJ NEW ENTRANT

36 Market Street, Stalybridge 0161 303 0304

'Magnificently balances a scrupulously clean kitchen, friendly and knowledgeable staff, interesting range, value for money and especially excellent cuisine. Akbari is a delight.' RW. Branch: Abdul's Balti House, 3 Corporation Street, Stalybridge 'caters more for the post-pub crowd. Clean and businesslike. Shammi was pretty good, shaslik was great.' RW

Stockport

(includes Chapel-en-Le-Firth, Heaviley, Heaton Moor, Marple, Offerton, Romiley, Whaley Bridge)

AL-MADINA NEW ENTRANT

38 Market Street, Whaley Bridge, Stockport 0161 432 0579

'People flock from far and wide and in constant steady numbers. Cooking and hygiene standards are of the highest order, staff are always friendly and courteous above and beyond the call of duty and we often choose to order on site as it's a pleasure to be there. Food is excellent, both in taste and value.' WV.

KUSHOOM KOLY ©

6 Shaw Road, Heaton Moor, Stockport 0161 432 9841

Meaning 'flowerbud', Mrs Kulsum Uddin's 80-seater with bow window and an open kitchen has been in the same family since it opened in 1971, with Fakuk front of house. The 8 rooms are decorated in pastel shades of peach and blue with carved teak screens on the walls. Sami and Kashim in the kitchens will cook Bengali fish dishes to order. 'A group of business consultants in Stockport consulted the *Guide* for reviews. Maturity, family ownership and positive reports prompted us to try on Thursday (busy) night. As taxi pulled up, impressed with garden exterior, trailing flowers.

Primed with beautifully fresh Popadoms and exceptional pickles but no Cobra. Starters: Onion Bhajia – crisp, Sheek Kebab – lean, no fat, Samosa – pastry not crispy, all with salad, overall good start. Main courses: CT Bhuna – superb, Chicken Rogon Josh – very good, Beef Bhuna – the best ever! Sag Aloo – tasty, Pullao Rice – fluffy and tasty, Nan – sweet roasty taste and "proper chips" as Farouk called them! Portions generous, absence of hot-plates, delicious dishes, service attentive. Lives up to its reputation.' LL. Takeaway 15% off. Delivery. Hours: 5pm-1am (2.30am on Sat.). Branch: Kaya Koly Takeaway, Heaton Road, Heaton Moor, Stockport.

MERSEYSIDE

Area: North West
Population: 1,415,000
Adjacent Counties: Cheshire, Lancs, Greater Man

Liverpool

ASHA RE-ENTRANT

79 Bold Street, Liverpool **0151 709 4734**

'The oldest Indian restaurant in Liverpool, established 1964, and I don't think the decor has changed since. Welcome, service and food fine.' H&DRC.

GANDI NAME CHANGE

18 Stanley Street, Liverpool **0151 236 3456**

'Unusual decor, through the door walk over a bridge over an indoor pool, past fountain to the bar area, down steps to dining area. Chingy Achari £9.95, marinated king prawns, strong spicy, sour – superb.' PS. 'As airline crew we had a night stop in Liverpool and were lucky enough to stumble across this curry house (hence I don't have the full address). Staff very courteous, seating cosy, food wonderful. Yummy Peshwari Naan, and lovely Cauliflower and Carrot Bhaji.' DC. Business lunch £3.50. Hours: Mon. to Fri. 12-2pm / 5pm-12am (1am on Fri. & Sat.).

©	Curry Club Discount	U	Unlicensed
V	Vegetarian	ANP	Alcohol not permitted
e-a-m-a-y-l	Eat as much as you like	BYO	Bring your own alcohol

GULSHAN TOP 100 AWARD WINNER ©

544-548 Aigburth Road, Liverpool L19 0151 427 2273

One look at M and S Rahman's venue tells you that it is likely to be good. Along its three-shop frontage is a white fascia, supported by twelve pillars, above each of which resides an attractive uplighter resembling an ice cream cone. Between each light is a small canopy that crowns each of the tinted, partially-curtained windows below, beyond which one can see an inviting restaurant scene. There's a smart lounge complete with leather Chesterfields, and the 76-seater restaurant, in 3 rooms, with equally impressive leather-backed chairs. The toilets are very expensively fitted out and they're spotless. The 'ladies'powder room'contains hairspray, perfumes, deodorants, hand-creams, cotton-buds and its very own resident resplendent black elephant. Sorry, chaps, no can see, not even if you're Lily Savage in full drag. DR says 'you could eat your dinner in there'– you're welcome, Denise, and we get your drift, but the Toilet Tikka has limited appeal, no matter how long the queue. The waiters wear striped waistcoats, and the tables are all well-dressed too, with crisp linen and decent cutlery. 'Even before we started to study the menu, complimentary Papadoms and chutneys were discreetly served … why doesn't every Indian restaurant do that?' asks GB. This is clearly a caring restaurant. They give a nuts-warning where relevant and are great with kids. Several regulars have remarked that the prices, though a little high, have hardly varied in several years, indeed we can confirm that they are the same now as in 1998. Starters include Chicken Tikka £4.30, Samosa and Onion Bhajia both £3.75. Gulshan Special, £5.75 contains king prawn, Chicken Tikka, Lamb Tikka, tomatoes, coconut and mushrooms in a cream and wine sauce, topped with egg soufflé and cheese. Chicken Zeera, £4.95 is chicken chunks cooked with cummin. 'Definitely a TOP 100. Took the Guide's advice and had a Mustard Balti Chicken, £4.95 cooked with mustard and wine, and Green Balti Masala, £4.95 containing puréed coriander, tamarind, green chilli and green herbs. Great when places experiment, thoroughly satisfied and went to the good pub opposite, then braved Liverpool's occasional public transport.' RDL. 'Recommended. Delighted to go.' RC. 'Very, very good, especially, as recommended, the Chicken Zeera and Green Balti Massala.' LH. The imaginative use of wine is rare in Indian restaurants and, done well as it is here by owner-chef M Rahman, it gives traditional dishes an unexpected and subtle lift. Established in 1986. Seats 72. Specials include: Green Balti Massalla (chicken, lamb or prawns prepared with freshly pured coriander, tamarind, mint, green chillies and balti herbs and spices) £6.95. Price check: Papadam complimentary, CTM £6.95, Pullao Rice £1.95, Peshwari Nan £1.95, Lager £2.90. Takeaway: 30% discount. Hours: 5-11pm. Stocks Cobra.

INDIAN DELIGHTS NEW ENTRANT

83 Renshaw Road, Liverpool 0151 709 1722

'A firm favourite among Liverpool's curry-eating population, especially the large student contingent. With its reasonable prices and friendly service, it does a roaring trade, particularly at weekends. Cuisine is first rate, from the impeccably crisp papadoms to the wide selection of main courses. Chicken Madras is typically hot and spicy but has a sharp twang of lemon that makes it a very distinct variant of the dish. Open up to 2.30am on Friday and Saturday nights.' BW.

LIGHT OF BENGAL NEW ENTRANT

286-288 Aigburth Road, Liverpool 0151 728 7030

'Smart, brightly lit restaurant, friendly waiters. Interesting specialities. Starters were mushrooms generously stuffed with spicy keema and fried in breadcrumbs, and Lamb Tikka, tender and pretty hot. Green Goan Chicken main course was oozing with fresh coriander and highly spiced. Dishes were delicious but so generous that we had to take most of main course home in a doggy bag. I heartily recommend an evening here.' LE.

MADHARI NEW ENTRANT

552 Migburth Road, Liverpool 0151 494 1134

'My husband and I eat here regularly, food is consistently excellent. Friendly and helpful staff, always happy to oblige with any special requests. We customise their Stuffed Nan by adding coriander. Last night, we started with Popadoms, then Chicken Dopiaza, Chicken Green Mossalla with Mushroom Pullao Rice. The chicken is juicy and sauce tasty. Portions generous. Cobra on draught. We recommend to everyone we know.' CF.

NOOR TANDOORI TAKEAWAY NEW ENTRANT

284 Aigburth Road, Liverpool 0151 726 0060

Established in 1996. Specials: King Prawn Zafran £5.95 – king prawn tikka, fairly hot spicy sauce. Chicken Kalia £4.25 – sliced chicken tikka cooked in butter and fresh cream curry sauce. Price check: Papadam 35p, CTM £4.25, Pullao Rice £1.10, Peshwari Nan £1.15. Hours: 5-11pm.

THE PARADE TANDOORI NEW ENTRANT

5 The Parade, Northway, Wavertree, Liverpool 0151 722 8533

Takeaway established in 1989. Recently refurbished. Specials: Rezella £5.30. Do special banquets. Price check: Papadam 35p, CTM £5.10, Pullao Rice £1.30, Peshwari Nan £1.40. Hours: 4.30-11.30pm. Stocks Cobra.

Newton-le-Willows

TASTE OF INDIA ©

56 Market Street, Newton-le-Willows 01925 228458

Akhlaqul Ambia's 80-seat Taste's house specials include: Balti Exotica – meat, chicken, lamb and king prawn, medium spiced. Balti Ruhabja – tikka cooked in mincemeat, highly spiced. Balti Garlic Chicken – tikka with fresh garlic and green peppers. Takeaway: 15% discount. Sunday buffet £7.95 between 3pm and 10pm. Hours: 5pm-12am. Branch: Haydock Tandoori, Kenton Lane, Haydock. Stocks Cobra.

St Helens

PALACE BALTI HOUSE NEW ENTRANT

59 Duke Street, St Helens 01744 225000

TJ tells us: 'St Helens up to now was forever associated with Pilkington glass and Sir Thomas Beecham. Now it has its Palace. Palace Indian is a very spacious, well accommodated eating house with impressive and extensive menu. Brilliant Special Palace Nawabi Murghi £8.35, Keema Pullao Rice £1.90 and Shahi Murghi £7.55, aromatic and has edge of mustard in medium hot sauce. I single out the rhapsodic Murghal Kulchi Lamb Masala £49.95 (four persons), whole leg of lamb cooked slowly and richly rewarding. Ample waiting staff to see to every need. Premises are well appointed, good wheelchair access, and a disabled loo. Many customers are regulars, it is obvious why.' RG. 'Interesting menu additions for you to try: Garlic Coriander Nan £1.65. The whole atmosphere is very civilised and welcoming, service is attentive without being intrusive. Chicken chaat was a meal in itself.' TJ. Minimum charge: £7.00. Price check: Papadam 50p, CTM £7.35 (inc: Pullao Rice or Nan), Pullao Rice £1.65.

Wirral

The Wirral is neither a town nor a county and, until 1965, was part of Cheshire. Since then the northern part – a small, digit-like, curry-rich peninsula between the rivers Mersey and Dee – has been part of Merseyside. Ellesmere Port (q.v.) remains in south Wirral but is in Cheshire. Our choice of Merseyside Wirral curryhouse towns are in alphabetical order:

Birkenhead, The Wirral

DHAKA TAKEAWAY NEW ENTRANT

344 Wood Church Road, Prenton,
Birkenhead, Wirral 0151 609 0782

Established in 1993 by Amin Qureshi, with chef Odud. Price check: Papadam 30p, CTM £5.95 (including Pullao rice), Pullao Rice £1.30, Peshwari Nan £1.50. Hours: 4-11.55pm; closed Tues.

Moreton, The Wirral

EASTERN STYLE TANDOORI NEW ENTRANT ©

11 Upton Road, Moreton, Wirral 0151 677 4863

Shahan and Miah manage and cook respectively at this takeaway only. Price check: Papadam 35p, CTM £4.40, Pullao Rice £1.20. Hours 5pm-12am.

SURMA TANDOORI ©

271-273 Hoylake Road, Moreton, Wirral 0151 677 1331

Jamshed Ullah's first-floor restaurant seats 52 diners. 'Good food, tasteful decor and friendly service. Side dish of Matter Paneer and the Chappati were excellent.' RK. Takeaway 20% discount. Takeaway: 20% discount. Hours: 5.30-11.30pm. Stocks Cobra.

New Brighton, The Wirral

LUCKY BALTI NEW ENTRANT

243 Rake Lane, New Brighton, Wirral

'Pleasant well lit restaurant. Service polite and attentive. 'Chicken Tikka Bhuna on Puris and Chicken Tikka Dhansak are out of this world. Chicken Korma had a little too much sauce. Breads excellent. Everything I have tried has been excellent. Can highly recommend.' DB.

Wallasey, The Wirral

BANGLA VAJON NEW ENTRANT BYO

285, Wallasey Village, Wallasey, Wirral 0151 639 9889

'Decor pleasant and light. Service attentive. No license – so BYO. Onion Bhajia – smallest in the world. Chicken Tikka Biryani – good portion, tasty but Rice slightly overdone. Good Jalfrezi. CTM, slightly sweet. Nans and Popadoms adequate.' DB.

TANDOORI MAHAL NEW ENTRANT

24-26, King Street, Wallasey 0151 639 5948

'Staff gave us their usual warm welcome. Popadoms and Chutneys OK – only mango and onion. Good starters of Mixed Kebab and Onion Bhajia. Chose the 'New' Chicken Chilli Masala, out of this world, a touch too many chillies sprinkled on top but superb.' DB. [And I thought you liked it hot, Dave!] 'Had craving for Chicken Chilli Masala. Popadoms, Chutneys, Samosas were wolfed down by all in anticipation of CCM, arrived looking splendid. My fellow diners thought it excellent but I was disappointed – different chef. Chicken Chat came with Big Puris and were tasty if on the mild side for me. [I was right!] For a late night curry – more than acceptable.' DB.

West Kirby, The Wirral

ROYAL BENGAL NEW ENTRANT

150 Banks Road, Kirby, The Wirral 0151 625 9718

'Recently been refurbished and now most 'un-Indian like', in Mediterranean style. Management are aiming (and succeeding) to attract evening clientele, rather than the 'late night after the pubs shut'brigade. Large, filling portions, service good. Will be back there in the near future.' PS. 'The restaurant has been transformed into a bright light cafe-bar style eatery. Popadoms warm and fresh, Onion, mango Chutney and Raitha lacked imagination. We five [men?] all had Garlic (loads of it – girlfriend hasn't spoken to me for 2 days). Chilli, varying strengths. My Vindaloo strength was excellent, not as hot as waiter advised. Rice and Breads very good. Only criticism, small portions and large Cobra £4.' DB. [Dave, what I want to know is, are your mates a bad influence on you or is it the other way around?] Takeaway: 10% discount. Price check: Papadam 50p, CTM £7.25, Pullao Rice £1.75, Peshwari Nan £2.15.

COBRA GOOD CURRY GUIDE
County Index, see page 5 Town Index, see page 614
A to Z of the Curry Menu, page 41 Contributors Key, page 604

MIDDLESEX

Area: All part of Greater London (west of London)
Population: 1,000,000
Adjacent Counties: Berks, Bucks, Herts GL, Essex GL, London NW & W and Surrey GL

The county of Middlesex is very ancient. It once contained most of London, though this distinction became diminished when central London became autonomous during Victorian times. What was left of the county (located west and north of London) was completely 'abolished' when Greater London was formed in 1965, a move unpopular with Middlesex residents. Confusion exists because the Post Office still use Middlesex as a postal county. Postcodes add to the confusion. Enfield, for example, is EN1, EN2, EN3 *in postal Middlesex but is in (Hertfordshire) GL county. Potters Bar* EN6 *is the same. Barnet is in postal Hertfordshire with* EN4 *and* EN5 *codes. It used to be in geographical Middlesex but is now a GL borough! There is talk of reviving the county of Middlesex. Wouldn't that be interesting! It would certainly help beleaguered guide editors!*

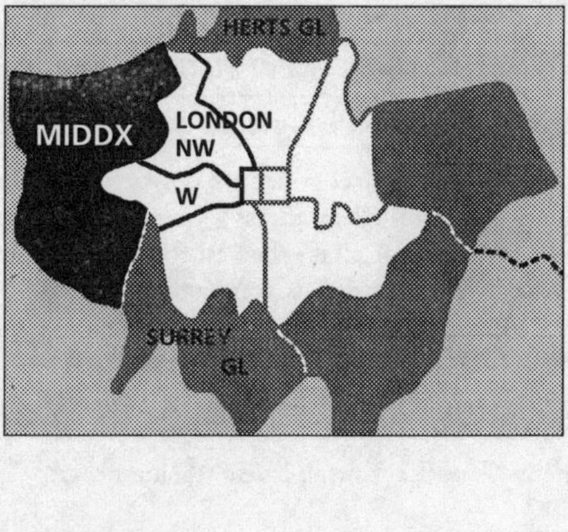

Ashford

SHAPPI OF ASHFORD NEW ENTRANT

7 Church Parade, Ashford 01784 258389

'Clean and ordinary looking, service quick and friendly. Lamb tikka rezalla was okay but re-coloured. I wouldn't go out of my way for a return visit, but would stop if I were already in Ashford.' RH.

©	Curry Club Discount	U	Unlicensed
V	Vegetarian	ANP	Alcohol not permitted
e-a-m-a-y-l	Eat as much as you like	BYO	Bring your own alcohol

TAMANNA'S NEW ENTRANT ©

15a Station Road, Ashford 01784 420720

Opened in 1998 by Azizuk Rahman. Seats 70 diners in a clean, modern restaurant with cane furnishings and wooden blinds. Specials: Bengal Fish Zafrani £10.95 – freshwater fish from Bangladesh served on a bed of baby spinach with lime and butter sauce, topped with fried shallots and spring onions, garnished with Karari Bhindi (sliced okra tossed in gram flour, fried until crispy). Sunday lunch: £6.95. Takeaway: 20% discount. Price check: Papadam 50p, CTM £6.95, Pullao Rice £1.90, Peshwari Nan £1.80, Lager £3 pint, House wine £8.95 bottle. Hours: 12-2pm/5.30-11.30pm. Stocks Cobra.

Eastcote

EASTCOTE TANDOORI NEW ENTRANT

134 Field End Road, Eastcote 020 8866 2989

'Menu offers a good choice. Quite busy with a fair number of Asian customers. Satisfied with quantity and quality of food. Service attentive.' RM.

Edgware

CANNON TANDOORI NEW ENTRANT

7 Station Parade, Whitchurch Lane, Edgware 020 8952 2501

'A best-kept-secret type of place. When we go it's always packed, has great atmosphere (lively yet dignified), waiters genuinely good fun, decor is fine, parking excellent. But most of all it's the best food of this kind that I've ever had. You can actually see each dish is completely individual.' SF.

RAJ MAHAL TANDOORI NEW ENTRANT

295 Hale Lane, Edgware 020 8958 9832

'Fairly basic menu. A pleasant meal, lovely restaurant.' CC.

Greenford

SUNDARBAN

3 Odeon Pde, Sudbury Heights Ave, Greenford 020 8900 0988

Opened in 1984 by Mr Abdul. Bangladeshi curries on the menu. Hours: 12pm-2.30pm/6-11.30pm. Branch: Pinner Tandoori, Pinner. Stocks Cobra.

Hampton

MONAF'S NEW ENTRANT

119 Station Road, Hampton 020 8979 6021

Named after its owner, Mr A Monaf, we hear good things about this restaurant, and its Sheesh Mahal sister. Monaf's is a well run, popular local. Sunday buffet. 10% discount on takeaway. Delivery 3-mile radius. Hours: 12-2,30pm/5.30pm-12am.

Harrow

WEALDSTONE TANDOORI NEW ENTRANT

30 Headstone Drive, Harrow 020 8427 8044

'It has recently changed hands and the food and service are now of an exceptionally high standard. Would recommend it to anyone.' GM.

Hayes

ASHA NEW ENTRANT

60 Station Road, Hayes 020 8573 4717

Established in 1977. Fully licensed and air-conditioned. 'It's a regular port of call when we stay at Heathrow overnight, and we've always been warmly welcomed and enjoyed an excellent meal (even when we've arrived just before 6pm!). Tikka Tandoori was a large sizzling platter with fresh salad, then Jeera Chicken which is excellent there – dry and flavoursome. Third visit this year. Menu includes several different dishes and they are prepared to provide anything requested. Excellent use of fresh ginger in their dishes.' GM.

THAMOULINEE SRI LANKAN RESTAURANT

128a Uxbridge Road, Hayes 020 8561 3723

We are often asked what makes a good restaurant, and by all our own yard-sticks, Thamouline shouldn't! But, as any regular visit to the subcontintent will vouch, dirt and decor are not in the frame over there. It's service and good food which matter, so welcome back Thamouline, and there are precious few Sri Lankan eateries in the UK. But, what's this? Anthony and Jasmine Hyacinth have finally retired and passed Thamouline into new hands. Mercifully nothing has changed, the awning having been repaired before the Hyacinths left (though Anthony predicted it will be torn again soon unless the landlord replaces the ever-slipping roof tiles). Presumably this don't-fix-it-unless-it's-broken precept has been passed onto the new owners. As ever, we parked at the bus stop, like everyone else does around 8pm. We were promptly and cheerily greeted and seated in an empty restaurant – no change there, then. Oh yes, there is a change – its former pale-pink decor is now pale blue, but the bar is still decorated with coloured Xmas tree lights and the carpet remains filthy. The menus are the same (and I mean by that they have been in service, stains and all, presumably since Roman times). We lamented the demise of the bustling Mrs H peering through the hatch – it's an all male domain now, but the hatch is still much in use for the new cooks to peer through and examine their customers. We decided to order the same food as our last visit, and held our breath waiting to see if standards had dropped. Delighted to report that the food is still very good – they can still cook. With our usual bottle of red wine (£5.95) we nibbled Papadams, still the lightest we've ever tasted, with mango chutney, mint raita and a red-tinged coconut chutney. Then our usual Mixed Special starters: Vadai, Mutton Roll, Crab Claw and Prawn Kebab, with a green-tinged coconut chutney and tomato sambol all fresh, and enjoyed, still for just £2.50. I ordered my usual Kothu Rotti, chopped chapatti prepared with mutton, egg, onions and spices. It looks unpromising, but at £4.10 it's a huge, filling portion – dry, spicy and a lovely change to wet curries. Pat's Thamoulinee Special Crab Curry, two crab shells, legs and claws, packed with meat, smothered in rich hot gravy, lived up to expectations at just £3.90. Special Fried Rice £2.80, was huge, with more coconut, tomato sambols and Achcharu (mixed pickle). This time, I didn't check out the services, but I do not imagine any change on the non-shutting door, the wood having warped too badly last time. Price check: Papadam 35p, Pullao Rice £1.25. Takeaway: 10% off. Hours: 12-2.30pm/6pm-12am; Tues. closed. Cash and cheques only. Stocks Cobra.

Heathrow Airport

NOON OF TASTE OF INDIA ADDRESS CHANGE

Terminal 3, Landside Area Mezzanine, Heathrow Airport

No phone – no booking at airports, just turn up. Says MW: 'On my way to Iceland, and ever willing to put my stomach at the disposal of The Curry Club, I sought out Noons to find they have decamped from Terminal I to T3. Unfortunately, I didn't have time to try them out. They are now one of several self-service counters on the mezzanine food court.' Mr GK Noon owns a vast Greenford state-of-the-art factory which churns out millions of curry ready-meals annually for the likes of Sainsbury's and Waitrose, as well as under the Noon name. One spin-off is to supply this factory mass-produced food to what Noons originally hoped was to be a national chain, though nothing has come of it over the last four years. All day you can have beverages, snacks and meals, Indian and western. The menu is the same, though the prices seem to have increased as much as petrol prices. We've not retried it since the move, but our TI trial was made with hopeful expectations, particularly following its nomination by Egon himself as the best UK airport caterer. On that occasion, we ordered Papadams which came with three chutneys (Royal's range – another Noon brand). We followed with Masala Dosa with Sambar then £3.45, now £4.75. It lacked south Indian tastes and textures. The dosa was greasy, as though it has been reheated, the potato was hard, and though curry leaves were in evidence, the sambar was a near miss of tastes. Raan Sandwich (then £4.95, now £5.95), thin slices of roast lamb, spread with curry paste sit on two small nans (no tandoori oven cooking for these breads) also spread with paste (coriander?). No traditional spiced-to-die-for, fall-off-the-bone Raan this! The Goan Prawn, £7.50, came in a thick, almost gluey sauce which tasted of little more than creamed coconut and tomato with, doubtless, starch and factory 'stabilisers', accompanied by turmeric-dyed, over-salted, not-basmati, slightly-starchy rice. Cobra lager 330ml £2.25, and £3.50 for a very good glass of Shiraz were expensive, but it is Heathrow! Naively we expected a great Indian meal, after all Mr Noon is Indian. The food was none other than Noon ready-meals. We detest such products, and unless you happen to like supermarket curries, be warned! Pity – with so much expertise available in nearby Southall, this could be showcase Indian food. As for the Ronay nomination, it says more about the state of the other airport caterers, and possibly the limit of Egon's currinary knowledge, than the excellence of Noon's, which is only here (in the *Guide*) because it's there (at the airport). If one must eat there, I suppose Noon's is it. Hours: 7am-11pm. Serves Cobra.

Hillingdon

HILLINGDON TANDOORI NEW ENTRANT

16 Byron Parade, Uxbridge Road, Hillingdon 020 8561 7055

'Has a number of nooks and crannies to allow very private tables. Complimentary starter – lentil dough deep fried with mint and yoghurt – was very good. Sarga chicken main course arrived after a 25-minute delay and was not a dish that I would recommend.' RH.

©	Curry Club Discount	U	Unlicensed
V	Vegetarian	ANP	Alcohol not permitted
e-a-m-a-y-l	Eat as much as you like	BYO	Bring your own alcohol

Hounslow

HOUNSLOW BRASSERIE ©

47-49 Spring Grove Road, Hounslow 020 8570 5535

Open-plan restaurant owned and managed by Naveed Sheikh. Chef Ali cooks Pakistani curries and side dishes. Specials: Zeera Chicken, cooked with ground cummin, fairly dry £6.25. Karahi Lobia, black-eye beans, herbs, spices, onions, capsicum and tomatoes £4.25. 'Meat Samosas, £1.50, are absolutely outstanding, the holy grail of samosas!' TE. 'A very quiet Thursday evening, and there were no other diners until I left at 20.30 hours. Samosas were fantastic, certainly the best I can recall. Chicken Tikka was very good with a smoky flavour and nice use of ginger as a garnish. Rice was fine. Three bored waiters gave okay service. Worth another visit if they stay in business.' RH. Takeaway: 5% off. Hours: 12-3pm (Fri. closed lunch)/6pm-12am.

KARAHI MASTER LAHORE TANDOORI BYO ©

795 London Road, Hounslow 020 8572 2205

Pakistani (Halal) 40-seater opposite Hounslow Bus Garage. Taken over this year by Mohammad Akmal. Specials include: Roast Lamb Leg £17.50, or, if celebrating with friends, Stuffed Whole Lamb £100 sounds great. Lunchtime specials for £5.95, please ask. BYO is allowed, 1 bottle per person. Price check: Papadam 10p, CTM £4.50, Pullao Rice £1.50, Peshwari Nan £1.25. A free drink to Curry Club members from Mr Akmal – cheers! Delivery: £15 minimum (6 free Papadams), 4-mile radius. Hours: 12pm-12am. Stocks Cobra.

Northolt

EMPRESS OF INDIA

40-42 Church Road, Northolt 020 8845 4361

Est. 1974, Ali, Zaman and EH Khan's a/c 52-seater serves popular curries. Butter Chicken Masala and Murghi Masala are specials. Sunday lunch buffet – 12-6pm £5.95. Takeaway: 10% discount. Delivery, free: £12.50 minimum, 3-mile radius. Hours: 12-2.30pm/6pm-12am. Specials include: Butter Chicken Massalla, CTM, Balti dishes. Hours: 12-2.30pm/6pm-12am; Sun. 12pm-12am. Stocks Cobra.

Northwood

ROYAL COTTAGE NEW ENTRANT ©

59-61 Green Road, Northwood 01923 824444

First opened in 2000. Seats 85. Specials: Papadam Spring Roll £3.50 – papadoms roll filled with minced chicken or prawns. Chicken Bhutuwa £7.95. Mari Chicken £7.95 – peppercorn and green chillies. Price check: Papadam 60p, CTM £7.95, Pullao Rice £1.95, Peshwari Nan £2.20, Lager £2.50 pint. Hours: 12.30-2.30pm/6-11.15pm. Stocks Cobra.

SHANTI ©

48 High Street, Northwood 01923 827856

Established in 1984, this 60-seater was taken over by Mofiz Miah in 1994. Decorated with carved wooden art hanging on white walls. Specials: Lamb Shahjanee – lamb tikka cooked with spicy kebab mince and sautéed onions served with rice or naan. Sunday buffet: 12-3pm, £7.25 adults, £4.25 children (under 10). Takeaway: 15% discount. Delivery: £10 min, 3-mile radius. Hours: 12-2.30pm (Sunday buffet £7.25 to 3pm)/6pm-12am. Stocks Cobra.

Ruislip

RICE N SPICE TAKEAWAY ©

73 Station Approach, South Ruislip 020 8841 5498

Kaizer Ahmed Chowdhury has agreed a drink for CC members as their discount at his (unlicensed) takeaway. Chef Cherag Ali's specials include: Chicken Tikka Mushroom Korai £4.30 and Peshwari Chicken or Lamb. Delivery: £12 minimum, 3-mile radius. Hours: 12-2pm/5-11.30pm.

RUISLIP TANDOORI ©

115 High Street, Ruislip 01895 632859

This air conditioned venu is an old friend of this *Guide*. It's a 52-seat Nepalese restaurant in black and white with flowering trees, Nepalese handicraft, pictures and a beautiful golden Buddha, which is, we're told, 'the main attraction apart from the Nepalese food'. Owner KB Raichhetri enjoys explaining about his Nepalese house specials on the menu. Takeaway: 10% off. Minimum charge: £8. Sunday buffet £6.95. Price check: Papadam 55p, free chutney, CTM £5.90, Pullao Rice £1.70. Delivery: £15 minimum, 2-mile radius. Hours: 12-2.30pm/6pm-12am. Stocks Cobra.

Shepperton

IVORY TUSK NEW ENTRANT

78 High Street, Shepperton 01923 246899

Red flock wall paper is as far removed from this venue as the Miah space station. Its new, though now much implemented decor style is by A La Carte Interiors of Ashford. Its stark white walls, expensive Scandinavian wooden floor, high back chairs in turmeric, paprika and chilli colours, and white starched linen give a trendy, airy feel. As to the food, we have a number of contented diners, and would welcome more reports.

Southall

From a single acorn (see Maharaja), there is an ever-growing number of sweet/snack centres, cafés and restaurants to be found, mostly on the Broadway, the main artery through Southall. The expansion westwards continues, where its unexpected bonus is a pleasing growth of Sri Lankan suppliers. Others are on South Road, and the Green. These places cater primarily for their indigenous Asian population, a generally peaceful mix of Indian and Pakistani, Sikh and Punjabi carnivores, enhanced by East African Asians. If you are none of these, do not feel inhibited from entering. Everyone is treated equally and all are welcome. However, if you are looking for lush decor, candlelight, carnations for the lady, etc., etc., you will not find them in most Southall venues. You'll find 'halal' not 'haute cuisine', nor curryhouse, nor alcohol in most. But you will find good, authentic cuisine in straightforward, functional eating houses, at realistic prices. The food is served from early morning to late night fast and fresh, whether in self-service cafés or in sit-down restaurants. One or two correspondents have bemoaned the use of the microwave to heat the food. We point out that a microwave is merely a heater, which has gained a poor reputaion because it cannot heat pastry well (samosas for example). It is not to be despised, and does not demean the food it heats. Better that than unhygienically keeping the food warm in bainmaries for hours on end. Below we examine our (and our correspondents') favourite eating holes.

BALTI & TANDOORI WORLD NEW ENTRANT U

185- 187 The Broadway, Southall 020 8867 9991

'There is no such thing as Balti,' I was earnestly told by a wealthy Indian lawyer who lives in Southall. Readers of these pages will know I'm always being told that by Indians. When I queried this restaurant with him, he poo-pooed it, telling me 'it's not a place I'd visit'. Strange, isn't it, how often people form opinions without ever trying the goods. Fortunately our inquisitive scribes try everything, and they like this one. 'World,' is the focus word at this newly emerged venue in the westward expansion, mentioned above. Not only does it do Balti dishes, aka Karahi by the Punjabis, and

Tandoori items, it does a fascinating mix of dishes from the culinary subcontinental world: Representative dishes from Gujarat, Punjab, Kenyan Asia, and north and south India are all on offer. 'Service is very quick and informative. Waiters kindly fetched beer and soft drinks from the adjoining off-licence. Customers can try their hand at cooking their own dishes. All dishes were of a high standard and were more authentic Indian-style cooking than some other restaurants we've visited. A memorable evening.' SF. Hours: 11.30am-11.30pm.

BOMBAY NEW ENTRANT

177 The Broadway, Southall 020 8560 4646

'We had planned to eat at the Maharajah, but for some reason (not known to us) it was closed – so instead of getting back into the car and undoing the security locks (such a pain, time consuming – but I mustn't get started on my "bring back hanging" campaign) we decided to eat at the Bombay which is just a few doors up the road. This restaurant has been around for a few years and has breathed fresh air into the "formica cafes" of Southall – it looks very modern and trendy inside and out – all black and white paint and stained wood. There is a bar on which to prop yourself up (if you can elbow the proprietor's friends out of the way who seem to treat the place like their local pub), a big TV for entertainment, many framed pictures of "stars" and a party room which always seems to be full of beautifully saried ladies having a roaring time with a booming disco and disappearing trays of steaming food being carried upstairs by some gormless youth. The menu is small but that's OK, with all you really need listed. The waiter noticed me gawping at the TV, turned over to Eastenders and put on the subtitles – how kind! Papadams are good with an excellent chutney tray – definitely handmade, lovely. Curries are well above average but with one critisicm, they are a little salty for my taste. Good value wine list. Enjoyable.'

BRILLIANT TOP 100 AWARD WINNER ©

72-74 Western Road, Southall 020 8574 1928

Owned by Kewel and Davinder (Gulu) Anand since 1975, who settled in the UK, having been forced to flee from troubled Kenya. An expansion plan has added the next-door venue onto the main room, installed a/c, and increased the seating to 180, plus there is a first-floor party room, with its own bar and music equipment (for discos etc) which seats 80. Despite the expansion and being above average in price (and really high for Southall), still the place is always full to bursting, being especially popular with happy, chattering Asian families, with rather more reserved whites in smaller groups. It simply proves that when something is really good, price is not the all-important criterion. It also indicates that Southall wants more luxury licensed restaurants than it currently has. The tables are large, and groups of 10 to 20 are the norm. Half of these will be kids, and Asian kids are always well-behaved at the restaurant, loving the experience as much as their parents. The restaurant has many large tables, laid out banquet-style, white linen cloths and burgundy paper napkins. Small matching chandeliers and wall-light fittings, padded velvet chairs. On busy nights you may find yourself sitting next to an unknown dinner companion, but conversation soon flows, as does the Punjabi cuisine, which is deliciously robust and spicy but not necessarily hot. Carrot and mint home-made pickles are on the table, Masala (only) Papadams, which can be either fried or roasted, will be served while you peruse the not overly large menu. You say: 'Visited many times! An exceptional restaurant! Standard of food, the way it's served, atmosphere, beyond compare. Cannot enthuse about enough! Well worth a 280-mile round trip from Weymouth! Vegetable Keema, CTM and Kofta are all wonderful. In fact, I might just drive up there now!' RC. And we thought our 80-mile trip heroic. Can anyone beat Roger's distance record? 'Terrific restaurant with a nice atmosphere, my favourite in the whole of Southall. Chilli Chicken, Egg Curry, Pullao Rice and Naan, all superb.' RL. 'Easy to find, difficult to park. Very popular with the locals. Friendly and helpful service. Enormous helpings.' R&NT. Specials are served in decorative copper beaten pots with serving spoons to match, balanced on individual heaters. 'The Anand signature dishes remain their most popular. Chilli Chicken, Butter Chicken, Jeera Chicken £15 whole bird or £7.50 half, on the bone, finger lickin' good, leaves the Colonel at the starting gate' DD. 100 parking spaces opposite in Featherstone High School. Price check: Papadam 50p, CTM £8, Pullao Rice £3.50, Peshwari Nan £3.50 Lager £3 pint. Takeaway: 10% discount. Free delivery only to regular customers. Hours: 12-3pm Tues.-Fri (no lunch Sat. & Sun)/6-11.30pm (12am on Fri. & Sat.); closed Mon. and all August. Stocks Cobra.

GIFTO'S LAHORE KARAHI AND TANDOORI BYO

162-164 The Broadway, Southall 020 8813 8669

Asif Rahman's Gifto has for many years operated one of Southall's best-stocked Asian grocery stores (at 115-119 The Broadway). Mr Rahman also takes a stand at the BBC Good Food Show cooking and selling his food at the exhibition. He has recently added 'Gifto's' to the name of his well-established and extremely popular restaurant' a few doors down from the shop, on the other side of the road. Its huge plate-glass window with sliding doors dominates the front of the 120-seater. The open stainless-steel kitchen runs down one side, the tandoor oven being in view from the street. Watch the chefs prepare Pakistani curries and accompaniments, with a noisy tossing of karahis and thumping of nan bread-making accompanying the beat of the Bangra background (make that foreground) music. Sit at simple formica tables at the front, or at the back in more 'glamorous' ones with high-backed padded seats. It's all pure show business, and it's good business, as the crowds of young Asians prove. Kebabs are most popular, though the food, uncompromisingly Punjabi, is all of very high quality. Specials include: Niharhi – spicy leg piece with spicy gravy £5.50, Paya – lamb trotters with thick gravy £5.50, Haleem – crushed lentils and lamb £5.50. There is also another counter with cold savoury items, Paan and sweets. Gifto's is rare in Southall for serving Bhel Puri (see A to Z of the Curry Menu). 'My favourites include: Dhai Vada, Alu Tikki and Chana Masala £1.80, Bhel Puri £1.90, Papri Chat £1.70 – Yum Yum! Waiters have a leisurely approach to service but are happy about it.' DBAC. Price check: Papadam: complimentary. Delivery is free locally. A further room upstairs holds 350 for weddings etc. Hours: 12pm-11.30 (Sat & Sun to 12am).

GLASSY JUNCTION NEW ENTRANT

97 South Road, Southall 020 8574 1626

Drive north over Southall railway station bridge, observing the tiny (and excellent) kebab house on its brow on the left and ahead you can't miss the amazing vista of Glassy Junction. It's a pub, whose exterior is clad with gigantic Hindu figures. And that name Glassy Junction is a pun which has got even this diehard editor impressed. And just why I've not included it in the *Guide*, search me. But here, at last, it is. Being a pub, it serves booze just like any other pub. Its clientèle is largely young trendy Asian, the like of which abounds in Southall. Bangra and Hindi movie music blares out. Add the chattering, and the noise is more deafening than a migrating flight of starlings. As to the food, there's a splendid selection of tandoori and curry items.

KARAHI TANDOORI KABAB CENTRE ANP

161-163 The Broadway, Southall 020 8574 3571

Owner AF Choudhury and Manager Dalawar delightedly tell us that their venue, known locally as TKC, was an original of the genre, founded in 1965, early days in Southall's currinary development, and that there have been numerous copiers, not least the ones dead opposite. And what is the genre? Firstly, it is and was uncompromisingly Asian in food style and service, though all are welcome, of course. In 1965, few whites visited it; now things have changed, and they are as taken for granted as the Asian clientèle. The venue is open-all-hours, and the price is right – inexpensive, and designed to attract regular local custom several times a week at breakfast, lunch, tea or dinner. Next, standard shop full-length windows ensure that when walking past, you are immediately attracted to the display cabinets containing all sorts of tempting snacks such as Pakora, Bhel Poori, Gol Goppas, Jeera Pani (cumin water), Tikki, Samosa, Indian sweets, etc. Alongside, and equally on show are the chefs, under head chef Farooq, and they soon learn to show off, much as do Tepiyakki chefs in the Japanese equivalent. Their freshly cooked Tandooris, Kebabs and breads, Punjabi Karahis and curries are cooked to order, and are quite delicious. Inside is a clean and tidy, no frills café-style restaurant, seating 66, with formica tables, and waiter-service. Head chef Farooq's menu says 'please specify your taste of chillies when ordering'. His Appetisers include: Reshmi Spring Lamb Boti, tender succulent pieces of lamb marinated in double cream roasted in the tandoor £3.50. Paneer Tikka, chunks of vegetarian cheese marinated with spices and baked in tandoor £3. Main courses: Nehari, shank of lamb served in a spicy sauce £4. Zeera Chicken, made with butter and cummin seeds £5. Sarson Ka Saag, mustard and spinach leaf £3.50. House Specialities: Chargha, fully roasted and tenderly spiced, free-range chicken, a recipe from the inner Punjab £6.50. Chappal Kebab, beaten mince steaks cooked and served on a sizzler, a speciality from the North-West Frontier Province £4. Try the Kulfi Faluda, a Pakistani version of the Knickerbocker Glory £1.80. Pinad Da Buffet £6.99. All food is prepared with Halal meat. Alcohol is strictly prohibited. Price check: Papadam complimentary, CTM £4.50, Pullao Rice £2, Peshwari Nan 60p. Hours: 10am-11pm. I wish this were the formula all over the country, rather than the exception in the various Asian communities. No wonder it gets very busy with all age groups, from the pensioners, mums and babes in the day to the young trendy ebullient fun-loving Asians at night and weekends. Hours: 9am-12am. Branch: Tandoori Express on Jalebi Junction, 93 The Broadway, Southall.

MADHU'S BRILLIANT TOP 100 AWARD WINNER ©

39 South Road, Southall 020 8574 1897

Opened in 1980 by JK, KK, Sanjay and Sanjeev Anand, nephews of the great Mr Anand of the Brilliant (see entry). The restaurant seats 94 on two floors, the upper floor, toilets and second bar being reached by a large spiral staircase at the front of the restaurant. You will often find Sanjay in the restaurant, welcoming diners as old friends – you will know which one he is, because of his very distinctive laugh. Our *Guide* was the first to recognize this restaurant, back in 1984, when the clientèle was mostly Asian. Today, and dozens of awards later, there are as many non-Asians as Asians enjoying the food and ambience here. The latter has been totally revamped at considerable expense. 'It is now absolutely amazing and would not look out of place in the West End. Walls are a creamy buttermilk, squares of gold leaf have been hand-brushed onto one wall making for a very dramatic look. All chairs have been replaced and upholstered in a heavy brocade style material, green and cream. Indian art and lighting is discreet. It has to be the poshest restaurant in Southall.' DBAC. Cooking is led by brother Sanjeev (affectionately called Mint). The food is typical Punjabi and far removed from the Bangladeshi curry house formula. We say this every time, that the food is authentic, and not formula, and we continue to get disappointed comments. Sorry to say, it says nothing for those people's judgement, so I'm not running them again. The Anand signature dishes, Butter Methis and Jeera Chicken, all £6.60 for half a chicken on the bone, are an absolute must when dining here. House specials: Mniahma Chommah – spring lamb ribs seasoned and marinated and cooked in tandoor. Machuzi Kuku – spring roaster – on the bone, in a thin curry, medium-spiced, a Kenyan speciality – three-person portion £16. Boozi Bafu – spring lamb chops from Kenyan Boozi, cooked authentically in a spicy medium sauce, highly recommended – three person portion £18. We get plenty of reports from those who can tell good Indian food from mediocre, for example: 'Never had better meal. It was quite different from the usual place.' PE. 'I ate here and can confirm its status in the Guide. Food a little pricey, but probably reflects London effect and reputation. Wonderful atmosphere as it was crowded with the local Asian community. Only 30 minutes from Heathrow, so good place to eat between flights. Parking can be difficult.' PAW. Price check: Papadam 50p, CTM £6.50, Pullao Rice £2, Peshwari Nan £2. House wine £8, mineral water £3. Lager £2.25 pint. Takeaway: 10% discount. Hours: 12.30-3pm (Sat. & Sun. closed)/6-11.30pm; closed Tues. Stocks Cobra.

MAHARAJA ©

171-173 The Broadway, Southall 020 8574 4564

Southall's very first Indian restaurant opened in 1955. Owned by AA Sandhu, since 1972. Managed by HS Sandhu. 'I like this restaurant, nicely decorated, seats 90 and is an oasis for those who like a pint of beer or a glass of wine with their meal, as I do. It is surrounded by fabulous Pakistani eateries, which are an alcohol desert. Northern Indian food is on the menu, all your regular favourites are there and cooked well.' DD. 'What an excellent choice, Mixed Grill (about £9), easily enough for two. Jalfrezi, in my top ten. Chana Masala, possibly a little heavy on the ginger. Two young waiters, very pleasant.' SW. 'Even my carnivorous, fussy sister actually likes it. In two phrases, I'd describe the Maharaja as the formula done better, and an ideal starting place for those unsure about the delights of Southall. Our meal for three with drinks cost £42.' DBAC. Takeaway: 10% discount. Price check: CTM £6.95, Pullao Rice £2.10, Peshwari Nan £2.25. House wine £7.95, mineral water £2.80. Hours: 12-3pm/6-11.30pm; closed Mon. Stocks Cobra.

OMI'S TOP 100

1 Beaconsfield Road, Southall 020 8571 4831

Owner-chef Mykesh Kharbanda cooks north Indian and Kenyan curries at Omi's off South Road, on a side street, and with just 42 seats, it gets harder to find a space, especially in the evenings. The shop front stands slightly back from the pavement, making room for parking for 4 vehicles. A short menu above the counter describes what is on offer, along with the Specials of the Day. The most popular dishes are Ginger Chicken and Palak Chana. Since we were taken here years ago by Indian journalist KN Malik ('I want to show you Indian food at its best'), we can safely say this is the Indians' Indian restaurant. We love his food and adore Mykesh's idiosyncrasies. The place doubles for van-hire. So one phone call can order you lovely, soft, delicious Garlic Nan and noisy diesel-fumey Transit Van! It has the usual plastic tables and chairs, making for a clean and tidy restaurant, but it's the freshly-cooked food you go for. Price check: Papadam 50p, CTM £4, Pullao Rice £1.75, Peshwari Nan £1.20. Set meal £4 (served till 6pm). House wine £1.50 glass. Delivery: small charge. Hours: 11am-9pm (Fri. & Sat. to 9.30pm).; closed Sun. Remains in our TOP 100. Stocks Cobra.

PALM PALACE NEW ENTRANT

80 South Road, Southall 020 8574 9209

Now in its fourth incarnation in as many years, and mercifully still Sri Lankan/south Indian, a scarce resource in the UK, and unique in Southall. Gone are the front samosa/sweet counter, and the noisy TV with its Hindi movies. The place is now simply decorated, licensed and all restaurant. And this seems to be working. It is now busier than we have seen before, not over full, mind you – Southall's Asians are a conservative lot – but the if-it-ain't-Punjabi-it-ain't-edible view is hopefully changing. And, as we say everytime, so it should. My benchmark crab curry from an early ownership has never been matched, but it's still an exciting dish, especially fired up to incendiary level for those of us who cannot do without chilli. There's nothing like picking and sucking out crab meat from legs and shell and dousing it in rich Sri Lankan gravy. Messy shirt-sprinkling stuff, yes, but a slow pleasurable experience, which is a contender for my desert island luxury.

PUNJABI KARAHI ©

175 The Broadway, Southall 020 8574 1112

Chef Khurrum Choudhry's restaurant seats 150 and he warns that parking after 6.30pm is 'thin on the ground'. Pakistani and Balti dishes are his speciality, including Mixed Grill £10, Kebabs 60p, Chicken legs £2.60 and Tandoori Batera (quail), £2.90 for starters and Methi Chicken £5.40, Paya – lamb trotters in a spicy sauce £5. Price check: Papadam 15p, CTM £5.40, Pullao Rice £1.80, Peshwari Nan £1.50. Hours: 11.30am-11.30pm (12am on Sat.).

NEW ASIAN TANDOORI CENTRE TOP 100

114-116 The Green, Southall 020 8574 2579157

There is nothing new about this venue. It began trading in 1959. Indeed it is still known as The Roxy, although its English transport caff namesake closed over four decades ago. In its place came an Asian version of the same – one of those long-standing restaurants which serve the local community morning, noon and night. Founders Mr Sagoo and Mr Thakhar strategically set up two such venues, located at either end of Southall; they have finally retired and sold their 157 The Broadway venue to the next door halal butcher, who has renamed it The Kashmir. When you enter the Roxy, there may be a queue, even outside the door, but it won't take long before it's your turn. Long glass counters display tempting Indian sweets and savoury snacks (Bhajias, Kebabs, Samosas, Aloo Tikki, Dahi Vasa, etc.), curries (Murgh Masala, on the bone, Bombay Potato, Sag Paneer, Sag Gosht and more, all cold but will be reheated in the microwave on request), Channa Dal, Rice (Plain, Pullao and Biryani) and breads. 'Pick up a tray and tell the chap behind the counter what you want and whether you are eating in or taking out. Portions are generous and I have to restrain myself from over-ordering. When you have paid (cash or cheques only), take your tray to the other room and seat yourself.' DBAC. 'The absolute curry experience, should be compulsory for all members to visit! Sample the vast range of dishes on offer, all authentic and served up in a no-nonsense style. We ate vast quantities of food, including Pakoras, Dall (black bean), Chicken and Meat Curries, Rotis and rice. Service with a smile, staff friendly. Highly recommended, must be very high in the TOP 100.' DB. They also serve a wonderful chutney, sticks of carrot, slices of onion, embalmed in a tamarind and yoghurt sauce, delicious, I can't get enough of it. You can BYO (but please ask), which all makes for a great meal out. Fresh fruit juice and Lassi are available. Hours: 10am-10.30pm (11pm on Fri.-Sun.). It is high in our TOP 100. Stocks Cobra.

SHAHANSHAH VEGETARIAN V ©

60 North Road, Southall 020 8574 1493

Gill Baljinder (manager) and Johl Sarbjit, have since 1984 specialised in cooking from north and south India at their vegetarian restaurant, which seats 30 diners. Samosas and other snacks are the most popular items ordered. Indian sweets are made on the premises, so you can be sure they are fresh. Set dinner £5. Sunday lunch £4. Price check: Papadam 30p, Pullao Rice £1.50. No credit cards. Hours: 10am-8pm. Branch: Shahanshah Vegetarian, 17 South Road, Southall.

TANDOORI EXPRESS ON JALEBI JUNCTION ©

93 The Broadway, Southall 020 8571 6782

Owner Abdul Chaudhury, manager Mr Shauket, and head chef Rassaq's bright and colourful venue appeals to the local young and trendy population. It is often full of chattering, bright young Asians babbling on in animated Southall cockney accents. A richly painted and decorated rickshaw can be seen outside on the wide pavement which enhances the environment. Also a cook makes Jalebis, those crispy, deep-fried squiggles, immersed in syrup, right there on the pavement. You can't get fresher than that, and if you've not seen it done, here's the only place in Britain we know of that does it on view. Great Pakistani curries and fresh breads are a big pull, along with snacks such as Samosas, Pakoras, etc. There is also a vast sweet counter to pile on the pounds (weight that is, not the bill). Starters include: Club Sandwich, finest chicken and lamb BBQ fillings £3. Shami Kebab, mince meat and lentil burger 50p. Dehi Bhalla, lentil flour doughnuts soaked in yoghurt £1.50. House specials: Masaladaar Raan, whole leg of lamb roasted in the tandoor with all the natural juices and flavours sealed within, a Moghul dish from Lakhshmi Chauk, Lahore, £15. Alcohol is strictly prohibited. Price check: Papadam 50p, CTM £4.50, Pullao Rice £2, Peshwari Nan £80p. Hours: 9am-11pm. Branch: Karahi Tandoori Kebab Centre, 161-163 The Broadway, Southall.

Sudbury

GHUNGHAT NEW ENTRANT

763-765 Harrow Road, Sudbury 020 8904 2636

Taken over July 1999 and managed by Mr Karim, with Ms Pervin in the kitchen. Seats 100 in very relaxing surroundings – like sitting in a Rajasthani village with thatched roofing with puppets, colourful mirror-work hangings and baskets decorating the walls. Specials: Chilli Paneer £2.95 – home-made cheese, deep-fried and tossed in fresh green chilli. Deep Fried Chilli Wings £2.75. Masala Fish £6.95 – fillets of Tilapia cooked in rich red masala with coriander leaves and green chillies. Takeaway: 10% discount. Hours: 12-2.30pm/7pm-12am. Stocks Cobra.

Teddington

BENGAL BRASSERIE ©

162 Stanley Road, Teddington 020 8977 7332

Established in 1986. Managed by Ali Kausar, head chef Sufian Khan. Air conditioned, seats 44, decorated with Indian and Bangladeshi art on the walls and fresh carnations on the tables. House specials include: Chicken or Lamb Balaka, marinated, cooked with potato, egg, green chilli, red wine, spicy hot. Jeera Chicken, marinated, cooked in cummin. Bangladeshi style Rezela and Jeera Chicken. Minimum charge £8.50. Collected takeaway: 10% discount. Takeaway: 10% discount. Delivery: £20 minimum, 2-mile radius. Hours: 6pm-12am. Stocks Cobra.

BILAS NEW ENTRANT

4 Broad Street, Teddington 020 8977 1529

'Food very good quality and quantity, service fine.' AJ.

MODERN NEW ENTRANT

196 Stanley Road, Teddington 020 8977 8679

'We have eaten here countless times and always find both food and service excellent. Far and away the best. Strongly recommended.' MR&MRS RB.

Twickenham

NAZ CUISINE NEW ENTRANT

20 Church Street, Twickenham 020 8744 9181

'Very helpful and welcoming staff, service quick. Fun music with popular hits played on traditional Indian instruments. Papadoms crispy and hot. Portions good-sized. Dishes are not over oily, hot and very tasty. Methi Mazz is always good. If in the mood for a Balti, there's none finer in Twickenham, we reckon.' A&BG.

PALLAVI SOUTH INDIAN NEW ENTRANT

Unit 3, Cross Deep, Court Heath Rd, Twickenham 020 8892 2345

Specialises in South Indian Keralan cuisine, with dishes from the cities of Cochin, Malabar and Travancore. Hot is the norm in Kerala but they cool it for 'western tastes'! So if you want to up the chilli strength, tell them and the kitchen will be more than happy to oblige. Contrary to popular belief, meat, chicken and fish dishes are the norm there. Try Lamb Cutlets: patties made of minced lamb and spices covered with breadcrumbs and fried. Served with tomato sauce and salad. Malabar Chicken is cooked with coconut, curry leaves, garlic and mustard. Fish Mollee is a classic dish, so mild and gentle in its coconut base that even the Raj allowed it at table. Cochin Prawn with the ubiquitous coconut, this time with tomato, is another. Chemeen Poriyal-King Prawn Fry: king prawns marinated in ginger, garlic, spices and sliced coconut, fried in seasoned oil. All the now-familiar vegetarian south Indian rice-based offerings are here, such as Masala Dosa (crispy, potato curry-stuffed pancake), Uthappam (an intriguing rice-flour, crisp disc, baked with a spicy topping), Vellappam (like rice noodles), Paripu, Sambar (lentil dishes) and Rasam, peppery soup and those wonderful coconut chutneys. Other less familiar vegetarian offerings include a Keralan crumpet made of flavoured rice and served with vegetable stew. Spinach Vadai: fried crunchy doughnut of channa dal, green chillies, onion, ginger, curry leaves and fresh spinach served with a variety of chutneys and for pud Banana Leaf Cake: made of rice with a sweet filling of grated coconut, banana and jaggery wrapped in banana leaf and steam cooked. 'Visited on return from Kerela, S. India. Authentic food and very good quantity and quality. The waiters came from the region, which makes it better. Kerelans are charming people with a special mannerism all their own! On leaving we were given a bag with information from Kevela Tourist Board.' RH. Hours: 12-3pm/6pm-midnight.

RAWALPINDI TANDOORI GRILL NEW ENTRANT

62 King Street, Twickenham 020 8892 3082

'The only restaurant in this area that compares with the best in London (I moved here from Central London 15 months ago). We've had countless meals, mainly takeaways (we have a baby!) – always excellent. Quantities are enormous, menu very well varied (all the usual stuff plus a lot of Persian speciality dishes). Every chicken dish we've had has been superb – always well marinated. Papadoms very good, likewise chapatis and other breads. Service is exceptionally friendly and courteous. Free home delivery or takeaway (15% discount). Exceptionally highly recommended.' AJ.

SHEESH MAHAL NEW ENTRANT

21 London Rd, Twickenham, Middlesex 020 8892 5471/3303

White and blue frontage this 66-seater (upstairs too) has been owned and managed by A Monaf, since '82. It describes itself as, 'nice and simple, for us and the customers'. Yes, you've guessed it, Chicken Tikka Masala is the most ordered dish. Takeaway 10% discount. Sunday lunch buffet £6.95. Price check: Papadam 50p, CTM £6.25, Pullao Rice £1.95. Delivery: £10 minimum, 3-mile radius. Hours: 12-2.30pm/5.30pm-12am. Branch: Monaf's, 119 Station Road, Hampton.

Uxbridge

INDIA INDIA TAKEAWAY NEW ENTRANT

61 Belmont Road, Uxbridge 01895 252341

Its modern frontage encourages customers, who tell us they like the India India's food and reasonable prices.

Wembley

Rapidly gaining ground as the second Southall. Unlike Southall, its large Gujarati/East African population gives Wembley food a different (predominantly vegetarian) taste from Southall. As with Southall, there are many good sweet/snack shops/cafés and restaurants crammed with Indian goodies. Here are your favourites:

ASIAN KARAHI NEW ENTRANT

272 Ealing Road, Wembley 020 8903 7524

Small venue (25 seats) which exudes careful service and thoughtful cooking. The usual range of Karahi style cooking is available all week, but at the weekend, they offer some really authentic stuff, not for the faint-hearted: Niharhi – marinated leg piece (shank) of lamb served with a spicy gravy, Paya – lamb trotters with thick gravy, Haleem – an almost gruel-like mash of crushed wheat and lamb and Haandi dishes all of very high quality. Spicing is done to taste – mild, medium and hot.

CHETNA'S BHEL PURI TOP 100 V

420 High Road, Wembley 020 8903 5989/8900

A large, very popular vegetarian licensed restaurant with vegan dishes. 'You often have to queue here. We waited on the pavement until they called out our number, but it is well worth it. They do deluxe Masal Dosas, and a great

Vegetarian Thali main course. Their Bhel Puri is gorgeous, with its crispy, crunchy textures, and its tart, hot and savoury tastes, and there is a variant called Alloo Papdi Chaat.' JM. Alongside dishes from Gujarat and south India, they serve pizzas, reflecting the craze, not only amongst Wembley Asians, but continuing to sweep Delhi and Bombay! Hours: 12-3pm/6-10.30pm.

CLAY OVEN NEW ENTRANT

197 Ealing Road, Wembley 020 8903 8800

We were invited to a fund-raising awards ceremony for disabled children with a party upstairs in one of their banqueting suites. Parking behind the building was organised by stewards. The main room is quite huge and very nicely decorated – wall to wall carpet and chandelier – you could believe that you are in some expensive hotel on Park Lane. Stage for awards and bangra disco dance floor. The food was served buffet style; I queued behind a man who told me he was starving and needed two plates – well, that will teach you for not eating lunch! A large selection of snacks and curries with breads and chutneys – all very good and in generous portions. Waiters need some training re: clearing up unless this was a hint for us all to go home. A great venue for weddings or other rave ups!

CURRY CRAZE TOP 100 ©

8-9 The Triangle, Wembley Hill Road, Wembley 020 8902 9720

Owned by Mr and Mrs SK Malhorta, she is also the head chef, specializing in East African/Punjabi food. See the Brilliant (Southall) for more information. Opened in 1980 and proving to be a reliable restaurant. 'Excellent, each year there is a conference for diving instructors in London; for the past two years it has been in Wembley and both times our party has gone to the Curry Craze – we have not been disappointed yet. After eating our fill of Papadoms, we started the proceedings with Jeera Chicken. Good value in terms of standard of cooking.' SN. When there is a concert or football match at the Stadium, a set dinner buffet is provided. 'Dishes were full of spices and excellent. Service was very friendly. Certainly worth its place in the TOP 100.' MF. Recommendations: Butter Chicken, Jeera Chicken – half £6.50, whole £13 and Chilli Chicken – whole £15, Methi Chicken – whole £14. 'Worthy of TOP 100.' RL, Service 10%. Price check: Papadam 50p, CTM £6.25, Pullao Rice £1.95. House wine £7.55. Hours: 6-11pm; Tues. closed.

KARAHI KING — U BYO

213 East Lane, Wembley — 020 8904 2760

'KK to those in the K (know) has been expanded and a redec has been undertaken. Such dangerous things haven't changed my favourtite haunt. Except it's getting even busier, and is still too good for you to put it into the Guide.' DD. Fabulous food, Kenyan Asian curries. 'Try the Mogo Bhajiia, a pakora of sweet potato complete with a super imli (tamarind) chutney, or the fabulous tandoori (including the breads), curries for meat-eaters and vegetarians. Methi Murgh divine.' DD. Hours: 12pm-12am. No credit cards. No corkage, so BYO.

KARAHI RAJA — U BYO

195 East Lane, Wembley — 020 8904 5553

Established in 1993 by Mushtaq Ahmed. Restaurant seats 150 diners between two rooms. Pakistani-styled curries cooked by B Hussain. House specials include: Haandi Chicken – chicken on the bone cooked with herbs, tomatoes and spicy thick sauce £4.95. Paya – lamb trotters Lahori style £4.95. Vegetarian dishes: Karahi Egg, scrambled egg, tomatoes, coriander and green chillies £4. BYO allowed, no corkage. Hours: 12pm-12am.

MARU'S BHAJIA HOUSE — V ANP

230 Ealing Road, Alperton, Wembley — 020 8903 6771

Opened by Maru over 20 years ago, itprovides superior family unique style of vegetarian curries and accompaniments from East Africa. Their Bhajias are the real thing, and they are even spelt correctly, rather than the formula Bhaji. Try their Potato Bhajias, besan-batter-coated, deep-fried and served with tamarind (imli) chutney as a real treat to die for. Hours: 12-9.30pm.

MARUTI BHEL PURI — V

238a Ealing Road, Wembley — 020 8903 6743

A vegetarian restaurant serving inexpensive melt-in-the-mouth delights, such as Dosas with Sambar and, of course, the namesake Bhel Puri. Try their Karahi Corn-on-the-Cob. 'All fantastic stuff for the lucky residents of Wembley. I wish I lived nearer.' DC. Hours: 12-10pm; closed Tues.

ONE EIGHTY TWO CLUB NEW ENTRANT

182 Preston Road, Wembley 020 8908 6040

'Visited this club/restaurant with some Asian friends who had dined here several times and said it was the closest restaurant food to home cooking that they had ever had. Decor was first class, like sitting in your own dining room, and the room was full of Asian families. We enjoyed exceptional spring rolls, fried mogo, kebabs, tandoori prawns and delicious pakoras, and first class main courses. Following my first earlier visit, I invited some work colleagues to try this new concept of a "private club/restaurant". Food, service and ambience was first class. For a Monday night it was very busy, with a mixture of Indian families and businessmen. Once again the Fish Pakoras were first class and excellent value for money. I urge you to visit.' DL. Stocks Cobra.

PALM BEACH

17 Ealing Road, Wembley 020 8900 8664

A licensed Sri Lankan and south Indian restaurant, but this doesn't mean there is no meat on the menu. Alongside the Dosas, Vadias and Hoppers, you will find Mutton Ceylon Curry, tender lamb, steeped in a richly spiced, meaty, juicy gravy. Decorations are relaxed, with batiks and wood carvings. Hours: 12pm-3pm/6-11.30pm; closed Tues. Branch: Palm Beach, 18 The Avenue, Ealing, London W13. Stocks Cobra.

POOJA COTTAGE NAME CHANGE ©

305 Harrow Road, Wembley Triangle 020 8902 4039

Established in '85 by T Moniz, as Wembley Cottage, this 45-seater is one of the few Nepalese restaurants. Baban in the kitchen cooks up unusual delights which include Mariz (pepper) Chicken £5.95, Nepalese Chicken Bhutuwa – highly spiced £6.25. Chicken Chowla – cooked in tandoor, mixed with ginger and garlic £5.95. 'Not terribly impressed with the food.' RM. 'Recommended to me by so many of my colleagues.' CT. Price check: Papadam 40p, CTM £5.95, Pullao Rice £1.90. Hours: 12-2.30pm/6-11.30pm. Stocks Cobra.

SAKONI V ANP

119-121 Ealing Road, Alperton Wembley 020 8903 9601

Alcohol is not allowed at Sakoni, which to some (including Asians we know) is a shame, but which seems not to detract from its popularity and its expansion (see branches below). The founder branch is now enormous, with its conservatory extension serving that Asian of Asain delights, Paan (see A to Z of the Curry Menu). It's family-run by Gujarati Kenyans who know about the food and tradition. But they offer variety to their regular Asian customers (of whom there are many) – dishes such as Chinese vegetarian noodles and Bombay Sandwich, white sliced bread with spicy spreading, a kind of relic of the Raj, the like of which you still, amazingly, find in Indian public schools and army messes. Such things make a change, but I for one prefer Sakoni's authentic Indian items (Dosai, Vadai, Uthappam et al, in a pleasant and informal atmosphere). 'Service good and quick. Generous portions. Chutneys are freshly prepared and not removed from the table every few minutes, which makes a change from most other Indian restaurants. Recommended.' RM. Hours: 11am-11.30pm. Branches: 116 Station Road, Edgware; 6 Dominion Parade, Station Road, Harrow.

WEMBLEY TANDOORI NEW ENTRANT ©

133a Wembley Road, Wembley 020 8902 2243

First opened in 1984, taken over by Mr D Chhetry in 1999 and given a Nepalese menu. Specials include: Momo, Simi Soup, Nepalese Chicken Bhutuwa, Nepalese Vegetable, Aloo Tama. Price check: CTM £6.50, Pullao Rice £2.25, Peshwari Nan £2.20, Lager £2.60 pint. Takeaway: 10% discount. Delivery: £16 minimum, 2-mile radius. Hours: 12-2.30pm/6-11.30pm; Sat. 6pm-12am.

WOODLANDS TOP 100 V ©

402a High Street, Wembley 020 8902 9869

A branch of Mrs Sood's well-liked, licensed, small chain of licensed southern Indian vegetarian restaurants. Back in March Pat was demo-ing on the QE2 as part of the world cruise and I went along as his able assistant! Flew to Singapore to meet the ship. Had two days in town so went to the Woodlands branch. After an appalling Japanese meal (Pat chose the restaurant) the previous night, I decided we would have lunch at Woodlands and I am thrilled to report that it was fantastic. On the main drag in a basement site. The restaurant was very quiet, but that's OK – we got good service! Immediately checked out the services – Singapore very humid and I had sticky fingers (which I detest). Can report that they were very clean. Ordered crispy Papadams with chutneys, Masala Dosa's brilliant with tasty Sambar and hot Rasam Soup, all washed down with bottle of red wine – great food and so was the price about £20. What is remarkable about this review, is that, apart from the climate, Woodlands is the same in San

Francisco, India and Singapore as it is in London and Wembley, whose House specials include Cashewnut Pakora, spicy batter coated and deep-fried, £2.75. Kancheepuram Idli, soft rice puffs with chilli, spices and cashewnuts, £3.25. Eight varieties of Dosa, £3.50 to £4.95. Service 12.5%. Price check: Papadam £1, Pullao Rice £3.50, House wine £9 bottle. Hours: 12-2.45pm/6-10.45pm. UK Branches: SW1 and W1. Stocks Cobra.

West Drayton

PALACE TANDOORI NEW ENTRANT

113 Station Road, West Drayton 01895 431206

'Each visit has left me in no doubt that this my no. 1 restaurant. Each dish I've tried has been of the utmost quality and of good size portion. The atmosphere is always friendly and deserves recognition.' AD. 'Complimentary mini-pakoras were delicious with excellent spicing and a very nice tomato chutney. Service was very fast at all the right points but not rushed and with good style.' RH. Stocks Cobra.

SIPSON TANDOORI NEW ENTRANT

5-7 Sipson Rd, Harmondsworth Rd, West Drayton 01895 435515

Established in 1997. Seats 76 in two rooms. 'In a "downmarket" neighbourhood, but its clientele and food is upmarket. Rezala Gosht was an excellent balance of spices within a cream sauce. Modest prices, good service and good food.' RH. Price check: Papadam 50p, CTM £5.80, Pullao Rice £1.80, Peshwari Nan £1.80, Lager £2.40 pint. Delivery: £12 minimum, 3-mile radius. Hours: 12-2.30pm/6-11.30pm. Stocks Cobra.

NORFOLK

Area: East
Population: 793,000
Adjacent Counties: Cambs, Suffolk

Great Yarmouth

BOMBAY NITE ©

25a King Street, Great Yarmouth 01493 331383

First opened in 1995. Seats 60. Raza is the owner and Louise Hughes is manager. We hear well of the Roast Chicken Massala and the Sylhet Supreme. Minimum charge £12.50. Service 10%. Takeaway: 10% discount. Delivery: £15 minimum. Hours: 6pm-12am. Stocks Cobra.

King's Lynn

INDIA GATE ©

41 St James Street, King's Lynn 01553 776489

Air conditioned. Taken over in August '97 by A Miah (manager) and S Ahmed (head chef). Bangladeshi curries and Balti. 'Called in at lunch time, to see if reservation was necessary for evening. I was told that after 9pm would be alright. At 9pm we arrived to be told very abruptly that they were full up. Explained earlier conversation, head waiter remembered me and we were duly seated within 5 minutes – no thanks to the waiter who "greeted" us and nearly lost our custom! Comfortably seats 50, nicely decorated pink and blue, drapes and glittery Indian pictures. Complimentary Popadoms (3) and Pickles. Onion Bhajia £1.85 – two flat, startling red appearance, accompanying Raita luminous orange. Sheek Kebab (2) large, tasted fine with crisp salad garnish. Chicken Dhansak £4.40 – plentiful, thickly sliced chicken fillets, tasty sauce. Murgh Nawabi £6.60 – lightly spiced, egg and tomato content equalled the chicken. Mixed Vegetable Bhajee £2.30 – formula stuff. Peshwari Nan – disappointing, sickly sweet. However, good formula curry. Full marks for the water test! Portions on the right size of average, prices average. Pleasant atmosphere until younger, noisier and worse for drink came in.' MW. Minimum charge: £5.95. Takeaway: 10% discount on orders over £12.50 (cash only). Price check: Papadam 40p, CTM £6.35, Pullao Rice £1.65, Peshwari Nan £1.75. Hours: 12-2pm/6pm-12am.. Stocks Cobra.

Norwich

ALI TANDOORI ©

12-14 Magdalen Street, Norwich **01603 666874**

Originally the Bombay, then Ali Tandoori then an'Owner Ali is a superb host and manager, his brother is an excellent cook. Crowds are flocking, have to book for a table virtually every day of the week. King Prawn Korai, superb. Chicken Dupiaza delicious and Chicken Makhani to be tried again. Overall exceptional. Well-drilled waiters.' GTC. 'Service efficient and very friendly – newspaper brought to my table while I was waiting. Chicken Biryani – good, meat tender and lots of it. Vegetable curry OK. Shahi Raita – excellent, smooth and creamy. Prices average.' JR. Stocks Cobra.

BENGAL SPICE NEW ENTRANT

38-40 St Benedicts Street, Norwich **01603 613444**

'Recently opened, spacious restaurant. Service good. Several new dishes to me. Can recommend "Hash e Hash" – on a par with a Jajfrezi or a Madras. Aiming to go back to try Jingo Khondan.' PS. 'Superb food, friendly service. I rate the Chicken Jalfrezi highly and the Mixed Vegetable Bhaji side dish is excellent, containing a good wide mix of veggies.' PM. Stocks Cobra.

NAZMA ©

15 Prince of Wales Road, Norwich **01603 616101/618701**

Glad to report that Mohabbat Ali's 1996 Nazma venture is thriving: PM says 'Recommended by locals. A delightful meal. Except we had three bad bottles of red wine in two nights. The restaurant staff handled the matter perfectly, but we were wary about returning a third time, as we got no pleasure from sending back wine.' [I presume you mean it was corked, Peter, and it is becoming a monster problem. Tesco is typical of the supermarkets in saying that some 15% of their wine is corked. Their master of wine also says that many people are not aware of what corked wine is, and simply drink it. It is always a tiresome business to have to reject wine, but it is also an excellent test of a restaurant's serving staff, especially when they themselves do not drink alcohol. -Ed]. Price check: Papadam 35p, CTM

£3.05, Pullao Rice £1.40. Minimum charge £5. Open daily for lunch and dinner. Branch: Nazma, 15 Magdalen Street, Norwich. Stocks Cobra.

NORWICH TANDOORI ©

98 Magdalen Street, Norwich 01603 621436

Kuti Meah is the managing owner. His 50-seater restaurant has: 'A straightforward comfortable interior. Lamb Pasanda best tried so far in the city. Chicken Tikka Pasanda, mildly creamy, cooked with butter, almonds and sultanas, exceeded expectations.' TW. Hours: 12-3pm/6pm-12am. Stocks Cobra.

Thetford

SAFFRON INDIAN CUISINE NEW ENTRANT ©

17 St Giles Lane, Thetford 01842 762000

Established in 1999. Seats 30. Specials include: Bengal Chicken Jelfrezi £7.50 – with onions, peppers and crushed Bengali chillies, Madras hot. Achari Chicken £5.75 – in thick sauce with pickle. Delivery: £10 minimum, 5-mile radius. Takeaway: 10% discount. Price check: Papadam 40p, CTM £5.50, Pullao Rice £1.60, Peshwari Nan £1.95, Lager £2.95 pint. Hours: 6pm-12am.

Wroxham

STAR OF INDIA

The Bridge, Norwich Road, Wroxham 01603 784243

'Tucked away between a supermarket and the obligatory gift shop very close to the river – beware, the small entrance is easily missable. Hearing that my wife was Belgian, the owner went to great lengths to discover her tastes and went on to explain the dishes that would appeal to her. We paid two visits and tried and can recommend the Prawn Special, King Prawn Ceylon, Chicken Tikka Biriany and the Vegetable side dishes. Keema and mushroom rices were extremely good and the Kulcha Naan was truly delicious. £20 for two.' B&DT. 'Greeting most friendly and cheerful. Unusual to find a pork dish on the menu, Special Pork £7.50 – pork steamed in tandoori sauce with cream and other trimmings. Can also recommend the Prawn Garlic Special, King Prawn Ceylon and Chicken Tikka Biriani. Truly delicious Kulcha Nan.' BT. Price check: Papadam 40p, CTM £5.25, Pullao Rice £1.30, Chutney 40p per person. Hours: 12-2.30pm/6pm-12am. Stocks Cobra.

NORTHAMPTONSHIRE

Area: Central
Population: 620,000
Adjacent Counties: Beds, Cambs, Leics, Oxon

Brackley

JAYPUR II NEW ENTRANT

8 Banbury Road, Brackley 01280 706922

'Good dishes, especially for an out-of-town place.' LMcC.

PRINCE CALCUTTA NEW ENTRANT ©

36 Market Place, Brackley 01280 703265

First opened in 1994, taken over by Azizul Islam in 1998. Seats 50. Chicken Moricha £5.95 – barbecued chicken with green chillies, fairly hot. Lamb Bakera with Pullao Rice £7.50 – chicken tikka, minced meat in rich medium sauce. Price check: Papadam 40p, CTM £5.95, Pullao Rice £1.45, Peshwari Nan £1.50, Lager £1.95 pint. Hours: 5.30-11.30pm; Fri., Sat. & Sun. 12-2.30pm/6-11.30pm. Stocks Cobra.

Kettering

MONSOON BAR & INDIAN NEW ENTRANT ©

Ebenezer Place, Kettering 01536 417421

Established in 1998 by P Sadrani. A colourfully painted Tudor style restaurant, seating 90. Specials: Jeera Tikka Masala £5.95 – marinated chicken or lamb cooked with cummin, onion, capsicum and herbs. Punjabi Masala £5.85 – Chicken or lamb flavoured with green chillies, yoghurt, capsicum and fresh coriander. Price check: Papadam 45p, CTM £6.75, Pullao Rice £1.70, Peshwari Nan £1.70, Lager £2.20 pint. Takeaway: 20% discount. Delivery: 4-mile radius. Hours: 5.30pm-12am. Stocks Cobra.

THE RAJ ©

50 Rockingham Road, Kettering 01536 513606

Established in 1991. Seats 110 in two rooms. Goyas Miah has newly refurbished in modern style – wooden floor, marbled walls, chrome downlighters. 'This Bangladeshi restaurant has had such a transformation – I thought I was in Brick Lane. Not only the appearance, the food is much better, more tasty, however with fewer colourants, which has got to be better for the consumer! Very friendly staff and helpful, have good knowledge of their indigenous food! What a wonderful time.' FAV. 'Just to let you know about a wonderful restaurant. Took my drummer and my wife; he was absolutely "gobsmacked" with food and service.' AB. Specials include: Muktaj, Sharabi, Batera, Chittol. Price check: Papadam 50p, CTM £6.45, Pullao Rice £1.75, Peshwari Nan £1.75, Lager £2.20 pint. Takeaway: 15% discount. Delivery: £7.50 minimum, 3-mile radius. Hours: 12-2pm/5.30pm-12am; Sun. 12pm-12am. Stocks Cobra.

Kingsthorpe

BOMBAY PALACE ©

9-11 Welford Road, Kingsthorpe 01604 713899

Abdul Ahad's restaurant first opened in 1988 and seats 40 diners. Of chef Abdul Husian's curries, CTM is the most ordered. 'Arrived without booking, offered a choice of smoking or non smoking area (excellent). Jayne, my girlfriend says this is the best Chicken Malaya in Northants! Jayne given rose as we left! (Nice touch). Well worth trying – don't be put off by the location.' DL. '20% off all meals including takeaway, Sunday to Thursday. Service was attentive and friendly. Popadoms fresh and crispy. The whole meal was excellent, with fresh vegetables and not a hint of unnatural spices. Cracking restaurant!' DL. Price check: Papadam 40p, CTM £6.75, Pullao Rice £1.75, Peshwari Nan £1.75, Lager £2.60 pint. Takeaway: £3 discount on minimum £10 order. Delivery: £10 minimum, anywhere in Northampton and surrounding villages of Kingsthorpe. Hours: 5.30pm-12am. Stocks Cobra.

Northampton

FAR COTTON TANDOORI ©

111 St Leonards Road, Far Cotton, Northampton 01604 706282

'Far out' wrote a local scribe (IM) of the three Alis: chef Haruni, Ansar and

Soub's above-average takeaway in the southern outskirts of town. Specials include: Mint Lamb, tikka meat, mint and almond. Chicken Dhakna, medium spiced, tomatoes, capsicums, fried garlic and mushrooms. Hours: 12-2pm/5-10.30pm (Sat. to 11pm, Sun. to 10pm). Stocks Cobra.

GULSHAAN NEW ENTRANT

18b Sheep Street, Northampton 01604 250995

'Highly individual restaurant in upstairs location close to city centre. Menu with large selections of duck, venison and fish dishes. Excellent duck starter served sizzling then transferred to plate with side salad. Superb venison main course with well balanced sauce with almonds and cream and a delicate blend of spices. Equally good Bombay Allo, compliments of the house. A rising star and highly recommended.' RW. Stocks Cobra.

IMRAN BALTI HUT BYO

285 Wellingborough Road, Northampton 01604 622730

Fully licensed (BYO welcomed) and air-conditioned. 'Having booked for 8pm, I knew the place was popular; we duly turned up to find a queue to people who had also booked in advance waiting for tables! Entrance area was full and chaotic. After 30 minutes we got a table, too small for our party. Food and service was exceptional, quality and large portions. Family Nan £2.50 were excellent. BUT the experience was ruined by front of house lack of organisation. Can't fault otherwise.' DJL. 'If you can get inside the door of this extremely popular restaurant and push through the crowds of people also trying to get a seat you are guaranteed an excellent meal. Always best to book [see above -Ed]. At the weekend people queue out of the door! Simply decorated, pleasant waiters. A large vegetarian choice. After papadoms and chutneys, don't order starters unless you have a particularly huge appetite, though a must is the family Naan – 2 feet by 18 inches – a highlight. Can BYO for a small corkage charge.' SS. Price check: Papadam 25p, CTM £4.20, Pullao Rice £1.05. Hours: 5.30pm (Fri. & Sat. 5pm)-1am. Stocks Cobra.

MAHARAJAH NEW ENTRANT

248 Wellingborough Road, Northampton 01604 637049

'This restaurant is one of many on this road, who are involved in a 'half price' curry war! Seven days a week all food is half-price before 10.30pm! The offer attracts all types of people with different requirements, but despite this the quality of service and food is not diminished. I particularly enjoyed the Tandoori Chicken and Sheeh Kebab served with Thali.' DL.

RAJPUT BALTI ©

224a Wellingborough Road, Northampton 01604 637336

Taken over in 1996 by Shahab Uddin. Seats 50, serves Bangladeshi formula curries, cooked by chef Shofor Ali. Set dinner £8.95. Free bottle of wine with orders over £20. Delivery: £8 minimum. Hours: 12-2.30pm/6pm-12am. Stocks Cobra.

STAR OF INDIA ©

5 Abington Avenue, Northampton 01604 630664

Fully licensed and air-conditioned 50 seater, established in 1964, and taken over by Abdul Noor in 1983. Managed by Bodrul Islam. Parking opposite on race course . 'Quality of food, service etc just gets better and better. Popadoms excellent, served with fresh chutneys and pickles. Tandoori Shahjahni £2.95 and Murgh Pakora £2.30, both super, served with a tasty sauce in a silver jug. Batak Mossaladar £7.50 – lean meat, not fatty, with a subtle sauce, gorgeous. Star Mixed Thali £8.95 – incredible, too much even for me to eat!! washed down with chilled Cobra, served with Pullao Rice and Roti Khasta. Excellent – deserves an award. Booking advisable.' DJL. 'Having dined here many times, we decided to try their 24-hr notice Murgh Mossala, a complete meal for 4 including a bottle of Indian red wine (£25 per person, min 4). After crisp Popadoms, with the usual accompaniments, were starters, including Onion Bhajis, Samosas and Tandoori Shah Jahni. Main course, two whole chickens marinated and stuffed with spices and two whole boiled eggs! and Special Fried Rice – did not disappoint!' DL. Tandoori dishes and Vegetarian dishes can be ordered in half-portions – what a great idea. Price check: Papadam 40p, CTM £5.95, Pullao Rice £1.50, Peshwari Nan £1.50, Lager £2.50 pint. Takeaway: 25% discount. Delivery: £9.50 minimum, within Northampton. Hours: 12-2.15pm/5.30pm-12am (1am on Fri. & Sat.); Sun. 12pm-12am. Stocks Cobra.

Rushden

SPICE OF LIFE TAKEAWAY NEW ENTRANT

169 Wellingborough Road, Rushden 01933 411122

Established in 1997. Specials: Jhinga Makhanwalla £7.90 – king prawns marinated in tandoori spices, grilled and finished in a creamy tomato, yoghurt and butter gravy. Price check: Papadam 35p, CTM £4.95, Pullao Rice £1.35, Peshwari Nan £1.40. Hours: 5.30-11.30pm daily.

©	Curry Club Discount	U	Unlicensed
V	Vegetarian	ANP	Alcohol not permitted
e-a-m-a-y-l	Eat as much as you like	BYO	Bring your own alcohol

Wellingborough

BALTI KING NEW ENTRANT

31-33 Midlands Road, Wellingborough 01933 222522

'Best Balti house outside of Birmingham, apart from the toilets! Menu interesting and varied. We will go back again very soon.' DL. Stocks Cobra.

EASTERN SPICE NEW ENTRANT

56-60 High St, Irthlingborough, Wellingborough 01933 650044

Established in 1993. Seats 100 in four rooms. Specials: Murgh Lasni £5.95 – chicken with garlic paste, onions, capsicums, tomatoes and potato, served with salad. Murgh Dil Bahar £5.95 – chicken with rich coconut, cashew, green chilli sauce. Price check: Papadam 40p, CTM £5.65, Pullao Rice £1.50, Peshwari Nan £1.60, Lager £2.15 pint. Takeaway: 10% discount. Delivery: £10.95 minimum, 6-mile radius. Hours: 12-2.30pm/6-11.30pm. Stocks Cobra.

NORTHUMBERLAND

Area: North East
Population: 310,000
Adjacent Counties: Borders, Cumbria, Durham, Tyne & Wear

Bedlington

FRONTIER KARAHI HOUSE NEW ENTRANT ©

46-48 Front Street, West Bedlington 01670 820222

Established 1997. Seats 66. New, modern decor. Specials include: Balti as well as Karahi. 'Discovered by accident on an evening trip for petrol. A considerable amount of thought and effort has gone into the decor and ambience. Presentation of food and quality were excellent. Best Tandoori King Prawns that I have ever come across. Proprietor Nazir is a wine buff – excellent wine list.' AMcC. Price check: Papadam 50p, CTM £6.95, Pullao

Rice £1.95, Peshwari Nan £1.75, Lager £2 pint. Takeaway: 20% discount. Delivery: £10 minimum. Hours: 5.30pm-12am; closed Mon. Open for lunches in the month leading to Christmas. Stocks Cobra.

Berwick-upon-Tweed

MAGNA NEW TO OUR TOP 100 ©

39 Bridge Street, Berwick-upon-Tweed 01289 302736

Free car park 100 yards from restaurant. Jahangir Khan's 80-seater family business is a pretty restaurant with smartly dressed black-tie waiters. It has been in our *Guide* since we started it in 1984. 'And no wonder.' says CC member Michael Fabricant, MP. The food, which is the standard formula stuff beloved by all curryholics, is as well described on the menu as it is cooked. It's a port in a storm right there on the A1-Scottish border, with the ghosts of Lindisfarne not far behind. 'Most pleasing and memorable way to spend an evening with friends.' GFB. Says WA 'Being a B&B House, we are pleased to send out guests to recommended restaurants. The feedback we receive on the Magna is excellent to say the least, not only for the high standard of Indian cuisine, but also the warm, friendly welcome and very cosy surroundings. Clean, comfortable restaurant, friendly and helpful staff, superb food, generous portions. It's always been well looked after by the family. We feel Mr Khan is well justified in his quest for being in the TOP 100.' WA. [And so do we – Ed] Specials include: Murghi Mossalla, Ash de Bash and Chandee Dishes, very mild with fresh cream and mango from £7.50. Shim Dishes, cooked with green beans from £7.50. Price check: Papadam 40p, CTM £6.95, Pullao Rice £1.90, Peshwari Nan £1.95, Lager £2.20 pint. Takeaway: 20% discount. Hours: 12-2pm/5.30pm-12am. Stocks Cobra.

Corbridge

CORBRIDGE TANDOORI ©

8 Market Square, Corbridge 01434 633676

SM Shahjahan's small restaurant hidden above a shop was est. in '89. Specials: Murghi Masala, succulent cubes of chicken tikka, cooked with mincemeat £6.95. Takeaway: 15% discount. Lamb Karaya, marinated diced tender lamb, barbecued over charcoal then cooked in a slow process in a pot called a karaya with garlic £6.70. DR MH continues to dine here regularly (though he lives in Wales) 'It is as good or better than the Valley.' [see entry below] 'and I go to both. If you want excellent decor and different dishes, go to the Valley. If you want excellent "standard" dishes, come here. It has only two drawbacks: it is small and can get stuffy and hot when busy, and it does get busy, especially at weekends. I cannot recommend it highly enough.' Price check: Papadam 50p, CTM £6.95, Pullao Rice £1.95. Hours: 12-2.30pm/6-11.30pm. Stocks Cobra.

THE VALLEY TOP 100 ©

The Old Station House, Corbridge 01434 633434

Corbridge station building, in the beautiful Tyne valley, was built in 1835 for Stephenson's railway. It is no longer used as a station although it is on the important Newcastle-to-Carlisle railway line. Trains stop at Corbridge station throughout each day, but passengers do not use the old building any more. That is, until Daraz (Syed Nadir Aziz) turned it into a stylish, up-market Indian restaurant. A feature of which is a unique service, for parties of 10 to 80 at £20 a head, including return travel. Uniformed restaurant staff welcome you at Newcastle Central Station and escort you by train to The Valley. En route, choose four courses from the à la carte menu. The order is rung through on a mobile. Your starter is awaiting your arrival. 'It beats ordering a taxi.' GM. Of course, individuals can make their own way here and back by scheduled train – but beware a fairly early last train. Or, there is parking for 12 cars. Why not book your takeaway by phone en-route, collect, pay and eat it, without leaving the train? As for the restaurant, there is a reception room and 80 seats in four connecting rooms (one of which opens onto the eastbound platform). Decor is lush and Indian, though a total interior refurbishment is 'expected'. And the food? Chef Abdul Khalick's menu contains all the CC (currinarily correct) favourites plus some good specials. Chingri Moslai, prawns with garlic and mustard. Macher Bora, tuna fish kebab. Luari Mangsho, medium hot lamb dish, cooked with tomatoes, green pepper and fresh coriander £7.25. Rajha Chingri Sagwala, king prawns cooked with fresh spinach, coriander and green chilli £9.95. Dhai Baigon, large grilled aubergine stuffed with spicy mixed vegetables, topped with yoghurt £6.50. 'I decided to visit having read the Guide write-up and was not disappointed. Food superb, one page devoted to house specialities, none of which I had ever come across before. An absolute must.' TOC. 'Continues to maintain a very high standard, and deserves TOP 100 rating.' DAD. Established in 1991. Seats 80, car parking for 20 directly outside. Refurbished in July 1999. Price check: Papadam 50p, CTM £7.95, Pullao Rice £2.95, Peshwari Nan £2.25, Lager £2.20 pint. Takeaway: 20% discount. Hours: 6-10pm; closed Sun. Branch: Valley Junction 397, The Old Station, Archbold Terrace, Jesmond, Newcastle. Remains high in our TOP 100. Stocks Cobra.

Cramlington

LAL QILA ©

Dudley Lane, Cramlington 01670 734268

Established '86 by Sabu Miah. Seats 60, serves formula curries. Red brick building, with private parking for 20 cars. Framed Indian art hangs, padded yellow and blue chairs, yellow tablecloth, red patterned carpet, flowery wallpaper and curtains, makes for quite an eyefull. Baingan Pakora, deliciously spiced, deep-fried aubergine served with minted sauce. Samba Gosht, lamb fairly hot, spiced cooked with lentils and fresh coriander. Specials include: Ajwan Chicken – fillet of chicken with braised ajwan, onion, peppers, served on sizzler. Restaurant owns parking area for 40. Business lunch Mon.-Fri. £2.50 and £6. Takeaway: 20% discount. Hours: 12-2pm/6-11.30pm. Stocks Cobra.

Hexham

ABBEY TANDOORI ©

28 Priestpopple, Hexham 01434 603509

Miah Sahid's 44-seat Abbey restaurant is plainly decorated but neat and tidy. A good selection of tandoori dishes on the menu with, as they call them, 'supporting dishes' and four different Nans. 'We found ourselves snowbound in Hexham en route to Essex from Scotland. Naturally we had our trusted *Good Curry Guide* in the car, and found the Abbey Tandoori. Meal was superb. King Prawn Vindaloo and Chicken Pathia. Naan bread one of the best I've tasted, crispy on the outside but beautifully light and fluffy on the inside. Too few king prawns in my Vindaloo. I'd have happily paid more for a few extra prawns.' S&KT. Hours: 12-2pm/6-11.30pm; Sun. 6-11pm only. Stocks Cobra.

DIWAN-E-AM NEW ENTRANT ©

4-5 Country Mills, Priestpopple, Hexham 01434 606575

Established in 1983. Seats 86. 'Pleasant decor and environment, friendly and helpful staff. Menu extensive, but no curry house inventions such as vindaloo here. Starters include the excellent Diwan Khata Mita Soup (garlic and lentils) and Mathu Vortha (grapefruit with chilli and coriander). Main course selection includes a wide range of duck and fish dishes. More expensive than the usual curry house, but good value given the high standard of the meals.' CF. Produce house-style cuisine on demand for regular customers. Price check: Papadam 60p, CTM £7.25, Pullao Rice £2.30, Peshwari Nan £1.95, Lager £2.50 pint. Takeaway: 20% discount. Hours: 5.30-11pm; Sun. 6.30-10.30pm. Stocks Cobra.

Morpeth

MANZIL NEW ENTRANT

2b Oldgate, Morpeth 01670 515405

'Especially impressed. Service friendly with no great fussiness. Wide menu, excellent value. Started with Chicken Chat – done their own way and very good. Chicken Korai, most distinctive and very fresh chilli taste, hot without being peppery.' PN. Hours: 12-2.30pm (Sun. closed)/6pm-12am. Stocks Cobra.

TANDOORI MAHAL ©

17 Bridge Street, Morpeth 01670 512420

60-seater, owned by chef Afrus Miah whose menu gives very good descriptions of every dish. Specials include Murgh Masala, spring chicken off the bone, soaked in spiced cream, roasted and served with Basmati Rice £8.50. Sabzi Ka Khazana contains Bhindi Bhaji, Milijuli Sabz, Dal Masala, Palak Bhaji, Chwal and two chapatis. 'An absolutely first-class establishment. Prices fair, service good, decor of a very high standard, parking no problem.' MB. Manager Surot Miah has promised to give a discount to Curry Club members at lunchtimes. Takeaway: 10% discount. Hours: 12-2.30pm/6pm-12am. Stocks Cobra.

Prudhoe

THE PALACE TANDOORI NEW ENTRANT

Front Street, Prudhoe 01661 833355

'Open for just over a year, this restaurant has quickly gained a reputation for the quality of its food, and would propose that you include it in your next guide. I was previously a big fan of the Valley, Corbridge, to which you awarded the "Best Curry Restaurant in the North", but I have switched allegiance to The Palace because of their consistent quality.' AM. Stocks Cobra.

NOTTINGHAMSHIRE

Area: East Midlands
Population: 1,043,000
Adjacent Counties: Derbs, Leics, Lincs, Yorks

Newark

NEWARK TANDOORI NEW ENTRANT

6 Balderton Gate, Newark 01636 610923

We have received many reports from Phil, telling of this, his local takeaway. It shows that a popular local curry house, like the local pub, has an important place in the community, and indeed in this *Guide*. 'My regular takeaway. Phone service was good, friendly conversation, arrived in 35 minutes. Containers all generously filled to the top. Chicken Korma £3.45 – thick, sweet, mild sauce, coconut and cream came through deliciously, topped off with almonds; Meat Joypuri £3.50 – a fantastic deep red-brown colour, sour, hot and very, very fruity topped with a sprinkling of coriander, very fragrant and appetising, meat just flaked apart in the mouth – a delight – my favourite, could eat this curry every day of the week! Pullao Rice £1.30 – fluffy and fragrant, Nan £1.10 – large and tasty, perhaps a little doughy. Bombay Aloo £1.90 – not very spicy, thick rich sauce. The meal came with free onion salad and Popadom. Best for miles.' PA. 'Paratha and mixed vegetable bhaji were delicious.' ANON

Nottingham

(includes Basford, Beeston, Mapperley, Radford, Sherwood and West Bridgford)

ANILA'S NEW ENTRANT

23 Goldsmith Street, Nottingham Centre 0115 948 3036

'Greeted with welcoming smile. Chicken Tikka Kastoon with masalla sauce was very tasty, Chicken Tikka Karali was delicious, Keema Pullao Rice was the best I've had.' JW. Stocks Cobra.

©	Curry Club Discount	U	Unlicensed
V	Vegetarian	ANP	Alcohol not permitted
e-a-m-a-y-l	Eat as much as you like	BYO	Bring your own alcohol

CURRY CLUB

BEESTON TANDOORI ©

150-152 High Road, Beeston, Nottingham SW 0115 922 3330

S Choudhury's cosy 40-seater. Chef recommends Uri and Muki Specials, described as fairly dry but well-spiced. Hours: 12-2.30pm/6pm-12am. Stocks Cobra.

BOMBAY BICYCLE SHOP TAKEAWAY ©

511 Alfreton Road, Basford, Nottingham NW 0115 978 6309

Takeaway only, interior in shades of grey, exterior red and yellow. Specials include: Chicken de Goa, fresh cream, flaked coconut, mango sauce £4.95. Sag Alloo Paneer £2.50. Garlic Chappati £1.20. 6 parking spaces behind takeaway. Credit cards not accepted. Delivery: £8 min. Hours: 5.30pm-12am.

CHAND TOP 100 ©

31 Mansfield Road, Nottingham Centre 0115 947 4103

38-seater, jointly owned by Mohammed Shanaz, front of house, and chef Mohammed Riaz. The menu contains a very good selection of vegetarian dishes. Dhava Thaum £2.20 – garlic mushrooms served on a thin bread, and Mixed Vegetable Karahi £5.15. There are plenty of meat, fish and fowl dishes, too. 'Food excellent, owner and staff always extremely friendly, very good choice of menu, comfortable and clean, very good sized portions. I highly recommend it to all my friends.' SW. And says TA: 'Finest of fine restaurants. Onion bhajiis are simply the best I have tasted anywhere in the world, truly mouth watering and the perfect introduction to the delights to follow. Chandni Murgi Tikka was sublime, a perfect balance of subtle flavours in a rich sauce. I can wholeheartedly recommend the Chand to anyone who hankers after delicious eating experiences'. TA. And BH: 'We've been eating here for many years, and whether it be meat or vegetarian dishes, the food is still the best we have eaten, made better with relaxed and pleasant atmosphere and very friendly and helpful staff. Large portions, and good value for money.' BH. 'A marvellous Punjabi restaurant. Despite being in the TOP 100, the food was relatively inexpensive. Next time we must try the Punjabi dishes, for which I gather Mr Shawaz has a reputation for perfection. The only thing that marred the day was that Brighton lost to Mansfield by two goals!'. BP-D. Takeaway 15% discount. Pickle Tray £1.20 – [expensive!] Paradise Balti, chicken, lamb, prawn and vegetables, all in one medium-spiced sauce with a mesh of omelette £7.50. Price check: Papadam 50p, CTM £7, Pullao Rice £1.50. Hours: 12-2pm (Sun. closed)/5.30pm-12.30am (1am on Sat.). Stocks Cobra.

THE INDIAN COTTAGE ©

5-7 Bentinck Road (off Alfreton Road),
Radford, Nottingham W 0115 942 4922

Pretty black beams, white frontage and inviting curtained windows at Naj Aziz's 40-seater in 2 areas (smoking and non-smoking). Very stylish restaurant, un-Indian, unfussy, light and bright, Wedgwood blue ceiling and magnolia walls. Walls are decorated with hanging carpets and back-lit fretwork, tiled floor, large palms in white pots. We hear that the food is family-style. 'Aubergine Paneer and Garlic and Mushroom Baji for starters, served with crisp salad. Murgh Makhani, Chicken Tikka cooked with garlic, coriander and brandy, and I can honestly say it was among the best curries I have ever eaten. Rice portions were large. Staff extremely friendly and food is outstanding.' CY. 'I feel compelled to write to you, having recently indulged in a remarkable gastronomic experience! A little 'oasis' in the middle of Radford, our first impression of The Indian Experience was a deep feeling of India. A veritable wealth of dishes, many quite original. From the papadoms right through to the coffee, the flavours were exquisite, presentation faultless and service wonderful. Hard to single out the best part of meal, and probably unfair to do so, but Peshwari Naan, which arrived dripping in honey, was an absolute delight. I urge you to pay a visit!' D. 10% service charge for parties of 6 or more [why???]. Takeaway 10% off. Sunday lunch £16. Hours: 6-10.30pm Tues.-Sat. Closed a week at Christmas and two weeks in the summer. Stocks Cobra.

JEWEL IN THE CROWN

25 Bridgford Road, West Bridgford,
Nottingham S 0115 981 1645

Owned by M Ibrahim, since 1995. Tells us that his air-conditioned restaurant is, 'nicely decorated, top class outside sign'; that his 'customers enjoy the meals' and that he is 'a very busy restaurant.' Specials: Jinga Sharab, king prawns are taken out of their shells, dipped in a tandoori sauce made from fresh cream, yoghurt, mint and tandoori spices, roasted in the Tandoor,. blended in a sauce prepared with white wine, delicious! Delivery: £10 minimum, 3-mile radius. Pay by credit card over the phone. Hours: 12-2pm/5.30pm-12.30am. Branch: Pavilion, 1a Radcliffe Road, West Bridgford.

KASHMIR BYO ©

60 Maid Marian Way, Nottingham Centre 0115 947 6542

At AD Satti's 100-seater, BYO allowed, no corkage. [Hooray!] 'Service was very good and friendly. Food excellent. Relaxed atmosphere. Have visited for many years, always had enjoyable time.' ANON. 'A star place! consistently efficient and friendly service, brilliant and inexpensive. No pressure to eat and leave – a huge bonus.' CN. 'Good variety, some unusual dishes, always good.' JH, 'Attentive, keen and efficient service. Cosy atmosphere. Decor needs some improvement. Good value for money.' AW. 'Freshly cooked food, always more than enough, prices very competitive.' ANON. Price check: Papadam free, CTM £6.50, Pullao Rice £1.40, Peshwari Nan £1.30. House wine £6.50. Hours: 6pm-1am (Sat. from 2pm, Sun. from 1pm). Stocks Cobra.

LAGUNA ©

43 Mount Street, Nottingham Centre 0115 941 1632

Taken over in '85 by manager Tony Ranjit Verma. Seats 62, serves Northern Indian curries, cooked by Bharat Desai. 'Very efficient, food well above average. Laguna Special, a sort of Tandoori Masala sauce is good, its vegetarian counterpart is potatoes in the same sauce, but is curiously called Bombay Aloo. Many vegetarian dishes and beautifully cooked.' PT. Service 10%. Takeaway: 10% discount. Hours: 12.30-2pm/6.30-11pm. Stocks Cobra.

MEHRAN ©

948 Woodborough Road, Mapperley, Nottingham N 0115 955 1005

Taken over in '98 by Mr and Mrs Mohamad Akram Khan. Balti – chicken balti most popular – restaurant seats 80. 'Excellent restaurant, good service. Very original recipes such as Chicken Sommerhand (made with strawberries, cherries, cream and pistachio nuts). Unfortunately it appears to be going through a bad patch, not helped by being situated next door to Nottingham's most established Chinese restaurants.' DE. Despite the above sounding like a fruit salad, we do know this restaurant, and have always heard well of it. So forget Chinese, and report please. Price check: Papadam 65p, CTM £8.50, Pullao Rice £2.30. House wine £7.50. Delivery: 2-mile radius. Hours: 6pm-12am (2am on Fri. & Sat.). Stocks Cobra.

MILAAP TANDOORI ©

67 Chilwell Road, Beeston, Nottingham 0115 925 4597

Owner chef Pervaz Iqbal seats a snug 28 diners and cooks Pakistani curries. All prices include Papadom, rice and chutney. 'A welcoming smile and friendly banter from manager Yousef (or "Chippy" as he is better known) makes the journey seem worthwhile. The Makhani Chicken Tikka is the mouth-watering combination of boulders of fresh moist chicken served in an indescribable tandoori sauce – truly magnificent!!!!!' PB. 'The clientele are welcomed as part of a family, and many people who have met over a meal have become good friends. Whatever I choose, I am never disappointed. The quality of the ingredients, and the care taken in the kitchen never vary.' CF. 'Whilst the food is excellent, the service is second to none.' PB. ' Pervez is an excellent cook, who manages to combine just the right amount of spiciness with the subtle flavours of Indian cuisine.' JB. 'We visit here frequently and can honestly say that we have never had a disappointing meal in over 10 years. The staff are always friendly and welcoming, take a pride in the food that they serve, are willing and able to give advice about food on the menu, and remember customer preferences. Food is always good and reasonably priced.' S&BA. Minimum charge £8.50. Hours: 5.30pm-12am (12.30am on Sat). Stocks Cobra.

MOGAL E AZAM ©

7-9 Goldsmith Street, Nottingham Centre 0115 952 8777

The Mogal was opened in 1977 by Mr SN Miah, and seats a huge 300 diners on ground and 1st floors, and serves very good, very popular formula curries, CTM the most popular dish ordered. 'Like the Taj Mahal inside, with arches and minarates built into walls and hallway, marble-effect look, creamy white in colour, with large brass bric-a-brac as decor.' SNM. Recommended by the student son of friends of ours. Portions enormous, well presented, good decor but pricey. Wonder how students afford it? Varied menu, slightly larger than most. Service excellent – they try very hard.' SJ. Specials include: Bengal ka Boul, Bangladesh fish £11.95. Hours: 12-2.30pm/ 5.30pm-1am. Stocks Cobra.

PARAMOUNT HOTEL AND BALTI HOUSE
NEW ENTRANT

328 Mansfield Road, Sherwood, Nottingham N 0115 962 1621

'This restaurant is in the dining room of a hotel. Standard menu. Popadoms with Mango Chutney and Onions were average. Mixed Kebab included Onion Bhajia, Shami and Reshmi Kebabs were very good and spicier than I've had before. Chicken Madras – sauce acceptable but Korma – insipid. Nans and Chapattis particularly good, rice portion small.' DB. Could be a good overnight stop over. More reports please. Stocks Cobra.

ROYAL CLAY OVEN TAKEAWAY NEW ENTRANT

21 Goose Gate, Nottingham Centre 0115 950 5070

Serves a range of authentic kebabs all with fresh Nan. Indian Pizzas – Tandoori Chicken and Chicken Tikka with green chillies and garam masala from £4.50. Chicken Tikka Kebab £3, Sheesh Kebab £3.

SAAGAR TOP 100 ©

473 Mansfield Road, Sherwood, Nottingham N 0115 962 2014

Mohammed Khizer opened his Victorian-styled 98-seater on two floors in 1984. Front of house is managed by Imtiaz Ahmed, leaving Mr Khizer to do his thing in the kitchen, assisted by Amjaid Parvaiz. This time we had a 'hated it' report from one scribe (MR) but all other reports are happy. 'Everything it is cracked up to be, expensive but worth it. Vegetarian Thali for two is not just a tray but a seemingly endless train of small bowls provided as fast as you can eat.' PT. 'The pops and picks were gorgeous. My Mixed Kebabs £4.90 were tasty. Chicken Kaallan £9.10 was very sweet, yet very sour too, with tender chicken cooked in a south Indian style, with mango, coconut and yoghurt. My girlfriend was brave enough to tackle Chilli Chicken Tikka Masala £9.50 incl. rice, and our Garlic and Tomato Naan £1.95 was excellent, covered in fresh tomato chunks. Everyone felt the food had been made freshly, and it was cooked to perfection. It makes a nice change to come to a decent restaurant which has the edge over others because of little things that just make a difference, like fresh flowers at every table, proper lemon-squeezers, spotless toilets, etc.' NH. Discounts for CC members at lunchtimes. £5.50 half carafe. Price check: Papadam 40p, CTM £9.10, Pullao Rice £2.30, Peshwari Nan £1.95, Lager £2.40 pint. Hours: 12-2.15pm/5.30pm-12.30am (closed Sun. lunch). Stocks Cobra.

Southwell

SANAM BALTI HOUSE ©

15-17 King Street, Southwell 01636 813618

Early Victorian listed building, established as the Taj Mahal in 1990, and taken over by Khalid Mahmood in 1994. The 50-seater boasts a spendid spiral staircase with original stain. All rooms are open plan with ornate Moghul style arches to doorways. Beautiful jade colour, lighting subdued crystal reflecting the traditional Indian art. All tables are covered in fine contrasting linen, sparkling silverware and fresh flowers. Centre of attention has to be a 26-cubic-feet fish tank, which is set within an existing chimney and can be viewed from both rooms. Chef-owner Khalid Mahmood or 'Chef Saab' as he is known to staff and customers, originates from Pakistan's Kashmir. 'Tastefully decorated. All food was hot, excellent Pullao Rice and Peshwari Nan.' LW. All main curry dishes include rice, pops and picks. Specials include: Makhani Tandoori Chicken, Marinated Tandoori Chicken with Makhani Sauce (green peppers, onions, tomatoes, methi, garlic sauce), Sanam Special (prawn, chicken and meat in bhuna sauce). Price check: Papadam 50p, CTM £7.50, Pullao Rice £1.50, Peshwari Nan £1.80, Lager £2.40 pint. Hours: 5.30-11.30pm.

Stapleford

MOUSHUMI NEW ENTRANT ©

124 Derby Road, Stapleford 0115 939 4929/ 917 0170

Established in 1993. The Moushumi is a tastefully decorated 70 seater decked out in sea greens and stained wood. Large and expensive engraved glass panels divide the restaurant. Proprietor Sanawor Ali is a romantic soul. His Valentine's Night at £25 per couple, with free cocktails for her and champagne for him, sounds good. No reports on proposals. Specials: Dakeshwari Murgh, chicken in cream and yoghurt £4.95. Car parking for 50 at side of restaurant. Price check: Papadam 60p, CTM £7.50, Pullao Rice £1.90, Peshwari Nan £2.10, Lager £2.45 pint. Takeaway: approximately 20% discount. Delivery: £10 minimum, 3-mile radius. Hours: 12-2.30pm/6-11.30pm. Branch: Amrit Takeaway, Mapperley Top, Nottingham. Stocks Cobra.

Sutton-in-Ashfield

HUTHWAITE TANDOORI NEW ENTRANT ©

17 Market Street, Huthwaite, Sutton in Ashfield
01623 557716

Established in 1990. Seats 80, parking for 30 at front. Specials: Rish Rosha £6.20 – marinated trout cooked in the tandoor, served with thick sauce. Kufta Khana £5.70 – minced lamb rolled into balls, roasted and served with spicy sauce. Price check: Papadam 40p, CTM £5.90, Pullao Rice £1.50, Peshwari Nan £1.50, Lager £1.90 pint. Takeaway: 10% discount. Hours: 12-2.30pm/6pm-12am. Stocks Cobra.

Worksop

NEW ROYAL BRASSERIE NEW ENTRANT

32 Carlton Road, Worksop 01909 477520

'Table was pre-booked, main courses arrived within 20 minutes of ordering. Comfortable restaurant. Well cooked rice, light and fluffy though not overly fragrant. Lamb Chilli Shobug – new to me – onion, tomatoes and halved red peppers, very thick, dark brown sauce, fairly hot, earthy texture – most enjoyable. Nan bread was thin, crispy, not exactly to my liking but very tasty none the less. Enjoyable meal.' PA.

OXFORDSHIRE

Area: Central
Population: 619,000
Adjacent Counties: Bucks, Berks, Glos, Middx, Northants, Warks, Wilts

Banbury

SHEESH MAHAL ©

43 Oxford Road, Banbury 01295 266489

M Khalid is the owner-chef here, and has been since 1986. It's a 64 seater, managed by M Manwar, and it serves standard formula curries. 'Decided to visit on a friend's recommendation. Tandoori Fish for starters, very good. Chicken Moghlai, excellent, Naan breads were massive. Coffee pot and cream were left on our table so we could help ourselves.' JSK. 20 private car parking spaces to rear. Specials include: Dahi Chicken, Lamb Pasanda, Sag Chicken, Makani Chicken £6.95. Price check: Papadam 50p, CTM £7.25, Pullao Rice £1.95, Peshwari Nan £1.95, Lager £2.95. Takeaway: 25% discount. Hours: 6pm-12am (Sat. to 1am). Stocks Cobra.

Bicester

BICESTER TANDOORI ©

15 Market Square, Bicester 01869 245170

The Sahana was taken over in 1994 by Mrs Dilwara Begum. Decorated in pink with a blue marble bar, seats 40. Formula curry house.Delivery: £15.95 minimum, 3-mile radius. Hours: 5.30-11.30pm (12am on Sat.). Stocks Cobra.

Chinnor

CHINNOR INDIAN ©

59-61 Lower Road, Chinnor 01844 354843

Saidur Rahman has been the owner of this 60-seater since '97 'The food is superb. A great evening. I can't fault them. Highly recommended.' MS. Decorated in green with artifical plants, to look like a garden, bamboo chairs, apricot table linen. 'Having eaten in many curry restaurants and having spent a great deal of my working life in Dhaka, Bombay and Delhi, as well as over 60 other countries in the world, I can safely say the food offered here ranks with the best I have ever tasted. Tandoori dishes are freshly made, curry dishes are subtle, chicken is succulent, lamb tender and well marinated, presentation is superb. Hospitality is warm and welcoming.' JR. 'My wife, children and I are always assured of a warm welcome from all the staff. Everything we have tried is excellent. Prices are very reasonable and the portions good value for money. On the rare occasion when we have had a problem with misunderstood orders or, more rarely, with a disappointing dish, corrective action is cheerfully taken. We can unreservedly recommend it (and often do) to anyone wanting a special Indian meal.' GB. 'I recommend it to all my friends.' DGG. Parking for 30 cars – side entrance. Price check: Papadam 50p, CTM £6.50, Pullao Rice £1.70, Peshwari Nan £1.80. House wine £6.90. Hours: 12-2.30pm/6-11.30pm. Stocks Cobra.

Chipping Norton

ANARKALL ©

6 West Street, Chipping Norton 01608 642785

'Good selection on menu, good-sized portions. Best-ever Naans, light and fluffy. Onion Bhajees out of this world. Bank Holiday weekend was busy but manager still had time to talk to us.' PA. Proprietor A Uddin. Hours 12-2.30pm/6-11.30pm. Stocks Cobra.

Didcot

SUNKOSHI TANDOORI NEW ENTRANT

226a Broadway, Didcot 01235 812796

'Hasina Kebabs and Chicken Chats were incredible, served piping hot and full of flavour. Karai Mixed Grill, Chicken Karai wonderfully cooked and huge portions. Service excellent. Having never knowingly eaten at a Nepalese restaurant before, we were very impressed and will return again very shortly.' DL. Stocks Cobra.

Faringdon

AZAD TANDOORI AND BALTI NEW ENTRANT ©

14 Coxwell Street, Faringdon 01367 244977

30-seater owned by Rabia Khanom Ali, since '95. 'Nicely decorated since he took it over.' RK. Serves Bangladeshi formula curries, Tandoori dishes are very popular. Takeaway: 15% discount. Price check: Papadam 50p, CTM £6.25, Pullao Rice £1.70, Peshwari Nan £1.75. House wine £6.95. Delivery: £10 minimum, 4-mile radius. Hours: 5-11.30pm; Sun. 12-11.30pm. Stocks Cobra.

Henley-on-Thames

GAZAL ©

53-55 Reading Road, Henley-on-Thames 01491 574659

Gazal means gentle Indian love songs. It has nothing to do with guzzling. ('I hope that puts one reporter right, who told me that's why he came here in the first place – to get big portions!' PJ.) He loves the place, though, visiting whenever he's in town. Hours: 12-2pm/6-11pm.

NAJMAH PALACE NEW ENTRANT

58-60 Bell Street, Henley on Thames 01491 410071

'A great deal of patience has been paid to the decor, flowers, linen which contribute to a light, clean, brasserie style. Busy with locals and tourists. Swift service, fresh Popadoms and Pickles, lean minced lamb in Meat Samosa, magnificently smoked chicken from the tandoor and fragrant Pullao Rice. Prices average – £20 with drinks.' AIE. Takeaway: 10% discount. Price check: Papadam 55p, CTM £6.95, Pullao Rice £2.00. Hours: 12-2.30pm/5.30-11pm. Stocks Cobra.

RAJUS NEW ENTRANT

21 Reading Road, Henley on-Thames 01491 572218

'Excellent food and friendly service.' AR.

Oxford

AZIZ TOP 100 ©

228-230 Cowley Road, Oxford 01865 794945

Smart 90-seater, white with gold lettering on exterior. Inside, very well decorated, cane chairs, plants, subdued lighting, upmarket, sophisticated. Named after its owner, Azizur (Aziz) Rahman, this restaurant is one of Oxford's best. 'Our third visit this year and it just seems to get better. Service as usual, swift and polite. Popadoms and naans in handy size pieces. Keema Somasas superb. The sauces in the Chicken Patia and the King Prawns with Red Pumpkin and Green Chillies were wonderful. I rate the cooking here amongst the best anywhere and I can't recommend it enough. Suggest booking beforehand, it's so popular.' MS. Aziz is one place where you will find the Bangladeshi curry house formula done as well as it can be. 'My no. 1 favourite.' JCC. 'Excellent quality, charming service. Very comfortable and relaxing atmosphere.' RT. 'Immediately impressed. Tables simply but elegantly set with crisp white linen. Good vegetarian selection on menu. Generous quantities and delicately flavoured. Emphasis on subtlety. A splendid meal.' WC. 'Impressive reports confirmed. Mid-week the place was packed. Decor is upmarket and smart, the food well prepared and served in generous quantities. This is where the middle class, the academics and well-off students of Oxford eat and entertain. Service was slow but the place was very busy. Parking can be a problem.' PAW. Arramba – to begin, Maach Bora, fish cake with potato, eggs and green chillies £3.50. Chott Pottie, chickpeas, egg and potatoes spiced with coriander £2.75. House specialities: Murgh Jal Frajee, stir-fried chicken in batter, with fresh chillies – hot £6.15, Jerre Koligi, lamb livers with cummin £6.15. Chitol Bhuna, Bangladeshi fish rolled into Kofta £6.65, Galda Chineri Kodu, king prawns with red pumpkin and green chillies £7.50. Dimm Dall, eggs and red lentils with coconut milk £4.50. Takeaway: 15% discount. Takeaway: 15% discount. Sunday buffet 12-5.30pm, £7.50 per person, children £3.75. Price check: Papadam 45p, CTM £6.25, Pullao Rice £1.85, Misti Nan £2.15. Hours: 12-2pm/6-11.30pm; Sun. 12-11.30pm; closed New Year's Day. High in our TOP 100.

KASHMIR HALAL ©

64 Cowley Road, Oxford 01865 250165

Opened in 1970 by Said Meah and seats 50 diners. A comprehensive menu listing all your favourite curries and accompaniments. Halal meat. Tandoori dishes a speciality of the house. Delivery: £10 minimum, 3-mile radius. Hours: 12-2.30pm (Fri. lunch closed)/6pm-12am. Stocks Cobra.

SHIMLA PINKS ©

16 Turl Street, Oxford 01865 243783

Formerly the Taj Mahal which was established in 1937 on the first floor above Whites, making it Britain's third ever Indian restaurant. It was taken over and renamed Shimla Pinks to form another of the Oriental Group's venues. Unfortunately, as we write, the group is in administration. For Shimla Pinks style and branches, see London EC2. We sincerely hope the group and this venerable restaurant survive. Reports please.

Thame

DE WANI SHAH'S ©

8 Swan Walk, Thame 01844 260066

Daytime this 28-seater is a coffee shop, found behind the Swan Hotel. At night it becomes De Wani (hall of assembly), a licensed Indian restaurant. Nural Isam is owner and chef. DK liked the 'leave-it-to-us' set meal at £9.99. Takeaway: 10% off. Delivery: £10 minimum, 5-mile radius. Hours: 5.30-11.30pm; Tues. closed.

THAME TANDOORI NEW ENTRANT

19 High Street, Thame 01844 212175

'Another knockout meal. Kicked off with Kingfisher lagers. Always book a table, it's very popular. The Shamee kebab and Reshhi kebab were enormous and very filling but totally delicious. Prawn Puri, delicious sauce – even let me try a bit, there was so much! Considering the smiling, swift service, super grub with excellent coffee to follow, I can continue to recommend this restaurant as one of the best, certainly one of my favourites.' MS. Minimum charge: £8.50. Chicken breast: 50p extra. Sunday lunch buffet: 12.15-3pm – £6.30, children £4.50. Takeaway: 10% discount. Price check: Papadam 70p, CTM £6.50, Pullao Rice £1.85, Peshwari Nan £1.90. Stocks Cobra.

RUTLAND

Britain's smallest county
Area: East Midlands
Population: 50,000
Adjacent Counties: Cambs, Leics, Lincs

Leicestershire's bureaucratic loss is Rutland's gain. Back again after decades of non-existence, it is once again Britain's smallest county – it is geographically smaller than the city of Birmingham.

Oakham

RUTLAND BALTI HOUSE ©

18 Mill Street, Oakham 01572 757232

Owned/managed by Abdul Khalique, since '95. Formerly Oakham Tandoori, plain white artex walls and ceiling, seats a cosy 32 diners, serves Bangladeshi formula curries. Takeaway 15% discount if orders over £15. Hours: 5.30pm-12am (12.30am on Sat.); Sun. 12-3pm/5.30pm-12am. Stocks Cobra.

SHROPSHIRE

Area: Welsh Border
Population: 431,000
Adjacent Counties: Cheshire, Clwyd, Hereford, Powys, Staffs, Worcs

Bridgnorth

EURASIA

21 West Castle Street, Bridgnorth 01746 764895

The 65-seater Eurasia is well-established, having opened in 1975. It changed hands in 1987 to Azadur Rahman and I Miah. East meets West classic decor. Specials include: Ayer Fish in Garlic Sauce, Makni Chicken, Jalfrezi and Tikka most popular. Price check: Papadam 50p, CTM £8.50, Pullao Rice

£1.95, Peshwari Nan £1.85, Lager £2.20 pint. Takeaway: 10% discount. Hours: 12-2pm/6pm-12am; Sun. 1pm-12am. Stocks Cobra.

Church Stretton

ALIMA'S NEW ENTRANT

5 The Square, Church Stretton 01694 724949

'Quite a small restaurant although we were OK without booking. We ate in and had a takeaway and were very impressed on both occasions.' AK&KW. 'Food we had was excellent – formula with a difference! I had King Prawn Korma £6.10, my wife Lamb Sagwalla £4.45 – we shared a Tarka Dhal £2.10. Quantities were ample and service prompt. Restaurant is small, comfortable, good lighting.' AJC. Price check: CTM £5.75, Pullao Rice £1.95, Peshwari Nan £1.95. Hours: 5.30pm-12am. Stocks Cobra.

Ludlow

SHAPLA BALTI BYO ©

58 Broad Street, Ludlow 01584 875153

Owner and manager Shalim Miah with chef Muzibur Rahman of this 1992 50-seater are 'enthusiastic and keen to help.' Specials include: Balti Sag Paneer (fresh chicken or lamb cooked with fresh spinach garnished with home made cheese, onion and tomatoes. Balti Sag, delicious – you wanted it to go on and on. Naans, massive. Price, very reasonable. The restaurant also does kebabs and cheeseburgers for philistines!' SR. And Donner Kebabs, including a Donner Chicken Tikka Kebab (£3.25). 'After 11pm, busy restaurant but looked after a large group of us very courteously and efficiently. Great Chicken Jalfrezi – very warm indeed. Recommended.' IB. BYO is allowed, no corkage. Price check: Papadam 50p, CTM £5.45, Pullao Rice £1.60, Peshwari Nan £1.60. Hours: 12pm-12am daily. Stocks Cobra.

Newport

SHIMLA ©

22 St Mary's Street, Newport 01952 825322

Set takeaway meals are excellent value at Nurul Islam's restaurant. Balti includes Papadam with mint sauce and onion salad, Tandoori Mix Kebab, Chicken (or Lamb) Tikka Balti, Sag Aloo, Pullao Rice (half-portion) or Nan, and sweet or coffee. Minimum charge £10. Hours: 6pm-12am.

Oswestry

RAJ MAHAL NEW ENTRANT

26 Leg Street, Oswestry 01691 652566

Established in 1983. Seats 60, serves Northern Indian curries and Baltis, with CTM being the most ordered dish. Price check: Papadam 50p, CTM £6.45, Pullao Rice £1.50, Peshwari Nan £1.50, Lager £2.25 pint. Takeaway: 10% discount. Hours: 12-2pm/6pm-12am; Sat. 6pm-1am. Stocks Cobra.

SIMLA ©

42 Beatrice Street, Oswestry 01691 659880

Sufu Miah's Simla has been trading since 1976, and seats 100. We'd like more satisfied reports about the food, prices and service. Hours: 12pm-12am daily. Branch: Simla, 5 Grapes Hill, Llangollen, Clwyd. Stocks Cobra.

Shifnal

ROYAL BENGAL NEW ENTRANT

28-34 Broadway, Shifnal 01952 460522

First opened in 1979. Seats 50, decorated in dusky shades of pink, ornate plaster work on walls and ceiling, real tableclothes. Serves Bangladeshi formula curries. Special: Drumstick Chicken Masala with Pullao Rice £8.95. Price check: Papadam 40p, CTM £7.95, Pullao Rice £1.75, Peshwari Nan £1.85, Lager £2.40 pint. Takeaway: 20% discount. Hours: 12-2pm/5.30-11.30pm; Sat. 5.30pm-12am. Stocks Cobra.

SHIFNAL BALTI NEW ENTRANT

20-22 Broadway, Shifnal 01952 460142

'My favourite. You are greeted by an authentic Indian Emperor who opens the door and welcomes your trade.' TE.

Shrewsbury

RAMNA BALTI HOUSE NEW ENTRANT

33 Wyle Cup, Shrewsbury 01743 363170

One of the Shrewsbury Balti houses to survive the terrible winter 1998 floods. Situated in a scenic part of town, it was the perfect setting for a

Christmas Eve curry on a crisp, wintery night. Never yet have we had a bad meal there. Small, inviting and beautifully decorated. Baltis had rich, fiery sauces, liberally infused with meat and green chillies, naans enormous and absolute heaven. Generous portions and efficient service.' sw. Stocks Cobra.

Whitchurch

EASTERN SPICE NEW ENTRANT

Brownlow Road, Whitchurch 01948 667776

Established in 1998. Seats 52. Specials: Chicken Tikka Sandwich £2.80. Chicken Samba £4.30 – chicken tikka with lentils, slightly hot. Price check: Papadam 40p, CTM £5.80, Pullao Rice £1.80, Peshwari Nan £2, Lager £2 pint. Takeaway: 20% discount. Hours: 5pm-12.30am. Stocks Cobra.

TASTE OF PUNJAB TAKEAWAY NEW ENTRANT

20a Mill Street, Whitchurch 01948 662282

Formerly the Nice'n' Spicy takeaway established in 1996 by manager Abdul Mozid: 'we like to think that all our dishes are special and reasonably priced.' Nicely decorated, comfortable sofa. Chef's Special: Bombay Chicken, cooked with whole boiled egg and potato £4.30. Price check: Papadam 40p, CTM £4.55, Pullao Rice £1.40 large container only. Hours: 5pm-12am.

SOMERSET

Area: West Country
Population: 493,000
Adjacent Counties: Bristol, Devon, Dorset, Glos, Wilts

Bath

CURRY 2000 NEW ENTRANT

31 Belvedere, Lansdown Road, Bath 01225 789666

Owned by the Choudhury family. Takeaway: 10% discount. Price check: Papadam 50p, CTM £6.50, Pullao Rice £1.80, Peshwari Nan £1.40. Hours: 12-2pm/6-11.30pm. Stocks Cobra.

DESH TAKEAWAY NEW ENTRANT

10 Chelsea Road, Weston, Bath 01225 314413

Established in 1991. Seats 34. Chef Shipu cooks up Bangladeshi formula curries – guess what's most popular? Price check: Papadam 40p, CTM £5.20, Pullao Rice £1.50, Peshwari Nan £1.50. Takeaway: 10% discount. Hours: 12-2pm/5.30pm-12am. Stocks Cobra.

THE EASTERN EYE NEW TO OUR TOP 100 ©

8a Quiet Street, Bath 01225 422323

140-seater, owned by Suhan Choudhury, pink and blue with most impressive Georgian interior, in one large room with three domes. 'Average high-street curry house it is not! It's a spectacular, huge and most impressive first-floor restaurant. Soft lighting, pink and blue colours, restful atmosphere. Tableclothes and cutlery are of good quality, even the hot towels are so thick they could almost have been squares of carpet! Stuffed pepper £3.90 – whole green stuffed with spicy diced chicken, barbecued, nicely blackened, delicately spiced, interesting but filling starter. Onion Bhajia £2.20 – two round bhajias, the best we have tasted for a long while, light, crispy and spicy. Prawn Puree – excellent, large succulent prawns, tangy sauce. Good, fresh and varied salad ganishes. Chicken Tikka Masala – most ordinary, standard offering. Chicken Mon Pasand £7.90 – excellent, different, mild, yoghurt based sauce, very herby. Lamb Jalfrezi £6.90 – large tender chunks of lamb, thick dark sauce, hotness hits you after first couple of mouthfulls. Vegetable Bhajee £2.80 – good variety of diced vegetables, nicely spiced and enjoyable. Peshwari Nan and Pullao Rice were both good, nan not sickly and rice contained smattering of diced vegetables to make it interesting. Prices slightly above average, but for decor and type of restaurant, very reasonable. Service efficient and friendly. 10% CC discount. An excellent meal in an elegant restaurant, must be knocking on the door of TOP 100.' MW. Service charge: 10%. Specials include: Mon Pasand – slightly hot, enlivened with herbs and yoghurt £7.50, Shah Jahani – chicken breast, slightly spiced, shallow fried in ghee, blended with homemade cheese and cream £7.50, Sultan Puri Pilau – from Uttar Pradesh, spiced rice with lamb and cashew nuts, served with a gravy £8.95. Bangladeshi food nights, seafood buffet. Price check: Papadam 50p, CTM £6.90, Pullao Rice £1.80, Peshwari Nan £1.80, Lager £2.95 pint. House wine £7.95. Service 10%. Minimum charge: £9. Takeaway: 10% discount. Hours: 12-2.30pm/6-11.30pm. Fax: 01225 482557 Website: www.easterneye.co.uk. It's been more than knocking on the door for some time. Welcome to our TOP 100. Stocks Cobra.

©	Curry Club Discount	U	Unlicensed
V	Vegetarian	ANP	Alcohol not permitted
e-a-m-a-y-l	Eat as much as you like	BYO	Bring your own alcohol

RUPOSHI TAKEAWAY ©

3 Sussex Place, Widcombe Parade, Bath 01225 337294

A safe bet, reasonably priced lunch and dinner takeaway-only, managed by Gous Ali. Price check: Papadam 30p, CTM £4.90, Pullao Rice £1.20. Branch: Ruposhi, 110 Mount Road, Bath.

Bridgewater

TASTE OF INDIA

31-33 Penel Orlieu, Bridgewater 01278 446660

At the former Simla, Biriani is apparently the most popular dish. £6.95 wine. Takeaway: 20% discount. Price check: Papadam 50p, CTM £5.45, Pullao Rice £1.75. Parking for 20 cars at back of restaurant. Hours: 12-2pm/5.30pm-12am. Stocks Cobra.

Cheddar

CHEDDAR COTTAGE NEW ENTRANT

Union Street, Cheddar 01934 742331

Established in 1994. Seats 50. Specials: Golap £5.75 – chicken cooked with fresh green chillies, garlic, ginger, peppers and tomato in rich very hot sauce. Table Nan £4.95 – large, £2.55 – medium. Price check: Papadam 40p, CTM £5.35, Pullao Rice £1.65, Peshwari Nan £1.55, Lager £2.20 pint, House wine £5 a bottle. Takeaway: 10% discount. Hours: 12-2pm/5.30-11pm. Stocks Cobra.

Clevedon

MOGHULS TANDOORI ©

33 Old Church Road, Clevedon 01275 873695

'Started with Chicken Tikka, big, succulent. Followed by Tandoori King Prawn Masala, lovely sauce with cream. Excellent Pullao Rice with chopped almonds and fried onions. Delicious Mixed Vegetable Curry, green peppers, cauli, beans, onion and mange-tout.' MS. Hours: 12-2pm/6pm-12am. Stocks Cobra.

Midsomer Norton

SHAPLA ©

43 High Street, Midsomer Norton 01761 410479

Tiny, seats 24 diners, serves formula curries, CTM is most popular. 'I especially liked their Dandag (*sic*) and had not previously heard of their Chicken, Lamb or Prawn Dim (*sic.*) – "cooked with egg in a sauce".' [Neither have we!] Takeaway 15% off. Delivery. Hours: 12-2pm/5.30pm-11.30pm. Branch: Tandoori Mahal, 13 Sadler Street, Wells. Next door is Shapla Indian Takeaway (tel. 01761 411887).

Taunton

MARINA INDIAN CUISINE NEW ENTRANT

18 Paul Street, Taunton 01823 335299

Fully licensed. 'Recommendation from some local work colleagues. Welcome and service very friendly, food exceptionally good. Have been eating curries for 25 years and like seriously hot curry. Had the Chicken Phall, full of flavour, very hot. Value for money – £30.80 for three.' SM. Sunday lunch special: £7.95. Takeaway: 20% discount. Delivery: 3-mile radius, £10 minimum. Price check: Papadam 40p, CTM £6.25, Pullao Rice £1.70, Peshwari Nan £1.80. Hours: 12-2pm/6pm-12am. Stocks Cobra.

Wellington

TASTE OF INDIA ©

2 North Street, Wellington 01823 667051

Naz Choudhury's Taste is a cosy little a/c 30-seater, which serves, for example, 'home-style: Fish Kurma, Murgee Razzla, Vegetable Kebabs, Achar Gust, Pilaw, chutney and pickle for four £55'. Buffet £9.95. £7.20 wine, also have off-license for takeaway trade. Hours: 12-2pm/6pm-12am; Tues. closed. Branch: Tandoori Spice, 12 Higher Street, Cullompton, Devon. Stocks Cobra.

Weston-super-Mare

AVON TANDOORI ©

16 Waterloo Street, Weston-super-Mare 01934 622622

Opened in May '88, seats 49 diners, managed by A Hoque, formula and Balti dishes. Specials: Tandoori King Prawn Zalfarazai, lemon juice, capsicum, onion, hot green chillies £10.95. Minimum charge: £7 per person. Takeaway: 10% discount. Hours: 12-2pm/6pm-12am; Sat. 6pm-12.30am; Sun. 6-11.30pm. Stocks Cobra.

CURRY GARDEN ©

69 Orchard Street, Weston-super-Mare 01934 624660

Seats 65, in two dining rooms, Bangladeshi curry house. Owned by Miah and Ali. Price check: 'Empty when we arrived at 7.30pm, seething by 8pm – book a table if you go, don't take a chance like we did. Chicken Tikka Masala was the best so far this year'. MS. Takeaway: 10% discount. Minimum charge: £5. Hours: 12-2pm/6pm-12am. Stocks Cobra.

VICEROY

57 Whitecross Road, Weston-super-Mare 01934 628735

Thank you, John, for your report which enables me to retain one of my favourite gags for another year! JG. says: 'Large, elegant restaurant – pond with Koi carp. Very quiet Monday evening. Excellent three course meal with drinks, about £16 per head. Food very tasty. Attentive service. Would definitely return.' JG. And the gag? ... the Viceroy's main claim to fame – its visit by *Silence of the Lambs*' Anthony Hopkins (bringing a whole new meaning to Chef's Special!). Stocks Cobra.

STAFFORDSHIRE

Area: North Midlands
Population: 1,066,000
Adjacent Counties: Cheshire, Derbs, Shrops, W Mids, Worcs

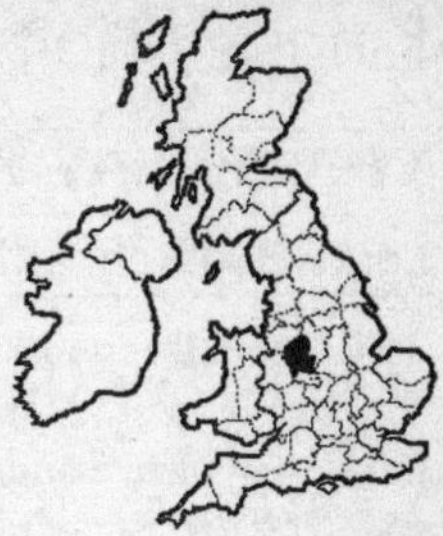

Cannock

JASMINE — BYO ©

125 Hednesford Road, Heath Hayes, Cannock — 01543 279620

N Islam's 50-seat Jasmine. Balti Special. Prawn, King Prawn and Lobster is £9.75. BYO, no corkage. Minimum charge: £5. Takeaway: 15% discount. Price check: Papadam 40p, CTM £7.25, Pullao Rice £1.40. House wine £6.95. Delivery: £10 minimum, 3-mile radius. Hours: 5-12.30pm; Sat. 5.30pm-1am. Stocks Cobra.

SANAM BALTI HOUSE — BYO

193 Cannock Road, Chadsmoor, Cannock — 01543 573565

'Excellent food and very friendly service. Book or be prepared for a long wait at weekends. It allows you to BYO. Our bill for ten was £64!' Price check: Papadam 35p, Balti CTM £4.95, Pullao Rice £1.10. Hours: 5.30pm-1am (2am on Fri. & Sat.).

Hednesford

BENGAL BRASSERIE — ©

44 Market Street, Hednesford — 01543 424769

Owner Kuti Miah's formula curry house seats 60. Specials: Chicken Keema Matter – succulent pieces of marinated chicken cooked in a spicy minced lamb sauce with chickpeas. Delivery: £15 minimum, 3-mile radius. Hours: 6pm-12am. Branches: Royal Indian Brasserie, Albion House, New Quay, Dyfed. Bay of Bengal, Crackwell Street, Tenby. Dilshad Brasserie, Whitford Street, Holywell, Clwyd. Stocks Cobra.

Kingsley Holt

THORNBURY HALL RASOI TOP 100

Lockwood Road, Kingsley Holt 01538 750831

This unusual restaurant is approximately 10 miles east of Hanley (off the A52) in a renovated Grade II listed building, once a manor house. Since 1994 it has been owned and managed by Mr and Mrs Siddique, who have brought style and Pakistani food to this beautiful area. It has three public areas, including a conference room. The main restaurant leads from the bar and is decorated in gold and terracotta, ceramic floor, open fire for winter evenings. The Shalimar room, named after gardens in Pakistan, is decorated in green and gold, large windows and doors leading to garden. Dance floor, sparkling globe and sound system. Lahore dining room, large, elegant, richly decorated Georgian plaster ceiling, swagged curtains and a brass teapot, it nearly reached the ceiling! Pakistani delicacies are on the menu. 'Could be tricky to find, but my in-laws live close by. The main hall is very grand, but not always open. Other areas are elegant and comfortable. Service good, including some staff from the village in Pakistani dress. Excellent flavours and quality. Sensible portions.' DRHM. 'Fantastic restaurant. Magnificent settings in a listed building. Kumbi Pullao Arasta Rice cooked with mushrooms was out of this world. Karahi Mogulai, pieces of lamb cooked with cream, egg, ground nuts, garnished with almonds, superb. Karahi Murgh Jalfrezi, cooked in green chilli, ginger, garlic, yoghurt and spices, the best my husband has ever tasted.' MR&MRS C. We're pleased to promote it to our TOP 100. Price check: Papadam 50p, CTM £6.50, Aloo Jeera £3.50, Plain Rice £1.50. Hours: 12-2.30pm/6-11pm (11.30pm on Fri. & Sat.). Stocks Cobra.

Leek

BOLAKA SPICE NEW ENTRANT ©

41 Stockwell Street, Leek 01538 373734

'Primarily a formula curry house, but two features make it stand out – the Haandis menu and a small specials board. Keema Motor is an outstanding and rich mix of lamb, chick peas and spices. At Christmas, a divine Turkey Tikka Masala with vegetables. Aubergines in a Sweet Sauce is Wow! Service polite and efficient.' PK. Stocks Cobra.

PABNA ©

16-18 Ashbourne Road, Leek 01538 381156

Formerly India garden, Fazz Meah took over in March '98 and completely refurbished. Formula curry house, Rogan Josh most popular, seats 80. 'Average Prawn Bhuna, excellent Tarka Dall.' PK. Price check: Papadam 45p, CTM £6.25, Pullao Rice £1.45. Lager £2.25 pint, house wine £7.25. Minimum charge: £7.50. Takeaway: 15% discount. Hours: 5.30pm-12am. Reports please.

Lichfield

EASTERN EYE TOP 100 ©

19b Bird Street, Lichfield 01543 254399

Abdul Salam's venue represents a Swat valley house, right up in Pakistan's northern mountain ranges (just a nan nudge from Baltistan). It is famous for its forests and ornate wooden carved furniture, showing Buddhist influences going back 2,000 years. The beams, pillars and window are from Swat. The bar front is from neighbouring Afghanistan, the chairs are Rajasthani and the table tops are from 150-year-old elm. 'Count the rings,' enthuses Mr Salam. The toilets are a 'must-see' on your list. The theme is Agra's Red Fort – probably India's best example of a Moghul residence. The food is well spoken of. Specials include Murgh with Apricot, marinated chicken with apricot yoghurt sauce, cream and fresh coriander. Rajasthani Paro Breast – pigeon. Michael Fabricant, MP, MCC (member of the Curry Club) continues regularly to take his seat at the Eye as a loyal local, rating it highly, as do so many other reports we get, e.g. 'From entering you know it'll be good. Decor reminded me of Putney's fine Ma Goa's (London SW15). In a mild mood, had Murgh Special with apricot which was delicious. My friend loved his Eastern Eye Mixed Massala (king prawn, lamb and chicken).' RL. 'Still my favourite. Mr Salam still very much in charge, evolving the menu and new dishes. Cooking excellent – far superior to average curry fare. Chicken and Banana, Chilli Chicken, Special tandoori Masala (inc chicken, lamb, king prawns) are all excellent. Amazingly light Naans. Wine list still consists of an armful of bottles placed on your table to take your pick from – a tradition I hope will remain and includes good examples from Spain and Australia. Deserves to be in the TOP 100.' PJ. ' The food was unusual and beautifully presented on huge oval china plates. Will definitely try it again if we're ever in the area.' K&ST. Discounts for CC Members on Sundays. Price check: Papadam 40p, CTM £6.95, Pullao Rice £1.70. House wine £6.95. Hours: 12-2.30pm (Sat. only)/ 5pm-12am. Stocks Cobra.

LAL BAGU ©

9 Bird Street, Lichfield 01543 262967

Formula curry house, seats 70, proprietor Masum Ahmed Chowdhury. Special: Shorti – chicken, lamb or prawn – cooked with chat masala, slight hot and sour, finely chopped green chillies and fenugreek £4.25. £6.25 wine. Price check: Papadam 40p, CTM £5.95, Pullao Rice £1.60. Delivery: £10 minimum. Sunday lunch £6.95. Takeaway over £20, free wine, papadam, salad and raita. Hours: 12.30-2.30pm Sun. only/5.30pm-12am. Stocks Cobra.

Newcastle-under-Lyme

BILASH ©

22 Highland Keele Road, Newcastle-under-Lyme 01782 614549

Established by Mrs D Choudhury's curry house in 1988, seats 90 in three dining rooms. Specials: Bangladeshi Rezala. Keema and Garlic Nan. Takeaway: 20% discount. Hours: 5pm-12.30am. Stocks Cobra.

OSSIES BYO ©

39 Ironmarket, Newcastle-under-Lyme 01782 662207

Formula (CTM is most popular) curry house seats 86 in two dining rooms. Formerly Ali Baba, taken over in late '96 by M Arshad. BYO no corkage. Hours: 6pm-1am (3am on Fri. & Sat.). Stocks Cobra.

Rugeley

BILASH ©

7 Horsefair, Rugeley 01889 584234

At Chowdhury, Rofique and Uddin's 90-seater: 'our favourite.' N&GD (party room 48). The specials include Chilli Chicken Tikka, with red and green chillies, served with salad. Takeaway 10% off. Hours: 12-2.30pm/ 5.30-11.30m. Stocks Cobra.

Shenstone Woodend

THE LODGE BYO ©

Lodge Cottage, 24 Birmingham Rd, Shenstone W 01543 483334

Shenstone Woodend is a small green-belt village on the W Mids border,

4 miles north of Sutton Coldfield. Jamal and Imam Uddin's 70-seater Lodge, established in 1996, is beautifully appointed, with carpet and pine floors, simple chandeliers, white ceiling-roses, arches and cornices, and magnolia walls. 'My family eats as often as possible in this luxurious restaurant. Smart, efficient waiters remember customer names and preferences, and they adore children. Chef Shanur Ali excels with a wide variety of Indian cuisine.' RLP. Parking in front for 32 cars, with CCTV. Takeaway: 15% discount. Delivery: £10 minimum, 4-mile radius. Hours: 5.30pm-12am; Sat. & Sun. 12-2pm. Branch: Streetly Balti, 188 Chester Road, Sutton Coldfield.

Stafford

CURRY KUTEER NEW ENTRANT ©

231 Greengate Street, Stafford 01785 253279

Established 1968. Seats 80. Specials: Hyderbadi Keema Masala £5.95 – minced lamb, green peas and potato. Vegetable tray £6.50 – three vegetable dishes of your choice (good value). Price check: Papadam 40p, CTM £6.70, Pullao Rice £1.80, Peshwari Nan £1.80, Lager £2 pint. Takeaway: 25% discount. Hours: 12-2pm/6pm-12am (Sat. to 1am). Stocks Cobra.

ROSE OF KASHMIR NEW ENTRANT

56 Foregate Road, Stafford 01785 225772

Established in 1992. Seats 58. Set meal: 3 courses £9.00 – Papadam, Mixed Starter, Balti (choice) with Nan or Rice. Price check: Papadam 50p, CTM £6.25, Pullao Rice £1.60, Peshwari Nan £2. Takeaway: 10% discount. Delivery: £1 charge, 3-mile radius. Hours: 5pm-12am.

Stoke-on-Trent

(including Burslem and Hanley)

ASHA TAKEAWAY NEW ENTRANT ©

42 Broad Street, Hanley, Stoke-on-Trent 01782 213339

Where (I believe) Robbie Williams comes from. Established in 1991. Specials: Keema Chat £1.65. Tandoori Steak £7.50. Coriander Nan £1.50. Price check: Papadam 25p, CTM £4.80, Pullao Rice £1.30, Peshwari Nan £1.60. Hours: 5pm-12am.

BOSTON CHICKEN & PIZZA HUT NEW ENTRANT ©

42 Broad Street, Hanley, Stoke-on-Trent 01782 213339

Established in 1995. Price check: Papadam 25p, CTM £4.80, Pullao Rice £1.30, Peshwari Nan £1.60, House wine £5.99 bottle. Hours: 7pm-3am. Stocks Cobra.

MONZIL ©

44 Broad Street, Hanley, Stoke-on-Trent 01782 280150

A Matin's Monzil's 1977 formula curry house, taken over by Mrs Chowdry in 1996 and seats 80. Chef's Special: chicken, meat, prawn, mushroom and tomato with spices and boiled egg. Takeaway: 10% off. Hours: 7pm-3am (2am on Sun.). Branch: Bilash, Newcastle, Staffs. Stocks Cobra.

NASEEB NEW ENTRANT

131 Etruria Vale Road, Hanley, Stoke-on-Trent 01782 212240

'Happily found the Naseeb while on a canal holiday. Looks like just another takeaway from the outside, but it's a smart and clean-looking fully licensed restaurant with friendly staff. Takeaway food freshly made for us to our taste in heat. Both main courses (Chicken Sambar and Karhai) sang out with fresh flavours and leftovers were eaten cold the next day – delicious.' CL. Stocks Cobra.

Uttoxeter

KOHI NOOR BYO ©

11 Queen Street, Uttoxeter 01889 562153

S Miah's 70-seater is 'difficult to find – it's at the back of Sketchley's Cleaners – and parking limited on site. Interesting decor. Food was good. Good value. It's never going to be a TOP 100 place but it is the archetypal English curry house – the backbone of curry houses in this country. Long may they live.' PW. Specials include Chicken Sath, lemon flavoured vegetables (Shatkora), coriander, garlic herbs and spices, £5.95. 'Interesting decor, early curry house style, red velvet chairs and '70's carpet. Food good. Good value.' PAW. CC members in parties of 10 or more will get a percentage off the bill, so gather up friends and family! Allows BYO, no corkage. Delivery: £20 min, 3-mile radius. Hours: 5.30pm-12am (1am on Fri. & Sat.). Stocks Cobra.

SUFFOLK

Area: East
Population: 675,000
Adjacent Counties: Cambs, Essex, Norfolk

Brandon

BRANDON TANDOORI ©

17-19 London Road, Brandon 01842 815874

Arjad Ali's 70-seater opened here in 1991, just a runway length from USAF Lakenheath. But the roar of the F111's is drowned out here by the roar of the tandoor, and the roar of approval from the locals. Our aero-med colonel pilot has retired back to the Midwest corn-bowl of America but still writes that he and his Suffolk wife miss their curries: 'I got my wings on Phantom jets, and again on the Brandon's Chicken Garlic Chilli, £6.10. It's hotter than my bird's jet pipe!' (We don't think he's referring to his wife!) 'The food is always of a wonderful quality, quickly and cheerfully served, and you can always rely on it when taking friends from India. My mouth waters at the memory of the last Murghi Massala, marinated spring chicken, cooked with mincemeat, peas, potato and tomato, £6.10. Book well in advance especially on Saturdays!' RE. Takeaway: 10% off. Minimum charge: £10. Hours: 12-2pm/6-11pm.

Bury-St-Edmonds

MUMTAZ INDIAN ©

9 Risbygate Street, Bury-St-Edmunds 01284 752988

Formula curry house, seating 44, opened in 1974 by Syed Nurul Haque, who tells us that during the Falklands War, he was asked to cook curries for the soldiers. His food was flown out by military aircraft and he believes that because the troops ate his food they won the war! Who am I to argue? Special Set Thai dinner: Onion Bhajai, Vegetable Curry, Chana Masala, Tarka Dal, Pullao Rice, Puri and curry sauce. Takeaway: 10% off. Minimum charge £6.50. Delivery: £10 minimum, 12-mile radius. Hours: 12-2.30pm/ 6-12am (12.30am on Sat.). Stocks Cobra.

©	Curry Club Discount	U	Unlicensed
V	Vegetarian	ANP	Alcohol not permitted
e-a-m-a-y-l	Eat as much as you like	BYO	Bring your own alcohol

Felixstowe

BOMBAY NITE ©

285 High Street, Walton, Felixstowe 01394 272131

Standard curry house, serving the formula. Owned and managed by Mahbub Alam. Seats 60 in three rooms, seating divided into booths. Decorated in cream and green. Takeaway: 15% discount. Hours: 12-2.30pm/6-11.30pm.

Hadleigh

ROYAL BENGAL

51 High Street, Hadleigh 01473 823744

'Small restaurant, well-lit, warm and comfortable. Chicken Tandoori Biryani, £8.50, good quality and flavour; Chicken Tikka Madras, £6.75 approx, was too mild, unmemorable; Nan very good, Onion Bhaji £1.80 very good.' NS. [Better order Phal next time, Nigel!]

Halesworth

RUCHITA ©

26 Market Place, Halesworth 01986 874524

E Miah and Z Allam run this 60-seater, with able assistance from John Gomez in the kitchen, whose handiwork is highly regarded. Try the King Prawn Re Jala, in cream with dry fruits, very mild spices £6.95 or the Chicken Patiwala, £6.95, diced chicken cooked with cheese, yoghurt, garlic, garnished with stuffed tomato and capsicum. Price check: Papadam 40p, CTM £5.20, Pullao Rice £1.30. House wine £5.85. Hours: 12-2.30pm/ 6-11.30pm. Stocks Cobra.

Ipswich

GULSHAN TAKEAWAY NEW ENTRANT

9 Stoke Street, Ipswich 01473 692929

Taken over in 1998 by Akikur Rahman (chef) and Abdul Jahid. Serving Balti meals and yes – CTM is most popular! Delivery: £10, 4 mile radius. Price check: Papadam 45p, CTM £5.75, Pullao Rice £1.50, Peshwari Nan £1.50. Hours: 5pm-12am.

TAJ MAHAL ©

40-42 Norwich Road, Ipswich 01473 257712

Established in 1964, making it Ipswich's first. Taken over by Syed Robbani in 1987. Seats 64. Serves formula curries, but 'anything can be arranged.' Special: Achar Chicken Masala, with pickled spices. CC members will get 10% off the bill. Takeaway: 20% off. Hours: 12-2pm (no lunch Fri.)/6-11.30pm.

Lowestoft

AHMED ©

150 Bridge Road, Oulton Broad, Lowestoft 01502 501725

Boshor Ali's cute little restaurant has just 28 seats. 'Brilliant.' says PJ. Hours: 12-2.30pm/6-11.30pm. Branch: Jorna Indian Takeaway, 29-33 Wherstead Road, Ipswich.

ROYAL BENGAL NEW ENTRANT ©

69 High Street, Lowestoft 01502 567070

Established in 1997. Seats 38. Specials include: Makari (chicken or lamb, two layers, the bottom cooked in tomatoey and slightly spicy sauce, and the top a mild creamy sauce), Dikush (a medium strength dish from the district of Sylhet, made with diced chicken/lamb, cooked in a special mosala sauce). Price check: Papadam 50p, CTM £6.50, Pullao Rice £1.70, Peshwari Nan £1.75, Lager £2.20 pint. Takeaway: 15% discount. Delivery: £12 minimum. Hours: 12-2pm/6-11.30pm. Stocks Cobra.

SEETA ©

176 High Street, Lowestoft 01502 574132

Sita is the Indian goddess of beauty and love. Alternatively, the Sitar is the melodic Indian stringed instrument. Now you'll remember the name! Either way, you like the Seeta. It's a pretty restaurant, with dusky pink walls, white ceiling, ornate plaster cornice and ceiling rose. Ceiling fan and brass light fittings, green velvet chairs, napkins, white table linen. It has the usual curries and accompaniments on the menu including, we're told, fresh scampi on request in the curries. But we think this is unique . . . You may order the 'Staff Curry' but please order the day before, so head chef Motin Uddin, can make extra portions. Takeaway: 10% discount. Hours: 12-1.30pm/6-11pm; closed Tues. Stocks Cobra.

Stowmarket

ROYAL TANDOORI INTERNATIONAL ©

16-18 Tavern Street, Stowmarket 01449 674392

M Ahmed and S Miah's 60-seater is situated in a white Georgian building, in two blue and pink rooms with matching curtains and carpet. Formula curry house, seats 60. 'Waited fifteen minutes for our takeaway in well-lit restaurant. Good decor, pleasant ansd efficient service. Food excellent, generous portions and reasonable prices. The Maya Khalia Chicken was worth the extra cost, tasty and highly flavoured. Very comprehensive menu which we would like to work our way through.' NDS. 'Food is gorgeous.' PJ. 'Once I got used to the idea of curry gravy with Chicken Jalfrezi, it was decidedly delicious.' LG. Thursday: 10% discount in restaurant, 20% takeaway. Price check: Papadam 60p, CTM £6.95, Pullao Rice £1.60. Lager £2.50 pint. Hours: 12-2.30pm/6-11.30pm.

Woodbridge

ROYAL BENGAL TOP 100 ©

6 Quay Street, Woodbridge 01394 387983

Mr Malik's 52-seater remains in our TOP 100, simply because it is CC (currinarily correct) in all departments. Amazingly, in all these years we have never had a complaint (we tempt fate with this comment each time). It must be the only TOP 100 not to have had one. The venue is spotlessly clean, including the toilets. The welcome is warm. The service is efficient, friendly, accurate, and positive. The untoward is handled with experience and tact, such as late arrivals, customer ordering error, spillages and small things that can become big things, such as a corked bottle of wine, spotted by the waiter and removed before comment was needed by the clients. There is nothing over-remarkable about the items on the attractive menu. But everything is here, and everything is cooked well, and everything is above average. Even the departure is handled well. Customer care is uppermost. A curryhouse should be a place where locals can be comfortable, unwind, enjoy and not feel overcharged. This restaurant is all of these things. And if other restaurants modelled themselves on these simple rules everyone would be a TOP 100 restaurant, but then I suppose there would be no need for our Guide at all. Congratulations to you, Mr Malik and your staff. Here's just one of many comments received: 'Of the restaurants in your guide, this is the restaurant I enjoyed the most.' SS. Price check: Papadam 45p, CTM £6.95, Pullao Rice £1.50. Lager £2.70 pint. Hours: 12-2pm/6-11pm.

SURREY

Area: Home Counties (south of London)
Population: 1,057,000
Adjacent Counties: Berks, Hants,
Kent, London, Sussex

Parts of Surrey were absorbed by Greater London in 1965. We note affected boroughs with the letters GL.

Ashtead

MOGHUL DYNASTY ©

1 Craddock Parade, Ashtead 01372 274810

Established in '86, managed by Adbul Mannan. Nicely decorated in cream with white pillars, table linen, green plants, wooden chairs with blue velvet seating, colonial fans. Formula curry house, CTM being most popular. Takeaway: orders over £12, 10% off. Minimum charge: £8.50. Hours: 12-2.30pm/5.30-11pm.

Bookham

SAFFRON GARDEN NEW ENTRANT

Guildford Road, Bookham, Leatherhead 01372 459256

'Building was originally a red brick house and later adapted, can hardly been seen from the Road, and is pretty unprepossessing, car parking is limited, can only be entered by the service road running parallel to the main Leatherhead/Guildford Road, (A246). Outside looks very uninteresting, but the interior is all beams and attractive furniture. Extensive menu, but usual dishes. Food well above average overall, Brinjal Bhaji excellent, Meat Bhuna disappointing. Probably the best Indian restaurant in our immediate vicinity. Visited with a friend who professed not to like curry, frog-marched in. The one waiter was marvellous and made us welcome and lots of cheerful humour. Full marks – wish there were more like him. The food was excellent. Couldn't dissuade our guest from starting with Prawn Cocktail but did manage to tempt him to a Chicken Korma. I think we won, he ate it all and declared it very good. Danny's Butter Chicken was superb, my KP Special, very rich mild sauce with Malibu liqueur, hardly traditional but very successful.' H&DRC. 'Set well back from the street, is difficult to see until you are almost on it. Interior has been fitted out in a kind of mock-Tudor style with timbering. I was struck by how well ordered and inviting everything looked. Freshly laundered tablecloths and napkins. Manager and waiter pleasant and friendly. Onion Bhajia quite outstanding, followed by Madras meat, Brinjal Bhajee and Pullao Rice, all excellent. On the debit side, glass of house wine (drinkable plonk) had the capacity of not much more than a couple of after-dinner coffee-cups, which at £2.50 a time I thought a rip-off. Despite this, restaurant deserves to be in the *Guide*.' CB.

Burgh Heath

A217 TAKEAWAY NEW ENTRANT

9 The Parade, Bright Road, Burgh Heath 01737 359400

Alix Ali opened his takeaway in 1999 and serves Bangladeshi formula curries. Specials: Sali Boti £5.95 – lamb with dry apricot in medium curry sauce. Battered Aloo £2.10. Coconut Rice £2.20. Delivery: £10, local. Takeaway: 10% discount over £12. Hours: 5.30-11pm.

Byfleet

RED ROSE OF BYFLEET ©

148-150 High Road, Byfleet 01932 355559

An attractively decorated restaurant, with plaster cornices and dado rails. Ivy and palms divide tables and chandeliers hang from the ceilings. King Prawn dishes are house specialities. Average prices. Managing partner, Shuel Miah, enjoys giving a red rose to the lady on departure. Hours: 12-2.30pm/6-11.30pm. Branches: Gaylord, Weybridge; Red Rose, of Surbiton, Red Rose of Chessington.

Camberley

ANCIENT RAJ NEW ENTRANT

9 The Parade, High Street, Frimley, Camberley 01276 21503

'First visit – parking no problem. Very spacious, large restaurant – looks like two shop units knocked into one – very busy. Full of groups who were clearly well known to the staff. Menu extensive, nice to see new things to try like Roshneys. Kingfisher on draught £3.20 a pint – ouch! Food well cooked and presented but service a little slow as they were very busy. Gill tried

Green Vegetable Cashewnut Korma £6.50 – very good. We will return as we like the choice on the menu, food good and staff friendly and well trained.' SM. 'A great many regular customers, myself included. Excellent vast menu, each dish tastes and looks as described and never varies, generous portions, good value for money.' HH. Stocks Cobra.

FRIMLEY TANDOORI TAKEAWAY ©

47 High Street, Frimley, Camberley 01276 685537

Bengali takeaway established '85 by Hassan Ahmed (manager) and Hussain Ahmed (chef). 'As ever the service was impeccable. Vegetable Madras was beautifully spiced, naan bread was light and fluffy, sag aloo superb. I challenge you not to be delighted by your overall experience! If you are a vegetarian like I am, it is refreshing to have a restaurant who are willing to create a curry to your requirements. A restaurant which clearly values its customers' loyalty. To date I have received nothing but exemplary service coupled with outstanding food. Staff are always willing to tailor dishes to your palate, and as a vegetarian I find their helpfulness very refreshing. Nothing less than outstanding. WS. Popular lunch specials: Chicken Tikka Roll or Kebab Roll. Luncheon Vouchers accepted. Hours: 12-2pm/6-11.30pm.

NEW DIWAN-EE-KHAS NEW ENTRANT

413 London Road, Camberley 01276 20359

One of our regular prolific reporters tells us many times how much he and his partner love this place, which is fine by us (we can never hear these things too often), so let's tell you. MG says: 1. 'My favourite local. Robbie had a Methi Gosht which he thought was better than his mum makes (Robbie is Indian). I had a good old Lamb Madras – stunning. Get it back in the guide!' 2: 'Lovely fresh dips with papadoms. Excellent starters, Prawn Puree was meal in itself.' 3: 'There's no doubt about it, being a regular in a favoured curry house does mean you get better treatment and food. On the other hand, fate will definitely decree that not everything is always hunkydory. 'Two further visits proves this point: 'On one occasion my main dish was disappointing. And on another occasion we had to wait 40 minutes for our main course because they were giving priority to takeaway customers.' 4: 'Spicy, pungent and honest food served by a friendly efficient staff at very reasonable prices. Plus they do an all-day Sunday buffet at £4.95.' 5: 'Achieved Nirvana. Popadoms were followed by a Prawn Patia and Chicken Tikka, both very nice, but no reason to write to the *GCG* – but the mains were extraordinary. My Lamb Methi Gosht was the best yet, vast and smouldering, tastes of clove and fenugreek, garlic and something else, kind of burnished. Definitely Olympian. Linda's Chicken Murgh was red and oniony and deliciously different. Service impeccable. We staggered out more stuffed than a Paratha!' 6: 'Back to the New Diwan e Kas for a Methi Gosht from paradise. Stupendous 2 course meal for five with Indian lager came to £68. You can't beat this place. TOP 100.' 7: 'Staggering Chicken Tikka at £2.75 (Linda didn't like the cloves in her two Samosas!) – Picky. Best Lamb Madras ever at £4.30, hot and succulent – loads of it. Boiled rice and two enormous chapathis completed my meal. Linda's vegetable Thali was uneven but over all very good – she loves their dhall.' M&LG. Stocks Cobra.

RAJ TANDOORI NEW ENTRANT

366 Yorktown Road, College Town, Camberley 01276 33224

'A nice meal in relaxed surroundings. Lots of novel items on the menu, like Kulcha Chicken or Lamb. Our only thumbs down was the Veggy Biriani.' S&GM. Stocks Cobra.

RAJPUR ©

57d Mytchett Road, Mytchett, Camberley 01252 542063

Manager Abdul Motin tells us his 46-seater is 'plush with Bengali paintings, comfortable cushioned seating, and a bright interior.' You tell us: 'Service and food is always of the highest standard. Quantities on large side. Comfort, decor, reception, service and ambience very good, thoroughly recommended. Best in area. CC Discount given even though we didn't ring before or book a table.' RGB. 'Had the phone put down on me twice when trying to book. Never did succeed in booking! Turned up anyway to find the restaurant is one of five takeaways/restaurants/off licences all sharing a tight parking area immediately in front. Unable to find anywhere where I felt I could safely park, I went to Tariq's instead! I am sure the restaurant would have lived up to its Guide entry had I been able to enter!' S&GM. 'Have tried to get in here, but parking a problem. Solved by going on Sunday lunchtime for buffet. Quite well patronised, buffet selection varied and frequently topped up. Chutneys and relishes fresh. Nice to see restaurant appealed to the older generation – which I think says a lot for its atmosphere and service. One criticism – food could have been hotter.' SM. Special: Bangladesh Style Tandoori Masala, tandoori chicken, boneless, thick mild spicy sauce. Banquets Weds. evenings £9.95. CC members 10% discount. Takeaway: 10% off. Sunday buffet lunch £6.50, £3.95 kids. Hours: 12-3.30pm/6-11pm.

COBRA GOOD CURRY GUIDE
County Index, see page 5 Town Index, see page 614
A to Z of the Curry Menu, page 41 Contributors Key, page 604

TARIQ'S INDIAN BRASSERIE

369 London Road, Camberley 01276 66441

'As a brasserie we had expected it to be more "westernised", but we were pleasantly surprised to find it tastefully decorated in traditional curry house style. Service good, quality of the food excellent and well presented. Particularly liked the Channa Dhal side dish.' S&GM. Home-delivery service available.' WPS. Price check: Papadam 35p, CTM £6.20, Pullao Rice £1.60. Hours: Mon.-Sat. lunch & dinner; Sun. dinner only. Stocks Cobra.

Carshalton GL

ROSE HILL TANDOORI ©

320 Wrythe Lane, Rose Hill Carshalton 020 8644 9793

A wee 30-seater, est. 1982, owned by Salequr Rahman, manager Mr E Rahman, and unusually at a formula curry house, a lady chef, Mrs Rahman – a family business. And I bet if you ask she'll cook really authentic Bangladeshi food. I see Confederates' Coffee, made with Southern Comfort – nice one! Delivery: £12 minimum, 1½-mile radius. Minimum charge: £7 per head. Hours: 12-2pm/5.30pm-12am. Stocks Cobra.

Cobham

COBHAM TANDOORI NEW ENTRANT

12c Anyards Road, Cobham 01932 863842

Well established, popular and competent curry house enjoyed by its locals. Service, customer care and food are all above average, without being over-priced. Stocks Cobra.

SPICY CHIMNEY NAME CHANGE ©

40 Portsmouth Road, Cobham 01932 863666

Abdul Alam and PH Choudhry's 72-seater is in two rooms of a quaint old building with lots of little alcoves, wooden beams decorated in peach and dusky apricot with rich damask tablecloths with matching napkins, and a fresh flower on each table. Chef Shaid Miah's 'menu is marvellous. Popadoms and relishes very good, one Popadom provided with the compliments of the waiter. King Prawn Suka, a large prawn pan-fried with a lovely thick, rich, slightly sweet and very oniony sauce. Onion Bhajias, four smallish spheres, very well spiced and not too stodgy. Butter Chicken, excellent. Pullao Rice, lovely texture. Nan, circular, quite light and deep. Salmon Kedgeree, unusual and good, very large plateful, spoiled by a large pile of inappropriate salad, served with thick lentil dhal. Brinjal Stuffed, two small aubergines, split, spread with spices and served in a rich creamy sauce, very good, not seen before. Service was absolutely first class, a very personable young waiter with a large smile, a full knowledge of the menu and competence added a great deal to the evening.' HC. Sunday lunch £7.95. £8.95 wine. Delivery: £15 minimum order, 3-mile radius. Hours: 12-2.30pm/6-11.30pm. Stocks Cobra.

Cranleigh

CURRY INN ©

214 High Street, Cranleigh 01483 273992

Bangladeshi formula curry restaurant, smart, bamboo chairs, palm trees, sugar pink table linen. Seats 93 diners, Bhel Puri dishes are most popular, well spiced with lemon, mint, bay leaves, methi (fenugreek) and dallcani (cinnamon), from £6. 16 car parking spaces at back of restaurant. Curry Club members: 10% discount. Sunday lunch £6.95. Hours: 12-3pm/6-11.30pm. Stocks Cobra.

Croydon GL

(Includes Addington Hamsey Green, Selsdon and Shirley)

BANANA LEAF ©

27 Lower Addiscombe Road, Croydon 020 8688 0297

Taken over in '97 by Mr D Sitha Raman. Masala Dosa is the most ordered dish. 'Not very familiar with South Indian food, decided to experiment. A small restaurant, tidy, clean and fresh. Friendly waiters. Pappadams, huge, crisp and fresh served with a variety of dips and onion salad. Bonda, hot, crisp, sensitively spiced with a small bowl of curry sauce. Onion Dosai , freshly cooked with golden onions and fresh coconut chutney. King Prawn Fried, certainly had a good kick. I paid by credit card and when the slip was presented to me the bottom line had been filled in, pleased me tremendously!' LH. We had a lovely meal – Idle, Masala Dosai and a Mushroom and Spinach Dry Masala but my partner decided to have a pint of draught Cobra with his meal. Foolishly we did not check the price and were astounded at £3.50.' JD. Hours: 12-2.30pm/6-11pm. Stocks Cobra.

THE DEANS BYO

241 London Road, Croydon 020 8665 9192

The Deans opened in 1993 and is named after its chef-owner Salam Ud Din and manager Zaka Ud Din. It is a massive, fully-licensed restaurant seating over 150 diners in two dining rooms, decorated in white with the 'sparkly' mosaic mirror Indian arches to be found in the Moghul palaces. It has a small but typically authentic Pakistani Punjabi menu, serving tandoori items and well-spiced curries. RE tells us of four visits: 1: 'A large busy restaurant favoured by Asians. Also does a very brisk takeaway. Apart from the papadoms (they are grilled which I don't like), the food is excellent. Lamb Nihari was "special" – very tender, quite hot with a distinctive ginger flavour. Lovely dish.' 2. 'Happy to go back as I was in the area. Seekh Kebabs freshly cooked and spicy, Chicken Tikka fresh and moist. Service is efficient and friendly.' 3. 'Third time is supposed to be lucky – not this time. Seekh Kebabs and Chicken Tikka were fine, but the Dhall Gosht, so good last time, was awful – undercooked meat in a pale, tasteless sauce. A chap on the next table was complaining that his curry was far too salty. A shame. I will (eventually) go back, but not for some time.' 4, 'After a culinary disaster last time, I decided to give Deans one more try – Glad I did. Seekh Kebabs were great, in a hot iron plate with fried onions. Haandi Dhall Gosht – very good, hot, spicy, full of flavour and very tender meat. Service good and friendly, busy with families. Slight moan – 660ml Cobra £4.' Specials: Handi dishes, chicken £4.90, Methi Gosht £5. Handi Aloo Chana £3.50, Dhal-stuffed Karela (bitter gourd) £5. BYO no corkage. Price check: Papadam 30p, CTM £5.50, Pullao Rice £1.50. House wine £7.50. Delivery: £10 min, 3-miles. Hours: 12-2.30pm/6-11.30pm (10.30pm on Sun.). Stocks Cobra.

KHYBER NEW ENTRANT

284-288 High Street, Croydon 020 8686 1729

Fully licensed and air conditioned. 'Friends' recommendation. First impressions – very polite staff, clean, separate smoking area. Four Popadoms were served with Mint Raitha and Onion Chutney – no lime pickle. Starters – Aloo Chat £2.95 – OK, but nothing special – bread greasy. Begum Masala £2.95 – excellent, aubergine not sour, the batter soft but not greasy. Main course – Lamb Pasanda £5.95 – tender, but gravy not almond sauce, Gosht Deccan £4.50 – very tender, slightly spiced, recommended, Bombay Aloo £2.25 – could not be faulted, Pullao Araske Dehlvi £1.60, Garlic £1.35 – not enough garlic and Peshwari Nan – superb, fresh, hot and sweet – were all served onto your plate – with no plate warmers thus was piled up onto your plate – very poor show. Hot towels provided.' MPW. Price check: Papadam 50p, Pullao Rice £1.60, Peshwari Nan £1.35. Hours: 12-2.30pm/6pm-12am (Sun. to 11.30pm). Stocks Cobra.

PANAHAR NEW ENTRANT ©

316 Limpsfield Road, Hamsey Green, Croydon 020 8651 9663

First opened in 1999 with a fund raising dinner attended by over 100 guests, making over £6,500 for the Mayor of Croydon's charities. Seats 120. Price check: Papadam 45p, CTM £6.25, Pullao Rice £1.55, Peshwari Nan £1.85, Lager £3.15 pint. Takeaway: 10% discount. Hours: 12-2.30pm/6-11pm. Stocks Cobra.

PLANET SPICE NEW ENTRANT **NEW TO OUR TOP 100**

88 Selsdon Park, Addington, Croydon 020 8651 3300

This trendily named 90. seater opened in 1999 and, being owned by Emdad Rahman of London SE23's TOP 100 Barbur, it has a lot going for it, especially with cooking by chefs Hardev Bhatty ex Chutney Mary and Kirti Rawat, ex chef to the President of India. A modern looking restaurant with bright, contemporary decor and furniture – not Indian at all. Speciality starters include: Patra £2.50 – arvi leaves layered with a spicy chick pea paste, steamed, sliced and deep-fried. Aloo Choff £2.50 – mashed potatoes and vegetables rolled in cashew nuts then fried till golden. Main courses include: Sali Jardaloo £5.95 – pieces of lamb with apricot and honey sprinkled with potatoes. Shugati Masala £5.95 – chicken with masala sauce, coconut and white poppy seeds. 'I rate very highly, though it is pricey i.e: £30 a head. Pianist playing light background music.' CC. Live music with Graham Jones, Monday, Tuesday and Wednesday evenings. Sunday brunch £9.95 adults, £5.95 for kids age 7 to 12, free for kids under 7 – let their regular magician entertain the whole family. Price check: Papadam £1, CTM £7.25, Pullao Rice £1.95, Peshwari Nan £1.95, Lager £3.50 pint. Takeaway: approximately 15% discount. Delivery: 2½ miles. Hours: 12.30-2.30pm; 6.30-11.30pm. Fax: 020 8651 4400 or www.planet-spice.com. Branch: Barbur, SE23. Stocks Cobra.

RUPEES TAKEAWAY ©

184 Wickham Road, Shirley, Croydon 020 8655 1866

Enamul Karim Khan and chef Chand Miah's takeaway offers a view of the clean, tidy, well organised open kitchen. Specials: Lamb Chop Bhuna. Chilli Nan. Delivery: £8 minimum, 4-mile radius. Hours: 5-11pm.

SHEESH MAHAL NEW ENTRANT ©

10 Lower Addiscombe Road, Croydon 020 8688 6239

Established in 1963. The current owner Mr Islam has been serving to three generations of customers. Head chef is an award winner of the Croydon Curry Chef of the Year Competition both in 1998 and 1999. Seats 32. Price check: Papadam 45p, CTM £5.20, Pullao Rice £1.55, Peshwari Nan £1.65, Lager £3.50 pint. Takeaway: 10% discount. Delivery: £9.50 minimum, 3-mile radius. Hours: 12-3pm/6pm to late. Stocks Cobra.

SURUCHI NEW ENTRANT ©

120 Headley Drive, New Addington 01689 841998

Established in 1995. 50-seater formula curry house, run by Aklis Miah, with manager Junel Ali. Specials: Lamb Shah Jahani £6.50 – thin slices of lamb seasoned with crushed pistachio nuts, onion and peppers. Chicken Tikka Nan £1.70. Set Dinner: £9. Sunday lunch £6.95. Price check: Papadam 45p, CTM £6, Pullao Rice £1.50. Delivery: £9 minimum, 3-mile radius. Hours: 5.30-11.30pm. Sun. 12-3pm/5.30-11pm. Stocks Cobra.

ZARA'S KITCHEN NEW ENTRANT BYO

60 South End, Croydon 020 8688 0782

'We rather like this restaurant. BYO, tasty vegetarian dishes and friendly service – very popular.' JD.

Dorking

NEW CURRY GARDEN NEW ENTRANT

41 South Street, Dorking 01306 889648

'Decor very striking, minimalist and modern, plain wood floor, bright walls and unusual squiggly light fittings. Food outstandingly good. Only one niggle, on main course did not come with the rest – caused manager great concern and much animated ticking-off of the staff. Excellent service – very enjoyable experience.' H&DRC.

MOGHUL

187 High Street, Dorking 01306 876296

The best in town, says PW: 'Wide choice of meals consumed, all up to usual high standards.' Stocks Cobra.

©	Curry Club Discount	U	Unlicensed
V	Vegetarian	ANP	Alcohol not permitted
e-a-m-a-y-l	Eat as much as you like	BYO	Bring your own alcohol

CURRY CLUB

East Molesey

GOLDEN CURRY ©

19 Hampton Court Parade, East Molesey — 020 8979 4358

A Aziz's traditionally decorated 52-seater has been going since 1967. Three generations of regulars go for a stable, quality operation and friendly service, led by head waiter Abdul Karim. Sunday lunch £4.95. Minimum charge: £6. Takeaway: 10% off. Hours: 12-2.30pm/6pm-12am. Stocks Cobra.

NEW ANARKALI NEW ENTRANT

158-160 Walton Road, East Molesey — 020 8979 5072

Serves delights such as Goshtaba – a Kashmiri dish of (paté-like) meat balls in light curry gravy. Bengal Roop Chanda – pomfret curry. Peswari Chicken – chicken cooked in the tandoor and served with a curry sauce of garlic, ginger, coriander and yoghurt.

PALACE INDIAN CUISINE ©

20 Bridge Road, East Molesey — 020 8979 1531

E Eshad's 60-seater is yards from Hampton Court Palace. 'It's a wonderful place for a leisurely meal in a conservatory, perfect for warm summer evenings.' DD. Chef's special: Murag Tikka Rajella, yoghurt based, spicy cooked with massala sauce and fresh garden mint. Minimum charge: £8. Takeaway: 10% discount. Delivery: £12 minimum, 2-mile radius. Hours: 12-2.30pm/6-11.30pm. Stocks Cobra.

Epsom

EPSOM BALTI HOUSE NEW ENTRANT

26 South Street, Epsom — 01372 747425

Fully licensed and air conditioned. 'Restaurant excellent, nice decor and large round tables for four people. Attentive service without being annoying, traditional style Indian dishes – excellent. Popadoms crisp and hot. Shami Kebabs £2.50 – small, nothing special. Prawn Puri £2.95 and KP Butterfly £3.50 – excellent. Main courses well presented. Meat Thali, superb. Colleagues spoke highly of Chicken Chilli Masala £5.95 and Balti Chicken Shashlik £5.95. Food washed down with ice cold Cobra. Well worth a visit!' DJL. Takeaway: 10% discount. Price check: Papadam 45p, CTM £5.95, Pullao Rice £1.75. Hours: 12- 2.30pm/6pm-12am (Sun. to 11.30pm). Stocks Cobra.

LE RAJ TOP 100

211 Firtree Road, Epsom Downs 01737 371371

Owner chef Enam Ali's 110 seater Le Raj is in outer Epsom (it's on the A240/A2022) in a line of shop fronts. To put the record straight, my report in our last Guide upset Enam because in my well-meaning attempt to credit him with the building up and chairmanship of the Guild of Bangladeshi Caterers, I mistakenly stated that it was the rival 'other' organisation. This also upset Mr Choudhury of the BCA and they both accosted me at an industry launch at La Porte des Indes to tell me that the 1999 Guide was full of errors. Other than the above, which was careless of me, and for which I have apologised in print, they were unable to tell me what those errors were, so we remain in the dark, I fear. I also said last time that Enam's cooking helped by chef Ajaib Kahn is 'light and innovative', and I returned Le Raj to the TOP 100, because of this. And, although we have received not a single report on Le Raj in the last 24 months, I'm keeping it there in the TOP 100. Incidentally, ask for it spicy if that's how you like things. Specials include such dishes as Bahar E Sammunder, Bangladeshi fresh water fish cooked with fresh herbs, Murgh E Shandan, delicate strips of supreme chicken in a hot fragrant sauce. Sabzi Halim, mixed vegetable cooked in lentils, lime juice and chilli. Minimum charge: £15. Hours: 12-2.30pm/5.30-11pm.

Farnham

BANARAS

40 Downing Street, Farnham 01252 734081

Established in 1990, MA Rahman's smart 60 seater is decorated in pink and white. 'All the food we had was more than acceptable, but the decor was the best thing about the restaurant and the service was a particular let-down.' HJC. Special: Karahi Duck Tikka, marinated in a thick sauce, cooked and served in a cast iron dish £9.95. Minimum charge: £10.50. Sunday lunch £8.95. Price check: Papadam 45p, CTM £7.95, Pullao Rice £1.95, Peshwari Nan £1.95, Lager £3.25 pint. House wine £7.50. Hours: 12-2pm/6-11.30pm. Sun. Buffet lunch: 12-2.30pm. Branches: Darjeeling, Farnham, Surrey. Viceroy, High Street, Hartley Witney, Hampshire. Stocks Cobra.

DARJEELING ©

25 South Street, Farnham 01252 714322

MA Rahman and S Islam's 46-seater is stylishly decorated, with mahogany wood panelling everywhere, brass plates decorate the walls and there is a large brass peacock in the window. 'Everything about this restaurant is good. The decor is subtle, low light, tropical fish. Good carpeting and sumptuous table linen and crockery. The menu is extensive. Service is very good. Waiters are friendly but unobtrusive. Food is excellent, subtly spiced, generous portions, excellent quality. Continues to be our favourite restaurant.' JW. Special: Garlic Chilli Chicken. Takeaway: over £15, 10% off. Set dinner £26 for two. Minimum charge: £15. Hours: 12-2pm/6-11.30pm. Branches: Banaras, Farnham. Viceroy, Hartley Witney, Hants.

Fetcham

FETCHAM TANDOORI RE-ENTRANT

248 Cobham Road, Fetcham 01372 374927

'What a lovely surprise. Good atmosphere, excellent and friendly service and really good food. Extensive menu, usual dishes, interesting vegetables. Full marks for fish curry being made with boal. All sensible portions, well cooked. Mango Sorbet, very good.' HJC.

Guildford

CINNAMONS NEW ENTRANT

4-5 Chapel Street, Guildford 01483 300626

'A great year 2000 addition to dining in Guildford. Decor very open, light and modern, could be any cuisine. Menu very appealing. Good, friendly service, all young men dressed in identical blue shirts and trendy ties. Food outstandingly good, attractively served in white china dishes and in sensible rather than generous portions. Only grumble, delivery of food unacceptably slow. They did apologise and offered free liqueurs. Espresso coffee served with good quality chocolates. No Indian desserts. Definitely wish to return.' HC. Takeaway: 20% discount. Price check: Papadam 60p, CTM £6.95, Pullao Rice £1.95, Peshwari Nan £2.25. Website: www.cinnamons. co.uk. Hours: 12-2.30pm/6-11.30pm.

CURRY CORNER NEW ENTRANT ©

86 Haydon Place, Guildford 01483 453437

Established in 1998. Seats 40. Banquet nights: Tues. and Thurs – from £15.95 for two. Specials: Chicken Achari £6.25 – a fiery dish, chicken in hot and sour sauce made from dry red chillies and vinegar. Price check: Papadam

50p, CTM £6.25, Pullao Rice £1.75, Peshwari Nan £1.95, Lager £2.50 pint. Delivery: £10 minimum, 5-mile radius. Hours: 12-2.30pm/5.30-11.30pm. Stocks Cobra.

MERROW DYNASTY NEW ENTRANT

261 Epsom Road, Merrow, Guildford 01483 562190

'Just popped in for small meal Sunday lunchtime. Had wonderful tasting prawn and meat dhansaks, with fragrant rice and aloo sag. Their buffet wasn't up and running although they offered to serve it at the table for the same price (£7.95). Wish we were hungrier. Will definitely go again.' M&LG.

RUM WONG THAI NEW ENTRANT

16 London Road, Guildford 01483 536092

One of the few Thai restaurants to be in the *Guide*, and this one is an exceptional restaurant. It not only does superb Thai food, it has a Thai grocery/cookware shop attached (though the shop is only open 9am-5pm, but not Sun and Mon). It is advisable to book a table; whenever we have been it has always been well patronised. Traditionally dressed in silk dresses, the Thai waitresses welcome you and show you to a table – smoking and non-smoking sections. One of my particular favourites is their mixed starters where you can try about four different starters – these are not advertised on the menu, so please ask. Two other dishes which Pat and I must have are Tom Yum soup – hot and sour with prawns or chicken and Pad Thai – rice noodles with bean sprouts, peanuts, palm sugar, prawns and crab meat – delicious! both done true to Thai form. But then I love their curries, and their salads and everything!

Haslemere

MAYAS NEPALESE NEW ENTRANT

64 Weyhill, Haslemere 01428 653568

Opened in 1999 on the site of the Krishna. Completely refurbished and very smart, with red deep-pile carpet, Nepalese art, discreet lighting and cane chairs. Nepalese food on offer, try the Bara £3.50 – ground black lentils with spices, pan-fried served with Achar (pickle) – very good, spicy. Aloo Achar £3.25 – cubes of potato, cucumber, green peas mixed with light curry sauce, served cold – not to everyone's taste, though I liked it very much. Momo £4.25 – minced pork wrapped in flour dough and steam cooked, served with

Achar – rather like dim sum, again perhaps not to everyone's taste but interesting. There are no curry house formula curries on the menu, just fabulous Nepalese food. Tarai Kukhura £7.95 – from the southern borders of Nepal, chicken with mustard and black pepper sauce – Pat likes this dish. Mayalu Kakhura £7.50 – boneless chicken with tomato sauce and cream – rather like CTM only much nicer, though a little mild for me. Khorsani Kukhur £6.75 – hot and spicy with fresh green chilli, tomato and fenugreek – another dish Pat likes. But one we didn't was Garlic Khasi Khorsani £7.75 – battered fried lamb with garlic, ginger, onion, pepper and chilli garlic sauce and soy – an unauthentic cross of Chinese and Indian flavours, it didn't work for us – but perhaps it will for you. The Rato Seeme £3.50 – red kidney beans in 'Zimbu' herbs was lovely, as was the Patina Roti (mint bread) £2.25 – which came to the table sliced with shredded fresh mint leaves sprinkled on top. Delivery: 5-mile radius, £15 minimum, no delivery on Mon. or Sun. Takeaway: 15% discount. Price check: Papadam 60p, Boiled Rice £2.25, Gulio Roti (sweet nan) £2.50. Hours: 12-2.30pm/5.30-11.30pm.

Horley

THE CURRY INN NEW ENTRANT

5 Central Parade, Massetts Road, Horley 01293 784888

'Attentive staff keen to advise on the menu. Food was excellent. I particularly recommend the Curry Inn special main dish – an exotic concoction based on chicken tikka but with fresh and tasty spices added. I notice that Sussex is poorly represented in the latest guide, and urge you to include this establishment in the next issue.' MSJ. Done, sir, but Horley is in Surrey (on the border), so I can't help with boosting Sussex with this one! [Reports from diners will help.] In fact I've been to the Curry Inn myself for a desperation curry after a highly delayed flight finally landed at Gatwick at 10pm. I scraped in late, very near closing time, but was welcomed with friendly service and a thoroughly admirable formula curry with all the perks. Stocks Cobra.

FORT RAJ BALTI RESTAURANT ©

74 Victoria Road, Horley 01293 822909

Established in 1995, Shah Ali Athar and Abdul Khan's Fort is a 74-seater (party room 32). Chef Ali Mokoddus's Specials include Balti Chicken or Lamb Tikka Shankapuri (£6.95), whose sauce contains coconut and red wine, and Tava Murg (a light and healthy stirfried dish, delicately cooked with special herbs and spices, and flambéed with white wine). 'Portions large and well-presented. Service very friendly. Decor is tasteful.' MR&MRS DNL. Minimum charge: £6.50. Price check: Papadam 50p, CTM £7.95, Pullao Rice £1.75, Peshwari Nan £1.75, Lager £3.20. Takeaway: 15-20% discount. Delivery: £15 min, 3-mile radius. Hours: 12-2.30pm; 6pm-12am. Stocks Cobra.

Kew GL

ZARANJ NEW ENTRANT

279 Sandycombe Road, Kew 020 8332 0754

'I am surprised that the Zaranj is not in your book. We enjoyed it many, many times when we lived in Richmond.' KLJ. Reports please from those who still use it.

Kingston-upon-Thames GL

MONTYS TANDOORI ©

53 Fife Road, Kingston 020 8546 1724

70-seater Nepalese restaurant, owned by Kishor Shrestha. South Indian face-masks decorate the white walls and hang from cream drapes. Hand-painted silk pictures of Indian scenes cover the walls, the floor is tiled. Specials: Nepalese Murgh Masala, chicken on the bone. 'Service is excellent, unobtrusive, polite and no mistakes. Food is plentiful and piping hot.' ST. Takeaway: 10% off. Hours: 12-2.30pm/6pm-12am.

Leatherhead

LAL QILLA TANDOORI NEW ENTRANT

207a Kingston Road, Leatherhead 01372 376715

'We went to the Lal Qilla years ago, and returned recently to a restaurant double the size. Menu is fairly extensive but nothing very unusual. Food took ages to arrive and Danny was not at all impressed with his Butter Chicken. But I think all the other dishes were more than adequate in quality and quantity. Prices fairly average. No quibbles about anything except the slow service, but I think this could be rectified easily with a few more staff.' H&DRC.

Morden GL

INDIAN VILLAGE NEW ENTRANT ©

10 Morden Court Parade, London Road, Morden 020 8640 8556

44-seater, fully licensed and air conditioned, established in 1998, whose decor includes fruit trees and flowers. Specials: Salmon Samosas £2.95. Stuffed Coco Yam Leaves £2.95 – patra leaves spread with a spicy paste, rolled and steamed, sliced and deep-fried (Pat particularly likes this dish). Boal £7.45 – a fresh water fish marinated in coriander sauce. 'My wife and I took our four daughters for a special occasion night, owner treated us so very well. Food really cooked well and portions just right. £128 for six (inc Champagne)' RL. Delivery: £15 minimum. Price check: Papadam 50p, CTM £5.95, Pullao Rice £1.65, Peshwari Nan £1.65, Lager £2.50 pint. Delivery: £15 minimum. Hours: 5.30-11.30pm; closed Mon. Stocks Cobra.

Motspur Park GL

MOTSPUR TANDOORI ©

365 West Road, Motspur Park 020 8949 4595

Established in 1982. Seats 70. Plans to refurbish in 2001. Specials include: Machley Jhol £6.99 (fish cooked in an authentic style with fresh coriander and onions, and with a blend of light spices). Price check: Papadam 55p, CTM £6.99, Pullao Rice £1.95, Peshwari Nan £1.75, Lager £2.95 pint. Takeaway: 10% discount. Delivery: £12 minimum, 3-mile radius. Hours: 12-2pm; 6-11.30pm. Stocks Cobra.

New Malden GL

CHARLIE'S INDIAN CUISINE NEW ENTRANT ©

276 Burlington Road, New Malden 020 8949 7476

Established in 1975, taken over by Mr Faruque and Mr Hoque in 1998. Previously called Shannon Tandoori. Seats 42. Air conditioned. Specials: Murgh Rezala £5.50 – chicken with green chillies, hot. Peshwari Chicken £5.50 – hot and fruity. Price check: Papadam 50p, CTM £5.50, Pullao Rice £1.75, Peshwari Nan £1.85, Lager £2.50 pint. Takeaway: 10-15% discount. Delivery: £12 minimum, 3-mile radius. Hours: 12-2.30pm/5.30-11pm; closed Mon. Stocks Cobra (£1.90 small, £3.50 large).

Newdigate

ALI RAJ NEW ENTRANT

Parkgate Road, Newdigate 01306 631664/631057

A very pleasant find in a small village, run by Laikat Ali, whose branches in Kent are equally enjoyed by their local regulars. Service, customer care and food are all above average, without being at arm-and-leg prices. Branches: Bombay Cuisine, 61 High Street, West Malling, Maidstone, Kent and Planet Spice, 5 Sevenoaks Road, Borough Green, Kent.

Oxted

GURKHA KITCHEN AWARD WINNER AND TOP 100

111 Station Road, East Oxted 01883 722621

Oxted town is divided by the railway, like Woking, which is very irritating. We drove up and down Station Road West twice before we realised about the other Station Road, not so easily reached by car, on the other side of the tracks. We arrived at 8pm and our coats were taken immediately by the waiter, who sat us in the reception/waiting area. The bench-style sofa was made very comfortable by large Nepalese patchwork and embroidered cushions; we ordered aperitifs. The floor is boarded, which makes it slightly noisy, but the whole look is very elegant. Beautiful hand-forged black steel chairs, the seat and back were wickered, the seat then covered in a small patterned carpet with a fringe on two sides. White linen tablecloths and napkins, large, fragile wine glasses, drinking receptacles for the connoisseur, their slender stems making a lovely bottle of Argentinian Norton red wine the more enjoyable. I asked our waiter if a lot get broken. 'Yes,' he said proudly, 'and I break the most.' At the back of the restaurant an area is decorated with a small roof as in a Nepalese village, fishing net and basket hanging from the wall. The food is perfectly cooked Nepalese fare. But it isn't earthy village food. It's slightly evolved and modern, yet indisputably Nepalese. 'The accolade by the (1999) *Guide* prompted this visit, and yes, it's spot on. Extremely interesting menu with not one dish that appears on a standard high street curry house menu. We had first class starters: Bhutuwa (excellent melt-in-the-mouth chicken livers stir fried in a delicately spiced light sauce served in a small wafer basket), Vegetable Khaja (filo pastry wrapped up like spring roll, but not so thick with vegetable filling and mint and mustard dressing £2.30. They were cut in half, diagonally, a small green salad with the dressing decorating the centre of the plate, the Khaja in four corners. Extremely mild, but tasty. Main dishes (Mooli Chicken, Piro Lamb and Hariyo Machha – monkfish wrapped in spinach prepared in a mild, dry fruit sauce £7) were all superb, with the flavouring of each being totally different and distinct from the others. Portions not large, but sufficient. Prices marginally higher than average. Waiter could have looked a bit happier.' MW. 'Nepalese cuisine served here in sophisticated modern surroundings. 'A mystery into the unknown as nothing whatsoever on the menu was familiar. However, fortified by large bottles of Kathmandu beer, we chose dishes that sounded good. Couldn't remember what they all were, nicely spiced and tasty. Only the breads were disappointing but perhaps they were meant to be like that – who knows! Well worth a visit, helpful, friendly waiters. Only £60 for three – worth every penny!' CS. 'Palungo Sag, steamed spinach sautéed with fenugreek seeds £2.60; the spinach was fresh. Gurkha Aloo, diced delicately, prepared in turmeric and cummin seeds £2.60, mild potato cubes fried a little brown on the sides. Rashilo Bhat, rice cooked with bay leaf, cardamom, garnished with brown onion £1.95, light, fluffy and flavoursome. Joano Patre, bread with carom seed £2, just like a Nan really, quartered, very good. Golbeda Ko Achar, fresh tomato pickle £1.25, spicy, a good accompaniment to all dishes. Everything was delivered in seperate white china dishes, the plates hot. All the waiters are smartly dressed and polite. For the surroundings, food, aperitifs I was expecting a bill of something around £60, but I was pleasantly surprised at a total of £43.45, service not included' DBAC. A TOP 100 restaurant. No-smoking. Sunday buffet 1-10pm. Hours: 12-2.30pm/6-11pm (11.30pm on Fri. & Sat.).

Purley GL

ROYAL TANDOORI NEW ENTRANT

10 Brighton Road, Purley 020 8763 9960

Beautiful interior by designers Fitch. Menu includes all popular favourites. Stocks Cobra.

Redhill

EXOTICA TANDOORI ©

18 Cromwell Road, Redhill 01737 778624

Chef/owner Ali Shazid's 30-seater is decorated in dark cherry, matching carpet, green plants. Specials: Chicken Chat, small juicy pieces of chicken, cooked in a hot and spicy sauce. Passanda, sliced meat cooked in fresh cream, cultivated yoghurt and ground nuts. Minimum charge: £10. Delivery: 4-miles. Hours: 12-2.30pm/5.30-11.30pm (12am on Fri. & Sat.). Stocks Cobra.

COBRA GOOD CURRY GUIDE
County Index, see page 5 Town Index, see page 614
A to Z of the Curry Menu, page 41 Contributors Key, page 604

Reigate

VILLAGE BRASSERIE ©

10 West Street, Reigate 01737 245695

40-seater fully licensed and air-conditioned curry house owned by MDA. Rashid. It has some South Indian specials, Mossala Dosi (sic.), pancake filled with delicious spicy vegetables, served with salad £2.10. Specials include: Bengal Chicken or Lamb £5.75 – cooked with citrus lemon. Chicken or Lamb Rezala £5.75 – cooked with mince. Green Kebab, spinach, cottage cheese, garlic and ginger cakes £2.50 and Choti Poti, chickpeas, potato, egg, garnished with Bombay Mix £2.50. Sunday buffet £7.25 – kids under twelve £3.25. Banquet Night: every Thursday evening £9.95. House wine £6.80. Sunday lunch £7.25. Delivery: 2-mile radius, £10 minimum. Takeaway: 10% discount. Price check: Papadam 50p, CTM £5.25, Pullao Rice £1.50, Peshwari Nan £1.50. Hours: 5.30-11.30pm; Sun. 12.30-3.30pm/5.30-11pm. Stocks Cobra.

Richmond-upon-Thames GL

LICHFIELD BRASSREIE NEW ENTRANT

13 Lichfield Terrace, Sheen Road, Richmond 020 8332 6704

Restaurants come and restaurants go, in particular, it seems, in Richmond. But one which has stood the test of time is this one, whose welcome extends to the sign over the front door. 'It's one of our locals. It's three miles to walk, so we often drive. Parking is hell though there are parks nearby. But once inside you get a warm welcome and sensible grub. It probably doesn't classify to be in your Guide. It's just a typical curry house, where nothing out of the ordinary takes place on the menu or off it, nor would you want it to.' RL Just the sort of place this *Guide* adores, actually, Ronnie. Stocks Cobra.

Staines

ANCIENT RAJ ©

157 High Street, Staines 01784 457099

Owner-chef Syed Joynul's restaurant is 'appropriate for all occasions, from takeaways to family celebrations'. A stylish setting. Moghul swordsmen decorate the walls. 'I tried a Wednesday evening when the full, standard menu is replaced by a slightly smaller banquet menu – fixed price for a starter, main course, side dish and rice or naan. Aloo chat was very tasty with a good balance of spices, jeera chicken excellent, matter paneer was disappointingly covered in a thick red-coloured sauce.' RH. 'We are impressed with the consistently high standard of well-presented and hot food. Reasonably priced.' SR. Hours: 12-2.30pm/6-11.30pm. Stocks Cobra.

Surbiton GL

AGRA TANDOORI ©

142 Ewell Road, Surbiton 020 8399 8854

Owner-manager HK Paul runs a good and reliable curry house, serving competent curries and their accompaniments. Hours: 12-2.30pm/6pm-12am. Stocks Cobra.

AJANTA ©

114 Ewell Road, Surbiton 020 8399 1262

Rubel Ahmad will help you to find all your favourites. 'Set meal for four, looked good value and so it proved. Huge quantities, good selection of starters, sensitively spiced Lamb Dupioza.' CJC. Hours: 12-2.30pm/6pm-12am. Branches: Shapla, Bristol Road, Selly Oak, and Stratford Road, Shirley, Birmingham. Stocks Cobra.

RAJ ©

163 Ewell Road, Surbiton 020 8390 0251

Aziz Miah's curry house seats 58 and 'offers the best value for money, excellent food, good-sized portions, attentive yet not overbearing waiter service and tasteful decor in clean and comfortable surroundings.' SH. Chef's Choice: Special Garlic Chicken, tikka cooked with garlic, onions, green peppers, in garlic sauce £5.85. Fully licensed and air conditioned. 'Looks very ordinary from the street, but highly rated by the locals. We were a group of fourteen at lunchtime, two waiters and chefs deserve praise for the service and food, delicious.' HC. Starters include: Kolijee Puri £2.30 – lightly spiced chicken liver stir-fried, served on bread. Main courses: Chicken or Lamb Cashew Nut Tikka £5.85 – cooked in a creamy sauce with cashew nuts. Chilli Nan £1.50. Takeaway: 10% discount. Sunday buffet – £5.95 adults, £3.95 children – from age 1 to 6. Takeaway: 10% discount. Delivery: £15 minimum. Price check: Papadam 45p, CTM £5.85, Pullao Rice £1.60, House wine £6.95. Hours: 12-2.30pm/6pm-12am; Sun. 12pm-12am. Stocks Cobra.

Tadworth

BURGH HEATH TANDOORI NEW ENTRANT U

1 The Parade, Tadworth 01737 371716

Established in 1999. Price check: Papadam 50p, CTM £4.95, Pullao Rice £1.60, Peshwari Nan £1.60. Takeaway: 10 % discount on orders collected over £12. Delivery: £10 minimum. Hours: 5.30-11pm.

Tolworth GL

JAIPUR ©

90 The Broadway, Tolworth 020 8399 3619

The external decor makes this venue unmissable. Its huge pink stone pillars make it stand out, a fact not unnoticed by the local council, who in the early days spent a considerable amount of time, and presumably money, trying to force owner SU Ali to remove them. Fortunately bureaucracy lost, and the pillars remain; indeed, they continue inside, giving a very Indian feel to the interior. India's Jaipur is the pink city, where every building is made from pink sandstone. Naturally the Jaipur's theme is pink too, with 'an amazing sugar-pink decor, with friezes of dancing ladies seemingly sculpted out of the wall.' DD. 'Thoroughly enjoyable.' DRC. 'One of my regular haunts.' PD.

Virginia Water

VICEROY OF INDIA ©

4 Station Approach, Virginia Water 01344 843157

MS Ali's Viceroy remains very popular. 'Popular curry house with good atmosphere and friendly staff.' CP. 'Restaurant empty (Wednesday lunchtime). Brusque waiter. Chicken Chilli Masallah and Meat Madras – nice spicing, especially the rice. OK value at £25 for two.' MG. Perhaps MG needs to contact AF, whose email tells us: 'Closed down at the end of last year for six weeks – complete refurbishment, three times the size, food even better. GCG 1999 – one line entry 'Remains very popular' must rank alongside 'Mostly harmless' *Hitchhikers Guide to the Galaxy* as the biggest example of understatement yet known in the history of the English language. This is a seriously excellent restaurant. Everyone I take there ABSOLUTELY REFUSES to go anywhere else and insists on going back. Chilli Chicken Masala ranks as historic and their Dhansak cannot be bettered.' Price check: Papadam 60p, Pullao Rice £1.95, Peshwari Nan £2.50. Stocks Cobra.

Walton-on-Thames

ORIENTAL CURRY CENTRE NEW ENTRANT ©

13 Church Street, Walton 01932 222317

Established in 1968. Taken over by manager Asif Iqbal in 1999. Seats 70. Specials include: Balti and Bangladeshi special dishes. Price check: Papadam 50p, CTM £5.95, Pullao Rice £1.95, Peshwari Nan £1.95, Lager £2.45 pint, House wine £7.50 bottle. Delivery: 4-mile radius. Hours: 12-2.30pm/6pm-12am. Stocks Cobra.

Weybridge

GOLDEN CURRY ©

132 Oatlands Drive, Weybridge 01932 846931

Good reports still received about owner Enayeth Khan's golden curries. Stocks Cobra.

THE HUSSAIN ©

47 Church Street, Weybridge 01932 844720

All reports speak well of the food and the service at M Suleman's Hussain. 'Garlic chicken was memorable, even next day, according to one wag.' HC. Branch: The Curry Corner Tandoori, Hersham, Surrey.

Whyteleafe

CURRY GARDEN ©

242 Godstone Road, Whyteleafe 01883 627237

An effort is made at Akhlaqur Rahman and Moynoor Rashid's 54-seater air-conditioned restaurant. On the ground and first floor, it's decorated in 'light blue wallpaper, silk plants, with a superb bar.' Special: Vegetable Malai Kofta, minced vegetables made into balls and cooked in cream £4.50. Sunday buffet 12-3pm, £5.95 adult, £3.95 children. Minimum charge: £6. Service: 10%. Takeaway: 10% discount. Delivery: £13 minimum order, 3-mile radius. Hours: 12-3pm/6pm-12am. Stocks Cobra.

Woking

GURU NEW ENTRANT

48 Westfield Road, Old Woking 01483 724440

'After sampling what must be well over 100 restaurants, we believe this one to be the most outstanding. And we're very lucky having it close enough to be regular patrons. Chef is always happy to oblige in cooking me Balti Chicken Dhansak. Quantities and quality of dishes was outstanding, every time. Very, very popular with the locals.' J&AK.

JAIPUR TOP 100

49 Chertsey Road, Woking 01483 772626

This elegant 60-seater, established in 1993, is owned by Nizam Ali and his two delightful sisters, Reggi and Sophi, all of whom I met in their gorgeous Sylheti home, during a monsoon storm a few years ago. 'The ambience (of the restaurant) is smooth and peaceful. The bar on the right invites you to enjoy a relaxing drink, while the huge pillars in their subdued tones of pink make you feel you are in India. Service is superb headed by manager Shahab Uddin. The food is always an adventure, spiced with care and forethought by long-standing chef Rupa Kumar, who was crowned Woking Curry Chef of the Year, 1999. The whole meal was outstanding.' DBAC. 'Basically traditional menu with a few interesting items. Food served with a smile. Chicken Dupiaza very light on onions. Could not fault the food but ordinary.' MP. 'We started with King Prawn Butterfly and Meat Samosa (both excellent). We followed with Sali Boti (sliced lamb with apricots) which was mild and beautifully cooked. The Nan bread (slightly crispy and buttery on top) was sensational. Service was perfect and this is definitely a worthy TOP 100.' AF. Minimum charge: £6.95. Business weekday self-serve buffet lunches £5.95, Sunday e-a-m-y-l buffet: £6.95 adult, £3.95 kids. Price check: Papadam 75p, CTM £6.95, Pullao Rice £2.50. Takeaway: 10% discount. Delivery: £10 min, 5-miles. Hours: 12-2.30pm/6-11.30pm. Stocks Cobra.

KHYBER PASS ©

18 The Broadway, Woking 01483 764710

It's a standard curry house, green decor and Hindi arches. 'Food is always good. Of particular interest to us is the lime pickle on the chutney tray.' DRC. Manager Jafar Abdul Wahab promises to give a generous discount to Curry Club members. Branches: Khyber Pass, 12 Lower Guildford Road, Knaphill and 54 Terrace Road, Walton-on-Thames. Stocks Cobra.

LOTUS OF BENGAL NEW ENTRANT ©

45 Goldsworth Road, Woking 01483 766226

Established in 1984, taken over by Mostaque Rahman in 1996. Seats 44. Parking at front of restaurant after 6pm. Banquets every Thurs. night. Price check: Papadam 60p, CTM £6.95, Pullao Rice £1.95, Peshwari Nan £1.95, Lager £2.90 pint. Takeaway: 10% discount. Delivery: £15 minimum, 3-mile radius. Hours: 12-2.30pm/6-11.30pm; Sun. 1-11pm.

Worcester Park GL

MEGHNA NEW ENTRANT

23 Cheam Common Road, Worcester Park 020 8337 3917

Mr Zaman Ahmed's long-standing, competent and popular curry house is the type of place enjoyed by its local regulars. Service, customer care and food are all above average, without being silly prices. Stocks Cobra.

SUSSEX

Area: South
Population: 1,487,000
Adjacent Counties: Hants, Kent, Surrey

For the purposes of this Guide we combine East and West Sussex.

Barnham

PASSAGE TO INDIA NEW ENTRANT

15 The Square, Barnham 01243 555064

Set in a small village, Mr Muhammed Yousuf Islam's 58-seater is a well established, popular and competent curry house enjoyed by its locals. Service, customer care and food are all above average, without being over-priced. Special: Butter Chicken £5.70. Seats 58, ample parking for 60. Spacious, air-conditioned. Price check: Papadam 50p, CTM £6.50, Pullao Rice £1.80, Peshwari Nan £1.80, Lager £2.50 pint. Takeaway: 10% discount. Hours: 12-2.30pm/6-11.30pm. (12am on Fri. & Sat.). Stocks Cobra.

Bexhill-on-Sea

SHIPLU ©

109 London Road, Bexhill-on-Sea 01424 219159

At Abdul Kalam Azad's Shiplu 'service couldn't be bettered, all dishes were well cooked and presented in adequate quantities.' DJB. Hours: 12pm-2.30pm/6pm-12am. Stocks Cobra.

Bognor Regis

MAGNA

3 Argyle Street, Bognor Regis 01243 828322

'Arrived at 6.30ish. Restaurant deceptively large, smart though typically colours clashed. Clean and well maintained. We were the first customers, but others soon appeared and takeaways doing a good trade for a Wednesday. Smart and polite waiters. As we sat a small plate of Bombay Mix was delivered, very fresh and crunchy, certainly no other hands had been rummaging in it. We virtually demolished this while we looked at the menus. Started with two very crispy pops and picks. CT, at least eight generous pieces, fresh and succulent on a bed of sautéed onions £1.95. Onion Bhajia – two flattish discs, spicy and moist £1.60. Taste of Sylhet Sat Kora Chicken – a type of lime, with potato and plenty of freshly sliced green chillies £4.65, made a good change. Side orders of Tarka Dal – topped with fried garlic £1.95. Specials include: Bangladeshi fish – Rui Mas and Boal Mas both £8.95. With a bottle of French red wine and an extra portion of rice the bill was a very reasonable £32.70 plus tip. I visited the toilets and can report that they score 9 out of 10.' AC. Hours: 12-2.30pm/5.30-11.30pm.

Brighton

BALTI HUT

2 Coombe Terrace, Brighton 01273 681280

30-seater, est. '97 by Dost Mohammed, serving formula curries and Balti specials from £4.80. 'Informative menu, with plenty of unusual delights. I used my naan to mop up every last trace of my Tandoori Nowab, excellently cooked and very delicious. Forget location prejudice.' N&D. Price check: Papadam 50p, CTM £6.80, Pullao Rice £1.45. House wine £7. Service 10%. Takeaway: 10% off. Delivery: £8 minimum, 3-mile radius. Hours: 6-11.30pm (12am on Sat.).

©	Curry Club Discount	U	Unlicensed
V	Vegetarian	ANP	Alcohol not permitted
e-a-m-a-y-l	Eat as much as you like	BYO	Bring your own alcohol

BAYLEAF

104 Western Road, Brighton 01273 773804

Established in 1998. Seats 87. 'Bingo, an oasis in the wilderness of mostly mediocre formula curry houses in Brighton. Bills itself as an Indian Brasserie and it's certainly different from yer average eaterie. Light airy room with tiled floor, polished wood tables and a cool blend of jazz and blues background music. Not a Balti, Pakora or Vindaloo in sight – about 12 starters and 12 mains, of mostly unusual dishes. The price for mains (about £6.90 per dish) was inclusive of side dishes of Dahl and Vegetable of the Day, so it was pretty good value. Food was uniformly excellent. Chicken Chaat gets a special recommendation – a really good interpretation of what is rapidly becoming in some places a very hackneyed (and oily- ugh!) dish.' SM. 'An unusual and refreshing different menu, although for the unadventurous some standard curries are available. I had Chicken Chaat followed by a Bayleaf Khasi – fresh lamb pieces with onion and red chillies, which came with Dal and a Vegetable Curry. Good quantities and the quality of food was excellent. Offered a drink on the house.' MK. Specials include: Chicken Nilgiri (chicken cooked with spinach and mint), Jeera Pullao (cumin flavoured basmati rice). Price check: CTM £6.95, Pullao Rice £1.45, Peshwari Nan £1.85, Lager £2.60 pint. Takeaway: 15% discount. Delivery: £10 minimum, 3-mile radius. Hours: 12-3pm/5.30-11.30pm; Sat. 12pm-12am. Stocks Cobra.

BOMBAY ALOO

39 Ship Street, Brighton. 01273 776038

'Vegetarian buffet meals all day, every day. A bargain, but I felt hungry again two hours later!' BP-D. 'Has improved over the last four years. The restaurant is comfortable and service fine. Main dishes are all a little similar to each other but they do provide good value at £4.95 per person. Rice, Nan and Onion Bhajias are all good and the Tarka Dal is also fine. Overall, for the price you can't complain!' AGS. 'We loved it, wanted to share it, and hope that many more vegetarian curry lovers can satisfy their craving without too many shekels leaving their pockets. Vegetarian Buffet meal (14 dishes) £4.50 eat 'til you burst. Buy 11 buffet meals and have the 12th on us.' SK&LD.

INDIAN OCEAN NEW ENTRANT

12 Preston Road, Brighton 01273 778721

'Appetising Prawn Puri with fresh salad. Tangy Chicken Dhansak, with half portion of Dall and half portion of Vegetable Curry included in the prices of £5.95. Nan – good size, well done as I had asked for. Overall excellent quality fresh food, tasty, very enjoyable. Service pleasant and unhurried. Decor brightly coloured, not cramped.' MK.

NOORIS NEW ENTRANT

70-71 Ship Street, Brighton 01273 329405

'Although it was full of Stag and Hen parties and right in the middle of Brighton festival, we managed to get a table. Staff were cheerful and helpful despite the over exuberance of some of the other diners. Food arrived in reasonable time. While we waited we got through some large bottles of Cobra and munched through some complimentary Popadoms. Chicken Tikka Dhansak and Prawn Korma, good, Nan just right. Perfectly acceptable for £30.' CS. 'Plain and spicy Popadoms served with condiment tray. Prawn Puri – served in a wooden bowl which made it a little awkward to cut puri. Chicken Dhansak – lean white meat with Aloo Bhajiee – well seasoned slices of potato and Pullao Rice. Average quantities, overall quite good. Service unsmiling. Kitchen roll in the toilets to dry your hands.' MK. But RE was less impressed: 'was in my top 4 at one time ... Chef change and not as good'. RE. Or an off-night? Reports please.

POLASH BYO ALLOWED ©

19 York Place, Brighton 01273 626221

Formula 60-seater, owned and managed by Nosir Ullah. Licensed but BYO, no corkage. Takeaway: 10% off. Delivery: £10 minimum. Hours: 12-2pm/6pm-12am. Stocks Cobra.

VICEROY OF INDIA

13 Preston Street, Brighton 01273 324733

Established in 1985 by Mohammed Wasid Ali. Seats 48 (soon to be 66). Specials: Jeera King Prawn £8.45. Lamb Pasanda £6.45 – prepared in red wine sauce, yoghurt, almonds and creamed coconut. Price check: Papadam 55p, CTM £5.85, Pullao Rice £1.75, Peshwari Nan £1.75, House wine £7.95 bottle, £1.95 glass, lager £2.50 pint. Takeaway: 10% discount. Hours: 12-2.30pm/5-11pm. Stocks Cobra.

Burgess Hill

SHAPLA NEW ENTRANT

226 London Road, Burgess Hill 01444 232493

'No airs and graces at this restaurant, but boy did the curry hit the spot. It was marvellous. Chicken Tikka Massala and Karai Chicken were exceptional.' N&D

Chichester

MEMORIES OF INDIA

Old Bridge Road (A259), Bosham Roundabout, Chichester 01243 572234

Abdul Jalil's formula curryhouse is nicely decorated, peach walls, tablecloths and napkins, and blue carpet. Separate bar, highly polished floor, cane chairs and tables, green plants. 'Had a takeaway and despite the decor which made us think it would be expensive we found it to be very reasonable. My only complaint, Sag Paneer was made with cheddar. Helpful staff, despite being busy.' SW. Specials: Lamb Podina, thin lamb with garlic, fresh mint and coriander £6.95. Ayre Jalfrey, Bengali fish cooked with chillies, garlic, peppers in a hot spicy sauce £7.95. Takeaway: 15% off. Minimum charge: £13.50. Hours: 12-2.30pm/6pm-12am. Stocks Cobra.

SHAPLA TANDOORI RE ENTRANT

Eastgate Square, Chichester 01243 775978

Formerly The Peacock. 'On second floor above old swimming pool. Very functional feel with bright pink emulsion painted walls. Usual menu with handful of unusual dishes – King Prawns in Mustard Sauce. Food well spiced, good chunks of garlic, chilli and excellent Nan bread. Service was a bit "dump it all on the table and run". Still worth including.' CC. 'Visited here twice before. Both times just before visiting the Festival Theatre for a Russian ballet performance. It is indeed painted in bright pink – but never mind, the food is typical curry house fayre but done passably well. I enjoyed their Chicken Dhansak (quite hot) and yes the Nan bread is excellent. Good value for money too.' DC. JR was less impressed.

Crawley

CROWN OF INDIA NEW ENTRANT

7 Pound Hill Parade, Crawley 01293 539007

Established in 1998. Seats 74. Parking for 15 cars at front. Price check: Papadam 50p, CTM £6.95, Pullao Rice £1.90, Peshwari Nan £1.95, Lager £2.95 pint. Takeaway: 20% discount. Hours: 12-2pm/6-11pm. Stocks Cobra.

RAJ TAKEAWAY ©

8 Broadfield Barton, Broadfield, Crawley 01293 515425

SU Ahmed has a loyalty discount scheme: collect stars for a free meal. As well as the goodies, chef A Ali does curry sauce and chips, kids' favourite. Hours: 5.30-11pm.

RUBY MURRAY

4-7 Orchard Street, Crawley 01293 417417

One shopfront does takeaway and delivery service. The menu covers a wide range of curries with other foods: Donner, Burgers including Chilli and Pizzas (Bombay Mix – curry sauce, Meat Tikka, Chicken Tikka, cheese, tomato, onion, mushroom, sweetcorn, green peppers). 'Meat Vindaloo, as always hot, with a wonderful sauce. Quick to arrive – free delivery in half an hour. Staff helpful and food inexpensive.' GT. The Ruby Murray stocks a selection of canned and bottled lagers, but their licence says these are strictly delivered with food to customers over the age of 18 and before 11pm. The other shopfront is the restaurant, formerly called Sultan's. 'We'd arrived back at Gatwick at midnight from lands afar, with huge withdrawal symptoms. B Khan's 100-seater Sultan was doing a good sit-down trade. Standard fare, but wonderful under the circumstances. 'Eight of us – relatives – met at this local. Menu fairly standard – Chicken Jalfrezi – quite hot, but we shared main and side dishes, which included CTM, Malaysian Chicken (with pineapple) and Chicken Dhansak. Some of the food could have been a little warmer. Quantity and quality very good. Service friendly and attentive. One waiter took some photographs for us.' MK. Special: Lamb Sheryan – minced lamb, coconut, raisins, cashew nuts and cream, served with special fried rice £11.95. Minimum charge: £10. Price check: Papadam 50p, CTM £6.95, Pullao Rice £1.95. House wine £7.45. Corporate functions welcome. Multi-storey parking opposite. Hours: 12-2.30pm/5pm-1am.

ZARI NEW ENTRANT

214 Ifield Drive, Ifield, Crawley 01293 553009

'The Zari is wonderfully different – up market, classy, clean, subtle light, dimmer switches, high back light wood chairs. Generous portions – two Rice and Sag Aloo £2.30 for three people. Although not advertised I often order a portion of masala sauce for my veggie daughter. Takeaway for four £39.95.' BW. Starters include : Machli Papeta na Pattice £2.95 – flakes of fish, mashed potato, herbs and spices. Murgh Tikka Mariali £2.95 – spicy green chicken tikka. Main courses: Zari Jhalak Machli £8.50 – crunchy pomfret on bed of crispy fried onions and aubergine salad, served with tangy sauce. Assorted Vegetable Tikka Chat £5.50 – vegetable cutlets marinated in yoghurt and fresh spices then barbecued in the tandoor. Disabled access. Price check: Papadam 60p, CTM £6.50, Pullao Rice £1.75, Peshwari Nan £1.75. Hours: 12-2.30pm/6-11.30pm.

Crowborough

BENGAL SPICE NEW ENTRANT

24 Crowborough Hill, Jarvis Brook 01892 661881

Fully licensed and air conditioned. 'Has been completely decorated, 44 covers, basket type furniture and greatly improved. Service excellent, attentive without being pushy. Food good, ample portions. Three of us had Popadoms and Chutneys 40p each, CTM, Chicken Vindaloo, Lamb Dopiaza £4.80, Pullao Rice, Special Fried Rice £2.70, Sag Aloo £2.60, Mushroom Bhajie £2.50, Naan Bread and two Chapaties 90p with two double whisky's and 4 pints of Bangla (stronger than Cobra). [What a lot of food – you must have been stuffed full!]. A good all round meal in clean and pleasant surroundings and definitely no. 1 in the small town of Crowborough.' BP-D, Kent. 'One of our favourites. We love it here. Waiters very polite and friendly, food excellent. £40 for two. Peshwari Nan the best we have ever tasted. Portions so big. Sag Paneer £2.60 is great.' MR&MRS RL. Price check: Papadam 50p, CTM £6.20, Pullao Rice £1.70, Peshwari Nan £1.85. Hours: 12-2.30pm/6-11.30pm. Stocks Cobra.

East Grinstead

SHAPLA TAKEAWAY

94 Railway Approach, East Grinstead 01342 327655

AK Azad Chuta's takaway deserves to get an honourable mention because, we always hear, the food is of good quality, it's plentiful and service, from initial phone order to hand-over, is efficient and pleasant.

Eastbourne

HURRY & CURRY NEW ENTRANT

52 Seaside Road, Eastbourne 01323 503483

Established in 1999. Takeaway only. Specials include: Bounty, so-called because it is very 'coco naughty' (King prawns cooked with exotic coconut milk, cream, garlic, onion, in a rich thick sauce with a touch of Malibu). Price check: Papadam 50p, CTM £5.95, Pullao Rice £1.60, Peshwari Nan £1.50. Delivery: £15 minimum. Hours: 6pm-2.30am; Sun. 6pm-1am; closed Mon.

INDIAN PARADISE ©

166 Seaside, Eastbourne 01323 735408

A Khalique's bright restaurant has been serving competent curries and accompaniments to a local following for the last 15 years. Delivery. Hours: 12pm-2.30pm/6pm-12am.

Hastings

SPICE OF INDIA NAME CHANGE ©

177a Queens Road, Hastings 01424 439493

Formerly the Shiplu, it is 'tastefully decorated and clean. Service on the slow side but friendly. Pops warm and crisp, Onion B large, could not be beaten. Phall not on the menu but asked for it. Very hot as it should be.' BP-D. 'Visited many times. Comfortable, unpretentious. Nothing very ambitious but always acceptable. Excellent Sag Gosht. Prices cheap.' JR. 'We found the food excellent. My partner was particularly pleased with the Lamb Madras, claiming it as one of the best he has ever had.' AK&KW. Hours: 12-2.30pm/6pm-12am. Stocks Cobra.

Haywards Heath

CURRY CONNECTION TAKEAWAY NEW ENTRANT

13 The Broadway, Haywards Heath 01444 413021

First opened in 1991, taken over by SM Iqbal in 1999. Takeaway only. Specials: Chicken Tikka Korai Balti, served with Nan £6.45. Chicken or

Lamb Kashmiri £5.95 – mild, creamy with banana and lychee. Price check: Papadam 45p, CTM £5.95, Pullao Rice £1.75, Peshwari Nan £1.75. Delivery: £6 minimum for inner areas; £15 minimum for outer areas. Hours: 4pm-12am.

CURRY INN ©

58 Commercial Square, Haywards Heath 1444 415414

At Abru Miah's 60-seater with blue and green marble effect bar, pillars, plants and chandelier lighting, Korma is the most popular dish. Hours: 12-2.30pm/6-11.30pm (12am on Sat.).

Heathfield

CURRY INN NEW ENTRANT

Hobby Way, Station Approach, Heathfield 01435 864930

Fully licensed and air-conditioned. 'Situated in large straggling market village. Mango Chutney with large chunks of fruit, Lime Pickle nice and sharp, Chicken Vindaloo £3.75, Madras £3.75, Lamb Dopiaza £3.90 – my wife, not a curry eater, said it was the best she had ever had, Saag Aloo £2.00, Pullao Rice and Keema Nans £1.55. Food just right in every way and in good sized portions. Service, considering the number of people present, was 1st class. Well decorated with traditional Indian pictures on the walls. Loos tiled from floor to ceiling and scrupulously clean. £40.10 for three inc drinks.' BP-D. Price check: Papadam 40p, CTM £6.25, Pullao Rice £1.60, Peshwari Nan £1.50. Hours: 5.30-11pm (Fri. & Sat. to 11.30pm). Stocks Cobra.

Hove

ASHOKA ©

95-97 Church Road, Hove 01273 734193

100-seater owned by Bashir Meah and Rafique Miah. 'Nice roomy restaurant, clean and comfortable. Onion Bhaji, small but good and tasty. Chicken Ceylon with Pilau Rice and Nan, hot, as it should be, nicely served and plenty of it! Bill allowed for 10% discount to Curry Club member, but offset by service charge.' BP-D. Madras most popular. Service 10%. Sunday lunch: £6.95. Hours: 12-3pm/6pm-12am. Branch: Bombay, Preston Street, Brighton. Stocks Cobra.

CURRY MAHAL NEW ENTRANT ©

171 Portland Road, Hove 01273 779125

First opened in 1970, taken over by Muazzam Hussain Malique in 1999. Seats 70 in two rooms. 'Reported to be the oldest original Indian restaurant in the area. The passing of time has certainly not taken its toll on the interior. However, it may not have been so benevolent in regard to the managerial disposition. The menu described every dish as either being tasty or having a very tasty sauce. In our opinion we would have to disagree. Although the free coffee was certainly tasty.' N&D. Specials include: Chatga Prawns, Murgh Sunam, Basha Prawns, Murgh Sylhety. Price check: Papadam 45p, CTM £7.95, Pullao Rice £1.75, Peshwari Nan £1.75, Lager £2.80 pint. Takeaway: 10% discount. Hours: 12-2.30pm/5.30-11.30pm. Stocks Cobra.

EVEREST NEPALESE NEW ENTRANT

244, Portland Road, Hove

'Nepalese new to Hove – much better food, quality and quantity than the better known traditional "Indians" in Church Road. Aloo Tarma £2.50 very good. Hope the *Brighton Argus* article attracts a few more customers, they will be in for a treat.' CH. Reports please.

GANGES ©

93 Church Road, Hove 01273 728292

Established 1992 by Abdul (front) and Karim (kitchen) who run an attractive restaurant decorated in white and green. Seats 100. Specials: Brandy King Prawn, served with Pullao Rice. Takeaway: 10% discount. Hours: 12-2.30pm/6pm-12am. Stocks Cobra.

HOVE TANDOORI ©

175 Church Road, Hove 01273 737188

Shofir and Shahed Ahmad's 42-seater. 'Very good menu, although fairly standard. Chicken Vindaloo good and hot, Chicken Madras enjoyable. Naan breads fluffy but a little charred. Onion Bhajis good and crisp. The only complaint was the decor, tatty and overdue for replacement. Walls of the passage to the lavatories were in a shocking state (paper and plaster peeling off), but we don't eat there do we?!' BP-D. [You need to ask, Bill?]. Hove Special: chicken, meat, prawn cooked with garlic, ginger, tomato, mushroom, onion, green pepper, coriander, green chilli in a thick sauce, served in a Korai with Rice £7.95. Takeaway: 10% off. Price check: Papadam 40p, CTM £4.75, Pullao Rice £1.30. House wine £4. Delivery: £8 minimum, 3-mile radius. Hours: 12-2.30pm/5.30pm-12am.

IKARIM'S TANDOORI ©

15 Blatchington Road, Hove 01273 739780

Formula curry house, traditionally decorated, seats 38. Balti dishes available. Minimum charge: £7.95. Service 10%. Delivery: £8 minimum order. Hours: 6-11.30pm (12am on Sat.). Branch: Balti House, Coombe Terrace, Brighton.

KASHMIR ©

71 Old Shoreham Road, Hove 01273 739677

Established way back in '78, by Subab Miah, who is a busy chap, being manager and head chef. Seats 45. Traditional decor, formula curries. 'The food is always delicious, the service courteous and friendly.' HF. 'A consistently high standard of cooking and preparation.' JHW. 'Mr Miah and family provide excellence at all expectations.' CRC. 'I've been coming since it opened. The seating and bar are very pleasant. The curries are delicately spiced and individual.' LH. Specials include Balti dishes. 'This restaurant being staunch supporters of Brighton Hove and Albion, saw that we were in a hurry to get to the match, and acted fast. Food excellent and good portions. Seemed au fait with the GCG coupon scheme and I got 10% discount.' BP-D. Price check: Papadam 45p, CTM £5, Pullao Rice £1.80. House wine £7. Delivery: Hove area. Hours: 12-3pm/6pm-12am.

Lewes

SHANAZ ©

83 High Street, Lewes 01273 488038

Taken over in '97 by Mrs LB Salim, her 98-seater (party room 44) is decorated cottage-style with varnished wood panelling. 'Best in Lewes. Food consistent. Chicken Nababi – large quantities of chicken tikka and minced lamb in a spicy, rich sauce – yum! Vegetable Pasanda – sweet and boozy. A useful eating place.' JR.'On the way to watch football, my son remarked he could "murder a curry". I replied that I could slaughter one any time, so we stopped at the Shanaz. What a surprise we got when we were led downstairs to a room resembling a jungle – tropical plants. Pleasant and relaxing ambience. Staff friendly and awake. Served food of excellent quality, quantities quite large. We would both like to come back and have a meal in the evening and enjoy the surroundings more.' and 'Gorged on the best of Indian food – Lobster curry. Had to book a week in advance. Lobster obtained from nearby Newhaven was presented to us in the form of Jalfrezi £9.95. One of the best curries we've ever had, big chunky wads of beautifully tasting lobster, hot spices accentuated the flavour. The meal, although, not cheap – what do you expect for REAL lobster – worth every penny. 10% CC Discount.' BP-D. Price check: Papadam 55p, CTM £4.95, Pullao Rice £1.65, Peshwari Nan £1.95. Hours: 12-2.30pm/6pm-12am.

Midhurst

NAVA THAI NEW ENTRANT

Hamilton Arms, School Lane, Stedham, Midhurst 01730 812555

Housed in the Hamilton Arms pub, now bedecked in Thai appurtenances, the conventional pub-style bar remains, and has Thai snacks on offer. Alongside is a recently extended (60 seat) restaurant. The venue is owned by a Thai (Mrs Surapee Karnasuta) and a Bangladeshi, Suhail Hussain. We went unbooked on a Wednesday evening, and there was ample parking space, and despite an it's-advisable-to-book spin, ample space in the restaurant. We perused the menu, which offered all one would expect, except a mixed starter platter. We asked the waiter if he did this. 'No we don't,' he said, 'but I can order them from the bar snack menu for you.' A straight 'yes' would have been better than this eyebrow-raising contradiction, since the bar is all of 10 paces, and is served by the same kitchen. Pat ordered his favourite Tom Yam Kung (prawn soup), and requested 'very hot'. 'If you like hot,' said the waiter, 'I recommend the Chilli Prawn as a main course.' Dom ordered Gaeng Ped Nua – (Red Beef Curry) thinly sliced prime beef in a red spicy hot curry sauce and Pud Thai – fried rice noodles with egg, prawns, crab meat, ground peanut and chopped salted turnip, and Mee Krob (crisp noodles drizzled with palm sugar). 'Sorry, they've been off for two days' and fried rice. The bar snacks (£7.50) provided five filling pairs of crispy tasty items. The curry was boosted with more bamboo shoot (not a Thai ingredient) than beef, though it had a medium pleasant coconut-based red sauce, and the Tom Yung Kung, had 2 Kung and 10 unannounced button mushrooms (not a Thai ingredient) floating on the surface. Hot it was not, neither were the chilli prawns, boosted with too much green pepper. The Pad Thai noodles were a weird artificial pink colour, and there was no evidence of the all-important crab. Asked why the food was not hot, the same waiter said 'You should have asked for Thai hot!' I said I did, but he went on undeterred: 'We used to serve the dishes hot, but the customers sent them back.' The venue and the ambience was good, and so too was the service. The waiter's answer-for-everything attitude was irritating – tantamount to complaiscency. Of course they can cook properly. Adding chilli heat is really simple, but Thai food without chilli veers towards baby food – sweet and toothless. Pander to your soft-tongued clients, if you must. But don't assume all clients like such watering down. Customers should not have to ask for Thai food as it should be (indeed as it is done in nearby Petersfield and Guildford – River Kwai and Rumwong respectively, both *sic*, where Thai is Thai and hot is hot, and where padding with cheap ingredients is not done.) Our bill with wine was £45. Despite shortcomings, we tipped (£5).

Newhaven

LAST VICEROY ©

4 Bridge Street, Newhaven 01273 513308

AS Ahmed's 40-seater is divided into smoking and non-smoking zones and has a separate entrance for t/a customers and an off-licence – cigarettes can be delivered to your table! Specials: Garlic Duck Masala. King Prawn Zafrani. 'Our favourite, always offering good food and friendly service. Ample portions, very enjoyable.' BJMCK. Kid's half-price menu. Sunday, free starters with main meal, eat-in only. Minimum charge: £10. Takeaway: 30% off. Delivery: £10 min. Hours: 12-2.30pm/6-11.30pm. Stocks Cobra.

Newick

NEWICK VILLAGE TANDOORI NEW ENTRANT

7-9 Church Road, Newick 01825 723738

'This should definitely be in the guide. Attractive and comfortable decor, Outstanding service. Food very good. Sag Gosht, large quantity of top-quality lamb. Paneer Pasanda very good. Prices higher than average – you get what you pay for.' JR. Stocks Cobra.

Nutbourne

TAMARIND AND MOONLIGHT EXPRESS NEW ENTRANT

Main Road, Nutbourne 01243 573149

Opened Sept '98 but who do you agree with? 'Myself and two colleagues were all disappointed. Diet Coke flat, as was the replacement; service was very slow and the waiters seemed uninterested; my Chicken Biryani was fine, but just as I was finishing I was presented with the vegetable curry which consisted of diced carrot, sweetcorn, green beans and potato in a non-descript dark brown, very non-Indian curry sauce, obviously out of a tin. Next time we will return to the excellent Ashoka next door.' TJB. 'Our takeaway order was good, and we were very impressed with our subsequent dining-in. Extensive menu. My wife had Patrani Machli (salmon fillets with mild spices baked in foil), and she said it was among the best fish dishes she has ever had. I had the Goa Machli Curry also made with salmon and also excellent. Tarka Dhal and boiled rice were OK. Definitely a TOP 100 candidate.' RH

Petworth

VICEREGAL LODGE

East Street, Petworth 01798 343217

Seats 36 in two rooms. 'Excellent! Service friendly and competent. Popadoms warm and crisp and onion relish nicely chilled. Chicken Rezala consisted of pieces of breast fillet in a spicy plum-tomato sauce with garlic and coriander. Prawn Jalfry equally good, a spicy lesson in oral aerobics. Very good Tarka Dal, Madras Sambar and Sag Aloo. Fresh and fragrant Pullao Rice, Nan and Chapatis.' CT. Hours: 6pm-12am. Reports please to stay in the *Guide*.

Polegate

VICEROY NEW ENTRANT

5 Grand Parade, Lewes Road, Polegate 01323 485248

'Very clean and efficient all round, waiters pleasant and friendly – particularly one who recognised me. Food excellent and well presented. Plain Popadoms with large variety of Chutneys and Pickles, Raitha and Salads. Chicken Phall was very hot and good portion! accompanied by Keema Nan £1.75 – large and fluffy. Cobra £3.75 a large bottle – a bit pricey. Overall a pleasant restaurant with quality food. £30 for two.' BP-D. Takeaway: 10% discount over £10. Price check: Papadam 45p, CTM £5.50, Pullao Rice £1.75, Peshwari Nan £1.75. Hours: 12-2pm (Sat. to 2.30pm & Fri. closed)/6-11.30pm (Fri. & Sat. to 12am). The menu includes Fried Chicken, Scampi and Chips for the morons. Branch: Last Viceroy, 4a Bridge Street, Newhaven, East Sussex.

Ringmer

RINGMER TANDOORI ©

72 Springett Avenue, Ringmer 01273 812855

Balti dishes feature on owner, MA Uddin's, menu along with the favourites. Hours: 12pm-2.30pm/6pm-12am. Stocks Cobra.

St Leonards-on-Sea

BENGAL CURRY HOUSE

7 Marine Court St Leonards 01424 465076

Established in 1992. Seats 40. 'Some remarkably cheap prices on the menu, possibly reflected in the smallish size of main course portions and the use of broken basmati for the Pullao Rice. Flavours up-front and rich – well-flavoured Chicken Dhansak and Meat Bhuna.' JR. 'My friends and I have been dining here for five years. Food superb, excellent value and a warm welcome from Naz and his staff.' RIW. 'Impressed with the sincerity and careful attention of the proprietor to his guests, coupled with his sense of humour, makes it very special and unusual in this age of disregard for the personal touch.' LG. Price check: Papadam 40p, CTM £3.20, Pullao Rice £1.45. Hours: 12-2.30pm/6-11.30pm. Stocks Cobra.

Seaford

BENGAL PALACE ©

30 Church Street, Seaford East 01323 899077

Air-conditioned, traditional decor, saris hang on walls, engraved glass screens divide tables. Managed by Eleas Hussain, formula curries, seats 48. Sunday lunch £7.95. Delivery: £10 minimum. Hours: 12-2.30pm/6pm-12pam. Stocks Cobra.

Shoreham-by-Sea

MILLAN NEW ENTRANT

Upper Shoreham Road, Shoreham-by-Sea 01273 440699

'Outside it doesn't look particularly attractive so the interior came as a very pleasant surprise. Pale green with etched glass panels, separating different areas. Good atmosphere, most tables occupied. Competent kitchen.' HC.

Southwick

RAJAH NEW ENTRANT

1 Windmill Road, Southwick 01273 593636

'All very impressed with friendly and helpful service. Waiters looked clean and smart – a credit to the restaurant. Food is exceptionally good with main courses served in very generous portions. I sampled the sauces of all dishes and can say they were all very different and all delicious. Tandoori King Prawns as good as I have had anywhere. Small niggles: no pomfret, only trout or salmon, and panir was Cheddar type. Two Anglicised versions definitely not to be encouraged. Restaurant and takeaway were busy all evening, a very good sign. Black mark: including service and then leaving the credit card slip open.' HC.

Uckfield

RAJDUTT NEW ENTRANT

Eastbourne Road, Uckfield 021825 890234

Established in 1999. Seats 64. 40 car-parking spaces to front and side. Specials include: King Prawn Silsila (cooked with fresh garlic, herbs and oriental spices) £9.25. Price check: Papadam 50p, CTM £6.25, Pullao Rice £1.55, Peshwari Nan £1.75, Lager £2.40. Takeaway: 10% discount. Hours: 12-2pm/6-11pm; Sat. 12-2pm/5.30-11.30pm.

Worthing

GURKHA NEW ENTRANT

121-123 Rectory Road, Worthing 01903 266384

'Nepalese food – very nice flavours. Vegetable Curry for the Biryani could be made hot as you liked. Very good flavours.' ND.

INDIAN OCEAN TAKEAWAY NEW ENTRANT

66, Teville Road, Worthing 01903 528888

Yusuf Khan is not the only owner to get all his customers to write to us. Here's a few of their comments: 'Tikka Masala, lots of cream, not too spicy. Too much though, neither I nor my partner could finish! Comfy sofa to wait on and very friendly service.' HB. "All traditional dishes available, good selection of side dishes. Pleasantly surprised at large chunks of chicken in

Dupiaza. Pullao Rice – nice and fluffy.' PK. 'Exceptional quality. Service with a smile. Watch TV while you wait.' RA. 'Reasonably priced.' BJH. 'Superb quality, all fresh – the following day we received a phone call to see if we liked it. We will always use this takeaway.' YM. 'Chicken Pakon, mountain of tender meat, medium hot sauce, spicy. Loyalty card entitling customers to enjoy a free meal once six have been purchased.' JS. Delivery. Hours: 5-11pm.

MA'HANN TOP 100 ©

179-181 Montague Street, Worthing 01903 205449

Established in 1984. Seats 150 after extension (to next door) and refurbishment. Pat and I visited for a re-launch party a year or two ago. Mahaan obviously cares about its regular clients very much, we heard nothing but praise for the host and his staff. After eating we were told the chef had created something special. Pat pointed out that we had just eaten and we were quite full, but to no avail, the special was packed up and we were also given a bottle of Champagne. Well, that's the best takeaway I've ever had!! 'Food and standard of service has not faltered over the last five years. Waiters have a friendly attitude no matter how busy they are.' PAH. 'I praise the consistent quality of food, menu choice and politeness of staff.' RDL. 'Food always excellent, matched equally by Abdul's staff. Not the cheapest but one would expect to pay more for top quality cuisine. Simply the tops.' M&S. Specials include: Murgh Sylhety, Chatga Prawns, Murgh Bhazzan, Murgh or Beef Sunam. Remains in our TOP 100 as a formula curry house doing the job as well as it can be done. Price check: Papadam 45p, CTM £6.95, Pullao Rice £1.95, Peshwari Nan £1.95, Lager £2.30 pint. Takeaway: 10% discount. Hours: 12-2.30pm/5.30-11.30pm. Stocks Cobra.

SHAFIQUE'S ©

42 Goring Road, Worthing 01903 504035

Shafique Uddin decribes his 48-seater as '30s colonial'. Special: Bangladeshi Mass, fish curry, hot. Takeaway: 10% discount. Delivery: £1, 3-mile radius. Hours: 12-2.30pm/5.30-11.30pm. Stocks Cobra.

TASTE OF BENGAL TAKEAWAY ©

203 Heene Road, Worthing 01903 238400

Owned by Faruk Kalam (chef) and Salik Miah since '84. Formula takeaway. Special: Murgi Mossallam, spring chicken cooked in mild spices, almonds, minced meat, fruit and eggs, served with saffron rice. Delivery: £7 min, 5-miles, charged at 95p! Hours: 12-2pm/5.30pm-12am.

TYNE & WEAR

Area: North East
Population: 1,127,000
Adjacent Counties: Durham, Northumberland

Gateshead

(includes Bensham, Bill Quay, Low Fell and Shipcote)

BILL QUAY TAKEAWAY ©

78 Station Road, Bill Quay, Gateshead 0191 495 0270

Est. '87 by Syed Amir Ali. Bangladeshi curry takeaway, CTM most popular. Price check: Papadam 35p, CTM £3.95, Pullao Rice £1.10. No credit cards. Hours: 6pm-12am.

CURRY GARDEN TAKEAWAY ©

53 Coatsworth Road, Bensham, Gateshead 0191 478 3614

Owned by Abdul Malik Choudhury since 1996, 'splendid from decor to menu,' serves formula curries. Special: Tandoori Bhuna Masala with Pullao Rice. Delivery: £5 minimum order, 3-mile radius, £1 charge. Hours: 12-2pm (Sun. closed)/6pm-12am.

THE LAST DAYS OF THE RAJ ©

218 Durham Road, Shipcote, Gateshead 0191 477 2888

A takeaway-only establishment serving Bangladeshi curry house food. Price check: Papadam 55p, CTM £5.95, Pullao Rice £1.75. Hours 12-2.30pm/6pm-12am.

LAST DAYS OF THE MOGUL RAJ

565 Durham Road, Low Fell, Gateshead 0191 487 6282

Run by Ali and Ali. Formula curry house. Special: Raj Lamb and Cabbage £4.95. Price check: Papadam 55p, CTM £5.95, Pullao Rice £1.75. Hours: 12-2pm (Sun. closed)/6pm-12am. Stocks Cobra.

©	Curry Club Discount	U	Unlicensed
V	Vegetarian	ANP	Alcohol not permitted
e-a-m-a-y-l	Eat as much as you like	BYO	Bring your own alcohol

CURRY CLUB

THE LAST DAYS OF THE RAJ TOP 100 ©

168 Kells Lane, Low Fell, Gateshead **0191 482 6494**

Athair Khan's up-market 100-seater has stylish decor – pure 30's Art Deco, complete with grand piano. Live music Thursdays. Crisp linen tablecloths laid on beautifully presented tables, brass light-fittings, ceiling-fans, trellis-climbing plants, and fresh flowers. Luxurious surroundings, with friendly and efficient waiters. The bar is spacious and well stocked. This restaurant must have one of the biggest and most comprehensive menus in the country; it is quite a delight. You will find all the regular formula curries with some regional and authentic dishes including recipes from the British Raj – Country Captain £7.25, a dry dish cooked with chicken breast, onion, ghee, chillies, ginger, garlic, turmeric and salt. Raj Lamb and Cabbage (£7.25) is cooked with yoghurt, poppy seeds, lemon juice, green coriander, garlic, onion, fresh coconut, green chillies, ground coriander, ginger, cinnamon and cumin with ghee and chilli. You will also find on the menu a few dishes with an oriental flavour, such as Dim Sum £3.25, Oriental King Prawn Rolls £3.75 and Butterfly Breaded Prawn £3.75, and there is a Pizza or two – quite fabulous, definitely a TOP 100 restaurant. Handi Murgh £7.15, King Prawn Garlic Chili £10.55. There is one dissenting couple among a lot of praise: T&KM found chicken tasteless with no marinated or tandoori flavour at all.' Price check: Papadam 75p, CTM £7.85, Pullao Rice £2.55. Sunday buffet £10.95. Hours: 12-2.30pm (closed Sun.)/6-11.30pm. Branch: Last Days of the Raj, Durham Road, Gateshead. Stocks Cobra.

Newcastle-upon-Tyne

(Includes Denton Burn, Forth Banks and West Jesmond)

ASHA RAVAL NEW ENTRANT

Princes Wharf, 27 Queen Street, Quayside, Central Newcastle **0191 232 7799**

'Superb and it isn't even in the guide. Leaves most of the TOP 100 that I have tried for dead. Murghi Handi Lazeer is a lovely tasty variation on the standard CTM.' AN.

KASTURI NEW ENTRANT

1 The Side, Central Newcastle **0191 222 1714**

70-seater opened in 2000 by Syed Azur Ali and Nizam Choudhury, in the street beside the Cathedral (yes there is one), opposite the Empress pub.

Kasturi is named after Dhaka's best restaurant (yes there is one) to be found in the Motijeel area of the city, and a must visit if ever you find yourself in that interesting city. Newcastle's version is also worth a visit, and serves the regular curryhouse cast list of pops, picks, bhajis and chicks (chicken that is), and some innovations – duck with bamboo shoots, and Crab Sholay flambéed with sambuca. Reports please.

KOMAL BALTI HOUSE NEW ENTRANTS

227 Stanhope Street, Newcastle W 0191 226 1726
14 Brentwood Ave, West Jesmond, Newcastle N 0191 281 4878

Small unpretentious Balti restaurant situated in unfashionable West End along from the hospital. Basic decor, informal atmosphere, but very friendly. Food is always freshly made, and the quality leaves some of the region's more prestigious, and considerably more expensive, restaurants in the shade. Owner now has a second Komal in Brentwood Avenue, with a slightly different atmosphere, and higher prices, but food very good.' DAD. Stocks Cobra.

LEELA'S NEW ENTRANT ©

20 Dean Street, Central Newcastle 0191 230 1261

Established in 1990, owned by Paul and Leela. Seats 60, serves South Indian food. 'Leela welcomes you, takes your order, even makes your order for you if you'll give them a free hand. She suggested a vegetarian feast that was flawless. Food preparation is supervised by her husband Paul. Best treat in Newcastle, and is the best. Deserves to be extremely popular!' WH. 'Since moving to London I have sampled over 40 of your TOP 100s. I therefore know a TOP 100-standard restaurant when I see it. So it had me reaching for the Prozac when I discovered that not only was Leela's not a TOP 100, but also, it wasn't in the guide at all (get it in Pat).' [Tim must have had the '98 *Guide* – it was in the 99 edition.] 'Leela is charismatic and ever present. Masal Dosa is herbaceous, Kathrika Chuttathu is orgasmic, and Kerala Meen superb. What a place!' TJ. 'Special: Paper Dosa, lentil and rice pancake with savoury sauce £3.95. Chemmen, marinated prawns stir-fried with cashew nuts £5.50. Irachi Thoran, strips of lean lamb, soaked in almond sauce and stir-fried £4.95. All sounds great! Price check: Papadam 50p, Pullao Rice £2.50. House wine £10.95. Hours: 12.30-2.30pm/6-11.30pm; Sun. closed. Stocks Cobra.

SACHINS TOP 100

Old Hawthorn Inn, Forth Banks,
Central Newcastle 0191 261 9035

As ever, contented reports come in about Sachins. It stays comfortably on our TOP 100, for, as ever, being spot on, unpretentious, non-exhibitionist, and well above average. Among the popular starter and main course favourites is Paneer Pakora, curd cheese deep-fried in a gram flour batter, Murgh Pakora, chicken pieces deep-fried in a gram flour batter, Murgh Marchi Masala, like a Chicken Tikka Masala but with fresh green chillies to give it a bite. 'Thoroughly enjoyed my Muglai Akbari.' FD. Scottish owner Liam Cunningham adds to the flair. Continue reporting please. Stocks Cobra.

SHIKARA ©

52 St Andrew's Street, Central Newcastle 0191 233 0005

Established in 1992. Bodrul Haque's Shikara seats 100. Chef Tipu Sultan's specials include: Murg Tandoori Masala Panjabi Style, Mirchi Kurma Kashmiri Style, Jinga Goa Style. 'Great value for money.' MS. 'Impressive menu.' DC. Takeaway: 15% discount. Hours: 12-2pm (except Sun.); 6pm-12am; Sat. 6pm-12.30am. Stocks Cobra.

SOLOMON'S

Thorntree Farm, West Road, Denton Burn,
Newcastle W 0191 274 2323

Not much farming remains in this busy area, nor is much left of Hadrian's Wall whose course runs along West Road. Now the barbarians are into bhajis, not battlements, and the hoards are hungry not hostile, ravenous not rampaging. Gags aside, it's a good restaurant in a converted farmhouse. TOC tells of visits to his parent's house: 'First problem, the menu: I have read shorter novels. Chose Punjabi Murgh Tikka, very spicy. On clearing the table, the waiter jokingly commented that I would have stomach problems in 2 hours!! – I didn't. Three main courses, superb. Angoori Chicken had grapes in the sauce. Paratha appeared to be a fried Nan. No dessert, by this stage the (no problem) stomach is sufficently full. The menu warned me that my starter was spicy, and it was. My Singapore Curry was a little bit different. Why didn't this place exist when I lived at home?' TOC.

THALI NEW ENTRANT ©

44 Dean Street, Central Newcastle 0191 230 2244

Established in 1995. Seats 52. Recently redeorated. Specials: Dahi Baigon £3.25 – grilled aubergine stuffed with vegetables and topped with yoghurt. Dali Gosht £6.95 – diced lamb with lentils, sweet and sour sauce. Murgh Zhal Roshun £7.50 – spring chicken with garlic and green chillies. Price check: Papadam 60p, CTM £7.95, Pullao Rice £2.50, Peshwari Nan £2.50, Lager £2.80 pint. Hours: 12-2pm/6pm-12am; Sun. 6pm-12am. Stocks Cobra.

VALLEY JUNCTION 397 TOP 100

397 The Old Station, Jesmond, Newcastle N 0191 281 6397

Daraz and his brother Locku have a penchant for purchasing old railway things and making money from them. First they spend a great deal to get the decor right. This one was formerly the Carriage Pub. The carriage in question was built for the Great Northern Railway at Doncaster in 1912. Numbered 397, it was a saloon for 'wealthy families to hire for their journeys'. Now incorporated into the restaurant, it is decked out in greens and golds, and still earns its keep for the well-heeled. Like its sister restaurant, it has quickly earned a reputation for good food, indeed the menus are identical. Says RL: 'A delightful dining experience. (For those not familiar with the area, it is next to Jesmond Metro station, down a subway. Our table was in the old railway carriage – a tight squeeze, so a lot of 'scuse me's.) Chringri Moslai delicious, Chicken Kebab great too. One minor quibble would be the phone ringing, and the waiters calling through to the bar.' Chingri Varkee, grilled green pepper stuffed with spicy prawns £3.50. Tandoori Dhakna, chicken wings marinated in fresh herbs and spices, served with minty yoghurt sauce £2.95. Murgh e Khazana, breast of chicken cooked mainly with mild spices and honey, in a creamy sauce £7.50. Mangsho Pesta Ke Shadi, top side of beef cooked with a blend of mild spices and pistachio nuts. £7.95. Reports please. Branch: The Valley, The Old Station House, Station Road, Corbridge, Northumberland. Safe bet TOP 100.

VUJON TOP 100 ©

29 Queen Street, Central Newcastle 0191 221 0601

Established in 1990 by Matab Miah. 'Stylish restaurant, upmarket surroundings, seats 90 on two floors, party room 40. Comfortable, well-lit and very clean. No standard curries, but starter and main courses proved interesting and a good choice.' KDF. 'Most luxurious surroundings in

Newcastle. Excellent tandoori starter, main course a little disappointing.' T&KM Remains in our TOP 100, and gives discounts. Price check: Papadam 60p, CTM £8.90, Pullao Rice £1.90. House wine £8.90. Hours: 11.30-2.30pm/6.30-11.30pm. Stocks Cobra.

South Shields

SAFFRON BALTI HOUSE ©

86 Ocean Road, South Shields 0191 456 6098

Abdul Kadir's 56-seater has 'light modern decor with traditional pictures on the walls, comfortable seating with tables for 2 to 8 people.' Sunday lunch £3.95. Takeaway: 15% off. Hours: 12-2.30pm (Fri. closed)/6pm-12.30am (2am on Fri. & Sat., 12am on Sun.). Stocks Cobra.

STAR OF INDIA ©

194 Ocean Road, South Shields 0191 456 2210

The first curry house in South Shields, it opened in 1960, and was taken over by M Faruque in 1972. Seats 60, light gold and white wall coverings, burgundy seats, alcove seating on both sides of restaurant. 'Standard restaurant and menu in very competitive area. Good service, excellent food and extremely cheap. Great value for money, no frills, good portions, not spotlessly clean, but I'll be back.' IB. Specials: Chicken Tikka Jalfrezi and Chilli Pilau. Takeaway: 15% off. Hours: 12-2.30pm/5.30pm-12am. Branch: Royal Bengal, Prince Regent Street, Stockton. Shapla, 192, Northgate, Darlington. Stocks Cobra.

Sunderland

MOTIRAJ NEW ENTRANT ©

6-7 Church Lane, Sunderland 0191 565 6916

Established in 1974. Seats 90. Parking for 20-25 cars outside main entrance. Fully refurbished in their Silver Jubilee Year (1999). Specials: Gobi Musallum £2.05 – spicy cauliflower, coconut and cashew nuts. Price check: Papadam 50p, CTM £5.80, Pullao Rice £1.90, Peshwari Nan £1.50. Takeaway: £1 off all main dishes. Hours: 6pm-12am. Stocks Cobra.

Wallsend

MODERN TAKEAWAY NEW ENTRANT

178 High Street, Wallsend 0191 212 4437

Established in 1979. Takeaway only. Price check: Papadam 50p, CTM £4.85, Pullao Rice £1.70, Peshwari Nan £1.80. Hours: 12-2.30pm/6-11.30pm.

Whickham

JAMDANI ©

3 The Square, Front Street, Whickham 0191 496 0820

Opened in 1988 by Mr A Miah. Try the Chicken Saffron or King Prawns – delicious. Hours: 12-2pm/6-11.30pm. Stocks Cobra.

MOTI JHEEL TAKEAWAY NEW ENTRANT ©

9 Front Street, Whickham 0191 488 0851

First opened in 1982, taken over by MM Rahman in 1990. Specials: Bamboo Shoot Bhajee £1.80. King Prawn Bhajia £2.60. Great selection of rice dishes: Onion Pullao £1.80, Lamb Tikka Pullao £3.20, Aloo Pullao £1.80 and Chilli Pullao £1.80 to name just a few. Price check: Papadam 35p, CTM £4.50, Pullao Rice £1.40, Peshwari Nan £1.40. Delivery: £1 within 2-mile radius. Hours: 12-2pm/6-11.30pm; Sat. & Sun. 6pm-12am.

Whitley Bay

HIMALAYA ©

33 Esplanade, Whitley Bay 0191 251 3629

Reliable curry house. Owner is Abdul Goffar. Hours: 12-2.30pm/5.30pm-12am. Stocks Cobra.

KISMET ©

177 Whitley Road, Whitley Bay 0191 297 2028

First opened in 1968, taken over in 1996 by Shohid Ahmed. Seats 45. Specials include: Chicken Tikka Massala Punjabi style, Lamb Shahi Tukra. 'The best Indian restaurant we have been to.' KW. Price check: Papadam 55p, CTM £5.95, Pullao Rice £1.85, Peshwari Nan £1.95, Lager £2 pint. Takeaway: 10% discount. Hours: 12-2pm (Fri. closed)/6pm-12am. Stocks Cobra.

SHAHENSHAH ©

187-189 Whitley Road, Whitley Bay 0191 297 0503

Established 1988 by Abu Taher, 'good-looking' decor. Bangladeshi formula curries cooked by A Hannan.'Food first-class. Chicken Tikka terrific, full of flavour.' MB. 'My local for a year.' SN. 'We found the restaurant busy in a quiet and efficient way. Cobra the perfect accompaniment.' PP. Hours: 12-2.30pm/6pm-12am. Stocks Cobra.

TAKDIR ©

11 East Parade, Whitley Bay 0191 253 0236

Majibur Rahman's reliable 70-seater. Minimum charge £10. Hours: 5.30pm-12am. Branches: Akash, 3 Tangier Street, Whitehaven, Cumbria; Al Mamun Takeaway, 5 John Street, Cullercoats, T&W. Stocks Cobra.

WHITLEY BAY TANDOORI NEW ENTRANT

40 Esplanade, Whitley Bay 0191 252 9483

Established in 1996. Seats 42. Specials include: King Prawn Peli Peli, King Prawn in thick lentil sauce with cooked red chillies. Price check: Papadam 75p, CTM £5.95, Pullao Rice £1.85, Peshwari Nan £1.55, Lager £2.20 pint. Takeaway: 10% discount. Delivery: £7 minimum, 3-mile radius. Hours: 12-2pm/6pm-12am. Stocks Cobra.

Winlaton

BALTI HOUSE ©20%

18a The Garth, Front Street, Winlaton 0191 414 2223

Established in 1996. Seats 42. Specials include: King Prawn Peli Peli. Owner F.I. Khan promises to increase his takeaway discount from 15% to 20% for CC members. You can't get fairer than that! Hours: 6pm-12am. Branch: Balti House, Newcastle. Stocks Cobra.

WARWICKSHIRE

Area: Midlands
Population: 506,000
Adjacent Counties: Derbys, Shrops, Staffs, W Mids, Worcs

Alcester

CELLAR

7 Market Place, High Street, Alcester 01789 764635

Formerly Balti Cellar. M Hussain's 60-seater, traditional vaulted historical cellar. Specials: Crab and Duck dishes. Hours: 6pm-12am.

Coleshill B46

POLASH BALTI CUISINE

85 High Street, Coleshill, B46 01675 462868

A chapatti throw from the NEC, and just inside the Warwickshire/W Mids border, is Coleshill. And much, it seems, to the delight of the locals, is this 32 seater cosy curry house, first opened in 1997. Taken over by in 98 by Adbul Mannan, it is decorated in cream, blue velvet chairs and carpet, with engraved glass screens dividing the seating. Car parking for 30 to rear of restaurant. Chef Taj Ullah cooks up the curries. Special: Bengal Fish Masala, Bangladeshi fish on the bone, cooked with herbs, coriander, served with rice £8.95. 'What an experience! Such attention, such luxury, such choice and such cooking! Our congratulations and thanks to the Polash.' HFC. Price check: Papadam 40p, CTM £5.50, Pullao Rice £1.70, Peshwari Nan £1.80, Lager £2.25 pint. Takeaway: 10% discount. Delivery: £15 minimum, 3-mile radius. Hours: 5.30pm-12am. Stocks Cobra.

Kenilworth

THE COCONUT LAGOON NEW ENTRANT

149 Warwick Road, Kenilworth 01926 851156

Opened early 1999 within the Peacock Hotel, Kenilworth. In its previous incarnation, it was known as Balti Towers and Kenilworth Lodge Hotel, respectively. The departure of Basil may raise less smiles, but I'll bet the staff are getting less ribbing now. The clue is in the name of this new venture. There is a superlative leisure resort of that name in India's deep south. Hardly had it opened before it was brought to our attention that this restaurant serves dishes from four regional cuisines of South India. 'All is very fresh and carefully cooked. It is an astonishingly good restaurant, as good as any in London and big surprise for the provinces, where genuinely Hindu "Indian" establishments are so few. I feel confident it will be an immediate candidate for your "TOP 100".' DC. We adore this style of cooking, so hard to find outside London, and it is to be encouraged. Deluge us with reports. Stocks Cobra.

RAFFLES

57 Warwick Road, Kenilworth 01926 864300

'Ultra expensive, top-quality, extremely upmarket restaurant. Choice of Malaysian Malay, Malaysian Chinese or Malaysian Indian. Curry Puff, triangular samosa shaped pastry but very different inside, exquisite taste. Ikin Kelaph, plaice in a crumb coating, which included coconut, deep-fried and very crispy, served with stir-fried asparagus, carrots, sweet potatoes and a spicy dip, most enjoyable. Sambal Ikan, magnificently spicy fish in a beautiful sauce, quite superb! Ais Kacing, shaved ice, condensed milk, rose water, bits of jelly, assorted colours. Very cold; as it melted, I fished around and got bits such as red kidney beans, very unusual. Superb service.' GGP&MP.

SEETAR NEW ENTRANT

55 Warwick Road, Kenilworth 01926 851585

Established in 1988. Seats 80. Price check: Papadam 70p, CTM £7.25, Pullao Rice £2.10, Peshwari Nan £2.10, Lager £2.30 pint. Takeaway: 20% discount. Hours: 5-11.30pm; Sat. 5pm-12am; Sun. 12.30-2pm. Stocks Cobra.

SUNAM BALTI HOUSE BYO

57 Abbey End, Abbey Court, Kenilworth 01926 863070

Amin Uddin's 62-seater. Northern Indian food on the menu. Licensed, but you are welcome to bring your own wines, strictly before 9.30pm (25p corkage per person). House special is Garlic King Prawns £6.50. Price check: Papadam 40p, CTM £4.95, Pullao Rice £1.50. Lager £1.90 pint, House wine £6.50. Takeaway: 10% off. Hours: 5-11.30pm.

Leamington Spa

BALTI VHUJOH TAKEAWAY NEW ENTRANT

509 Queen Street, Leamington Spa 01926 423828

Established in February 2000. Takeaway only. Specials include: Tandoori Jinga Massala (King sized prawns Tandoori roasted, and cooked with mild spices, cream and a touch of butter), £7.95. Price check: Papadam 35p, CTM £4.95, Pullao Rice £1.40, Peshwari Nan £1.35. Delivery: £10 minimum, 3-mile radius. Hours: 5.30-11pm; closed Sun.

BOMBAY TANDOORI ©

38-40 Regent Street, Leamington Spa 01926 420521

Opened in 1990 by chef Anar Ahmed. Serves Bangladeshi and north Indian curries. House specials: Khata Masli (Bangladeshi fish steaks in tangy spicy sauce) £6.75, Kooris Lamb (whole leg of spring lamb spiced, marinated for at least eight hours, roasted tandoori-style, garnished with mincemeat and served with Vegetable Bartha and Pillao Rice) £58.50 for four. Minimum order £5.50. Takeaway: 20% off. Price check: Papadam 50p, CTM £5.95, Pullao Rice £1.50. House wine £6.25. Delivery: £12 minimum, 3-mile radius. Hours: 6pm-1am (3am on Fri. & Sat.). Stocks Cobra.

PAPRIKA NEW ENTRANT

22, Regent Street, Leamington Spa 01926 428272

Formerly Balti Mela. 'Decor very fresh, bright and modern. Attentive staff. Food very good, tasty, visually attractive and ample portions, prices quite reasonable.' FWB. Price check: Papadam 45p, CTM £5.60, Pullao Rice £1.70, Peshwari Nan £1.50. Hours: 6pm-12am (Fri. & Sat. to 1am). Stocks Cobra.

PUNJAB NEW ENTRANT

41 Bath Street, Leamington Spa 01926 425184

Established in 1972. Seats 40. Specials include: Karahi chicken or lamb dishes with special spices. Price check: Papadam 50p, CTM £5.50, Pullao Rice £1.95, Peshwari Nan £1.95, Lager £2.25 pint. Delivery: £10 minimum. Hours: 6pm-1am. Stocks Cobra.

Nuneaton

RAJDHANI ©

1 Cambourne Drive, Horeston Grange, Nuneaton 01203 352254

Surat Miah's 56-seater. Opened in 1985. Unusual specials: Tikka Paneer Jalfrezi, cooked with tomatoes, onion and green chillies, £6.95. and Tandoori Quail or Trout. Minimum charge £12. Takeaway: 20% off. Hours: 5.30-11pm.

Rugby

BENGAL SPICE NEW ENTRANT

318 Hill Morton Road, Rugby 01788 540222

Established in 1995, taken over by Rehan Uddin in 1998. Previously called Paddox Balti. Seats 60. Special buffet supper every night. Price check: Papadam 40p, CTM £5.95, Pullao Rice £1.50, Peshwari Nan £1.50, Lager £2.30 pint. Takeaway: 10% discount. Delivery: £10 minimum, 3-mile radius. Hours: 5-11pm. Stocks Cobra.

DILRUBA TANDOORI

155-157, Railway Terrace, Rugby 01788 542262

Liaquat Ali owns this popular 54-seater. 'Saturday evening, staff gave very friendly welcome. Popadoms and the tray appeared quickly. Impressive menu, diversity of dishes, some new to us. Cobra and Kingfisher on draught, these exotic lager beers were priced the same as others, which I thought was fair. [It is not a question of being fair, it is only right, these lager beers are not exotic, they are brewed over here.] Shared a marinated fish starter, sufficiently good to remind us of the fish curries we had in beach cafés in Goa several years ago. Main courses arrived as soon as the starter plates had been whipped away. Balti Chicken Shashlik – new to me, packed with chicken, wasn't as much onion as I expected, overpowering tomato sauce. CTM tasty, minimum amount of ghee.' AT. 'Surprised to read in the Club Magazine of poor report. [Rugby's LW told us she had two disappointing meals here.] We have been going at least once a week for many years. Pleased to see new additions to menu. I chose Massala Fish £3.50, my wife Onion Bhajia £2.00, shared CTM £7, Prawn Bhuna £5, Peas Pullao Rice and Plain Nan. As usual, very enjoyable,very comfortable, friendly, staff helpful. £28 for two.' D&LC. Price check: Papadam 60p, CTM £6.50, Pullao Rice £1.60. Takeaway: 10% off. Delivery: £10 minimum. Hours: 6pm-1am (2am on Sat.). Stocks Cobra.

TITASH INTERNATIONAL BALTI NEW ENTRANT

65 Church Street, Rugby 01788 574433

'Rather more upmarket than traditional plastic chair/formica table/BYO Balti house, but is good value and serves excellent curries. Small reception area, friendly welcome, etched glass panels and marble-top tables. Service polite and efficient, high quality food. Particular favourites: Tandoori Mixed Kebab and Lamb Spare Ribs. Baltis are delivered to the table on a trolley and vigorously heated to serving temperature over a gas burner, aromas make for a mouthwatering experience. Chicken Tikka Chilli Masala is highly recommended. Wines have increased in price in short space of time. One of my favourite places for a tasty, no-nonsence curry experience.' PJ. Stocks Cobra.

Stratford-upon-Avon

LALBAGH BALTI ©

3 Greenhill Street, Stratford 01789 293563

Opened in 1989 by Abdul Aziz, who is also to be found in the kitchen as head chef. 46 seater, decorated in maroon with patterned wallpaper, green carpet and Bangladeshi pictures on the wall. Specials: Mushroom on Puri, and Fish Kebab. 'Conventional menu. Excellent comfort. Polite and reserved service. Papadoms served with delicious sauce and onion relish, very good. Lalbagh Special Chicken, large quantity, wholesome chicken, quality ingredients.' GG&MP. Takeaway: 10% discount. Hours: 6pm-12.30am; Fri & Sat. 6pm-1am.

RAJ ©

7 Greenhill Street, Stratford 01789 267067

Owner/manager Nurul Zaman Khan. Decoration: mixture of burgundy and cream colours. Special: Chicken Sath Lemon Sylheti, diced chicken cooked in medium spiced sauce with sath lemon (shakora). Delivery: £15 min, 4-mile radius. Hours: 12.30pm-12.30am; Sun. lunch closed. Stocks Cobra.

THESPIAN'S INDIAN CUISINE ©

26 Sheep Street, Stratford 01789 267187

Opened in 1996 by chef-proprietor Habibur Rahman. 45 seat, air-conditioned with Bangladeshi food featuring on his menu. For an interesting change, try Boal Biriani for a starter – fillets of Bengal boal, lightly spiced. House specials include Lobster Beruda, aubergine-flavoured sauce, served with Pilau Rice. Fish Bhuna Bengal Style (just as it is cooked in India, says Mr Rahman). 'Very wide menu, unusual choices. Predominantly pink lounge with mock tudor bar. Very comfortable with pleasant surroundings. Variable quality and quantity.' GG&MP. Minimum charge £10.95. Takeaway: 10% discount. Delivery: £12 min, 3-miles. Hours: 5.30-11.30pm. Branches: Knowle Indian Brasserie, Knowle; Stockland Balti Takeaway, Marsh Lane, Erdington, Birmingham. Stocks Cobra.

USHA INDIAN CUISINE NEW ENTRANT

28 Meer Street, Stratford — 01789 297348

First opened 1968, taken over by Nazrul Isuam in 1995. Previously called the Kashmir Restaurant. Seats 56. The takeaway menu even gives a mobile number! – now there's a restaurant keen not to miss any business! 'With one and a half hours to kill before the theatre, we found this delightful restaurant by chance. Service and food first class. Popadoms crisp, mango chutney and lime pickle "simply wonderful". Starters: Chicken Pakora and Persian Tandoori Kebab – excellent portions and taste. Main courses: Chicken Sag Balti – breast and Special Mixed Balti – full of meat, prawns, sauce a little watery with Keema Nans – arrived already sliced, like pizza, a nice touch.' DJL. Takeaway: 15% discount. Price check: Papadams 40p, CTM £6.95, Pullao Rice £1.70, Peshwari Nan £1.70. Lager £2.50 pint. Hours: 5pm-12am (Sat. to 12.30am); Sun. 6pm-12am. Stocks Cobra.

Warwick

VERANDA NEW ENTRANT

24 Smith Street, Warwick — 01926 491736

'Nice welcome, very plush, seating on a verandah overlooking the bar area, toilets clean, service friendly and efficient, good quality food served hot. Would certainly return when in the area.' JAG. Stocks Cobra.

COBRA GOOD CURRY GUIDE
County Index, see page 5 Town Index, see page 614
A to Z of the Curry Menu, page 41 Contributors Key, page 604

WEST MIDLANDS

Area: Midlands
Population: 2,638,000
Adjacent Counties: Staffs, Warks, Worcs

West Midlands was introduced as a county in 1965 and contains the conurbations from the Black Country at its west, through to Coventry in the east. At its hub is Birmingham city.

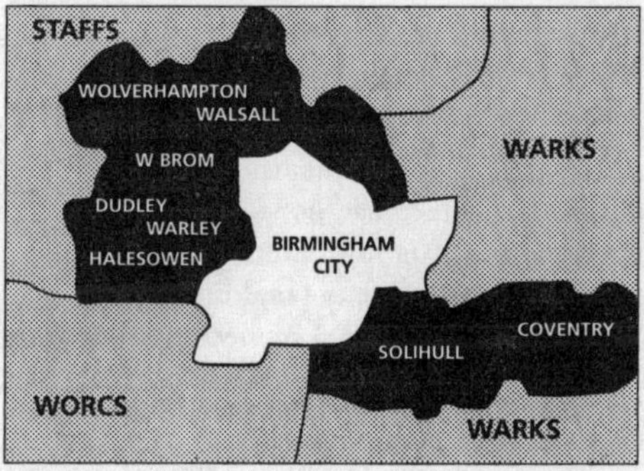

BIRMINGHAM CITY

Birmingham postcodes, B1 to B46
Population – 1,018,000

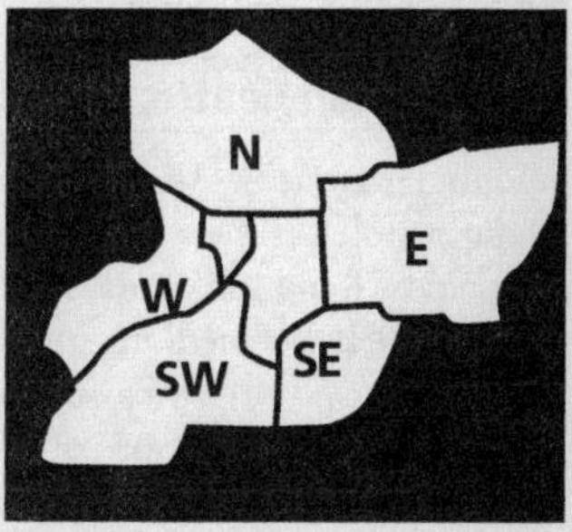

Unquestionably Britain's number two city, Brum has come vibrantly alive with investment in its infrastructure. For the purposes of this Directory, we divide the city into geographical areas, in which are grouped postcode zones B1 *to* B48 *although, as ever, there is no sequential logic to postcode numbering. They are frankly a jumble. But it is the system which exists, and to help narrow things down, we have divided the city, using major roads as our arbitrary boundaries. We start with Birmingham Central, then go south to the adjacent Balti Zone, next North of the city, then East, South East, South West, and West. Further* B *postcodes,* B62 *(Halesowen) to* B93 *(Solihull) follow, listed alphabetically by their suburb name.*

©	Curry Club Discount	**U**	Unlicensed
V	Vegetarian	**ANP**	Alcohol not permitted
e-a-m-a-y-l	Eat as much as you like	**BYO**	Bring your own alcohol

Birmingham Central
Postcodes B1 to B5
(restaurants listed in alphabetical order)

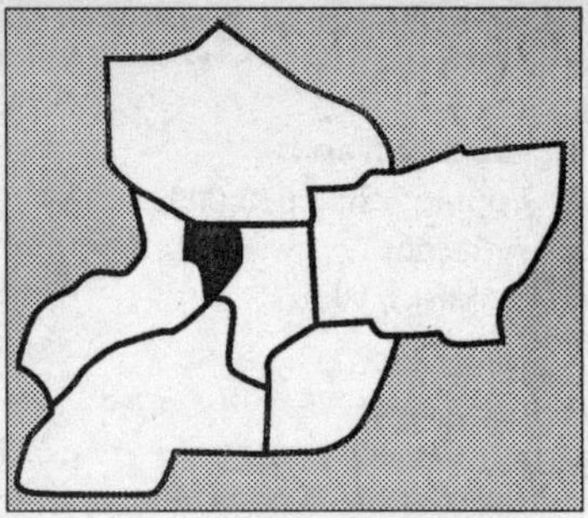

ALOKA

6-8 Bristol Street, Digbeth, Birmingham B5 — 0121 622 2011

In 1960, Birmingham centre had just one curryhouse. It was at the above address. I know because I always came here from as far afield as Coventry, where I lived and worked, which had none. I really don't remember if it was called the Aloka then, but it is now. During the 1960s, the spread of the curry house was as prolific as the city's building. Now it's Birmingham 280, Coventry 40. So here's to the Aloka, a pioneer indeed. Stocks Cobra.

BOMBAY SPICE NEW ENTRANT

28 Essex Street, Digbeth, Birmingham, B5 — 0121 236 8664

Established in 1959, taken over by A Shiraz in 2000. Previously called Bombay Restaurant, until 1999. Seats 110. Fully refurbished. Price check: Papadam 45p, CTM £5.95, Pullao Rice £1.95, Peshwari Nan £1.95. Takeaway: 10% discount. Delivery: £7 min. Hours: 6pm-4am. Stocks Cobra.

FESTIVAL BALTI ©

204 Arcadian Centre, Birmingham B5 — 0121 622 6289

'Mojibul Haque's 48-seater is chic and modern and packed with smart young people on the night we looked in. Chef Abdul Ali's specials include Chicken or Lamb Shatkora, made tangy with the Sylhetti lemon (£5.95) and Seafood Delight, medium-spiced with fish, prawns and scampi. Pops and free chutney. Lamb Tikka sparse, Fish Pakora good size. Very nice Chicken Rogan Josh. Presentation of food excellent. Restaurant clean and tidy.' GG&MP. I am pleased to see this restaurant mentioned in the guide. Standards seem to have generally been maintained. Superb onion/herb relish, excellent Sheek Kebab, really superb Chicken Tikka Garlic Balti. On a separate visit I ordered Chicken Shashlik which, although nicely marinated and very tasty, was barely warm and badly presented – a shame as the chicken itself tasted great.' CT. Minimum charge £5. Hours: 5-11.30pm, Fri. & Sat. lunch 12-2pm. Stocks Cobra.

MAHARAJAH AWARD WINNER AND TOP 100

23 Hurst Street, Birmingham B5 0121 622 2641

N Bhatt's Maharajah is a small place (62 seats on two floors) and booking is recommended. The food is Indian, cooked by Gurmaj Kumar and Jaskarn Dhillon. The menu looks a little ordinary, but the food is still always spot on. Ask about the Special Dish of the Day. I recall this restaurant serving Biriani topped with edible silver leaf (vark) when it first opened in 1971. It was the first time I'd seen it used in Britain, though traditionalists in India would not contemplate the dish without it. It was a Moghul fetish, of course, the emperor permitting a gold leaf garnish only on the food for himself and the chosen member of the harem (the dish of the day!), while his wives had to make do with silver leaf. They believed it to be an aphrodisiac. It is not for me to comment on the validity of this claim and, with the EU ban on vark (because of aluminium adulteration), neither can the Maharajah's diners – they no longer serve it, sadly. Service is mature and careful, and the place is often full to bursting. Waiting bookers are deftly dispatched to the downstairs bar. Such competence is rare and welcome. We continue to receive plentiful reports on the Maharajah, and just one snorter (from MRS JJB). Stays in our TOP 100. Price check: Papadam 70p, CTM £6.80, Pullao Rice £2.20, Plain Nan £1.40, Lager £2.40. Hours: 12-2pm/6-11pm; closed Sun. & bank holidays. Stocks Cobra.

MILAN INDIAN CUISINE ©

93 Newhall Street, Birmingham B3 0121 236 0671

Dhirendra Patel's 120-seater, established in 1989, is decorated in pastel shades, giving it a light and airy feel. The bar area is typically Indian with beaten copper drinks tables and large coffee pots. Chef Balbir Malhi's menu features all the usual curry house favourites from Korma to Jalfrezi but there is also an extensive vegetarian section. Paneer Tikka £2.25, spicy paneer cooked in the tandoor. Stuffed peppers filled with coconut, potatoes and coriander £1.95. Reshmi Mattar Paneer £4.50, homemade cheese with herbs, spices, peas, cashews and corn. Price check: Papadam 70p, CTM £6.50, Pullao Rice £1.95, Peshwari Nan £1.95, Lager £2.50 pint. Minimum charge £8.50. Hours: 12-2pm/6pm-12am; Sat. 6pm-12am; Sun. closed. Branches: 129 Stoney Lane, B11, 238 Soho Rd, Handsworth B21, and 296 S Abel Street, Milpitas, nr San José, California, US. Stocks Cobra.

MOKHAM'S OF DIGBETH U ©

140 Digbeth High Street, Birmingham B5 0121 643 7375

Of Naz Khan's venue AM says 'Mokham's pride themselves on their cooking so you may have to wait as all the food is freshly prepared. Tandoori Sheeksh Kebab is certainly one of the best I have ever tasted. Balti Exotica is meat, chicken, prawns, mushroom and pasta, without doubt unique in my experience. A very substantial dish, served up in the traditional black bowl, it was beautifully spiced and the pasta blended superbly but when combined with my Nan bread it left me feeling like Pavarotti.' And RW says: 'Small but smart genuine Balti house in the city centre. Very friendly, family run. Extensive menu. Fresh papadoms, light and well cooked chat, tender Lamb Tikka cuts in a mild to medium sauce. Light and fluffy naans buttered and pleasantly sweet.' Hours: 12-2.30pm/6pm to late.

RAJDOOT ©

12 Albert Street, Birmingham B4 0121 643 8749

MS Gill manages this 84-seat branch of Des Sarda's Rajdoot (the others are in Bristol, Manchester, Dublin and Fuengirola, Spain). He opened this one in 1972. As are all the Rajdoots, it is fully air-conditioned and tastefully and authentically decorated. Des is an architect and knows a thing or two about style. The chefs here are Nepalese (head chef Basu Mali) and their cooking is as delicate as you'll find. 'Absolutely superb, we find this establishment to be extremely reliable. Fish Tikka starter exquisite as usual as was the Chilli Chicken Tikka, generous portions. King Prawn Chilli Garlic was a favourite amongst our group again but I decided to try the Lamb Punjabi Massalla this time and what a good choice!! Meat extremely lean and well spiced, served in a dark onion and tomato gravy finished with balsamic vinegar and red wine. We ordered the usual side dishes, dal of the day, Bombay Allo Jeera and Sag Paneer as well as Pillau Rice and Peshwari Nan, all of which were fresh and cooked to perfection.' CT. I regret to say that like the other Rajdoots (see entries) we do get complaints. Service charge 10%. Hours: 12-2.30pm (not Sun.)/6.30-11.30pm. Stocks Cobra.

SHAH'S BALTI TANDOORI NEW ENTRANT

59 Station Road, B5 0121 643 5723

Established in 1993. Seats 56. Sharp, modern, minimalist decor. Price check: Papadam 65p, CTM £8.85, Pullao Rice £2.25, Peshwari Nan £2.20, Lager £2.80 pint. Hours: 6pm-12am; Sat. 6pm-1am; Sun. 6pm-12am. Stocks Cobra.

BIRMINGHAM – BALTI ZONE

Consists of B10 to B13

(restaurants listed in alphabetical order within postcode)

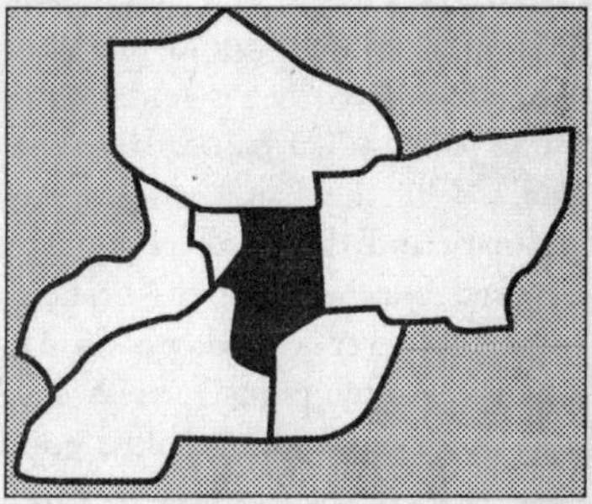

The Balti Zone starts about 2 miles south east of the city (follow the A34), and is thickly spread around the suburbs of Small Heath, Sparkhill, Sparkbrook and Moseley (B10 to B13). The population is largely north Pakistani, mostly from Kashmir's Mirpur, adjacent to which is the district of Baltistan, high up in the Pakistani mountains. You'll find recipes and more about this subject in my 'Balti Bible' (see page 624). Those who doubt the existence of Baltistan should visit K2 Baltihouse, upon whose walls is the biggest map of the region that I've seen, and it is from there that Balti originated. But for those who prefer to say it did so in a bucket in Birmingham, you are certain to get the nation's best Baltis here. There have been innumerable changes here over the last two years. Too many venues has led to empty houses, even at the weekend, and subsequent closures. One result is the e-a-m-a-y-l buffets, which, whilst value for money, never, in our view compare in quality to individually cooked baltis. Here are the views of the lucky scribes who live there, and those who visit:

Birmingham B11

Sparkbrook, Sparkhill

ADIL 1 AWARD WINNER AND TOP 100 BYO ©

148-150 Stoney Lane, Sparkbrook, B11 0121 449 0335

Mohammed Arif, Rashid and Abid Mahood opened here in 1975. Although they are not the first balti (it was a café called the Paris opened in 1973 by a Mr Ramzan, the former long-closed because the latter had retired back to native Baltistan before discovering that he had started an international cult). Arif is happy to claim to be first, and he is indisputably the longer at it. 'My grandfather' he says, 'ran a restaurant in Kashmir decades ago, called Adil meaning Justice. Customers chose their own fresh raw ingredients, and watched the entire cooking process. Apart from that, our Sparkbrook restaurant is identical.' Well, it was. There's been a sparkling modernisation recently, enlarging the place to 100 seats with 56 upstairs. The menu hasn't changed. It still offers 72 different Baltis, including their much-copied signature dish, meat 'chicken' mince with veg-dall-spi-chana. 'My birthday and what better, after a 7.30am champagne and Guinness breakfast in

©	Curry Club Discount	U	Unlicensed
V	Vegetarian	ANP	Alcohol not permitted
e-a-m-a-y-l	Eat as much as you like	BYO	Bring your own alcohol

London's Smithfield Market, than to travel to Birmingham for a Balti at Adil's. After the initiation course of Green Chilli Bhajis 70p, we settled down to enjoy Balti Chicken Tikka Veg-Dall-Spi-Chana £5.20, two massive Table Nans £2.90 and two portions of rice £1. My colleague Ian (two puddings) Hunter could not contain himself, unable to decide between Rasmali 90p, Barfi 60p and Kulfi £1.40, and ate all three. Simple as abc – Adil's for Balti Curry.' DB. 'If I'm anywhere near Birmingham I pilgrimage to Adil's. Oh! the Baltis! and so low a price. Avoid the starters, they are ordinary and the small portions make them poor value for money. Not licensed, but there is an off-licence next door run by his cousin. If you order a cab, the driver is another cousin! Family enterprise!' CD. Adil's own car park opposite. Often pioneers are best, although Adil's took a dive in popularity and quality recently: 'Looked good from the outside and was quite busy. Next door to the Al-Faisal so I thought the competition would ensure high quality food – wrong. I had to send back my Seekh Kebabs, the replacements were not much better. Tandoori Roti was OK, papadoms were oily. Won't bother going back.' RE. I am happy to see it begin to thrive again in its second-generation-same-family management. Accordingly I am not only restoring Adils to our TOP 100, I am giving it our 1999 Best UK Balti Award. Price check: Papadam 35p, Pullao Rice: £1. CTM £4.50. Delivery: minimum £10. 3-mile radius. Hours: 12am-12am (Thurs.-Sat. to 1am).

DESI KHANA — ANP

706 Stratford Road, Sparkhill, B11 — 0121 778 4450

RE said last time: 'This is my favourite. Decidedly Asian – European customers are rare – strict Muslim. Glass top tables and a shortish menu, but the food is good.' This time he says: 'Still great food. Sheeh Kebab freshly cooked on sizzling platter, excellent. Peshwari Gosht in a balti, had quality lamb pieces in a thick, tasty sauce. The price for one person was high by comparison with most others in the area, but the food is good.' [On a subsequent visit Ray reports that it has had a facelift, and food is still very good.]

MILAN SWEET CENTRE NEW ENTRANT — V

191 Stoney Lane, Sparkbrook, B11 — 0121 449 1617

A branch of the Milan restaurant in 93 Newhall Street, Birmingham B3 (see entry above). This is a takeaway venue for Indian sweets, and savoury snacks. The selection is huge and satisfying, at prices too cheap to ignore. Sister t/a branch at 238 Soho Road, Handsworth, B21.

ROYAL NAIM AWARD WINNER AND TOP 100 BYO ©

417-419 Stratford Road, Sparkhill, B11 0121 766 7849

Sadly, we've had three really bad reports about a venue we praise highly enough to have given it Best Balti Award twice. Yet we ourselves have visited here, unannounced, several times in the same period, and we haven't had the same experience. The place has been busy, though given the current state of competition in Baltiland, maybe less busy than before, but it was, in each case, a mid week visit. This is a *Guide* editor's dilemma. It seems so unlikely for the owners to change their ways for the worse, and no restaurant can make an instant change (for the better) because a restaurant critic turns up. We welcome your reports, but here is an amalgam of our own experiences. The Nazir brothers' restaurant is huge – 180 seats on two floors, yet it doesn't feel oversized. It's open all hours, of course it's BYO, and the prices are very reasonable. You can fill yourself for £5, and blow up for £10. You are made welcome and are served with prompt efficiency throughout. The portions are still huge, and more importantly, the food is as tasty as you can get in any style of 'Indo-Pak' restaurant. Order from the menu located under the glass table top. The selection is huge, with every Balti combination you can think of and some more. Then leave it to Chef Shaffique and his crew to get cooking, while your taste buds tingle. But before your choice arrives, get nibbling on a papadom, if for nothing else, to taste the lurid red delicious chutney that accompanies it. Unless your stomach is horse-sized, don't order more than one Balti, and don't eat too much before it arrives – it's a huge portion. Order rice if you must, but doing it the Pakistani way, with no cutlery, and huge naan breads to tear and scoop with is hugely satisfying. And then it arrives, served the Balti way, in 10" steel karahis (Balti pans) the food cooked in the pan, made black with thousands of hours of cooking. It's more than filling and great fun. The Naim also produce deep frozen Baltis for retail outlets and local schools. 'No wonder Birmingham's education standards are starting to rise!' AM. 'The atmosphere was building before we found the actual restaurant because of the community in which it is situated and the numerous other Balti restaurants surrounding it. The basic nature emphasized the excellent food. Owner very attentive and helpful. Returned a month later. Once you get the Balti in front of you and taste it you don't want it to end.' SR. 'Visited on a busy Saturday night. Standard of service, choice, quality of food and value for money is very high. Party of eight, four adults, four children, plenty of choice for all. Our large Naan £3 covered the table. Washed down with a jug of Lassi. Ras Malai for pudding is hard to beat. My children insisted I make a detour two days later on our return from Kendal to Suffolk to revisit the Royal Naim.' DB. Delivery: £10 minimum, 3-mile radius. Hours: 12pm-1am; Sat. 12pm-3am.

SHAHEHSHAH NEW ENTRANT

326 Ladypool Road, Sparkbrook, B11 0121 449 6463

'Shami Kebabs £1.00 – excellent value for money. Very good and very spicy. Generous portion. Chicken Masala Balti – sauce a little bland, but chicken of good quality. Menu extremely wide, variable quality, generous quantities, service very good. But we were all agreed that our meals were much too salty and this was passed on to the management. Overall verdict: absolutely superb'. GG&MP.

TY'S JAZZ & SPICE NEW ENTRANT

132 Stratford Road, Sparkhill, B11 0121 773 1632

Authentic Kashmiri cuisine here 'and excellent too' – AN. The clue's in the name. This place hums, literally, with its emphasis on live jazz on certain days. Established in 1999. Formerly the Kashmir Lodge. Seats 80. 'Very impressive decor, high ceilings, drape curtains, chandelier. Mixed Grill, Lamb Tikka, Chicken Tikka, Tandoori Fish, Sheesh Kebab at £3.50, wonderful mixture of flavours. Very large quantities, top-quality ingredients. Service slow with starters but these were obviously freshly cooked, so understandable.' GG&MP. Private car park for up to 30 cars with CCTV. Chic, modern decor. Price check: Papadam 50p, CTM £8.50, Pullao Rice £1.50, Peshwari Nan £2.10.

Birmingham B12

Balsall Heath, Sparkbrook, Sparkhill

AL-FRASH BYO ©

186 Ladypool Road, Sparkbrook, B12 0121 753 3120

Established in 1994, Mukhtar Ahmed's 180-seater is a 'Traditional curry house with old style decor. A little on the dark side perhaps. Customer care rating very high (they asked whether the person ordering the Meetha Ghosht was allergic to nuts). Succulent Mixed Grill, outstandingly melt-in-your-mouth Tandoori Fish, but undercooked Aloo Pakora and very poor Vegetable Samosas.' GG&MP . Starters include Onion Rings 65p, one of DBAC's favourites. It's one of Andy Munroe's Top 10: 'Starters to die for – the mushroom and aubergine Pakoras come highly recommended. For main course try the "white rose" house speciality which is not a steal from a Bradford curry house but a popular Lahore dish comprising chunks of chicken breast languishing in a cardamom flavoured sauce with cashew and cream. Alternatively try Meetha Gosht which is tender lamb in fried onions, sultanas, coconut and almonds, a great balance of a spicy back taste off-setting the sweetness. Mop it all up with voluptuous garlic Nan, although the coriander version takes some beating.' AM. Smart decor with authentic Kashmiri furniture. Specials include: Meetha Ghusht. Price check: Papadam 35p, CTM £5.20, Pullao Rice £1.40, Peshwari Nan £1.50. Hours: 5pm-1am.

ALI BABA — U BYO ©

250 Ladypool Road, Sparkbrook, B12 — 0121 449 4929

We like Mr Aslam's logo of a chap holding a sizzling Balti, sitting on a flying carpet (beats cars for home delivery?). 'Clean comfortable. BYO. Very good Sheek Kebab 70p, freshly cooked and spicy. Nice Roti. Lamb Bhuna, prepared with extra chilli, very accommodating.' RE.

IMRAN'S BALTI HUT — U BYO

264 Ladypool Road, Sparkbrook, B12 — 0121 449 1370

'Baltis, superb. Family Nan, unbelievable – 3 feet by 2 feet. BYO from "offy" next door. Excellent value for money.' RS. 'Claims to have been around at the time of the first-ever splitting of Balti bread in Brum. Spacious and includes in-view cooking for those who like to see a Sheeksh Kebab being cooked live. My main course Balti Chicken and Mushroom had an impressively spicy kick. Unusually you can also get a family Chapatti also Quail Balti (a dish which has now achieved almost protected status).' AM. 'Lamb Jalfrezi, meat tough and lacked depth of flavour. Chicken Korma – too hot for a Korma and for my wife.' RE. Hours: 12pm-12am.

KASHMIR KEBAB HOUSE — NEW ENTRANT

141 Ladypool Rd, Sparkbrook, B12

'A cross between McDonalds and a wine bar. Thriving takeaway. Food is all on display in glass cabinet. Food is very good and exceptional value for money.' RE.

KASHMIR LODGE

132 Stratford Road, Sparkbrook, B12 — 0121 773 1632

'Housed in a former bank – the sort of grandiose building used before such establishments became virtually an excuse for a hole in the wall. Prices remain at a credible street level. There is a good range of Baltis including Balti Tinda (sweet potato) and Balti Karele (bitter gourd).' AM. Hours: 12-2.30pm/6-12pm.

©	Curry Club Discount	U	Unlicensed
V	Vegetarian	ANP	Alcohol not permitted
e-a-m-a-y-l	Eat as much as you like	BYO	Bring your own alcohol

KHYBER U BYO

365 Ladypool Road, Sparkbrook, B12 0121 449 5139

'Cosy family restaurant where the sign should read "enjoy as much as you like". Tasty Tikkas and no-nonsense Balti just like mom used to cook 'em. Lovingly prepared so expect to wait a little for a true taste of Birmingham's unique Balti experience.' AM.

KING'S PARADISE U BYO ©

321 Stratford Road, Sparkhill, B12 0121 753 2212

Owned by Mahboob Hussain. 'Balti Tandoori Butter Chicken, very smooth-tasting, in bright red sauce with some onion in there. Peshwari Naan, large, tasty with just a hint of syrup.' GG&MP. Mushroom Naan sounds great! Hours: 12pm-2.30pm/5.30pm-12am. Private car parking.

KUSHI U BYO ©

58 Moseley Road, Birmingham B12 0121 449 7678

Messrs Mohammed and Haydur's 62-seat 'Kushi appears to have picked up just about every cup apart from the Jules Rimet. However, never mind the awards, try the food. Kushi's Kebab is one of the best of its kind as are the sizzling Shashliks. Wide choice of main courses including Kushi's new and highly valued range of "saffron" dishes. Good selection of Nans from Keema to Kulcha.' AM. 'All nine of us agreed that this was a magnificent Balti house.' GG&MP. Delivery: £10 minimum. Hours: 5.30pm-1am (2am on Sat.); Sun. 6pm-12am.

LAHORE KARAHI U BYO

357-363 Ladypool Road, Sparkbrook, B12 0121 449 9007

One of the pioneers of the Balti Buffet, now available at so many of the Zone's venues. But this one is probably the best of the buffet bunch. RE is a frequent customer, and here is an amalgam of his views. 'A large self-service, always bustling busy restaurant, with space for 300 diners. Small car park at the rear, but otherwise can be difficult. Many Moslem and Seikh customers. E-a-m-a-y-l – amazing variety of food for £5.95. Sheekh kebabs good and tasty, roti not too thick, lamb dall superb, mixed dall nice consistency, spinach lamb, on the bone really tender meat and delicious. Keema Peas – delightful. Great food and great value. The trouble with buffet style restaurants as good as Lahore is knowing when to stop eating. Having said that I then went for seconds! Highly recommended.' RE. 'Everything qualifying for the top melt-in-the-mouth award. Highly recommended. Booking is advisable at weekends.' MJB.

LAHORE KEBAB AND PAN HOUSE NEW ENTRANT U

187 Ladypool Road, Sparkbrook, B12 0121 440 3264

'You can't go much more down market than this. Predominantly a takeaway offering just seekh kebabs, fish massala, samosas, pakoras, tikkas etc. In other words no main courses. However, what they do serve is freshly cooked and very good. Worth going for a cheap snack.' RE.

PLAZA TANDOORI U BYO ©

278 Ladypool Road, Balsall Heath, B12 0121 449 4249

The food at this unlicensed (BYO welcome) 80-seater is more Southall than Sparkbrook or Balti Heath, since owners R Singh and GS Pank and chef Gurmit (1997 Birmingham Council Chef of the Year) are Sikhs who specialise in Northern Indian Punjabi food. This adds a different flavour to the cooking. 'I enjoyed my first visit so much that I have been back twice. Seekh kebabs as good as before, spicy chicken wings great taste and hot.' RE. Hours: 5pm-12am.

POPULAR BALTI U BYO

139 Ladypool Road, Sparkbrook, B12 0121 440 0014

'Small, slightly scruffy restaurant. Sheeh Kebabs not quite so good as on my previous visit (I suspect they may have been 'Blue Peter' kebabs – here are some we prepared earlier). Lamb curry very good indeed. This cafe/restaurant rates one of the best for value.' and 'Redecorated since last visit, but the bright green striped wallpaper takes some getting used to! Service quick and friendly. Seekh Kebabs were fresh cooked and spicy. Very good value, good food.' RE.

PUNJABI PARADISE BYO

377 Ladypool Road, Sparkbrook, B12 0121 449 4110

'Mohammed Shabaz's popular place. One of the Balti glitterati featured on more TV programmes than Ulrika Jonsson. However, the food backs up the image – fresh coriander laden Baltis, yeasty Nan breads with a frantic but friendly atmosphere. Their special chicken Kebabs are worth a stab. Even has its own garage for all its valued (and that's everybody) customers.' AM. 'Food very good.' RE. Minimum charge £6. Hours: 5pm-1am.

©	Curry Club Discount	U	Unlicensed
V	Vegetarian	ANP	Alcohol not permitted
e-a-m-a-y-l	Eat as much as you like	BYO	Bring your own alcohol

ROYAL AL FAISAL — U BYO

136-140 Stoney Lane, Balsall Heath, B12 — 0121 449 5695

Spelt Faisal, or Faisel, the other venerable Balti, contemporary with Adil's (1982) from whom it is a few doors away, is Mohammed Ajaib's smartly decorated restaurant in shades of green. Seats 150 diners, tables of four. This early leader is now following the buffet trend and is, we hear, as busy as ever. 'Celebrating a momentous victory for Northampton's Saints, away at Gloucester. On recommendation, pulled off M42 to visit Royal Al Faisal. 6.30pm – very busy. Now a Balti Buffet Restaurant. One price of £5.95 – all you can eat. Faced with a huge array of dishes. Starters: Tandoori Chicken, Onion Bhajia, Mushroom Bhajia, Sheek Kebabs with Popadoms and Chutneys plentiful. Main courses: wide range of Baltis, vegetarian and meat, Tarka Dal Balti – first class. Excellent value for money. Convenient shops nearby to purchase your own drinks.' DL. 'Food is good but I think the Lahore Karahi Buffet has the edge. Twice in one week is OK in the name of serious research! Must return again soon.' RE. Hours: 11.30am-12am.

SHANDOR — e-a-m-a-y-l

353 Ladypool Road, Sparkbrook, B12 — 0121 449 5139

'Very similar to Lahore Karahi Buffet next door, but on a smaller scale. Not so much choice, but what there was was excellent.' RE. 'Visited as result of write-up in *GCG*. Ethos has changed – to a buffet style – pay one price and e-a-m-a-y-l. Many other local restaurants have also changed to this style. A pleasant experience, none-the-less. My wife enjoyed it because she could try a bit of everything.' MR&MRS T. 'Incidentally it is licensed and £4.50 for a bottle of Sparkbrook's finest Liebfraumilch must make every hour a happy one.' AM. Private car parking. Hours: 12pm to late.

SHEREEN KADAH — U BYO

543 Moseley Road, Balsall Heath, B12 — 0121 440 4641

'Busy and cheerful. Large open barbecue by the window where the kebabs etc are freshly cooked to order. Sheeh Kebabs were excellent, balti meat superb. Unfortunately, my wife's Chicken Kurma was awful – too spicy and the sauce had curdled. To be fair they took it off the bill. Very good value.' RE. On subsequent visits RE reports: 'Food was excellent, service was brisk and friendly, the clientele was largely Asian. Back to a good standard after my disappointing visit.' 'In the display cabinet is a selection of Kebabs on an array of sharp skewers which look like a Zulu armoury after an attack on Rourke's Drift.' AM. Hours: 11am-12am.

Birmingham B13

Moseley

COSMOPOLITAN TANDOORI NEW ENTRANT **U BYO**

31 Woodbridge Road, Moseley, B13 0121 449 5793

Not a Balti, but a formula curry house which, for some, makes a pleasant change in Baltiland. Established in 1990. Seats 40. Specials: Ceylon Balti dishes with black pepper and lemon juice from £4.90, Malayan Balti dishes with coconut cream and pineapple from £4.90, Chicken and Lamb Shashlick £3, Balti Mix Extras (King Prawn, Chicken, Lamb and Mushroom) £6.90. Price check: Papadam 40p, CTM £5.25, Pullao Rice £1.35, Peshwari Nan £1.50. Hours: 6-11.30pm (Fri. & Sat. to 1am).

K2 ©

107 Alcester Road, Moseley, B13 0121 449 3883

N Pasha and M Niam's 58-seater is named after the highest mountain in Pakistan, shown on the biggest map of Baltistan (to prove it exists to the doubters) on one wall. Peppered Chicken £3.10, is Chino-Tibetan (a Baltistan influence) with its sweet and sour chicken prepared with a mixture of black and green pepper, ginger, soya sauce, sugar and lime. Balti Chicken and Mushroom £5.50, Nan £1.20. The favourite venue of more than one BBC Pebble Mill crew, but not of RE. Price check: Papadam served with mint sauce, 30p, CTM £6, Pullao Rice £1.30. Access and Visa accepted. Hours: 6-11.30pm. Stocks Cobra.

SPICE AVENUE

562-4 Moseley Road, Birmingham B13 0121 442 4936

In a corner-site on the fringe of the Zone, it's a smart licensed restaurant with rear car park 'which is handy. Attentive and friendly staff. Food OK. A bit overpriced [compared with the rest of the Zone].' RE. 'The Balti Ginger Chicken is a straightforward but excellent combination. However, the lamb Shahan is an excellent exotic alternative with tender lamb cutlets stuffed with garlic mushrooms. Accompanying onion kulcha will make your eyes and mouth water.' AM. Stocks Cobra.

BIRMINGHAM NORTH

Consists of B6, B7, B19 to B24, B35, B42 to B44

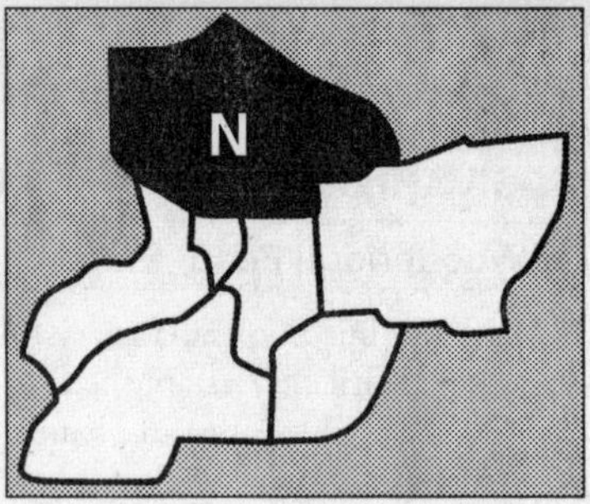

Birmingham B21

Handsworth

MILAN SWEET CENTRE NEW ENTRANT **V**

238 Soho Road, Handsworth, B21 0121 551 5239

A branch of the Milan restaurant in 93 Newhall Street, Birmingham B3 (see entry). This is a takeaway venue for Indian sweets, and savoury snacks. The seletion is huge and satisfying, at prices too cheap to ignore. Sister t/a branch at 191 Stoney Lane, Sparkbrook, B11.

Birmingham B23

Erdington

BALTI COURT NEW ENTRANT **U BYO**

Gravelly Lane, Erdington, Birmingham B23 0121 382 4200

'The food is excellent, the spices, flavour, everything. Must be the best in the area.' MR A. 'Excellent and varied menu with many new dishes. Service is always first class. Smoking is not encouraged.' SG. 'Excellent choice, substantial quantities, superb quality food, efficient and friendly staff.' SS. 'Have visited on many occasions and the food is consistently of a very high standard. A must.' LW.

SAMRAT TANDOORI **©**

710 Chester Road, Erdington, B23 0121 384 5900

Samrat means Emperor; established in '83, managed by Mr Dey, chef Mr Choudhury. Air-conditioned, seats 50, party room 30. Special: Spicy Fish £3.30. Kurzi lamb, served with Basmati rice £21 for two. Delivery: £6, 5-mile radius. Hours: 5pm-1am (2am on Fri. & Sat.).

STOCKLAND BALTI TAKEAWAY — U BYO ©

332 Marsh Lane, Erdington, B23 — 0121 377 8789

Owned and managed by Mrs Amina Begum since '93 serving competent curries to a regular crowd. Price check: Papadam 30p, CTM £4.10, Pullao Rice £1.05. Delivery: £10. Hours: 5pm-12am (1am on Fri. & Sat.).

Birmingham B44

Great Barr

BALTI SPICE TAKEAWAY — U ©

1240 Aldridge Road, Great Barr, B44 — 0121 366 6548

First opened in 1981, taken over by Nazrul Hussain in 1998 with Bilal Miah (manager). Chef Abdul Ahad's open kitchen allows customers to see their formula curries cooking. Coke, Fanta and mineral water available. Price check: Papadam 30p, CTM £4.95, Pullao Rice £1.20, Peshwari Nan £1.20. Takeaway: 10% discount. Delivery: £8 minimum, 3-mile radius; £12 minimum, 4-mile radius. Hours: 4.30pm-12am; Sat. 4.30pm-1pm.

BIRMINGHAM EAST

Consists of B8, B9, B25, B26, B33, B34, B36, B37, and B40 (NEC)

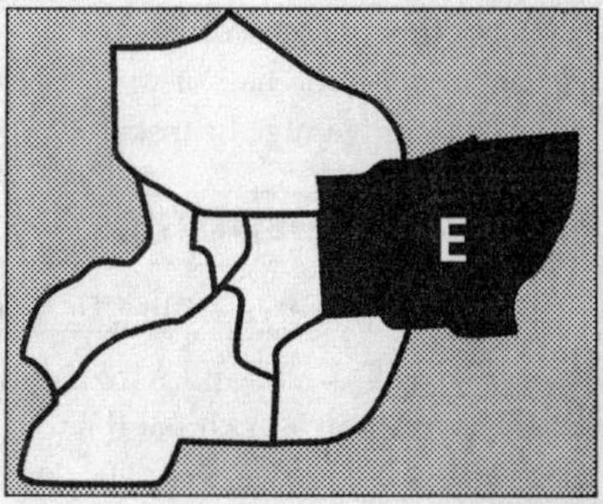

Birmingham B9

Small Heath

IIB NE GHANI — U BYO ©

264-266 Green Lane, Small Heath, B9 — 0121 772 8138

Competent curries and Baltis at Dawood Hussain's establishment. Hours: 5pm-1am; Fri. & Sat. 4pm-2am.

©	Curry Club Discount	U	Unlicensed
V	Vegetarian	ANP	Alcohol not permitted
e-a-m-a-y-l	Eat as much as you like	BYO	Bring your own alcohol

Birmingham B25

Yardley

YEW TREE COTTAGE ©

43 Stoney Lane, Yardley, B25 0121 784 0707

Opened in 1979 by Jamal Chaudhuri, this 40-seater curry house is in old cottage-style with oak beams. Takeaway services on the ground floor, restaurant on 1st floor. Gourmet Nights, four courses £9.95. Special starters: Tikka Sandwich, chicken tikka with nan, salad and dressing. Mixgrill Sandwich, chicken and lamb tikka, sheek kebab and Nan. Banana Chicken, medium spiced. Madras sauce. Vindaloo Sauce. Minimum charge: £15. Sunday buffet £9.95. Delivery: under £40, £2.50 charge, over £40, free, 3-mile radius. Hours: 5pm (Sun. 6pm)-1am (Sat. 2am). Stocks Cobra.

Birmingham B26

Sheldon

BENGAL FLAVA NEW ENTRANT

2065 Coventry Rd, Sheldon, B26 0121 722 3205

'Impeccable service. I ate there on two consecutive nights. All menus accidentally binned! All I can say is it's in a road on the way out of Birmingham about half a mile from Harry Ramsden's fish shop and the cheap Travelodge my cheapskate employers put me in!!!' PM. Stocks Cobra.

SHABAR TANDOORI ©

4 Arden Oak Road, Sheldon, B26 0121 742 0636

Angur Miah Qureshi and Mozamil Ali's Balti restaurant, seats 62. Special: Chicken or Lamb Zarzara and Table Naan. Spiced Banana in ghee. Sunday lunch: £5.95. Takeaway: 10% discount. Hours: 5.30pm-12am. Stocks Cobra.

TITASH INTERNATIONAL RE ENTRANT

2278 Coventry Road, Sheldon, B26 0121 722 2080

Away from home? Have to endure the dreaded catering, dispensed expensively and with a straight face at the neighbouring NEC, railway station, airport, and hotels of varying pretensions? Want to know of an alternative close to hand? That's what this Guide is for. Titash is a good standard, formula curryhouse, with ample on-street parking. Stocks Cobra.

BIRMINGHAM SOUTH EAST

Consists of B27 and B28

(Beyond this is Knowle and Solihull – see entries)

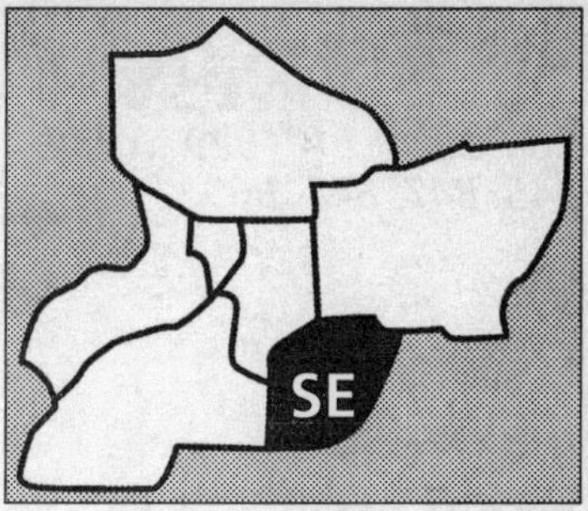

Birmingham B27

Acocks Green

DEVDOOT NEW ENTRANT ©

1st Floor, 37 Westley Road, B27 0121 706 4842

Seats 46. Specials: Persian Chicken Biriani £5.15 – with omelette and Malayan Chicken Biriani £5.15 – with pineapple. Price check: Papadam 35p, CTM £5.35, Pullao Rice £1.55, Peshwari Nan £1.65, Lager £2.20. Hours: 6pm-1am (Sat. to 2am).

MOGHUL ©

1184 Warwick Road, Acocks Green, B27 0121 707 6777

At Mr Hassan's mahogany and pink venue. Special starters: Tandoori Fish and Mushroom Garlic Fry. Takeaway: 20% discount. Minimum charge: £5. Hours: 5.30pm-12.30pm (1am on Sat.). Branch: Diwan Balti, Alcester Road, Moseley, Birmingham.

Birmingham B28

Hall Green

MIZAN ©

1347 Stratford Road, Hall Green, B28 0121 777 3185

Formerly J Jays, KA Rahman's curry house seats 66. Takeaway: 10% off. Minimum charge: £5. Special: Saag Kamal Kakri, spinach and lotus roots. Hours: 12-2pm/5.30pm-12am (12.30 on Fri. & Sat.). Stocks Cobra.

BIRMINGHAM SOUTH WEST

Consists of B14, B29 to B31, B45, B47, B48, B60

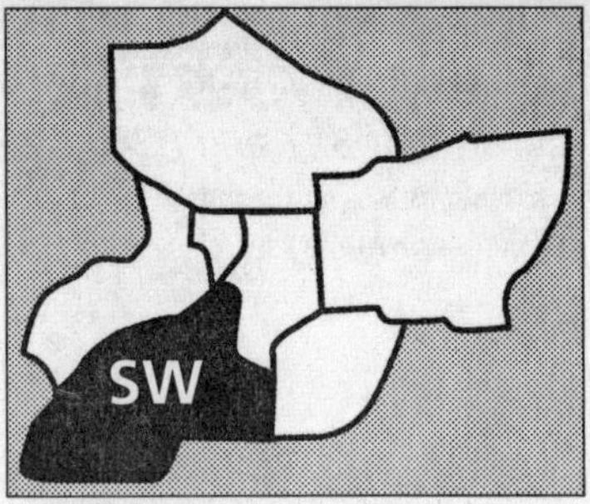

Birmingham B14

Hollywood, Kings Heath, Selly Oak

KINGS BALTI NEW ENTRANT

13-15 York Rd, King's Heath, B14 0121 443 1114

Owned and managed by Salim Miah. Specials: Panir Tikka, curd cheese dipped in gram flour and fried £2.05. Balti Chicken Tikka Naryl, delicate coconut sauce £4.95. Balti Chicken Dan Gali, cashew, sultanas, almonds, pistachio, fresh banana £4.95. Price check: Papadam 30p, CTM £4.95, Pullao Rice £1.20. Delivery: £8, 2-miles. Takeaway: 10% off. Hours: 5.30-11.30pm.

Birmingham B29

Selly Oak

DILSHAD INTERNATIONAL NEW ENTRANT

618-620 Bristol Road, Selly Oak, B29 0121 472 5016

Established in 1978. Seats 80. Specials include: Achar Gosth £6.10, Champa Koli Bahar £7.95, Fish of Bengal £7.65. Price check: Papadam 40p, CTM £5.95, Pullao Rice £1.45, Peshwari Nan £1.40, Lager £1.90 pint. Takeaway: 10% discount. Delivery: 3-mile radius. Hours: 5.30pm to late. Stocks Cobra.

Birmingham B30

Cotteridge, Stirchley

RAJPOOT ©

1831-1833 Pershore Road, Cotteridge, B30 0121 458 5604

Watir Ali's 94-seater does all your favourites. 'A glitzy little place with friendly service. All the family use it regularly.' JAD. Hours: 6pm-2am. Stocks Cobra.

COBRA GOOD CURRY GUIDE
County Index, see page 5 Town Index, see page 614
A to Z of the Curry Menu, page 41 Contributors Key, page 604

SPICE EXCHANGE

1845-1847 Pershore Road, Cotteridge, B30 — 0121 451 1007

'Startling decor – primary colours of varying hue.' [I believe restaurants call this modern, Graham]. 'Wide selection of imaginative choices. Outstanding quality – wonderful melange of flavours. Quantity more than adequate.' GG&MP. Tandoori Fish, served with salad £3.25. Gusthaba, a speciality from Kashmir, minced lamb, turmeric, black pepper, garam masala formed into meat balls, pan fried in sweet and hot tomato sauce £5.75. Cocktail Baltis – have your favourite balti cooked with French wine and brandy for £1.50 extra. Stocks Cobra.

YASSER TANDOORI — BYO ©

1268 Pershore Road, Stirchley, B30 — 0121 433 3023

A Hussain and Sarwar Khan's Yasser seats 80, and specialises in Pakistani and Kashmiri cooking. Special: Tandoori Fish. Balti Chef Special Tropical, prawn, chicken, meat, mushroom. Garlic Family Naan. BYO. Parking for 12 cars. Hours: 4pm-1am.

BIRMINGHAM WEST

Consists of B15 to B18 & B32

(Beyond this is Halesowen, Smethwick, Warley and West Bromwich – see entries)

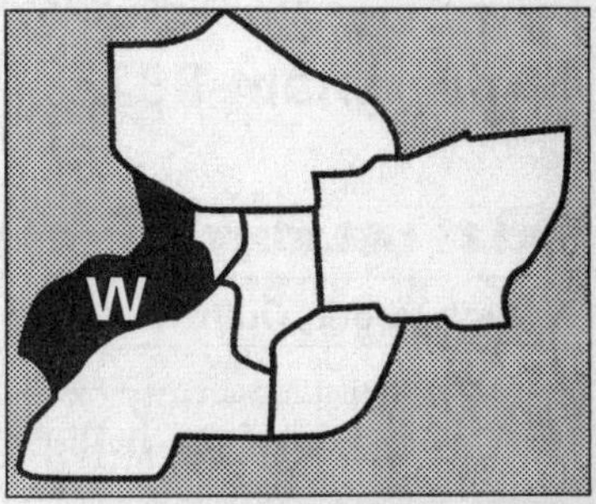

Birmingham B15

Edgbaston

SHIMLA PINKS

214 Broad Street, Birmingham B15 — 0121 633 0366

This was the first branch of a proposed franchise operation all over the UK led by Kal Dhaliwal's Oriental Group. As we write the Group is in administration, but we are keeping it in the *Guide*, although we anticipate new ownership, which may affect both its name and its branches. Just west of Central TV, this fully licensed, upmarket pricey pilot has established a

©	Curry Club Discount	U	Unlicensed
V	Vegetarian	ANP	Alcohol not permitted
e-a-m-a-y-l	Eat as much as you like	BYO	Bring your own alcohol

formula which appeals to some, but not others. 'Nans the best I've had. Bhuna Chicken particularly good. Service courteous. Plenty of space. Strange decor.' MJG. 'Minimalist decor. Food out of this world.' SR&LG. 'Unusual modern decor in agreeable surroundings. An upmarket restaurant, with good food, which on the whole is mildly spiced.' NR. 'A party from work attended and whoever was paying (not a curry regular) decided we would have one of their "banquets". I had been looking forward to the meal as I had heard a lot about it but I was very disappointed. Each dish tasted similar and the portions small. If that was a banquet I'm glad I didn't pop in for a quick snack! I'm glad that I wasn't paying as it came to over £350. All in all, very poor.' CS. Branches: Shimla Pinks Manchester M3. Oxford; Johnstone, Strathclyde and London EC. Stocks Cobra.

Birmingham B16

Edgbaston

J JAYS NEW ENTRANT

2 Edgbaston Shopping Centre, Five Ways, B16 0121 455 6871

Upmarket (Roman Villa) restaurant with marble everywhere, material tented ceiling. Serves north Indian curries and accompaniments. Stocks Cobra.

Birmingham B32

Quinton

BALTI DELIGHT TAKEAWAY NEW ENTRANT

32 High Street, Quinton, B32 0121 421 2646

'I frequently pick up a curry from this obscure takeaway. Quality is always very good and they do an excellent Sag Chana as a side dish. The portions are not generous but the food is always ready on time and the prices are reasonable.' NR.

SOHO INDIA ©

417 Hagley Road, West, Quinton, B32 0121 421 3242

Bangladeshi formula curry house, seats 50, established in 1985 by Mohammed Abdul Muquit. CC members will get 10% off their bill. Special: Village Special Soup £1.75. Lager £1.85 pint, one of the lowest prices in the guide. Price check: Papadam 35p, CTM £5.85, Pullao Rice £1.75. House wine £5.95. No takeaway. Minimum charge: £6.50. Hours: 5pm-12am. Stocks Cobra.

REMAINDER OF WEST MIDLANDS

Brierley Hill

WATERFRONT BALTI HOUSE — BYO ©

127-129, Dudley Road, Brierley Hill — 01384 76929

This is another reaason why Brum and surrounds are at the heart of economic growth. Brierley Hill has regenerated and some, with its Merry Hill shopping centre, complete with monorail and the Waterfront development, sitting astride the Dudley Canal. Between the two it's easy to spend hours shopping and enjoying the good life. But don't spend all your hard earned money. Save some for Mohammed Ashraf's nearby 80-seater. It is blessed with car parking for 40 to front and rear and serves Kashmiri-style curries and Baltis, including the try-it-and-see Balti Chef Special, £5.95. 10% off for students and nurses. Tuesday Balti night, 3-course meal £4.30. Price check: Papadam 30p, BCTM £4.80, Pullao Rice £1.30. Peshwari Nan £1.45. Delivery: £12 minimum, 3-mile radius. Minimum charge: £6.50. Delivery: £7. Hours: 5pm-1am; Sat. 5pm-2am.

Coventry

BENGAL DELIGHT NEW ENTRANT

166-168 Holbrook Lane, Coventry — 024 7668 6789

Recommended by Biren and the gang at Cobra. Reports please.

BOMBAY PALACE NEW ENTRANT

64 Earlsdon Street, Earlsdon, Coventry — 024 7667 7851

'Good quality food, average quantity and service. Decor very pink. We rate this no. 2 in the city.' GG&MP.

CAFE SPICE

244 Hipswell Highway, Coventry — 024 7665 9800

'Very luxurious, obviously a lot of money has been spent. Generally very good, but were it not for disappointing quantities of the main course, would put it high in the TOP 100. Popadoms 60p and chutney. Starters, Tandoori Chicken, beautifully presented and well marinated £1.95, Kebab Roll with salad, absolutely superb £2.20, huge. First class service.' GG&MP.

COUNDON INDIAN CUISINE NEW ENTRANT

61 Barker Butts Road, Coundon, Coventry 024 7659 0500

'An upmarket restaurant, although not as pricey as the Rupali (Coventry). Roupushi was too fiddly, but it had a very nice flavour. Stuffed pepper very tasty.' GG&MP

HOLLY BUSH PUB NEW ENTRANT

Holbrooks Lane, Coventry 024 7668 6923

'Nice relaxed pub atmosphere. I was amazed to be told it had been going since 1995. Balti Chicken Tikka was tasty. Generally, the meat was good, but the vegetables had not been properly marinated and the peas were tinned. Prompt service, but rather impersonal.' GG&MP.

L'IMRANS EXPERIENCE NEW ENTRANT e-a-m-a-y-l

14 Butts Lane, Earlsdon, Coventry 024 7623 1699

'This is the first restaurant to open in Coventry which is predominantly focussing on the buffet side of things. You have 2 hours to e-a-m-a-y-l for £7.95. We visited about three weeks after opening and were very impressed. There were fish, red meat, white meat and vegetarian alternatives for both starter and main courses. Air-conditioned and with a separate non-smoking section. Overall impression was an extremely favourable one.' GG&MP. The time limit is a new twist, and I wonder what they'd do if you run overtime?

MONSOON NEW TO OUR TOP 100 ©

20-21 Far Gosford Street, Coventry 024 7622 9651

Owned by J Raj and G Judge, since 1996. 'Modern, zazzy music.' Pakistani curries, 'Recently refurbished with many paintings now decorating the wall. This has greatly improved the look of the restaurant. Firmly established as my favourite. We were given a very generous discount with the voucher from the *CC Magazine*. As superb as ever with an excellent Chana Masala starter. Balti Chilli Chicken Masala £3.95 was a feast, wonderfully spicy with sumptuous chicken, Balti Mince £3.95 with vegetables including okra, pepper, chana, tomatoes, potatoes and courgettes was mouthwateringly good. Peshwari Nan £2.10. The bees' knees for Balti houses. An incredible amount of vegetables in the meals. Free popadoms. Once again absolutely top quality food, served in huge quantities, and with magnificent service. I simply cannot fault it. Please place in your TOP 100.' GG&MP. Done, Graham. Price check: Papadam 45p, CTM £5.55, Pullao Rice £1.50. Coriander Nan £1.90. Lager £2 pint, house wine £6.99. Takeaway 10% off. Delivery: £10 minimum, 4-mile radius. Hours: 6pm-12am (1am on Sat.).

PELE'S BALTI HOUSE AND PUB

1059 Foleshill Road, Coventry 024 7668 6394

Since we said last time that some 6,500 British pubs serve curry, the total has gone up by a further 2,500. Unfortunately, few do it well. Hoping that the word 'curry' will keep the punters in the pub rather than exiting to the nearest curryhouse, they are in a massive me-too scramble. Most buy in factory ready-meal curries, which are pale imitations of the real thing. This includes Moat House Hotels and Weatherspoons who have decided that branding their offerings Curry Club is good for business. Sure it is, but it does nothing for us. And if, heaven forbid, the discerning readers of this publication have tasted the product, they will know the Curry Club has nothing to do with it. Since many of you have asked us, they didn't ask our permission to use our trade-marked and registered name, nor do we earn a royalty for the use our name. Meanwhile, if you are tempted to try Wetherspoon's Curry Club food, think again, and seek out a decent curry. And one place you'll get one is at Pele and Jatinder Bains' whose origins are north India. Back in 1986, these experienced publicans tried a new idea at their 160-seater Coventry pub. They put only authentic curries on the menu. And guess what? From day one, it's been a resounding success. All the regular curries are there, with the cooking by Pele. Trouble is, since it changed its name from 'King William IV' and was taken over by a smallish brewery, with plans, we hear, to roll Pele's out as a brand in the Midlands area, we've received very mixed reports: 'Seems to have lost its way. Pretty awful meal. Service was vague and slightly rude. Rice was more like rice pudding.' ME. 'This meal was very cheap but this did not make up for the poor food and the severe disappointment. The main courses were awful.' MPW. 'There should be a Pele's in every town. Portions more than ample, prices very reasonable. And the food ... sensational. Chicken Pele Punjabi Balti was particularly superb – one of the finest curries I've ever tasted, and I've had a couple of hundred.' RL. 'An excellent meal was spoilt by the much too loud background music. The quality of the food was first class but if this extremely intrusive music continues I think you will have to review continuing to keep it in your list.' GG&MP. Price check: Papadam 30p, CTM £4.70. House wine £6. Hours: 12-2pm/6pm-10.30pm (Sun. 7-10pm).

QUICK STOP BALTI — BYO

80 Far Gosford Street, Coventry — 024 76632578

'Unlicensed and unpretentious restaurant. Fairly basic menu, service very good. Balti Chicken Jalfrezi, well marinated.' GG&MP.

ROYAL BENGAL NEW ENTRANT

172 Albany Road, Coventry — 024 7671 2345

Recommended by Biren and the gang at Cobra. Reports please.

RUPALI ©

337 The Hill Lane, Coventry — 024 7642 2500

'Ashik Ali's huge 200-seater was under refurbishment when MPW visited: 'Half of the restaurant was screened off by hanging sheets (with Indian print thereon), hiding refurbishments. However, this did not affect the food, service etc (except for the tell-tale grime in the gent's hand sink where the work force must have earlier washed up before starting to cook! Raita was superbly fresh and seemed to fizz on your tongue, excellent. Two spicy papadoms tasted stale. Lamb Stuffed Pepper very different, beautifully served, excellent. Special Chicken Jafrezi also excellent. Overall good food, biggish portions, slightly overpriced with polite, friendly service. Recommended but I don't think it justifies its TOP 100 position at this time – maybe after all building work finished!' MPW. The personable Chef Rois Ali can cook, and we are glad to hear from several reporters that the Rupali has increased its portion size, though prices are still at the high end. 'Naan were excellent as were the Popadoms and pickle tray. Two lagers and two soda waters came to £7 – scandalous!' DH. CC members 10% off, so plenty more reports please. Price check: Papadam 60p, CTM £8.95, Pullao Rice £1.95. Lager £2.50 pint, house wine £8.95. Takeaway: 25 % off. Sunday lunch: £7.95. Minimum charge: £9.95. Hours:5.30-11pm.

SHAHI PALACE ©

367 Foleshill Road, Coventry — 024 7668 8719

It's had a record four names in 10 years (Palace, Kashmir, Balti). Since 1995 it's been Iqbal Hussain's Shahi Palace, a licensed 90-seater, nicely decorated in greens. Special: slices of Bangladeshi boal fish in hot and tangy taste with green chilli and shatkora £7.95. Nawabi Murgh, pieces of chicken marinated cooked in mince lamb sauce and freshly garnished with chilli, coriander and egg £8.50. Daily banquets £5.95. Price check: Papadam 40p, CTM £5.50,

Pullao Rice £1.50. Minimum charge £10. Service 10%. Delivery: £10 minimum, 4-mile radius. Hours: 5.30pm-12.30am. Stocks Cobra.

SONARGAON NEW ENTRANT

153 Daventry Road, Coventry 024 7650 4670

Recommended by Biren and the gang at Cobra. Reports please.

THAI DUSIT

39 London Road, Coventry 024 7622 7788

'This, the first Thai restaurant in Coventry, is on the site of the former Samrat and Royal India. It has been beautifully refurbished and provides a tasteful and delightful sight on arrival. Polite and friendly staff. Wide and extensive range of Thai dishes. It is not cheap but overall provides a memorable experience.' GG&MP.

Dudley

BALTI 4 U NAME CHANGE BYO ©

63 Halesowen Road, Netherton, Dudley 01384 240230

At R Khan's small restaurant we continue to hear of the Happy Hour special menu from 6-9pm. Hours: 6pm-2am (3am at weekends).

Halesowen B62,B63 & B65

AMEENA ©

192 Hagley Road, Hasbury, Halesowen, B63 0121 550 4317

Hiron Miah's 78-seater (est. 1974). 'I've only tried this restaurant once. The food was good standard, and while I was waiting regulars were warmly welcomed.' NR. 'Have visited twice recently, on first occasion the food was exceptionally good – in particular the Chicken Tikka Buna and the fresh naan bread. Second visit was not so good, but still of a standard that I would choose to call again if in this area.' RJP. 'Slightly downmarket feel to the place but not the food! Prawn Bhuna is delicious with the sauce adding a tasty extra. Chicken Jalfrezi with thin strips of ginger laid on top lattice work fashion. Enjoyed the Sag Aloo. Cobra a pleasant fix. Waiters cheerful and attentive. In the guide and deserves it.' MS. Delivery: 3-mile radius, £10 minimum, 5.30-10pm. Hours: 5.30pm-12am (Fri. & Sat. to 1am). Stocks Cobra.

RED PEPPERS NEW ENTRANT

8 Hagley Street, Halesowen 0121 550 8588

'A bit pricey compared to its peers but the food is good. With so much local choice I don't tend to eat here very often, but when I do the quality does not vary.' NR. Established in 1990. Seats 46. Price check: Papadam 40p, CTM £5.95, Pullao Rice £1.50, Peshwari Nan £1.50, Lager £2.10 pint. Delivery: £10 minimum. Hours: 6pm-12am; Fri. & Sat. 6pm-1am.

Kingswinford

THE BALTI BYO

847 High Street, Kingswinford 01384 823111

Formerly Mr Daves. 'BYO, quite cheap, excellent standard of Balti. Chicken Pakora is the greatest we've ever had.' SR&LG.

Knowle

BILASH ©

1608 High Street, Knowle, B93 01564 773030

Mashud Uddin and Nowab Ali's Bangladeshi curry house seats 64, party room 40. Set in black and white surroundings, dating back to the 16th century. Special: Jeera Chicken Dilkush, spring chicken, coconut, jeera, tomato and mixed spices. 'Very good quality.' J&MCL. Takeaway: 10% off. Hours: 5.30pm-12am. Branches: Bilash, 82-90 Priory Road, Kenilworth. Bejoy Takeaway, 763 Old Lode Lane, Solihull, West Midlands.

KNOWLE INDIAN BRASSERIE ©

1690 High Street, Knowle, B93 01564 776453

Established in 1995, Hossain Miah's air-conditioned Bangladeshi curry house seats 45. Nicely decorated in cream and pale pink, plaster cornices and velvet upholstered chairs. Special: Fish Bhuna Bengal Style, chunks of Bangladeshi fish, cooked in medium sauce with spices, herbs and green chillies £6.75. 'Excellent. Good, helpful service. Food tasty, hot, prompt. Would definitely return and recommend.' J. 'Malai Kebab, chicken marinated in cream with herbs and spices and baked in a clay oven – very tasty. Chicken Tikka Sylhet, boneless chicken with minced lamb and egg cooked with spices and herbs – unusual mixture of mince and chicken, very spicy with good texture and flavours. Bombay Aloo, well-marinated potato although not as spicy as they promised in the menu. Quantities – enormous. Not as expensive as one might expect. A top-quality restaurant.' GG&MP. Price check: Papadam 50p, CTM £5.45, Pullao Rice £1.70, Peshwari Nan £1.80, Lager £2.10 pint. Takeaway: 10% discount. Delivery: £12 minimum, 3-mile radius. Hours: 5.30-11.30pm; Sun. 5.30-10.30pm.

Lye

BALTI BAZAAR BYO

1a Pedmore Road, Lye 01384 353800

Opened in 1997 by R Miah, with Ali Akbor managing front of house and Noor Miah as head chef. 'The service was prompt and pleasant, with a reassuring "quality check" by the staff midway through the meal. The food was above average.' LW. Hours: 5pm-12am.

PEPPER AND SPICE BYO ©

204 - 205 High Street, Lye 01384 893933

At Sabber Iqbal's 40-seater you can get these intriguing specials: Pepper Chicken, capsicum stuffed with tandoori chicken. Fish chat, fish in a sweet and sour sauce. Balti Chicken and Mushroom, Naan. Licensed but BYO allowed. Credit cards not accepted. Delivery: £7 minimum. Hours: 6pm-12am. Stocks Cobra.

SPICE OF LYEFE NEW ENTRANT

286 High Street, Lye 01384 823344

A clever name from the owner of this 100-seater, established in 1995. 'Low-lit warm environment and is so popular that there was already a queue by 6pm! Excellent, attentive and helpful service. I had a so-so Margis Kebab, but my wife had a magnificent plate of Onion Bhaji, which had clearly been individually spiced, since one piece was hotter than the other. Mushroom Puree was both exceedingly tasty and sufficient to feed an army. Main courses were genuinely spectacular! A sublime Balti Lamb Tikka Masala Tropical, where each mouthful seemed to become a new experience. A Tandoori Medium Naan which was enough for all four of us. It's still getting better. Locals rate it as the top place in Lye.' MT. Specials include: Chilli Chicken £5, Special Garlic Naan £1.95. Price check: Papadam 90p, CTM £4.45, Pullao Rice £1.50, Peshwari Nan £1.75. Delivery: £10 minimum, 3-mile radius. Hours: 6pm-12am.

ZAFRAN NEW ENTRANT

8 Stourbridge Road, Lye 01384 894780

'Car parking facilities available immediately outside the restaurant (and as everyone knows, Lye has double yellow lines throughout the town!). High quality food. King Prawn Madras was unbelievable, Gulubjaman for pudding was thoroughly enjoyable. Quantity could have been better, and waiters could have been more friendly. But well worth a visit.' DC.

Solihull B90 to B93

RAJNAGAR INTERNATIONAL NEW ENTRANT

256 Lyndon Rd, Olton, Solihull, B92 0121 742 8140

How come Rajnagar isn't in the *Guide*? It really is exceptionally good.' MM.

Stourbridge

NEEL AKASH BALTI AND TANDOORI ©

2F High Street, Wollaston, Stourbridge 01384 375919

Chef Mujibur Rahman's 60-seater. Bangladeshi formula curries including Bengal Masala and Bhoona Shashlik. Balti Chicken and Mushroom, Naan. Minimum charge: £5. Special: Acher Special, chicken, meat or prawn with pickles. Takeaway: 10% off. Delivery: £8 minimum, 3-mile radius. Hours: 5pm-12am. Stocks Cobra.

REDFORTE ASIAN CUISINE TAKEAWAY

70 Bridgnorth Road, Wollaston, Stourbridge 01384 835555

Takeaway only, situated next door to the village bakery. Owned by Shaun Hussain Shah (manager). Hours: 5.30pm-12.30am.

Sutton Coldfield B72 to B76

ASIAN GRILL

91 Park Road, Sutton Coldfield, B73 0121 354 7491

Opened way back in 1968. If you, or any other business for that matter, have survived that long, you must be good. Bangladeshi and formula curries on the menu including Balti Chicken Tikka with Naan. Seats 76. Minimum charge £8. Hours: 5.30pm-12am (1am on Fri. & Sat.). Stocks Cobra.

MOTHER INDIA BALTI NEW ENTRANT

60a Boldmere Road, Boldmere,
Sutton Coldfield, B73 0121 354 1923

Established in 1998. Seats 50. Chicken Jafrazi £6.95, Lobster Jamdani £10.95. Price check: Papadam 40p, CTM £5.85, Pullao Rice £1.75, Peshwari Nan £1.75. Takeaway: 20% discount. Hours: 5pm-12am.

RICKSHAW INDIAN TAKEAWAY NEW ENTRANT

121 Chester Rd, Streetly, Sutton Coldfield, B74 0138 423 3446

A very satisfied customer: 'My family and I have used their services for at least two years and in that time we have always had excellent food. Premises are very clean, staff very friendly. We always recommend this takeaway to all our friends and associates.' BBM. 'We would like to highly recommend the Rickshaw for both its quality of food and excellent standard of service. They have never failed to impress us whether they have been catering for a meal for two or helping us with larger parties of guests.' MR&MRS MB. 'The perfect balti house. The dishes are so mouthwateringly fresh that I can't wait for the next one.' IS. Price check: Papadam 50p, CTM £5.10, Pullao Rice £1.40, Peshwari Nan £1.50. Delivery: £10 minimum, 5-mile radius. Hours: 5-11pm; Sun. 5-10.30pm

SHAMOLI INDIAN CUISINE NEW ENTRANT

5-15, Maney House, Maney Corner,
Birmingham Rd, Maney, Sutton Coldfield, B72 0121 321 2446

'Above the Kwik-Fit Tyre Centre, near the Odeon Cinema. Large, one room restaurant seating around 80. I was early, being hungry after a rough day in the concrete jungle and ready to be well looked after, which I was. Went for Bhuna Prawn Puree – large amount of prawns, lovely thick sauce, sliced onions wrapped in a chapatti, no sign of the more normal fried bread or similar – never mind – it was delicious. Chicken Tikka Pathia – authentic hot, sweet and sour taste, again generous amount of chicken and sauce. Accompanied by Sag Aloo – not on the menu said waiter, but ours is the best around here try it – so I did and it was lovely! Ended with coffee and very talkative waiter offered a drink on the house – brandy! Ended a thoroughly pleasant evening.' MS. Price check: Papadam 55p, CTM £7.65, Pullao Rice £1.60, Peshwari Nan £1.60. Hours: 6pm-12am (Fri. & Sat. to 1am, Sun. to 11pm). Stocks Cobra.

Walsall

EAST END ©

9 Hawes Close, Broadway, Walsall — 01922 614800

Muhibur Rahman is proud of his veteran 1967 curry house. Special is Green Chilli Chicken Tikka Masala. Balti Chicken and Mushroom, Naan. Hours: 5.30pm-12am.

GOLDEN MOMENTS NEW ENTRANT

3 Ablewell Street, Walsall — 01992 640363

Established in 1993. Seats 100. 'Having eaten Indian food for 25 years this establishment must rate as the one of the best. Staff, service, surroundings and food are excellent.' BD. Specials: Betatawada £2.50 – mashed potatoes with herbs and spices, battered and deep-fried. White Chicken Tikka £2.95 – delicately spiced, wonderfully tender. Dhaba Gosht £6.25 – small cubes of lamb cooked in the Tandoor, finished in thick sauce. Price check: Papadam 40p, CTM £6.50, Pullao Rice £1.85, Peshwari Nan £2.30, Lager £2.40. Takeaway: 15% discount. Hours: 6pm-12am. Stocks Cobra.

KING BALTI BYO ©

89 Ablewell Street, Walsall — 01922 620376

48-seater owned by Dudu Miah. Chicken Tikka Jalfrezi most popular. Takeaway: 10% discount. Delivery: £12 minimum, 3-mile radius. Hours: 6pm-1am; Sat. 6pm-1.30am.

SAFFRON ©

42-43 Bradford Street, Walsall — 01922 627899

Fully licensed 130-seater, smart restaurant opened in 1963. New ownership. 'Superb genuine Balti house within easy (post meal) wobbling distance of the railway station. Excellent starter, Nargis Kebab £1.65 – spicy Scotch egg style, crisp salad, yoghurt sauce plus Popadoms 60p with usual chutney mix 45p. Mix Balti £4.75 – lovely medium thick sauce with a well balanced and mouth watering blend of spices, sizable chunks of lamb and chicken, plus some small but juicy prawns, medium hot. Lovely light Chappatis £1.10 a little on the dear side. Good service, real tablecloths.' RW. E-a-m-a-y-l buffet: £6.96 on Weds. & Thurs. evenings and Sun. lunch. Price check: Papadam 30p, CTM £4.70, Pullao Rice £1.45, Peshwari Nan £1.45. Hours: 5.30pm (Sun. 12.30pm)-12.30am (Fri. & Sat. to 1.30am).

Warley B65 to B68

AL MOUGHAL BYO ©

622 Bearwood Road, Smethwick, Warley, B66 0121 420 3987

100-seater managed by Mumtaz. Pakistani-style curries on the menu. 'Reasonably clean, down-market but cheap and cheerful. Chicken Karahi Tikka Massala Special and three Chapatis, waiter advised only two – spot on. Food competent and tasty. Tremendous value. If this place was a wine it would be a Blue Nun.' PAW. [Yuk! Let's settle for a 'Brown Nan' -Ed] Balti Chicken Tikka Aloo Jalfrezi. Onion Nan. BYO. Delivery: £10 minimum, 3-mile radius. Hours: 6pm-12am.

HAWELI NEW ENTRANT

509 Hagley Road, Bearwood, Warley 0121 434 4869

Established in 1993. Seats 68. Price check: Papadam 40p, CTM £5.25, Pullao Rice £1.65, Peshwari Nan £1.35, Lager £2.10 pint. Delivery: free for regular customers, 1-mile radius. Hours: 6-11.45pm; Sat. 6pm-12am. Stocks Cobra.

STANDARD ©

2 High St, Blackheath, Rowley Regis, Warley, B65 0121 561 2048

Kazi Ashafuz and Kazi Wahiduz Zaman's tiny 30-seater (pretty, green wallpaper and wood-panelling) serves formula curries. Special: Chicken Jaipur, creamy, egg and nuts £5.05. BYO. Price check: Papadam 50p, CTM £5.50, Pullao Rice £1.50. House wine £6. Takeaway: 10% off. Delivery: £10 minimum. Hours: 6pm-1am (2am on Sat.). Stocks Cobra.

Wolverhampton

(inc. Albrighton, Compton, and Wednesfield)

CABERET ANGELS NEW ENTRANT

Old Railway Station, Albrighton Road,
Albrighton, Wolverhampton 01902 441442

'The food, service, decor and atmosphere are second to none. The menu looks absolutely gigantic at first sight, but in fact it includes a lot of sensible set menus at special prices. Not short on choice. Delicious and highly individual dishes – no question that each one had been sauced and prepared separately' GD. Stocks Cobra.

©	Curry Club Discount	U	Unlicensed
V	Vegetarian	ANP	Alcohol not permitted
e-a-m-a-y-l	Eat as much as you like	BYO	Bring your own alcohol

DILRAJ NEW ENTRANT

3a Long Knowle Lane, Wednesfield, Wolverhampton 01902 306040

'Small restaurant, about eight tables, but the food is of a very high quality. Nothing is too much trouble for the staff. Only opened about 12 months, but deserves to do well. No Chicken Ceylon on the menu, but when I asked if they could do this they said no problem, even though the place was full.' PE.

JIVANS BALTI NEW ENTRANT

14 Broad Street, Wolverhampton 01902 427289

Recommended by Biren and the gang at Cobra. Reports please.

MEMSAHIB NEW ENTRANT

Swan Complex, Compton, Wolverhampton 01902 757555

'There is now a new chef (from London) and the improvement is outstanding! There is no change in the menu, but the quality and quantity of the food is now superb. Waiters seem much happier.' JT.

MOTHER INDIA NEW ENTRANT

136 Tettenhall Road, Wolverhampton 01902 750755

Punjabi cuisine. Specials: Chicken Tunda – deep-fried chicken with a lemon dipping sauce. Lamb Dhai – lamb with mint and yoghurt. 'Great samosas, followed by South Indian Garlic Chilli Chicken (tender chicken lumps, lashings of creamy spicy sauce), with enough rice to feed the Bengal Lancers. I loved it except the naan bread which was nearly as bad as the ones I try to cook. And not cheap. Other than this can recommend it.' MS. Stocks Cobra.

PURBANI NEW ENTRANT

41-43 Birch Street, Wolverhampton 01902 424030

Established in 1979. Seats 125. Major refurbishment in 1999. Specials include: Chicken Tikka curries. Price check: Papadam 35p, CTM £6.20, Pullao Rice £1.85, Peshwari Nan £1.55, Lager £2 pint. Takeaway: 10% discount. Delivery: £10 minimum, 5-mile radius. Hours: 5.30pm-12.30am; Sat. 6pm-12am; Sun. 6pm-12.30am. Stocks Cobra.

RANGA MATI NEW ENTRANT

75 Lichfield Road, Wednesfield, Wolverhampton 01902 307550

Established in 1997. Seats 60. Parking for 10 cars at front. Free bottle of wine with orders over £25. Price check: Papadam 35p, CTM £5.50, Pullao Rice £1.35, Peshwari Nan £1.35, Lager £2.15 pint. Delivery: £7 minimum, 7-mile radius. Hours: 5pm-12am; Sat. 5pm-1am.

WILTSHIRE

Area: Mid West
Population: 608,000
Adjacent Counties: Berks, Dorset, Hants, Oxon

Chippenham

AKASH TANDOORI AND BALTI ©

19 The Bridge, Chippenham 01249 653358

Established in '79 by Nurul Islam, an old friend of this *Guide*, having been in since our first edition. 46 seater, decorated in 'red dado and curtains with green plants and doors, incorporates framed pictures and tropical fish tank'. Special: Passanda, creamy fragrantly spiced dish £6.70. Specials include: Murgi Musala, for two (chicken marinated in the Chef's special recipe, roasted in the oven and served with an exotic sauce and special rice) £24.50. Price check: Papadam 50p, CTM £6.70, Pullao Rice £2.20, Peshwari Nan £2, Lager £2.90 pint, House wine £8.50. Takeaway: 10% discount. Hours: 12-2pm/6pm-12am.

TAJ MAHAL ©

51 The Causeway, Chippenham 01249 653243

'Cosy little restaurant. Standard dishes, plus a number of lobster and duck variations. The only small criticism of the whole meal is that the Bhajias came without any accompanying salad, looking very bare and plain on the plate. Sag and cauliflower was the best I've had for a long while. Portions all plentiful, service efficient and friendly, prices about standard for the area.'

©	Curry Club Discount	U	Unlicensed
V	Vegetarian	ANP	Alcohol not permitted
e-a-m-a-y-l	Eat as much as you like	BYO	Bring your own alcohol

MW. Established in 1989. Seats 40. Price check: Papadam 75p, CTM £6.75, Pullao Rice £2, Peshwari Nan £2, Lager £2.40 pint. Takeaway: 10% discount, £10 minimum. Delivery: £10 minimum, 8-mile radius. Hours: 12-2pm/6pm-12am.

Cricklade

ANCIENT RAJ NAME CHANGE

47, High Street, Cricklade 01793 752242

Two-roomed 44-seater formerly Golden Delight. Specials: Ginger Chicken £6.25, Mushroom Biriani £5.25. Price check: Papadam 60p, CTM £6.25, Pullao Rice £1.75. Lager £2.50 pint, house wine £6.75. Takeaway: 10% off. Hours: 12-2.30pm (Sun.-Fri.)/6-11.30pm (12am on Sat.).

Devizes

DEEDAR

2 Sidmouth Street, Devizes 01380 720009

Joshim Ahmed's 24-seater's kitchen is in full view. Chutney Deedar, chicken, lamb or prawn cooked with mango chutney and lime pickle £4.50. 'Appearance of this restaurant is basic and very simple, no frills with formica tables. A very welcoming atmosphere and the food is cooked in full view. Madras and Dhansak curries are full of flavour and the Peshwari Nan was plump and puffed up, dripping with melted butter – delicious.' PGN. Price check: Papadam 30p, CTM £4.80, Pullao Rice £1.30, Pickles 20p. House wine £7.50. Takeaway: 10% less. Hours 12-2pm/5.30-11.30pm. Stocks Cobra.

Ludgershall

MUGHAL ©

33 Andover Road, Ludgershall 01264 790463

'Of Mrs Bushra Rahman's 44-seater's curries, Tikka and Balti are the most popular. Menu, both content and quality, excellent. Very welcoming. Lamb sheek kebab starter tender and juicy.' PA. Special: Jhingi Kodv. Delivery: £15 min, 3-mile radius. Hours: 12-2.30pm/6pm-12am. Stocks Cobra.

Malmesbury

MALMESBURY TANDOORI NEW ENTRANT

49 High Street, Malmesbury 01666 822984

'Well established and popular. Chicken Patia nicely hot with plenty of flavour in a dark, rich thick sauce. Mixed dry vegetable curry had a good selection of veg and the cauliflower bhaji was also very good. Portions large and reasonably priced. Friendly service.' MW.

Melksham

MELKSHAM TANDOORI ©

26 Church Street, Melksham 01225 705242

Mr Mahammed Mayna's attractive Cotswold stone building is adjacent to a car park. Its bar/reception are in a long narrow room with 50 seats beyond. 'Chicken Tikka very well cooked, nice and succulent. Lovely mint sauce. Lamb Jalfrezi rich and loads of green chillies lurking for the unwary – I love 'em. Portions huge, cooking great and amazing value.' MS. Stocks Cobra.

Salisbury

ASIA

90 Fisherton Street, Salisbury 01722 327628

'Not the first time I have written about this thriving, always packed, splendid restaurant. Euphoria of our Friday evening family reunion curry has vigorously survived well into Saturday. House was full, glad we booked. Had variety of rich dishes – Patia, Dupazia, Madras, Butter Chicken, Chili Chicken and Balti. Curry sauces are smooth and rich, plenty of personality. Sag Bhaji was the best I've had – very spicy with guts and edge.' Stocks Cobra.

Swindon

BHAJI'S TAKEAWAY ©

76 Thames Avenue, Swindon 01793 533799

Owned by Iqbal Shishir. Special: Tandoori Garlic Chilli Chicken or Lamb £5.45, most popular. Established in 1997. Parking for 50 cars in front. Specials include: Tandoori Garlic Chilli Chicken or Lamb £5.75. Price check: Delivery: £10 minimum, 4-mile radius. Hours: 5pm-12am.

BIPLOB ©

12-14 Wood Street, Swindon 01793 490265

Rokib Alo and Fozlur Rahman's 60-seater has a separate lounge/bar area seating 20. Well explained menu. House specials include Tandoori Duck Tikka (£9.95, but worth it for a treat), and Tandoori Duck Bonani (cooked with cream, cashews and brandy – £10.50) and Fish Buzon – Bangladeshi river fish (£7.95) and Begun Bahar – chicken in a herby gravy, £6.95. Price check: Papadam 45p, Masala 50p, CTM £6.45, Pullao Rice £1.50. Minimum charge £10. Hours: 12-2.30pm/6pm-12am. Branch: Raja Takeaway, Cheltenham, Rajdoot, 35 Castle St, Cirencester, Glos. Stocks Cobra.

CURRY GARDEN ©

90 Victoria Road, Swindon 01793 521114

R Khan's large restaurant was established as far back as 1969. It seats 80, and judging from reports, these are often filled, so it's popular. Chef specials: Tandoori King Prawn Jalfrezi, with green chillies £9.95. CC Members will get a 10% discount. Takeaway: 15% less. Hours: 12-2pm/5.30pm-12am. Stocks Cobra.

GULSHAN ©

122 Victoria Road, Old Town, Swindon 01793 522558

Owned and managed by Abdul Kahhar. Seats 80 on two floors connected by a spiral staircase. 'Very smart decor, pleasant attentive waiters. Extensive menu, mainly Bangladeshi. Muglai Paneer, cheese, mixed fruit, almond, sultanas, fresh cream in mild sauce served with Onion Bhajias and beer, cost £9.40. A nice idea was the revolving sweet tray with the bill.' DS. Sunday all-day buffet £7.50. Takeaway: 15% discount. Hours: 12-2.30pm/6pm-12am;. Sat. 6pm-1am. Stocks Cobra.

LALBAGH NEW ENTRANT ©

171 Rodbourne Road, Swindon 01793 535577

Established in 1997. Seats 60. Specials: Moonlight Chicken £6.90 – with cauliflower, mushroom and brandy in medium sauce. Tarana Chicken £6.90 – with potato, egg, green chilli and red wine in spicy hot sauce. Begana Lamb £6.90 – with mixed fruit, cream, white wine in mild sauce. Spiced Nan £1.70 – with garlic and chilli. Price check: Papadam 50p, CTM £6.50, Pullao Rice £1.70, Peshwari Nan £1.70. Takeaway: 10% discount. Delivery: £10 minimum, 3-mile radius. Hours: 12-2.30pm/6-11.30pm. Stocks Cobra.

COBRA GOOD CURRY GUIDE
County Index, see page 5 Town Index, see page 614
A to Z of the Curry Menu, page 41 Contributors Key, page 604

RAFU'S TANDOORI NEW TO OUR TOP 100 ©

29-30 High Street, Highworth, Swindon 01793 765320

Opened in 1982 by Mr Rafu as the Biplob; renamed to prevent confusion. It remains popular. 'Menu large and varied choice. Complete satisfaction. Best Jalfrazi in the West. Good service, pleasant atmosphere, superb location. Everything nice except the prantha (too greasy).' ZI. 'Menu had wide variety and choice. Quantity more than adequate. Service very courteous and polite. Atmosphere very convivial. Very good quality meal and good value.' KS 'We visit weekly. Extensive and varied menu. Generous quantities. High quality. Outstanding service. Excellent Bangra. Hasina Chicken – best in Europe!' IG&JN. 'The wine list is very good for an Indian restaurant. Whenever we go to Rafu's we know we are going to have a top-class meal, with friendly people, in pleasant surroundings.' JS. Price check: Papadam 50p, CTM £6.95, Pullao Rice £1.80, Peshwari Nan £1.80. Hours: 12-3pm/6pm-12am. Hours: 5pm to late.

SPICY AROMA ©

144 Cricklade Road, Gorse Hill, Swindon 01793 488700

Established in 1996, Abdul Rouf Ali's Aroma now seats 64 in two dining rooms decorated with 'mahogany effect with cream background, with a classic wooden effect bar'. Specials: Scampi Chilli Masala (304) £9.95 – thick onion, ginger and garlic sauce. Takeaway menu reads 'please order by number' – rather like a Chinese takeaway, is it a first for an Indian or before my time? Price check: Papadam 50p, CTM £6.75, Pullao Rice £1.95. Peshwari Nan £1.95, Lager £2.50 pint. Minimum charge: £6.95. Sunday lunch buffet: £7.95. Takeaway: 10% discount. Delivery: £12 minimum, 5-mile radius. Hours: 5pm-12.30am; Sat. 5pm-1.30am. Stocks Cobra.

Warminster

AGRA

32 East Street, Warminster 01985 212713

Mr M Rahman's 1984 ownership of this 50-seater coincided with the publication of our first *Guide*, in which it appeared. We've always regarded it as a useful currying hole in an otherwise devoid area. Special: Duck Jhalferezi, with fresh green chillies, £7.95. Price check: Papadam 30p, CTM £7.95 (incl. rice), Pullao Rice £1.95. Lager £1.90 pint, House wine £6.95. Minimum charge: £9. Takeaway: 10% off. Hours: 12-2.30pm/6-11.30pm. Branch: Assam Takeaway, East Street, Warminster.

SALAAM NEW ENTRANT

32a George Street, Warminster 01985 212064

Owner chef is Miff, 23, and he's proud to tell you that he is the winner of the 1999 BBC Network East Chef of the Year. His 1998 restaurant benefits from this, and we hear that it is already popular in the town. Reports please. Branch: Salaam, Winchester.

Wootton Bassett

MEMORIES OF INDIA NAME CHANGE

21 High Street, Wootton Bassett 01793 852365

Situated opposite the Curriers' Arms! Formerly Salik's. 'Bhajia £1.95 and Samosa £1.95, freshly made, nicely presented and delicious! Fragrant, fluffy Pullao Rice. Lots of meat in Keema Nan £1.65. Massive portion of Chicken Biryani £4.95. Chicken Tikka Bhuna £4.65, lots of well-marinated breast meat.' TE. 'This little gem deserves a mention. Extraordinary food, quality and service at a low price.' AE. Price check: Papadam 40p, CTM £5.25, Pullao Rice £1.55. Delivery: free on orders over £10. Hours: 12-2.30pm/6pm-12am (1am on Fri. & Sat.). Stocks Cobra.

WORCESTERSHIRE

Area: Midlands
Population: 476,000
Adjacent Counties: Glos, Hereford, Shrops, Warks, W Mids

Bewdley

THE RAJAH OF BEWDLEY ©

8 Load Street, Bewdley 01299 400368

Anwar Uddin's 34-seater is in a grade 2 listed cottage with soft lighting and exposed beams. 'Food excellent, the people extremely friendly, offering a high standard of customer service.' SH. Special: Tandoori Lobster. Price check: CTM £5.95, Pullao Rice £1.50. House wine £6.95. Takeaway: 10% off. Minimum charge: £4.95. Hours: 5-11.30pm.

COBRA GOOD CURRY GUIDE
County Index, see page 5 Town Index, see page 614
A to Z of the Curry Menu, page 41 Contributors Key, page 604

Bromsgrove

TANDOORI INDIAN NEW ENTRANT

11 Crown Close, Market Street, Bromsgrove 01527 870333

'Good varied menu. High quality food. Service excellent. Well worth a visit.' PF.

Droitwich

MOGHUL TANDOORI NEW ENTRANT

17 St Andrews Street, Droitwich 01905 794188

First opened in 1988, taken over in 1992 by A Matin, S Ali, K Miah and S Ahmed. Seats 46. Ample parking to front and rear. Specials: Tandoori Fish £5.25 – marinated, gently spiced, over charcoal. Price check: Papadam 40p, CTM £6.25, Pullao Rice £1.75, Peshwari Nan £1.50, Lager £2.20 pint. Takeaway: 10% discount. Delivery: 1 meal minimum, within Droitwich area. Hours: 5.30pm-12am (Fri. & Sat. 5.30pm-1am). Stocks Cobra.

Kidderminster

EURASIA TAKEAWAY ©

Unit 1, 19, Stourbridge Road, Kidderminster 01562 825861

First opened in 97, taken over by Syed Hussain Ahmed in 99. Specials include: Jamuna (a hot dish cooked with chicken, meat, prawn and a selection of oriental spices, herbs and green chilli, garnished with an egg) £4.90. Price check: Papadam 40p, CTM £4.75, Pullao Rice £1.30, Peshwari Nan £1.50. Delivery: £10 minimum, 4-mile radius. Hours: 5pm-12am.

NEW SHER E PUNJAB ©

48 George Street, Kidderminster 01562 740061

Evenings only at Puran Singh's restaurant which has been open a long time (since 1971). Stocks Cobra.

PARADISE BALTI HOUSE NEW ENTRANT

32 The Horsefair, Lower Mill Street, Kidderminster 01562 60479

'An excellent Balti house. We always get a great feed (Papadoms, starter, main course, Naans) for about £8 per head. Very friendly staff'. SH. 'I have tried many dishes from their menu and have enjoyed all of them. However,

I must emphasise that their Naan Breads are something else!' KP. 'Food here is excellent, staff are efficient and the atmosphere very congenial. I highly recommend Chicken Jalfrezi and the Naans are enormous.' PL. Well, let's hear it for the Naans!!! Stocks Cobra.

SPENNELLS TANDOORI TAKEAWAY NEW ENTRANT

3 Warble Place, Kidderminster 01562 748484

Established in 1998. Specials: Nawabi £4.90 – mild dish of rich sauce, banana, pineapple, lychees with butter and fresh cream. Price check: Papadam 25p, CTM £4.25, Pullao Rice £1.25, Peshwari Nan £1.45. Delivery: £8 minimum, 5-mile radius. Hours: 5-11pm; Sun. 6-11pm.

SPICE EMPIRE NEW ENTRANT

17 High Street, Kidderminster 01299 270419

'A superb meal – the best in the area. Service wonderful. Prices reasonable.' SS-L. Stocks Cobra.

Redditch

BALTI SPICE TAKEAWAY NEW ENTRANT ©

65 Popular Road, Batchley, Redditch 01527 596802

First opened in 1984, taken over in 1999 by Mastakin Miah. Previously called Pipasha Takeaway. Specials: Murghi Baburchi Walla £5.25 – medium spicy, Tandoori Chicken, eggs and minced meat. Family Nan: from £2.40 to £3.00. Price check: Papadam 30p, CTM £4.95, Pullao Rice £1.20, Peshwari Nan £1.20. Delivery: £8 minimum, 3-mile radius; £12 minimum, 4-mile radius. Hours: 5pm-12am; Sat. 5pm-1am.

NAWAB

17-21 Unicorn Hill, Redditch 01527 464594

Ajaib Hussain's 60-seater's Lamb Tikka Specials are noted e.g. Lamb Tikka Jeera, marinated and roasted in the tandoor, with onions, fresh tomatoes, fenugreek, coriander, cummin and spring onions £5.50. 'Conventional menu. Service above average. Lamb Tikka Ginger too bland and lamb chewy and tasteless, but Lamb Tikka Jafrezi Balti was plentiful, nicely balanced and complimented the Peshwari Naan superbly.' GG&MP. Minimum charge: £4.95. Credit cards not accepted. Price check: Papadam 40p, CTM £5.50, Pullao Rice £1.35. Delivery: £12 min, 3-miles. Hours: 5.30pm-12am. Stocks Cobra.

Tenbury Wells

SHAMRAJ BALTI HOUSE ©

28 Cross Street, Tenbury Wells 01584 819612

Owned by Mr Rahman, seats 60, party room 14, formula curries, 'marble-effect painted interior, light blue'. Takeaway: 15% off. Hours: 12-2.30pm (Sat. & Sun.)/5pm-12am. Stocks Cobra.

Upton-on-Severn

PUNDITS NEW ENTRANT

9 Old Street, Upton-on-Severn 01684 591022

'Reasonable Piazi for my starter, but my wife found her Aloo Chop too spicy for her taste. Excellent Chicken Tikka Shathkora and my wife enjoyed her Chicken Tikka Keema Massalla. Service somewhat slow since all food freshly cooked to order with excellent complimentary naan bread. Pricey for small town restaurant but good value in terms of the food and cooking standards. Should be included in the *Guide*.' RJP. Stocks Cobra.

West Hagley

SHENAPUR NEW ENTRANT

86 Worcester Road, West Hagley 01562 884867

'Everything superb. Large, air-conditioned, comfortable seating, service quick and cheerful. Lamb stuffed pepper delicious and filling, chicken Jalfrezi was the best I've had for ages. Plates untouchably hot. It isn't cheap but worth it. If you're in the area make a detour, I'm sure you won't be disappointed – the onion relish alone would be a good reason! This restaurant merits a TOP 100 position.' MS. More reports could get it there.

Worcester

BOMBAY PALACE ©

38 The Tything, Worcester 01905 613969

Abdul Rob tells us his 40-seater has 7 parking spaces at the back. Specials include: Kebabi Kofta, Chi Tik Pudina, Chicken Tikka Dhareswari and Tam Shami Moss. Generally good reports except one blaster from RJP. Takeaway: 10% off. Delivery: £10 min. Hours: 6pm-12am; Sat. 6pm-1am. Stocks Cobra.

©	Curry Club Discount	U	Unlicensed
V	Vegetarian	ANP	Alcohol not permitted
e-a-m-a-y-l	Eat as much as you like	BYO	Bring your own alcohol

MONSOON NEW TO OUR TOP 100

35 Foregate Road, Worcester 01905 726333

White painted angled pillars and wooden stained concertina doors make this 120 seater restaurant stand out on Foregate Road. Established in 1999 by Rahman (manager), Choudhury and Choudhury. Reception has been painted in a creamy colour with comfortable sofas upholstered in paprika. The restaurant has a light and airy feel, with bleached wooden flooring, paprika and cinnamon painted walls; original art hangs sparingly on the walls with matching chairs in paprika, cinnamon, turmeric and indigo. Natural wooden tables are economically laid with crisp white linen napkins and generous wine glasses. Specials: Tangri Kebab £2.95 – drumstick marinated in cashew nuts, spices and served with tamarind chutney. Achar Wali Machi £4.25 – salmon steak pickled in spices, served cold with salad. Parsi Jinga £9.25 – tiger prawns in mint, turmeric, garlic and tamarind juice. Lamb Shikampuri £9.25 – mince lamb balls stuffed with coriander, ginger, onion, raisins in curry gravy. Daal Panchmela £5.75 – a mix of five varieties of lentils. Many good reports allow us to place this restaurant into our TOP 100. Takeaway: 10% discount. Price check: Papadam 50p, CTM £6.50, Pullao Rice £2.25, Peshwari Nan £2.25, Lager £2.20 pint, House wine £6.95 bottle. Hours: 6pm-12am (Fri. & Sat. to 1). Branch: Cheltenham Tandoori, 2 Great Norwood Street Cheltenham, Gloucs. Tel: 01242 227772. Stocks Cobra.

ROYAL BALTI NEW ENTRANT

50 The Tything, Worcester 01905 25694

'Consistently good specialities, also good naan bread. Should be included in your guide and is far better than many in the town.' RJP. Stocks Cobra.

SPICE CUISINE NEW TO OUR TOP 100 U BYO

39-41 Bromyard Road, Worcester 01905 429786

Hidden away behind Birmingham Midshires Building Society, just over the river bridge from Worcester Town, it has been owned by the same family for years, Muslims from Pakistan. RE has been visiting regularly each week for years. Some excerpts follow: 'Staff are so friendly. My favourite main course is the chef's own recipe from Pakistan, Balti Chicken Special, but I have it with lamb. Superb – chunks of tender lamb in a thick spicy sauce. My wife's Chicken Kurma is exactly right. I tried Balti Apock and thoroughly enjoyed it – lamb, very tender in a thick spicy sauce. She-Who-Likes-Only-Baby-Curry had her favourite, Chicken Kurma – mild without being bland, and cooked to perfection. The manager's mother had sent some home cooked chicken curry, on the bone, as a treat for me. It was superb, but don't expect it on the menu! Prawn Puri was tasty with abundant prawns. Can't keep away. My weekly visit – this time for a traditional Sunday Curry. A really great place and a well kept secret from the passing punter.' [not any more Ray!] 'Saved me a fresh fish curry, but not really to my taste. I shared their Staff Curry Supper, lamb back chops, on the bone, in a rich, thick spicy sauce. I could eat it forever. Once again, service very good. I had Keema Balti and Tandoori Roti – both tasty and lots of it. What made tonight special was that I was presented, free of charge, a "Valued Customer Membership Gold Card". This entitled me to a 10% discount every time I visit. I was very touched. Our 34th wedding anniversary. Restaurant was heaving – good job we booked. My daughter said the Chicken Aloo Balti was the best Balti ever. Heaving – word has got around. Had our usual – Chicken Kurma, Seekh Kebabs, Lamb Special – and we were not disappointed. Seekh kebabs not so good this time. Staff curry main course made up for it – chicken on the bone and spinach in an almost too tasty sauce. Their regular Tandoori chef has gone – left for Pakistan for good. The washer-up has been promoted but thank goodness, the manager, Masteen and his cousin Israr are good teachers. So the Seekh Kebab standard is maintained... and Roti still done as I like it. Every time I go it seems to get better – friendly service and good food. Food as always excellent. A new Tandoori chef poached from Birmingham – excellent. My birthday, and they had made a lamb on the bone special which was excellent. Unfortunately their new Tandoori chef tried too hard and over-spiced the Seekh Kebabs. But Chicken Pakoras, Chicken Kurma, Aloo Balti and Naan all good. My friend Amrik (a Sikh) and his wife are both strict vegetarians and had Balti-E-Khas, the chef's own recipe of mushrooms, channa and alloo. They also had Tarka Daal. The verdict – very good indeed. Difficult to fault this place, and by the way they deliver takeaways. Firmly lodged as my number two favourite after London E1's Lahore Kebab House. I just love their food, love it, love it, love it.' RE We'd never have guessed, Ray!!! And just for you it goes into our TOP 100.

NORTH YORKSHIRE

Area: North
Population: 748,000
Adjacent Counties: Cumbria, Durham,
Lancs, E & W Yorks

1997 county changes returned 'Cleveland' south of the Tees to North Yorks. At the same time, the changes created a 'new' Yorkshire county by transferring territory and towns from 'North Humbs' into East Yorkshire. This restored Yorkshire as Britain's biggest county. Because the area is so large, we deal with these four counties in their current administrative formats and in compass order, N, E, S, W.

Filey

FILEY TANDOORI NEW ENTRANT

16a Bellevue Crescent, Filey 01723 515992

Established in 1998. Seats 32. Specials: Chana Gousht £4.25 – lamb with chick peas, garlic, tomato and fresh coriander, medium hot. Price check: Papadam 45p, CTM £6.25, Pullao Rice £1.65, Peshwari Nan £1.75. Delivery: £10 minimum, 4-mile radius, £1 charge. Hours: 6-11pm.

Harrogate

RAJPUT

11 Cheltenham Parade, Harrogate 01423 562113

Opened in 1992 by Mrs Perveen Khan – head chef, Mr Khan front of house. 'Food was excellent and the restaurant full. The service was also good and polite. I recommend the Rajput.' RA. Stocks Cobra.

RAJ RANI TAKEAWAY ©

235 Skipton Road, Harrogate 01423 529295

Ahad Miah, the proprietor of this takeaway only, is offering Monday and Tuesday CC customers 15% discount on collected takeaways over £15. Special Lamb Tikka, sliced lamb tikka, keema, peppers, onions, herbs and coriander. Delivery: £8.50, 4-miles. Hours: 5.30-11.30pm (11pm on Sat., 10.30pm Sun.).

Knaresborough

SPICE MERCHANT NEW ENTRANT

Market Square, Knaresborough 01423 861777

Opposite the Police Station. 'Excellent decor, comfortable, good service, not rushed, superb menu – many dishes incorporating fruit. Very good value for money.' HH. And another report for one of our regular reporters. 'The newest in Knaresborough. Spacious on one level. Staff very pleasant, chatty. We were asked if we wanted any drink (alcoholic), we declined, without prompting waiter produced jug of water. I chose Chicken Korai £4.95 – to compare with my favourite 'Bradford Dish'; it was surprisingly good. Mixed Kebab Cocktail £5.10 – blend of chicken, lamb, and meat balls, marinated and barbecued, the sauce very tasty. Meal nicely presented, warm plates, towels to wipe our mitts.' JMFP. Price check: CTM £4.25, Pullao Rice £1.50, Garlic Nan £1.45. Hours: 5.30pm-12am (Fri. & Sat. to 1am). Stocks Cobra.

Malton

RAJ TANDOORI ©

21 Church Street, Norton, Malton 01653 697337

S Islam's friendly 34-seater has dusky pink and petrol blue walls, white cornices, Indian art, pink and white linen and spotlights. Special: Akhini Chicken, pineapple, almond, sultanas, peas and rice, served with vegetable curry £6. 'Has been a satisfying experience following their progress, to what is now a very good restaurant.' AT. Takeaway: 20% off. Delivery: £1.50 min. Hours: 5.30pm-12am; Mon. closed except bank holidays. Stocks Cobra.

Middlesborough

CLEVELAND TANDOORI ©

289 Linthorpe Road, Middlesbrough 01642 242777

First opened in 1991, taken over by owner-chef Abid Hussain in 1996. His 32-seater serves formula curry, but there are some Pakistani gems: Shalgum Gosht is meat with turnip and Lahori Gosht, meat with okra. There is a range of Haandi dishes. For the yet-to-be-converted-to curry, try Abid's Anglo Indian Coronation Chicken, created in 1953 by London's Cordon Bleu school in honour of QEII's Coronation: diced chicken cooked with apricots in a creamy sauce. E-a-m-a-y-l Sunday, Monday, Tuesday. Delivery: £6 minimum, 3-miles. Hours: 6pm-12am (2.30am on Fri./Sat.). Stocks Cobra.

Ripon

MOTI RAJ ©

18 High Skellgate, Ripon 01765 690348

I was hosting a cooking theatre at an ethnic exhibition, which William Hague officially opened (for posterity, when our great-grandchildren are reading yellowing, curry-stained copies of this tome, he was Tory opposition leader at this time). When I asked him if he liked curry 'er yes I do actually' and when I asked where was his fav rest, he said 'er the Moti Raj Ripon'. I quote the 'er', but he did say Moti Raj without hesitation, and he is more or less a local. Abdul Malik's restaurant is indeed a local to a good many scribes who inform me of its qualitites. Abdul's philosophy is: 'the only path to good food, like good wine, is time.' And what he means is, relax and enjoy your evening. Special: Sliced Chicken Tikka with Keema. 'For main course I had Chicken Karahi, served in a proper cast iron karahi and piping hot. One of my friends had Prawn Bhuna, not on the menu, but not the slightest trouble for them to provide. Total bill (for 3) came to £24. .' JMFP. Takeaway 10% off. Delivery: 3-miles. Hours: 5.30pm-12am.

Scarborough

EASTERN TANDOORI NEW ENTRANT

5 St Helens Square, Scarborough 01723 375227

Formerly Tandoori Nights. 'A very small but cosy restaurant and very polite staff. Rezala was not highly spicy but had large chunks of tender lamb cooked with cinnamon. Keema Rice was tasty and fluffy.' MR&MRS DB. Stocks Cobra.

Settle

SETTLE TANDOORI NEW ENTRANT ©

9 Commercial Courtyard, Duke Street, Settle 01729 823393

Established in 1998 by Abdul Rob. Seats 50. Palm trees in middle of restaurant. Specials: Garlic Chicken £4.70. Chicken Tikka Balti £6.50. Price check: Papadam 40p, CTM £5.80, Pullao Rice £1.50, Peshwari Nan £1.50, Lager £1.80 pint. Takeaway: 10% discount. Hours: 5.30-11.30pm. Stocks Cobra.

Skipton

AAGRAH TOP 100 ©

Devonshire Place, Keighley Road, Skipton 01756 790807

Established in 1989 and managed by Mostafizur Rahman, this 52-seater is the third of seven very popular Aagrahs (so booking advisable) (See Shipley, W Yorks for detailed comment). Pakistani food, more gutsy and robust than the Bangla formula, sometimes attracts criticism (T&KM didn't like it, for example) but this doesn't mean it should be demoted from our TOP 100. Specials include: Achar, Hydrabady and Masala dishes. Price check: Papadam 40p, CTM £6.90, Pullao Rice £1.50, Peshwari Nan £1.80, Lager £2.10 pint. Takeaway: 10% discount. Hours: 6pm-12am; Sun. 6-11pm. Stocks Cobra.

RAJ BALTI HOUSE

11 Keighley Road, Skipton 01756 795697

'Better than the Aagrah' say T&KM about owner-manager Mastab Ali's 42 seater restaurant. Special: Balti Tikka £7.95, Chicken Passanda £7.95. Takeaway 15% off. Price check: Papadam 40p, CTM £6.10, Pullao Rice £1.60. Hours: 6pm (Sat. & Sun. 5.30pm)-12am (1am on Sat., 11.30pm on Sun.). Stocks Cobra.

Tadcaster

AAGRAH TOP 100 ©

York Road, Steeton, Tadcaster 01937 530888

Managed by Aagrah boss, Mohammed Aslam, this 120-seater, which opened in 1996, is the sixth of seven very popular Aagrahs. It's on the A64 near York, with easy parking. See Aagrah Skipton, above. 'Very large, pleasantly decorated and comfortable restaurant. A bit pricey, but good service, even when very busy on buffet night. Good portions and excellent Murgh Chana and Stuffed paratha.' IB. Specials include: Achar, Hydrabady and Masala dishes. Price check: Papadam 40p, CTM £6.90, Pullao Rice £1.50, Peshwari Nan £1.80, Lager £2.10 pint. Takeaway: 10% discount. Hours: 6-11.30pm. Sun. 6-11pm. Stocks Cobra. All the Aagrahs are rated with a collective TOP 100 cachet. (See Shipley, W Yorks, for fuller comment.)

Whitby

WHITBY INDIAN TANDOORI NEW ENTRANT

6 Whitby Quays, Station Square, Whitby 01947 820871

'Situated in the entrance to Whitby Station. Saturday night on a bank holiday was busy, and the six waiters were rushing about trying to cope with the orders, although not always successfully. But we were served efficiently enough. Comprehensive menu of all the standard dishes. Onion Bhajis solid but acceptable. Prawn Patia was prawns in a rather insipid watery sauce. Dhansak was quite tasty and reasonably hot. Portions adequate. Marginally above average prices, but having a monopoly in a holiday town is perhaps not surprising.' MW. Stocks Cobra.

Yarm

BALTI HOUSE

49 High Street, Yarm 01642 788998

Say T&KM: 'The tandoori dishes had a smokey flavour which I do not enjoy.' But we are not delisting this place because of this, since tandoori dishes have a barbeque flavour by definition. Besides, Yarm is a favourite place of mine. In the mid-1960s I used to fly over tiny Yarm, landing RAF jets at Middleton St George, now Teesside Airport, but there wasn't a curry house there then, nor indeed anywhere within a 50-mile radius. Now there are over 100 in that area, and even two in Yarm. We hear that Johir Uddin's 80-seater is a curry house with a difference, decorated rather like a pub, great idea. Special: Beef Munro, mild dish cooked with garlic sauce, ground almonds, served with Pullao Rice £8.95. Price check: Papadam 40p, CTM £6.95, Pullao Rice £1.50. House wine £8.95. Takeaway 10% off. Minimum charge £6.95. Hours: 12-11pm (2am on Fri. & Sat.). Stocks Cobra.

York

AKASH ©

10 North Street, York 01904 633550

Established in 1983, chef/owner JU Ahmed hasn't upped his prices since our last *Guide*. His 38-seater does a set dinner for £9.50. Specials: Kabuli Chicken or Lamb, chickpeas, tomato and fresh coriander £6.20. Price check: Papadam 50p, CTM £6.20, Pullao Rice £1.50. Peshwari Nan £1.40. Takeaway 20% off. Delivery: £8 min, 3-miles. Hours: 5pm-12am. Stocks Cobra.

BENGAL BRASSIERE NEW ENTRANT

21 Goodramgate, York 01904 640066

Established in 1999 by Dobir Malik and Iqbal Chowdury, a 100-seater that is typical of the new style contemporary decor being applied by restaurants of all nationalities. Hard polished wooden floors, brightly coloured upholstered chairs, wrought iron stair casing, spot lighting, and white walls. Price check: Papadam 40p, CTM £6.25, Pullao Rice £1.70, Peshwari Nan £1.70. Takeaway: 20% discount. Hours: 5.30-11.30pm. Sat. 12-2.30pm/5.30-11.30pm; Sun. 12-10.30pm. Branch: Bengal Brasserie, York Business Park, Mifield Lane, Nether Poppleton, York, 01904 788808.

BILASH TAKEAWAY NEW ENTRANT

1 Bromley Street, Leeham Road, York 01904 653660

'Situated in a mean backstreet on the outskirts of the city. My previous experience of takeouts has not been good, as invariably the food has been greasy and bland. But here the food was outstandingly good and tasty and is must for GCG. What also surprised us was not only the quality and quantity of the food, but the extremely low prices (meal for three was £14.45).' BP-D.

GARDEN OF INDIA NEW ENTRANT

5 Fawcett Street, York 01904 645679

Established in 1992. Seats 50. Price check: Papadam 50p, CTM £6.70, Pullao Rice £1.60, Peshwari Nan £1.40, Lager £1.85 pint. Takeaway: 15% discount. Delivery: £5 minimum, 3-mile radius. Hours: 6pm-12am. Stocks Cobra.

JAIPUR SPICE NEW ENTRANT

103 Haxby Road York Road, Easingwold, York 01904 673550

Refurbished Garth Hotel off the A19 and is able to seat 140 in smoking and non-smoking areas. Fully licensed. Air conditioned. Ample free parking. 'The service is smart and exemplary, with a high degree of training evident. The food was more than appetising, and we left feeling well satisfied.' RL. Stocks Cobra.

JINNAH BALTI NEW TO OUR TOP 100 ©

105-107 Micklegate, York 01904 659999

Saleem Akhtar's chain of restaurants is growing, reflecting each branch's popularity, in an area which has previously not been known for currinary excellence. Decor, including conservatory extensions, smart logos, menus and staff, 'all contribute to a good experience, which is very different at lunch time to evening. We've been at both times of day, to all of Mr Akhtar's restaurants. Each has its own atmosphere, but you can tell they are in the same ownership'. ED. 'I started with the Seekh Kebabs and thought I was going to be disappointed with the place as the Kebabs were of the red-colouring variety and possibly microwaved (the best I've tasted were at Bharat in Bradford). However, the main course, Jinnah Special Balti which was chicken, lamb, prawn and mushrooms was excellent.' RC. However, JR found ' the Jinnah Special Biryani flavouring unadventurous, ditto the vegetable curry accompaniment, but everything else OK.' JR. Price check: Papadam 45p, CTM £6.95, Pullao Rice £1.95. Hours: 12-2.30pm/6pm-12am. Branches: Jinnah, A64 Malton Road, Flaxton, York; Viceroy of India, 26 Monkgate, York; Jinnah, 845 York Road, Leeds; Jinnah Takeaway, 18 The Village, Haxby; Taj Mahal and Viceroy of India, York. Stocks Cobra.

KINGS RANSOM TANDOORI NEW ENTRANT

12a King Street, York 01904 632886

'Attractive looking restaurant situated just off the waterfront. Service friendly, promptly seated, but pretty indifferent during the meal. Mutton in Mutton Tikka was very, very chewy, Chicken Chilli Massala was disappointing, but Prawn Patia was spot on. Boiled rice and naan excellent. In summary, a good competent place.' PW. Stocks Cobra.

TAJ MAHAL

4 Kings Staith, York 01904 653944

'Good value, service excellent, comfort good. Vegetable dishes to be recommended.' JW. 'Food and prices excellent.' AA. Hours: 12-2.30pm/6pm-12am.

EAST YORKSHIRE

Area: North
Population: 800,000
Adjacent Counties: Lincs, N S & W Yorks

1997 county changes created this 'new' Yorkshire county by transferring territory and towns here from 'North Humbs'.

Beverley

NASEEB ©

9-10 Wednesday Market, Beverley — 01482 861110

Established in 1988 by Abdul Muzir, seats 44 diners, Bangladeshi formula curries. Very pretty restaurant, Indian painting, white walls, arches, ceiling fans, blue tablecloths and napkins, velvet chairs and curtains. Roshoon Mirch Murgh, hot, thick sauce, fresh garlic, green chillies, green pepper, chopped tomatoes and fresh coriander leaves £6.10. Delivery only available to Nasseeb club members, ask for details. Takeaway: 10% discount. Hours: 6-11.30pm. Stocks Cobra.

Hessle

LIGHT OF INDIA ©

27 The Weir, Hessle — 01482 649521

Saiful Islam Tarafdar's Light is under the shadow of the fabulous bridge, and does 'fabulous takeaways only' KY. Special: Indian Burger, pitta bread with spicy kebab and salad £1.90. Curry Sauce and Chips £1.90! Delivery: £7 minimum, Hessle area and £10 minimum local area, possibly small charge! Hours: 5pm-12am (12.30am on Sat.).

Hull

MAHARAJAH

245 Holderness Road, Hull — 01482 224647

Established in 1995, Abdul Hamid's 46-seater does: 'Good quality food and service.' JF. Side Dish Specials: Peeled Plum Tomato Bhajee £2.40, Yellow

Split Pea Bhajee £2.40, Garlic Chilli Sag Bhajee £2.40. Price check: Papadam 40p, CTM £5.25, Pullao Rice £1.65, Peshwari Nan £1.70, Lager £2.40 pint. Takeaway: 15% discount. Delivery: £1.10 charge. Hours: 12-2pm/6pm-12am. Sat. 6pm-1am. Stocks Cobra.

RAJ PAVILION NEW ENTRANT

56a-58, Beverley Road, Hull 01482 581939

'50 yards from the Champanile Hotel and Hull Daily Mail buildings. Walk or go by taxi – it's double yellow lines. I and colleagues went by taxi, since we expected to and did consume copious quantities of lager – Lal Toofan on draught; it's wet but a bit anaemic and I think the dreaded Carlsberg is also available. Doesn't look much from the outside, but inside all black and chrome trimmings – quite impressive. Service full of smiles and attentive. Started with King Prawn Butterfly £2.95 – two bashed flat and breadcrumbed. Popadoms still not consumed when starters arrived so loads of onion Cachumber etc to jolly things along. Nicely presented, portions not over generous – enough I suppose but no more. Colleague tried my Chicken Jalfrezi £4.75 – I saw spoon go into the bowl and come out with chicken and at least three chillies, which I told him about when he descended from the ceiling ten minutes later! He said that he was very doubtful that I had any parents! Have never watched anyone devour a Kulfi with such relief. My colleague said he hated me even more the following morning – can't think why! £49 for two including six pints (we did a lot of talking which is thirsty work as you know).' MS. Yes, Maurice, we know EXACTLY what you mean. Delivery. Special: Murg Nan £1.45 – stuffed with chicken. Price check: Papadam 35p, CTM £4.95, Pullao Rice £1.30, Peshwari Nan £1.45. Hours: 12-2.30pm/6-11.30pm (Fri. & Sat. 12am).

TANDOORI MAHAL ©

589 Anlaby Road, Hull 01482 505653

Abu Maksud and Mizanur Tarafder's 64-seat restaurant is one of RK's favourites. 'Have been regular customers for over three years. We have always received first class service and excellent food.' PT. Kurzi Lamb £45. Set dinner £16.95. Hours: 6pm-12am. Stocks Cobra.

SOUTH YORKSHIRE

Area: North
Population: 1,306,000
Adjacent Counties: Derbys, Lincs, Notts, E & W Yorks

Barnsley

INDIAN GARDENS

16 Peel Square, Barnsley 01226 282612

RA Rahman's 60-seat curry house, first opened in 1981. 'The staff are very friendly and attentive. Specials marginally more expensive than standards, but are superior. Naans wonderfully light, but on the small side. Personal favourite Chicken Karahi comes to the table sizzling in a blackened cast-iron karahi on a wooden base.' NW. Other specials include: Begon Took, fried aubergine bathed in tangy sauce of yoghurt and gram flour paste £1.60. Palong Sag, spinach, lentils and fresh coriander £3.70. Even hotter than a Vindaloo, comes the Sindalo, cooked with Chinese dry chillies, from £3.50. Hours: 6pm-12.30am; Sat. 6pm-2am. Stocks Cobra.

JALSA ©

7 Pitt Street, Barnsley 01226 779114

Emdadur Rahman established his Jalsa in 1992. It is a comfortable, smart, 50-seater with a delightful reception area and bar. And we know it's popular. Specials include: Chrigri Sizzler £6.90 (Farons Bengal Tiger Prawns steamed with baby tomatoes, mushrooms and stir fried, served with salad). Takeaway 15% off. Price check: Papadam 50p, CTM £7.25, Pullao Rice £1.70, Peshwari Nan £1.90, Takeaway: 15% discount. Hours: 6pm-12am. Stocks Cobra.

K2 ©

5 Royal Street, Barnsley 01226 299230

Kashmiri Balti takeaway-only establishment. 'Excellent.' TH. Price check: They don't do lunch and we're not surprised, owner/manager/chef Ditta must be exhausted with these hours! 10% off for students before 10.30pm. Hours: 6pm-3am (4am on Sat., 12.30am on Sun.).

©	Curry Club Discount	U	Unlicensed
V	Vegetarian	ANP	Alcohol not permitted
e-a-m-a-y-l	Eat as much as you like	BYO	Bring your own alcohol

TANDOORI HUT NEW ENTRANT **BYO**

Wakefield Road, Mapplewell, Barnsley 01226 390037

'Seats 30, owned and managed by Mr Farouk. Has gained popularity due to excellent reputation and quality food served in large portions. My favourite is an excellent Chicken Methi, which is cooked to taste by chef Ali.' SL. BYO: no corkage. Delivery: 4 miles. Price check: Papadam 30p, CTM £5.60, Pullao Rice £1.20, Enormous Nan £1.

Bawtry

DOWER HOUSE INDIAN NEW ENTRANT

Market Place, 19-21 Copley Road, Bawtry 01302 719696

'Open since 1992, upmarket, seats approx. 80. Small menu but any dish requested will be endeavoured to be cookeds. Quality of lamb and chicken exceptional, and all the sauces are fairly dry, better than a lot of the sloppy sauces served in cheaper restaurants. Methi Ghost cooked madras hot is my favourite. All waiters very competent, friendly and efficient. My partner and I consider it to be the best restaurant we've ever visited.' PS. Stocks Cobra.

Doncaster

AAGRAH TOP 100 AWARD WINNER ©

Great North Road, Woodlands, Doncaster 01302 728888

Opened in 1995, the fifth of seven very popular (so booking advisable) Aagrahs. This 90-seater is a franchise run by cousin Liaquat Ali. Like its sisters, it is awarded a collective TOP 100 cachet. 'I would put it at no. 1 in Doncaster, and there's a lot of competition.' JF. (See Shipley, W Yorks for detailed comment.) Specials include: Achar, Hydrabady and Masala dishes. Takeaway: 10% discount. Hours: 6-11.30pm; Fri. & Sat. 6pm-12am; Sun. 6-11pm. Stocks Cobra.

INDUS ©

24-26 Silver Street, Doncaster 01302 810800

Long-established (1968) 175-seater, owned by Karim Din, with manager M Ilyas. Modern, upmarket Anglo/Indian decor. 'A sophisticated restaurant.' DC. 'Is and always has been our favourite in Yorkshire.' WHH. Takeaway: 10% discount. Delivery: £20. Sun. buffet £12. Hours: 12-2pm/6.30-11.30pm. Stocks Cobra.

TAJ MAHAL NEW ENTRANT ©

32 Hallgate, Doncaster 01302 341218

Established in 1989. Seats 78. Specials include: Lahore King Prawns, £6.45. Price check: Papadam 50p, CTM £6.50, Pullao Rice £1.70, Peshwari Nan £1.90, Lager £1.90 pint. Takeaway: 10% discount. Delivery: £10 minimum, 3-mile radius. Hours: 5.30pm-12.30am (Fri. & Sat. 5.30-1am). Stocks Cobra.

Rotherham

MUGHAL CURRY CENTRE NEW ENTRANT ©

1 Bellows Road, Rawmarsh, Rotherham 01709 527084

Established in 1993. Seats 48. Karahi dishes are most popular. Monday, Tuesday and Thursday: two for one. Price check: Papadam 40p, CTM £5.20, Pullao Rice £1.50, Peshwari Nan £1.90, Lager £2.40 pint. Takeaway: 10% discount. Hours: 6pm to late; Sat. 6pm-3am. Stocks Cobra.

Sheffield

ASHOKA NEW TO OUR TOP 100

307 Ecclesall Road, Sheffield 0114 268 3029

Established in 1967 by Mrs M Ahmed, this 38-seater is managed by Mr Ahmed. 'The best Indian restaurant we have been to, including many in the London area and Birmingham. We went back to it every night of the week [while attending a scientific meeting in Sheffield]. We cannot praise its delicate and distinct flavours too highly, and the friendly, efficient service. You should add it to your excellent Curry Club book.' J&AF. OK Jack and Anna, but it first entered the Guide last time. Anyway, yours is one of many contented reports, so we feel it's time for this well-established and well run venue to join the elite TOP 100. Most ordered dish Bhel Puri – £2.95, Liver Puri – chicken livers, stir-fried in masala, served on bread £2.95. Price check: Papadam 70p, CTM £7.25, Pullao Rice £1.75. Lager £2.60 pint, House wine £8.90. Takeaway: 10% off. Hours: 6 (Sun. 7)-11.30pm.

BENGAL SPICE NEW ENTRANT ©

457 Manchester Road, Sheffield 0114 288 8666

Established in 1998. Specials: Musca £4.70 – tikka with bananas, pineapple and fresh cream, fruity. Haryali Murgh £5.50 – marinated chicken in sauce of spinach, mint and coriander leaf. Price check: Papadam 30p, CTM £4.70,

Pullao Rice £1.30, Peshwari Nan £1.50. Delivery: £10 minimum, 4-mile radius. Hours: 5-11pm/Sat. 5-11.30pm.

BILASH TAKEAWAY

347 Sharrow Vale Road, Sheffield 0114 266 1746

Established by chef Abdul Jahir in 1986. Specials: Chicken Tikka Jalfrezi £4.30, King Prawn Sag £5.50. Price check (unchanged for years): Papadam 30p, CTM £3.95, Pullao Rice £1, Peshwari Nan £1.15. Hours: 5.30-11.30pm.

DILSHAD NEW ENTRANT ©

96 The Dale, Sheffield 0114 255 5008

Established in 1995. Seats 48. Specials: Shahi Chicken or Lamb £4 – with mincemeat, eggs, onions, peppers and tomatoes, medium. Gatta Special £4 – chicken, meat, prawns and fruit, medium. Investigate the set meals – there is something for everyone. Price check: Papadam 45p, CTM £6.95, Pullao Rice £1.60, Peshwari Nan £1.90, Lager £1.90 pint. Takeaway: approximately 15%. Hours: 6pm-12am; Sat. 6pm-12.30am. Stocks Cobra.

ELINAS NEW ENTRANT ©

282 Sharrow Road, Sheffield 0114 267 9846

First opened in 1993, taken over by Mrs Reba Khan in 1999. Seats 40 in two-tone lime green marble effect walls. Specials: Chicken Shobuz Masala £4.40 – fresh coriander and green chillies, hot. Sag Tikka £4.30 – with spinach. Price check: Papadam 50p, CTM £6.90, Pullao Rice £1.95, Peshwari Nan £1.90, Lager £2.10 pint. Takeaway: 15% discount. Delivery: £10 minimum, 3-mile radius. Hours: 5.30-11.30pm; Sat. 5.30pm-12am. Stocks Cobra.

EVEREST TANDOORI NEW ENTRANT ©

59-61 Chesterfield Road, Sheffield 0114 258 2975

First opened in 1978, taken over by NM Raja in 1998. Seats 76. Specials: Bhattak Masalla £7.95 – duck, marinated, spices, fresh onion, tomato, rich masala sauce. Chicken or Lamb Razalla £5.95 – with onion, tomato, fresh green chillies, thick spicy sauce, very hot! Price check: Papadam 40p, CTM £4.95, Pullao Rice £1.60, Peshwari Nan £2, Lager £2.20 pint. Takeaway: 10% discount. Delivery: 2-mile radius. Hours: 6pm-1am; Thurs. 6pm-2am; Fri. & Sat. 6pm-3am. Stocks Cobra.

HAMID'S BALTI HOUSE NEW ENTRANT

983 Eccleshall Road, Sheffield 0114 266 0155

Established in 1995. Specials: King Prawn Madrasi £5.30 – with green chilli, hot. Chicken Satay £4.60 with Korma sauce. Butter Chicken £4.60 – in butter and cream sauce. Egg Pullao £1.35. Price check: Papadam 30p, CTM £4.60, Pullao Rice £1.10, Peshwari Nan £1.35. Takeaway: 10% discount. Delivery: £9.50 minimum, 3-mile radius. Hours: 5.30-11.30pm.

IJAFLONG ©

182 Northfield Road, Crookes, Sheffield 0114 266 1802

A cosy Bangladeshi formula curry house, seating just 36 diners. Balti dishes on the menu, from £3.50. Special: Jahangir Bhuna Prawn, medium, onions, tomatoes and mushrooms £4.20. Hours: 6pm-12am (1am on Fri. & Sat.).

NEW INDIA GARDEN RE ENTRANT

659 London Road, Heeley, Sheffield 0114 250 0059

'I cannot believe this is no longer in the 1999 *GCG*. Nothing has changed except the premises have been redecorated. It deserves a TOP 100 listing.' AG. Blame the owners, Andy. If they had returned their 1999 *Guide* entry form they wouldn't have been delisted. They haven't bothered to return the 2001 form either, but just for you we'll reinstate them. As for TOP 100, plentiful good reports from known readers, and the next *Guide* form from New India might, just might get them this accolade! Stocks Cobra.

NIRMAL'S TOP 100 ©

189-193 Glossop Road, Sheffield 0114 272 4054

Mrs Nirmal Gupta is the owner chef, with the front going to Mr PL Gupta. But Nirmal is no retiring backstage person. She makes appearances on the restaurant floor and 'enjoys talking about food' PM. She is a huge personality and has no hesitation in telling customers like William Hague and Jamie Lee Curtis such snippets as 'curry is an aphrodisiac'. But not all her clients are stars. She opened in 1981 near the University 'to feed hungry students', indeed many of her regulars work and study there. Mrs Nirmal's has virtually doubled in size since we first reported on it, and now has a reception area, cocktail bar and 80 seats on two floors. Its famous Special Board, upon which are chalked the dishes of the day, fortunately remains. The technique would hardly merit a mention in 1001 bistros up and down the land, but it is rare in the world of curry. I mentioned this back in 1984, and I'm still waiting for the formula wallahs to cotton on! The menu is northern Indian with, on the face of it, just standard Tandoori, Tikkas, Kormas, Bhunas, Madrases, Vindaloos and the rest. 'But do not expect one-sauce cooking here.' RS. 'All is cooked superbly, as at an Indian home.' GA. Of those specials: 'Nirmal's Potato Chops £2.25, are amazing mashed potato rissoles with a central stuffing of spicy lentils topped with almond tikka. The vegetable dishes prove the point that this is exceptional cooking. The paneer is always light and fresh, and stuffed Bhindi (okra) is always the test of a good chef – they can so easily go sappy! I've not seen that happen here.' BR. 'She is a magician with lentils.' SG. Price check: Papadam 45p, CTM £6.95, Pullao Rice £1.95. Tomato Paneer, £4.95. Parsnips with peppers and tomatoes £4.50. Aubergine Green Pepper £4.95. Gourmet Buffet night on Tuesday, £9.95 from 7.30-11pm. Sun. buffet £9.95. Service 10%. Hours: 12-2.30pm/6pm-12am. Nirmal's stays firmly in our TOP 100. Stocks Cobra.

WEST YORKSHIRE

Area: North
Population: 2,125,000
Adjacent Counties: G Man, Lincs, N & S Yorks

Batley

BOMBAY PALACE BYO ©

3 St James Street, Batley 01924 444440

Location: off the A652 Bradford Road from Dewsbury, easily accessed from M1 junction 40. Balti 74-seater in an old converted bakery, with many features still apparent, such as the dough mixers; opened in 1992 by G Maniyar and Shahid Akudi. Brick walls display Moghal paintings, open fire. 'Upstairs with a light industrial theme, very pleasant surroundings which includes a separate family room. Popadoms are complimentary after giving your order. Food excellent, every dish has its own flavour. As the level of hotness tends to be gauged higher than most restaurants, this will suit the fire eaters. Portions are generous, one rice is enough for two. Staff extremely friendly and efficient.' PVI. 'My wife and I have been regulars since it opened. Our current favourites are Seekh Kebabs – beautifully spicy, not too hot, fresh and tasty. Nargis Kebabs – full of flavour with a velvety texture. For special occasions there are banquet menus, which again represent excellent value for money.' TN. Specials include: Shikari dish £6.90, Achari dish £6.90, and Palace Raan, whole leg of lamb, marinated for 24 hours in herbs, yoghurt, almonds and cashews, cut into slices, plenty for 4, £60. Price check: Papadam 20p, CTM £7.50, Pullao Rice £1.50, Peshwari Nan £1.70. Takeaway: approximately 10% discount. Delivery: £10 minimum, 3-mile radius, £6 minimum, 2-mile radius. Hours: 6pm-12am.

SPICE GARDEN BYO ©

2 Market Place, Birstall, Batley 01924 471690

Specials at Abrar Hussain's Pakistani 74-seater include the Grand-Slam – it's four different meats, vegetables, prawns, massive portion – so now you know! Takeaway: 10% off. Delivery: £7, 3-miles. BYO. Hours: 5pm-12am.

Bradford

(inc. Baildon, Chapel Green, Great Horton, Idle, Manningham and Thornbury)

Bradford has a high pedigree curry background, with its very well-established, largely-Pakistani population. This means Halal meat and few veg at the many unlicensed cheap n' cheerful spit n' sawdust caffs. Since many are strict Moslems, not all welcome BYO. In such establishments, please check with the staff that you may BYO, and even if 'yes', always drink discretely and in moderation. The restaurants, sweet shops and cafés are much more widely spread around than, say, Southall. Curryholics must locate them, for their excellent, uncompromising ethnic food at real value-for-money prices. With more curry establishments (160) per head of the population (475,000) than in any other city in Britain (the ratio is 1:2968) Bradford remains Curry City UK (see Leicester and Glasgow).

ASHA ©

31 Cheapside, Central Bradford 01274 729358

Special Feast Night on Sundays and Thursdays at owner Abdul Anwar's Asha. Hours: 6pm-12am. Stocks Cobra.

BOMBAY BRASSERIE

1 Simes Street, off Westgate, Central Bradford 01274 737564

Established in 1983. Taken over in 1998 by Ali Shan. The building was once a Presbyterian church and makes a fantastic venue, seating 150 in smoking and non-smoking areas. 'Great atmosphere, and food, indeed a memorable occasion, and something quite out of the Bradford norm.' AN. Price check: Papadam 35p, CTM £7.50, Pullao Rice £1.50, Peshwari Nan £1.70, Lager £2.20 pint. Hours: 5.30-11.30pm; Fri. & Sat. 5.30pm-12.30am; Sun. 12.30-11pm. Stocks Cobra.

INTERNATIONAL TANDOORI

40 Manville Terrace, off Morley Street, Central Bradford 01274 721449

'I have been eating at Bradford curry houses for over 20 years, and my favourite has been the Kashmir. However, having had a couple of disappointing meals there recently, I decided to try somewhere new. The International was recommended and I have returned on three occasions since. The food, while not being particularly sophisticated, is excellent. I'm not able to report on a wide range of dishes since I've tended to stick to classic curry house dishes, but I can vouch for old favourites like the Shami Kebabs and the Kemma Vindaloo.' MB.

KARACHI

15-17 Neal Street, Central Bradford 01274 732015

Limited menu but others can be asked for, provided no long preparation is required. Proudly home run with friendly and unflappable staff. Cheap, cheerful and excellent food. To round off a cracking meal I had a homemade Pistachio Kulfi, frozen solidly, but melting into a sweet and spicy mush.' RW. 'Food is good quality, service is friendly. Decor reminded us of a school canteen, and the guide is correct – the toilets are dreadful. Goes without saying that in Bradford it came with three chapatis. However, this was its undoing, as they were too thick meaning that you left feeling bloated.' HR.

KASHMIR

27 Morley Street, Central Bradford 01274 726513

Restaurant holds about 200 on two floors, downstairs – formica tables, upstairs – carpeted, tablecloths. 'Downstairs restaurant has been extended since last visit – 40 seats added. After sitting down it was some five or ten minutes before a member of staff approached our table – I had time to wonder if the management had over extended or perhaps the ordering system had changed and I was supposed to go to the counter. My wife's Chicken Kashmiri £3.90 and my Chicken Masala £3.60 looked very similar but the difference in taste was obvious. We both enjoyed our brief stop-off meal but left thinking that it wasn't as good as I remembered – rose tinted memories? A very popular restaurant with its local clientele.' AT. 'Seekh Kebabs 60p very good flavour, Meat Roghan Josh £ 3.90 – not as spicy as other dishes but still good. Good service, pleasant staff.' L&CH. Price check: Papadam 20p, CTM £3.90, Fried Rice £1.00, Garlic Nan £1. Hours: 11am to 3am. Branch: Kashmir, 858 Leeds Road, Bradford Centre. 01274 664357 (near the hospital).

MUMTAZ PAAN HOUSE NEW ENTRANT

386 Great Horton Road, Great Horton, Bradford SW 01274 571861

Says PS: 'Noted as being the place to go in Bradford; also as the place not to go if you like "Europeanised" curries because they serve only the real thing! With this in mind we went looking forward to a decent curry night out, but came away rather disappointed, not because of the food, but other things: patchy service, we were affected by smokers on surrounding tables, menu is not as extensive as in other restaurants, hard to check your bill due to payment method (the waiter leaves a copy of your order at the table inside a folder which you take to the cash desk, where codes are entered into the till, and you are uncertain whether service charge has been added). Despite all above, food was superb, and I shall return (better prepared!).' PS. 'In my view and the view of many friends in Leeds, this is one of the finest curry houses in the country.' AF. We hear of its plans to expand to 450 covers to make it biggest in Europe. Watch this space.

OMAR'S BALTI NEW ENTRANT

46 Great Horton Road, Great Horton, Bradford SW 01274 414188

'We keep returning to Omar's. My favourite, the nicest curry ever, the Kashmir Chicken. Incredible value at £4.50 with chapatis. Naans are £1.70, but enough for four. The best thing about Omar's is that it gives a 15% discount to regulars. I have a card that I simply hand over when I pay. The only bad thing is that a large TV plays MTV non stop – unnecessary and destroys the atmosphere.' HR.

PAZEEKAH BYO

1362 Leeds Road, Thornbury, Bradford E 01274 664943

Ex bus driver Mazhar-ul-Haq's tells us he likes to change the decor and the menu regularly, 'because that's what customers want to see.' Successful Pakistani restaurant, seats a considerable 130 diners. Chef/manager is son

Mohammed Jamil. Hours: 4pm-12.30am (1.30am on Sat.).Also own an 18,000 sq ft Asian Superstore, selling Asian food, and utensils at 91 Edderthorpe Street, off Leeds Road, Bradford. Reports please.

RAWAL BYO ©

3 Wilton Street, off Morley Street,
Central Bradford 01274 720030

Owner Chef Abdul P Butt cooks Pakistani curries in his open kitchen, Mobin Iqbal manages the 50-seater and promised a 10% discount to CC members. Special: Grand Slam, mixture of meat, chicken, keema and fresh vegetables, served with Pullao Rice £5.70. Zam-Zam Special, meat, chicken, king prawns, and chick peas, served with Pullao Rice £5.70. Rawal claims 'Once tried never forgotten'. DC says it is indeed true: 'Great price, great food'. Takeaway: 10% off for students, 3 chappatis or boiled rice with each order. Hours: 5pm-2am (3am on Fri. & Sat.); closed Mon.

ROTI NEW ENTRANT

16 Duckworth Lane, Bradford 01274 482700

A pleasing restaurant to look at, and by all accounts pleasing to its band of regulars, who swear by it since it opened a couple of years ago. Cooking by Arshad Mahmood is Kashmiri, and well liked, we hear. More reports welcomed.

SHAH JEHAN ©

30 Little Horton Lane, Central Bradford 01274 390777

Aka Ormar's Shajehan or just Omar's, after their owner/chef Omar Gulzar Khan. His three branches have identical menus. The Horton Lane branch seats 150 and is spread over three rooms. It is stylish and luxuriously decorated, with lovely leather sofas to relax on, while waiting for a takeaway, and pretty red chairs for your table. Goods comments on all three branches, usually: 'An extremely smart and well laid out restaurant with friendly service throughout. We had the whole leg of lamb ordered 24 hours in advance. Superb. Highly recommended.' CT. 'Very, very, very good.' LH. But one downer: 'Slightly disappointing – have had better meals here in the past. Has won several awards from various bodies, and it's possible that staff are not trying as hard as before the restaurant became "famous". But Meat Pathia very tasty.' L&CH. Hours: 12-2.30pm/5.30pm-12am. Branches: 6 North Gate, Baildon, Bradford N; 726 Manchester Road, Chapel Green, Bradford S. Stocks Cobra.

SHIRAZ BYO ©

133 Oak Lane, Manningham, Bradford N 01274 490176

Owned by Mohammed Gulbahar, with Mohammed Aslam managing and Mohammed Afzal cooking competent Kashmiri curries and Baltis. Hours: 4pm-2am. Closed Christmas Day and for Muslim festivals.

SHISH MAHAL BYO ©

6 St Thomas Road, Central Bradford 01274 723999

Mohammed Taj's 54-seater 'is next door to one of the best pubs in Britain, The New Beehive – tremendous real ale with genuine character. The food at this BYO restaurant is nothing short of marvellous. Flavour literally explodes in the mouth. Sensational garlic chicken. Friendly and informal service.' SL. Hours: 4pm-3am.

SWEET CENTRE

110 Lumb Lane, Central Bradford 01274 731735

At the counter you order savouries and sweets by the pound. I know because way back, I purchased 120 samosas here for a CC function, and we all found the measuring process a wee bit complex. Eventually they settled for 15p each and the sams were worth the sum! The sit down's fun too: 'Unlicensed all-hours cafe, cutlery on request. Asian clientele. Food cheap.' DC. 'Excellent. The service is good and the food very tasty.' SL.

TASTE OF BENGAL ©

79 Bradford Road, Idle, Bradford N 01274 618308

First opened in 1980. Abdul Subhan took over in '98 and it's a cosy restaurant, decorated in, 'simple, plain wallpaper, minty colour, Axminster carpet' has just 28 covers, so book at weekends, or be disappointed or have a takeaway. Abdul Qayum runs the front with Uddin Khan in the kitchen. Balti and Bengal Specialities feature on the menu with a Dine Bangladeshi-Sylhet Special – cooked in a thick blend of spicy sauce with king prawns, mixed vegetables and (more) prawns. Jaflong dishes, Niralee dishes, Sylhet special dishes. Takeaway: 10% discount. Hours: 6pm-12am; Sat. 6pm-12.30am. Branches: Moghul, Horsforth, Leeds and Ilkley. Stocks Cobra.

Castleford

KING'S BALTI NEW ENTRANT

2 The Square, Castleford 01977 668880

'One of nine Indian takeaways in Castleford. All excellent here, especially the chicken pakora. My husband thought the chicken curry one of the best he had tasted and my korma had a lovely flavour but the muddy colour could have been a bit off-putting for some. Peshwari naan was much too aniseedy for my taste.' JH-T

Dewsbury

MOONLIGHT BYO

Springwell House, 14 Halifax Road, Dewsbury 01924 462222

'Delighted to see the Moonlight featured in the 1999 GCG following our recommendation. Pleased to report that the owner, Raf Hussain, told us with great pride that he has had several people coming to the restaurant armed with the GCG, most of whom are now regulars. Deservedly so, it remains Dewsbury's best value in Indian food with consistently high standards. Karahi dishes are to die for!' L&CH. Linda and Chris returned and say: 'We had a buffet style party to celebrate my 40th birthday. We did not quite manage to eat everything, but everyone agreed that it had all been one of the best meals they had eaten.' All main courses are served with three Chapattis, Rice, Chips or Nan Bread – what a wonderful deal!. Delivery: 3-mile radius, £5 minimum. Price check: Papadam 30p, CTM £4.70, Pullao Rice £1.10, Peshwari Nan £1.60. Hours: 5pm-1am (Thurs to 2.30am, Fri. & Sat. to 3am, Sun. to 2am).

ZAM ZAM TAKEAWAY NEW ENTRANT ©

5 North Road, Ravensthorp, Dewsbury 01924 469677

First opened in 1980, taken over by Perwaiz Khan in 1994. Samosas and Shami Kebabs are great value at £1.30 for two. Main dishes are served with either three Chapatis, Rice or Chips. Pizzas also available from £2.80 for 12" thin crust and from £3.80 Large deep pan. Price check: Papadam 20p, CTM £4.20, Pullao Rice £1.20, Peshwari Nan £1.50. Delivery: £5 minimum, 3-mile radius. Hours: 6pm-12.30am; Sat. 6pm-2.30am; Sun. 6pm-1am.

Garforth

AAGRAH TOP 100 ©

Aberford Road, Garforth 0113 287 6606

Nephew Wasim Aslam manages this 175-seater, opened in 1993, and the fourth of the very popular Aagrahs. (See Shipley entry.) Car parking for 90. Specials include: Achar, Hydrabady and Masala dishes. 'Excellent' says PW. Takeaway: 10% off. Hours: 6-11.3-pm; Fri. & Sat. 5.30-11.30pm. Stocks Cobra.

Halifax

CROWN TANDOORI NEW ENTRANT ©

31-33 Crown Street, Halifax 01422 349270

Established in 1995. Seats 62. Onion Bhajia's and Samosas are great value at £1.30 each for two. Specials: Full Tandoori Chicken with Vegetable Curry £8. Chicken Tikka and Chips £4.25. Outrageous Pickle Tray £1.50. Price check: Papadam 30p, CTM £5, Pullao Rice £1.20, Peshwari Nan £1.50. Delivery: £8 minimum, 3-mile radius. Hours: 6pm-1am; Sat. 6pm-3am. Stocks Cobra.

Haworth

HAWORTH TANDOORI NEW ENTRANT

14 Mill Hey Road, Haworth 01535 647879

A corpse at Hawarth Tandoori! This phall deed ensures you've heard it all now. And how could we not enter this to the *Guide*? Of course it wasn't a real murder, it was even more bizarre. It's the title of a new detective mystery by Robert Barnard, with bodies in the car park (dead and alive), and shananigans in the Shami department. Restaurant owner Fotik Miah was delighted to gain all the publicity that the book and its launch produced. As this is the land of the Brontë sisters, and the Moors, it already gets a fair share of tourists, so we welcome reports of your visits please. Stocks Cobra.

Heckmondwike

SPICE COTTAGE NEW ENTRANT

10 Union Street, Heckmondwike 01924 400600

'Seekh Kebabs and Chicken Pakoras very good, Meat Balti was very tasty. Staff very friendly and service good. We will definitely be returning.' L&CH

Huddersfield

BALOOSHAI NEW ENTRANT

The Old Silk Mill, Meltham Road, Honley,
Nr Huddersfield 01484 660360

'Seekh Kebabs – well presented, good flavour. Starters: Cheese and Spring Onion Fritters – unusual, very nice. Main courses: Chicken Karahi – very good, nice and spicy. Cheese and Onion Nan – very good, soft. Bailey's Kulfi – ideal way to end a very good meal. Only let down by indifferent service from not very interested staff!!' L&CH. Stocks Cobra.

SERENA ©

12 St Peters Street, Huddersfield 01484 451991

Ihsan Elahi's 'modern and chic' Pakistani formula curry house, established in 1993, seats 62, the party room, 40. Chef Khalid Hussain's specials include Balti and Karahi dishes, and Hawahan Muragh, chicken with pineapple, cream. 'Good quality, well prepared dishes. Value for money, service excellent.' JT. Service 10%. Takeaway: 15% off. Hours: 6-11.30pm. Stocks Cobra.

Ilkley

EXOTIC TANDOORI NAME CHANGE ©

10 Church Street, Ilkley 01943 607241

Shah Marshal Alom's traditionally decorated 50-seater has golden arches and hanging plants. Special: Boul Mas, Bangladeshi fish £7. Price check: Papadam 30p, CTM £5.95, Pullao Rice £1.40. House wine £3.95 half-litre. Takeaway: 10% off. Hours: 5.30pm-12am. Stocks Cobra.

SABERA ©

9 Wells Road, Ilkley 01943 607104

This old friend of the *Guide* first opened in 1974. Taken over by Abdus Sattar in 1998, it is, we hear: 'A clean restaurant with pine panelling and 48 seats. I enjoyed my Kalajee Gurda Dil and will return to try some of their other dishes.' DM. Specials include: Murgi Mossaala £10.95, Korahi dish £7.95. Price check: Papadam 45p, CTM £7.50, Pullao Rice £1.50, Peshwari Nan £1.50, Lager £2 pint. Delivery: £10 minimum, 2-mile radius. Hours: 5.30pm-12am. Stocks Cobra.

Keighley

KEIGHLEY TANDOORI NEW ENTRANT ©

Unit 3 Park Way House, Worthway, Keighley 01535 691818

Established in 1995 by Mohammad Hanif. Seats an intimate 24. Samosa Special £2.50 – served with chick pea curry. All main dishes are served with three Chappati, Boiled Rice or Chips – the choice is yours! Burgers from £2.20. Price check: Papadam 25p, CTM £4.50, Pullao Rice £1.20, Peshwari Nan £1.25. Delivery: £7 minimum, 3-mile radius. Hours: 6pm-1am.

BALTI HOUSE BYO

1 Russell Street, Keighley 01535 611600

Managed by Mr Akhtar. Secluded cabins, pleasant atmosphere. 'Portions are good and prices are cheap, but I do feel that many of their dishes are cooked and spiced in a very similar manner. No reason to remove it from the guide, but more variety in the dishes would help.' MB. Delivery: £8, 5-miles. No credit cards. Hours: 6pm-12.30am (1.30am on Fri. & Sat.).

SHIMLA SPICE BYO ©

14 South Street, Keighley 01535 602040

Opened in 1998 by Mohammed Ayub and his two brothers, who had their 70-seater built from scratch on a useful corner site. Interior is decorated beautifully, ornate plasterwork on ceiling and walls, colonial fans, large chandelier, 'Tiffany' lamps and cane furniture.'We've become regulars. Staff are always polite and helpful, menu is excellent.' BD&FH. 'I eat here at least once a week either on my own after working late, or with family or friends. Excellent quality of food, very friendly and prompt service, attractive decor. Extensive menu including a very wide choice of vegetarian meals. Portions generous, flavours well blended, dishes include a variety of fresh vegetables and herbs. The top of our list.' JB. 'I eat here more than any other restaurant. Starters are excellent, especially the Shami Kebabs, Chicken Pakora and Fish Masala. Main course favourites are the Chicken and Meat and Chicken and Keema Balti dishes, the Tandoori Bemisaal and the Achari dishes. The price of such a good meal is surprisingly reasonable. I feel this is a restaurant on a par with many in your Top 100.' MB. Specials include: Fish Masala £2.50, Murgh Jaipur £5.95, Achri Gosth £5.75, CTM £6.25, Murgh Makani £5.75, Lamb Jallfrazi £5.50. Price check: Papadam 30p, CTM £6.25, Pullao Rice £1.45, Peshwari Nan £1.40. Takeaway: 10% discount. Delivery: £8 minimum. Hours: 6pm-12.15am (Sat. to 1.15am).

Knottingley

JEWEL IN THE CROWN e-a-m-a-y-l ©

110 Weeland Road, Knottingley 01977 607233

Pakistani curries at Manager Adnan Miraf's 40-seater. 'Excellent food at reasonable prices. Service friendly and efficient. Recommend the Punjabi (Tandoori) Mixed Grill.' IB. E-a-m-a-y-l £8. Takeaway: 20% off. Delivery: £8, 2-mile radius. Hours: 6pm-12am.

Leeds

(inc. Headingley, Horsforth, Kirkstall, Oakwood, Morley and Stanningley)

AZRAM'S SHEESH MAHAL NEW ENTRANT

348 Kirkstall, Road, Leeds NW 0113 230 4161

First opened in 1987, taken over by Azram Chaudhry in 1990. Seats 76 with a further room for 38. Up the road from YTV studios, Azram's, as the locals know it, set on its prominent corner site, has recently been refurbished and expanded. Specials include: Kofta Special, Balti Murgh, Murgh Punchabi Masala. 'Highly recommend the food, service and ambience. All dishes reasonably priced. Azram is a first rate host, well liked by clients. Welcomes children and family groups.' EP. Price check: Papadam 30p, CTM £5.20, Pullao Rice £1.50, Peshwari Nan £2.20, Lager £2.30. Hours: 5pm-12am (open for lunches from Nov. to end Jan.). Stocks Cobra.

CHILLI PEPPERS NEW ENTRANT

629, Roundhay Road, Oakwood, Leeds NE 0113 240 1010

'Oh what a joy! A refuge from the hotel carvery in Leeds (in fact, the hotel manager recommended Chilli peppers!). In 1998 young couple Mohan and Smita Patel converted old dry cleaning shop into new, attractive restaurant peach and blue decor. Chef, Mr Akhray from Bradford, quickly established sound reputation. Pops and Pickles 90p – great lime. Followed by Meat Samosa £1.50 – lean filling, Onion Bhajia £1.50 – crisp, and enormous Pakora Platter £3.75 – Glasgow colleague demolished. Main courses: Chicken Tikka Bhuna – exquisite, Chicken Jalfrezi £4.90, Pullao Rice, Sag Aloo £2.40 and Nan Bread £1.50. Gigantic portions, good quality, freshly spiced. Home made Kulfi – lovely texture. Great value for money with personal service.' AIE. Price check: Papadam 40p, CTM £5.50, Pullao Rice £1.50. Hours: 6-11.30pm (Sat. & Sun. from 5.30pm). Stocks Cobra.

CHIRAAG BALTI NEW ENTRANT ©

30-32 Chapel Hill, Morley, Leeds S 0113 253 5720

40-seater, taken over in February '97 by T Hussain. Fully licensed. 'Excellent Seekh Kebabs £1.60, Very tasty Balti Lamb Rogan Josh £4.95. Service good, staff very pleasant.' L&CH. 'Consistently excellent spicy dishes.' PW. Specials: Fish Pakora £2.50. Mushroom Pakora £1.95. Sweetcorn and Mushroom Biryani £4.60. Price check: Papadam 30p, CTM £5.80, Pullao Rice £1.50. Takeaway: 15% off. Delivery: £8, 3-mile radius. Hours: 6pm-12am (Fri. & Sat. to 1am); closed Tues. Stocks Cobra.

COOKY'S NEW ENTRANT

27 Kingwear Road, Leeds 0113 231 1909

Established in 1991 by Mr Lohn managing front of house with Mrs Yasmin Lohn heading the kitchen brigade. Seats 28. New exterior in 1998. Specials: Chicken Tikka Balti £5. Cheese and Keema Nan £1.80. Burgers from £2.30 for a ¼lb, Southern Fried Chicken from £2.70 and Donner Kebabs from £2.30 also available. Price check: Papadam 20p – one of the cheapest, CTM £4.60, Pullao Rice £1.20, Peshwari Nan £1.50. Delivery: £5 minimum, 3-mile radius. Hours: 6pm-1am.

DARBAR TOP 100

16-17 Kirkgate, Leeds Centre 0113 246 0381

A turbaned doorman welcomes you at 'a very ordinary street-level door, but upstairs the decor is a revelation.' HJC. It's exotic, with traditional Moghul paintings and an antique Hawali (palace) door, specially brought from India. 'Has a very impressive interior. Room is large and the decor promotes the Indian Palace feeling – spacious yet warm and elegant'. AG 'Excellent restaurant, especially at lunchtime, self service buffet. Probably deserves TOP 100, although I am always slightly suspicious of Indians with grandiose decor.' RC [You'd be suspicious of India then, Robert! -Ed]. 'Very good service and cooking. And, the decor is marvellous.' SL. 'Overall this restaurant is superb and complements the Shabab very well. Indian food-lovers in Leeds are very fortunate to have two such restaurants.' HJC. Special: Murgh Lahori, bone-off spring chicken, tangy spices, green coriander, cream, yoghurt, tomatoes and ginger £7.25 (t/a). Daal Mash, white lentils cooked in butter with ginger, garlic and fried onions £2.50 (t/a). Strawberry Lassi (large jug) £3.75. Price check: CTM £8.50, Pullao Rice £1.50. House wine £11.95. Minimum charge: £16 eves. Lunch e-a-m-a-y-l £4.95. Hours: Mon.-Sat. 11.30am-2.30pm/6-11.30pm; Sun. closed. Stocks Cobra.

HANSA'S GUJARATI VEGETARIAN V ©

72-74 North Street, Leeds Centre 0113 244 4408

Owned by Mr and Mrs Dabhi. 'I particularly enjoyed the crunchy, spicy flavour of the Shrikhand.' DM. 'As a non-veg I went with an open mind. Food was fine but portions small.' DB. 'Exquisite Lassi, portions small.' DO'R. Reports please. Hours: 12-2pm/6-11pm. Stocks Cobra.

KASHMIR BYO ©

162a Woodhouse Lane, Leeds N 0113 245 3058

Unlicensed, 72-seater restaurant, managed by T Mahmood. Price check: Papadam 20p, CTM £4.60, Pullao Rice 95p. Hours: 12pm-3am.

MOGHUL BALTI HOUSE

8-9 The Green, Town St, Horsforth, Leeds,NW 0113 259 0530

Abdul Aziz's Bangladeshi curry house seats 40 and has a new menu with Balti Dishes, Moghul Specialities, Niralee Dishes, Dine Bangladesh, and Vegetarian Dishes. 'Was staying in a nearby national chain hostelry – you know one of those without catering – you're advised to use the nearby no-skill-food place in the same ownership. Not fancying such an experience, I turned to my trusty *Guide* to save the day, and not a tava throw away it told me of the Moghul. I suspect I'd have enjoyed it if it were abysmal. But it was marvellous, and is firmly went into my Filofax.' JR. Takeaway: 10% off. Price check: Papadam 30p, CTM £6.40, Pullao Rice £1.20. House wine £6.95 litre. Hours: 6pm-12am. Stocks Cobra.

POLASH NEW TO OUR TOP 100 ©

103 Town Street, Stanningley, Leeds W 0113 256 0989

M Arif's huge 150-seater is popular, it seems. 'Recently I had a family party at home and asked the Polash to cater for me. The resultant banquet was beyond praise.' EF. 'Our daughter, 14, says that the Polash Chicken Korma is her favourite, even though she has tried others in many other Indian restaurants.' BT. 'We were impressed. Food tasty. Service a little stretched at busy times.' IEF-E. 'How much we enjoy our visits. Excellent food, courteous staff.' MG. 'Always welcoming and courteous, high standard, always consistent, always start with Chicken Tikka followed by King Prawn Khass.' JS. 'Combination of service and freshly cooked food, makes the Polash our favourite.' MH-R. 'Very smart inside. Good mix of standard and unusual dishes – Chana Aloo Puri was superb. Friendly attentive service.' M&SR.

'Excellent restaurant. Best starters we have tasted anywhere.' MM. 'For several years we have been patrons of the Aagrah at Thornbury, but for nearly two years now changed to Polash. Standard of food and service is superb. Choice is tremendous, carefully prepared, garnished and served with a smile. Reasonably priced – half the cost of the Aagrah!' MR&MRS DH. 'We tell all our friends of the Polash.' MC. 'Spacious restaurant in dis-used Conservative Club. Tandoori Mixed Grill £7.95 – an enormous plate full of Tandoori Chicken, Chicken and Lamb Tikka, Lamb Chops, Seekh Kebab, Liver and fresh salad with a Vegetable Curry (does anyone actually finish that lot?). Gold Card Scheme – £25 a year, member and up to five guests 20% discount (except on Saturday). Very popular facility.' RW. 'Speciality curries are our firm favourites: Nagisi Kofti £7.95 (inc. Mushroom Rice), Murgh Keema Aloo £7.25 (inc Lemon Rice) and Garlic Chicken Balti £8.20 (inc Pullao Rice) – truly excellent.' DF. 'Proprietors are always on hand to oversee, spotless kitchen.' PJS. 'Well presented, tasty, freshly prepared and served food. Meat is lean – important to us.' DA. So much praise – we'll promote the Polash to our TOP 100. Price check: Papadam 30p, CTM £4.95, Pullao Rice £1.40. Hours: 5.30-11.30pm (Mon. & Sun. to 11pm). Stocks Cobra.

TARIQ'S ©

12-16 St Michaels Road, Headingley, Leeds 0113 275 1881

'Windies were playing England and it was stopped by rain. After waiting till early evening in hope, there was a stampede down to Tarriq's just round from the cricket ground. Got there first, luckily – they were queuing within minutes. Superb meal made up for a wet day.' IB. Owned and managed by Bobby Sharma, this Balti House seats 64 . Special offer meal deal, Thursday and Sunday before 10pm. Dining in – free papadams and chutneys – nice touch. Price check: Papadam 20p, CTM £4.90, Pullao Rice £1.20. Lager £2 bottle, House wine £6.50. Delivery: £6, 3-mile radius. Hours: 5.30pm-2.30am (3am on Sat., 12.30am on Sun.). Stocks Cobra.

Mirfield

SPICE OF BENGAL NEW ENTRANT

100, Greenside Road, Mirfield 01924 490745

'Onion or Vegetable Pullao Rice and Cheese Nan, divine, very good and yummy. Staff attentive, deserves to do well.' L&CH. Price check: Papadam 30p, CTM £5.95, Pullao Rice £1.35. Hours: 5.30pm-12am (Sun. 6-11.30pm).

SUBRAS NEW ENTRANT

8, Knowl Road, Mirfield 01924 491414

'Menu states that all main curry dishes are served with either three Chapattis, Boiled Rice, Nan or Chips. Mixed Starter (Samosa, Seekh, Shami, Onion Bhajia with salad) – large portion!! all very tasty. Samosa £1.20 – crispy outside, well filled inside, not greasy. Garlic Nan £1.50 – excellent, soft and fluffy. Free Popadoms and yoghurt. Seekh Kebabs and Chicken Pakoras were very tasty. Excellent Chicken Rogan Josh and good size garlic naan. Decent portions, very friendly staff, prices very reasonable. Well worth a visit. Only two minutes drive from home – our favourite local.' L&CH. What do you mean – two minutes drive – you should both walk! Delivery: 3-mile radius, £5 minimum. Hours: 5pm to late.

Otley

JEWEL OF INDIA

1 Bridge Street, Otley 01943 467138

Seats 35. 'Excellent quality and generous portions of Chicken Madras (sauce a little too thick) and Keema Rogan Josh. Melt in the mouth Peshwari Nan. Pleasant staff, well turned out in traditional dress.' JMFP. Hours: 6pm-12am (1am on Fri. & Sat.). Stocks Cobra.

Pontefract

ROTI ©

North Baileygate, Pontefract 01977 703915

Arshad Mahmood's 110-seater (party room 40) is bright and airy with tented ceiling, beams, cream-with-green napkins, marble table tops, wicker furniture. Abdul Aziz's kitchen on view behind glass. Pakistani food. 'Excellent quality, bordering on the expensive.' KH. Hours: 5pm-12am. Stocks Cobra.

VICEROY ©

6 Front Street, Pontefract 01977 700007

First opened in 1990, taken over by Chef Akram Hussain Lohn in 1994. He cooks Pakistani food at his 60-seater, managed by Susan Ruckledge. Mushroom Pakora a speciality. Karai (including rice, chips or three chapatis). Takeaway: 30% discount. Delivery: £6 minimum. Hours: 5pm-1am. Stocks Cobra.

Pudsey

AAGRAH **TOP 100 AWARD WINNER** ©

483 Bradford Road, Pudsey 01274 668818

Located midway between Bradford and Leeds, the second Aagrah is Head Office, as well as a 72-seater managed by Arshad Mahmood opened in 1986. Car parking for 25. Specials include: Achar, Hydrabady and Masala dishes. Price check: Papadam 40p, CTM £6.90, Pullao Rice £1.50, Peshwari Nan £1.80, Lager £2.10 pint. Takeaway: 10% discount. Hours: 6-11.30pm; Fri. & Sat. 6pm-12am; Sun. 12.30-11.30pm. Stocks Cobra.

Shipley

AAGRAH **TOP 100 AWARD WINNER** ©

27 Westgate, Shipley 01274 594660

Today there are seven Aagrahs, all in Yorkshire, and all TOP 100s in this guide. It was here in 1977, refurbished in 1999, that this 50-seater was opened by Mohammed Sabir. The notion to expand came from son Mohammed Aslam (then a London bus driver) assisted later by brother Zafar Iqbal, who now runs this one. It is notable for its Kashmiri-style decor with attractive block-print table linen and those fabulous hand-made, hand-painted colourful lacquered chairs with the cute tinkly bells, especially commissioned in Pakistan (£60 each). Gradually Aslam encouraged his extended family to join the enterprise as managers, staff and cooks. With increasing impetus the other branches have been brought on-stream, as stylish and up-market restaurants. We hear contentedly from many regulars who visit twice or more a week, and visitors from afar. Their average age is over 25 (no after-pub teenage louts here). Their average spend of £15 gives the chain a turnover of *c.*£2 million. The food is Pakistani, which self-taught cook Aslam has insisted that all family members also learn, training in both the kitchens and out front to NVQ level. This way the service and food in all the Aagrah restaurants is of equal standard. There is ample choice in the identical menus. Starters includeYahknee £1.80, spicy chicken soup, and Panir Pakora £2.20, Indian curd cheese fritter. Balti Liver £5.90, is a main-course dish, with garlic, ginger, chillies, tomatoes and coriander. There are many meat, chicken and fish dishes. Aslam's current *pièces de résistance* are Murgh Hydrabady, spring chicken, tangy spices, coriander, cream, yoghurt, tomatoes, ginger, £6.95. Balti Bhindi Aloo Paneer, curd cheese, bhindi and potato, onions, ginger, garlic, coriander, £5.90. Family Nan £2.80, Cheese and Onion Nan £1.80. Takeaway: rice and 3 chapattis free. Specials include:

Achar, Hydrabady and Masala dishes. Price check: Papadam 40p, CTM £6.90, Pullao Rice £1.50, Peshwari Nan £1.80, Lager £2.10 pint. Takeaway: 10% discount. Hours: 6pm-12am. Fri. & Sat. 6pm-1am. Branches: Garforth, Pudsey, Wakefield, W Yorks; Skipton Tadcaster, N Yorks; Doncaster, S Yorks. Stocks Cobra.

Wakefield

AAGRAH TOP 100 ©

108 Barnsley Road, Sandal, Wakefield 01974 242222

The seventh of seven Aagrahs, a 100-seater, opened in 1986. Parking for 40 cars. Like its sisters, it is justifiably very popular and good enough to be awarded a collective TOP 100 cachet. (See above entry for detailed comment.) The Aagrah is also able to offer accommodation – so don't drink and drive, just stay over at the Sandal Court Hotel. Specials include: Achar, Hydrabady and Masala dishes. Price check: Papadam 40p, CTM £6.90, Pullao Rice £1.50, Peshwari Nan £1.80, Lager £2.10 pint. Takeaway: 10% discount. Hours: 6-11.30pm; Fri. & Sat. 5.30-11.30pm; Sun. 6-11pm. Stocks Cobra.

RAJPOOT

134 Kirkgate, Wakefield 01924 371215

Ashik Miah's 52-seater is a small, cosy restaurant on one of Wakefield's main roads, and very close to Kirkgate railway station. 'Good menu selection, huge quantities, excellent service within comfortable surroundings.' AKD. 'Mulligatawny soup (thick dall soup with good chicken stock, garlic, rice, onion and some pineapple) was delicious and very satisfying. Main Biryani was equally good, with fluffy basmati rice, well scented and not greasy. Real ale is an unusual offering, with beer supplied from the local Clark's brewery.' RW. 'I ate the Gurda Kaleja, which does not feature on the takeaway menu. I was brought up to appreciate offal and I am pleased to see it is included in Indian cuisine. Worthy of its entry.' DM. 'I have had the pleasure of eating here on several occasions and have never been disappointed. Chicken Chaat a delight.' AKD. Mashuk Miah holds court in the kitchen where his specials include: Chicken Tikka Biryani £5.95. Takeaway: 10% off. Monday and Tuesday – 3-course meal £5.95. Price check: Papadam 35p, CTM £5.95, Pullao Rice £1.30. House wine £7.50. Delivery: £12, 3-mile radius. Takeaway: 10% off. Hours: 5.30pm-12am (1am on Fri. & Sat.); Sun. 2pm-12am. Branch: India Palace, 36 Smyth Street, Wakefield. Stocks Cobra.

THE ISLES AND ISLANDS

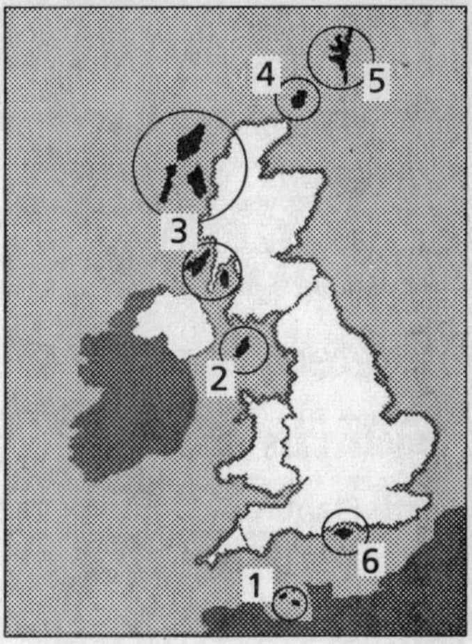

When he failed to capture the British Isles, Napoleon dismissed us as a nation of shopkeepers. Were he around today, he might observe that we are now a nation of curry house keepers. Some isles, including Lundy, the Isles of Scilly, Uist, Mull, etc., have no curry houses but, for neatness, we group those that do together. For those who delight in collecting useless information, Lerwick, capital of the Shetland Isles, contains the nation's most northerly curry house (and still probably that of the whole globe). It is 600 miles from London and 800 miles from our most southerly curry house in St Helier, capital of Jersey.

CHANNEL ISLANDS

1 on the map

Alderney

NELLIE GRAYS INDIAN CUISINE

Victoria Street, Alderney 01481 823333

Established 1996, owned by Matin Miah (formerly the head chef of Jersey's Bombay Brasserie), and managed by Ashraf Makadur. Seats 50 in two dining rooms. Two parking spaces at rear of building. Jalfrezi most popular, chef's special Tarkari £6.95. Price check: Papadam 50p, CTM £7.75, Pullao Rice £1.75. House wine £6.95. Set dinner: £14.95. Sunday lunch buffet: £9.95. Service: 10%. Hours: 6-11pm; Sun. 12-2pm. Stocks Cobra.

Guernsey

L'Eree

TASTE OF INDIA

Sunset Cottage, St Peter, L'Eree 01481 264516

Owned and managed by Tony Fernandes, who is from Goa, since 1989. Pink stone wall design with maroom seating for 60 diners. Chef Paltu Bhattachajee holds court in the kitchen serving specialities such as Sardines on Puri £2.95, Tandoori Lobster and Bhuna – market price and subject to availability. Takeaway: 10% discount. Set lunch: £10.95 and £24.95 (for two). Pickle Tray a very expensive £1.50. Price check: Papadams 40p, CTM £8.95, Pullao Rice £2.50, Peshwari Nan £2.20, Lager £2.20 pint, House wine £9 bottle. Hours: 6-11pm; closed Mon. Branch: Taste of India, St Peter Port.

St Peter Port

SAWATDI NEW ENTRANT

North Plantation, St Peter Port 01481 725805

'Thai restaurant, serving excellent curries and most definitely worthy of a wider audience. Very busy on a Bank Holiday weekend, but staff were bright, cheerful and helpful. Downstairs restaurant is small, but bigger area upstairs with low tables, floor cushions and views across the harbour – lovely for a party or celebration meal. Lots of excellent seafood dishes, but the star of the evening was a fabulous Thai Green Curry – each mouthful was an absolute delight. Ask for the special vegetarian menu (dishes not on main menu) – a delicious peanut and pineapple Muslim style curry.' CC.

TAJ MAHAL

North Esplanade, St Peter Port 01481 724008

Mujibul Hussain's 60-seater is located in the heart of St Peter Port opposite the main public car park. 'Beautifully decorated with tables in canopied booths. Charming and attentive staff. Interesting menu – imaginative main courses and unusual vegetable side-dishes (Uri Besi, mangetout and butter beans; Balar Aloo, mashed potatoes with garlic). Special main course vegetarian section including Baygoon (aubergine, spinach and chickpeas) which was sampled by non-veggies with some envy! Delicious Chicken Sholay arrived flamed in brandy. All food was fragrantly spicy with subtle differences between each dish.' CC. Hours: 12-2pm/6-11.30pm (12am on Sat.). Stocks Cobra.

TASTE OF INDIA

2, Mill Street, St Peter Port 01481 723730

Established in 1990. Seats 50. Owned and managed by Tony Fernandes. Decorated in maroon. Specials: Bamboo Shoot Masala – a dry curry. Takeaway: 10%. Hours: 6-11pm; closed Mon. Branch: Taste of India, L'Eree.

Jersey

St Aubin

SHAPLA

Victoria Road, St Aubin 01534 746495

Decor high standard with rich reds, golds and blues. Hasna Kebabs, lamb marinated in yoghurt, tandooried with onions, peppers and tomatoes, really tasty. Chicken Jalfrezi, aroma terrific. Simply perfect Lamb Rogan Gosht. Polite and helpful waiter.' MB. Hours: 12-2pm/6pm-12am. Stocks Cobra.

St Brelade

BENGAL BRASSERIE NEW ENTRANT

11 La Pulente, St Brelade 01534 490279

Formerly Taj Mahal. 'Menu has some very interesting and inventive dishes, including Fish Jalfrazi, salmon and even lobster curries. Favourite dish is the Chef's Balti – like no other – chicken, lamb, prawns, egg, kidney beans, mange tout, you name it. Portions more than adequate. Service best on the island, staff very friendly. Al fresco in the summer. Only 30 yards from St Ouens beach. Best place to see the sunset.' GL. Hours: 12-2pm/6-11.30pm.

St Helier

NEW RAJ

8 Burlington Parade, St Saviours Road, St Helier 01534 874131

Owned and managed by Kass Malik since 1984. Decorated with tented ceiling. Seats 60 in two dining rooms. 'Apart from cramped seating, the decor was pleasant. Starters arrived before we had finished papadoms, but we then had to wait over half an hour for our main course. Onion Bhaji was good, Chicken Chat not so good, being insipid and needing some salt. Chicken Dhansak was well spiced, my wife's CTM was rated the best she has had for some time. After a nice meal came the not so nice bill. Charged for wine which we hadn't had, and £1.70 for water (we hadn't been given the choice of bottled rather than tap, or the option of carbonated or still). Deducted from the bill, so nearly £15 less than originally charged. All in all a mixed evening. The rather uncomfortable seating, poor timing of serving and overcharging were fortunately offset by a good meal.' MW. Beef currys on the menu from Korma to Pal from £4.50. Price check: Papadam 40p,

CTM £5.95, Pullao Rice £1.95,Service 10%. House wine £6.25. Takeaway: 7-10% discount. Hours: 12-2pm/6pm-12am. Stocks Cobra.

SHEZAN

53 Kensington Place, St Helier 01534 22960

A small restaurant seating 40. 'Meal very good. A bit expensive, but worth it.' SC. 'Owner, Shani Gill, is always the gentleman. His endeavours to satisfy all his customers have made him many friends.' GDM.

TAJ MAHAL CENTRAL

La Motte Street, St Helier 01534 20147

'Classy and luxurious restaurant. You are surrounded by running water and tropical fish. Had best ever Tarka Dal.' TM.

ISLE OF MAN

2 on the map

Douglas

SAAGAR TANDOORI ©

1 South View, Queens Promenade, Douglas 01624 674939

Mr and Mrs Chowdhury and Mr Jaigirdar's 60-seater is 'the best I've been to.' RR. 'One time we tried the special Kachee Biriani – 12 hours' notice is required to prepare it. It's partially cooked Basmati rice layered over meat marinated in spices, yoghurt and herbs then cooked in the oven – perfumed with saffron. £25 for two. Delicious. Next time we brought friends and tried Kurzi Lamb – 24 hours' notice is required for this extravaganza (£48 for four). We've yet to try £70 whole leg of lamb marinated in fresh ground spices with lamb mince meat cooked in the oven. Mixed starters, side dishes, rice and breads for four are also included.' AN. Hours: 12-2pm/6pm-12am.

Ramsey

SPICE OF LIFE

8 Peel Street, Ramsey 01624 816534

'We enjoyed the food, and would have done had it been in Manchester' GB. 'Bizarre note on the door, *We do not serve drunks*.' DMcC.

SCOTTISH WESTERN ISLES

3 on the map

Isle of Bute

INDIAN PAVILION

7 Argyle Street, Rothesay, Isle of Bute — 01700 504988

Est. 1993 by Bobby Mahey, 30-seater. Dave Mahey cooks north and south Indian and Goan food. Delivery charge 95p. Hours: 5pm-12.30am.

Isle of Lewis

STORNOWAY BALTI HOUSE NEW ENTRANT

24 South Beech, Stornoway — 01851 706116

First opened in 1991, taken over in 1996 by Abarok Ali. Previously called Ali's Takeaway. Seats 46. Specials include: Chicken Tikka Balti £7.50, Chicken Korma £5.95. Price check: Papadam 60p, CTM £6.95, Pullao Rice £1.90, Peshwari Nan £2.10, Lager £2 pint. Takeaway: 10% discount. Hours: 12-2pm/5-11.30pm;. Sat. & Sun. 5-11.30pm.

Isle of Skye

SPICE HUT INDIAN NEW ENTRANT (NAME CHANGE)

Bayfield Road, Portree — 01478 612681

Formerly the Ghandi. 'Difficult to find – at the rear of the big car and coach park near the Tourist Information Centre. A bizarre experience. We turned up at 1pm to find "Closed" on the door. However, we tried the door anyway and it opened. Two bored looking Asian teenagers were folding napkins, and one lethargically showed us to a table in the otherwise totally deserted restaurant. He took our order with his now customary lack of charm, and we prepared for the worst. However, the food arrived very promptly and was actually delicious. Vegetable Rowghon was fragrant and packed with fresh tomatoes. Garlic Chicken Tikka was equally good. It is an enormous shame that a clearly excellent chef is having his hard work marred by a front of house crew displaying such shameless amateurism.' cc. Stocks Cobra.

ORKNEY ISLANDS *4 on the map*

Kirkwall

MUMTAZ

7 Bridge Street, Kirkwall 01856 873537

'Comfortable and modern restaurant. All food very tasty. Service good and efficient.' PAWW. Hours: 12pm-12am.

SHETLAND ISLANDS *5 on the map*

Lerwick

RABA INDIAN

26 Commercial Road, Lerwick 01595 695554

'Warm decor. Well-cooked Indian cuisine at reasonable prices. Samosas, Bhajia and Chicken Tikka Masala were all delicious.' AIE. Hours: 12-2pm/4.30pm-12am. Sunday buffet: 1pm-11pm. Adults £7.50/Kids £5 (à la carte also available). Stocks Cobra.

ISLE OF WIGHT *6 on the map*

Cowes

COWES TANDOORI ©

40 High Street, Cowes 01983 296710

At Ashid Ali's 64-seater DB 'loves the Podina Gusht and Garlic Chicken' and L&CH found 'Tasty Sheek Kebabs'. Hours: 12-2pm/6pm-12am. Stocks Cobra.

Newport

NABAB PALACE ©

84 Upper Street, James Street, Newport 01983 523276

'Jila Miah's 54-seater serves good, competent curries and accompaniments at reasonable island prices, eased by his offer to give a 10% discount to CC members. Well deserved place in *Good Curry Guide*. Nizami Chicken delicious.' L&CH. 'Pleasantly surprised. Decor clean and comfortable, service efficient. Starters: King Prawn – fresh and well cooked. Chana Puri – well spiced. No vegetarian main courses but prepared a Vegetable Dhansak without a problem and it was good. Tarka Dal very good. Garlic Nan – plenty of fresh garlic. Well worth the money. £30 for two.' AG. Hours: 12-2pm/6pm-12am. Stocks Cobra.

NORTHERN IRELAND

Population: 1,600,000

Curry still hasn't grabbed this part of the world in the way it has on the 'mainland'. We have just 25 establishments on our database all over the province. Compare this with Bradford W Yorks and you'll get the picture. There are fewer curry establishments per head of the population than in any other place in Britain (the ratio is 1:64,000). However, the number of curry restaurants has more than doubled in the province in 3 years. That's a good statistic for the media. We'd dearly love more reports, please.

Belfast

ARCHANA

53 Dublin Road, Belfast 028 9032 3713

'Menu very comfortable. Vindaloo very hot, excellent. Balti Chicken Chilli, also excellent. Decor and comfort good. Value for money.' JP. Stocks Cobra.

ASHOKA ©

363-367 Lisburn Road, Belfast 028 9066 0362

Ravi and Ms Sonal Chawda's 130-seater is an elegant, pillared dining room (apparently the only Indian restaurant in Northern Ireland with an Indian chef – Ishtiaque Khan). Frequented by politicians and celebrities, including Ian Paisley, David Trimble, members of U2 and Liam Neeson. Specials: Lobster dishes (prices vary), Baltis £10-15.95. Takeaway: 20% off. Hours: 5.30-11.30pm. Stocks Cobra.

GHANDI NEW ENTRANT

701c Lisburn Road, Belfast 028 9066 6833

'The food took a fairly long time to arrive, but this proved to be more of a case of care being taken with every dish than sloppy service. One immediately noticeable feature of the entire meal was the restrained use of ghee for which the chef is be commended. Each dish was fresh and light with its own distinctive taste well brought out. The top of my list of Belfast curry houses.' DMcD. Any agreement on this? Reports please. Stocks Cobra.

JHARNA

133 Lisburn Road, Belfast 028 9038 1299

Large a/c 110-seater. 'We found the Tandoori Crayfish superb and different £11.95.' CD. Price check: Papadam free, CTM £8.95 inc Pullao Rice, £1.50. Set menu £4.95 (3 courses). Hours: 12-2pm/5.30-11.30pm. Branch: Tamarind, Carrickfergus; Bithika Takeaway, Belfast. Stocks Cobra.

MOGHUL NEW ENTRANT

62 Botanic Avenue, Belfast 028 9032 6677

Established 1984 and taken over in 1998 by H Sirpal. Formerly Maharaja. Seats 80 diners. Specials: Tikka Special £7.95 – marinated chicken, mild sauce with mangoes and banana. Pakora Curry £5.95 – fairly hot, with yoghurt, gramflour and Punjabi spices. Paneer Makhani £6.95 – chef's own paneer, mild buttery sauce. Kebabs (delivery only): Donner, Sheesh, Chicken Tikka etc available from £3 and Chicken Burger with salad £2.50. Delivery: £1 charge. Price check: Papadam 40p, CTM £7.95, Pullao Rice £1.60, House wine £8.95 bottle. Hours: 12-2pm/5pm-12am. Stocks Cobra.

Carrickfergus

TAMARIND

32-36 West Street, Carrickfergus 01960 355579

Popular with its locals, we hear. Price check: CTM £5.95, Pillau Rice £1.20. Hours: 12-2pm/5.30-11.30pm. (Sun. to 11pm). Delivery. Stocks Cobra.

Lisburn

HIMALAYA ©

13 Bachelors Walk, Lisburn 01846 660044

Feroz Talukder's 48-seater has 10 parking spaces out front. 'The Jalfrezi £6.95 is outstanding.' GR. Price check: Papadam: 40p, CTM £6.50, Pullao Rice £1.40. Delivery: free over £40, £1 within 3-miles. Hours: 12-2pm/5-11.30pm; Sun. 5-11pm. Branch: Gandhi, Belfast. Stocks Cobra.

SCOTLAND

In 1965, much to the Scots' disgust, the age-old mainland Scottish shires and counties were amalgamated into nine large counties (or regions). In 1997 new changes resulted in only three staying totally unchanged (D&G, Fife and Highland). Two others have the same boundaries but new names: Borders became Scottish Borders, while Central once again became Stirling. Tayside is no more, being split into two (Angus and Perth & Kinross). Part of Grampian has been retained, with its western part returning to Moray. Northern Strathclyde has become Argyll & Bute, while the rest of Strathclyde, and the whole of Lothian have been split into sixteen Unitary Authorities, administering the larger cities and surrounds. For the time being, and until Scotland itself takes all these changes for granted, we retain in this Guide, the nine former counties (listing their ancient shires and/or new names within them, as relevant). Scotland's population of just over 5 million (less than that of central London) occupies a land mass nearly half that of England, though most of her curry houses are in and around the large cities. We'd adore a huge postbag of Scottish reports for our next Guide please.

BORDERS

Now called Scottish Borders
(Inc. Peebles and Roxburgh)

Area: Southeast Scotland
Population: 107,000
Adjacent Counties: D & G, Lothian, Northumberland, Strathclyde

Galashiels

SWAGAT NEW ENTRANT

36 Market Street, Galashiels 01896 750100

'Well lit, comfortable little place. Service is good. Very tasty Jalfry.' GMCG. Helpful and polite waiter on telephone. Hours: 12-2pm/5-11pm.

Hawick

SHUGONDA BALTI HOUSE

4 Station Building, Dove Mount Place 01450 373313

BM Talukder's 50-seater Bangladeshi curry house has 10 car parking spaces. Specials: Harsa Mossalla Chi, Masooru Dall Chi, Bengal Begun Mushroom Jal. Hours: 12-2pm/6-11.30pm. Reports please. Stocks Cobra.

©	Curry Club Discount	U	Unlicensed
V	Vegetarian	ANP	Alcohol not permitted
e-a-m-a-y-l	Eat as much as you like	BYO	Bring your own alcohol

CENTRAL

Now called Stirling – i.e. the former Stirlingshire
Area: Mid Scotland
Population: 276,000
Adjacent Counties: Lothian, Strathclyde, Tayside

Bridge of Allen

ASHOKA

23 Henderson Street, Bridge of Allan 01786 833710

'Food good in all aspects, especially the Garlic Nan and side dishes.' AGJ.

Denny

OMAR KHAYYAM

1 Church Walk, Denny 01324 825898

First opened in 1980, taken over by M Riaz in 1985. Seats 70. Specials include: Chicken Tikka Zilzia – spices, onions, peppers with a dash of Indian lager for a unique flavour (sounds rather strange!) £8.50 including rice. Snack menu: Kebabs – served with salad, sauce and pitta bread from £3, Burgers from £1.60 and Chapati Rolls with salad from £3 also available. Price check: Papadam 90p, CTM £9, Pullao Rice £2.10, Peshwari Nan £3, Lager £2.10 pint. Takeaway: 20% discount. Hours: 12-2pm/4.30pm-12am (to 1am Sat.)

Drymen

DRYMEN TANDOORI NEW ENTRANT ©

5-7 Stirling Road, Drymen 01360 660099

Established in 1994 by Sohail Wahid. Seats 65. Car parking for 14 cars. Specials: Samosas £3.25 – filling choice of vegetable, mince, cheese and potato. South Indian Garlic Chilli £7.95 – fresh garlic, chilli sauce with coriander and a touch of crispy red chilli. Pizzas also available from £4.50. Price check: Papadam 60p, CTM £7.95, Pullao Rice £1.75, Peshwari Nan £2.45, Lager £1.95 pint, House wine £9.95 bottle. Takeaway: 10% discount. Delivery: £10 minimum, 5-mile radius. Hours: 12pm-12am.

Dunblane

INDIA GATE

Fourways, Perth Road, Dunblane 01786 825394

This branch of Archie Sharrif's Peppermint Group is located at a corner site with useful parking, in a purpose-built modern bungalow. The exterior is reminiscent of those colonial Indian buildings, which still thrive in the sub-continent, indeed bungalow is an Indian word. KH went on a 'Wednesday night 9pm for the Buffet (£9.95) which looked appetizing, but turned out to be lukewarm, but apart from that quality was OK.' KH. 'Lots to eat, lots of taste, but not lots of price.' SH. See also Modern India, Regent Street, Glasgow, Indian Cottage, Kirkintilloch, Glasgow and Cafe India, Paisley.

DUMFRIES & GALLOWAY

Area: Southwest Scotland
Population: 148,000
Adjacent Counties: Borders, Cumbria, Strathclyde

Castle Douglas

MERRICK HOTEL

193 King Street, Castle Douglas 01556 504469

'Outside distinctly unprepossessing. A useful place in a culinary desert.' ME. Hours: 12-2pm (closed Sun. lunch)/5-11pm. Stocks Cobra.

Dumfries

JEWEL IN THE CROWN ©

48-50 St Michael Street, Dumfries 01387 264183

Manager A Muhit. 'Attentive staff. Bombay Mix on the table as we perused menu. Pops & pics immediately ready. Good starters – Vegetable Pakora and Mix Kebab. Chicken Dhansak and Chicken Methi reasonable. Good value.' AY. Hours: 12-2.30pm/6-11pm. Stocks Cobra.

FIFE

Area: East Scotland
Population: 351,000
Adjacent Counties: Lothian, Tayside

Dunfermline

VICEROY NEW ENTRANT

1 Queen Anne Street, Dunfermline 01383 622600

'Marvellous atmospheric restaurant. Attentive staff. Chicken Chaat was one of the best consumed to date, a hot combination of spices with small but juicy chunks of chicken on a melt in the mouth puri. The Sharabi was unusual as it contained single malt whisky in addition to the hot spices, capsicum and chillies. Top notch food at top notch prices. Business lunches available during the week at attractive prices.' RW. Well, those business lunches must be popular; I rang and could hardly hear the waiter for the noise on a Thursday afternoon (it was 2.30pm). Hours: 12-2pm/5-11pm.

Glenrothes

NURJAHAN ©

Coslane, Woodside Road, Glenrothes 01592 630649

Manirul Islam's 110-seater. Decorated in pinks to a very high standard. Roomy carver-chairs at all the tables. Striking menu with photographs of spices, dishes of curry and breads. 'Truly magnificent meal. Decor tastefully outstanding and spotless. More than generous quantities. The best quality we have ever tasted. A superior restaurant in every aspect.' MAJF. Waiter very polite and helpful when I rang for their opening hours, even though he had to repeat himself since the restaurant was very noisy with diners and I could hardly hear him. Hours: 12-2pm/5-11pm (Fri. & Sat. to 12am); Sun. 4-11pm.

Rosyth

TASTE OF INDIA

130 Admiralty Road, Rosyth 01383 413844

'Starters set a high standard of promises to come – the main courses let down. Raita that accompanies the Pakoras was made with yoghurt, mint and mango, very tasty.' NS. When I rang to enquire about their opening hours, the waiter told me that they did open for Sunday lunch – 'if anyone turns up' but that Sunday's 'the day we do lots of cleaning ready for the evening', about which he told me 'we're very busy'. So, people of Rosyth, if you are not having the traditional Sunday roast – what could be better than a curry at the Taste of India!, and hey, where's the navy? Hours: 12-2pm/5.30-11pm (Fri. & Sat. to 11.30pm).

St Andrews

NEW BALAKA BANGLADESHI
TOP 100 AWARD WINNER

Alexander Place, Market Street, St Andrews 01334 474825

Even before you enter Abdur Rouf's up-market and sophisticated 52-seater, note the frontage floral display. He has won awards for it. The unique feature is the huge kitchen garden at the rear, in which Mr Rouf grows all his own herbs and many vegetables. More foliage inside with palms dividing tables and hand-stitched Bangladeshi tapestries on the walls. Unusual dishes on the menu include Mas Bangla – salmon marinated in lime, turmeric and chilli, fried in mustard oil, garlic, onion, tomato and aubergine. I had the privilege of being trained to cook this dish by chef Abdul Monem which I reproduced at a lecture at St Andrews University for the Chemical Soc and all of Mr Rouf's friends. I hope they enjoyed it as much as I did. We then moved on to the restaurant for a fabulous meal. Amazingly the restaurant has no tandoor, which is detectable in the flavours of the breads and tikkas. But that aside, Mr Rouf's team continues to provide outstanding food in superb surroundings. We have lots of contented customer reports. All show a friendly, caring patron, and here's proof: 'Is still excellent.' M. 'We dined here with a large party of friends from the Netherlands and around the world. The evening was a tremendous success – wonderful food and service.' TGM. It seems to me it's always busy, and if you are really lucky you might just see Sean Connery on the nearby golf course. Please book your table. Meanwhile price check: Papadam 60p, CTM £7.85, Pullao Rice £2.75. Delivery: Local only, £1.75. Hours: Sun.-Thurs. 5pm-1am; Fri. & Sat. 12am-1am. Open Christmas Day. Comfortably in our TOP 100. Stocks Cobra.

GRAMPIAN & MORAY

Inc. Aberdeenshire, Banff, Kincardine and Morayshire

Area: North Scotland
Population: 537,000
Adjacent Counties: Highland, Tayside

Aberdeen

JEWEL IN THE CROWN NEW ENTRANT

Crown Street, Aberdeen 01224 210288

'This restaurant really is a jewel. The food is consistently of the highest quality and flavour, and the staff are unfailingly helpful, friendly and polite. We live 35 miles from Aberdeen and cannot always take the time to eat there. If we are combining it with a shopping trip we phone the day before and have a takeaway prepared. It is always painstakingly carefully packed. I asked them once where they obtained their bunches of coriander as I couldn't find any and from then on they have enclosed a bunch of coriander in the order. The owner, manager and staff are a great bunch.' JF. Now, that's an extra special takeaway.

NAZMA TANDOORI NEW ENTRANT

62 Bridge Street, Aberdeen 01224 211296

Established in 1990. Seats 150. 'Very impressed with all aspects. Chicken Chaat best yet. Veg, rice and naan bread all very good quality and quantity.' AKD. Specials include: Lamb Sardari £9.30, Ryhani Lamb £9.30, Akbori Makani £10.50. Price check: Papadam 70p, CTM £9.30, Pullao Rice £2.10, Peshwari Nan £2.50, Lager £2.50 pint. Takeaway: 10% discount. Hours: 12-2pm/5-10.30pm. Stocks Cobra.

SERENA INDIAN BRASSERIE e-a-m-a-y-l ©

75 Holburn Street, Aberdeen 01224 213355

Zafar Iqbal's 120-seater has 18 parking spaces, and specialises in Pakistani curries. Nightly e-a-m-a-y-l, £10.95, 6-10pm. Delivery: Minimum order £15, free within 4-mile radius, otherwise £1.50. Takeaway: 10% off. Hours: 5pm-12am Stocks Cobra.

Buckie

NEMAT TANDOOR ©

52 West Church Street, Buckie 01542 832653

Nemat Ali's 80-seater specialises in Balti, Pakistani and Southern Indian cuisine. Takeaway: 10% discount. I rang to check opening hours, the waiter told me that they opened the restaurant at 5pm but if I wanted to come in earlier then I was to give him a ring – how sweet! Hours: 12-2pm/5pm-12am.

Elgin

AL BAHAR NEW ENTRANT

156 High Street, Elgin 01343 545000

'Service was faultless. Chicken Khyberry was fantastic.' IW.

QISMAT ©

202-204 High Street, Elgin 01343 541461

Established in 1987 by Liaquat Ali. Seats 100 diners in a modern and brightly decorated restaurant with wooden polished floor, palms, coloured seat pads and air-conditioning. Specials: Chicken Tikka Achari £8.40 – cooked with tangy pickle, fresh green chillies and coriander. Chicken Rice £2.60. Garlic and Green Chilli Nan £2.20. 'Not very impressed by the service. Waiters seemed very uninterested in the customers, they had mastered the art of throwing the meals onto the table whilst staring at the ceiling. On the plus side there was lots of chicken in the Dhansak and the service was the quickest I have ever had.' IW. Price check: Papadam 55p, CTM £8.70, Pullao Rice £1.70, Peshwari Nan £2.20, Lager £2 pint. Takeaway: 10% discount. Delivery: £10 minimum, within Elgin only. Hours: 12-2pm/5-11.30pm; Sun. evening only. Branch: Qismat, 1b Millburn Road, Inverness.

Ellon

NOSHEEN ©

5 Bridge Street, Ellon 01358 724309

Established in 1989. Owned by Khalid Ahmed. Restaurant decorated rather lavishly in crimson ceiling and chairs, cream walls, green tablecloths and brass light fittings. Seats 92. Banquet A: £14.50 – Papadams and Spiced Onion, Pakora, Bhoona or Korma, Patia, Pullao Rice and Nan – for two.

Price check: Papadam 60p, CTM £8.50, Pullao Rice £1.95, Peshwari Nan £2.75. Takeaway: 10% discount. Delivery: £12 minimum in Ellon, £18 minimum outside Ellon. Hours: 5-11.30pm (Sat. to 12am).

Fraserburgh

RAJ TANDOORI NEW ENTRANT ©

69 Broad Street, Fraserburgh 01346 512220

Established in 1987 by Mrs G Soni, who manages front of house. Seats 48. Specials include: Murg Basanti (chicken tikka cooked in a sauce blended with onions, tomatoes, green peppers and a touch of Achari Masala) £7.45, Murg Chamak Challo (chicken cooked with tropical fruits and mushrooms) £7.45. Price check: Papadam 50p, CTM £6.95, Pullao Rice £1.95, Peshwari Nan £2.50, Takeaway: 10% discount. Delivery: £21 minimum, 4-mile radius. Hours: 11.45am-2pm/5-11.30pm (Sat. to 1am); Sun. 5-11.30pm.

Inverurie

BANANA TANDOORI NAME CHANGE ©

56 Market Place, Inverurie 01467 624860

Formerly Alo Chaya. Remains a well-established restaurant, owned since it was opened in 1987 by Syed Mujibul Hoque. 'Waiters efficient and friendly. Buffet night is worth a visit.' AMCW. Open 12-2.30pm/5.30-11.30pm.

NAZMA TAKEAWAY

42 West High Street, Inverurie 01467 629100

A takeaway-only establishment. 'Has a large TV as you enter, so you can see what's going on in the kitchen. Spotless.' RK. See next entry.

Peterhead

NAZMA TANDOORI

22a Queen Street, Peterhead 01779 478898

One of a chain of four restaurants in the area run by the four Ullah brothers. Established in 1989, seats 60. Special: Murgh Massala, chicken on-the-bone cooked in medium spicy sauce with mince and fresh coriander, garlic and ginger. 'Our local favourite for years. Service courteous and efficient. Food of consistently high standard.' DL. Hours: 12-2pm/5-11pm.

Stonehaven

TANDOORI HAVEN ©

54 Allardice Street, Stonehaven **01569 762793**

Shofiqul Hoque's 68-seater has a special menu for children which includes Herby Fish-Fry, Indian-style fish and chips. Sunday lunch buffet: £9.95. Takeaway: 10% off. House wine £7.90. Hours: 12-2pm/5-11pm. Stocks Cobra.

Turriff

SHOMI NEW ENTRANT

24 Balmellie Street, Turriff **01888 562636**

'Quality, quantity and presentation are fantastic, and I cannot speak highly enough of the service. Book Friday, Saturday and Sunday nights when they have their buffet banquet. Having my own business and having travelled all over Britain, I would certainly put this curry house up with those in Aberdeen, Glasgow, Edinburgh, Birmingham and London.' BS. 'We have been regulars here since it opened. Whenever we have an Indian meal elsewhere, even in the most expensive city restaurants, we realise just how superior the Shomi is. I would thoroughly recommend the Shomi Tandoori for the most prestigious awards and honours available.' SR. Stocks Cobra.

HIGHLAND

Inc. Caithness, Inverness, Nairn, Ross & Cromarty and Sutherland

Area: North Scotland
Population: 211,000
Adjacent Counties: Grampian, Strathclyde, Tayside

Aviemore

ASHA

43 Grampian Road, Aviemore **01479 811118**

'Our first impression of the menu was that it seemed expensive, but most main courses included rice. Katta Murgh Masala was very tasty with a tang of lime.' EO'D. Hours: 12-2pm/5.30-11.30pm.

©	Curry Club Discount	U	Unlicensed
V	Vegetarian	ANP	Alcohol not permitted
e-a-m-a-y-l	Eat as much as you like	BYO	Bring your own alcohol

Dingwall

CAFÉ INDIAN BRASSERIE NEW ENTRANT

Lockhart Hse, Tulloch Sreet, Dingwall 01349 862552

Established in 1984. A really pretty restaurant with luxurious red swathes of material on the ceiling – rather like a tent with palm trees and bamboo chairs – very nice. Seats 60-70. Buffet and Balti nights. Specials: Green Herb Chicken £6.50 – garlic fried chicken, onion, tomato, green chilli, fresh coriander leaves. Tandoori Vollaile £6.95 – half a corn-fed chicken marinated and grilled in tandoor. Price check: Papadam 60p, CTM £8.50, Pullao Rice £2.60, Peshwari Nan £1.95, Lager £2.30 pint, House wine £9.50 bottle. Takeaway: 10% discount. Hours: 12-2pm/5-11pm. Stocks Cobra.

DINGWALL TANDOORI NEW ENTRANT

4 High Street, Dingwall 01349 861917

'Friendly service from Abdul, a local celebrity, and his staff. Popadoms were perfection itself. Hot and spicy sheek kebabs were crudely coloured, and the tasty chicken massala was a little too soft. Good quality lamb. A warming delight after a day in the Scottish Highlands.' PW.

Inverness

QISMET TANDOORI NEW ENTRANT ©

1b, Millburn Road, Inverness 01463 716020

Established in 1998 by Liaquat Ali; your host is pictured on the takeaway menu. Restaurant seats 100 and is brightly decorated, polished wooden floor and chairs, white tablecloths, palm trees, spot lighting. Specials: Chicken Tikka Sonali £8.75 – with finely chopped ginger, green chillies and onion, medium hot. Mazedar £8.40 – lamb tikka with Worcestershire sauce, lemon juice, cream and cheese. Price check: Papadam 55p, CTM £8.70, Pullao Rice £2. Takeaway: 10% discount. Hours: 12-2pm/5-11.30pm. Stocks Cobra.

Nairn

AL RAJ ©

25 Harbour Street, Nairn 01667 455370

Mobarok Ali's 70-seater has built up a good reputation with helpful waiters. Even Nick Nairn himself has been seen here. Hours: 12-2pm/5-11.30pm.

COBRA GOOD CURRY GUIDE
County Index, see page 5 Town Index, see page 614
A to Z of the Curry Menu, page 41 Contributors Key, page 604

LOTHIAN

Area: Mid Eastern Scotland
Population: 774,000
Adjacent Counties: Borders, Central, Fife, Strathclyde

The region of Lothian has been disbanded, the larger cities and surrounds split into a number of Unitary Authorities. For the time being, we are sticking to the old Lothian in this Guide.

Edinburgh

Inc. Blackhall, Dalry, Greenhill, Roseburn, Stockbridge and Viewforth – Leith is entered separately

ANN PURNA NEW ENTRANT V

45 St Patricks Square, Central Edinburgh 0131 667 4432

A vegetarian restaurant serving delights from South India and Gujarat. Specials: Patra (one of Pat's favourites) – steamed green Arvi leaves layered with a spiced gram flour paste. Ann Purna Baingan (aubergine) and Bhindi (okra) Masala are popular favourites. Stocks Cobra.

BOMBAY BICYCLE CLUB NEW ENTRANT

6a Brougham Place, Central Edinburgh 0131 229 8839

'Been here several times, always excellent. Innovative menu, massive, tasty portions (especially the vegetarian main dishes). A treat!' MH.

FAR PAVILION TOP 100 ©

1-12 Craigleith Road, Stockbridge, Edinburgh W 0131 332 3362

Est. 1987, this 85-seater in two rooms is 'no ordinary curry house. It's sumptuous outside and in, bar and lounge areas decorated in brown and blue, complete with stained glass windows.' GR. *The Scotsman's* Gillian Glover says 'the walls bore dimpled panels of buttoned velvet. Even the staff were upholstered.' Owners Wasim and Aasim Chaudhry say 'the aim of true Indian cooking is never simply to bring a flush to the face and take a layer of skin from the tongue. We prefer to call each dish a presentation'. Chef Abdul Aziz's 'chilli-rated' menu is a well-worded presentation in its own

©	Curry Club Discount	U	Unlicensed
V	Vegetarian	ANP	Alcohol not permitted
e-a-m-a-y-l	Eat as much as you like	BYO	Bring your own alcohol

right. Eye-catching specials range from Kashmir to Goa with goodies like Masala Roast Lamb and Prawn Amottik – hot and spicy. 'I had my favourite Pala Gosht from Punjab, £8.25, and it had the correct Pakistani flavour, and the suggested Tarka Dhal was gorgeous in authenticity – wafts of garlic, loads of flavour.' PL. Expect to spend £20 a head plus drinks, and watch those extras. The Pickles Tray is £2.50, for example! But that said, this restaurant rermains in our TOP 100. The CC discount eases the bill as does the e-a-m-a-y-l Tuesday 6.30-10pm, £11.95 and lunchtime buffet. Price check: Papadam 55p, CTM £8.95, Pullao Rice £2.25. Takeaway: 10% off. Hours: 12-2pm (weekdays)/5.30pm-12am; closed Sun. except December. Have voice-mail to take table bookings. Reports please. Stocks Cobra.

GURU BALTI — BYO ©

9, Dundee Terrace, Viewforth, Edinburgh SW — 0131 221 9779

First opened in 1995, taken over by manager Mustafa Iqbal in 1998. Seats 45. 'Tiny restaurant in quieter part of city. Refreshing menu with lots to experiment with. Paid £10.95 for starter, Balti and sweet. Huge portions – had to leave half of Nan and sweet! Nice decor and music – great!' MM Specials: Balti Drumsticks £2.60 – chicken drumsticks, medium sauce with salad. Pickle Tray: £1.40. Thursday Balti Night: four course, £10.95. Sunday Family Night Special: kids eat free. Tuesday Night: Guru Banquet – four course set menu £9.95. BYO (no corkage – please ring for confirmation). Price check: Papadam 60p, CTM £7.95, Pullao Rice £2.25, Peshwari Nan £2.25, Hours: 5pm-12pm. Stocks Cobra.

HIMALAYA — RE ENTRANT

171 Bruntsfield Place, Greenhill, Edinburgh S — 0131 229 8216

'Used to be in the guide some years ago and I honestly don't know why it dropped out.' [Because no one, including the Himalaya communicated with us about it. Normally if a restaurant can't be bothered to return our entry forms, we delist them. Just for you then, Martin, but we need reports please, and the next guide form returned to continue this entry.] 'Very busy, very tasty vegetable dishes, quick service and quite the biggest naan I've ever had.' MH.

JAIPUR OF INDIA — NEW ENTRANT ©

16 Marishchal Road, Blackhall, Edinburgh — 0131 467 7773

Established in 1994 by AH Boksh. Modern decor, with leather sofas and chandeliers. Specials: Murgh Risotto £6.76 – chicken with mushroom, pineapple, medium sauce, served with Nan. Takeaway only. Price check:

Papadam 50p, CTM £5.35, Pullao Rice £1.85, Peshwari Nan £1.80. Delivery: free if over £18, otherwise £1.75. Hours: 5-11pm.

KALPNA V

2-3 St Patrick's Square, Central Edinburgh 0131 667 9890

This vegetarian restaurant, established in 1983, remains very popular, under the auspices of owner-chef Ajay Bhartdwaj. It serves a mix of Gujarati, Bombay and south Indian items, such as Bhel Puri and Dosas (see glossary), with some distinctive Moghul non-meat items too, such as Aloo Dom – Kashmiri stuffed potatoes. Wednesday evening buffet. I rang to confirm opening times – restaurant very busy and noisy on this Thursday lunchtime, waiter helpful and polite. Hours: 12-2pm/5-11pm. Stocks Cobra.

KHUSHI'S NEW ENTRANT

32c Broughton Street, Central Edinburgh 0131 556 8092

'Small, intimate, smart, clean, efficient and friendly restaurant. Large starter was cooked to perfection, main course was a delightful combination of lamb and mushroom with succulent and tender meat in a spicy but well balanced sauce. I returned again within two days and was again very pleased with my meal.' RW. Hours: 5-12pm. (Fri & Sat to 1am).

KHUSHI'S BYO

16 Drummond Street, Central Edinburgh 0131 556 8996

No relation to the above Kushi's. 'Nice short menu, good helpings, very good meat, perfectly marinated. Fair service, nice Italian waiter. Clean, light-painted decor, very clean toilets. Good comfort on padded benches and formica tables. Excellent big starters. No alcohol, but most people brought big jugs (2-3 pints) of beer from the pub next door. Madras was now a Vindaloo; Bhuna and Korma could have been Madras.' NC. Branch: Khushi's of West Lothian, Mid Calder. Waiter very helpful and polite. When I telephoned to ask for opening hours, he replied 'when would you like to come?' Hours: 12-3pm/5-10pm. Closed Sundays except during Festival.

KING'S BALTI U BYO

79 Buccleuch Street, Central Edinburgh 0131 662 9212

100-seater, managed by Nunir Abu with chef Ibrahim Ali. 'This is where Edinburgh University is alongside, so academics and students go for their Indian cuisine. Our family re-visited the King's Balti last week, to celebrate my student daughter's 22nd birthday and we came away bursting at the seams and with increased enthusiasm for the place due to their swift service, high quality cuisine and low prices.' TE. Unlicensed (the waiters nip round to the off-licence next door for you!). Delivery service. Hours: 12-2pm/5pm-12am; Fri. & Sat. 12pm-12am.

LANCERS BRASSERIE TOP 100

5 Hamilton Place, Central Edinburgh 0131 332 3444

70-seater opened in 1985 by Wali Udin JP, managed by Alok Saha, head chef Badrul Hussain. Beautifully decorated, stylish restaurant for business and special occasions. Pink suede on the walls, tiled floor, highly polished tables. 'Went for lunch. Very attractive decor. Papadoms were sadly not accompanied by pickles – so annoying that. I tried Sabzi Kofta Massallam, mixed vegetable balls in a mild, cream sauce. Tasty enough, but not something I'd have again too soon. Worth visiting.' RL. 'Lovely food with courteous service.' T&KM. Downstairs is a private dining room for 12 diners. Chippendale-style furniture, banquet-style Raj prints decorate the walls. A small but selective menu. Set Dinner: £15.95. Takeaway: 20% off. Delivery: £15, 4-mile radius. Hours: 12-2.30pm/5-11.30pm. Stocks Cobra.

MAHARAJAH'S

17-19 Forrest Rd, Old Town, Central Edinburgh 0131 220 2273

Magnificently designed, with hand-painted murals, to resemble a tented pavilion set within a beautiful palace garden, and right in the heart of the university area (10% discount for students and nurses). 'Lots of medics from the nearby Royal Infirmary pop in here for quick fix. Very reliable, tasty food.' MH. Buffet on Monday and Tuesday. Hours: 12-2pm/5.30pm-12am. Stocks Cobra.

SHALIMAR NEW ENTRANT

29 West Maitland Street, Central Edinburgh 0131 225 3199

Established in 1995. Seats 50. Decorated in green, gold and plum. Specials: Karahi Bhoona £6.95 – prepared in cast iron pot, onions, capsicums, tomatoes, fenugreek leaves, fresh ginger and garlic, flambéed in cognac. Price check: Papadam 50p, CTM £7.50, Pullao Rice £1.95, Peshwari Nan £1.95, Lager £2.25 pint. Takeaway: 25% discount. Delivery: £10 minimum, 2-mile radius. Hours: 12-2pm/5-11.30pm; Sun. 3-11pm. Stocks Cobra.

SHAMIANA TOP 100 AWARD WINNER

14 Brougham Street, Central Edinburgh 0131 228 2265

First opened in 1977, taken over in 1992 by co-owner brothers Nadim (manager) and Mohammed (head chef) Butt. Seats 37. Specialising in Pakistani Kashmiri cuisine. Mohammed was awarded the Best Chef Award in the 1998 *Good Curry Guide*. 'I have been a regular customer of your excellent restaurant for around seven years and have been consistently impressed by the quality of your food. I also appreciate the professional manner in which your restaurant is run, and that last orders are taken at 10pm, thus restricting clientele to genuine curry enthusiasts.' TN. 'I went here when it boasted an award-winning chef, but my last visit a few months ago will be my last. It still claims to have its honoured chef, but my contacts in the trade tell me that he moved on some time ago. This was evidenced when I ordered a Pakora starter and received some small, soggy vegetable balls. Chicken Tikka wasn't much better. Bad food, poor service and a greasy-spoon sort of ambience are not worthy of a mention in your esteemed publication.' GR. Well, grumpy Greg, I am afraid that you are out-numbered. Here are some more glowing reports. 'The food at Shamiana is excellent and the standard during the last ten years has been first class' A& AM. 'Another excellent meal. My business colleagues look forward to further frequent visits now that our office headquarters are located around the corner' TAS. 'We hadn't booked, it was midweek, it was packed, we got the penultimate table. Popadoms crispy, good chutney tray, but naughty, naughty – don't put tomato ketchup in the cachumber ever again! Samosa was shaped like a spring roll, but tasted very good. Main course portions good. Pat ordered his beloved Methi Chaman Gosht, with spinach, fenugreek, fresh oriental herbs and hot spices – £4.95, and pronounced it authentic and delicious. I had the Pakistani equivalent of CTM – Kashmiri Chasni Tikka, spicy, and equally good. Rice and breads enormous.' DBAC. Great to see Kulfi Pista, Gulab Jaman and Garjar Halwa on the dessert menu. Specials include: Shahi Murgh (spiced whole roast chicken created in the kitchens of the Great Maharajah of India, serves 4, 24 hours notice required, £30). Price check: Papadam 40p, CTM £6.85, Pullao Rice £1.95, Peshwari Nan £2.50, Lager £2.10 pint. Hours: 6-10pm. Stocks Cobra.

SINGAPORA ©

69 North Castle Street, Central Edinburgh 0131 538 7878

Malaysian-Singaporean 65-seater owned and managed by chef C Pang. Decor is 'dominant decorative wood and high ceiling reminiscent of colonial-style romance, the waitresses in national dress.' AG. Satay: Chicken,

Beef, King Prawn or Tofu, marinated, skewered and chargrilled, served with a delicious peanut sauce (five sticks). The Malay Kari – chicken, beef, or vegetables in a coconut base, and Redang Beef, the national dish curry. Takeaway: 10% off. Delivery. Hours: 12-2.30pm/6-10.30pm; Sun. closed winter.

SURUCHI ©

14a Nicolson Street, Central Edinburgh 0131 556 6583

Unique at Herman Rodrigues' 70-seater is his careful selection of his own beautiful photographs of India which hang on the walls. Suruchi means, in most Indian languages, good taste, an apt name when considering the decor has been imported from India, and is clean and smart. Jaipur blue/turquoise tiles adorn the walls. Table linen is vegetable-dyed pink and tableware is beaten coppered brass. It serves real home-style Indian food. Well-situated for a pre-theatre (which is opposite) curry dinner. Regional Indian food festivals held monthly. Specials: Shakuti, from Goa with coconut and black pepper, and Upperi, shredded cabbage with coconut and mustard seeds. Most ordered dish: Kumbhi Narial, mushroom with coconut. Takeaway: 33% discount. Hours: 12-2pm/5.30-11.30pm. Stocks Cobra.

TIPPOO SAHIB ©

129a Rose Street, Central Edinburgh 0131 226 2862

A Pakistani restaurant opened in 1982 as the Shanaz by the Parvez family. In 1996 Anjam Parvez renamed the 60-seater. Tippoo Sultan ruled south India in the late 17th century. His battle collaborations with the French caused the British severe problems, but left Tippoo's name a legend. Tippoo's Tiger, his famous favourite mechanical 'toy', is now housed in the V&A Museum, and his portrait by Sir David Wilkie is in the Scottish National Gallery. It was Edinburgh's Wild Macrea's regiment who defeated Tippoo. The colourful murals at the restaurant depict the story. Chicken Mancharry, tandoor-cooked, with freshly grated chilli, garlic and ginger, Chicken Nentara, cooked with onions and methi, and Massalidar Gosht, meat cooked with pickles, and Karella Gosht meat with bitter gourd. 'First class quality food, staff and atmosphere. Reasonable prices.' RC. Hours: 12-2pm/5pm-12am; Sat. 12-11.30pm; Sun. 5-11.30pm.

VERANDAH TOP 100 ©

17 Dalry Road, Dalry, Edinburgh W 0131 337 5828

44-seater opened in 1981 by Wali Tasar Uddin, MBE, JP, and his nephew, Foysol Choudhury, who describes it as 'reassuringly low-key' serving northern Indian and Bangladeshi cuisine. It's a pretty, relaxing restaurant with cane chairs and bamboo-slatted wall blinds, a clever and effective illusion. A very popular and well-established restaurant. But we've had a blaster: 'Very disappointed with the food.' MR&MRS MS. 'Prompt service as we'd got in just before the rush (it was the Scotland v South Africa rugby match). Chilli Garlic Chicken wasn't bad, quite well spiced with good chunks of chicken. But not too far above the standard you'd expect from a good Indian.' RL. Knowing the care Foysol puts in we find this surprising, but since the *Guide* gets the blame, we felt obliged to report it. Not everyone agrees anyway: 'Lovely food with courteous service.' T&KM. We dearly wish to keep our old friend the Verandah in our in our TOP 100, and we will, this time. Your reports please will determine this. House specials include Amer Murghi, mild chicken cooked with mango pulp and cream £6.95 and Chilli Garlic Chicken £6.95. Price check: Papadam 60p, CTM £7.25, Pullao Rice £2.25. Set menus £5.95 and £6.95 for lunch and £16.95 for dinner. The wine list is very much above average, and includes a drink-what-with-which-curry-guide. Delivery: £15. Hours: 12-2pm/5pm-12am. Stocks Cobra.

Leith

BRITANNIA SPICE NEW TO OUR TOP 100 BEST IN SCOTLAND ©

150 Commercial Street, Britannia Way, Leigh 0131 555 2255

A superb new venue (est. 1999) with a nautical theme from Wali Uddin, MBE. Seats a considerable 150 diners in a dining room with blue chairs, polished wooden tables and floors, brass railings and blinds that look like sails. A perfect stop off after you have visited Ocean Terminal where the former Royal yacht *Britannia* is docked – though I think Glasgow should have got the ship, since they built it, or Pompey, cos they sailed it for five decades. However, their loss is Wali's gain. Incidentally, the yacht is now home to ITV 'This Morning's Chef of the Year, Tony Singh; though 'continental-trained' he's unlikely to change ships from one *Britannia* to another. The menu includes popular favourites, starters such as Pakora and Samosa. Main courses include Sag Gosht and Tikka Masala but there are some Thai specialities – Tom Kha Gai £3.75 – chicken soup and Gaeng Kiew Waan £8.25 – green chicken curry and Pad Ho Ra Pa Kub Nua £8.50 – beef stir-fry. Also includes authentic Bangladeshi dishes – Shatkora Gosht £8.95 – lamb with citrus fruit and chilli. There is also a short list of Nepalese main courses – Himalayan Momo £8.95 – minced meat mixed with flour and cooked in the traditional way of the mountains of Nepal. Though if nothing excites you and you wish to stay with something you know then choose from the Northern Indian section – Ginger Murgh £7.35 – tender chicken, hot spices, made into kebabs with ginger and coriander sauce. Aloo Gosht £6.95 – lamb with potato, garlic, herbs and spices. For the totally unadventurous there is a small choice of English dishes – steak, roast chicken etc. Buffet banquet lunches: Mon.-Fri. 12-2.15pm £7.95. Takeaway: 15% discount. Delivery: £50 minimum, 5-mile radius. Price check: Papadam 70p, CTM £7.95, Pullao Rice £2.75, Peshwari Nan £2.75, Lager £2.95 pint. Hours: 12-2.15pm/5-11.45pm. Stocks Cobra.

GULNAR'S PASSAGE TO INDIA TOP 100 ©

46 Queen Charlotte Street, Leith, Edinburgh 0131 554 7520

'Over the last ten years Leith has evolved from a derelict dock area into a tasteful commercial area surrounded by designer flats and yacht marina, and now the Royal Yacht *Britannia*. Another attraction is Mohammad Ridha Saleh's 82-seater Passage, not only for north Indian and Kashmiri food. 'Many are the nights I've spent there feeling like a desert king, being fed the most amazing food under the drapes that give the establishment the air of a Bedouin tent. One Arabic dish at Gulnar's especially emphasises this feeling: Helahil, chicken cooked with sweetcorn, onion, fresh coriander and chilli, served on a bed of rice with salad, a superb dish with a wonderful mix of flavours. Two new introductions are: Halabcha, spiced and roasted aubergine cooked in the tandoor with chicken, yoghurt, tomatoes, onions, garlic, chilli and coriander, a hot dish that tantalises the tastebuds; and Onion Sambal, combined with Chicken Tikka is an incredible edible experience.' GR. 'Recommended by several people, but to be honest we thought it sounded a bit too good to be true. We soon realised that all that accolade was not exaggerated. We went for the atmosphere mainly, but were very thrilled with the variety and quality of the exotic food. A great cheer to a marvellous place which had given us one of the best nights out in the UK for a long, long time.' FA. 'Free papadoms, nice dips. My dining partner thought the Chicken Tikka was the best she'd tasted, but my Jhal Frezie was not so good – too bland. Service was good and fast.' GMcG. What you need to do, Gary, is ask for a plate of fresh green chillies – as Pat does – that will hot things up a bit. Specials include Aloobora – spicy potato balls filled with minced lamb £2.10. Potahari Sangam – minced lamb fried with fresh herbs and spices, garnished with coconut, wrapped in a puri £2.50. Rooflifter £6.75, lamb and chicken marinated, tandoor-cooked and prepared with mint, nuts and spices. Such delights promote Gulnar's to our TOP 100. Price check: free Papadams, CTM £6.25, Pullao Rice £1.80. Delivery: Leith area. Hours: 12-2pm/5.30pm-12am (1am on Sat.). Stocks Cobra.

SAAGAR NEW ENTRANT

9 Commercial Quay, 92 Commercial Street, Leith 0131 553 1518

Fashionably modern restaurant down a short marble staircase with brass handrails. Lloyd Loom styled chairs, painted in white, black and red. Specials: Cashew nut Roll, Chicken Chat. Branch: Joypur, 114 High Street, North Berwick. Reports please. Stocks Cobra.

RAJ

91 Henderson Street, Leith, Edinburgh 0131 553 3980

Benefiting from Leith's reincarnation, Tommy Miah's restaurant is still very popular with local residents, business people and visitors to Leith retaining its Victorian architecture. It continues to offer meals at 1983 prices on Sundays and Thursdays. Bangladeshi cuisine is consistently good, however... Tommy, please invest in some hot plates! 'I like to eat the last of my curry while it is still hot.' TE. 'Wonderful restaurant, but often busy and service painfully slow.' T&KM. Own-labelled products – eg: Mango Chutney for sale.

Musselburgh

SHISH MAHAL ©

63a, High Street, Musselburgh 0131 665 3121

Established 1979, Idris Khan's and manager Shezad's 40 seater is decorated with original Pakistani wall hangings. Chef Tariq's specials include Shajaman Murgh, half barbecued chicken, on- or off-bone, in medium curry sauce, £9.50, Specials include: Shish Garlic and Chilli £7.50, Kashmiri Kebab Curry £8.50, Shish Kebab Murgh £7.50, Nawabi Bhindi Gosht – okra with lamb £8.50 and Sabzi Pasanda, all vegetables £7.50. Buffet Tuesday. 'The food is outstanding. I live 10 miles from Musselburgh but it is worth the trip as the food is always superb. My favourite in Scotland.' LW. Price check: Papadam 75p, CTM £7.50, Pullao Rice £1.95, Peshwari Nan £2.25, Takeaway: 10% discount. Delivery: £10 min. Hours: 5pm-12am. Stocks Cobra.

Penicuik

CLIPPERS NEW ENTRANT

26 High Street, Penicuik 01968 679977

Clean lines and no clutter make for a smart restaurant to dine in. Crimson walls, highly polished wooden floor, chairs and tables. Specials: Kathmandu

Murgh – chicken Tikka with garlic, ginger, whole spring onions and lentils. Fangash Dupiaza – fish with green beans. Polite and helpful waiters. Hours: 12-2pm/5.30-11.30pm (Fri. & Sat. to 12am). Stocks Cobra.

STRATHCLYDE

Inc. the former counties of: Argyle, Ayrshire, Dunbartonshire, Lanarkshire and Renfrewshire

Area: Central west Scotland
Population: 2,255,000
Adjacent Counties: Borders, D & G, Central, Highland, Lothian

Note: For this edition at least, we are maintaining the old region of Strathclyde here, but we point out that Northern Strathclyde has become Argyll & Bute, while the rest of Strathclyde is divided into a number of Unitary Authorities, administering the larger cities and surrounds.

Ayr

BOLLYWOOD CUISINE

242 Prestwick Road, Ayr 01292 611221

'If you are anywhere nearby and don't know where to go for a fix – this is it. The food is so good. Chicken Nimbo and Samosas for our starters – both different, both great. Lamb Minty and Lamb Budda (the sauce had port in it) next, superb quality lamb. Can't fault it.' MS.

Coatbridge

PUNJAB EXPRESS ©

22 West Canal Street, Coatbridge 01236 422522

Opened in 1993 by the Dhanda brothers, Kally and Tari. The Punjab Express is part of the former Coatbridge Central Station House. Built in 1899, the building still has many of the period features. The station was closed by Lord Beeching in 1963 and the restaurant is situated in what used to be the station master's accommodation. Downstairs, in the former ticket office, is the Pullman Lounge. Reports please. Stocks Cobra.

GLASGOW

Inc. Battlefield, Finnieston, Hillhead, Muirend, Nitshill, Pollockshields, Scotstoun, Townhead

Glaswegians are at pains to tell us that Glasgow curries are 'the real thing, the best anywhere' ... 'everywhere else is a pale imitation, especially the pakoras', writes one person frequently. The other thing they lay claim to is that Glasgow is the curry city of the world! As to the first claim, what they've got, lucky people, is a largely Pakistani population, and this means gutsy, spicy Kashmiri/Punjab-style curries, as are found in Southall and Bradford, which are quite removed from the Bangladeshi curry house formula. Put another way, Glasgow's curries are the authentic thing, once tasted, never forgotten. As to 'curry city' sorry lads and wee lassies, you are still number three, measured by the number of curry restaurants to the number of citizens. At 132 to 700,000 (1:4375), this puts you behind Bradford and Leicester. But Glasgow is not standing still. It has some very entrepreneurial high-flyers, whose new-wave, large restaurants are leading Britain in size, popularity and style.

ALISHAN TANDOORI

250 Battlefield Road, Battlefield, Glasgow S 0141 632 5294

Established in 1987, MA Qureshi's 48-seater has an extensive range of specials. Basanti, tandoori items in a creamy sauce with a tangy touch of pickle; Nashilee, ditto with wine; Nashidar, with brandy, all £9.50. 'Chicken Tikka Chasni had to be one of the best main course meals I have ever had! The taste was fantastic, the sauce rich, and the serving had plenty of fully cooked tender meat. But disappointing Peshwari Naan – thinner crust and smaller than ones seen elsewhere. Service was polite and courteous. Very enjoyable and highly recommended.' SL-J. Price check: Papadam 60p, CTM £7.50, Pullao Rice £1.50, Peshwari Nan £2.50, Lager £2.50 pint. Takeaway: 10% discount. Delivery: £10 minimum. Hours: 12-2pm/5pm-12am; Sun. 5pm-12am. Stocks Cobra.

AMBALA SWEET CENTRE ANP ©

178 Maxwell Road, Pollockshields, Glasgow S 0141 429 5620

'Lamb Bhoona is amazing!' DF. This is a franchise operated by Mrs S Ahmad. (See Ambala, Drummond St, London, NW1.) As well as the counter takeaway sweets and snacks, chef Akmal cooks a small range of curries for the 26-seat restaurant. BYO not allowed. No credit cards. Price check: Papadam 40p, CTM £4, Pullao Rice £1.90. Hours: 10am-10pm.

THE ASHOKA TOP 100

108 Elderslie Street, Central Glasgow 0141 221 1761

Originally opened 1968, it was taken over in 1995. Owned by brothers Bhpoinder and Parminder Purewal, who assure you that their Ashoka has no connection with the many other Ashokas in the area. Ashoka, incidentally, was an Indian emperor from centuries ago. Recently 110 seats in two dining rooms. Had a £250,000 facelift by restaurant designer Harris Khan. Critics have described it as 'Baroque into fantasyland' and 'rich opulence'. What do you say about that and chef Alexandré Paaeschi's cooking? The new menu has plenty of play on the words 'spark' and 'flame' (Old Flame for example are the old favourites like CTM). 'This restaurant oozes class, little wonder it was voted "Best in Scotland". The decor, service, presentation and food are excellent.' MC. Price check: Papadam 80p, CTM £7.95, Pullau Rice £1.95. Lager £1.95 pint, House wine £9.95. Takeaway: 10% off. Hours: 12-11.30pm; Sun. 5pm-11pm.

ASHOKA ASHTON LANE NEW ENTRANT

19 Ashton Lane, Hillhead, Glasgow W 0141 357 5904

There have been Ashoka restaraunts in Glasgow since 1968. Balbur Singh Sumal grew the number to six during the 1980s (including the original at Elderslie Street, noted abov,e which is one is no longer part of the group). The remainder, listed together here, are now part of Charan Gill's Harlequin Group of several Ashokas in and around Glasgow, and one in Johnstone. The rebranding has added location to the titles, which certainly helps identify one from the other. The menus are the same at each branch, and the service is, we hear: 'exemplary, the food as good as ever from the old days.' IMcT. This one is near Hillhead underground station, and Uni land.

ASHOKA AT THE MILL NEW ENTRANT
NEW TO OUR TOP 100

500 Corselet Road, Nitshill, Glasgow SW 0800 195 3195

This Ashoka is novel, and the clue is in the name. It is indeed located in an old mill, and is now Charan Gill's flagship, containing 'head office'. The location is off the M77 at J3 – go west half a mile along the A726, turn left and follow the signs, and suddenly you've left industrial Glasgy behind. Gill had to do a huge refurb job on the premises, and he let his fantasy run a wee bit. There is a Scotland the Brave, neo-Medieval look to the place, with bare stone contrasting with plaster walls, boarded floor and silver/electric-blue decor. The chairs look a bit spindly, but probably cost a fortune, branded cattle ranch-style, with the letter 'A'. The large venue (225 seats) is not dwarfed by its central feature – a tree trunk painted blue ('it was there so I used it' said designer David Roulston). The tree continues on upstairs in the mezzanine section. Large windows ensure plenty of daylight. The food, according to IMcT: 'is not all Indian, but it's all at the Ashoka standard worth travelling for.' Specials include Goanese fish and prawns, Kala Mirch Masala, sliced chicken breast in a peppery, tangy herbal sauce. Average spend is £15, and we welcome more reports. Meanwhile on the strength of what we have we are pleased to put the Mill in our TOP 100. Stocks Cobra.

ASHOKA SOUTH SIDE RE ENTRANT

268 Clarkston Road, Muirend, Glasgow S 0141 637 5904

Another long-standing branch which has appeared in this *Guide* over the years.

ASHOKA WEST END RE ENTRANT

1284 Argyle Street, Central Glasgow 0141 339 0936

This Ashoka appeared in our first (1984) *Guide* when it was a Vegetarian restaurant It is no longer veggie, and has the same menu as the other Ashokas. Charan Gill first became a partner here in 1985, and with his cousinn Gurmhil Dhillon he started to build up his group. Other Harlequin Group branches: Kama Sutra, Murphy's Pakora Bar, Mr Singh's, Glasgow, Ashoka Johnstone.

CAFÉ INDIA TOP 100

171 North St, Charing Cross, Central Glasgow 0141 248 4074

Described (by its owner Abdul Sattar) as 'Britain's first-ever designer buffet restaurant'. It certainly has changed since it opened in 1979, its seating by 1999 having reached a monumental 500, and two years on 560. This makes it Britain's biggest. Sattar again: 'it's arty decor, attracts young clientele.' The exterior tells you that. The ground floor is open-plan and bright. The seats are expensive high-backed pale wood with pink or blue upholstery, depending which zone you are in, and there are some alcove tables. The area called the galleries in the lower floor is moody, with darker reds and wrought iron. There is provision for self-service via a smart counter. Both floors have eye-catching artwork and light fittings. Suddenly this style of decor is already dated, being installed up and down Britain as fast as red flock in the 60s. Young clientèle love it though and their set meals, which are a speciality, and the Friday/Saturday e-a-m-a-y-ls (at £12.50). Specials:

©	Curry Club Discount	U	Unlicensed
V	Vegetarian	ANP	Alcohol not permitted
e-a-m-a-y-l	Eat as much as you like	BYO	Bring your own alcohol

South Indian Garlic Chilli Chicken (£8.90), Lobster £18.90, Lamb Redfort £8.90. Sattar it seems is proud of the fact that he served 1160 diners in a single day. But size and numbers aren't everything, and we hope this, the only report received in two years is an exception: 'I appreciate I may have dined on a "bad night" and that my experience may not be typical, but the service or lack of it, was really poor. The wrong drinks were brought, and we had to get up and ask waiters to clear our table between all courses. In terms of the food, the selection and quality was poor, and the desserts in particular were a major disappointment.' WMA. We made you a TOP 100 last time, and this time we'll hold you there, but we'd like a raft of happy reports please. If writing is out for the 'young clientèle' you can use our email. (see last page). Price check: Papadam 70p, CTM £8.95, Pullao Rice £1.60. Lager £1.90 pint, House wine £1.90 (glass). Takeaway: 10% off. Hours: 12pm-12am; Sun. 3pm-12am.

CHAPATI I ©

2017 Dumbarton Road, Glasgow W 0141 576 0118

Chain of 11 takeaways, est. 1983 by Iqbal S Gill each of which has its own personnel, but are overseen by Deepa Gill (service) and Harnak Singh (chef). Curries, Kebabs and Pizza. Prices are not cheap for takeaway: Onion Bhajia £2.25, Mango Chutney 70p, Potato and Cauiflower Curry £3.50. Most ordered dishes: Karahi Chicken and Chicken Jullander. Hours: Sun.-Thurs. 4pm-12.30am; Fri. & Sat. 4pm-1.30am. Branches: (All Glasgow area) Chapati 2, 1576 Dumbarton Rd, 0141 954 3154; Chapati 3, 339 Dumbarton Rd, Partick, 0141 337 1059; Chapati 4, 20 Byres Rd, 0141 334 4089; Chapati 5, 354 Paisley Rd W, 0141 427 6925; Chapati 6, 468 Dumbarton Rd, Dalmuir, 0141 952 9210; Chapati 7, 182 Paisley Rd W , Renfrew, 0141 885 2313; Chapati 8, 5 Lennox Dr, Faifley, 01389 879914; Chapati 9, 3 Greenock Rd, Bishopton, 01505 862 222; Chapati 10 39 Main St, Busby, 0141 644 1971; Sajjan, 2372 Dumbarton Rd, Yoker, 0141 951 1839. Neelim, 1590 Dumbarton Road, Glasgow, 0141 959 6265.

CHARGHA'S FOOD CLUB NEW ENTRANT ©

2-4, Glebe Street, Townhead, Central Glasgow 0141 886 5161

Established in 1996. Specials include: Tikka Masala, Chicken or Lamb Bohana and Korma. Price check: Papadam 50p, CTM £5.20, Pullao Rice £1.30, Peshwari Nan £1.95. Hours: 3.45pm-12am; Sat. 3pm-1am.

LA CREME DE LA CREME NEW TO OUR TOP 100

1071 Argyle Street, Finnieston, Central Glasgow 0141 221 3222

Café India's boss, Abdul Sattar (see above) bought La Creme from Bubther Purewal for £22m in the spring of 2000. Along from Central Station, it's another giant – 400 seats, this time in a former cinema aiming up-market, former stalls and dress circle in use. No expense has been spared, creating a style reminiscent, in parts, of London's Bombay Brasserie. 'Food good, service poor.' BG. 'Service superb. Prices dear, but portions large.' DMCK. 'Tried the buffet, my first experience of this type of spice inhalation. All reasonable.' CW. Weekday lunch prices 20% off until 3pm. Balcony evening e-a-m-a-y-l buffet served 6-10pm, £8.95 weekdays, £11.95 weekends. Hours: 12pm-12am. At your request, it goes into our TOP 100. Stocks Cobra.

KAMA SUTRA NEW ENTRANT

331 Sauchiehall Street, Central Glasgow 0141 332 0055

A relatively new acquisition by Charan Gill's Harlequin Group (see Ashoka above). As the Ghandi, this restaurant was an entrant in our 1992 *Guide*. Gill has created a really stylish venue. The smoked full-height glass windows allow you to look inside. The doorway's sleek curves look like they're carved from stone, its double copper doors inviting you inside. There you find the ultra modern, right down to the basement bar. Of course, Crafty Charan chose the name to get maximum effect. ME on her travels 'wondered whether the food would be an aphrodisiac, but who cared, I was tired, hungry, ready for anything, and it was good – and they cared for me, a single female diner, in a full house, as if I were their boss.' Stocks Cobra.

KOH I NOOR TOP 100 e-a-m-a-y-l

235 North St, Charing Cross, Central Glasgow 0141 204 1444

Glasgow's earliest Indo-Pak opened in 1961, and boasts to be the originator of the famous e-a-m-a-y-l buffet nights (Mon.-Fri. 7-9pm). Authentic Indian and Pakistani design with authentic Asian decor, with hanging rugs, arches etc. 'Fabulous decor.' DBAC. Northern Indian formula curries. Its 150 seating is now small in comparison with other Glasgow venues, but is still big considering the national average of 50, and it's still very busy. 'Not only was the service friendly and helpful but the food arrived very promptly, considering the number of people there. The Chicken Dansak was excellent and the naan breads terrific (and large for the price).' RA. 'Excellent. Samosas so filling, had to leave most of my main course!' SF. 'Starters very impressive, quantities large. Garlic Nan not for the faint-hearted: beautiful. Chicken

Tikka Chasini and Chicken Nentara memorable.' HB. 'Absolutely superb. In a class of its own.' BS. Price check: Papadam 85p, CTM £9.25, Pullao Rice £1.95, Peshwari Nan £2.75, Lager £2.40 pint. Hours: 12pm-12am. (Fri. & Sat. to 1am). Stocks Cobra.

MODERN INDIA NEW ENTRANT

51 West Regent St, Charing Cross,
Central Glasgow 0141 331 1980

One of Archie Sharrif's Peppermint Group, right there in the middle of Glasgow's shopping drags. Drag of course, is the wrong word these days. It's investment like this which has lifted Glasgow, and Glasgow's curry scene to new economic heights. It's 'deliciously smart, with polished wood floors, white plaster pillars, and a neo-classic look to it. Prices are average, but the lunchtime 50% discount makes it really good value. However, we do take issue with Archie's cheeky publicity which claims that Modern India has three stars in the *Good Curry Guide*. Strange that, since this is the first time Modern India has appeared in this *Guide*, and we don't use a star-rating system. To stay in the *Guide*, Archie, we need reports, please, from you about this, and all your branches, and reports from you, the diners too please. See also India Gate, Dunblane, Indian Cottage, Kirkintilloch, Glasgow and Café India, Paisley.

MISTER SINGH'S INDIA NEW TO OUR TOP 100

149 Elderslie Street, Central Glasgow 0141 204 0186

Satty Singh owns this restaurant, as its eponymous title suggests, and like other Glasgow restaurants, as part of Charan Gill's Harlequin Group, it benefits from group marketing and purchasing muscle. At this 90-seater, decor combines ethnic and traditional Scottish. Manager Jamil Ahmed, and the waiters wear kilts and the girls wear salwars; Younis Ahraf (who wears chef's whites, by the way) does curried Haggis! And we hear that there's a French influence at work in the kitchens too. 'Without question the best I have visited! Vast menu. Fantastic food, good portions. Booking essential, even mid-week. Brandy-drinkers beware. They have a 200-year-bottle of Napoleon's brandy at £35 a shot!' GD. 'For me, it is a 'must' when I am travelling to Glasgow! The food is so good and tasty, particularly the Chilli Garlic Chicken.' RA. Price check: Papadam 60p, CTM £8.95, Pullao Rice £1.85. Takeaway: 10% off. Hours: 12-3pm/5-11.30pm; Sun. 2.30-11.30pm. Stocks Cobra.

MURPHY'S PAKORA BAR NEW TO OUR TOP 100 ©

1287 Argyle Street, Central Glasgow 0141 334 1550

Like Mr Singh's above, now part of Charan Gill's Harlequin Group, it still retains its owner Teresa Doherty, herself, with as much of an eye to sound bites as Charan. That's fortunate for us 'cos we can run the old gags one more time: Doherty says 'We Scots are a fiery race!' [We Scots? Doherty? Murphy? Sounds like a bit of the blarney to me!] 'It was love at first bite! As we sank our baby teeth into our first chunk of pakora, there were loud karahis of more mum!' [groan] 'The word Pakora, to a Scot, slips off the tongue as easily as haggis, neeps and tatties. It's one of those snacks that can be eaten at any time of day or night ... one bite is never enough.' At Murphy's the chef's a Scot (R McGregor) which is why there's Haggis Pakora. 'Beam me up, Scotty.' CW. And there are 30 others including Chilli. 'Handkerchiefs supplied, but be warned, you'll be dumb struck ... or is that struck dumb?' [Oh ha! ha! But what happened to the fiery race?] Or there are Pizzas – traditional or with an Indian twist. Of course, it is a licensed bar, selling, well Murphy's of course! Price check Pakoras from £3.15. Takeway: 10% off. Hours: 12pm-12am (1am on Fri. & Sat.). Stocks Cobra.

NEELIM ©

1590 Dumbarton Road, Scotstoun, Glasgow, W 0141 959 6265

Iqbal Gill is a well-known Glaswegian curry restaurateur. Well, to be exact, he also owns, with partners, all those 'Chapati' takeaways (see above) plus one called Sajjan and one restaurant. Harachan Singh manages this 60-seater and of chef Deepa Gill's north Indian curries, the most ordered dish is Chicken Jullander, the staff's favourite, with Punjabi spices, £7.50. Price check 60p, CTM £6.95. Pullao Rice: £1.45. Service 5%.Takeaway: 10% off. Free delivery. Hours: 5pm-12am.

SHALIMAR NEW ENTRANT ©

23/25 Gibson Street, Central Glasgow 0141 339 6453

Rahmat Ali's 96-seater, opened in 1971. ('Time it was in the *Guide.*' AN). Quite right! Specialises in Pakistani dishes. Nightly buffet. Price check: Papadam 50p, CTM £7.25, Pullao Rice £1.80. Takeaway: 20% off. Delivery: £1. Hours: 12-2pm/5pm-12am; Sat. 12pm-12am; Sun. 5pm-12am.

SHISH MAHAL TOP 100 BYO ©

66-68 Park Road, Central Glasgow 0141 334 7899

Glasgow's second oldest opened in 1964 in Gibson Street as a family business with five tables. Following its move in 1994, today it is a 95-seater in two dining rooms currently under the direction of brothers Ali Aslam and Nasim Ahmed. The real Shish Mahal is Lahore's 300-year-old palace of mirrors, built to enthral the Mohul emperors. It was once Glasgow's finest, but took a dive when all the smart young places started opening. But, following its move, it has regained its reputation for very good Pakistani/Punjabi food served well. Last time we asked you should we reinstate it to our TOP 100? And a lot of you said we should, e.g. JL's compelling request: 'I urge you to reinstate Glasgow's Shish Mahal to your TOP 100. I have eaten curry there more than anywhere else – literally hundreds of times – and have been disappointed on only a couple of occasions.' Price check: Papadam 75p, CTM £7.95, Pullao Rice £1.50. Takeaway: 10% discount if under £20 order, 20% discount if over £20 order. You may BYO, corkage £2. Hours: 12-2pm/5pm-12am. Stocks Cobra.

SPICE OF LIFE NEW ENTRANT

1293 Argyle Street, Central Glasgow 0141 334 0678

One of Charan Gill's Harlequin Group. See Ashokas, above. Stocks Cobra.

Hamilton

MANZIL TAKEAWAY ©

5, Shopping Centre, Hill House Road, Hamilton 01697 457111

This Pakistani takeaway was taken over in 1999 by A Wahis and is hygenically decorated with white tiled walls with stainless steel. Most ordered dish: Chicken Tikka Jaipuree. Delivery: £1 charge. Price check: Papadam 50p, CTM £6.75, Pullao Rice £1.30. Hours: 4pm-12am.

Irvine

GULAB ©

2 Stanecastle Road, Irvine 01294 279141

Tandoori restaurant. Seats 100 with 30 car parking spaces. Loyalty takeaway: 10% discount, min order £10. Hours: Mon.-Thurs. 12pm-1.30pm/4.30pm-12.30am; Fri. 4.30pm-12.30am; Sat. 12pm- 1.30am; Sun. 4.30pm-1am.

Johnstone

ASHOKA

3 Rankine Street, Johnstone 01505 322430

'The day has started for me in Plymouth and was running ever later, and it was clear I wouldn't get to Glasgow till very late. When the last Heathrow shuttle was delayed, I was glad I'd decided to cancel my expensive hotel booking in Glasgow centre, instead taking a punt at the nearest cheap-and-cheerful hotel to Renfrew airport, which turned out to be a Travel Inn. Told the car hire manager I was gasping for a fix, and he recommended the Ashoka. Will do that again.' ME. Same menu as at the Glasgow branches. Set meals are good value for money. Branches: Ashoka Ashton Lane, Glasgow; Ashoka West End, Glasgow. Stocks Cobra.

SHIMLA PINKS

4 William Street, off Houston Square, Johnstone 01505 322697

Modern restaurant. Polished floors, tubular stainless steel chairs arranged round black tables. Branches: East Indian Company and Varsity Blues, Stirling, Central; Killermont Polo Club, Glasgow; Shimla Pinks, Birmingham B15, West Midlands. Reports please. Stocks Cobra.

Kirkintilloch

INDIAN COTTAGE NEW ENTRANT

10 Kilsyth Road, Kirkintilloch 0141 777 8884

A few miles NW of Glasgow this attractive restaurant is one of Archie Sharrif's Peppermint Group. The room's vaulted roof and arched windows are attired in cream and pastel pink with matching chairs and split level dining to catch the eye. The food 'equally attractive' AN. See also India Gate Dunblane, Modern India, Regent Street, Glasgow, and Café India, Paisley. Stocks Cobra.

Largs

KOH I NOOR ©

84 Gallowgate Street, Largs 01475 686051

Established in 1989, this 52-seater is situated on the shorefront and has a good view. Managed by Sukhdeep Johal, but he tells us 'everyone knows me as Sunny.' 'Varied menu, good-sized quantities, quality of meal very good.' ww. Price check: Papadam 50p, CTM £7.25, Pullao Rice £1.35, Peshwari Nan £2.25, Lager £2.30 pint. Delivery: Local, £1.80 if order under £10, otherwise free. Hours: 5-11.30pm; Fri. & Sat. 2pm-12.45am; Sun. 2-11.30pm.

Paisley

CAFE INDIA NEW ENTRANT

8 New Street, Paisley 0141 887 6877

Archie Sharrif, owner of the Peppermint Group of restaurants, always achieves a sophistication and tranquillity in his decor that the multi-coloured minimalist modernist should learn from. This Café India (it's a popular name round this area) is up to the standard of all of Archie's others. Reports please. See also India Gate, Dunblane, Modern India, Regent Street, Glasgow, and Indian Cottage, Kirkintilloch.

SHEZAN ©

82 Glasgow Road, Paisley 0141 887 2861

Established by Manjit Singh in 1987. Open plan with 45 seats. Privilege card entitles customer to 25% discount. Takeaway: 20-30% off (depending on times). Delivery 90p charge. Hours: 12pm-12am; Sun. 5pm-12am. Stocks Cobra.

Prestwick

TAJ ©

141 Main Street, Prestwick 01292 477318

Rabinder Singh's Taj seats 136 diners. Specials: Chicken Jira, Chicken Manana, Chicken Noorpuri. Delivery: free, £9 minimum. Hours: 12-2pm/5-12.15am; Fri. & Sat. 12pm-1.15am; Sun. 4.30pm-12.15am.

Renfrew

CHAPATTI 7 TAKEAWAY

182 Paisley Road, West Renfrew 0141 885 2313

See Glasgow Chapatti I for details.

TAYSIDE

(inc. Angus, Kinross and Perthshire)

Area: East Scotland
Population: 394,000
Adjacent Counties: Central, Fife, Grampian, Highland, Strathclyde

Broughty Ferry

GULISTAN HOUSE ©

Queen Street Halls, Broughty Ferry 01382 738844

'Impressive decor. Some meals excellent. Tandoori dishes are normally very good.' FC. Owner is MA Mohammed. Hours: 5pm-12am.

Perth

MANZIL ©

13 York Place, Perth 01738 446222

Rana Ali's 85-seat curry house. The most popular dish: South Indian Garlic Chilli. Takeaway: 10% discount. Delivery: free local. Hours: 12-2pm/5-11.30pm. Branch: Tandoori Knights, Princess Street, Perth (takeaway only).

SHALIMAR

56 Atholl Street, Perth 01738 634204

The Shalimar first opened way back in 1983. Its current owner, Bal Krishan, took over the restaurant in 1996. 'The best I have found in years!' NC.

TANDOORI NIGHTS NEW ENTRANT ©

12, Princes Street, Perth 01738 441277

Established in 1998. Seats 38. Indian Specialities: Chicken Nashedar £5.45 – barbecued chicken or lamb in a spiced cream based sauce with cashew nuts and flavoured with brandy. Lamb Tikka Achari £5.45 – strong, spicy dish, slightly sour, cooked with tangy pickle, fresh green chillies, lemon and fresh coriander. Menu also has Turkish kebabs, Italian Pizzas and European Dishes. Price check: Papadam 50p, CTM £6.50, Pullao Rice £1.50, Takeaway: 10% discount. Delivery: free in Perth. Hours: 5pm-12am. (Sat. to 1am).

©	Curry Club Discount	U	Unlicensed
V	Vegetarian	ANP	Alcohol not permitted
e-a-m-a-y-l	Eat as much as you like	BYO	Bring your own alcohol

CURRY CLUB

WALES

As with England, the Guide runs alphabetically in county and town order. In 1997 a large number of Unitary Authorities replaced the six Welsh counties (regions) which had themselves replaced the age-old shires and smaller counties in 1965. To provide a convenient geographical division of Wales in this Guide, we retain the six former counties (listing their shires within them). With a population of under 3 million (nearly matched by Greater Manchester alone) and only 270 curry restaurants in the whole of Wales (there are more in London SW), we cannot say Cymru is big on the nation's favourite food. And we would very much welcome a plethora of Welsh reports for next time.

CLWYD

(Inc. Denbighshire, Flintshire and Wrexham)

Area: North Wales
Population: 421,000
Adjacent Counties: Cheshire, Gwynedd, Powys, Shrops

Colwyn Bay

BENGAL PALACE ©

The Clock House, 55-57 Abergele Rd, Colwyn Bay 01492 531683

Manager AM Khan's large, air-conditioned restaurant is spread over two rooms, seating 85 in one and 40 in the other. Reliable curries, we're informed. Hours: 12-2.30pm/6-11.15pm.

Deeside

BENGAL DYNASTY TOP 100 ©

106 Chester Road East, Shotton, Deeside 01244 830455

Opened in 1991 by Mohammed Monchab Ali, with Rico managing, seats 92 with an additional lounge area for 40, in air-conditioned, purpose-built, airy and elegant, luxurious surroundings. Chef Foyzur Rahman's north Indian and Bangladeshi specials include Kashir Rezala, £7.95, Chicken Bondhuk,

£8.95, Satkora Gosth, £8.55, Bengal Fish Curry, £7.95. 'Truly exceptional place. The food was just the business. This restaurant is well worthy of its Best in North Wales rating.' MW. 'Immense size of restaurant – huge. Politely greeted and guided to bar. Can see why this restaurant features so highly in the Guide.' MW. 'Outstanding.' WAJ. The Dynasty's Bangladeshi food festival in May was raved over by locals, as were the cookery demos from three of the industry's greatest chefs (Manzoor Ali from London's Tabaq, Mohammed Ali from Yorkshire's Agra, and Monchab himself) and the superb menus. Price check: Papadam 60p, CTM £6.95, Pullao Rice £1.95, House wine £6.50, Peshwari Nan £2.75, Lager £2.40. Takeaway: 15% discount. Delivery: £10 minimum, 5-mile radius. Hours: 12-2.30pm/5.30-11.30pm; Sun. 12.30-11pm. Branch: Bengal Dynasty, Llandudno, Gwynedd. Stocks Cobra.

PLAZA AMANTOLA ©

Welsh Road, Sealand, Deeside 01244 811383

Formerly Amantola International, Foysol Miah's Plaza, managed by Habibur Rahman, seats a vast 205. Chef Gous Ali's specials include the cutely-named Indian Summer (hot chicken), Jewel in the Crown (variety of spices), Himalayan Delight (very mild), Asian Love (tender pieces of lamb), and Bollywood Chicken (creamy with Keema), all £7.95. 'Nothing impressive from the outside. Huge inside, large lounge bar. Service was very helpful throughout. Huge menu, including Chinese selections. Excellent, enjoyable, good value.' JG. Price check: Papadam 60p, CTM £6.95, Pullao Rice £1.75, House wine £8.95. Takeaway: 25% off. Delivery: 5-mile radius, minimum charge £15. Hours: 12-2pm/5.30pm-12.30am. Stocks Cobra.

Hope

COUNTRY SPICE NEW ENTRANT

Asha House, Hawarden Road, Hope 01978 762330

Established in 1999. Seats 72. A high ceiling with oak beams which have been draped with swaithes of patterned fabric. Brasslights and fans also decorate the ceiling. Pink tableclothes and upholstered chairs. Chefs have cooked an Onion Bhajia weighing over 10 kilos and measuring 58cm across, also a Nan Bread measuring 77cm by 49cm – now that's a family Nan and a half. Price check: Papadam 60p, CTM £6.60, Pullao Rice £1.70, Peshwari Nan £1.85, Lager £2.20 pint. Takeaway: 15% discount. Hours: 5.30-11.30pm; Sun. 1-11.30pm (buffet). Stocks Cobra.

Llangollen

SIMLA

4-5 Victoria Square, Llangollen 01978 860610

Shofique Uddin has owned this 50-seater since 1982. 'Staff were smart, smiling and attentive. Tandoori Chicken Biryani, with egg-white laced over the presentation, plus Vegetable Bhoona, Tarka Dal, Chicken Tikka, Nan bread and chilli chutney. Superb evening.' DMD. Hours: 12-2pm/6pm-12am.

St Asaph

BENGAL VILLAGE TAKEAWAY NEW ENTRANT

Old Bank Building, High Street, St Asaph 01745 582323

This takeaway was established in 1996 by manager Abdul Noor. CTM and Korma are the most popular dishes. Price check: Papadam 50p, CTM £6.95 (inc. rice), Pullao Rice £1.50, Peshwari Nan £1.50. Hours: 4.30-11.30pm.

Wrexham

KHAZANA NEW ENTRANT

A4-83 Ruabon By-Pass, Wrexham 01978 822220

New restaurant recommended by Biren. Reports please. Stocks Cobra.

DYFED

(Inc. Cardigan, Carmarthenshire and Pembrokeshire)

Area: West Wales
Population: 356,000
Adjacent Counties: Glam, Powys, Gwynedd

Aberystwyth

ROYAL PIER TANDOORI

The Pier, Marine Terrace, Aberystwyth 01970 624888

'Something of a novelty, situated on the end of the pier. Mixed Tikka prepared at my request without the usual salad, cheerfully served.' JL.

Cardigan

ROSE OF INDIA NEW ENTRANT

30 Priory Street, Cardigan 01239 614891

'Decor pleasant, seating could have been a bit more comfortable. Service was efficient. Prawn Bhuna starter was good, Sheekh Kebab adequate, Prawn Rogan was tasty, but Chicken Tikka Jalfrezi could have done with more chillies in it. Overall we enjoyed our meal.' T&CV.

Carmarthen

TAJ BALTI ©

119 Priory Street, Carmarthen 01267 221995

Opened in 1995 by Lias Miah. 'My husband and I always enjoy their fare. Elegant decor, service excellent and friendly, with superb food. Muted traditional music, intimacy of individual booths, a special atmosphere. Tandoori Mixed Grill declared the best ever.' JF. Sun. e-a-m-a-y-l buffet. Hours: 6pm-12am.

Llandeilo

THE RED FORT ©

64 Rhosmaen Street, Llandeilo 01558 824224

Est. in 1998 by Bashir Miah. Newly furnished. Seats 38. Most popular dishes: Chicken Kurme, Bolti Tikka Mosolle, Murg Nobab.. Sun. buffet 20% for CC. Takeaway: 20% off. Hours: 5.30pm-12.30am; Sun. 3pm-12am.

Llanelli

BENGAL LANCER ©

43 Murray Street, Llanelli 01554 749199

78-seater fully licensed restaurant opened by Ahmed Ali in 1986. Muzaffar heads the cooking brigade. It's a very popular venue serving Bangladeshi and North Indian Tandooris, Curries and Accompaniments. Recently refurbished. Minimum charge £12.50. Takeaway: 10% off. Hours: 12-2.30pm/6pm-12am. Branch: Anarkali, Swansea. Stocks Cobra.

VERANDAH NEW ENTRANT ©

20 Market Street, Llanelli 01554 759561

Opened in 1985 by Mr A Khalique. Restaurant seats 64 diners and is about to be refurbished (by the time this *Guide* is out the new decor will be in place). The restaurant is to be brightly decorated with turmeric walls, indigo carpet and shelving with chilli-red and orange chairs and sofas. Specials: Charga Mossalla £4.75 (half spring-chicken, marinated, tomatoes, green peppers, red wine). Price check: Papadam 45p, CTM £4.75, Pullao Rice £1.50, Peshwari Nan £1.45. Hours: 6pm-12am (Sat. to 12.30am).

GLAMORGAN

Inc. the former West, Mid and South Glamorganshire

Area: South Wales
Population: 1,346,000
Adjacent Counties: Dyfed, Gwent, Powys

Note, in 1997, the counties of West, Mid and South Glamorganshire were disbanded in favour of 11 Unitary Authorities to administrate the 11 large towns (inc. Newport) in the area. For Guide convenience we have retained the former Glamorgan geography. For Newport see Gwent.

Aberkenfig

SIMLA TANDOORI NEW ENTRANT

83 Bridgend Road, Aberkenfig, Bridgend

'I have not visited this curry house but one of my fellow fire fighters has recently moved to this area and he raves about this one. Apparently the decor is quite good and has a nice informal feel to it. Seating comfortable and service good. Food described as delicious and excellent. My friend phoned the restaurant and asked if he could have flowers delivered and brought to the table for his girlfriend as this was a special occasion (his engagement, so this place must be good). He tells me that the staff could not have been more helpful and delivered the flowers to the table with style.' RE.

Barry

BARRY BALTI ©

10 Broad Street Parade, Barry 01446 7221717

Balti takeaway established in 1996 by Abdul Khan. Comments card for customer to complete in their own time and return to the restaurant. The comments we receive are favourable. Hours: 5.30apm-1am; Sat. 5.30pm-2am.

MODERN TANDOORI TAKEAWAY ©

290 Holton Road, Barry 01446 746787

First opened in 1982, taken over by A Akbar and re-opened in 1993. Try the Staff Special – three courses at £15.95 for two. Specialises in parties and Asian wedding catering. Hours: 5.30pm-12.30am; Sat. 5.30pm-1.30am. Branch: The Balti House Tandoori, 14 Crwys Road, Cathays, Cardiff.

Bridgend

THE RAJ BALTI HOUSE ©

59-61 Nolton Street, Bridgend 01656 647229

Northern Indian/Bangladeshi curries at S Rahman's 48-seater. Takeaway: 10% discount. Delivery: 3-mile radius, £15 min. Hours: 6pm-1am. Branch: The Rose Balti House, Station Road, Port Talbot. Stocks Cobra.

Cardiff

BALTI EMPIRE NEW ENTRANT

157 Albany Road, Cardiff 029 2049 1554

'Small but comfortable. Portions good and service friendly. Banquet Sunday lunch at £6.95.' JB.

BENGAL GARDEN NEW ENTRANT ©

186, Whitchurch Road, Heath, Cardiff 029 2062 1587

Established in 1972 by Faisal Ali. Restaurant decorated in cream and burgundy, plain though tidy, seats 42. CTM is their most popular dish. Delivery: £1. Price check: Papadam 40p, CTM £4.70, Pullao Rice £1.60, Peshwari Nan £1.60, Lager £1.70 pint, House wine £7.95. Hours: 7pm-12am. Stocks Cobra.

©	Curry Club Discount	U	Unlicensed
V	Vegetarian	ANP	Alcohol not permitted
e-a-m-a-y-l	Eat as much as you like	BYO	Bring your own alcohol

JUBORAJ 2 TOP 100

10 Mill Lane, The Hayes, Cardiff 029 2037 7668

'Fairly large, comfortable restaurant, good reputation, very popular. Visited by Tom Jones [wow!] CTM fine and the Chicken Biriani tasty. Rice wasn't coloured – I like that.' HS. 'A very good extensive menu, large portions, very good service, luxury surroundings. A bit on the expensive side, but well worth it.' PAH. 'Probably the only Indian restaurant in Cardiff City Centre and in my opinion, one of Cardiff's best. Another visit, and the food once again was excellent.' JB. Price check: Papadam 60p, CTM £7.35, Bombay Potato £2.95, Pullao Rice £1.95. Hours: 12-2pm/6pm-12am. Branch: Juboraj, 11 Heol-y-Deri, Rhiwbina, Glamorgan and Juboraj, Lakeside, Lake Road West, Cardiff. Remains in our TOP 100.

PREMIER INDIAN TAKEAWAY NEW ENTRANT ©

146 North Road, Cardiff 029 2061 9911

Established in 1999 by owner/manager Mohammed Al Hafiz. Restaurant cleanly decorated with floor-to-ceiling white tiles and red trim. Specials: Noka Chana £2.40 – spiced chickpeas with green peppers, medium. Goan Fish Biryani £6.99 – fresh fish, seafood, onions, peppers, served with salad. Delivery: £10 minimum, 5-mile radius. Price check: Papadam 35p, CTM £4.95, Pullao Rice £1.50, Peshwari Nan £1.50. Hours: 5.30-11pm.

STAR OF WALES ©

438 Cowbridge Road East, Canton, Cardiff 029 2038 3222

This 60-seater first opened way back in the 1960s. Managed by Diloar, its present owner, since 1987, is Kadir Miah who is also the chef. His specials include Jaipuri Chi, Murgi Mossalla, Lamb Bahar, and Anarkali Bahar. 'Nice polite staff. Good average portions. Keema Nan especially delicious.' HS. Takeaway: 15% off. Hours: 12-2.30pm/6pm-1am.

Merthyr Tydfil

NEW BALTI PALACE ©

1 Morlais Building, High Street, Merthyr Tydfil 01685 388344

Owned by Abdul Karim. Good prices all round. Free Papadams and Mint Sauce with takeaway orders over £7. Delivery. Hours: 12-2.30pm/6pm-1am.

Swansea

ANARKALI

80 St Helen's Road, Swansea 01792 650549

Fully licensed and air-conditioned 60-seater established by A Rahman way back in 1978. It serves Banglasheshi Cuisine, Baltis, Tandooris, Curries and side dishes, in other words, the nation's favourites. From the comments we receive, it's popular. Such long-standing gives it an assurance, experience and confidence with a long list of regulars. Hours: 12-2.30pm/6pm-12am.

BENGAL BRASSERIE NEW ENTRANT

47 Walter Road, Uplands, Swansea 01792 643747

'Great restaurant. Service was attentive and no short cuts were apparent in food preparation. Starter was an appealing combination of keema and rice wrapped in cabbage leaves. Main course was a beautifully balanced combination of spices that left a real zing in the mouth, particularly the ginger pieces on top. Naan was a little small.' RW.

BONOPHOL BANGLADESHI NEW TO OUR TOP 100 ©

93 Sterry Road, Gowerton, Swansea 01792 875253

Owned by Mohammed Al Imran since 1990, and managed by Moin Uddin, its name change from Gowerton Tandoori in 1996 to Bonophol gives it a unique and pretty name, meaning 'forest flower'. The exterior is elegantly picked out in attractive tones of green and gilt, and this theme continues inside, with contrasting burgundy seats. For those who like to know these things, the logo on the menu is a map of Bangladesh, in the national flag colours. What you get at this 40-seater fully licensed restaurant is 'fine Bangladeshi Cuisine, with all my favourites, done conscientiously and very well.' EG. 'Managed by a well-known pleasant and cheerful person known to all as Abdul – he has been around for years. Quality of food is very good, service also good. e-a-m-a-y-l for a fiver every day.' CMJ. Takes part in regular Bangladeshi food festivals with other Swansea restaurants. Special: Lobster, prawns, crabs etc. Buna in Bangladeshi style; vegetable thali for two £13.90. Starter for CC discount. Price check: Papadam 40p, CTM £5.90, Pullao Rice £1.40, Peshwari Nan £1.90, Lager £1.80 pint, House wine: £5.90. Takeaway: 10% discount. Delivery: £10 minimum, 4-mile radius. Hours: 5.30pm-11.55pm (Fri & Sat. to 1230am); Sun. 12pm-12am. Stocks Cobra.

LAL QUILA

480 Mumbles Road, Mumbles, Swansea 01792 363520

Formerly Ocean View. 'Completely refurbished, now has very attractive decor, waiters wear smart uniforms. Probably Swansea's most upmarket restaurant. Everything is spotless with quick and friendly service. I particularly like the Chicken Methi with lots of fresh fenugreek. Food generally good.' JD. Reports please.

MOGHUL BRASSERIE TOP 100

81 St Helen's Road, Swansea 01792 475131

58-seater, opened in 1989 by Shazan Uddin, who is also the chef, managed by Ashik Rahman. Bangladeshi and Balti cuisine. Special: Lamb/Chicken Kochi £6. Sunday e-a-m-a-y-l buffet £7 for adults, £4 for children, from the selection of lamb, chicken, prawn and tandoori delicacies and three different vegetable dishes plus bread and rice. 'Have been regulars for several years. Consistency is the key word for Mr Uddin. Efficient service in very pleasant surroundings. Excellent Chicken Tikka Karahi, Sali Boti and my favourite Pathia (prawn and chicken). Mr Uddin recently exhibited a wonderful Cockle Masala, at a Culinary Festival. Superb!' A&AP. 'We have never come across anywhere that comes even close to the wonderful cuisine served at the Moghul.' E&ME. Set menu – six choices ranging in price from £14-22. Takeaway: 10% off. Remains in our TOP 100. Hours: 12-2.30pm/5pm-12am (2am on Fri. & Sat.). Stocks Cobra.

NAWAB NEW ENTRANT

12, Christina Street, Swansea 01792 470770

Established in 1975. Seats 60. Chef's Tandoori Dinner: Sheek Kebab, Tandoori Chicken, Mutton and Chicken Tikka with Special Rice, Nan, Salad and a bowl of Masalla sauce – £16 for two, £30 for four. Price check: Papadam 50p, CTM £4.50, Pullao Rice £1.80, Peshwari Nan £2.10, Lager £1.95 pint. Takeaway: 10-20% discount. Delivery: £10 minimum, 2-mile radius. Hours: 5.30pm-1am (Sat. to 3am); Sun. 6pm-1am.

GWENT
(Monmouthshire)

Area: Southwest Wales
Population: 454,000
Adjacent Counties: Glamorgan, Gloucestershire, Herefordshire and Powys

In the 1997 reorganisation, Monmouthshire has been partly restored, and though Newport is now an independent Unitary Authority, we retain it here.

Abergavenny

THE RED ROSE

35 Frogmore Street, Abergavenny — 01873 854790

Specialising in Handi and Bengali cuisine. Change of ownership has been smooth enough to retain the Rose in the *Guide.* 'Curry very good, similar to last management. Good quantity of chicken, nice thick sauce. Excellent Pullao Rice. Good service, friendly waiters. Quiet and pleasant atmosphere.' PAH. 'Handi with good portions of chicken and vegetables in thick sauce, pullao rice well cooked with topping of crisp onions. £28.90 for 2.' PH.

SUNDARBON BENGAL CUISINE

7 Monk Street, Abergavenny — 01873 855785

'By far and away the best. Serving formula curries, standard of presentation much higher than the others. Very crisp and clean table linen, overall impression of a well-to-do establishment.' JL. 'Good quality and quantity in all dishes. Madras was excellent, Vegetable Rice a little oily but good taste.' and 'I have visited this restaurant many times this year. The quality of the food, service and welcome has always been first class, with the owner giving a personal service, being helpful and friendly.' PAH.

Bedwas

INDIAN COTTAGE ©

Bridge Cottage, The Square, Bedwas — 029 2086 0369

The foundations of Mohammed Riaz's cosy 28-seater were laid around the time that Queen Elizabeth I came to the throne. There is an interesting and detailed history of the building on the back of the menu. The cottage now dispenses 'very good, tasty' GR, Pakistani food. Delivery charges: Bedwas and Trethomas 80p; Llanbradach, Caerphilly, Machen £1.20. Hours: 6-11pm (12am on Fri. & Sat.).

Cwmbran

KHAN TANDOORI TAKEAWAY ©

6 Commercial Street, Pontnewydd, Cwmbran 01633 867141

Siraj Khan started his takeaway in 1984. Eleven types of bread are listed under the heading of 'good companions'. Delivery local area. Hours: 5.30pm-12.30am (1am on Fri. & Sat.).

MAHARAJA BALTI

6 General Rees Square, Cwmbran 01633 483627

76-seater owned by Mohammed Omar Sheik since 1992. Serves Pakistani and Balti curries. Delivery: £8, 6-mile radius, ordered by 12am. Hours: 12-2.30pm/6pm-1.30am (2.30am on Fri. & Sat.). Stocks Cobra.

Monmouth

MISBAH TANDOORI NEW TO OUR TOP 100

9 Priory Street, Monmouth 01600 714940

D Miah opened his 32-seater restaurant in 1990. This cosy, comfortable venue exudes customer care, but being so small, booking is advisable. Mr Miah's Misbah attracts celebs, and he's delighted to tell you about them (ask him – each one has a tale). Chef A Rahman does a good range of Baltis served with Nan bread ranging from King Prawn Balti at £9.95 to Vegetable Balti at £5.50. Special four-course Sun. lunch £6.95. Special: Bengal Fish Mossala (freshwater fish from Bangladesh cooked in tomato and onion, £7.95). Super stuff. Restaurants like this are what this *Guide* is all about. Welcome to our TOP 100. Price check: Papadam 45p, CTM £6.75, Pullao Rice £1.75, Lager £1.95 pint, House wine £6.95. Takeaway: 10% off. Hours: 12-2pm/6-11pm.

Newport

DILSHAD INTERNATIONAL CUISINE ©

30/34 Clarence Place, Newport 01633 254062

Mozadul Hussain and Moshaid Ali's 80-seater, est. 1989 has been recently refurbished, and has car parking for 20 cars. Chef Sirajul Islam cooks Bangladeshi and Balti curries, Rogon and Persian dishes such as Murug Zallander, Korahi. Takeaway: 10% discount. Delivery: £10, 4-mile radius. Hours: 6pm-1.30am (11.30pm on Fri., 2.30pm on Sat.).

INDIAN COTTAGE TAKEAWAY

18 Malpas Road, Newport 01633 821196

Del Ramzan assures us that his takeaway-only, established in 1985 does dishes 'clearly distinguishable from the others because of their distinctive features'. House special: Chilli Garlic Chicken Massalah. Specials include: Chicken Badam Pasanda. Delivery: £10 min in Newport, £12 min in Cwnbran area. Hours: 5pm-12am; Fri. & Sat. 4.30pm-1am.

THE KOH I NOOR ©

164 Chepstow Road, Maindee, Newport 01633 258028

Mrs L Khanan's venerable 60-seat Koh i Noor was established in 1978, and has appeared in most of our *Guides*. We've said before that nothing on the menu changes. Chef Tahir Ullah's curries are listed under such categories as mild, fruity, fairly hot, very hot, hottest and most favourite. In other words this is one of the early standard curry houses with its clutch of once-a-week regulars. Nothing wrong with that. Price check: Papadam 50p, CTM £5.40, Pullao Rice £1.90. (Well not quite everything on the menu is the same! The price check for 1984 was Papadams 15p, CTM £1.90, Rice 65p). Hours: 12-2.30pm/6pm-1am. Sun. 6pm-12am.

Usk

DIL INDIAN CUISINE NEW ENTRANT

6 Bridge Street, Usk 01291 673372

'Overall meal satisfactory, but rather expensive.' MS.

©	Curry Club Discount	U	Unlicensed
V	Vegetarian	ANP	Alcohol not permitted
e-a-m-a-y-l	Eat as much as you like	BYO	Bring your own alcohol

GWYNEDD

Inc. Anglesey, Caernarvonshire, Conwy and Merioneth

Area: North Wales
Population: 240,000
Adjacent Counties: Clwyd, Dyfed, Powys

Bangor

MAHABHARAT ©

5-7 High Street, Bangor 01248 351337

M Sholayman took over this 1968 curry house in 1990. 'Spacious and comfortable. Service very efficient except for the late arrival of the mint sauce which was supposed to accompany the starter. Portions very generous and food of a high standard.' IM. Free Papadams and dips with every takeaway order. Minimum charge £9. Hours: 12-2pm/6pm-12am.

Caernarfon

GANDHI

11 Palace Street, Caernarfon 01286 676797

'King Prawn Butterfly followed by Lamb Tikka Masala, Pilau Rice and Keema Nan. Bombay Potato, particularly spicy – excellent. A very pleasing meal all round, good portions.' JL. 'If you are ever in North Wales, do pay them a visit. The food is very tasty. An excellent restaurant.' HJ .Hours: 12-2pm, not Sun./5.30-11pm.

Holyhead

RAJA'S BENGAL CUISINE NEW ENTRANT ©

8 Newry Street, Holyhead 01407 760333

First opened in 1982, taken over in 1990 by Shiron Miah. Seats 70. Name change from Omar Khayyam, decorated with brass and chandeliers. Specials include: Raja's Special Balti (cooked in a traditional balti with special balti paste, garlic, ginger, fresh tomatoes, onions, capsicum and fresh coriander) £9.95. Price check: Papadam 60p, CTM £6.95, Pullao Rice £1.95, Peshwari Nan £2.25, Lager £2.20. Takeaway: 15% discount. Hours: 5.30-11pm. Stocks Cobra.

Llandudno

BENGAL DYNASTY TOP 100 ©

1 North Parade, Llandudno 01492 878445

Llandudno is a really fabulous seaside town with gorgeous Georgian buildings running in an arch along the waterfront. Lewis Carroll wrote *Alice in Wonderland* in this seaside resort. Established in 1988, the 86-seat Bengal Dynasty is situated upstairs in one of these fine buildings. 'I was about to settle for fish & chips when I saw it, upstairs above a shoe shop. I had Lamb Tikka to start and then Chicken Bhuna, which was excellent.' AG 'King Prawn Butterfly followed by my usual main courses. A very accomplished meal. Keema Nan was the highlight together with a homemade Kulfi. Gets my vote.' JL. 'Service was welcoming, prompt and polite. Pops and chuts fresh and crisp. Main meals were large, everything was hot and well presented. An enjoyable experience, but not outstanding.' SR. 'Menu was wide and varied. Papadoms and chutneys excellent. Raita exceptional. All meals were served piping hot with hot plates and the portions were satisfying. Waiters were very accommodating in making changes to dishes for our individual tastes. Smart, clean and tasteful surroundings. Highly recommended.' NC. 'An impressive restaurant – the carpet must have cost a fortune, restaurant and stairs with the restaurant name woven in. Comfortable and busy. Service slow. Food – all in all not bad, and should remain listed in the *GCG*.' AN. Specials: Chicken Bondhuk, Lamb Satkora Gost Macher Tarkari. Takeaway: 15% off. Hours: 12-2.30pm (4.30pm on Sun.)/ 6-11.30pm. Branch: Bengal Dynasty, Deeside, Clwyd.

Llangefni

MOONLIGHT ©

40 High Street, Llangefni 01248 722595

First opened in 1985 as the Gandhi, this 42-seater was taken over by owner-manager Emdadur Rahman, in 1991. It offers authentic Bangladeshi and northern Indian dishes using fresh ingredients and spices. Takeaway available until midnight. Takeaway: 10% discount. Hours: 12-2pm/5.30-11.30pm. Stocks Cobra.

Porthmadog

PASSAGE TO INDIA

26 Lombard Street, Porthmadog 01766 512144

Established in 1985. Seats 42. 'Tandoori Sheek Kebab was very spicy and dry and required nearly a pint of lager to get it down! The Chicken Shashlic was very good.' AG. Specials: Butter Chicken – boneless chicken, marinated with butter and grilled in Tandoor. Hours: 6-11pm. Stocks Cobra.

Pwllheli

POLASH BALTI NEW ENTRANT ©

28, Penlan Street, Pwllheli 01758 613884

Previously the Shapla until 1998 when taken over by Abdul Jalil. Seats 70. Specials include: Chingri Jhul King Prawn (cooked in a specially spiced curry sauce flavoured with oriental herbs and spices and served sizzling hot). Takeaway: 10% discount. Hours: 12-2pm; 6-11.30pm. Stocks Cobra.

POWYS

Inc. Brecknock and Montgomery

Area: Central East Wales
Population: 124,000
Adjacent Counties: Clwyd, Dyfed, Glamorgan, Gwent, Gwynedd, Herefordshire, Shropshire

Builth Wells

BALTI HOUSE

11 Market Street, Builth Wells 01982 551131

Owned by Rokib Ali since 1997. 'Pleasantly furnished and the staff most obliging and friendly. Chefs can be viewed from the dining area. Ate there three times while on holiday and each meal was better than the last.' JP. Northern Indian formula curries. Hours: Mon.-Thurs. 5.30pm-12.30am; Fri. & Sat. 12-2pm/5.30pm-12.30am; Sun. 5.30-11.30pm. Stocks Cobra.

Llansantfraid

TANDOORI PLAICE NEW ENTRANT

Waterloo House, Llansantfraid 01691 828152

Established in 1994 by manager Shoakoth Ali. Black ash coffee table with red chairs for waiting customers. Takeaway only. Specials include: Baltis £4.95, Mossalas £4.95, Tandoori dishes from £4.30. Price check: Papadam 30p, CTM £4.95, Pullao Rice £1.30, Peshwari Nan £1.30. Hours: 5-11.30pm (Fri. & Sat. to 12am).

Llanymynech

BENGAL SPICES NEW ENTRANT

Ashfield House, Llanymynech 01691 830170

'Excellent restaurant. The presentation sets it apart from other restaurants in the area. Try the Balti house speciality, or the Korai Keema Aloo, with Bombay Aloo and Keema Naan. Delicious.' NS. Stocks Cobra.

List of Contributors

This *Guide* is possible thanks to the many Curry Club members, and others, who have sent in reports on restaurants. Especial thanks to the following regular, prolific and reliable reporters (apologies for any errors, duplications and omissions).

A: Martin Abbott, Gloucs; Colin Adam, Kilwinning; Ray Adams, Kimberley; Meena Ahamed, London; W Aitken, Stoke-on-Trent; Firs Ali, Richmond; Paul Allan, Boston; Derek Allen, Yorks; Paul Allen, Chatham; Tony and Lesley Allen, Rugby; MF Alsan, Rugby; G Amos, Wirral; Capt R Ancliffe, BFPO 12; Apryl Anderson, Ponteland; W Anderson, Berwick-upon-Tweed; Karen Andras, Nottingham; Tim Andrews, Nottingham; Lisa Appadurai, Benfleet; Rebecca Armitage, W Sussex; Robin Arnott, Stafford; Mrs M Asher, Woodford Green; Dave Ashton, Warrington; Jo Ashton, Elland; Allan Ashworth, York; Berry Ashworth, Compton Bassett; Michelle Aspinal, Chester; Darius Astell, Southampton; Rachael Atkinson, Cheshire; Simon Atkinson, N5; Y Atkinson, IOM; Claire Austin, Stoke; DJ Austin, W13; Arman Aziz, N4; Philip Ayling, email.

B: GB, Lancs; Tom Bailey, Alresford; John Baker, Loughton; Kim Baker, Hatfield; Geoffrey Bamford, Chinnor; Mr & Mrs ML Banks, Enfield; Keith Bardwell, Hertford; Ian Barlex, Ilford; Trevor Barnard, Gravesend; Christopher Barnes, Ashton; Derek Barnett, Colchester; JF Barnett, London; Tony Barrel, Hounslow; Joanne Bastock, Saltash; Mike Bates, Radcliffe; Shirley Bayley, Worthing; Karin and Angela, Rugby; RG Bean, Frimley; Mr MJ Beard, Stafford; Joyce Bearpark, Murcia Spain; Dave Beazer, Cornwall; Mike Bedford, W Yorks; DJ Beer, Ross-on-Wye; Derick Behrens, Bucks; Ian Bell, Cheshire; Ian Bell, Cheshire; Matt Bell, Derbs; P Bell, Carlisle; Sam Bell, Coventry; Guy Belmont; Dudley; Steve Bennedin, Hampton; Mrs Rosemary Bennett, Leamington Spa; TW Bennett, Sherborne; Becky Benson, Worcs; John Bentley, Northampton; Ron Bergin, Gerrards Cross; Ian Berry, Goole; Martyn Berry, SE3; Kenneth Beswick, Lincoln; Ray Bettle, Saudi Arabia; DJ Betts, Bexhill; FW Bibby, London; Jonathan Bick, Cardiff; Brian and Anne Biffin, Fleet; Colin Bird, Welwyn Garden City; Giles Bird, London; BH Birch, Hyde; Jim Birkumshaw, Derbys; James Birtles, Manchester; Allan Black, Northants; Chris Blackmore, Bristol; Claude Blair, OBE, Surrey; Glyn Bolan, Lancashire; David Bolton, Lichfield; Mrs C Bone, Norfolk; Ian Booty, Peterborough; A Boughton, SE27; Dave Boulton, Nottingham; L Le Bouochon, Jersey; Mrs I Bowman, Rochester; Robert Box, Knottingley; Alan Boxall, Burwash; Sean Boxall, Andover; F Boyd, Stranraer; Iain Boyd, Wealdstone; Roderick Braggins, Peebles; Amanda Bramwell, Sheffield; Dave Bridge, Wallasey; Michael E Bridgstock, Northants; Sandra Brighton, Nelson; Judith Brindle, Bingley; Steve Broadfoot, Anfield; Mr & Mrs R

Broadhurst, Teddington; John and Susan Brockington, Sutton Coldfield; Paul Bromley, SE13; Robert Brook, London; Nigel John Brooks, Stoke on Trent; Bob Brown, Sheffield; David Brown, Leeds; Helena Browne, Surrey; IA Brown, Fernhurst; Mark Brown, Ellesmere Port and Scunthorpe; Steve Brown, Twickenham; DA Bryan, York; RC Bryant, Witney; Robert Bruce, Thornaby; Heather Buchanan, Inverness; Dr TM Buckenham, SW11; Dr TJ Buck, Hove; Mr PS Buckley, Wicklow, Ireland; Mrs J Buffey, Sutton Coldfield; LG Burgess, Berkhamsted; A Burton, Weston-super-Mare; Rory Button, Bucks.

C: D Cadby, Swindon; Barry Caldwell, Chesterfield; David Caldwell, Brownhills; Stan Calland, Kingsley; Hugh Callaway, Cleethorpes; Duncan Cameron, Fordoun; Frank Cameron, Dundee; HS Cameron, Wirral; Alex Campbell, Ramsey Campbell, Wallasey; Hartley Wintney; Mrs E Campbell, Harrogate; N Campbell, Edinburgh; Josephine Capps, Romford; David Carney, Helston; Lynn Carr, Surrey; L Carroll, Huddersfield; James Casey, Wiltshire; Peter Cash, Liverpool; Mark Caunter, Guildford; TM Chandler, Farnborough; Desmond Carr, N8; J Carr, Birkenhead; TO Carr, Warrington; BR Carrick, Wakefield; DL Carter, Huntingdon; Mrs M Carter, Colchester; Madeline Castro, Bury St Edmunds; Dr WF Cavenagh, Norfolk; David Chambers, Colchester; M Chambers, Cockermouth; Neil Chantrell, Warrington; Hilary and Danny Chapchal, Leatherhead; John Chapman, Leics; Paul Chapman, Leighton Buzzard; Mr & Mrs Chatfield, Wimborne; Rajender Chatwal, Bicester; Dr GT Cheney, Salhouse; Dave & Liz Cheney, Warks; Lee Chester, London; Paul Chester, Cuffley; Sqn Ldr PF Christopher, Ferndown; Alexis Ciusczak, Capistrano Beach, CA; Michael Clark, Kingston-upon-Thames; Craig Clarkson, Manchester; Patrick Clifford, Cambs; Peter Clyne, SW11; VA Coak, Penzance; Louise Coben-Sutherland, Enfield; CH Coleman, Sussex; Robin Collier, Mid Calder; Billy Collins, Wirral; Chris Coles, Kent; Mrs J Collins, Portsmouth; HF Collison, Shustoke; CJ Comer, Basingstoke; Rhys Compton, Cheltenham; A Conroy, Durham; Joseph Coohil, Oxford; Neil Cook, Royston; Mr LW Coombes, Devon; Alan & Margaret Cooper, Llansteffan; Kim Cooper, Basildon; DW Cope, Whitchurch; Dr JC Coppola, Woodstock; Will Coppola, Oxford; Nigel Cornwell, Orpington; John Costa, Tunbridge Wells; MJ Cotterill, Bristol; Stephen Cowie, SW16; Steve Cowling, Shrops; Mrs Mary Cox, Yorks; Julie Cozens, Oxon; CR Crawford, Fareham; Dr AM Croft, Cornwall; Mr Crofton, Marlborough; Roderick Cromar, Buckie; C Cross, Poole; Yasmin Cross, Huddersfield; Major & Mrs FJB Crosse, Salisbury; Robert Crossley, Huddersfield; Frank and Elizabeth Crozier, Redruth; Don Cuppitt, Cambridge; R Cuthbertson, Southampton.

D: S Daglish, Scarborough; P Dalton, Wirral; Jan Daniel, Felpham; Mr & Mrs PE Dannat, Eastleigh; Martin Daubney, Hitchin; Gary Davey, W4; Alasdair Davidson, Heswall; Adrian Davies, NW3; Gwyn Davies, Wirral; Mrs

JC Davies, Leeds; Josephine Davies, Swansea; Lucy Davies, Essex; Paul Davies, Chiddingfold; Mrs G Davies-Goff, Marlow; Colin Davis, Tatsfield; AK Dawson, Hyde; Ian Dawson, Mirfield; Mike Dawson, Ely; DM Day, Preston; Michael Day, West Bromwich; Peter Deane, Bath; Gary & Katy Debono, High Wycombe; David Dee, Ruislip; Elizabeth Defty, Co. Durham; David Delaney, Leominster; Neil Denham, The Netherlands; R Dent, Bishop Auckland; Les Denton, Barnsley; Richard Develyn, St Leonards; Nigel Deville, Uttoxeter; Ken Dewsbury, Somerset; Richard Diamond, Romsey; RC Dilnot, Broadstairs; Graham Divers, Glasgow; AK Dawson, Hyde; James Dobson, Burscough; S Dolden, Rochester; R Dolley, W11; Clive Doody, Surrey; Keith Dorey, Barnet; Rev Kevan Dorgan, Lancaster; Jane Doswell, Surrey; Neil Downey, Worthing; Sarah Dowsett, Swindon; Anna Driscoll, Cape Province; Mrs J Driscoll, BFPO; Diane Duame, Wicklow; Eric Duhig, Hornchurch; Sheila Dunbar, Pinner; James Duncan, West Kilbride; Mark Dunn, E18; Robin Durant, Brighton; Martin Durrant, Chester; Mr & Mrs JA Dywer, Birmingham.

E: A Edden-Jones, Bristol; Bruce Edwards, Norwich; Dave Edwards, Rugeley; CM Eeley, Witney; Rod Eglin, Whitehaven; Wendy Elkington; David Elliott, Woodborough; Ray Elliott, Worcester; PT Ellis, W'rtn; Mrs G Elston, Woodley; Tony Emmerton, Chorley; Lucy Evans, Liverpool; Mark Evans, Caersws; Mr & Mrs A Evans, Manchester; T Evans, Nr Barry; Brian Exford, Derbys.

F: Gary Fairbrother, Crosby; Barry & Sue Faircloth, Norwich; Hazel Fairley, Guildford; Mrs N Falloon, Warks; D Farrel, Yorkshire; Chris Farrington, Cherry Hinton; WH Farrow, Nantwich; Graham Faulkner, Dorking; John Fearson, Bucks; Denis Feeney, Glasgow; Kevin Fenner, Rothley; Stuart Ferguson, Haywards Heath; Bill and Laraine Field, Newcastle-upon-Lyme; Stephen Field, Norton; Mick Fielden, Glossop; AJ Finch, Enfield Wash; Duncan Finley, Glasgow; Maureen Fisher, Woodford Green; Bernard Fison, Holmrook; John Fitzgerald, Great Missenden; Merly Flashman, TN12; Colin & Toni Fleet, Dorset; Dr Cornel Fleming, N6; KD Flint, Kempsey; Shaun Flook, New Barnet; Fiona Floyd, Truro; Stephen & Elizabeth Foden, Lynton; Chris Fogarty, Enfield; Gareth Foley, Porthcawl; Neil Foley, Essex; IE Folkard-Evans, Manchester; Mrs J Fordham, Basingstoke; SR Tracy Forster, Beds; Rod Fouracres, Glos; Jack & Anna Fowler, London; Rosemary Fowler, Midhurst; John W Fox, Doncaster; Linda Foye, Barry; Theresa Frey, Fareham; Chris Frid, Hexham; Steve Frost, Kingston; Alan Furniss, email; June Fyall, Bronwydd; Mrs MAJ Fyall, Dyfed.

G: Stephen Gaines, Middlesex; MJ Gainsford, Burbage; Leo Gajsler, Geneva; Martin and Linda Gale, Hampshire; Martin Gale, Farnborough; Mrs FE Gaunt, Stonehouse; Phillip Gentry, Bexleyheath; Brian George, Wolverton; CM Gerry, Cyprus; G Gibb, SE21; Prof Robert Giddings, Poole;

Michael Gill, Leeds; Andrew Gillies, Edinburgh; AV Glanville, Windsor; Ms D Glass, Liverpool; Andy Glazier, London; A Glenford, Lincoln; Nick Goddard, Stevenage; Andrew Godfrey, Seer Green; Lesley Goldmann, W Sussex; Matthew Goldsmith, Burgess Hill; Mr & Mrs A. Goldthorp, Halstead; JA Goleczka, Wrington; John Goleczka, Pensford; Michael Goodband, Perhore; Bryn Gooding, Corfu; Dr G Gordon, Kidlington; Mrs J Gorman, Strood; Ian Gosden, Woking; Bill Gosland, Camberley; Isabel Gourlay, Highworth; David Gramagan, Formby; DC Grant, Enfield; Kathryn Grass, Wigan; Brian Gray, Yorks; Alan Gray, Erskine; DR Gray, SW11; A Greaves, Chesterfield; Andrew Greaves, Derbyshire; Rachel Greaves, Tavistock; Denise Gregory, Nottinghamshire; Jonathan Green, Cathays, Michael Green, Leicester; Nigel Green, Orpington; Richard Green, Gerrards Cross; Sheila Green, Barrow; A Gregor, Boston; Frank Gregori, NW10; Andrew Grendale, Ingatestone; A Griffiths, Milton Keynes; JK Greye, Bath; M Griffiths, Northampton; Dave Groves, Walsall; Lynda Gudgeon, Willenhall; Louis Gunn, Chelmsford.

H: Karen Haley, Telford; Hazel Hall, Surrey; John Hall, Cullercoats; Sarah Hall, Beds; Andrew Halling, Leigh; Stephen Hames, Bewdley; Alan Hamilton, Wakefield; Tina Hammond, Ipswich; Geoff & Janet Hampshire-Thomas, Kirkland; Neil Hancock, Derby; Ray Hancock, Chester; Dorothy Hankin, Fordingbridge; Mr & Mrs D Hannam, Yorks; Sharon Hanson, Derby; Glynn Harby, Knaresborough; Martyn Harding, Powys; Roger Hargreaves, Stoke; J Harman, Brentwood; Gerald S Harnden, Westcliff-on-Sea; Robert D Harper, Maidenhead; Dawn Harris, Dubley; Paul Harris, BFPO; Rick Harrington, Chichester; David Harrison, Dursley; Patrick Harrison, Cambridge; Steve Hartley, Ramsbottom; David Harvey, SE24; S Harwood, Lewes; John K Hattam, York; Sally Haseman, Surbiton; Christopher & Linda Haw, Dewsbury; Chris and Colin Hay, e-mail; Ann & David Haynes, Bournemouth; John Haynes, Saffron Walden; DI Hazelgrove, West Byfleet; M Hearle, Tunbridge Wells; Kevin Hearn, Newcastle; Bernice Heath, Nottingham; Luisa Heaton, Tarporley; Andy Hemingway, Leeds; Terry Herbat, Barnsley; Georgina Herridge, W9; J & J Hetherington, Preston; Victoria Heywood, Burton; Roger Hickman, N1; Pat & Paul Hickson, Chorley; Janet Higgins, Blackburn; Mrs S Higgins, Blackburn; Mrs B Higgs, Cotty; Dave Hignett, Newcastle-upon-Tyne; Alec Hill, Wigan; Carolyn Hill, Nottingham; Stephen Hill, Chesterfield; Barry Hills, Surrey; David Hindle, W5; Bharti Hindocha, Richmond; Daniel Hinge, Bishop Auckland; Mrs MJ Hirst, Kent; PA Hoad, W Sussex; SC Hodgon; Daniel Hodson, Abingdon; Peter Hoes, Bingley; P Hogkinson, Sheffield; BJ Holland, West Sussex; Duncan Holloway, Windsor; Kevin Hooper, St Austell; Linda Horan, Wirral; Peter Hornfleck, Farnborough; Jerry Horwood, Guildford; Dr & Mrs MP Houghton, Nr Rugby; Neil Houldsworth, Keighley; JK Howard, Enfield Wash; P Howard, Hornchurch; Mrs J Howarth, Oldham; Kathy Howe, Carlisle; Simon Howell,

Gillingham; Ken Howells, Selby; Bruce Howerd, Tongham; Lynn Howie, Sanderstead; Jan Hudson, Hemel Hempstead; Tom Hudson, Jarrow; Chris Hughes, Wraysbury; Paul Hulley, Stockport; SP Hulley, Reddish; HL & S Humphreys, Stoke-on-Trent; AG Hunt, Westcliff-on-Sea; John & Frances Hunt, Langport; Paul Hunt, Essex; Paul Hunt, Rayleigh; Roger Hunt, Sidmouth; Vince Hunt, Manchester; Penny Hunter, Brighton; Sheila Hunter, Dundee; Dr M Hutchinson, Gwynedd; Mrs V Hyland, Manchester.

I: DM Ibbotson, Sheffield; Nick & Mandy Idle, Ossett; Nigel Ineson, email; Mrs Tina Ingamells, Ivybridge; Brian Ingram, London; Ken Ingram, Leeds; G Innocent, Dawlish; Z Iqbal, London; Mrs G Irving, Redditch; Paul & Valerie Issott, Yorks; Robert Izzo, Horsham.

J: Dr AG James, Wigan; KL James, Marlborough; Nef Jandu, London; Tony Jannotti, Lathom; O Jarrett, Norwich; Sue Jayasekara, Essex; Sally Jeffries, Heathfield; Ian Jelley, Hatfield; L Jiggins, Dagenham; G John, Wirral; Colin Johnson, Southall; Maxine & Andrew Johnson, Leiden; Colin Johnson, Southall; Peter Johnson, Droitwich; Tim Johnson, Hounslow; Paul Jolliffe, Exeter; CML Jones, St Albans; Derek Jones, Chester; Gareth Jones, Tonypandy; Kate Jones, Leiden; RW Jones, N9; Shirley Jones, SE13; WA Jones, Flints; Wendy Jones, Clwyd; Michael Lloyd Jones, Cardiff; Carol Lorraine Jowett, Glos; Esther Juby, Norwich.

K: Tessa Kamara, W13; AD Kantes, Northants; Chris Keardey, Southampton; Anthony Kearns, Stafford; James Kellie, Hampshire; Russ Kelly, Seaforth; Prof. and Mrs Kemp, Royston; Mr & Mrs MJB Kendall, Hook; David Kerray, Akrotiri; John Kettle, Dover; JS Kettle, Banbury; Saul Keyworth, Essex; Stephen Kiely, N16; David King, Biggleswade; Mike King, Sussex; John & Jane Kingdom, Plymouth; Alyson Kingham, Oldham; Paul Kinsella, West Sussex; Frances Kitchen, Langport; Peter Kitney, Banbury; J & P Klusiatis, Reading; Drs Heather & Mark Knight, Oxford; Mrs UYS Knowles, Surrey; Drs MJ & A Krimholtz, SW14.

L: John & Sheila Lacey, S Willingham; Caz Lack, Kent; Martin Lally, Chester; RD Langridge, West Sussex; Alan Lathan, Chorley; Cass Lawson, Swindon; Jonathan Lazenby, Mamhilad, Gwent; Gary Leatt, St Brelade, Jersey; Andrew Lecomber, Durham; DH Lee, Waltham Abbey; Jackie Leek, Dartford; David Legg, Bristol; Simon Leng, Wakefield; David Leslie, Aberdeen; Russell D Lewin, NW2; A Lewis, Sherborne; D Lewis, London; Margaret Ann Lewis, Ashford; R Lewis, Rayleigh; Pat Lindsay, Hampshire; David Lloyd, Northampton; David Lloyd, Oswestry; Flt Lt Sion Lloyd-Jones, Uxbridge; Eleanor & Owen Lock, Geneva; Paul Logan, Kidderminster; Peter Long, Cheltenham; J Longman, Bodmin; John Loosemore, Orpington; DA Lord, Hove; Julia & Philip Lovell, Brighton; AP

Lowe, Tolworth; Mr and Mrs R Lowing, Sussex; Mr & Mrs DN Luckman, Horley; Jeremy Ludlow, Dorset; Steve Lumb, Yorkshire; Mrs H Lundy, Wallasey; Anthony and Anna Lunt, Reading; Graeme Lutman, Herts; Tim Lynch, Romford; Jamie Lyon, Burscough.

Mac/Mc: M Mcbryde, Watford; David Mackay, Twickenham; David Mackenzie, Darlington; Lin Macmillan, Lincoln; Deb McCarthy, E6; Patrick McCloy, N8; Vanessa McCrow, Teddington; David McCulloch, NW11; Michael McDonald, Ellesmere Port; David McDowell, Telford; Gary McGuire, Galashiels; BJ McKeown, Seaford; Ian McLean, Brighton; Dr and Mrs J McLelland, Mid Calder; Alan & Jean McLucas, Solihull; Dr FB McManus, Lincolnshire; Alan McWilliam, Inverurie.

M: Chris Mabey, Swindon; D & K Mackie, Portsmouth; Rakesh Makhecha, Harrow; Peter Mallinson, email; Richard Manley, Wirral; Cherry Manners, Hatfield; E Mansfield, Camberley; Clive Mantle; Michelle Markham, London; JF Marshall, Bedford; Geraldine Marson, Winsford; Colin Martin, Nuneaton; Derek and Pat Martin, Bucks; Jane Martin, SW19; PR Martin, Southend; DH Marston, Southport; DJ Mason, Cleveland; LJ Mason, Leeds; John Maundrell, Tunbridge Wells; Gilian and Colin May, Kent; Peter F May, St Albans; Yvette Mayes, W Sussex; Simon Mayo, Farnborough; David Meaden, London; Simon Meaton, Andover; John Medd, Nottingham; Tim Mee, Harrow; Sue & Alf Melor, Hanworth; Nigel Meredith, Huddersfield; Sujata Mia, Middlesex; H Middleton, Coventry; Simon Mighall, St Neots; PJL Mighell, Canterbury; Robert Miles, Hertfordshire; Catherine Millar, BFPO; DR Millichap, Horsham; BW Milligan; AJ Millington, Woodford; Sally Millington, N10; Mr & Mrs P Mills, Mold; Mary Mirfin, Leeds; Al Mitchell, Belfast; Jonathon Mitchell, Alton; F Moan, Cuddington; Sarah Moles, Buxton; Jon Molyneaux, Peterborough; Mrs SE Monk, Gisburn; AV Moody, Portsmouth; Christy Moore, Dublin; Christy Moore, London; Jonathan Moore, Newton Abbot; DM Moreland, Willington; S Morgan, Feltham; Simon Morley, Kent; Ian Morris, Bangor; TG Morris, Amsterdam; Audrey Morton, East Molesey; Peter Morwood, Wicklow; A Moss, Colchester; Caroline Moss, Solihull; Mrs L Muirhead, Glasgow; David Muncaster, Stoke; David, Muncester, Cheshire; Andy Munro, Birmingham; Joan Munro, Leyburn; Annette Murray, Thornton Cleveleys; JL Murray, Enfield; RG Murray, Carlisle; Simon Muth, Berks; Drs Heather & Harry Mycook.

N: Simon Nash, Cheshire; Mrs PG Naylor, Salisbury; Hugh Neal, Kent; Jeff Neal, Bolton; A Nelson-Smith, Swansea; Liam Nevens, Stockton; Tony Newman, Margate; Rebecca Newman, Hayes; Tony Newman, Margate; Clive Newton, Northwich; Jonathon Nichols, Nr Rugby; P & D Nixon, Basildon; James Norris, London; Mrs DA Nowakowa, Tiverton; Robert

Nugent, SE31; Canon Peter Nunn, Gloucestershire; Jody Lynn Nye, Illinois. **O**: Beverley Oakes, Essex; AM O'Brien, Worthing; Eamon O'Brien, Holland; Pauline O'Brien, London; Aidan O'Connor, Dublin; DC O'Donnell, Wetherby; Elise O'Donnell, Wolverhampton; Mary O'Hanlon, N Oliver, SE27; Helensburgh; Sheila Openshaw, Hampshire; David O'Regan, Leeds; Jan Ostron, Felpham; Judith Owen, SW6; Lucy Owen, London; William & Sue Oxley, Southampton.

P: Trevor Pack, Rushden; RH Paczec, Newcastle; M Padina, Mattingley; Melissa and Graham Paine, Coventry; Keith Paine, Tilbury; GJ Palmer, Gainsborough; RS Palmer, Norfolk; Mrs A Parker, Birmingham; Mr GM Parker, Birmingham; Graham Parker, Middx; John MF Parker, North Yorks; Bill Parkes-Davies, Tunbridge Wells; Bill Parkes-Davis, Kent; Chris Parkhurst, Surrey; Angela Parkinson, Clitheroe; M Parsons, Fareham; Roy Parsons, Richmond; Donald Paterson, East Grinstead; GM Patrick, London; Richard Patterson, Cornwall; PA Pearson, Bristol; Mrs G Pedlow, Hitchin; Mrs Barrie Penfold, Bourne End; J Penn, Southampton; AJW Perry, Bristol; Ian Perry, Essex; MJ Perry, E17; Ian Pettigrew, Edinburgh; Christopher Phelps, Gloucester; Adrian & Angela Phillips, Ammanford; Diane Phillips, Hyde; Jonathan Phillips, Saffron Walden; Steve Phillips, Wokingham; Colin Phipps, Scarborough; Sara Pickering, Northolt; Jack Pievsky, Pinner; Mike Plant, Essex; Susan Platt, Bury; D Pool, SE2; K Pool, Leyland; SR Poole, Runcorn; Tony Pope, Derbyshire; Des and Pat Portas, Boston; Steve Porter, Walsall; RL Power, Sutton Coldfield; Dave Prentice, Dartmouth; Dave Prentice, Devon; Steve Prentice, Devon; Eric Preston, West Yorks; Tim Preston, Barrow; Alison Preuss, Glencarse; Jeff Price, Bristol; J Priest, Harlow; Mr J Priest, Sawbridgeworth; Dr John Priestman, Huddersfield; D Pulsford, Marford; Janet Purchon, Bradford; Steve Puttock, Chatham; Julie Pyne, County Down.

Q: Sheila Quince, E11.

R: Mrs V Radbourne, Edgware; Diane Radigan, Welling; Clive Ramsey, Edinburgh; Steve Ransome, Backmill; Alison Ratcliff, Halstead; KJ Rayment, Hertford; RC Raynham, Chelmsford; CR Read, Epsom; Mark Read, Romford; Kim Reeder, South Shields; Debbie Reddy, W12; Francis Redgate, Nottingham; Steven Redknap, Ashford; I Reid, Fife; John Reid, Chinnor; Lorraine Reid, Edinburgh; Duncan Renn, Dursley; Julian Rhodes, St Leonards-on-Sea; Derek Richards, Bewdley; Sean Richards, Dover; Simon Richardson, Gainsborough; Brian and Pat Rides, Glos; Mike Ridgway, Buxton; Mathew Riley, SE3; Mrs S Rive, Epping; Hywel Roberts, Bradford; Lindsay Roberts, Lancaster; Margaret Roberts, Rubery; Peter Roberts, Shipston; Tony Roberts, Hemel Hempstead; Stewart & Anne Robertson, Leamington; Simon Roccason, Willenhall; Pat Roche, Chislehurst; J & P Rockery, Leicester; KG Rodwell, Harston; Malcolm

Rodino, Mattingley; Nicholas Ronan, W Midlands; R Ronan, IOW; John Roscoe, Stalybridge; Doreen Ross, Alberta, Canada; Brian Roston, Pontefract; John Rose, Hull; Ms SP Rowe, West Sussex; WJ Rowe; Steve Rowland, Matlock; Wade Rowlett, Lincolnshire; Mrs EM Ruck, Darlington; DC Ruggins, Chalfont; JA Rumble, Rochford; Paul Rushton, Nottingham; Greg Russell, Edinburgh; K Ruth, W1; Bob Rutter, Blackpool; EJ Ryan, Effingham; N Ryer, Mansfield.

S: George and Mrs J Sadler, Little Thetford; Suzanne St Clair, Bucks; MB Samson, Hertfordshire; Pauline Sapsford, Milton Keynes; MR Sargeant, Cornwall; Mark Sarjant, Guildford; Nigel Savage, Llangollens; GM Saville, Egremont; Mike Scotlock, Rayleigh; Mike Scott, Holmer Green; MJ Scott, SE26; Nicky & Don Scowen, Romford; Tim Sebensfield, Beeston; M Seefeld, W5; Patrick Sellar, Maidstone; Philip Senior, Liverpool; N Sennett, Hull; David Sewell, Aldershot; Mrs DA Seymour, Burnham-on-Sea; Richard Shackleton, Wakefield; Brian Shallon, Camberley; Jeane Sharp, St Albans; Howard & Mary Sherman, Upton-by-Chester; Mark Shaw, Swindon; Michelle Shaw, Ilford; Deborah Shent, Nottingham; Barrie Shepherd, Bishopston; Howard Sherman, Chester; Graham Sherwood, Waterlooville; David Shields, Bedfordshire; Theresa Shilcock, Derbyshire; Lyndon Silver, Hampshire; Mrs C Silvester, Guildford; Ewan Sim, Leeds; Carolyn Simpson, SE13; Jennifer Singh, Enfield; Jeff Slater, E6; William P Sloan, Camberley; Else & Harald Smaage, Sauvegny; David Smith, Norwich; David Smith, Swindon; Denis Smith, Swindon; EK Smith, Edinburgh; Caroline Smith, Kent; Gillian Smith, St Andrews; Hazel Smith, Llandrinio; Howard Smith, Cardiff; Jim Smith, Cork; LP & A Smith, Gibraltar; Mark Smith, Lancashire; Nora Smith, Cardiff; RB Smith, BFPO; Sue Smith, Northampton; Susan Smith, Devon; Peter Smyth, London; Colin Snowball, Glos; Tim Softly, Leigh; Robert Solbe, Surrey; Peter Soloman, Middlesbrough; M Somerton-Rayner, Cranwell; Maurice Southwell, Aylesbury; Gill Sparks, Halifax; Andrew Speller, Harlow; GD Spencer, Stonehaven; Mrs P Spencer, Norwich; Andy Spiers, Brighton; R Spiers, Wolverhampton; PJ Spence, Yorkshire; Chris Spinks, Ilford; CP Spinks, Church Langley; John Spinks, Hainault; Doug & Audrey Spittle, Gt Yarmouth; Martin Spooner, Wallsend; DJ Stacey, Cambridge; Mrs WL Stanley-Smith, Belper; Mr & Mrs M Stanworth, Haywards Heath; John Starley, Birdingbury; Nigel Steel, Carlisle; Avril Steele, Crossgar; Bob Stencill, Sheffield; John Stent, Liss; K Stevens, Faringdon, Oxon; Ian Stewart, Potters Bar; Tim Stewart, Norfolk; Susie Stockton-Link, Bewdley; Tina Stone, Illford; Brian Strachan, Furriff; Barry Strange, Kent; Rob Struthers, Brighton; Mrs MB Such; FD Sunderland, Plympton; FC Sutton, Poole; Mary Suwinsky, Virginia, USA; Andrew Swain, Sudbury; Carolyn Swain, Leeds; Gary Swain, Coventry; DL Swann, Parbold; Frank Sweeney, Middlesbrough; Gill & Graham Swift, Beeston; MS Sykes, Dorrington; Brian Sylvester, Maidenhead.

T: RT, Berkshire; Jon Talbot, Wrexham; Nigel & Gill Tancock, Newbury; Steve Tandy, Cleveleys; Bernard Tarpey, Failsworth; Andrew Tattersall, North Yorks; CB Taylor, Wolverhampton; Colin Taylor, Preston; Kevin Taylor, Sevenoaks; Ken Taylor, Sevenoaks; Peter Taylor, Kingston-upon-Hull; Philip & Vivien Taylor, Cromer; Roger Taylor, Hamela; Len Teff, Whaddon; Mrs PF Terrazzano, Leigh-on-Sea; RL Terry, Kent; Christopher & Niamh Thomas, Barnet; David Thomas, Gloucester; DL Thomas, Peterborough; Mrs J Thomas, Cumbria; Mark Thomas, Exeter; Nigel Thomas, Lincoln; Dr DA & AHE Thombs, Slimbridge; Alan Thompson, Clwyd; David & Lisa Thompson, SE10; Richard Thompson, Rainham; Bill Thomson, Ramsgate; Paul Thomson, Salford; J Thorne, South Benfleet; Richard & Nicki Tilbe, Wokingham; Mrs BM Clifton Timms, Chorley; Joan & Ken Timms, West Sussex; Mrs M Tindale, Beverley; Alan Tingle, Hayling Island; Andrew Tittershill, Leicestershire; Joan Tongue, Huddersfield; Graham Todd, Crawley; Joan Tongue, Huddersfield; Alex & Sarah Torrence, Cleveland; SR Tracey-Forster, Bronham; Bernard Train, Barton; Leigh Trevitt, Bishops Stortford; R Trinkwon, Ferring; Kevin & Sarah Troubridge, Chelmsford; Dr JG Tucker, SW17; Paul Tunnicliffe, Cleveland; Martin Turley, Belgium; Don Turnball, Geneva; Mrs SM Turner, Stroud; Brian & Danielle Turnock, Belgium; John Turton, West Midlands; R Twiddy, Boston; S Twiggs, Lower Kingswood; Jeremey Twomey, Leamington; John Tyler, Romford.

V: David Valentine, Forfar; Alan & Lesley Vaughan, Paington; D Vaughan-Williams, Penyffordd; Mrs B Venton, Chipstead; Wesley Vernon, High Peak; Richard Vinnicombe, Camberley; Mr & Mrs T Vhsimas, Crymyoh; Sarah Vokes, Dorking; Gordon Volke, Worthing.

W: Sharon and Philip Waine, Manchester; R Waldron, Oxon; Linda Wainscot, Rugby; Alison Walker, Droitwich; Andrew Walker, Aklington; DJ Walker, Bedfordshire; Dr JB Walker, Burnham; John Walker, Chorley; Dr PAW Walker, Wirral; William Wallace, West Kilbride; Alison Walton, North Shields; Mrs J Ward, Wakefield; Cathy Ward, Slough; Pamela Ward, Birmingham; Simon Ward, Croydon; John Warren, Lancs; Mrs G Warrington, Hyde; Ralph Warrington, Hyde; Nicholas Watt, Houghton; RG Watt, Bromyard; Andy Webb, Aberdeen; Peter Webb, Kelsall, Nr Tarporley; TG Webb, Peterborough; Nick Webley, Llandeilo; Dave Webster, Gateshead; Harry and Marina Webster, Nottingham; Andrew Wegg, SW16; Michael Welch, Reading; J Weld, Eastleigh; Dave Weldon, Hale; John Wellings, Edinburgh; AD West, Aylesbury; A West, Leicestershire; Laurence West, Torquay; Dr PJ West, Warrington; Mrs B Watkins, West Sussex; Joyce Westrip, Perth, Australia; Andrew Wheatcroft, Chesterfield; Sarah Wheatley, Leavesden; George Whilton, Huddersfield; Robert Ian White, East Sussex; Andy Whitehead, Swindon; Mr & Mrs DW Whitehouse,

Redditch; R Whitehurst, Bramhall; K Whiteside, Rossendale; Mrs S Whiting, Gedling; George Whitton, Huddersfield; Peter Wickendon, East Tilbury; Jennette Wickes, Fleet; PM Wilce, Abingdon; Malcolm Wilkins, Gravesend; Chris Wilkinson, Cumbria; Geoffrey Wilkinson, Orpington; Babs Williams, Bristol; Mark P Williams, Kent; P Williams, Cornwall; Raoul Williams, Cambridge; Ted Williams, Norwich; David Williamson, NW3; David Williamson, Stamford; BP and J Willoughby, Devizes; Bob & Eve Wilson, NW2; Dr Michael Wilson, Crewe; Major Mike Wilson, BFPO 140; Richard Winfield, Yorkshire; John Wirring, Swindon; Mrs AC Withrington, Hindhead; David Wolfe, SW1, Ian and Jane Wood, Tameside; W Wood, Hornsea; Louise Woodcock, Edinburgh; Caroline and Kim Woody, Harlow; John Woolsgrove, Enfield; Geof Worthington, Handforth; Alan Worthy, Matlock; Mrs C Wright, Glasgow; Mrs CF Wright, Stockport; Clive Wright, Halesowen; D Wright, Rotherham; John D Wright, St Ives; Georgina Wright, Nottingham; Lynn Wright, Newark; Sally Wrighter, Hitchens.

Y: Stephen Yarrow, NW11; EJ Yea, Cambridgeshire; Rev. Can. David Yerburgh, Stroud; Andrew Young, Cumbria; Andy Young, Penrith; Mrs B Young, Basildon; Carl Young, Nottingham; Mrs E Young, Ilmington.

To join this list, all you need to do is tell us about your favourite and least favourite restaurants.

See page 621 onwards for more information on how to contact us.

Town Index

About the Author

Pat Chapman was born in London's Blitz, with an addiction to curry inherited from his family's six-generation connection with India, the story of which is told in Pat's book *Pat Chapman's Taste of the Raj* (*see* page 624). Virtually weaned on his grandmother's curries, he was taken to his first curry houses – Veeraswamy in Piccadilly and Shafi's in Gerrard Street – at the age of six, at a time when there were only three such establishments in London, and six in the whole of the UK. Visits became a regular treat and confirmed in Pat a passion and a curiosity about the food of India. He was already a curryholic! Following education at Bedales and Cambridge, he did a short stint in the RAF, flying fast jets, then spent several years in industry.

He founded the now world-renowned Curry Club in 1982, at a time when the curry was just beginning to become nationally important, as a way of sharing information about recipes, restaurants and all things to do with spicy food. Soon a national network of curry restaurant reporters was established, whose voluntary contributions led to the publication of the first edition of this highly successful *Good Curry Guide* in 1984, and its prestigious awards to restaurants.

Assisted by his wife, Dominique, Pat frequently demonstrates at major food shows and appears on TV and radio, and they regularly stage cookery courses and events. His pioneering Gourmet Tours to India are now well-established holidays for *aficionados*.

With book sales exceeding 1.5 million, Pat is best known as a writer of easy-to-follow recipes. His succession of popular curry titles, some of which are listed on page 624, are published by Simon & Schuster, Hodder & Stoughton, Piatkus, Sainsbury's and the BBC.

the CURRY CLUB

Pat Chapman always had a deep-rooted interest in spicy food, curry in particular, and over the years he built up a huge pool of information which he felt could be usefully passed on to others. He conceived the idea of forming an organisation for this purpose.

Since it was founded in January, 1982, The Curry Club has built up a membership of several thousands. We have a marchioness, some lords and ladies, knights a-plenty, a captain of industry or two, generals, admirals and air marshals (not to mention a sprinkling of ex-colonels), and we have celebrity names – actresses, politicians, rock stars and sportsmen. We have an airline, a former Royal Navy warship, and a hotel chain.

We have 15 members whose name is Curry or Curries, 20 called Rice and several with the name Spice or Spicer, Cook, Fry, Frier or Fryer and one Boiling. We have a Puri (a restaurant owner), a Paratha and a Nan, and a good many Mills and Millers, one Dal and a Lentil, an Oiler, a Gee (but no Ghee), a Cummin and a Butter but no Marj (several Marjories though, and a Marjoram and a Minty). We also have several Longs and Shorts, Thins and Broads, one Fatt and one Wide, and a Chilley and a Coole.

We have members on every continent including a good number of Asian members, but by and large the membership is a typical cross-section of the Great British Public, ranging in age from teenage to dotage, and in occupation from refuse collectors to receivers, high street traders to high court judges, tax inspectors to taxi drivers. There are students and pensioners, millionaires and unemployed . . . thousands of people who have just one thing in common – a love of curry and spicy foods.

Members receive a bright and colourful quarterly magazine, which has regular features on curry and the curry lands. It includes news items, recipes, reports on restaurants, picture features, and contributions from members and professionals alike. The information is largely concerned with curry, but by popular demand it now includes regular input on other exotic and spicy cuisines such as those of Thailand, the spicy Americas, the Middle East and China. We produce a wide selection of publications, including the books listed overleaf.

Curry diners will be familiar with the Curry Club window sticker and restaurant quality certificate, which adorns the windows and the walls of the best thousand curry restaurants. As detailed elsewhere, Curry Club members form the national network of reporters, which leads to the selection of the restaurants in this publication, and to the prestigious awards to the top restaurants.

Obtaining some of the ingredients required for curry cooking can be difficult, but The Curry Club makes it easy, with a comprehensive range of products, including spice mixes, chutneys, pickles, papadoms, sauces and curry pastes. These are available from major food stores and specialist delicatessens up and down the country. If they are not stocked near you, there is the Club's associate, well-established and efficient mail-order service. Hundreds of items are in stock, including spices, pickles, pastes, dry foods, tinned foods, gift items, publications and specialist kitchen and tableware.

On the social side, the Club holds residential weekend cookery courses and gourmet nights at selected restaurants. Top of the list is our regular Curry Club gourmet trip to India and other spicy countries. We take a small group of curry enthusiasts to the chosen country and tour the incredible sights, in between sampling the delicious food of each region.

If you would like more information about The Curry Club, write (enclosing a stamped addressed envelope please) to:
The Curry Club, PO Box 7, Haslemere, Surrey. GU27 1EP.

Some of Pat Chapman's Best-sellers

PAT CHAPMAN'S CURRY BIBLE

This definitive, gorgeously illustrated book for all curryholics brings together a wealth of information on how to prepare the perfect Indian meal. All your favourite curry house dishes are arranged in menu order, with descriptions, recipes and pictures of every one. Some are compared with their authentic classic counterparts. All are easy to cook, giving superb results. Step-by-step colour sequences, ingredients, utensils, store cupboard list.

An illustrated A to Z of Spices. Menu suggestions.

'A truly authoritative book.' Max Davidson, Daily Telegraph

PAT CHAPMAN'S BALTI BIBLE

Definitive lavishly illustrated sister volume to the Curry Bible. Over 200 easy-to-cook recipes, including 120 Balti dishes, plus further recipes for starters, rice and bread, accompaniments and desserts. Descriptions, recipes and pictures of every favourite dish at the Balti House, plus step-by-step sequences, utensils, store cupboard list.

An illustrated A to Z of Ingredients. A must for the Baltiholic!!!

PAT CHAPMAN'S VEGETABLE CURRY BIBLE NEWLY PUBLISHED

Sister volume to the above Bibles. Equally definitive and beautifully illustrated. Over 200 easy-to-cook recipes, using vegetables, dairy, eggs, nuts and fruit, including soups, beverages, snacks, starters, 100 different curries, rice, breads, accompaniments and desserts.

Step-by-step sequences, store cupboard list.

An illustrated A to Z of Vegetables and Fruit. A must for the vegetarian and meat-eater alike.

PAT CHAPMAN'S NOODLE BOOK

Over 100 exciting recipes, and all the Noodler needs to know about a food growing fast in popularity.

PAT CHAPMAN'S TASTE OF THE RAJ

Pat tells the story of the amazing rise and inevitable fall of the British Raj. His in-depth look at its food gives probably the most critical analysis of the vitriolic cookbook writers of the era. Pat's curry-loving ancestors spent six generations in India. It's their story too, told anecdotally, with fun and facts and over 100 delicious spicy 'Anglo Indian' recipes, including a chapter on Raj curries.

Every spice lover will adore these many long-forgotten recipes.

PAT CHAPMAN'S THAI RESTAURANT COOKBOOK

120 mouth-watering favourite recipes, garnered from the world's best Thai restaurants, are bound to include your favourites – crispy starters, crunchy salads, sumptuous soups, fragrant meat, poultry, fish and vegetable dishes, Thai curries, rice, noodles and desserts.

Historical and background information. Menu suggestions. Glossary.

THE CURRY CLUB INDIAN RESTAURANT COOKBOOK

Pat's original book, now in its 16th reprint. 150 delicious recipes. That 'Indian restaurant flavour' in your own kitchen, with minimal effort and maximum enjoyment. Glossary, store-cupboard list, many useful tips. Ideal starter book.

THE CURRY CLUB BANGLADESHI CURRY COOKBOOK

With 90% of our curry houses Bangladeshi-owned, we felt it was time that authentic Bangladeshi curries were highlighted. Recognised by the Bangladeshi High Commission as the definitive book on its subject. Over 100 sumptuous authentic recipes. Background info, including a full history of the curry restaurant around the world.

2000 COBRA CURRYHOLICS DIRECTORY BRAND NEW IDEA

Compliments the Guide. The Directory is the first ever publication to list every curry restaurant in the UK, plus every curry product, and useful curry snippets.

A must for the curryholic!

What We Need to Know

We need to know everything there is to know about all curry restaurants in the UK. And there is no one better able to tell us than those who use them. We do not mind how many times we receive a report about a particular place, so please don't feel inhibited or that someone else would be better qualified. They aren't. Your opinion is every bit as important as the next person's.

Ideally, we'd like a report from you every time you dine out – even on a humble takeaway. We realize this is hard work so we don't mind if your report is very short, and you are welcome to send in more than one report on the same place telling of different occasions. Please cut out the forms on the last page. Or you can even use the back of an envelope or a postcard, or we can supply you with more forms if you write in (with an S.A.E., please).

If you can get hold of a menu (they usually have takeaway menus to give away) or visiting cards, they are useful to us too, as are newspaper cuttings, good and bad, and advertisements.

So, please send anything along with your report. Most reports received will appear, in abbreviated form, in the *Curry Magazine* (the Curry Club members' regular publication). They are also used when preparing the next edition of this *Guide.*

We do not pay for reports but our ever-increasing corps of regular correspondents receive the occasional perk from us. Why not join them? Please send us your report after your next restaurant curry.

Thank you.

Pat Chapman
Founder, The Curry Club
PO Box 7
Haslemere
Surrey
GU27 1EP

Fax it to: 01428 645045

email it to chapman.curry@virgin.net

CURRY CLUB MEMBERS'

DISCOUNT VOUCHER SCHEME

SAVE POUNDS ON DINING!

To make big savings on your curry meals or takeaways, you must become a Curry Club member. It's easy: contact us at the address below. Members get our colourful *Curry Club Magazine* three times a year. In it are six vouchers, so you get eighteen vouchers a year.

Each voucher is valid at any one of the restaurants that have agreed to participate in this scheme. To identify them look for the © sign at the top right hand of the restaurant's entry.

The actual discount each restaurant is willing to give varies from restaurant to restaurant. Some will give a free bottle of wine, or free starters, others 5% off the bill, and some are offering as much as 10%, or even more.

We have agreed with the restaurant owners that these discounts are available at the discretion of the restaurant, at their quieter times, and that each Curry Club member will book in advance when using a DISCOUNT VOUCHER.

To find out how much discount you can get, and when they will give it to you, please PHONE THE MANAGER. (Where possible we have given the name of the individual owner or manager who has agreed to give the discount in the participating restaurant's entry.) Then please BOOK.

There is no limit to the number of people Curry Club members may take. One voucher is valid for a discount on one meal, and must be handed over when paying the bill.

REMEMBER, YOU MUST BE A MEMBER OF THE CURRY CLUB TO GET YOUR VOUCHERS. SO JOIN NOW TO SAVE POUNDS.

More information about the scheme and the Club from:

THE CURRY CLUB, PO BOX 7, HASLEMERE., SURREY GU27 IEP

Please send an S.A.E.

RESTAURANT UPDATE INFORMATION

Even if you do not fill in a report overleaf, you may be able to give us vital information, such as that below. DO YOU KNOW OF ANY:

NEW CURRY RESTAURANT OPENINGS:

Restaurant name:

Street no and name:

Town: County:

Postcode: Telephone:

CURRY RESTAURANT CLOSURES OVER THE LAST FEW MONTHS,

Including any listed in this Guide

Restaurant name:

Street no and name:

Town: County:

Postcode: Telephone:

HYGIENE OR OTHER OFFENCES

Please back up with a local press cutting if possible

Restaurant name:

Street no and name:

Town: County:

Postcode: Telephone:

YOUR FAVOURITE RESTAURANT(S)

If possible, in descending order, best first

Restaurant name:

Street no and name:

Town: County:

Postcode: Telephone:

ANY OTHER CURRY RESTAURANT INFORMATION?

Please continue on separate sheets of paper if required

Please return your info to: The Curry Club, PO Box 7, Haslemere, Surrey. GU27 IEP
email: chapman.curry@virgin.net

RESTAURANT REPORT FORM

Whenever you have an 'Indian' meal or takeaway, The Curry Club would like to have your opinion.

Name and address of restaurant:

Telephone: Date Visited:

REPORT

Please tell us everything... your first impressions, the welcome, cleanliness, your table – was it appealing? nice things waiting for you on it? the menu, quantities, quality, service, background music, comfort, decor. The food? First visit? Been before? Would you go back/ recommend to friends? How were the toilets? Overall was the restaurant good, bad or indifferent?

If possible send us the restaurant takeaway menu and other information.

Do continue on separate sheets of paper if required.

Please return your report to THE CURRY CLUB, PO BOX 7, HASLEMERE, SURREY GU27 IEP
email: chapman.curry@virgin.net

RESTAURANT UPDATE INFORMATION

Even if you do not fill in a report overleaf, you may be able to give us vital information, such as that below. DO YOU KNOW OF ANY:

NEW CURRY RESTAURANT OPENINGS:

Restaurant name:

Street no and name:

Town: County:

Postcode: Telephone:

CURRY RESTAURANT CLOSURES OVER THE LAST FEW MONTHS,

Including any listed in this Guide

Restaurant name:

Street no and name:

Town: County:

Postcode: Telephone:

HYGIENE OR OTHER OFFENCES

Please back up with a local press cutting if possible

Restaurant name:

Street no and name:

Town: County:

Postcode: Telephone:

YOUR FAVOURITE RESTAURANT(S)

If possible, in descending order, best first

Restaurant name:

Street no and name:

Town: County:

Postcode: Telephone:

ANY OTHER CURRY RESTAURANT INFORMATION?

Continue on separate sheets of paper if required

Please return your info to: The Curry Club, PO Box 7, Haslemere, Surrey GU27 IEP
email: chapman.curry@virgin.net

RESTAURANT REPORT FORM

Whenever you have an 'Indian' meal or takeaway, The Curry Club would like to have your opinion.

Name and address of restaurant:

Telephone: Date Visited:

REPORT

Please tell us everything... your first impressions, the welcome, cleanliness, your table – was it appealing? nice things waiting for you on it? the menu, quantities, quality, service, background music, comfort, decor. The food? First visit? Been before? Would you go back/ recommend to friends? How were the toilets? Overall was the restaurant good, bad or indifferent?

If possible send us the restaurant takeaway menu and other information.

Do continue on separate sheets of paper if required.

Please return your report to THE CURRY CLUB, PO BOX 7, HASLEMERE, SURREY GU27 IEP
email: chapman.curry@virgin.net